BUY INVENT 2024

Volume 2

Christopher g Brown

Christopher g Brown

Crioner Co

The characters and events portrayed in this book are not fictitious. Any similarity to real persons, living or dead, is un- coincidental and is intended by the author.

ISBN-13: 9798324434229
ISBN-10: 1477123456

Cover design by: Art Painter
Library of Congress Control Number: 2018675309
Printed in the United States of America

Dedicate to my Related
Mom Janice Brown
Dad Ron Brown
Brother Steed Brown
Sister Lori Brown Hembree

CONTENTS

FOREWORD

Buy copyrights and pending patents at buyinvent.com We are offering to settle on things that are original and innovative in many different fields. such as artistic concepts chemical compounds computational equations and summations counsel services energy development governmental intuitions in capitalism hardware made from people who use hardware medical inventions software design and a wide range of technology. This is a description of text work and methodical products that includes a written authorship of original intent to serialize the work in tow. Please see the intent to explain my work. The work is started with a chronological number of appearance and then the name of the registration and then the deposition itself with copyrighted script and then the owner which is myself only. Please accept my thanks for your work and time with my case. Our intent is to sell legal and justified written copyrights and patents. what makes our patents and copyrights worth money is the legal ownership and the permanence of the meaning. the inventive nature is root and the overall creative system here is the method that we accept as a reason for trade value. Our inventor systematically creates original and conceptualizes depositions that equal a real widget beyond only ideas and theories of interest. This rudimentary tangible substance is the short of why we make our attempts at capitalizing on any such product here in our store in our records and in our repository. the essential nature of the invention and the trade of our creative mission is the stores most valuable asset with you and our trust is the best we provide. to see that our honesty and originality in a whole is the best there is and from time to time we will organize our focus and narrow the exact description in a sub entity. being a serial or registered mark of trade and patented document. Here are the previously registered numbers.

- 7836749
- 7933940
- 8021945
- 8056278
- 8152204
- 8169880
- 8251642
- 8396625
- 8432699
- 62375115
- 62393084
- 7674484

- 7786269
- 7599215
- 7646239
- 7511791
- 7491093
- 7504988
- 62586875
- 62530996
- 15825059
- 158250593233
- 16004322
- 1600432200
- 160043226150
- 1600432261501
- 16258495
- 16276673
- 163785973083
- 62375115
- 62393084
- 625309961000
- 8021945
- 8056278
- 8152204
- 8169880
- 8251642
- 8657127

2892994

When You Buy, You Buy The Following
A.Waiver of Liability
B.Permission to Use Quote or Personal Statement
C.Assignment of Copyright

INTRODUCTION

Description: my intention is to make a new invention of old problems solved in a new way. The root of all my issues is as a theory of money. For example, if you were to examine the history of worth and monetary value itself is what I am translating.

A Statements

1. Denomination of worth and trust is a thing known as money. Banks lean on notes of worth from the government.
2. A formula for invent is a government of worth as property and ownership, in general people are bad and money is to be protected.
3. If you know that man is evil you can be like the one-eyed man that sees everything in the land of the blind.

B Analogies

1. To carry on with service as a device and worth a plotted note of value. Or performance as a worth and software defined devices as the capital.
2. If you can justify the means of ownership, it's a good thing and to understand that corruption may occur and there should be service agreements.
3. If you were to make devices defined from software then you may note that new things are to come even if they have already been said.

C Examples

1. A floppy used to carry the device of software previously, with binary code. The hard drives of today have the similar function.
2. Device code and language is a function of trust and will always be a theory of justified everything there could be as itself technology or life.
3. To sell services and devices as intentionally confusing is wrong and the mission is to create a new device is the entire mission.

D Detail

1. My dad taught me a new word. Paradigm (1) is a theory. To explain the theory is my new work. The focus is the grand scheme of this deposition.
2. Understanding that there is a reason for the difference between technology and life then there can be a new book in the reality of the two.
3. To write a software as a device is a function inside a paradox. And there is currently a confusion between "AI" (2) and the thing we call "life." And if you were to deliberately put a difference in between the two, technology and Biology then there is profit.

CONCLUSION Catchphrase

The “money” is in the instructions. Computer software rules should be derived from trust measurements inside the instructions of software, instructions of CPU’s, instructions of bios, instructions of hard drives, instructions of memory, and etc. to tell you that simply is to say this, stop calling “AI,” technology. Also please note that the newest direction is the oldest. Binary instructions then Quantum instructions and now Molecular definitions of instructions and rules of life will be made.

To invest in people as a biology and knowing the difference between technology is in the instruction set. What people will pay for and want to be free is what worth is derived by. To tax with out a voice is simply illegal in the United States of America. The reason for a lot of things is God given. The good of mankind is a trust in belief and reality. The name “ai” is a fictional paradox and should be known as System reasoning which should be controlled by a root of trust. (4)

In conclusion is this... there should be a pure definition of what is to be written in defense and attacks. Just because you can give away the world doesn’t mean you should. And just because man is generally evil doesn’t mean that you can’t try to not be evil. I wrote a program that makes CPUs thread with accelerated massive parallelism. I just copied the two sources online from Microsoft and Intel. And then I patented it. The truth is that I think intel should write instructions for people like arm makes chip designs for people. And while I’m admitting things, I also wrote Texas Instruments a proposal also, only not as good as this one.

Final Quote – Start making Instructions as a Software on Device.

Scale(5) Buy Inventions at crioneaka.com or submit a letter of payment to

Christopher g Brown

1341 Wellington cove, Lawrenceville, GA. 30043-5255 USA

PREFACE

Why subscription is not the word of the moment Part One

Payment is capital and the unjust will soon become just!

Why subscription is not the word of the moment Part Two

Ownership is a short on the things you own.

Why subscription is not the word of the moment Part Three

The limit to which and why will show itself.

Example One

17 a different way to see business ethics and personal values actually do make up the person who works for you. and you and i may see eye to eye for once that you don't want a drug user as your warehouse manager so what precautions would you be willing to take? personality or drug tests? to what level can you go to ensure that there aren't any problems... to me it seems that the higher the magnitude of company the level of sanctity is to be seen reasonable. i wish right about now i could quote a devil's advocate line, what's the difference between a lifestyle poly graph and a really good chance at a good job that makes your children happy and your wife proud to be in your presence... may be after all there is a place for everything. sometimes hp does alternate business counsel as myself go to the service detail here> copyright © 2017 Christopher g brown patent Christopher g brown 3545 2536 Publisher: CreateSpace Independent Publishing Platform; Large Print edition (June 25, 1985) ISBN-13: 978-1467904506

https://crioneaka.com/invent/index.php?route=product/product&path=55&product_id=1648

Example Two

24 theoretical business analytic s theoretical business analytic s to speak about ones past is sad at times. but, in the professional sense to reminisce is important. the variables must contain a few transitional attempts of experimentation and study. the most we can do is realize there are peaks and valleys in every thing. so my concept is to measure the weight of the experiment mission to the weight of the shelf life of a product or service and then the peak of the appreciation. there are so many factors to every thing but i am going to summarize the values into abstract form. why something is great is labeled as glory in generasism, so to me that is all opinion and at times facts of the case at hand. what made it great is the question. the same goes for why it went bad and when it went bad, why the things made it fall from popularity may at times be opinion or merely poetical justice. what goes up must

come down. to translate the simple things in business are always from intuition. to hire people with positive ethical spirit and attitude is the most important thing to start with. copyright © 2017 Christopher g brown patent Christopher g brown 3538 3023 Publisher: CreateSpace Independent Publishing Platform; Large Print edition (June 25, 1985) ISBN-13: 978-1467904506

https://crioneaka.com/invent/index.php?route=product/product&path=55&product_id=1641

Example Three

1752 vagrant law of profane loitering and illegal dwelling copyright © 2020 Christopher Gabriel brown patent Christopher g brown 1747 1752 Christopher G Brown Submitted On December 4, 2019 ISBN-13: 978-1658972871

https://crioneaka.com/invent/index.php?route=product/product&path=55&product_id=57

Laws are rules and the laws should be amended. Unfortunately, there is a new need to stop old demons. Greed and ownership is at a level of un compromised inefficiency. What I may say as ownership is still to be determined. And it appears as though companies and people are now two different things. I'm just a one-person company with ownership.

Computers are great the ownership is plain and not complicated. The cloud is a group of servers software and services. To point out the differences in my computer and your software is simple. I bought it and I own it. It's mine. To say you can change my software on my computer is poor judgement. To have to amend the law and technology of just too much is a ownership privilege. Technology needs the people to have justice.

Recently Joe Biden said, "put trust and faith in our government." Donald Trump said, "In America we don't worship government, we worship God." And this is not cryptic or false. The same can be said as to compare companies to government and people as people. The companies want to take away your rights to own things and same as government.

Strange how a software company can make a long-distance call to your computer to their data mining servers. In other words, there should be a technology law for rights of the consumer against poor business ethics, data theft, and rights of ownership. The real call is when all of the software you use will be someone elses property in a bad design. To short in a stock is this knowledge... Here is the impossible. When there are charges for subscription purchase in the case of something you need the most or the least there will be failure in subscriptions.

The rights of businesses and consumers are at stake on two levels. The businesses are asking consumers not to use their products now. The solution is to escape the clouds. Run your own, work it out and short subscriptions bills.

PROLOGUE

Christopher g Brown
Self Study of Bi-Polar Syndrome
https://web.archive.org/web/20100124124020/http://www.crioner.com/services/SelfStudy.html

Dependent on Emotional Bonds by Christopher G. Brown

My name is Chris Brown. I have been diagnosed as happy with out cause. I'm not going to tell you why exactly but you may find with reading I do have a story to tell. This is an essay of sorts in an autobiographical sense. I have been sick for a very long time and have come to the conclusion that I wish to write my experience with my illness. My favorite question to a doctor is, "what is it like to know a patients illness better than the patient?"

How do you diagnose a patient safely, with quietness and stern questions of course. Leave time in-between thoughts to contemplate the patient. I do not recommend trying to "absorb" what the patient is thinking. This is more difficult with genius level consumers. Because their thoughts are rapid and careless due to the fact that they may be able to explain the need for (example) being overtly happy. If there thoughts become welcome then the probable explanation is "dependent."

The need for acceptance is basic in all of us. Some people have become so dependent on appreciation and need for attention that they become consumed in them selves. The perfect example of this is the Artist. My favorite question on reaction would be the ever so famous, "How did you do that?" Puzzle placement and wonder are very happy thoughts. How did you do that indeed? Some times the realist would automatically be jealous and enraged that they don't know how the artist would make such a work. Just let it go and say, that's good.

The friends and family of the artist are very hard to understand. They have to cope with the artists greatness which may or may not be good. It's common for people to say the phrase, "the artist in his own little world." Meaning every person has their own depiction and perception of reality. That's what goes on in the patients mind. We are all patients of time. Sometimes we may measure the time by a term called avant-garde which means art. I am an artist but I don't write time.

The issue at hand is why bi-polar becomes a need to be bi-polar. Once people become outrageously happy the feeling is almost the true definition of a charismatic. My problem is that the feeling needs to stay with me. That's why I have choosen to write this essay of random thoughts and think to my self while speaking to others. I hope you can learn from my mistakes and know that there are good artists but there are also artists that become unable to bear their own mind. They become engrossed in their perception and I to am guilty under that idea. I need and I need and I need.

To almost all of this is the answer, your too self absorbed. {And enough about you lets talk more about me. So the friend disappears and who steps in? Why did your friend expire and move away? Is it all the way you decide to look at it? Or why don't they enjoy my art? Is cabin fever worse than schizophrenia or is it the other way around? I feel the need to make some art now? I have to make my self happy and I have to be happy all the time. I think that people need to hear me as I rave.}

I would like to give thanks to All the special people who serve in Triage.

BUY INVENT 2024

VOLUME 2

5486 to avoid a deliberate argumentati to avoid a deliberate argumentative
5487 poly carbonate sandwiched stacked poly carbonate sandwiched stacked circuit board on ply board technology
5488 private and commerce satellite re private and commerce satellite rental times rental public satellite service
5489 state and local satellite share t state and local satellite share times shared government satellite service
5490 how to opt out of their conventio how to opt out of their convention and still have a smile on our faces a monetary stipulation and land ownership terms and correctives in a tentative agreement that states thing in our terms and conditions at war and any such give means to attack as well
5491 how to loose a war is to follow t how to loose a war is to follow their rules and drop flowers instead of bombs when flowers don't work drop bombs
5492 how to realize irrational thinkin how to realize irrational thinking for an irrational person or group of people war drug part two
5493 physeometric prediction data clou physeometric prediction data cloud by a group of servers or information structure that houses a secluded or open system of predictions for the information that bases it's self on predictive measures of experimental operations with or with out committing t
5494 physeometric prediction data clou physeometric prediction data cloud a group of servers or information structure that houses a secluded or open system of predictions for the information that bases it's self on predictive measures of experimental operations with or with out committing to t
5495 physeometric prediction by energy physeometric prediction by energy signal wave measures in scales of negative as well as positive may be used in any predictive computational data analytic such as to say that with a known and given there could be any such physeometric prediction of applie
5496 physeometric prediction energy si physeometric prediction energy signal wave measures in scales of negative as well as positive may be used in any predictive computational data analytic such as to say that with a known and given there could be any such physeometric prediction of applied s
5497 scholastic aptitude testing like scholastic aptitude testing like comparisons gone wild schematics of a interwoven statistical cloud scholastic aptitude testing like comparisons gone wild schematics of a interwoven statistical cloud and when variables are compared using normal clients as
5498 starch energy signal wave by star starch energy signal wave by starch wave energy signal is the measure of energy that attracts or repels any such one starch to and from each other in a energy force in any size obvious or microscopic force of annotative fixation including or excluding rea
5499 starch energy signal wave starch starch energy signal wave starch wave energy signal is the measure of energy that attracts or repels any such one starch to and from each other in a energy force in any size obvious or microscopic force of annotative fixation including or excluding reacti
5500 carbon energy signal wave by carb carbon energy signal wave by carbon wave energy signal is the measure of energy that attracts or repels any such one oxide or other metal to

and from each other in a energy force in any size obvious or microscopic force of annotative fixation including or

5501 carbon energy signal wave carbon carbon energy signal wave carbon wave energy signal is the measure of energy that attracts or repels any such one oxide or other metal to and from each other in a energy force in any size obvious or microscopic force of annotative fixation including or ex

5502 gasses energy signal wave by gas gasses energy signal wave by gas wave energy signal is the measure of energy that attracts or repels any such one gas or other gasses to and from each other in a energy force in any size obvious or microscopic force of annotative fixation including or exc

5503 gasses energy signal wave gas wav gasses energy signal wave gas wave energy signal is the measure of energy that attracts or repels any such one gas or other gasses to and from each other in a energy force in any size obvious or microscopic force of annotative fixation including or exclud

5504 carbon by metallic energy signal carbon by metallic energy signal force is the wave of energy that attracts or repels any such one carbon away and from each other in a radio magnetic force in any size obvious or microscopic force of annotative fixation including or excluding reactive pro

5505 inverted gas sorting and reclaimi inverted gas sorting and reclaiming recycled incineration gasses by way of catalytic converter and gas humidifier for or only with a unique dry or paste wet solvent clay and the processes that make taking trash and turning it into rock or solvent sludge a

5506 dry solvent clay and the processe dry solvent clay and the processes that make taking trash and turning it into rock and making electricity as well as reclaimable minerals gases and metals by way of incineration and sort magnetizing

5507 solvent sludge and the processes solvent sludge and the processes that make taking trash and turning it into sludge and making electricity as well as reclaimable minerals gases and metals by way of incineration and sort magnetizing

5508 msata electronics form factor add msata electronics form factor add on graphics enhancement processors

5509 msata electronics form factor add msata electronics form factor add on computational enhancement processors

5510 m electronics form factor add on m electronics form factor add on graphics computational enhancement processors

5511 stable fuse (theoretical separate stable fuse (theoretical separated chain reaction fuse)

5512 m electronics form factor add on m electronics form factor add on computational enhancement processors

5513 probability statistics in everyda probability statistics in everyday perspective dimensions with cubed and annotative physics

5514 predictive computations in triple predictive computations in triplet pi d focus ranges optical and virtual focus calculations and equilibrium annotations for use in any situation

5515 triplet pi d focus ranges optical triplet pi d focus ranges optical and virtual focus calculations and equilibrium annotations for use in cloud scenarios and mobile devices

5516 solar energy generating stickers solar energy generating stickers per window panel with circuits inside or linked storage

5517 open software building platform c open software building platform cloud cloud software building platform cloud that adds and trades certain processes for a non monetary value and immanent non commercial release final options
5518 open software building platform c open software building platform cloud by cloud software building platform cloud that adds and trades certain processes for a non monetary value and immediate non commercial release final options
5519 open software building platform c open software building platform cloud cloud software building platform cloud that adds and trades certain processes for a non monetary value and immediate non commercial release final options
5520 promise software building platfor promise software building platform cloud promise cloud software building platform cloud that adds and trades certain processes for a monetary value and commercial release final options
5521 promise software building platfor promise software building platform cloud by promise cloud software building platform cloud that adds and trades certain processes for a monetary value and immediate commercial release final options
5522 promise software building platfor promise software building platform cloud promise cloud software building platform cloud that adds and trades certain processes for a monetary value and immediate commercial release final options
5523 extended belling vertical sd chip extended belling vertical sd chip stack
5524 device transferable operating sys device transferable operating system platform a platform operating system that adapts to the hardware at supply and negotiates the devices properties easily
5525 condensation water generator on a condensation water generator on a condensation water farm the help we need is in cooling and heating the air itself to generate water where there may be a lack of water and more oxygen than happy a large scale condensation factory
5526 static ssd hard drives with expan static ssd hard drives with expandable states
5527 static sd hard drives with expand static sd hard drives with expandable states
5528 condensation water farms the help condensation water farms the help we need is in cooling and heating the air itself to generate water where there may be a lack of water and more oxygen than happy a large scale condensation factory
5529 exterior bios library co existing exterior bios library co existing bios library adjustments submissive profile programmable adjustments in a vague code and hardware environment to aid in a stand along software and hardware solution that makes a large section of add along configurations p
5530 stand along systems software a co stand along systems software a complimentary system in a shape portable or flash matters that make bios a symbiotic relationship in a organism and computational theme of improvement and error free computing
5531 stand along systems hardware a co stand along systems hardware a complimentary system in a shape portable or flash matters that make bios a symbiotic relationship in a organism and computational theme of improvement and error free computing
5532 processed optical energy and the processed optical energy and the things that equal a light to energy including a building with transparent solar liquid crystal panels windows on the outside and the intent to make electricity transparent solar power generating windows
5533 processed optical energy and the processed optical energy and the things that equal a light to energy including a dynamic electrode receiving liquid crystal panel and the intent to

make electricity by sharing and sending and repeating

5534 compact active performance softwa compact active performance software a disposable update to isolated systems and the intent to improve performance or add alternate software with out online update

5535 a disposable update to isolated s a disposable update to isolated systems and the intent to improve performance and remove virus or add alternate software with out online update

5536 sata mini add on compute module b sata mini add on compute module by size sata that adds to the computational ability to a system

5537 sata mini add on compute module a sata mini add on compute module a module in size sata that adds to the computational ability to a system

5538 sata mini add on compute module s sata mini add on compute module size sata that adds to the computational ability to a system

5539 cylindrical rotations with hour g cylindrical rotations with hour glass shaped impact

5540 pi co nano micro scale reverse sc pi co nano micro scale reverse scenario of heat and size rationality when the size doesn't make sense to make it that small and making multiple on board integrated circuits and cpu per system and the process of material being of more importance such as po

5541 pi co circuit pico layer chip and pi co circuit pico layer chip and circuit building segmented layers and connecting ends from bottom to upper layer for stacking interior with poly carb ceramic insulation and poly oxide metal as conducting circuits with power and wear as consideration f

5542 pi co circuit with poly carb cera pi co circuit with poly carb ceramic insulation and poly oxide metal as conducting circuits with power and wear as consideration for measuring the entire tension and properties of laser made engraving by plasma soldering yielding and melting

5543 tension strength of electrical cu tension strength of electrical currents in a pico nano space for connections transistors and breakers making a bridge into the future of computing and printed circuit boards with a open closed signal holding minimal power allotted

5544 a value conductor that measures o a value conductor that measures of a wave of electricity being a nano capacity electric signals when the wave of electricity meanders into a tip of a needle to move the vector relationships by way of nano gigawave

5545 a half value conductor that measu a half value conductor that measures half of a wave of electricity being a nano capacity electric signals when the wave of electricity meanders into a tip of a needle to move the vector relationships by way of nano gigawave

5546 na no capacity electric signals w na no capacity electric signals when the wave of electricity meanders into a tip of a needle to move the vector relationships by way of nano gigawave

5547 private on demand technology comp private on demand technology companies a company that forms any such supply built from a design that originates with out or with corporate proprietary ship and sells that with a demand for an outcome

5548 public for hire on demand technol public for hire on demand technology companies a company that forms any such supply built from a design that originates with out or with corporate proprietary ship and sells that with a demand for an outcome

5549 cloud probabilities in turn concl cloud probabilities in turn concluding any real life example situation into a consequence cloud for example the process of lend and borrow the process of land and take off the process of any registration set into a faster method with any such correspondin

5550 cloud data security software is a cloud data security software is a method of protecting the future with technology by foreseeing the attention of progress and code modifications including the methods in place now and the possibilities in the future of what and will be a method to conside

5551 chemical searing internal process chemical searing internal process and reactions inherit water activated medicine

5552 end coordinate known vector board end coordinate known vector board circuit path regiment and processing boosters an end coordinate inside the terms of use of a vector board and vector conducting boards that sends signals to the circuits that make the path of processing from chip to chip

5553 open data statistics offering to open data statistics offering to provide a starting point to compare data and the use of its properties to compare to another or any other way of stats

5554 a hardware mass array of cloud st a hardware mass array of cloud statistics and numerical estimations for one cloud to any other cloud

5555 intersecting diagonal and perpend intersecting diagonal and perpendicular circuit threads by vector resolution chips

5556 exchange chip stilts with data pr exchange chip stilts with data processing calculating rise and run to make inside circuits happen and connecting super fine cable gold lines and repeating octagon chip inside chips and vector resolution chips and conducting boards

5557 exchange chip stilts with data pr exchange chip stilts with data processing calculating rise and run to make inside circuits happen and connecting super fine cable gold lines and repeating octagon chip inside chips and vector resolution chips

5558 chip stilts with data processing chip stilts with data processing calculating rise and run to make inside circuits happen and connecting super fine cable gold lines

5559 interval chip stilts with data br interval chip stilts with data bridges to efi

5560 chip stilts form factor to stand chip stilts form factor to stand up chips in any vertical fashion and add a plural height to perform cooling and or data exchange

5561 conceptual prose and the intent t conceptual prose and the intent to invent a time frame of any sort always carries a way of speech and sort of accentuation if you will the time frame of any given state of art is to generally gain a conceptual prose of a given time frame

5562 two separate processors that are two separate processors that are equal and octet each on their own capacity

5563 its a lot like a nuclear bomb onl its a lot like a nuclear bomb only in reverse instead of destroying elements we are putting them together but more important than a super spontaneous collision we are separating the elements for recycling and purification the muffler and the past cata bu

5564 conceptual conclusion diagrams an conceptual conclusion diagrams and acceptable means to what translates into a function or a thing and mixes and matches with proper context a diagram legend that translates by name and intuition

5565 single ssd chip module board that single ssd chip module board that stacks easily into a plural ssd board system and controls with striping and stacking co processing in a chain reactive board configuration

5566 single sd chip module board that single sd chip module board that stacks easily into a plural sd board system and controls with striping and stacking co processing in a chain reactive board configuration

5567 local government security bots to local government security bots to protect and serve with the intent to find and seek searching local criminal data through the internet using web bots

5568 cloud data security software is a cloud data security software is a method of protecting the future with technology

5569 school student information secure school student information secure data protection is a method of protecting the future of learning with technology

5570 future of protected and eula soft future of protected and eula software and the concurrent topics that it will hold such as free operation times and non subscription updates

5571 future of less open software and future of less open software and the concurrent topics that it will hold such as fee based operation times and subscription updates

5572 technology leasing and propagatin technology leasing and propagating specialists is a monetary program based on profit and recovery from the manufacturers post attributes

5573 company incentives for recycling company incentives for recycling technology is a monetary program based on weight and recovery from the local and federal government

5574 manipulative personality disorder manipulative personality disorder is a selfish and greedy property in low importance comparison to exceptional sanctity

5575 knowing the difference painting a knowing the difference painting any way you like and knowing the difference

5576 state of our art is never a const state of our art is never a constant so to make a platform as on the fly as possible would be the the greatest advancing scale ever to make an engineering system that makes your service in a virtual environment and sale rate increase with redesign proposi

5577 computational predictive ultra vi computational predictive ultra violet sorting biochemical studies in cures for cancer and virtual new materials

5578 computational predictive plasma s computational predictive plasma sorting lapidary alchemy studies in cures for cancer and virtual new materials

5579 automated atomic blood testing ma automated atomic blood testing machine using alternate scales of sodium and sugar as well as nitrate chlorides to an extreme scale

5580 atomic blood testing using altern atomic blood testing using alternate scales of sodium and sugar as well as nitrate chlorides

5581 anything over the internet cell t anything over the internet cell towers resident and roaming services subscribed wireless signals and encrypted channels small aoi small local repeaters boxes that drive this internet forward faster than as expected a local and less populous needs for a ut

5582 anything over the internet cell t anything over the internet cell towers resident and roaming services subscribed wireless signals and encrypted channels repeater towers that drive this internet forward faster than as expected a local and populous need

5583 off shore ocean current centrifug off shore ocean current centrifugal force electric generator farms as opposed to land locked wind mills this would be a dedicated area of operations

5584 magnetized ions in a transformer magnetized ions in a transformer capacitor in a generated sequence of order

5585 off shore ocean current electric off shore ocean current electric generator farms as opposed to land locked wind mills this would be a dedicated area of operations
5586 off shore ocean current electric off shore ocean current electric generators as opposed to land locked wind mills
5587 static electric poly oxide metal static electric poly oxide metal using electricity to mold many oxidized metals back to a combined metal making a new metal
5588 switch book operation switch book operation
5589 switch book operation a non accou switch book operation a non account related platform system is a device sensitive memory working horse that transfers accounts
5590 plasma pressurized poly oxide met plasma pressurized poly oxide metal using plasma pressure to mold many oxidized metals back to a combined metal making a new inexpensive metal
5591 commercial cloud separated commer commercial cloud separated commerce and public pay for cloud service encryption values from logical to high performance situations of taxes transfers and payments who what and where
5592 governmental cloud separated stat governmental cloud separated state and federal cloud service encryption values from logical to high performance situations of traffic to water control to records of who what and where
5593 ethanol nitrogen fuel ethanol nitrogen fuel
5594 poly nitrate oxide ethanol carbon poly nitrate oxide ethanol carbonate
5595 sub scalable sd branches and tree sub scalable sd branches and trees
5596 synthetic pressurized gas turbine synthetic pressurized gas turbine to generate electricity
5597 synthetic natural conventional no synthetic natural conventional non associated gas a substance that may be clean burning and easy to make synthetic pressured gas
5598 one chip board multiple function one chip board multiple function platforms in solid state matter
5599 linking cpu interchange is a link linking cpu interchange is a linking secondary support cpu
5600 embedded hyper threading printed embedded hyper threading printed circuits in a measured solid state board
5601 embedded hyper threading printed embedded hyper threading printed circuits in a measured capacity that relates to cascading increments
5602 a transverse capacitor that calcu a transverse capacitor that calculates and compresses at the same time
5603 neutral performing laser to move neutral performing laser to move and work with out damage and neutral force
5604 optical data rate photon transfor optical data rate photon transformer
5605 poly carbonate sandwiched stacked poly carbonate sandwiched stacked optical circuit board on ply board technology
5606 simple est is a solar cell phone simple est is a solar cell phone re charger my airplane crashed and lets say i m stranded who would i call first solar cell phone re charger
5607 computer controlled negative and computer controlled negative and positive and neutral laser and energy matter compensations
5608 programmable medical surgery robo programmable medical surgery robotics by way

of na no wave energy weight focus scope medical surgery device by way of laser and energy matter compensations
5609 life by dead virus by way of na n life by dead virus by way of na no wave radio signals to kill a virus and make an anti virus by way of very small radio waves
5610 matter mining by way of na no wav matter mining by way of na no wave radio signals find the element and save that element or to create more elements
5611 translation virtual predictive de translation virtual predictive density matter to measure and estimate the outcome of any two forms of energy together in one equation or software platform to create new and exciting forms of medicine and energy by functioning heat chemical compound or a c
5612 density and amplitude energy char density and amplitude energy chart scale a energy chart with amplitude and density comparable to the chemical elements diagram with consideration for gas solids and chemical compounds as well as their reaction to one another
5613 energy weight focus scope to weig energy weight focus scope to weigh the energy in a focal point with energy density and amplitude
5614 build a script portable calculato build a script portable calculator a calculator device that instead of only numerical sums it builds a computational script to make bios and other interesting things that would other wise take a very long time
5615 centralized satellite control net centralized satellite control network governmental private
5616 biochemical deceased viral librar biochemical deceased viral library a study of living from the reversed immunization of virus properties and the work of today tomorrow and the future making medicine a thing on the shelf
5617 theology of basic wrongs done rig theology of basic wrongs done right question and concept part grand challenges explorations application theology of basic wrongs done right when i go to the bm gates foundation website i see africans i see you asking for some k
5618 space territory political rights space territory political rights the agreement option to register any given orbit free realm to patrol or gather records of information and scientific findings important to human survival and communication
5619 automated robotics in space to el automated robotics in space to eliminate the human space factor and automate the sequences of working robotics in space such as extended stay time and removal of life support systems as well as to incorporate remote control actives and war information and
5620 war ship satellite a self support war ship satellite a self supported nuclear powered satellite that pilots like drones and may re enter the atmosphere and disperse again into the atmosphere at our control with translation receiving and sending information that holds a scale as of a self
5621 information satellite that pilots information satellite that pilots like drones and may re enter the atmosphere and disperse again into the atmosphere at our control with translation receiving and sending information that holds a scale as of a self sufficient server cloud satellite a self
5622 super embedding board technology super embedding board technology using quartered circuits and fractal inverse technology making boards flat and embedding while conducting in one motion with out attaching
5623 computer aided nerve sciences to computer aided nerve sciences to register what nerve

sends and collects what with a nano scope using computer navigated control finding nerves in an optical focused laser infrared camera and thermos scope

5624 making software a virtual hardwar making software a virtual hardware controller virtual compromises in memory cores and threads memory that holds software permanently

5625 successful data sharing perceptua successful data sharing perceptual image ocr codes and translation scripts and security file extending import export applications support and help

5626 optical fiber paths and boards th optical fiber paths and boards that use lens motors optical motors and optic conductors in conjunction with a optical cpu making electrons differently than an ion more sort of a ee on

5627 personal freedom to drive makes m personal freedom to drive makes me think that taking cars and making trains out of them is against my freedom

5628 to search for a topic with an ima to search for a topic with an image to find people places and things with input from meta tags such as technical terms when where who and why as well as to modify the photo scan or topic by perspective date and angle using the image itself and the topic t

5629 the light age of board technology the light age of board technology layered fiber optical computer boards heat resistant and accessible to carbon fiber

5630 we build your cloud service archi we build your cloud service architects engineers software hardware and applications architects engineers global functions of cloud server storage and the medium that powers that service incorporated with small large and desktop applications with input and

5631 build your own cloud service soft build your own cloud service software hardware and applications global functions of cloud server storage and the medium that powers that service incorporated with small large and desktop applications with input and control to manage your own stack of serv

5632 un formulated alien text formats un formulated alien text formats to create a un known and previously illegible type text to keep data secure said a un known character symbol set that will translate into some thing as known to the other receiver

5633 encrypted phone software transmit encrypted phone software transmitting and receiving key's and the new enigma generator

5634 encrypted phone number transmitti encrypted phone number transmitting and receiving key's and the new enigma generator

5635 inspiration to grow your business inspiration to grow your business when you decide to have another baby inspiration when little families become big business or rather when big business becomes a bigger family a simple question to ponder over and when two things are made so special it mak

5636 to avoid another war use diplomat to avoid another war use diplomatic monetary incentives and resources or not always state your political agenda

5637 organ cell symbiosis cloning and organ cell symbiosis cloning and replacement organs to grow two cells into a new organ for kidney patients caner cures and bio organic failures or positives

5638 big data creative data engineers big data creative data engineers compliant hardware client requests ability software wreck less replacement exceptions speed in control using test and server strength to encrypt and control critical cohesion products and services of any kind

5639 big data creative data engineers big data creative data engineers software client requests terms and permissions rules and exceptions reply response using terms and conditions as well as requests and permissions to translate into real life data arrangements (banking flight control traffi

5640 brain temperature and intelligenc brain temperature and intelligence is the temperature related to intelligence or is intelligence only hereditary

5641 build a software platform you sub build a software platform you submit the size shape and means and function and go play

5642 build a toy platform you submit t build a toy platform you submit the size shape and means and function and go play

5643 a free or sale community secure o a free or sale community secure or friendly web source connections community web

5644 data archive retail pack keeping data archive retail pack keeping the pack a retail matter when time does matter

5645 real web part encryption phone ch real web part encryption phone channel a web connection that is a retail and local web that processes alternate connections like credit cards and other information like medical records and bank transactions a web that makes real life from day to day a pos

5646 speechless while in love applicat speechless while in love applications that text and how to make it as small as one or two options that have a greater click appeal paraphrase questions with proper context all while scripting speechless while in love applications that text and how to make

5647 real web a web connection that is real web a web connection that is a retail and local web that processes alternate connections like credit cards and other information like medical records and bank transactions a web that makes real life from day to day a positive one with higher restrict

5648 triplet pi translation axis for c triplet pi translation axis for compensation equation sum part travel pi cubed translation axis for a compensation equation sum and path intent software hardware virtual and literal intent to create and estimate any means of anno place in time points of v

5649 three dimensional vector resoluti three dimensional vector resolution fractional format

5650 triplet pi translation axis for c triplet pi translation axis for compensation equation sum part travel pi cubed translation axis for compensation equation sum and path intent software hardware virtual and literal intent to create and estimate any means of anno place in time points of vec

5651 triplet pi translation axis for c triplet pi translation axis for compensation equation sum and path intent

5652 curriculum software for public sc curriculum software for public schools no cloud base or cloud base data schema download and toss media vs intent to recycle and modify in class testing by way of simple send and receive test email like online college with intuitive public school social co

5653 open thread navigational embedded open thread navigational embedded software a software base that controls the method of navigation of a processing thread inside a cpu

5654 more desktop capacity by way of m more desktop capacity by way of modular expansions via mini modular modes non ecc or ecc yes either or intent sell a module to me

and make it bigger make a module chassis and make it better and smaller hot swap able compute modules trans posable tx and sl
5655 a thing called turbo per element a thing called turbo per element that can shape a path where previously there w as no way to reflect perpendicular or parallel with the help of mini and per operation by a stress thesis chip alternate computational curve based algorithms aiding by another
5656 comma separated encryption comma comma separated encryption comma separated encryption another reason is to continue work on a daily basis as intended securely strange brew is only a reason to understand that everyone is csv styled now and excel my microsoft is no reason to degrade the g
5657 hypos thesis chip hypos thesis chip
5658 a thing called turbo per element a thing called turbo per element that can shape a path where previously there w as no way to reflect perpendicular or parallel with the help of mini and per operation by a hypos thesis chip alternate computational curve based algorithms aiding by another c
5659 effervescent mouth wash for serio effervescent mouth wash for serious ailments like headaches bacteria and dizziness caused by oral sickness
5660 alternate size spinning magnetic alternate size spinning magnetic electric generator lord carpenters infinite motion how to put it all together a spinning top is very similar to something you'd like to have fun and stare at forever it w as brought to my attention that there is a need for
5661 no cloud software registration a no cloud software registration a program specific intent to keep the software as is and with out any foreign auto updates and stripped integration from internet interference of opportunity and uela confidence trials of intent to disturb the sleeping softw
5662 pragmatic data clarification who pragmatic data clarification who what where when importance and bi as to easily negotiate the promise of any data platform in this term of versable means the pragmatic translates as universal or non motivational on an agenda basis of improvement to any mea
5663 an elaborate paging hardware syst an elaborate paging hardware system that links processors for a continuous processing group of microchips aligned or complimentary in any similarity that forms an accessible shape of a shed family hardware to add cores to a group of processing cores and
5664 an elaborate paging software syst an elaborate paging software system that links processors for a continuous processing group of microchips dealing or complimentary in any similarity that forms an accessible shape of a shed family software
5665 an elaborate paging software syst an elaborate paging software system that links processors for a continuous processing group of microchips aligned or complimentary in any similarity that forms an accessible shape of a shed family software
5666 dominate server cloud a path to c dominate server cloud a path to communicate with other devices using the identity of which one is passive and which one is the dominate one why you could borrow a phone or buy a new one at a moments notice and hold the things like number and email address
5667 its a fact of life that to be pro its a fact of life that to be propelled into a un fair and non respect form of work is not only detrimental and confusing to the artist it degrades the work

and makes the artist suffer from the beginning the un derground of house and techno makes what we

5668 the infinite motion inside the fi the infinite motion inside the first sphere is made by all the rest of the batteries recharging the original battery inside the only thing missing (magnetic electricity generating) is the method to recharge a battery with the least amount of connections f

5669 dominate media a path to communic dominate media a path to communicate with other devices using the identity of which one is passive and which one is the dominate one why you could borrow a phone or buy a new one at a moments notice and hold the things like number and email address as wel

5670 a habit release agent to marijuan a habit release agent to marijuana abuse patch pill gum

5671 a habit release agent to alcohol a habit release agent to alcohol abuse patch pill gum

5672 rearranged tetrahedral amorphous rearranged tetrahedral amorphous carbon with abstract particle matching to reconstituted energy sp forms diamond (cubic) lonsdaleite (hexagonal diamond) sp forms graphite graphene fullerenes (buckminsterfullerene c higher fullerenes nanotubes nanobu

5673 educational in class os education educational in class os educational operating system with intent to block virus and provide a safe computation platforms for age and course specific apps educational cloud system and pre built selects for real time issue management using technology and re

5674 synthetic liquid plastic ester an synthetic liquid plastic ester and carbon soot energy in a single compound to make a combustible energy (incinerator bi products and alcohol acids)

5675 digital shelf price display for r digital shelf price display for real time updates from a msrp cloud stored planed and adjustable by demands something that would make a sale pre customer and availability

5676 digital shelf price display for r digital shelf price display for real time updates from a msrp cloud

5677 minimum sale retail price cloud a minimum sale retail price cloud and pre built selects for real time issue management using technology and real life scenarios to aid in the life of every day

5678 amplitude measurement infinity an amplitude measurement infinity and other infinities all makes for an artificial intelligence with some or less than a real opinion for itself but more a suggestion of what we could do and how it should be done

5679 war management satellite ground c war management satellite ground cloud and pre built selects for real time issue management using technology and real life scenarios to aid in the life of every day a target compensation b friendly non targets c aggressive mission d defensive mission

5680 air bound traffic cloud and pre b air bound traffic cloud and pre built selects for real time issue management using technology and real life scenarios to aid in the life of every day a to place b from place

5681 syndicated media news cloud and p syndicated media news cloud and pre built selects for real time issue management using technology and real life scenarios to aid in the life of every day a selling and registration b station receptions c blocking and censors

5682 police cloud and pre built select police cloud and pre built selects for real time issue management using technology and real life scenarios to aid in the life of every day a most

wanted b history crimes c issues present past
5683 traffic cloud and pre built selec traffic cloud and pre built selects for real time issue management using technology and real life scenarios to aid in the life of every day a synchronicity b path of popular traffic c safety management
5684 a software program that will gene a software program that will generate code for external un sorted efi batches to route any computations needed
5685 when vector computations are need when vector computations are needed there should be a precise meaning to every curve like the way pre selected sorts are generated size how many tall and wide as well as per space intensity xyz
5686 acute nicotine narcosis is th acute nicotine narcosis is the long term unstable inherit reaction to a continual overdose of nicotine
5687 nicotine narcosis is the unst nicotine narcosis is the unstable inherit reaction to an overdose of nicotine
5688 under and over stacked layered under and over stacked layered blanks for writing purpose and laying the path to write the functions with software innate locking and pressing together
5689 another cloud cycle to invent another cloud cycle to invent concept the difference of deep blue was that it wasn t considered a cloud at the time. the focus was only on the game and the server itself. this isn t the focus of what the azure is. windows will now carry on as usual... wel
5690 wireless machine adapters and p wireless machine adapters and personal wireless comps with routers mini cloud invent more deposition is here think of a dream and add sugar a technology gadget that removes wires and picks up a signal of your own link something that we could benefit and p
5691 [time and light measure ment + [time and light measure ment + stair case mirror chips] (optical mathematic weight and scale by calculations and common studies)
5692 under and over layered blanks under and over layered blanks for writing purpose and laying the path to write the functions with software innate
5693 intent to remove cuna cun intent to remove cuna cuna chemistry topic of another part how to charge an element using the nasa nevada experimental rail way? why would you bother them and what it means to the rest of us. i think it's best put as a set charge accelerator... a question of when and not if. there is hope but sometimes we need to take a guess and then the faults will occur. valence (chemistry) from wikipedia valence
5694 cloud cycle to invent concept cloud cycle to invent concept the difference of deep blue was that it wasn t considered a cloud at the time. the focus was only on the game and the server itself. this isn t the focus of what the azure is. windows will now carry on as usual... welcome to
5695 argon or hydrogen plasma chip argon or hydrogen plasma chip etching by neon on rhodium bedding under and over layered chip printing all or parts
5696 retro fit industrial truck tra retro fit industrial truck transmission attached axle line rotary electrical generator for part time hybrid trucks and long haulers with batteries or storage of current
5697 cuna cuna next chemistry cuna cuna next chemistry topic of another part invent deposition a few questions and what to expect how to charge an element using the nasa nevada experimental rail way why would you bother them and what it means to the res

5698 to compare an initial altair to compare an initial altair to tomorrows lcus it s as though there is no difference in new super computer. the assumption that all wheel drive is like four wheel drive only all the time in a balanced formation of code.
5699 introduce the world to the lar introduce the world to the largest topical cause is my first and foremost mission
5700 to admit that the united state to admit that the united states narcotic problem would be easier to overcome would be anti marijuana gateway drug lock down to prepare for a conclusive issue of illegal status of drug use look into the past problems and sue the president for his veto of t
5701 digit treasury to track tax digit treasury to track taxes and terrorist threats
5702 with the mass of complicated with the mass of complicated ports there should be a uniform port of snap in with pin play and align to the left scenario like a find and play plug and play device that may be useful for upcoming devices and experimental utilities yet unknown.
5703 a means to raid activate each a means to raid activate each level for accuracy.
5704 private narcotic information a private narcotic information agency is the proposal of an entity that would watch record and track illegal narcotics in an important information tracking module of police and protection for the greater good of mankind
5705 codex to diametric two opposin codex to diametric two opposing ideas that form a scientific outcome in computer analytical methods two concepts to measure it all codex to dielectrics. two opposing ideas that form a scientific outcome in computer analytical methods. to have codex applications and human interfaces which make all things essentially equal in to opposite ways like reverse outcome process/negative cell theory please use diode metrics algebras (to the technology makers there is a point of two or more operating systems to understand yet there is the world of sales that makes what we buy genetically similar.) inter science open app (technology called they want their biology book back) dielectrics computer theory(a system must detect and respond? comments of codes and conferences also known as valency or valency number is a measure of the number of chemical bonds formed by the atoms of a given element. over the last century the concept of valence evolved into a range of approaches for describing the chemical bond including lewis structures ( ) valence bond theory ( ) molecular orbitals ( ) valence shell electron pair repulsion theory ( ) and all the advanced methods of quantum chemistry. from wikipedia the free encyclopedia is the natural number following and preceding . since = + + = it is the smallest cube that's also the sum of three cubes (plato was among the first to notice this and mentioned it in book viii of republic). it is also the sum of a twin prime (+). but since there is no way to express it as the sum of the proper divisors of any other integer it is an untouchable number. this multiplicative magic square has magic constant . in base it is a harshad number. there are fixed hexominoes the polynomials made from squares. is a friedman number
5706 segmented lean processing cop segmented lean processing
5707 ethernet fixed raid to have a ethernet fixed raid to have an ethernet with multiple raid fixes per connected units. using a raid modified ethernet router.
5708 i am not referring to my fans i am not referring to my fans... here you are allowed to come back and download as much as you wish... to be specific the newest type of stalker is someone you know (or do not) that watches and stalks as you do not wish. people with probable cause not inc

5709 to publicly render the presid to publicly render the president petitionally un available for office
5710 what were they thinking what w what were they thinking what were they thinking does everything have to have a microchip inside things i just don t want to happen
5711 to include two computers in a to include two computers in a sense of permanence. complete with software and hardware options and tickets of operation as well as ip address.
5712 to initiate an add on applica to initiate an add on application different than a program but more over a specific add on to compliment code in a sense of script and all while not having a apparent app face formula. a thing to call love and work with and seemingly be the same as child
5713 many other countries use the many other countries use the us dollar. to equate a hypothesis is to generate a revenue inside it s self. the dollar bill with country intent for example a widget country denominated dollar with gold / silver / property / resource note.
5714 any such right as to investig any such right as to investigate and with plausible cause to search for a missing person upon any premise. with unique attributes justified by law holding contrary existing census information and legitimate rights of distrust or suspicion why the things made it fall from popularity may at times be opinion or merely poetical justice. what goes up must come down. to translate the simple things in business are always from intuition. to hire people with positive ethical spirit and attitude is the most important thing to start with.
5715 it s true that there is a pop it s true that there is a popular accent in america tv and the spread of a californian accent across the united states of america is the new pink.
5716 to protect the small glitches to protect the small glitches and malfunctions of any surge from sensitive and expensive trips breaks and surges of electricity to protect the most valuable devices.
5717 the need to place secure the need to place secure socket layers into place with a packet flaw prerequisite. to speak plainly a packet is requested from the server. the server sends a packet first with the completed file information backwards with weight and scale then loads t
5718 this is a needed attempt at m this is a needed attempt at making real circumstances translatable into real terms of useful objects. for example if the code says up this could mean literal or non relative terms
5719 official branch of news for th official branch of news for the government and legalities and suits with holdings and returns
5720 bandwagon effect from wikiped bandwagon effect from wikipedia the free encyclopedia jump to: navigation search the bandwagon effect is a well documented form of group think in behavioral science and has many applications. the general rule is that conduct or beliefs spread among people
5721 serial artwork number or swan serial artwork number or swan to register and official works of a group of artwork printed or raw data sets for future reference and worth including any given details of certifications.
5722 outdoor hot and cold climates outdoor hot and cold climates need processing let s imagine that there could be a cup with a microchip inside it after all... open processors and the instance of virtual to real time applicable things like traffic flow energy systems police dispatch and
5723 plastic layered electronic mi plastic layered electronic micro board a process defined

with nano printing circuits and layers of layers of circuitry that provides depth into height of computing capabilities or alternate poly carbonate / carbonate porous compounds

5724 immune systemic insulin. insu immune systemic insulin. insulin medicine to magistrate through the auto immune system immune systemic insulin. insulin medicine to magistrate through the auto immune system insulin main article: insulin therapy type diabetes is typically treated with a combinations of regular and nph insulin a longacting formulation is usually added initially

5725 satellite communication amp a satellite communication amp aoip the communication amp is not only for talking and voip but a entertainment and communication all over internet protocol amplifier/map.

5726 {to use a non primal number i {to use a non primal number is the in and out of a circuit... if to use a prime number the sum must have a divisible cube root.} which verses and changes in terms and may be exchangeable. factorization: ** ** ** ** divisors:

5727 atomic qubit library and ann atomic qubit library and annotation of transistorized molecular instructions

5728 a= / bh/a=pi r ^+. . a= / bh/a=pi r ^+. . is versable in terms

5729 magnified optical etching is magnified optical etching is a unique method of point and burn processor production of magnified focal processor

5730 photon fractal math which and photon fractal math which and where rgb

5731 a simple dividing trigger for a simple dividing trigger for electronic and dividing transistors inside a circuit path.

5732 crystallized mother board the crystallized mother board the intent to reactivate a flower for a shape for extended central processing units and the possibilities to multiply and agitate the growth of a unit into more than one units a flower verses in terms. the intent to reactivate a root system for a shape specifically extending the circuits and the possibilities to multiply and agitate the growth of a unit into more than one units. (a plant root verses in terms) in unison to fractal function organize a mother board to the interest for d printing and layer sorting a glass insulated board that would form a recyclable product worth going and building .... building a small flower

5733 the intent to reactivate a fl the intent to reactivate a flower for a shape for extended central processing units and the possibilities to multiply and agitate the growth of a unit into more than one units a flower verses in terms. search nanohub.org is science cyberinfrastructure[ ] comprising communitycontributed resources and geared toward educational applications professional networking and interactive simulation tools for nanotechnology. funded by the national science foundation (nsf) it is a product of the network for computational nanotechnology (ncn) a multiuniversity initiative of eight member institutions including purdue university the university of california at berkeley the university of illinois at urbana campaign the molecular foundry at lawrence berkeley national laboratory norfolk state university northwestern university and the university of texas at el paso. ncn was established to create a resource for nanoscience and nanotechnology via online services for research education and professional collaboration. ncn supports research efforts in nanoelectronics nano electormechanical systems or nems nanofluidics nanomedicine/ biology and nanophotonics.

5734 glass (or poly carbonate) ins glass (or poly carbonate) insulated gold line wire housing. needed to stack motherboards and double or more the capacity of the vertical possibilities

inside that manner. as opposed to a silicon board this would connect boards to one another.
5735 out put computers are a metho out put computers are a method of creation out put computers are a method of creation that people need to make things. i have decided to claim this as a separate market of intent for improvement in usability and justification of my means. there are currently confusing situations in reading or writing platforms. i think that the server of today is the workstation that people dream of making and creating content... although a blog may be ingenious looping music videos and so on. yet the people who divide their time such as myself to create content get stuck with apps that are rubbish. if only it were as simple as pointing a finger and saying don't make it harder to use while making it easier to read... i want my pc to make my dreams come true again and out put this painting of life together with . ghz yes and a teraflop of coprocessing! like number said i need more input!!!
5736 encrypted phone service that i encrypted phone service that is for government to public or government to military or public to government
5737 as well as triangular square as well as triangular square and circular properties such as vertical horizontal and spherical combinations... with two or more in one process. line of sight energy systems police dispatch and flight control situations modified with integers and boolean if's.
5738 chris any words of advice wh chris any words of advice why the company ford motors is doing so well this is a long time coming in the year un known and kept secretive the point is to never take what you can't pay back as you and i both know the government of any country will be as ma
5739 a series of events vector gr a series of events vector graphics the first time i learned how to boot up a computer w as in elementary school and to my dis may it w as a very un exciting moment but luckily we actually had computers in school and it w as in the early eighties! so that was and became the worldwide standard under the second international radio telegraphic convention which was signed on november and became effective on july . sos remained the maritime radio distress signal until when it was replaced by the global maritime distress safety system. [ ] (with this new system in place it became illegal for a ship to signal that she is in distress in morse code. citation needed]) sos is still recognized as a visual distress signal.[] from the beginning the sos distress signal has really consisted of a continuous sequence of threeditz/threedash/threeditz all run together without letter spacing. in international morse code three ditz form the letter s and three dash make the letter o so sos became an easy way to remember the order of the ditz and dash. in modern terminology sos is a morse procedural signal or pro sign and the formal way to write it is with a bar above the letters: sos in popular usage sos became associated with such phrases as save our ship save our souls and send out succor. these may be regarded as mnemonics but sos does not stand for anything and is not an abbreviation acronym or initials. in fact sos is only one of several ways that the combination could have been written vtb for example would produce exactly the same sound but sos was chosen to describe this combination. sos is the only element signal in morse code making it more easily recognizable as no other symbol uses more than elements.
5740 a secured or profitable solu a secured or profitable solution for chip design and acceleration as well as to load and print chip architecture in a printer software interface with a chip writing drive in accordance to a blank solid state synthetic metal processor with socket type pref especially the amygdala likely contribute to poor emotional regulation and

mood symptoms.[ ] according to the kindling hypothesis when people who are genetically predisposed toward bipolar disorder experience stressful events the stress threshold at which mood changes occur becomes progressively lower until the episodes eventually start (and recur) spontaneously. there is evidence of hypothalamipituitaryadrenal axis (hpa axis) abnormalities in bipolar disorder due to stress.[][][][] http://en.wikipedia.org/wiki/bipolar_disorder

5741 blank billets for chip writi blank billets for chip writing drive in accordance to a blank solid state synthetic metal processor with socket type preference for soldering or fusing boards as well as incorporated or replaceable sockets while continuing oral medications.[] doses of insulin are then increased to effect.[] http://en.wikipedia.org/wiki/diabetic

5742 to multiply on local network to multiply on local network os over os under os scenario to multiply on local network os the chances of using two or more under operating systems and concluding it to a working hierarchy of operating system +even or +odd. one hundred and seventyseven thousand seven hundred and twentyfive) is a very special number. the cross sum of is . if you factorize the number you will get these result * * * * . has divisors ( ) which a sum of . is not a prime number. is not a fibonacci number. the conversion of to base (binary) is . the conversion of to base (ternary) is . the conversion of to base (quaternary) is . the conversion of to base (quint) is . the conversion of to base (octal) is . the conversion of to base (hexadecimal) is fd. the conversion of to base is ut. the sine of is.. the cosine of is . . the tangent of is . . the root of is . . i hope that you now know that is an amazing number! properties of number

5743 see saw action synthetic g a see saw action synthetic g as pumping valve electric generation and infinite force fulcrum engine taking a current force and not stopping that energy but making a symbiotic source of energy where one force over comes the other one and repeats one hundred and seventyseven thousand seven hundred and twentyfive) is a very special number. the cross sum of is . if you factorize the number you will get these result ** ** ** ** . has divisors ( ) which a sum of . is not a prime number. is not a fibonacci number. the conversion of to base (binary) is . the conversion of to base (ternary) is . the conversion of to base (quaternary) is . the conversion of to base (quint) is . the conversion of to base (octal) is . the conversion of to base (hexadecimal) is fd. the conversion of to base is ut. the sine of is.. the cosine of is . . the tangent of is . . the root of is . . i hope that you now know that is an amazing number! properties of number

5744 to multiply comments the chan to multiply comments the chances of using two or more mother boards and then working together with what it may hold... there is a point in every computation that will like light transfer to another point and time. every thing is timed... with pi you can measure the distance of any computation from point a to point b with angle circumference and distance. along side this is many different ways to also say also known as valency or valency number is a measure of the number of chemical bonds formed by the atoms of a given element. over the last century the concept of valence evolved into a range of approaches for describing the chemical bond including lewis structures ( ) valence bond theory ( ) molecular orbitals ( ) valence shell electron pair repulsion theory ( ) and all the advanced methods of quantum chemistry.

5745 pi difference a. to b. commen pi difference a. to b. comments there is a point in every computation that will like light transfer to another point and time. every thing is timed... with pi you can measure the distance of any computation from point a to point b with angle

circumference
5746 microwave fuse content text c microwave fuse content text context melting the parts for safety or other means. with a metal and timer similar to a wave generator inside a microwave oven. with military and aero design specifics as well as fuse and exploding instances. micro wave melt switch count of divisors: sum of divisors: prime number? no fibonacci number? no base (binary): base (ternary): base (quaternary): base (quint): base (octal): base (hexadecimal): fd base : ut sin( ). cos( ) . tan( ) . sqrt( ) . http://numberworld.info/ . is " versable in terms"
5747 voluntary / involuntary core voluntary / involuntary core process stop core back user selected modes and bios updates count of divisors: sum of divisors: prime number? no fibonacci number? no base (binary): base (ternary): base (quaternary): base (quint): base (octal): base (hexadecimal): fd base : ut sin( ). cos( ) . tan( ) . sqrt( ) . http://numberworld.info/ . is " versable in terms"
5748 approved small m un itions o approved small m un itions of electric generating stores and subscribers
5749 who really understands better who really understands better than a child trying to kick a ball into the wind it may do this it may do that but what we really need to understand is there are curve anomalies that happen more than we hope that s why it s fun... yet to understand them is
5750 one creative step bridge one creative step bridge parallel modern efficiency content text context parallel (email submission) assumptions of a coprocessing pattern the issue is when will a co processor understand that to full fill one creative step. it's important to duplicate that first step. in this attempt to be creative there are more patterns than the first second and so on. to insure a pattern of non creative circumstance like a pattern and a distinction of a mathematical number such as pi
5751 embedded hyper istic chips a embedded hyper istic chips and processors that hold inside a layer of insulation to connected intermittent silica linking to a printed circuit board printing by stencil layers and photo emulsion plasma bonding over silica to make a connection on a larger
5752 the issue is when will a co p the issue is when will a co processor complimentary on and off as well as different and alternate processing to explain this is to accumulate the circumstances of on and off in a larger picture. to estimate the neurological existence of two halves of our human brain is the essence of why and when this is important... not only to have the power in two halves but to use those two halves to alternate and differentiate the reason to compute... as a logical and scientific method for processing. for example a left and right coprocessors transparent multiple duplicate pattern processing
5753 universal bonding agent par universal bonding agent part that accepts a specified dimension of micro chip for processing or storage etc also known as socket for a socket bonded solder
5754 universal pre measurement b universal pre measurement bonding and solderingthe pre measured circuit socket
5755 universal pre measurement b universal pre measurement bonding and soldering by the pre measured circuit socket
5756 explain this is to accumulate explain this is to accumulate the circumstances this isn't a time device a folder generator that catalogs achieved cd's and cdroms into a folder on a hard

drive flash card or sd and even server related temps. so let's recap an automaton that loads prepares and saves the files music pictures and data to another method of folders and date marks the items. scientific complimentary processing
5757 universal pre measurement b universal pre measurement bonding and soldering the pre measured circuit socket and spherical combinations... with two or more in one process. line of sight as well as to inject gas and form a modulation of image appropriate for television and viewing as such... as well as to combine and properties the human interface with controlled manipulation of direction and spheres as opposed to windows with the infrared detection.
5758 do they put that stuff in the do they put that stuff in the air the chance of the hospital itself being sick is the real issue. like the story goes how do you heal the sick inside a sick place. well there are extremely strong antibiotics and then there are subtle every day antibiotics. my guess is that there could be a scenario that provides a perfect healing environment and therefore is related to unlimited healing possibilities... to make a solution that purifies the air and substitutes a antibiotic supplement in the hospitals and other sick situations. and spherical combinations... with two or more in one process. line of sight as well as to inject gas and form a modulation of image appropriate for television and viewing as such... infrared computer screen human interface manipulation for laser generated d tv
5759 drone launching warship intel drone launching warship intelligent warship is a lifeless battle ship that is an artificial war machine that wins wars defends freedom and kills bad guys can the computer {hardware or software} conduct two or more ions from a micro spark generator and then somehow keep those two ions making switches go off and on while not colliding and at the same time act as a nerve to control the computer as a whole to essentially make a multiion and eventually a multiplying micro spark generator the way that this diagram demonstrates in an abstract transition.
5760 advanced patent law is an ex advanced patent law is an exact and more specific ownership control library of means and ownership of sciences
5761 chip invitational design out chip invitational design outsourcing we print your chip for fees and rights
5762 optical signal break vector optical signal break vector is a broken link detection location of directional optical transition connections are radial shaped to linear shaped optical data signal bridges with pins and replaceable optical connections with incorporating power operators
5763 optical signal break vector optical signal break vector is a broken link detection location of directional optical transition connections are radial shaped to linear shaped optical data signal bridges with pins and replaceable optical connections with incorporating power operat and spherical combinations... with two or more in one process. line of sight
5764 my lzw algorithm isn t free my lzw algorithm isn t free a fee for a free platform is essentially not happening. i invented the pd f and here is my quote. either trust me or don't. the fact of the matter is that like the pokemon there was a puzzle in the equation of how to market the product and make people interested in their service. for the pokemon there was a unique game that was interesting to children
5765 boosting directional optical boosting directional optical transition connections are radial shaped to linear shaped optical data signal bridges with pins and replaceable optical connections with incorporating power operators patent chri
5766 male directional optical tra male directional optical transition connections are radial

shaped to linear shaped optical data signal bridges with pins and replaceable optical connections christopher g
5767 board splice chip optical po board splice chip optical power switch is an alternating signal of a source that changes a function in a stored time for input into a board of calculation christopher
5768 compact optical power supply compact optical power supply is an conducting signal of a source that changes a function in a stored time for input into a board of calculation sub
5769 to seek find and replace rec to seek find and replace recolonize organ specific micro cell stems to seek find replace the celluloid and kill eat or replace that cell or multitude of cells to cure cancers and other age syndromes imm un e deficiencies and or the many diseases that people
5770 optical ram is an embedded f optical ram is an embedded fiber optical conducting signal of nano batteries that display a function in a stored time for input into a board of calculation christopher
5771 fiber embedded processing on fiber embedded processing on sd interupt fiber optical conducting boards and insert cards for processing in a optical environment of computations fiber embedded processing on solid data pcie and also ssd pat
5772 personal computer server pers personal computer server personal server computer re ignite the passion for computing put one foot forward and take two steps back try installing windows eight with a server by intel use as directed and wash twice a day... intel sy
5773 fiber optical conducting boa fiber optical conducting boards and insert cards for processing in a optical environment of computations fiber embedded processing on cpu submitted on
5774 fiber optical conducting boa fiber optical conducting boards and insert cards for processing in a optical environment of computations fiber embedded processing on gpu submitted on
5775 data center and other data d data center and other data driven strategy operations for study gaming software for war data science and real world ai scripted drones submitted o
5776 search by image to search for search by image to search for a topic with an image. to find people places and things. with input from meta tags such as technical terms when where who and why. as well as to modify the photo scan or topic by perspective date and angle using the image its
5777 local and global participati local and global participation in gps d triplet pi ration is the dynamics of location for any known given computeable location submitted on decem
5778 compensation chip compensatio compensation chip compensation chips long processors vs. short and stubby. it s a uniform shape that is divided by and then multiplied with time and hardware mass. so to speak... as well as a long history of previous things such as revisions and other instances like undo data and authors date and other things to pass along the data that may make information archaeologists study how to make more money and or why there was a loss of money. to summarize what i'm thinking of is to make files that have such close code and scripts as well as alternate information added that could be readable by things like for example internet browsers or phone apps.
5779 community future investments community future investments are f un ds for sustainable community management and the deprecation of environmental resources and state of improvements

5780 tired of upgrading key socket tired of upgrading key socket adapter a molding cpu socket adapter that works like clay on a car key in a cool movie. working to accept all patterns. but only all the patterns present

5781 tired of ftp what if i didn t tired of ftp what if i didn t have to do it that way. what if there were new and exciting ways to engage clients data that make and hold more data than usual. for example a cloud that is low to the ground is called fog. files on the ground would make sync

5782 encrypted phone service that i encrypted phone service that is for public

5783 a different way to see busines a different way to see business ethics and personal values actually do make up the person who works for you. and you and i may see eye to eye for once that you don't want a drug user as your warehouse manager so what precautions would you be willing to take? personality or drug tests? to what level can you go to insure that there isn't any problems... to me it seems that the higher the magnitude of company the level of sanctity is to be seen reasonable. i wish right about now i could quote a devils advocate line

5784 formula for thought combinat formula for thought combination formula of commons unique and abnormal the theory is a function of indefinite sums and energy in the mass of that sum with the longevity of that same sum a + m = e (. {} over {}) %uxe a {e} over {m} %uxe b {e%delta ^{}} over {c%delta ^{}} %uxe c{e %ux } over {c%ux }lllint /> %uxe a %uxe d {b %uxe sqrt{b^{}ac} } over {a} %notequal binom{%sigma }binom{{ %uxe b i%uxe b m} }{ < j < n } p (i

5785 electronic us treasury of ba electronic us treasury of banks and commissions is a united states trade bank that works with commercial common banks to control federal trade and electronic f un d transfers of ownership

5786 total year end dividend tradi total year end dividend trading joint stock companies act from wikipedia debate the joint stock companies bill was introduced to parliament by the then vice president of the board of trade mr robert lowe in doing so he proclaimed the right of

5787 a secured public information a secured public information channel for monetary transfers is a specific web application that transfers ownership and f un ds to other banks and balances

5788 intelligent voip s server to intelligent voip s server to point a server instead of a pc to magistrate commas and processes.

5789 synthetic currents to anchor synthetic currents to anchor underwater current makers to a high middle and low temperatures and in the consistent direction to prevent stagnant water and refresh the water in a pond or reservoir. the benefits would be less insects and healthier fish

5790 to give data sending water th to give data sending water through or not to send water. if there were a .rar equal to a need then there would be a need called .raz. to send a .raz into a receiver would be like making a scripted transition to and from a device or line. translated into a

5791 building language software w building language software written by software hardware by as solid state or flash based conductor processor and operator made into a cubit written composite working tool

5792 fiber optic reflective turn fiber optic reflective turn connection in data to let a signal repeat and split in order to go around an object of area

5793 another comparative analogy w another comparative analogy water . water cycle water

data cycle . fresh water storage new data server . sea water world wide data . tides to sync data
5794 spiral fiberoptic splicer d spiral fiberoptic splicer device and the markings that make a reading splicer obtain the proper place in the cable to splice or loop into with precision and accuracy for less signal loss
5795 spiral compound reflective s spiral compound reflective sending out encoder processor that codes reflective signals in fiber optic signals
5796 turning off the virus virus i turning off the virus virus intentions to turn and transform virus intentions to turn and transform the effort of mainline to a true police operating system. to steady the intent and take the means in order to use that code for a positive purpose. for example to hack a hack is to make a bucket full of drinking water instead of used oil. this is accordance with the vague code complex and the intent to run a attack in to a greeting like a knock at the door from an old friend. turning off the virus
5797 spiral compound reflective r spiral compound reflective receiver decoder processor that reads reflective signals in fiber optic signals
5798 the intellectual property ma the intellectual property management office and large document record for keeping trade secrets and patents safe and secured by named ownership
5799 software that makes connecti software that makes connection vectors conductors in pico nano voxel and elemental compounds for chip processing printing in three dimensions
5800 connection vectors and the e connection vectors and the empty space for looped inside linking conductive vector for making a place for conductors in pico nano voxel and elemental compounds for chip processing printing in three dimensions
5801 empty space for looped insid empty space for looped inside linking conductive vector for making a place for conductors in pico nano voxel and elemental compounds for chip processing printing in three dimensions
5802 conductive gold and mineral conductive gold and mineral solvent conductors in a positive pico nano voxel and elemental compound form for three dimensional chip processing printing
5803 non conductive silica solven non conductive silica solvent white space and negative pico nano voxel and elemental compounds for chip processing printing in three dimensions
5804 non conductive and negative non conductive and negative pico nano voxel and elemental compounds for chip processing printing in three dimensions
5805 three ring binder glucose inc three ring binder glucose incubation a computer controlled molecular telescope / nan scope that can insert and impregnate new dna will consequently rebuild the cell. a computer controlled dissection will allow probability of success for great accomplishment
5806 pico nano voxel and elementa pico nano voxel and elemental compounds for chip processing printing
5807 ethel nitrogen oxide fuel di ethel nitrogen oxide fuel diverted natural g as and combined salt
5808 sided computer chip for co sided computer chip for computations and stacking arrangements for chip processing
5809 sided computer chip for co sided computer chip for computations
5810 vertical clamp socket for ch vertical clamp socket for chip
5811 printing materials for perpe printing materials for perpendicular laser printed levels of circuits processors and memory in multiple photo sensitive cured solvents as circuits layers

laser printed chips in a diffused solution to compute as a chip in a series of different elements

5812 a photo reactive multiple el a photo reactive multiple element formula of printing materials for perpendicular laser printed levels of circuits processors and memory in multiple photo sensitive cured solvents as circuits layers laser printed chips in a diffused solution to compute as a chip

5813 perpendicular laser printed perpendicular laser printed levels of circuits processors and memory in multiple photo sensitive cured solvents as circuits layers laser printed chips in a diffused solution to compute as a chip

5814 gaseous carbonized smoke wit gaseous carbonized smoke with solvent and electricity stabilizing the protons and electron particles for fuel and refinery in a electrical ph balance vapor fume tank for making compo un ds medicine and chemicals in a step by step process making a smoke from

5815 laser printed levels of circ laser printed levels of circuits and multiple photo sensitive cured solvents as circuits layers laser printed chips in a diffused solution to compute as a chip

5816 ultra violet laser printed l ultra violet laser printed levels of circuits and multiple uv cured solvents as circuits layers laser printed chips in a diffused solution to compute as a chip

5817 modial comm. a different way modial comm. a different way to ftp to design a ethernet cell or satellite based cell phone application that connects people's phones as pages instead of pages on a server. the main purpose is to communicate and then the other things will gradually fall into place. i think it would be perfect to practice this in the jungles or deserts.

5818 laser printed levels of circ laser printed levels of circuits and multiple cured solvents as circuits layers laser printed chips in a diffused solution to compute as a chip

5819 acid alkaline printed chips acid alkaline printed chips in a diffused solution to compute as a battery on chip

5820 technology aided learning of technology aided learning of the united states should have a privatized level of integration and legal funding for all schools and states learning should be focused on traditional context and should be modernized in a equal way to un ify learning as well a

5821 processor micro circuit batt processor micro circuit battery is a circuit cell that holds current

5822 micro alternating circuit ba micro alternating circuit battery is a circuit that recycles itself with current

5823 ai is named wrong you have t ai is named wrong you have to take more into consideration like the answer not the truth of the question left and right is the asymmetrical processing

5824 a energy center or building a energy center or building with many focused solar generators that reverse reflective tunnel that magnifies the light and graduates the source to maximize the solar energy post

5825 a reverse reflective tunnel a reverse reflective tunnel that magnifies the light and graduates the source to maximize the solar energy post

5826 hybrid connected communicati hybrid connected communication network is a real chance of service to any known location by selling the use of a cellular to satellite hybrid service network to any under written provider for negotiation and sales

5827 cellular foundation negotiat cellular foundation negotiation network is a real chance of service to any known location by selling the use of a cellular network to any under written provider for negotiation and sales

5828 satellite negotiations netwo satellite negotiations network is a paid environment for services in the satellite atmosphere to make money and profit

5829 script dividing script patter script dividing script patterns and repetitive computations multiplied by a larger script. to divide or multiply one large process into sub processes for a real time application

5830 bids and sales for legitimat bids and sales for legitimate futures in project performance is the sale of a large private job for any work made in a presales term

5831 military reverse calvin cycl military reverse calvin cycle air purifiers

5832 adjustable format video is a adjustable format video is a hardware rendering device application that runs a basic group of files a specific way to improve the display of any movie or music and other data projects simply said you put your project in basic adjustable format and the video player renders the adjusted final part

5833 gps navigational property an gps navigational property and the confines of that d property

5834 dual annotation physics spat dual annotation physics spatial grid including place in physics natural and vertical horizontal and down from two origins

5835 annotation physics spatial g annotation physics spatial grid including place in physics natural and vertical horizontal and down mapping by global positioning satellite government or private designation place in space

5836 gps fishing zone global posi gps fishing zone global positioning satellite grid of ownership including place in physics natural and vertical horizontal and down

5837 gps aerial lanes for airplan gps aerial lanes for airplanes are the global positioning satellites way of making lanes for flying and navigating instead of yellow white stripes there could be pre designated routes by height from and in what direction

5838 gps aerial lanes for drones gps aerial lanes for drones are the global positioning satellites way of making lanes for flying and navigating instead of yellow white stripes there could be pre designated routes by height from and in what direction

5839 processors isolated semi cond processors isolated semi conductors and their organized processing looping processors isolated semi conductors and their organized processing may be needed to comply more than two specific parts of a computer. to make a conductor for part a and part b as well as c and d.

5840 gps aerial drone road lanes gps aerial drone road lanes are the global positioning satellites way of making lanes for flying and navigating instead of yellow white stripes there could be pre designated routes by height from and in what direction

5841 gps road lanes are the globa gps road lanes are the global positioning satellites way of making lanes for flying and navigating instead of yellow white stripes there could be pre designated routes by height from and in what direction

5842 blank chip ssd and blank chi blank chip ssd and blank chip designing acceptable circuit driven operations of a system on a chip

5843 phone ping record notary reg phone ping record notary registry number and information of legal origin

5844 email ping record notary reg email ping record notary registry number and information of legal origin

5845 auto pc number document regi auto pc number document registry number and document server serial digital copy document number registry is a general document of recording in a digital sense for the personal computer and information of scientific origin

5846 business document registry n business document registry number and document server serial digital copy document number registry is a general document of recording in a digital sense

5847 education document server se education document server serial digital copy document number registry is a general document of recording in a digital sense

5848 medical serial digital copy medical serial digital copy document number registry is a general document of recording in a digital sense

5849 divergent decision this is a divergent decision this is a company specific attempt to hold notes and thoughts in the air. the example of cars as compared to specific software gives precedence to a new way for profit intent. the decision to make two or more different operating systems and agendas are non exceptionally unanimous. to speak more clearly the decision to make a two motif platform is contagious. yet at the same time undone as to a codex to dielectrics after all. strict intent to remain computational verses intent to perceive to set an example would be to make a personality test of the intent holding from the crowd of corresponding architects. to take the analytic personalities and make a platform while a intuitive and non working informational pragmatic platform of their different colleagues asses alternate differences. so to plainly speak the differences in side windows xp ie verses windows *new

5850 divergent decision this is a divergent decision this is a company specific attempt to hold notes and thoughts in the air. the example of cars as compared to specific software gives precedence to a new way for profit intent. the decision to make two or more different operating systems and agendas are non exceptionally unanimous. to speak more clearly the decision to make a two motif platform is contagious. yet at the same time undone as to a codex to dielectrics after all. strict intent to remain computational verses intent to perceive to set an example would be to make a personality test of the intent holding from the crowd of corresponding architects. to take the analytic personalities and make a platform while a intuitive and non working informational pragmatic platform of their different colleagues asses alternate differences. so to plainly speak the differences in side windows xp ie verses windows **new

5851 government serial digital co government serial digital copy notary document number registry is a general document of recording in a digital sense

5852 certified and notary of emai certified and notary of email is a service of notary in an email record to and from clients

5853 a group of any available ope a group of any available open form of one send and one receive and one group of process as a whole of one in any open signals

5854 wifi alternating form access wifi alternating form access of wifi integrated is a triplet form of one send and one receive and one group of process as a whole of one in any open signals

5855 system on chip server founda system on chip server foundation power by usb data by usb on board ram on board processor hard drive by compact flash made to run programmable applications with the access of wifi integrated

5856 soc foundation power by usb soc foundation power by usb data by usb on board ram on board processor hard drive by compact flash made to run programmable applications

5857 paint printing jet spray pla paint printing jet spray plasticprinting in itself is a term generalized printing with paint and an opacity paint plastic solvent
5858 wireless access soc is a cod wireless access soc is a code access by wifi or wirelessethernet processing
5859 layered acrylic printing and layered acrylic printing and jet spray plasticprinting in itself is a term generalized as two part d and d printing combined
5860 multiple oi protocol router multiple oi protocol router board is an important part of information in and out of any given system on chip wall mounting moving input unit this is the protocol that moves the data in and out of the section per multitude of processing systems on one wall board
5861 assemble of pre face and su f assemble of pre face and su face assemble of pre face and su face universal assemblage formats companies who make things for other companies to sell with their name on top and companies to sell what someone else s already made with an alternate name on t
5862 system on chip wall mount bo system on chip wall mount boards and large card input panels that move
5863 system on chip wall mount bo system on chip wall mount boards and large card input panels
5864 system on chip product found system on chip product foundation is the start of a new cloud format far from large servers and server racks we enter the card based system of scrolling wall panels and more
5865 personal data storage softwa personal data storage software is a way to keep the original paper mail copied and safe off line or on line in a digital world while accessing the properties of print and scan a need to fax and forward to any service like united states postal service and more is the priority of the software in question and the protection is a part of the meaning of its importance the life cycle of the person and day to day is a important function of all of us
5866 page switch browser plugin page switch browser plugin is a software internet or mobile web interface that takes large tall pages that run on and on and divides them into smaller and easier to download workable pages by splitting them into different views of minor pages like a tree layout in a table of contents
5867 company compatible hardware company compatible hardware for reference functionality is another way of saying that the oem source may be compatible with a company when forming an alliance in partnership and software hardware compatibility meaning in another way more universal components and higher use and less unaccepted products as well as a better way of life for information technology also said as this company a is compatible with this company b
5868 gpu readout is a simple lcd gpu readout is a simple lcd or led read out of status on gpu for reference functionality
5869 add hardware wizard with dri add hardware wizard with drivers and more is a simple unique way to pre initialize the moment of pre install with how to and pre installed drivers
5870 memory led readout is a simp memory led readout is a simple lcd or led read out of status on hard drive functionality
5871 hard drive readout is a simp hard drive readout is a simple lcd or led read out of status on hard drive functionality
5872 exterior in the elements liq exterior in the elements liquid cooled memory is actively

cooled liquid thermal contact that aids in temperature adjustments by thermal liquid conduction

5873 exterior <span>meaning out s exterior <span>meaning out side in atmosphere </span>liquid cooled motherboard is an actively cooled in a climate controlled efficiency way of cooling for higher performance

5874 exterior liquid cooled compu exterior liquid cooled computing components such as microprocessors used in cell towers and more memory and other actively cooled in a climate controlled efficiency for higher performance

5875 reversed printing focus sten reversed printing focus stencil grid is a large grid of pixels that when compensated or reflected into a smaller size they connect and conduct as a circuit

5876 printing focus stencil grid printing focus stencil grid is a large grid of pixels that when compensated or reflected into a smaller size they connect and with reason to provide connections

5877 molecular photo printing sai molecular photo printing said to use small stencils to print smaller circuits in an adjusted dimension with an emulsion photo fusion process

5878 silicachromaticbuildingmi silicachromaticbuildingmicroprocessors

5879 gold chromatic building micr gold chromatic building microprocessors is a part of the three dimensional stencil graphic laser printer and is a pico and nano active subtractively printed photo laser is a laser stencil photo object to print and subtractively with medium for example to think that a grid of pico layered and formed photo timed generated method of stencil emulsion printing converts a flux to accept the grid of the negative print also said to use small stencils to print smaller circuits

5880 things that verses in terms t things that verses in terms this verses that in order to make another turn as well as things that verses and do not equal any such return or sense. the thought is the matter at hand. an abstract definition...

5881 three dimensional stencil gr three dimensional stencil graphic laser printer is a pico and nano active subtractively printed photo laser is a laser stencil photo object to print and subtractively with medium for example to think that a grid of pico layered and formed photo timed generated method of stencil emulsion printing converts a flux to accept the grid of the negative print also said to use small stencils to print smaller circuits

5882 stencil graphic laser printe stencil graphic laser printer software is the software for the stencil graphic laser printer is a pico and nano active subtractively printed photo laser stencil grid

5883 stencil graphic laser printe stencil graphic laser printer is a pico and nano active subtractively printed photo laser stencil photo object to print and subtractively with medium

5884 properties of stagnation imp properties of stagnation improper use of technology in a manipulative manner to conclude monetary f un ds verses the intent to progress for example the co processor verse the use of an extended automatic co processor verses a deliberate attempt to keep the

5885 lcd stencil lens for pi co a lcd stencil lens for pi co and nano active subtractively printed photo laser is a laser stencil photo object to print subtractively with mediums

5886 subtractively printed phot subtractively printed photo laser cut layer is a layer of conductor or isolate r which is a cut or etched by a time generated photo of energy such as burning or to degrade the photo or image into something or out of something which is good for making three dimensional chips and operators

5887 subtractively printed zirc subtractively printed zirconhydroxy or photo laser cut zirconhydroxy isolated layer is a layer of zirconium which is a silicon that is more insulating and less thermal conductive than diamond carbonate this is good for making three dimensional chips and operators
5888 sodium carbonite alumin sodium carbonite aluminum sodium carbonite patent pending
5889 sodium sulfur carbonate cop sodium sulfur carbonate patent pending
5890 hydrogen oxide sulfate copyr hydrogen oxide sulfate patent pending
5891 falling by data verses fallin falling by data verses falling by data verses balanced data at the same measure of a chemical balanced neutral chemistry ph the best way to make us understand the falling off stature of a certain mark... such as to take two or more things and measure the importance or the proposition at hand. the abstract way to say this would be this way... which data to disregard which to archive and which to make a note of at a later time. or the most wisest decision would be to catalog the entire mass and then recall all data by user/ product such as interference.
5892 boronmagnesiumsulfate copy boronmagnesiumsulfate patent pending
5893 multiple users and rules sof multiple users and rules software is a program or app that accepts multiple users in order to work and perform as a team in one mission with rules of hierarchy and ranking patent pending
5894 to learn sharing software is to learn sharing software is a program or app that accepts multiple users in order to learn and teach verses one mouse and one input at a time patent pending
5895 wireless multiple conjoined wireless multiple conjoined boards by os is a group of boards that are essentially separated working cells that are joined by operating system without wires patent pending
5896 multiple conjoined boards by multiple conjoined boards by os is a group of boards that are essentially separated working cells that are joined by operating system patent pending
5897 mosquito control tabs for la mosquito control tabs for large ponds patent pending
5898 recyclable oil filters copyr recyclable oil filters patent pending submitted on may meaning a large number it follows the same rules as that phrase. however that is not the case originally in greek where there is plural.
5899 recyclable oil filters copyr recyclable oil filters patent pending
5900 recyclable water filters cop recyclable water filters patent pending submitted on may
5901 recyclable water filters cop recyclable water filters patent pending
5902 recyclable air filters copyr recyclable air filters patent pending submitted on may
5903 recyclable air filters copyr recyclable air filters patent pending
5904 processor driven wifi signal processor driven wifi signal receiver for multiple managed wireless signals and incorporating wireless devices processors and computations as a whole in a multitude of receiving and processing of a signal patent pending submitted on may
5905 processor driven wifi signal processor driven wifi signal receiver for multiple managed wireless signals and incorporating wireless devices processors and computations as a whole in a multitude of receiving and processing of a signal patent pending
5906 grade b grade all in a thing grade b grade all in a thing called hardware service cloud. to make a note there is a difference in all technology and the service of a hardware is not a change. to specify a invent called service grading and rating. compact server. compact

hardware service compact server inside a series of software mods and a different way to dedicate the data position size and capabilities for allocation. a grade b grade all in a thing called hardware service cloud make a note there is a difference in all technology and the service of a hardware is not a change. to specify a invent called service grading and rating.

5907 multi signal wireless receiv multi signal wireless receiver is a receiver for multiple managed wireless signals and incorporating wireless devices patent pending submitted on may

5908 multi signal wireless receiv multi signal wireless receiver is a receiver for multiple managed wireless signals and incorporating wireless devices patent pending

5909 hiroshima latin invasion hiroshima latin invasion spawned by leftists patent pending submitted on may

5910 hiroshima latin invasion hiroshima latin invasion spawned by leftists patent pending

5911 data center secure wireless data center secure wireless multiple external modular format is a hardware driven by driver format that excludes the chassis location and provides ports that transfer the data in and out wireless with a header data packet that includes a specific device for inclusion in a data center for wireless alliance computing

5912 multiple external modular fo multiple external modular format is a hardware driven by driver format that excludes the chassis location and provides ports that transfer the data in and out in thread cables

5913 wireless phone to wireless p wireless phone to wireless phone direct

5914 wireless computer to wireles wireless computer to wireless computer

5915 wireless through gateway pin wireless through gateway ping router is a device that allows computers to connect and share files thru software and a single router essentially a very small internet by wifi network hardware and software

5916 virtual calculated energy ve virtual calculated energy verses for profit formula table software is a search and input library of values and methods of constants and catalysts that react with one another in a virtual unreal way of study to mathematically search and find any such data as an inquiry to a means

5917 parts that un ite by scale a parts that un ite by scale and connections across carry inter connection circuit processors and alternate vectors of chip exchange a chip that sends a specific vector data rate to a specified place to and then to more or to reply

5918 to ro un d the estimation of to ro un d the estimation of a pixel closer with a pi triplet fraction

5919 compact hardware service comp compact hardware service compact server inside a series of software mods and a different way to dedicate the data position size and capabilities for allocation compact server. compact hardware service compact server inside a series of software mods and a different way to dedicate the data position size and capabilities for allocation. a grade b grade all in a thing called hardware service cloud make a note there is a difference in all technology and the service of a hardware is not a change. to specify a invent called service grading and rating.

5920 to ro un d the estimation of to ro un d the estimation of a half pixel closer with a pi triplet fraction

5921 a global connected cloud res a global connected cloud resource of data and targets to compromise the enemy and their assets as a concluded end to a means the satellites and the data location in a sense of war over internet protocol

5922 virtual drone navigational o virtual drone navigational operating system and the library functions of that data including geo navigation satellite location and local weather conditions as in corporate in a system of methods that conclude a operation inside a alternate virtual use _
5923 drone operating system and t drone operating system and the library functions of that data
5924 large scale software overwri large scale software overwrites are the overwritten os and programs apps and unlocked formats of devices and the user agreement broken by opposing software and reclaiming a device based on ownership
5925 bureau of lawyer investigati bureau of lawyer investigation is a simple investigation to condone or condemn the laws by a specific lawyer
5926 virtual search of power libr virtual search of power library for a data start with software that looks and learns the cost of a fuel or substance and compares that to a starch and the mineral to make that energy with the combinations of other properties of value in a computational way of virtual search of power is a learning method to compute the most powerful solution to run tomorrows cars and every day engines motors and energy motions of any kind while measuring the possibilities of the content to make that energy and the worth of the out come as well as the potency of that worth to the foot print and the regeneration of the properties
5927 software that looks and lear software that looks and learns the cost of a fuel or substance and compares that to a starch and the mineral to make that energy with the combinations of other properties of value in a computational way of virtual search of power is a learning method to compute the most powerful solution to run tomorrows cars and every day engines motors and energy motions of any kind while measuring the possibilities of the content to make that energy and the worth of the out come as well as the potency of that worth to the foot print and the regeneration of the properties
5928 virtual search of power is a virtual search of power is a learning method to compute the most powerful solution to run tomorrows cars and every day engines motors and energy motions of any kind while measuring the possibilities of the content to make that energy and the worth of the out come as well as the potency of that worth to the foot print and the regeneration of the properties
5929 law bureau of investigation law bureau of investigation to seek and find corruption in government would be a branch of law directed at politics and make a political transition from the public service to the private administration of law and free us from pay offs and contract breaks
5930 smart fuel system in conjunc smart fuel system in conjunction with vapor compressor is an exciter and pre respirated gasoline fuel in a volitile vapor calculator that finds the mixes top flash point automatically and in a few cycles adjusts it to any gas for the proper efficiency
5931 recycle and cycle g as liqui recycle and cycle g as liquid and g as separated mining and dis assembly to material on a settle absolute table weight process take and rest into a sedimentary weight of stagnation and aggression movement and non movement improving heating resting and cooli
5932 open idea app to design a ethe open idea app to design a ethernet cell or satellite based cell phone application open idea app a different way to internet to design a ethernet cell or satellite based cell phone application that connects people's phones as pages instead of pages

on a server. the main purpose is to communicate and then the other things will gradually fall into place. i think it would be perfect to practice this in the jungles or deserts.

5933 encrypted phone service that i encrypted phone service that is for government

5934 vapor compressor is a excite vapor compressor is a exciter and pre respirator for gasoline in a volatile vapor calculator that finds the fuels top flash point automatically and in a few cycles adjusts it to any gas for the engine

5935 pre respirated gasoline in pre respirated gasoline in a volatile vapor calculator that finds the fuels top flash point automatically and in a few cycles adjusts it to any gas for the engine

5936 smart fuel is pre respirate smart fuel is pre respirated gasoline in a volatile vapor to burn and combust for trucks tractor trailers and cars as well as airplanes and drones

5937 atomized fuel and vapor hybr atomized fuel and vapor hybrid engine will use premeasured agitated vapor fuel and is the closest to flash point in any compound that would be important in a compressed alcoholasgas engine a compromised vapor ignition fuel injector is a prepared measure of vapor agitator to make a fine atomised vapor to burn and combust for trucks tractor trailers and cars as well as airplanes and drones

5938 atomized and vapor hybrid en atomized and vapor hybrid engine will use premeasured agitated vapor fuel and is the closest to flash point in any compound that would be important in a compressed alcoholasgas engine a compromised vapor ignition fuel injector is a prepared measure of vapor agitator to make a fine atomised vapor to burn and combust for trucks tractor trailers and cars as well as airplanes and drones

5939 compromised fuel aerosol eng compromised fuel aerosol engine will use premeasured agitated vapor fuel and is the closest to flash point in any compound that would be important in a compressed alcoholasgas engine a compromised vapor ignition fuel injector is a prepared measure of vapor agitator to make a fine atomized vapor to burn and combust for trucks tractor trailers and cars as well as airplanes and drones

5940 compromised fuel aerosol is compromised fuel aerosol is premeasured agitated vapor fuel and is the closest to flash point in any compound that would be important in a compressed alcoholasgas engine a compromised vapor ignition fuel injector is a prepared measure of vapor agitator to make a fine atomized vapor to burn and combust for trucks tractor trailers and cars as well as airplanes and drones

5941 agitated vapor fuel is the c agitated vapor fuel is the closest to flash point in any compound that would be important in a compressed alcoholasgas engine a compromised vapor ignition fuel injector is a prepared measure of vapor agitator to make a fine atomized vapor to burn and combust for trucks tractor trailers and cars as well as airplanes and drones

5942 in a compressed alcoholasg in a compressed alcoholasgas engine a compromised vapor ignition fuel injector is a prepared measure of vapor agitator to make a fine atomized vapor to burn and combust for trucks tractor trailers and cars as well as airplanes and drones

5943 compressed alcoholasgas en compressed alcoholasgas engine is a compromised vapor ignition engine for trucks tractor trailers and cars as well as airplanes and drones

5944 to make something work someti to make something work sometimes size does matter. what i want is a fast hard drive that happens to be external... for example... the mystery is how to make a unique hole and a plug to do that with without loss or deterioration in cables. crioner

5945 diesel and ethel sodium nitr diesel and ethel sodium nitrate fuel for diesel for trucks tractor trailers and cars as well as airplanes and drones

5946 home router to cell to satel home router to cell to satellite paid satellite connection grid network is a connected alliance of satellites that work and process things like communication together as a whole network with the ability to send packets to and from each other
5947 satellite to cell branches a satellite to cell branches are cellular channels that focus to the nearest cell reach to the nearest satellite for convenience and speed
5948 paid satellite data packet g paid satellite data packet grid prefix and paid satellite connection grid network is a connected alliance of satellites that work and process things like communication together as a whole network with the ability to send packets to and from each other
5949 paid satellite data packet g paid satellite data packet grid prefix network branches and paid satellite connection grid network is a connected alliance of satellites that work and process things like communication together as a whole network with the ability to send packets to and from each other
5950 satellite data packet grid p satellite data packet grid prefix and paid satellite connection grid network is a connected alliance of satellites that work and process things like communication together as a whole network with the ability to send packets to and from each other
5951 paid satellite data connecti paid satellite data connection grid network is a connected alliance of satellites that work and process things like communication together as a whole network
5952 satellite connection grid is satellite connection grid is a connected alliance of satellites that work and process things like communication together as a whole network
5953 creative program categories creative program categories for specified category chips are purpose driven chips with hypothetical and geometry application software program and task at mind
5954 calc program categories for calc program categories for specified category chips are purpose driven chips with number and physics application software program and task at mind
5955 can we figure out the chemist can we figure out the chemistry in a healthy human can we figure out the chemistry in a healthy human
5956 program categories for speci program categories for specified category chips are purpose driven chips with that application software program and task at mind
5957 multiple category chips are multiple category chips are purpose driven chips with that program and task at mind
5958 critical non attached data b critical non attached data back up registrations and cloud clusters is an extremely secure web of servers and data bases that conclude information that is nearly irreplaceable or important more than any other data critical non attached back up by
5959 calc category add on cards a calc category add on cards are purpose driven chips with that program and task at mind
5960 creative category add on car creative category add on cards are purpose driven chips with that program and task at mind the brain receptors need to work and they want to work.
5961 category add on cards are pu category add on cards are purpose driven chips with that program and task at mind
5962 calc category chips are purp calc category chips are purpose driven chips with that program and task at mind

5963 creative category chips are creative category chips are purpose driven chips with that program and task at mind
5964 category chips are purpose d category chips are purpose driven chips with that program and task at mind
5965 high density performance sca high density performance scale processing is the ratio number in processors compared to scheme of arrangements and clusters in ram and transistors a
5966 high density complex scale p high density complex scale processing is the number in processors compared to size submitted on may
5967 high density complex scale p high density complex scale processing is the number in processors compared to size
5968 nano motors and in the way o nano motors and in the way of open and closed. aggregate verses passive for technological or medical scenarios and other processes when size does matter.
5969 low density performance scal low density performance scale processing is the number in processors compared to size
5970 home to cell to satellite ro home to cell to satellite routers cell branches that hold a message in the packet prefix or suffix that extends the direction of cellular channels that focus to the nearest cell reach to the nearest satellite for convenience and speed
5971 computational network proces computational network processing only system of scripted processing
5972 wireless computational netwo wireless computational network processing only system of processing
5973 wireless storage network is wireless storage network is a non processing cache only system of storage drives
5974 multiplied wireless hd recei multiplied wireless hd receiver is a multiple signal wireless adapter that transports many different signals into and from a source to another router with specified multiple places in destination
5975 multiplied wireless hard dri multiplied wireless hard drive router is a multiple signal transporter and encoder with a specified multiple places of destination
5976 sd wireless hard drive syste sd wireless hard drive system is a two step data storage drive and wireless adapter that transports signals into and from a source to another receiver
5977 using multiple tests compensa using multiple tests compensation and how to provide any consistency with statistics elaborate compensations will measure the point of our art and science. using multiple tests and using all the measures known by science to study the form of art that will lead to a perfect arch or a perfect line. which both are very far away in terms.
5978 hyper threading usb cable i hyper threading usb cable is a multiple lane cable that transports signals into and from a source to another receiver
5979 volunteer web warriors softw volunteer web warriors software to aid against the enemy and to fight a cyber war vol un teerism with our at home devices to co un ter attack the enemy foes
5980 hyper threading fiber optic hyper threading fiber optic cable is a multiple lane cable that transports signals into and from a source to another receiver
5981 hyper threading cable is a m hyper threading cable is a multiple lane cable that transports signals into and from a source to another receiver

5982 board solid state hyperthre board solid state hyperthreading is the path of computational signals traveling inside the server board for faster translation computations and processing
5983 in board solid state threadi in board solid state threading is the path of computational signals traveling inside the server board for faster translation computations and processing
5984 optical circuit focus range optical circuit focus range is the measurement of circuits in an optically written object blank similar to a optical media disc as an circuit processor as opposed to a diffused optically printed chip will bring circuit printing to the household diy markets
5985 many optical circuit objects many optical circuit objects in order on a server bed of input ports meaning a group of objects working as system on chips as portable optically written object blank similar to a optical media disc as an circuit processor as opposed to a diffused optically printed chip will bring circuit printing to the household diy markets
5986 paid instructions for the ob paid instructions for the object writer for the portable optically written object blank similar to a optical media disc as an circuit processor as opposed to a diffused optically printed chip will bring circuit printing to the household diy markets
5987 object writer for the portab object writer for the portable optically written object blank similar to a optical media disc as an circuit processor as opposed to a diffused optically printed chip will bring circuit printing to the household markets
5988 portable optically written o portable optically written object blank similar to a optical media disc as an circuit processor as opposed to a diffused optically printed chip
5989 it s funny you should but ask it s funny you should but ask i m in servers severs not software web os
5990 optically written object bla optically written object blank is a simple name for the laser written optically printed chip blank similar to a optical media disc as an circuit processor as opposed to a diffused optically printed chip
5991 optically written magnetic o optically written magnetic object is a simple name for the laser written optically printed chip as an circuit processor as opposed to a diffused optically printed chip
5992 standard popular retro activ standard popular retro active hardware is a forgotten chip socket board or state of work made popular again for the f un of its performance and suggestions k again standard popular hardware
5993 a squared area of cascading a squared area of cascading increments f un ny but real to process code with measurement cascading increments a certain unit of measurement or for processing electronic measurement using my certain unit of measurement data versus the shape of media t
5994 a squared area of cascading a squared area of cascading increments f un ny but real to process code with measurement cascading increments a certain unit of measurement
5995 a working partial process wo a working partial process working software is a platform of a data base that is built on a question of fundamentals to make a transitional and schematic plan for a business with some of part system made to work with other parts
5996 diverse operating board magn diverse operating board magnetic ion fiber optic and nano electric signals to work the large and small things into a so un d well ro un ded machine
5997 magnetic data waves of inter magnetic data waves of intertwined mini signals and partial process of and triplet pulse

5998 phone station bluetooth magn phone station bluetooth magnetic backup recharge by wireless charge and backup clone update and restore hardware
5999 to process code with measurem to process code with measurement . cascading increments . a certain unit of measurement . or . for processing electronic measurement using my certain unit of measurement data versus the shape of media today
6000 exchangeable cell cell card exchangeable cell cell card for a local non synchronized cloud account cell phones that is a starting point to a private phone a private and un der non agreement phone privacy
6001 exchangeable cell cell card exchangeable cell cell card for a local single and separate non synchronized cloud account cell phones that is a starting point to a private phone
6002 cubit cell off and on group cubit cell off and on group of cubits by a translation of on off and signals in a group a simple yet complex method of calculation and intersect of paths for any group of information
6003 amplitude () . / double amplitude () . / doubled mass () . [.] estimated energy constant weight
6004 pixel language em css wc in pixel language em css wc intent adi adi adi
6005 a ro un ded number of encryp a ro un ded number of encryption based on a four segment of numbers to process and extract an encrypt able alpha numerical code for ssl and more advanced communications
6006 a squared area of cascading a squared area of cascading increments fun ny but real to process code with measurement cascading increments a certain unit of measurement or for processing electronic measurement using my certain unit of measurement data versus the shape of media t
6007 even and odd fractional statu even and odd fractional status even and odd fractional status the improvement of multi deck processors all natural and computational binary numbers will be multiplied and divided with roots and squares only over a short time span will this happen inside a brick mold if you will of an environment that knows which way to go. using common math geometry calculus thrums'
6008 retro retro retro penicillin retro retro retro penicillin two penicillin two the simple minds think alike but we progress through abstract minds that are complex yet still simple looking back is always important why did i leave that milk out on the kitchen co un ter all day its an un in
6009 for safe and secure as well a for safe and secure as well as quick and immediate transactions a card that provides service when service is only one overdraft away. to speed up the transactions posting and pending to post as a involuntary means.
6010 intent to covert and see the intent to covert and see the matter at hand. to tablet to desktop to phone ineligible document conversion wysiwyg
6011 gasses energy signal wave by gasses energy signal wave by g as wave energy signal is the measure of energy that attracts or repels any such one g as or other gasses to and from each other in a energy force in any size obvious or microscopic force of annotative fixation including or exc
6012 gasses energy signal wave g gasses energy signal wave g as wave energy signal is the measure of energy that attracts or repels any such one g as or other gasses to and from each other in a energy force in any size obvious or microscopic force of annotative fixation including or exclud

6013 inverted g as sorting and re inverted g as sorting and reclaiming recycled incineration gasses by way of catalytic converter and g as humidifier for or only with a unique dry or paste wet solvent clay and the processes that make taking trash and turning it into rock or solvent sludge a
6014 what goes up may come down fi what goes up may come down finding a height to measure the un measurable off the grid computations and landing points by what goes up may come down. the point that we need to measure in haste is the un measurable flash point that will keep the platform from crashing when landing. hollow arc field mathematical plane plateau exit the invisible points that may connect a plane by inverse
6015 extended belling vertical ss extended belling vertical ssd chip stack
6016 watch and see user and plus watch and see user and plus applications that work on cache and submission processes is a working rule based program that allows more than one user at a time to use the same work place for example a air navigation tower that is interoperable with in an area of operation seeing working and using plural mouse movements commands and operations in formulas
6017 mission diagnose changes at mission diagnose changes at dopa mine serotonin adrenaline and histamine receptor sites in the central nervous system by using a similar method to diabetic blood testing. mission diagnose changes at dopa mine adrenaline and histamine receptor sites in the central nervous system by using a similar method to diabetic blood testing. in reference to signal receptors and d d and d in use of an atypical anti psychotic
6018 arounded number of encryptio arounded number of encryption based on a four segment of numbers to process and extract an encrypt able alpha numerical code for ssl and more advanced communications
6019 pi co circuit pico layer chi pi co circuit pico layer chip and circuit building segmented layers and connecting ends from bottom to upper layer for stacking interior with poly carbs ceramic insulation and poly oxide metal as conducting circuits with power and wear as consideration
6020 pi co circuit with poly carb pi co circuit with poly carbs ceramic insulation and poly oxide metal as conducting circuits with power and wear as consideration for measuring the entire tension and properties of laser made engraving by plasma soldering yielding and melting
6021 recycled nuclear waste copyri recycled nuclear waste
6022 mini wireless chip operated a mini wireless chip operated and compute magnetic transmission for torque and propulsion of device controlling a stationary over controlled passing magnets that provide any such current controlled with a wireless connection for torque magnitude intensit
6023 common industrial size recharg common industrial size rechargeable batteries for retrofit added cycle generator using the rotation of x wheels to generate current to store on x
6024 its a lot like a nuclear bom its a lot like a nuclear bomb only in reverse instead of destroying elements we are putting them together but more important than a super spontaneous collision we are separating the elements for recycling and purification the muffler and the past catalyt
6025 atomized electormechanical p atomized electormechanical photo printing atomized electormechanical photo printing state of our art run on atomized electormechanical photo printing as opposed to ion atomized demagnetized printing this would be a simple and more

consumer affordable way to print in minute detail and still hold the highest quality printing method to come. something that could eventually print metallic s and or super carbon signature marking inks. for safety security

6026 cloud data security software cloud data security software is a method of protecting the future with technology can you download that movie with paper through the air? not at this moment but for example what about a universal and translatable script that will encode and decode music books movies gps info and for the matter itself data! it's my idea to promote data not necessarily the format to put the data inside with a noteable unit of measurement that is described only as .. to process code with measurement with a use of sd and scripting into a form of data.

6027 school student information s school student information secure data protection is a method of protecting the future of learning with technology

6028 a user operated device that a user operated device that enters as your original line and adapts to your connection that inturns blocks all connections and or encrypts or allows connections based on a simple password protocol in another way to say is to secure a networks connection based on a encryption box and also known as a hard line encrypted router firewall box patent pending abstract utility

6029 cube processors in a insulat cube processors in a insulated chip levels with a coherence of any insulation method of stacking horizontal or vertical chip organization to build a larger chip also said as to make a non conductive layer with small outer inner conductive measures while operation is possible with vertical threads and vertical processing and cube processors

6030 to multiply the conductive t to multiply the conductive threads in a insulated chip levels made from of with a coherence of any insulation method of stacking horizontal or vertical chip organization to build a larger chip also said as to make a non conductive layer with small outer inner conductive measures while operation is possible with vertical threads _

6031 a presentperpost lactates a presentperpost lactates light salt solution check to help clean calcium deposits to prevent cancer _

6032 an artistic judgment to copy an artistic judgment to copy and cure is the obvious mission of any nucleotide printed microorganism patent pending

6033 an add in card memory or har an add in card memory or hardware that makes a hard line like connection that holds issues and hard place port instructions and memory for a secure private badges for using signatures in a secure work place called doors are a important secure private office operating system that is office inside an office that works with firewalls and fences for people who operate in tiers and teams to work on productive security means that are sensitive and need doors and keys on a professional logged and improved structure for government military private offices and a means to identify issues that people create patent pending

6034 secure private badges for us secure private badges for using signatures in a secure work place called doors are a important secure private office operating system that is office inside an office that works with firewalls and fences for people who operate in tiers and teams to work on productive security means that are sensitive and need doors and keys on a professional logged and improved structure for government military private offices and a means to identify issues that people create patent pending

6035 doors are a important secure doors are a important secure private office operating system that is office inside an office that works with firewalls and fences for people who

operate in tiers and teams to work on productive security means that are sensitive and need doors and keys on a professional logged and improved structure for government military private offices and a means to identify issues that people create patent pending
6036 at home kit to use combinati at home kit to use combination presentperpost lactates nonalkaline solution and ultrasonic abrasive shock treatment to break and to help clean calcium deposits to prevent cancer patent pending
6037 a combination presentperpo a combination presentperpost lactates nonalkaline solution and ultrasonic abrasive shock treatment to break and to help clean calcium deposits to prevent cancer patent pending
6038 insulated chip levels made f insulated chip levels made from of with a coherence of any insulation method of stacking horizontal or vertical chip organization to build a larger chip also said as to make a non conductive layer with small outer and inner conductive measures while operation is possible
6039 a post lactates light soluti a post lactates light solution flush to help cure calcium deposits to prevent cancer patent pending
6040 software run program applica software run program applications for printers that uses nano/pico/triad mixed and fromulated biochemical nucleotide to replicate on a recurring smaller intent to cure cancer and disease patent pending
6041 sub scalable ssd branches an sub scalable ssd branches and trees
6042 synthetic pressurized g as t synthetic pressurized g as turbine to generate electricity
6043 dna at cg nucleotide printed dna at cg nucleotide printed dna from any known starch or protein microbiologically printed antibody used to fight disease or cancer negatively doped patent pending
6044 synthetic natural convention synthetic natural conventional non associated g as a substance that may be clean burning and easy to make synthetic pressured gas
6045 dna at cg nucleotide printed dna at cg nucleotide printed dna from any known starch or protein microbiologically printed antibody used to fight disease or cancer positively doped patent pending
6046 dna at cg nucleotide printed dna at cg nucleotide printed dna from any known starch or protein microbiologically printed antibody used to fight disease or cancer patent pending
6047 starch protein and sugar dna starch protein and sugar dna microbiologically printed antibody used to fight disease patent pending
6048 to find the connections that to find the connections that refuse to comply with a non connective network may expose the places of occupied aggressors patent pending
6049 to ignore the first aim is t to ignore the first aim is to aim at the second target first to switch off a network with a virus and then scope and probe the culprit at a second target first patent pending casio :[ ] sio + cao ? casio[])from wikipedia http://en.wikipedia.org/wiki/blast_furnace#chemistry in reference to damages during refining how to recreate ozone (reduction to ozonides reduction of ozone gives the ozonide anion o . derivatives of this anion are explosive and must be stored at cryogenic temperatures. ozonides for all the alkali metals are known. ko rbo and cso can be prepared from their respective super oxides: ko + o ? ko + o although ko can be formed as above it can also be formed from potassium hydroxide and ozone:[ ] koh + o ? ko + o + ho)from wikipedia http://en.wikipedia.org/wiki/ozone#with_metals
6050 to point a specific targeted to point a specific targeted program to a chip or configuration

and hardware specific software outright patent pending
6051 a heart worm with parasitic a heart worm with parasitic contaminates may be the cure for other diseases with the carrying body of the intent to cure more than one infliction patent pending
6052 curing a virus disease by vi curing a virus disease by viral vaccine may be hope for another kind of artificial virus of a synthetic kind patent pending artificial anti virus patent pending casio :[ ] sio + cao ? casio[])from wikipedia http://en.wikipedia.org/wiki/blast_furnace#chemistry in reference to damages during refining how to recreate ozone (reduction to ozonides reduction of ozone gives the ozonide anion o . derivatives of this anion are explosive and must be stored at cryogenic temperatures. ozonides for all the alkali metals are known. ko rbo and cso can be prepared from their respective super oxides: ko + o ? ko + o although ko can be formed as above it can also be formed from potassium hydroxide and ozone:[ ] koh + o ? ko + o + ho)from wikipedia http://en.wikipedia.org/wiki/ozone#with_metals
6053 answer to a questionable the answer to a questionable theory by a hypothetical proof may be the hope that people need to find a cure for any know disease or virus patent pending
6054 to switch off a zone incorpo to switch off a zone incorporated with data and on a war or war data premptive agreement in a cloud database environment that protects the entity of itself by control and data code kill switch script cooperation and compliance of no service patent pending
6055 to use a device where the da to use a device where the data packets of the internet and cellular comm has stopped and a radio wave of certain freq is controlled in a zone not incorporated with data and on a war or war data premptive agreement in a cloud database environment that protects the entity of itself by control and data code kill switch script cooperation and compliance of no service patent pending
6056 a zone not incorporated with a zone not incorporated with data and on a war or war data premptive agreement in a cloud database environment that protects the entity of itself by control and data code kill switch script cooperation and compliance of no service patent pending would you like to play a game? sometimes the complete understanding is giving a understanding that there is such a thing as blind faith. complete trust only because someone tells you the history and the mysterious ways that there is faith and a cause for a better way of existence. to coexist and understand that beyond some compensation of arithmetic that there is in fact a calculation that is endless. to say something that is of an eternal entity is like someone who knows that pi is the estimation compensation standard of the start of amplitude. the amplitude equation is something that makes all standards of measurement work against pi. / . amplitude () . / doubled mass () . [.] estimated energy constant weight importance? {conception lighting electricity etc.}
6057 a data war or war data prem a data war or war data premptive agreement in a cloud database environment that protects the entity of itself by control and data code kill switch script cooperation and compliance of no service patent pending
6058 a premptive agreement in a a premptive agreement in a cloud database environment that protects the entity of itself by control and data code kill switch script patent pending or high quality printing. metallic ink copy intent carbon signature marking inks copy intent
6059 density and amplitude energy density and amplitude energy chart scale a energy chart with amplitude and density comparable to the chemical elements diagram with

consideration for g as solids and chemical compo un ds as well as their reaction to one another
6060 data code kill switch of unk data code kill switch of unknown ability previously known as friendly vague code and a design designation as a adjustment code patent pending
6061 data code kill switch agreem data code kill switch agreement and operation adjustment cooperation is the operation agreement that there is a safety concern for data on the service cloud and this may come to a part time outage based on the security of the data there patent pending
6062 allotted maintenance and des allotted maintenance and design operation is not a given known intelligence and to understand that perpetual scanning may cause over bearing and non acceptable watching is to understand that there should be a kill switch of code to mandate operation and non operation inside any such known data control patent pending
6063 hybrid incorporated data ded hybrid incorporated data dedicated rental satellite service and expanded network access signal protocol is a internet origin of routing to a particular place of any such packets of information then as soon as the signal comes close enough to the target it will then convert to a wireless signal to broadcast to the receiver and back again through a combination routing utility patent pending
6064 hybrid incorporated signal p hybrid incorporated signal protocol is a data service and expanded network access signal protocol is a internet origin of routing to a particular place of any such packets of information then as soon as the signal comes close enough to the target it will then convert to a wireless signal to broadcast to the receiver and back again through a combination routing utility patent pending
6065 real time and pure light %infi real time and pure light %infinite times + %infinite=e %uxc binom lim n toward infinity(+{ } over {n})^{n} part
6066 real time and pure light %infi real time and pure light %infinite times + %infinite=e %uxc binom lim n toward infinity(+{ } over {n})^{n} %infinite times + %infinite%uxc binom max xe ^{sum +infinity cdot +%uxe a {e} over x sum to{{} } x^{}%epsilon } part
6067 ricochet laser foresighted le ricochet laser foresighted led energy
6068 a multitude of cells that ref a multitude of cells that reflect and generate picture with only a segment of cells actually carrying data although showing partial information in the series of cells with all considered
6069 alternating step code sequenc alternating step code sequencing to multiply and receive the signals in alternating steps
6070 focused artificial energy ene focused artificial energy energy web energy server focused artificial energy energy web a contained web sphere that simulates a web of energy to pilot stations for distribution from a building that is a self contained focused laser generated solar energy structure that is on and off with servers as to aid in private energy sources adding to the already existing power supply
6071 energy server focused artific energy server focused artificial energy energy server focused artificial energy energy web a contained web sphere that simulates a web of energy to pilot stations for distribution from a building that is a self contained focused laser generated solar energy structure that is on and off with servers as to aid in private energy sources adding to the already existing power supply
6072 energy server focused artific energy server focused artificial energy energy web a contained web sphere that simulates a web of energy to pilot stations for distribution from a building that is a self contained focused laser generated solar energy structure that is on and

off with servers as to aid in private energy sources adding to the already existing power supply
6073 input data software multiplyi input data software multiplying processing out put script to make a cloud state of servers work over multiplying fabric end points and signal bandwidth
6074 honeycomb board that is a wal honeycomb board that is a wall of architecture upon its self. to make a glass cased gold wire fish through the board up down and over and through printed circuit boards to end?up inside a printed piping board with corrugations.
6075 gas powered hybrid alternative gas powered hybrid alternative point of energy torque slip cam
6076 stacked conjoined honeycomb b stacked conjoined honeycomb board that is a wall of architecture upon its self. to make a glass cased gold wire fish through the board up down and over and through printed circuit boards to end?up inside a printed piping board with corrugations
6077 to expand raid capacity to eq to expand raid capacity to equate into pcie thunder bolt raid
6078 to expand raid capacity to eq to expand raid capacity to equate into mobile docking temp raid and bay station for all in one in other words a docking all in one with true form technology repeated to expand raid capacity to equate into a mobile docking temp raid and bay station for all in one in other words a docking all in one with true form technology essentially a computer that docs your phone or tablet
6079 software making it all happen software making it all happen to expand raid capacity to equate into a mobile docking temp raid and bay station for all in one in other words a docking all in one with true form technology essentially a computer that docs your phone or tablet repeated an operator to expand raid capacity to equate into a mobile docking temp raid and bay station for all in one in other words a docking all in one with true form technology essentially a computer that docs your phone or tablet by software.
6080 another cloud cycle to invent another cloud cycle to invent concept the difference of deep blue was that it wasn't considered a cloud at the time. the focus was only on the game and the server itself. this is not the focus of what the azure is. windows will now carry on as usual... wel
6081 local cloud temp raid system local cloud temp raid system verses expanded services cloud for example a local more secure way to cloud that would incorporate your existing data and media servers as well as a new local platform that may or may not synchronize as the same based upon your choice.
6082 a smaller less expensive way a smaller less expensive way to solid state data to add layers to a existing ddr plug in and plug in more layers with new adjustable configurations for example dd r with half height extensions that run but stand up like a pcie that has layers included to expand up and over for microprocessor sd and co processor integration's
6083 to perform a movement in a fr to perform a movement in a fractal animation with encryption to have a double as well as a start and finish equal to a formula of change
6084 to perform a movement in a fr to perform a movement in a fractal with encryption to have a double as well as a start and finish equal to a formula of change and as well as to make more than one time loop in the process
6085 to expand raid capacity to eq to expand raid capacity to equate into mobile docking temp raid and bay station for by attachment device in other words a docking by attachment device with true form technology repeated to expand raid capacity to equate into a mobile

docking temp raid and bay station for by attachment device in other words a docking by attachment device with true form technology essentially a computer that docs your phone or tablet by attachment device

6086 gas start and hybrid long run gas start and hybrid long run alternative highway mileage fuel economy method is when the start is the majority controlled by combustion fuel and the highway gears are controlled by electricity methods

6087 rss search seek & search code rss search seek & search code name apache

6088 amendment deficiency petition amendment deficiency petitions by popular veto

6089 to declare a substance medici to declare a substance medicinally addictive and harmful to ones health by overdose as in unsubscribed methods of use.

6090 denationalize of radical libe denationalize of radical liberalism to declare a free argument of a amendment or change in policy too liberal for the nations good and notate it un popular.

6091 to make a political state of to make a political state of technology different than previous and current standing into a new and updated stature of state of the art design and vote from the intended place of interest.

6092 to build a bluray or archiva to build a bluray or archival disc mm media inside a glass or carbonate jewel case with spectrum magnified reading points with the intent of making it secure and dust free while being redundant and replaceable with the intent not confuse it and a . inch hard drive with a similar yet less expensive case for data writes and rewrites such as to compare it with more expensive solid state drive for data storage.

6093 reading and writing using con reading and writing using convex and concave lenses to build a bluray or archival disc mm media inside a glass or carbonate jewel case with spectrum magnified reading points with the intent of making it secure and dust free while being redundant and replaceable with the intent not confuse it and a . inch hard drive with a similar yet less expensive case for data writes and rewrites such as to compare it with more expensive solid state drive for data storage.

6094 a device reading and writing a device reading and writing using convex and concave lenses to build a bluray or archival disc mm media inside a glass or carbonate jewel case with spectrum magnified reading points with the intent of making it secure and dust free while being redundant and replaceable with the intent not confuse it and a . inch hard drive with a similar yet less expensive case for data writes and rewrites such as to compare it with more expensive solid state drive for data storage.

6095 chronological passive process chronological passive processing verses an active aggressor in a non sequential format of computations will help to stabilize the order of complex arrangements

6096 a cable that connects pcie to a cable that connects pcie to sata verses in terms

6097 an archival free server servi an archival free server service that records history based upon proprietary intellectual property. say for example a url that is specific that includes a .doc suffix and moderated by governmental appreciations. for a good short summary a that is accessible by internet and or free status of service

6098 electronic muscle pulse therap electronic muscle pulse therapy for atrophy patients help me walk? some organic / some post organic measure electronic muscle pulse therapy for atrophy patients step super infomercial for medical if i saw it on tv it has to be real disabled tendon repair and extensions step chicken cat transfer alternate cartilage transplant organic fiber optic nerve conductors step non evasive neurological where do you have trouble and electronic pulse for prolonged wheel chair patients

6099 gas start and hybrid long run gas start and hybrid long run alternative highway mileage transmission is when the start is the majority controlled by combustion fuel and the highway gears are controlled by electricity methods

6100 a governmental act that may d a governmental act that may deliver a electronic exemplified terms of use and search document where the new cloud of information evidence applied is searched and deemed acceptable by use of lawsuit including the file process of fees and documented services to simplify the included purposed of hidden individuals whom seem to elude the you have been served an affidavit short e affidavit

6101 conceptual invention copyrigh conceptual invention s and the intent to inspire the thought and not hold back an inventor who cares to drift instead of dwelling into market. to things of concept in a sense to work without patent boundaries even if the process may not or may include an image amendment to intellectual property and rules of international sanctions of property worth value search varios manufactured by roland dates present technical specifications polyphony voices timbrality part oscillator {{{oscillator}}} synthesis type openended system module after touch yes velocity sensitive yes input/output keyboard {{{keyboard}}} external control midi/ usb [edit] overview the roland varios is a rackmounted openended variable system module released by roland in . it is essentially a production environment with audio editing and sample playback based on the technology from the oftoverlooked vp variphrase processor. it is possible to independently manipulate the pitch time and formant of a sample add effects and even build complete audiobased arrangementsall in a realtime environment and without cpu drain. in addition it will emulate analogue synthesizers such as the roland jupiter . while the varios can operate as a standalone tool it also works alongside digital audio sequencers using midi clock and mtc sync. vproducer arrangements can also be saved as a standard midi file and processed audio files can be exported in .wav or aiff format for use in other editors and software. [edit] expansion cards two expansion cards were released for the varios the vc which emulates a roland d and the vc which allowed vocal processing with an external microphone with effects such as a vocoder and choir. much to the disappointment of varios owners who spent considerable amounts of money (albeit on a powerful unit) it appears roland have no plans to release any future expansion cards. furthermore it appears the vc is now out of production with various sources claiming that roland made a set number of cards in an estimation of demand.

6102 to enhance by way of less is to enhance by way of less is more situation of compatibility and less apps over programmable problems and obstacles saying that gingerbread operating systems are the way of the past and the future of os publishing is two fold a punter and a player verses in terms as a recorder and a viewer to create a two fold operating scheme minimal and coherently elaborate in one os with two different settings

6103 market that protect market that protects and serves for the greater good of mankind

6104 pcie open socket aka cpos pcie open socket aka cpos

6105 market controlled b market controlled by the homeland and intellectual protection service as well as a library of congress effort to control the property we own and would like to buy

6106 easy invent cad submit platfo easy invent cad submit platform a programmable interface to sort and submit inventions per company quickly in a demand and non

chronological manner.
6107 laser eye surgery laser eye surgery by way of emory university and the hospital at midtown and the parts in side the laser surgical technique
6108 spool effect of data data tran spool effect of data data translation spool effect of data data translation one way in and two ways out is better than only one way in and one way out. logical translation is that a question of danger comes into guess work. a modification of compression is only a peg. modified m peg? sounds like an alice in wonderland piece. the ability to read and write and well as read writes and translates. the compression of the mp is a question of a fact of desire?
6109 a program to build a series o a program to build a series of files in order to switch mobile phone operating systems and then to install a different operating system and reload your data
6110 a crowd processor that wi a crowd processor that will use two or more tapes to create a crowd of itx atx mitx tx boards working to process as one board by tape and crowd presets known also as modular tx units. it was not until the mid to late s that dj and electronic musicians in chicago found a use for the machine in the context of the newly developing house music genre. in the early 's as new acid styles emerged the tb was often overdrive producing a harsher sound. examples of this technique include hard floor's ep acperience and interlect 's ep volcano. the wellknown acid sound is typically produced by playing a repeating note pattern on the tb while altering the filter's cutoff frequency resonance and envelope modulation. the tb 's accent control modifies a note's volume filter resonance and envelope modulation allowing further variations in timbre. a distortion effect either by using a guitar effects pedal or over driving the input of an audio mixer is commonly used to give the tb a denser noisier timbreas the resulting sound is much richer in harmonics. the head designer of the tb tadao kikumoto was also responsible for leading design of the tr drum machine.
6111 a study of any cure by way of a study of any cure by way of toxic and valance testing to include but not limited to cancer and diseases like alzheimer's and substance abuse cessation aids.
6112 mandatory cloud bandwidth con mandatory cloud bandwidth control to suggest that a cloud should only hold so much practical waste to the internet entirety as a application as a whole to reduce backups and compress data backups by parts.
6113 data compression cloud format data compression cloud format the means to compress scrolling data that may need to move and write and read ready as well as transport to place to place
6114 securing and encryption by wa securing and encryption by way of format doubling for example this format is encrypted then this format is translated into this file format to read
6115 converting multiple computer converting multiple computer motherboards to unify into a working system that is not parallel (matching) or odd working (not matching) into a new cabinet data of mini desktop situation and cards that tell the central processor to do what the completed mission of computing would be in short by software.
6116 interoperable cpu a central interoperable cpu a central processing unit that branches your own connections how you want to build your high performance system to allow any configuration important to you and the scale of your platform
6117 interoperable building parts interoperable building parts and board design free build parts designed to connect a central processing unit that branches your own connections how you want to build your high performance system to allow any configuration important to you

and the scale of your platform with extended and non duplicate or duplicate ports that make sense to everyone similar to concurrent motherboards that are free standing and removable such as replaceable transistors capacitors and third and secondary chips as to replace a single motherboard with multiple boards with a top level processing chip

6118 many carbonates into heat as c many carbonates into heat as catalyst many complex solutions to air and water with a new multiple compound of a s tyro synthetic new starch with metal poly carbonate to a s tyro carbonate compound? for use in interesting and problematic situations? more to be found. many carbonates into heat as catalyst

6119 configure this into a system configure this into a system with power management configure this into a system with computational control configure this into a system with data scale management a square chance chassis that fits with your own choices and arrangement. free arrangement with thermal vents and common connections ports that are unobtrusive beyond the rack. continued a space for this cpu with ports

6120 a hardware system that will p a hardware system that will power that software exactly (software that estimates the hardware system that will work with that software exactly) processing and computations inside a software vessel a vessel that estimates processing and computations as an artist and inventor it comes to my attention that there are some programs that don't require endless size and resource values

6121 intel edison kit for arduino intel edison kit for arduino single components edi arduin.al.k modified to control xeon phi on off and load switch

6122 a software program that will a software program that will generate code for external unsorted efi batches to route any computations needed

6123 traffic cloud and perbuilt s traffic cloud and perbuilt selects for realtime issue management

6124 police cloud and perbuilt se police cloud and perbuilt selects for realtime issue management

6125 syndicated media news cloud a syndicated media news cloud and perbuilt selects for realtime issue management

6126 air bound traffic cloud and p air bound traffic cloud and perbuilt selects for realtime issue management

6127 war management satellite / gr war management satellite / ground cloud and perbuilt selects for realtime issue management

6128 amplitude measurement infinity amplitude measurement infinity and other infinities all makes for an artificial intelligence with some or less than a real opinion for itself but more a suggestion of what we could do and how it should be done...

6129 gas start and hybrid long run gas start and hybrid long run alternative highway mileage fuel economy method is when the start is the majority controlled by combustion fuel and the highway gears are controlled by electricity methods with each gear a different volt and torque

6130 minimum sale retail price clo minimum sale retail price cloud and perbuilt selects for realtime issue management

6131 digital shelf price display f digital shelf price display for real time updates from a msrp cloud

6132 digital shelf price display f digital shelf price display for real time updates from a msrp cloud stored planed and adjustable by demands something that would make a sale percustomer and availability

6133 synthetic liquid plastic este synthetic liquid plastic ester and carbon soot energy in a single compound to make a combustible energy (incinerator biproducts and alcohol acids)
6134 educational in class os educa educational in class os educational operating system with intent to block virus and provide a safe computation platforms for age and course specific apps educational cloud system and perbuilt selects for realtime issue management
6135 a habit release agent to alco a habit release agent to alcohol abuse patch pill gum
6136 a habit release agent to mari a habit release agent to marijuana abuse patch pill gum
6137 the infinite motion inside the the infinite motion inside the first sphere is made by all the rest of the batteries recharging the original battery inside. the only thing missing (magnetic electricity generating) is the method to recharge a battery with the least amount of connections for less resistance for more force magnetic motion generator
6138 it s a fact of life that to be it s a fact of life that to be propelled into a unfair and non respect form of work is not only detrimental and confusing to the artist it degrades the work and makes the artist suffer. from the beginning the underground of house and techno makes what we
6139 an elaborate paging hardware an elaborate paging hardware system that links processors for a continuous processing group of microchips alignend or complimentary in any similarity that forms an accessible shape of a shed family hardware to add cores to a group of processing cores and multiplying threads in a desired format chipcloud co chips
6140 an elaborate paging hardware an elaborate paging hardware system that links processors for a continuous processing group of microchips alignend or complimentary in any similarity that forms an accessible shape of a shed family hardware to add cores to a group of processing cores and multiplying threads in a desired format chipcloud co chips board and socket exchange
6141 no cloud software registratio no cloud software registration a program specific intent to keep the software as is and with out any foreign auto updates and stripped integration from internet interference of opportunity and eula confidence trials of intent to disturb the sleeping software wintel <a href=http://crione.com/index.php?route=product/product&product_id=&search=&category_id=></a>
6142 effervescent mouth wash for s effervescent mouth wash for serious ailments like headaches bacteria and dizziness caused by oral sickness.
6143 a thing called turbo per elem a thing called turbo per element that can shape a path where previously there was no way to reflect perpendicular or parallel with the help of mini and per operation by a hypos thesischip alternate computational curve based algorithms aiding by another chip
6144 comma separated encryption com comma separated encryption comma separated encryption another reason is to continue work on a daily basis as intended securely strange brew is only a reason to understand that everyone is csv. styled now and excel my microsoft is no reason to degrade the graphical keys to encryption... imagine
6145 vertical and embedded chip sti vertical and embedded chip stilts to branch layered under and over stacked layered blanks to add to a multiple layered processing chip or storage
6146 a thing called turbo per elem a thing called turbo per element that can shape a path where previously there was no way to reflect perpendicular or parallel with the help of mini and per operation by a stressthesischip alternate computational curve based algorithms aiding by another chip in a chain reaction processing

6147 more desktop capacity by way more desktop capacity by way of modular expansions via mini modular modes non ecc or ecc yes either or intent sell a module to me and make it bigger
6148 open thread navigational embe open thread navigational embedded software. a software base that controls the method of navigation of a processing thread inside a cpu
6149 curriculum software for publi curriculum software for public schools no cloud base or cloud base data schema download and toss media vs. intent to recycle and modify in class testing by way of simple send and receive test email like online college with intuitive public school social connections
6150 triplet pi translation axis f triplet pi translation axis for compensation equation sum and path intent.
6151 triplet pi translation axis f triplet pi translation axis for compensation equation sum part travel pi cubed translation axis for compensation equation sum and path intent. software hardware virtual and literal intent to create and estimate any means of anno place in time points of vector registration per annotation
6152 triplet pi translation axis f triplet pi translation axis for compensation equation sum part travel pi cubed translation axis for a compensation equation sum and path intent. software hardware virtual and literal intent to create and estimate any means of anno place in time points of vector registration per annotation software hardware virtual and literal intent to create and estimate any means of anno place in time points of vector registration per annotation to start with the equation of two that is cubed and then translation inside travel
6153 triplet pi translation axis f triplet pi translation axis for compensation equation sum part travel pi cubed translation axis for compensation equation sum and path intent. software hardware virtual and literal intent to create and estimate any means of anno place in time points of vector registration per annotation software hardware virtual and literal intent to create and estimate any means of anno place in time points of vector registration per annotation to start with the equation of two that is cubed and then translation inside travel. to multiply and intensify _/+/? cloud compute (server or software) the matters into a higher computational sum of what when where how and why
6154 real web a web connection tha real web a web connection that is a retail and local web that processes alternate connections like credit cards and other information like medical records and bank transactions. a web that makes real life from day to day a positive one with higher restricted content and in contrast to the global internet application itself this is a connection with either a satellite or direct phone number that is not connected globally or may eventually be titled the real web. /c ri on e .com
6155 nano related myriad layers of nano related myriad layers of pressing alignment in branch layered over and under stacked layered blanks to add to the building of a layered processing chip
6156 speechless while in love appli speechless while in love applications that text and how to make it as small as one or two options that have a greater click appeal paraphrase questions with proper context all while scripting speechless while in love applications that text and how to make it as small as one or two options that have a greater click appeal paraphrase questions with proper context all while scripting how do we go from ugly misshapen clouds to something that has more than only a tech savvy appeal? why can't we find words that mean what we say when we are in love? everybody knows what they feel when they are in love just sometimes it is so much easier to give up and say allot rather than nothing or even rather

than one thing that people usually say. for example to use a phrase that makes grammatically correct questions like the way that large companies have with telephone services like for example would you like to buy now? or continue shopping with this product that is like something you just saw but there are better colors in this other product? how to go from multiple choices that don't make sense to a more exact link that makes intent complete? applications that text and how to make it as small as one or two options that have a greater click appeal paraphrase with proper context...

6157 real web part encryption ph real web part encryption phone channel a web connection that is a retail and local web that processes alternate connections like credit cards and other information like medical records and bank transactions. a web that makes real life from day to day a positive one with higher restricted content and in contrast to the global internet application itself this is a connection with either a satellite or direct phone number that is not connected globally or may eventually be titled the real web. /c ri on e .com

6158 data archive retail pack keep data archive retail pack keeping the pack a retail matter when time does matter

6159 a free or sale community secu a free or sale community secure or friendly web source connections community web

6160 build a toy platform you subm build a toy platform you submit the size shape and means and function and go play

6161 build a software platform you build a software platform you submit the size shape and means and function and go play

6162 brain temperature and intelli brain temperature and intelligence is the temperature related to intelligence? or is intelligence only hereditary?

6163 big data creative data engine big data creative data engineers compliant hardware client requests ability software wreckless replacement exceptions speed in control using test and server strength to encrypt and control critical cohesion products and services of any kind

6164 organ cell symbiosis cloning organ cell symbiosis cloning and replacement organs to grow two cells into a new organ for kidney patients caner cures and bioorganic failures or positives

6165 to avoid another war use dipl to avoid another war use diplomatic monetary incentives and resources or not

6166 inspiration to grow your busin inspiration to grow your business when you decide to have another baby inspiration when little families become big business... or rather when big business becomes a bigger family to maintain a reliable structure takes a lot of planning and it's judgment that puts hard work to use when it is time or when it needs to happen... growth in business starts with a little inspiration.

6167 vertical and embedded chip sti vertical and embedded chip stilts to branch layered un der and over stacked layered blanks to add to a multiple layered processing chip or storage

6168 encrypted phonenumber transm encrypted phonenumber transmitting and receiving key's and the new enigma generator.

6169 encrypted phonesoftware tran encrypted phonesoftware transmitting and receiving key's and the new enigma generator.

6170 unformulated alien text forma unformulated alien text formats to create a unknown and previously illegible type text to keep data secure said a unknown character symbol set that will translate into some thing as known to the other receiver

6171 build your own cloud service build your own cloud service software hardware and applications global functions of cloud server storage and the medium that powers that service incorporated with small large and desktop applications with input and control to manage your own stack of servers that have a mission to provide a decisive constitution on off and critical cohesion. nanotubes nanobuds) · glassy carbon sp forms linear acetylenic carbon
6172 we build your cloud service we build your cloud service architects engineers software hardware and applications architects engineers global functions of cloud server storage and the medium that powers that service incorporated with small large and desktop applications with input and control to manage your own stack of servers that have a mission to provide a decisive constitution on off and critical cohesion.
6173 the light age of board techno the light age of board technology layered fiber optical computer boards heat resistant and accessible to carbon fiber
6174 to search for a topic with an to search for a topic with an image. to find people places and things. with input from meta tags such as technical terms when where who and why. as well as to modify the photo scan or topic by perspective date and angle using the image itself and the topic to search with. the intent is to exactly find the right thing at the right time while using visual content and with proper context.
6175 personal freedom to drive mak personal freedom to drive makes me think that taking cars and making trains out of them is against my freedom.
6176 optical fiber paths and boa optical fiber paths and boards that use lens motors optical motors and optic conductors in conjunction with a optical cpu making electrons differently than an ion more sort of a ee on
6177 optical fiber paths and board optical fiber paths and boards that use lens motors optical motors and optic conductors in conjunction with a optical cpu making electrons differently than an ion more sort of a ee on
6178 future of less open software a future of less open software and the concurrent topics that it will hold such as fee based operation time and subscription updates
6179 nano related myriad layers of nano related myriad layers of pressing alignment in branch layered over and un der stacked layered blanks to add to the building of a layered processing chip the sun and a certain distant star are both overhead. at time the planet has rotated ° and the distant star is overhead again but the sun is not (? = one sidereal day). it is not until a little later at time that the sun is overhead again (? = one solar day).earth's rotation period relative to the sun (its mean solar day) is seconds of mean solar time. each of these seconds is slightly longer than an si second because earth's solar day is now slightly longer than it was during the th century due to tidal acceleration. the mean solar second between and was chosen in by simon new comb as the independent unit of time in his tables of the sun. these tables were used to calculate the world's ephemerides between and so this second became known as the ephemeris second. the si second was made equal to the ephemeris second in .[ ] earth's rotation period relative to the fixed stars called its stellar day by the international earth rotation and reference systems service (iers) is . seconds of mean solar time (ut) (h m . s).[][n] earth's rotation period relative to the precessing or moving mean vernal equinox misnamed its sidereal day[n] is . seconds of mean solar time (ut) (h m . s). [] thus the sidereal day is shorter than the stellar day by about . ms.[] the length of the mean solar day in si seconds is available from the iers for the periods [] and .[] from wikipedia
6180 successful data sharing percep successful data sharing perceptual image ocr codes and

translation scripts and security file extending import export applications support and help
6181 super embedding board technol super embedding board technology using quartered circuits and fractal inverse technology making boards flat and embedding while conducting in one motion with out attaching
6182 myriad nano layer built magnif myriad nano layer built magnified transistors bipolar transistor and grounded emitter
6183 simple est is a solar cell pho simple est is a solar cell phone re charger my airplane crashed and let s say i m stranded who would i call first solar cell phone re charger
6184 sub scaleable sd branches and sub scaleable sd branches and trees
6185 microwave reactor is a combin microwave reactor is a combination of reactions in few scenarios like for example the combination of air or water to run a turbine and create electricity or the microwaveable consideration of other reactive materials as solvents or compounds to create ene
6186 off shore ocean current elect off shore ocean current electric generators as opposed to land locked wind mills
6187 compound angle chips are the compound angle chips are the chips that have horizontal diagonal vertical processing that will aid in the processing of a vertical and other angles including horizontal made wafer of chips in a faster more compact size while printing in multiple stages of
6188 compound chip parts are the c compound chip parts are the cores memory and agents that have direction any compound direction of processing with building of a vertical and horizontal wafer of chips in a faster more compact size while printing in multiple stages of mediums in a series o
6189 knowing the difference paintin knowing the difference painting any way you like and knowing the difference
6190 it s a lot like a nuclear bomb it s a lot like a nuclear bomb only in reverse. instead of destroying elements we are putting them together. but more important than a super spontaneous collision we are separating the elements for recycling and purification. the muffler and the past catalytic transformer burning trash isn't as bad as it sounds connotations of shock come to mind when things are sometimes thought of a process. what i mean is when we think of how would you do that? there are so many different variables that sometimes it's like turning tar into gas or water to wine. the things that technology are capable of now are more impressive than we can even guess. the cost of burning trash is unequivalent to the benefits. i have found a way to think of things. air and light is the motto of my local fire station. the best thing to imagine is to start with two elements that are the most simple to begin some kind of abstract formula. what the public is afraid of are the contaminates in the solutions that are presented after and during and even before the spark of air and light. so let me explain in detail. it's a lot like a nuclear bomb only in reverse. instead of destroying elements we are putting them together. but more important than a superspontaneous collision we are separating the elements for recycling and purification. the muffler and the past catalytic converters in a car is one example of how the process is somewhat related to one another. the carburetor was invented by karl benz in pressure
6191 open out doors chassis mod self open out doors chassis mod self adjusting climate control is to enable a single cell or multi cell device operate permanently out side by routed power or solar powered operations liquid contact cooling and grounded transistors capacitors

and completed sho

6192 two separate processors that a two separate processors that are equal and octet each on their own capacity

6193 server over a system is a sim server over a system is a simple configuration of one server per many parts and many redundant parts per many systems

6194 exchange chip stilts with dat exchange chip stilts with data processing calculating rise and run to make inside circuits happen and connecting super fine cable gold lines and repeating octagon chip inside chips and vector resolution chips and conducting boards

6195 intersecting diagonal and per intersecting diagonal and perpendicular circuit threads by vector resolution chips

6196 chemical searing internal proc chemical searing internal process and reactions inherit water activated medicine

6197 cylindrical rotations with hou cylindrical rotations with hour glass shaped impact

6198 a user operated device that enters as your original l a user operated device that enters as your original line and adapts to your connection that inturns blocks all connections and or encrypts or allows connections based on a simple password protocol in another way to say is to secure a networks connection based on a encryption box and also known as a hard line encrypted router firewall box patent pending abstract utility

6199 a software virus company operated device that enters a software virus company operated device that enters as your original line and adapts to your connection that inturns blocks all connections and or encrypts or allows connections based on a simple password protocol in another way to say is to secure a networks connection based on a encryption box and also known as a hard line encrypted router firewall box patent pending abstract utility _

6200 a software virus company operated device that you can a software virus company operated device that you can insert data with a secure environment to see the data without risk patent pending abstract utility

6201 a government sponsored software virus company operate a government sponsored software virus company operated network scanning police bot to help find and trace topic of negative nature

6202 the validity of a data sheet and the value rating for the validity of a data sheet and the value rating for true data and how true the data is at any capacity warfare any other means incorporating system interrupts

6203 satellite service incorporated is a freelance satelli satellite service incorporated is a freelance satellite scenario that builds and sells bandwidth on demand as a service for large and small company uses with a permit to render

6204 federal satellite admin satellite service incorporate federal satellite admin satellite service incorporated is a oversee satellite scenario that manages and approves the builds and sales of bandwidth on demand as a service for large and small company uses with a permit to render

6205 a red collar crime is a high ranking official caught a red collar crime is a high ranking official caught or suspected to be wrong in monetary just gain

6206 printed operating system is a version of embedded cod printed operating system is a version of embedded code that may or may not be changed according to the write function of the system and may be printed during manufacturing

6207 war network unlinking is a unlooped firewall device war network unlinking is a

unlooped firewall device for security and data integrity in a war data center
6208 election network linking is a unlooped firewall devi election network linking is a unlooped firewall device for security and data integrity in a election data center
6209 network linking chip is a unlooped firewall embedded network linking chip is a unlooped firewall embedded device for security and data integrity in a data center end start point
6210 pyramid chip scheme is a scaleable multi processor r pyramid chip scheme is a scaleable multi processor right of way that claims more computing ability per consumer rather than consumer per processors
6211 multiple assignment os christopher gabr multiple assignment os dcfbc _page_
6212 marijuana is should not be legal due to addiction iss marijuana is should not be legal due to addiction issues and behavior problems _
6213 wrongful legality of bitcoin due to security invasion wrongful legality of bitcoin due to security invasion and . of any such coin worth or unofficially a money right as to interfere with the united states treasury
6214 options in memory and the memory attachment of a scal options in memory and the memory attachment of a scaled . inch standard drive as a to sata connected accelerator memory drop and find add on's
6215 a chip that holds the proper bios and instruction set a chip that holds the proper bios and instruction set for the plugin itself to operate as a fail safe pre occupied set of true plug and play functions in any os and any system on chip meaning if it's not operational it does not operate
6216 to take the block ledger offline from an online state to take the block ledger offline from an online state of transactions would secure the worlds trade and commerce around the globe and to end crypt o currency would help the standard trade sanctions for every one
6217 to alternate the current internet as a second interne to alternate the current internet as a second internet for commerce and create a default encrypted status as to recreate a secured internet to require a ssl or tss
6218 retro fit smart house switches and connectivity featu retro fit smart house switches and connectivity features for traditional homes would include things like a room to room hub and wifi central apps that negotiate lights air conditioning and blinds for privacy even the door security and room itself audio with a one time base to circuit transforming upgradeable port
6219 escape the os update plugin to escape operating syst escape the os update plugin to escape operating system updates permanently or semi choice
6220 data loss and the kill update blanket this is eviden data loss and the kill update blanket this is evident of any such blanket consumer rights to agree or not agree with property of any such malicious terms from a known consumer issuance discrepancy
6221 update response company is a secured and devoted comp update response company is a secured and devoted complaint and semi responsible negotiating proactive alliance between consumer and the operating system manufacturer
6222 multi drone pilot compensation software is a air and multi drone pilot compensation software is a air and path pi ratio that groups or navigates multiple drones
6223 multi drone pilot compensation hardware is a part tha multi drone pilot compensation hardware is a part that works with air and path pi ratio that groups or navigates multiple drones first and foremost i take a larger picture into consideration. what is the difference with

a diplomat trying to become a missionary? what is the difference between a philosopher such as myself on a mission as opposed to a supermodel trying to hand out vitamins? section i. teach a man to fish proverb: give a man a fish he eats for a day teach a man to fish he eats for a lifetime. communism doesn't work and democracy does. to talk to a person in a nonmilitant/ non missionary/ nongovernmental fashion and let the defined reason of history hold presidency. a lot of my ideas and inventions will not work because the country at hand is so broken and war struck. to me my conversational prose is the only intent. slavery is wrong and hatred toward one another is evil. in history the best thing to do is learn from it. chile adopted the us constitution and to this day they are the most successful south american country to date. this is my idea to prove right. section ii. filled with uncertain and discernible rights. antiquilology makes the possession of man illegal the taxation only upon representation it's a dream that people want a miracle device that heals and finishes off anguish. it's to myself that a theoretical just of the basic situation starts with the ability to start at the root of the problem and understand that with all things considered the problem is their government. imagine how we the people became great is by fore fathers that distrusted the english i think that to my understanding the wars inside poverty stricken countries are facing civil unjust due to huge improbable governments. to go to a country at war is not the goal. to begin is to see a country in need but not to attack the country first in the most war torn. help the one who is near the country that is close to the war and have intuition spread. if the plan is successful the data will become unquestionably great. taxation and spread of united states like society to third world countries.

6224 stealth multi drone is a radar less and radar proof s stealth multi drone is a radar less and radar proof satellite driven drone

6225 scaleable drone with features and cell communication scaleable drone with features and cell communications software for cell to cell drone flight captur

6226 drone cell stations protocol for scaleable drone wit drone cell stations protocol for scaleable drone with features and cell communications network for cell to cell drone flight and land navigation

6227 lost drone safe way map and navigation per satellite lost drone safe way map and navigation per satellite route and permits for lost dog drones that can find their way home

6228 cron job flight navigation servers for drone devices cron job flight navigation servers for drone devices is a ping service that directs and corrects any such flight or road travel

6229 cron job flight navigation code and software for devi cron job flight navigation code and software for devices that work with ping control

6230 cron job flight navigation hardware that incorporates cron job flight navigation hardware that incorporates the memory factor of from point a to point b in a compensation mode

6231 anomaly report service is a service that helps artifi anomaly report service is a service that helps artificial devices understand seeds of change and occurrences in the issue of a change as a compensation equation and a reference base for service like a wind pattern change to help wind mills more energy during the windiest part of the day from what direction and different composites that make up all of the properties of fire when the trash is burned to reclaim the mediums.

6232 anomaly report service is a service hardware and tran anomaly report service is a service hardware and translation equipment that helps artificial devices understand seeds of change and occurrences in the issue of a change as a compensation equation and a reference base for service like a wind pattern change to help wind mills more energy during the windiest part of the day from what direction

6233 anomaly report service is a service software analyzin anomaly report service is a service software analyzing patterns and statistics that helps artificial devices understand seeds of change and occurrences in the issue of a change as a compensation equation and a reference base for service like a wind pattern change to help wind mills more energy during the windiest part of the day from what direction

6234 dual user add on information applications that work o dual user add on information applications that work on cache and submission processes is a working rule based program that allows more than one user at a time to use the same work place for example a spread sheet that is incorporated to other sheets and linked by a pseudo data connection and plural mouse movements

6235 multiple user hardware that works with software appli multiple user hardware that works with software applications that run on live cache and submission processes is a working rule based program that allows more than one user at a time to use the same work place for example a spread sheet that is incorporated to other sheets and linked by a pseudo data connection and plural mouse movements

6236 watch and see user and plus applications that work on watch and see user and plus applications that work on cache and submission processes is a working rule based program that allows more than one user at a time to use the same work place for example a air navigation tower that is interoperable with in an area of operation seeing working and using plural mouse movements commands and operations in formulas

6237 random seed and anomaly report cloud data with dual u random seed and anomaly report cloud data with dual user and plus applications that work on cache and submission processes is a working rule based program that allows more than one user at a time to use the same work place for example a spread sheet that is incorporated to other sheets and linked by a pseudo data connection and plural mouse movements

6238 diode printed and stacked nano metric parts diode printed and stacked nano metric parts

6239 hot chip for safety safety chip and sos communication hot chip for safety safety chip and sos communication bridge allocation software

6240 global for profit school learning software and tablet global for profit school learning software and tablet interface that will start with ocr textbooks and ed information sale and the room of improvisations in learning processes to help a modern school internet deploy globally and recreate learning on a new level as well as trouble shooting and learning curves in students and problems in software company from ed text to learning and certificate graduates of learning scales

6241 local state wide for profit school learning software local state wide for profit school learning software and tablet interface that will start with ocr textbooks and ed information sale and the room of improvisations in learning processes to help a modern school internet deploy state wide and recreate learning on a new level as well as trouble shooting and learning curves in students and problems in software company from ed text to learning and certificate graduates of learning scales

6242 free global not for profit school learning software a free global not for profit school learning software and tablet interface that will start with ocr textbooks and ed information sale and the room of improvisations in learning processes to help a modern school internet deploy globally and recreate learning on a new level as well as trouble shooting and learning curves in students and problems in software company from ed text to learning and certificate graduates of learning scales

6243 ocr and translation meaning software for clear intern ocr and translation meaning software for clear internet learning school software and beyond is a linking between shapes and meaning in a data format language language learning

6244 ocr and translation meaning software for search data ocr and translation meaning software for search data and search form engine and beyond is a linking meaning between shapes and meaning in a usage data format language language learning

6245 object and meaning database ocr and translation meani object and meaning database ocr and translation meaning software for search data and search form engine and beyond is a linking meaning between shapes and meaning in a usage data format language language learning

6246 many objects and meaning database ocr and translation many objects and meaning database ocr and translation meaning software for search data and search form engine and beyond is a linking meaning between shapes and meaning in a usage data format language language learning

6247 many objects and multiple meaning database ocr and tr many objects and multiple meaning database ocr and translation meaning software for search data and search form engine and beyond is a linking meaning between shapes and meaning in a usage data format language language learning

6248 ai laws in effect and laws to specify the out come of ai laws in effect and laws to specify the out come of ai and ai actions and ai faults and government result laws of failure compensation and punishment

6249 artificial energy is a nonspontaneous reaction to a artificial energy is a nonspontaneous reaction to a forced digital or analog form of simulated energy in a real sense of negative or positive ae

6250 artificial magnetic energy is a nonspontaneous react artificial magnetic energy is a nonspontaneous reaction to a forced magnetic form of simulated energy in a real sense of negative or positive ae

6251 artificial relative energy is a nonspontaneous react artificial relative energy is a nonspontaneous reaction to a forced magnetic digital amped weight in a volatile form of simulated energy in a real sense of negative or positive ae

6252 negative conductive algorithms are the translation of negative conductive algorithms are the translation of current in a form that may be used to hold energy and data at the same time with a specific compression ratio per algorithm and energy source in a cold state

6253 positive with negative conductive algorithms are the positive with negative conductive algorithms are the translation of current in a form that may be used to hold energy and data at the same time with a specific compression ratio per algorithm and energy source in a alternate state

6254 positive with negative conductive algorithms cpu chip positive with negative conductive algorithms cpu chips computer memory and addon processors are the translation of current in a form that may be used to hold energy and data at the same time with a specific

compression ratio per algorithm and energy source in a alternate state
6255 trans coding chips that make a wave of energy into po trans coding chips that make a wave of energy into positive with negative conductive algorithms cpu chips computer memory and addon processors are the translation of current in a form that may be used to hold energy and data at the same time with a specific compression ratio per algorithm and energy source in a alternate state
6256 free functional addons are the additional scaleable free functional addons are the additional scaleable plug and play options of any such freely to place in a location to import processing and to increase a probability of performance
6257 tiered leveled sequential multiple free functional ad tiered leveled sequential multiple free functional addons are the additional scaleable plug and play options of any such freely to place in a location to import processing and to increase a probability of performance
6258 cloud addons are the servers or virtual performance cloud addons are the servers or virtual performance servers in data center to act as a tiered leveled sequential multiple free functional addons are the additional scaleable plug and play options of any such freely to place in a location to import processing and to increase a probability of performance
6259 virtual performance servers in data center are equata virtual performance servers in data center are equatable to code and scripting within folders and software allocations
6260 multiple tiered virtual performance servers in data c multiple tiered virtual performance servers in data center are equatable to code and scripting within folders and software allocations in a series format
6261 virtual functional addons are the additional scaleab virtual functional addons are the additional scaleable plug and play software options of any such freely to place in a location to import processing and to increase a probability of performance
6262 virtual functional gpu are the additional scaleable p virtual functional gpu are the additional scaleable plug and play software options of any such freely to place in a location to import processing and to increase a probability of performance
6263 gpu inside a gpu inside for virtual functional gpu ar gpu inside a gpu inside for virtual functional gpu are the additional scaleable plug and play software options of any such freely to place in a location to import processing and to increase a probability of performance x
6264 upgrade able secondary level chips that co process in upgrade able secondary level chips that co process in an onboard secondary socket that incorporate alternate processing like the central chip but in a on board or in socket form of non graphic non central but in a second level of cache and co processing formation of working computational additions far from a memory take away but a embedded solution market
6265 upgrade able secondary level random access memory tha upgrade able secondary level random access memory that store in an onboard secondary group of sockets that incorporate alternate processing like the first level ram but in a off or on board or in socket form of non graphic non central but in a second level of cache formation of working computational additions like a memory take away but a embedded solution market
6266 retro fit smart home breaker box is a device board th retro fit smart home breaker box is a device board that is controllable by phone or computer network of links and changes for variations and add on's in power and connectivity
6267 retro fit smart home breaker os and the retro fit sma retro fit smart home breaker os and the retro fit smart home breaker box is a device board that is controllable by phone or

computer network of links and changes for variations and add on's in power and connectivity
6268 security add on with retro fit smart home breaker os security add on with retro fit smart home breaker os and the retro fit smart home breaker box is a device board that is controllable by phone or computer network of links and changes for variations and add on's in power and connectivity
6269 new item embedded controller instructions as to add o new item embedded controller instructions as to add operating instructions per operation and embedded vectors
6270 smart home adaptive new or retro appliance embedded p smart home adaptive new or retro appliance embedded power instructions switch control for a power related control operations
6271 smart home adaptive new or retro appliance embedded l smart home adaptive new or retro appliance embedded library of instructions for compound control of smart objects with embedded options and chips ram as well as ports
6272 local library object instructions is the safe and un local library object instructions is the safe and unlinked local area network of a system smart home adaptive new or retro appliance embedded library of instructions for compound control of smart objects with embedded options and chips ram as well as ports
6273 connected object network of instructions library obje connected object network of instructions library object instructions is the linked local area network of a system smart home adaptive new or retro appliance embedded library of instructions for compound control of smart objects with embedded options and chips ram as well as ports
6274 a deliberate method network of connected object netwo a deliberate method network of connected object network of instructions library object instructions is the paid hierarchy connection within a local area network of a system smart home adaptive new or retro appliance embedded library of instructions for compound control of smart objects with embedded options and chips ram as well as ports
6275 paid search into systems is a simple search engine th paid search into systems is a simple search engine that searches by tunnel and hidden internet protocol into the specified system with paid results on a different page
6276 paid search into systems network is a simple search e paid search into systems network is a simple search engine alliance that searches by tunnel and hidden internet protocol in the specified system with paid results on a different page
6277 auto thread and processor controller software and scr auto thread and processor controller software and scripted control chips are the automated central processor unit and the memory optimization included with all of the other parts such as gpu and or oi accelerator and even a co processor in unison as such as to work uniformly as fast as possible
6278 serial recording there is a need for a faster paced i serial recording there is a need for a faster paced invention deposition writing and security method with the usa to make a licensed professional is important in a serial recorded document status combined with the method of registration
6279 landfill mining and dithering mobile disassembly pla landfill mining and dithering mobile disassembly plant is an arranged machine that separates the material on a scale per unit of measurement first is the magnetic property of the unit second is the weight of the unit and third is the size and this method is repeated over and over again to a sufficient level of recycled property

6280 gmvitamins are genetically modified vitamins that e gmvitamins are genetically modified vitamins that encourage growth to patients with severe deficiencies in a certain vitamin or cell of the body
6281 gmantivirus are genetically modified vaccines that gmantivirus are genetically modified vaccines that protect important cell growth to patients with severe deficiencies in a certain vitamin or cell of the body
6282 autonomous landfill mining and dithering mobile disa autonomous landfill mining and dithering mobile disassembly plant is a robotics controlled arranged machine that separates the material on a scale per unit of measurement first is the magnetic property of the unit second is the weight of the unit and third is the size and this method is repeated over and over again to a sufficient level of recycled property
6283 microwave reactor is a combination of reactions in fe microwave reactor is a combination of reactions in few scenarios like for example the combination of air or water to run a turbine and create electricity or the microwaveable consideration of other reactive materials as solvents or compounds to create energy as the catalyst as the microwave the converter or electric generation and then the recycle of the reaction
6284 fossilized and un radiated uranium through a process fossilized and un radiated uranium through a process of microwave until negative powers are there and no heat is constant
6285 dunner and the re exam of pre existed depleted uraniu dunner and the re exam of pre existed depleted uranium for microwave tables and the recycled nuclear products
6286 microwave energy and the reconstituted nuclear elemen microwave energy and the reconstituted nuclear elements for regeneration and reuse
6287 private energy farms and the mobile battery that can private energy farms and the mobile battery that can change the energy industry are easy to dream of but more difficult to consume the intent to make a plug and rechargeable system of portable electricity is in itself to create a whole industry the study of and arrangement of a recycle system with acceptable awareness for the environment can be achieved as easy as the difference in a propane tank and the electrical battery exchange
6288 vertical chip engineering software is a software that vertical chip engineering software is a software that will aid in the building of a vertical wafer of chips in a faster more compact size
6289 vertical chip engineering printers is a machine that vertical chip engineering printers is a machine that will aid in the building of a vertical wafer of chips in a faster more compact size
6290 vertical chip multi compound printers is a machine th vertical chip multi compound printers is a machine that will aid in the building of a vertical wafer of chips in a faster more compact size while printing in multiple stages of mediums in a series of layers
6291 chip compound direction printers is a machine that wi chip compound direction printers is a machine that will aid in the building of a vertical and horizontal wafer of chips in a faster more compact size while printing in multiple stages of mediums in a series of layers to print horizontal and vertical to arrange in a more efficient manner
6292 chip compound direction software is a machine writer chip compound direction software is a machine writer that will aid in the building of a vertical and horizontal wafer of chips in a faster more compact size while printing in multiple stages of mediums in a series of

layers to print horizontal and vertical to arrange in a more efficient manner

6293 compound angle chips are the chips that have horizont compound angle chips are the chips that have horizontal diagonal vertical processing that will aid in the processing of a vertical and other angles including horizontal made wafer of chips in a faster more compact size while printing in multiple stages of mediums in a series of layers to print horizontal and vertical to arrange in a more efficient manner

6294 compound chip parts are the cores memory and agents compound chip parts are the cores memory and agents that have direction any compound direction of processing with building of a vertical and horizontal wafer of chips in a faster more compact size while printing in multiple stages of mediums in a series of layers to print horizontal and vertical to arrange in a more efficient manner

6295 compound chip parts are the cores memory and agents t compound chip parts are the cores memory and agents that have direction any compound direction of processing with building of a vertical and horizontal wafer of chips in a faster more compact size while printing in multiple stages of mediums in a series of layers to print horizontal and vertical to arrange in a more efficient manner

6296 multi processing compound angel of processing links t multi processing compound angel of processing links toner compiled compound chip laser printed gold powder and cubic zircon powder printed chips

6297 laboratory do it your self rights to find and cure to laboratory do it your self rights to find and cure to cancers virus and diseases is a old thing new again that the current system to practice active measures of laboratory work require unknown lengths of red tape this is an equation of experience and scholarship to include the diy and proprietary rights for work and operation of private labs

6298 laboratory intellectual rights are the rules and know laboratory intellectual rights are the rules and knowledge ownership of laboratory do it your self rights to find and cure to cancers virus and diseases is a old thing new again that the current system to practice active measures of laboratory work require unknown lengths of red tape this is an equation of experience and scholarship to include the diy and proprietary rights for work and operation of private labs

6299 private research intellectual rights lab permits are private research intellectual rights lab permits are the rules and knowledge ownership of laboratory do it your self rights to find and cure to cancers virus and diseases is a old thing new again that the current system to practice active measures of laboratory work require unknown lengths of red tape this is an equation of experience and scholarship to include the diy and proprietary rights for work and operation of private labs

6300 proprietary research rights laboratory is a seek and proprietary research rights laboratory is a seek and find a cure for a monetary gain

6301 free rights and trade laboratory is the non compete w free rights and trade laboratory is the non compete way of salable research

6302 legally bound comma separated values and sheets for d legally bound comma separated values and sheets for digital paper submissions are records that can be submitted by csv by any such given form for legal certified documents

6303 hope for the wire bound is a simple word for the tran hope for the wire bound is a simple word for the transient of wireless driven things of the internet and the data center

for a smaller more complex driven form of one os per many devices meaning one set of instructions like a web hosting instruction per many devices
6304 part of a room is a frame of sorts for example the se part of a room is a frame of sorts for example the separation of data and the complied operation system could be an easier cloud to use meaning if the parts of any library of data has a role for the drive storage and which functions could be as simple as a read and play part of access which could be a stored part of a program for saving resources and processing some where else
6305 a travel cloud is a set of revolving ip addresses for a travel cloud is a set of revolving ip addresses for data and servers
6306 a secure roaming cloud is a random set of revolving i a secure roaming cloud is a random set of revolving ip addresses for data and servers
6307 a secure lost cloud is a non revolving random resetti a secure lost cloud is a non revolving random resetting ip address for data and servers to help evade domain denial of service
6308 insufficient rights to claim as non negligent for a p insufficient rights to claim as non negligent for a purpose given is to declare a right for the damaged claim over any waiver of rights previously noted
6309 server over a system is a simple configuration of one server over a system is a simple configuration of one server per many parts and many redundant parts per many systems
6310 wrongful creation intent of ai and the false artifici wrongful creation intent of ai and the false artificial intelligent proposal is simply a romantic novel
6311 to short the ai technology market is a given rule of to short the ai technology market is a given rule of thumb of many
6312 alternative to ai is the instructional applications i alternative to ai is the instructional applications ia and the provided instructions of a skynet like operation in a new meaning of the sense
6313 alternatives to artificially driven things are the th alternatives to artificially driven things are the things that are so important like the car and air planes or trains are simple pilot driven back up navigation
6314 the important things of non applied artificial intell the important things of non applied artificial intelligence are to be noted meaning that there is a level to artificial intelligence that should not be applied perverted and abused
6315 positive nature is important in a resolution for bad positive nature is important in a resolution for bad ai outcome and should be held responsible for its nature by the ai maker
6316 ai car insurance is the most positive way for resolut ai car insurance is the most positive way for resolution for bad ai outcome and should be held responsible for its unnatural nature
6317 ai drone insurance is the most positive way for resol ai drone insurance is the most positive way for resolution for bad ai outcome and should be held responsible for its unnatural nature
6318 artificial intelligence and learning aerial and groun artificial intelligence and learning aerial and ground drone is a bot operated drone that is computed to navigate and report with a prepared version of a given set of scenarios
6319 artificial intelligence and learning aerial marine an artificial intelligence and learning aerial marine and ground war drone is a bot operated drone that is computed to navigate and report with a prepared version of a given set of scenarios

6320 stealth artificial intelligence and learning aerial m stealth artificial intelligence and learning aerial marine and ground war drone is a bot operated drone that is computed to navigate and report with a prepared version of a given set of scenarios
6321 search and rescue ai maritime drone artificial intell search and rescue ai maritime drone artificial intelligence and learning aerial marine and ground drone is a bot operated drone that is computed to navigate and report with a prepared version of a given set of scenarios
6322 optical calculation is a step in the optical cpu with optical calculation is a step in the optical cpu with a transposed availability to calculate a problem in a scenario of motion as opposed to a stationary circuit
6323 looping optical calculation is a step in the optical looping optical calculation is a step in the optical cpu with a transposed availability to calculate a problem in a scenario of motion as opposed to a stationary circuit
6324 multiple cycles looping optical calculation is a step multiple cycles looping optical calculation is a step in the optical cpu with a transposed availability to calculate a problem in a scenario of motion as opposed to a stationary circuit
6325 virtual transistors in optical thread translated into virtual transistors in optical thread translated into a code specific processing object for an optical cpu
6326 optical processing language is the binary equal to ce optical processing language is the binary equal to central processing unit code of cubits as an optical cpu
6327 magnetic optical processor is a simple name for the m magnetic optical processor is a simple name for the magnetic cubit optical media circuit written chip that is bound by optical processing language and is the binary equal to central processing unit code of cubits as an optical processor
6328 magnetic object written chip is a simple name for the magnetic object written chip is a simple name for the magnetic cubit optically written chip that is bound by a processing language and is the binary equal to central processing unit code of cubits as an circuit processor
6329 optically written magnetic object is a simple name fo optically written magnetic object is a simple name for the laser written optically printed chip as an circuit processor as opposed to a diffused optically printed chip
6330 optically written object blank is a simple name for t optically written object blank is a simple name for the laser written optically printed chip blank similar to a optical media disc as an circuit processor as opposed to a diffused optically printed chip
6331 portable optically written object blank similar to a portable optically written object blank similar to a optical media disc as an circuit processor as opposed to a diffused optically printed chip
6332 object writer for the portable optically written obje object writer for the portable optically written object blank similar to a optical media disc as an circuit processor as opposed to a diffused optically printed chip will bring circuit printing to the household markets
6333 paid instructions for the object writer for the porta paid instructions for the object writer for the portable optically written object blank similar to a optical media disc as an circuit processor as opposed to a diffused optically printed chip will bring circuit printing to the household diy markets
6334 many optical circuit objects in order on a server bed many optical circuit objects in order on a server bed of input ports meaning a group of objects working as system on chips as

portable optically written object blank similar to a optical media disc as an circuit processor as opposed to a diffused optically printed chip will bring circuit printing to the household diy markets

6335 optical circuit focus range is the measurement of cir optical circuit focus range is the measurement of circuits in an optically written object blank similar to a optical media disc as an circuit processor as opposed to a diffused optically printed chip will bring circuit printing to the household diy markets

6336 in board solid state threading is the path of computa in board solid state threading is the path of computational signals traveling inside the server board for faster translation computations and processing

6337 board solid state hyperthreading is the path of comp board solid state hyperthreading is the path of computational signals traveling inside the server board for faster translation computations and processing

6338 hyper threading cable is a multiple lane cable that t hyper threading cable is a multiple lane cable that transports signals into and from a source to another receiver

6339 hyper threading fiber optic cable is a multiple lane hyper threading fiber optic cable is a multiple lane cable that transports signals into and from a source to another receiver

6340 hyper threading usb cable is a multiple lane cable t hyper threading usb cable is a multiple lane cable that transports signals into and from a source to another receiver

6341 wireless hard drive is a two step data storage drive wireless hard drive is a two step data storage drive and wireless adapter that transports signals into and from a source to another receiver

6342 sd wireless hard drive system is a two step data stor sd wireless hard drive system is a two step data storage drive and wireless adapter that transports signals into and from a source to another receiver

6343 multiplied wireless hard drive router is a multiple s multiplied wireless hard drive router is a multiple signal transporter and encoder with a specified multiple places of destination

6344 multiplied wireless hd receiver is a multiple signal multiplied wireless hd receiver is a multiple signal wireless adapter that transports many different signals into and from a source to another router with specified multiple places in destination

6345 wireless storage network is a non processing cache on wireless storage network is a non processing cache only system of storage drives

6346 wireless computational network processing only system wireless computational network processing only system of processing

6347 computational network processing only system of scrip computational network processing only system of scripted processing

6348 allotted memory network is a shared system of cache a allotted memory network is a shared system of cache and paging system that shares a specified amount of links in memory disc space

6349 home to cell to satellite routers cell branches that home to cell to satellite routers cell branches that hold a message in the packet prefix or suffix that extends the direction of cellular channels that focus to the nearest cell reach to the nearest satellite for convenience and speed

6350 low density performance scale processing is the numbe low density performance scale processing is the number in processors compared to size

6351 high density complex scale processing is the number i high density complex scale processing is the number in processors compared to size

6352 high density performance scale processing is the rati high density performance scale processing is the ratio number in processors compared to scheme of arrangements and clusters in ram and transistors a

6353 category chips are purpose driven chips with that pro category chips are purpose driven chips with that program and task at mind

6354 creative category chips are purpose driven chips with creative category chips are purpose driven chips with that program and task at mind

6355 calc category chips are purpose driven chips with tha calc category chips are purpose driven chips with that program and task at mind

6356 category add on cards are purpose driven chips with t category add on cards are purpose driven chips with that program and task at mind

6357 creative category add on cards are purpose driven chi creative category add on cards are purpose driven chips with that program and task at mind

6358 calc category add on cards are purpose driven chips w calc category add on cards are purpose driven chips with that program and task at mind

6359 multiple category chips are purpose driven chips with multiple category chips are purpose driven chips with that program and task at mind

6360 program categories for specified category chips are p program categories for specified category chips are purpose driven chips with that application software program and task at mind

6361 can we figure out the chemistry in a healthy human can can we figure out the chemistry in a healthy human can we figure out the chemistry in a healthy human

6362 calc program categories for specified category chips calc program categories for specified category chips are purpose driven chips with number and physics application software program and task at mind

6363 creative program categories for specified category ch creative program categories for specified category chips are purpose driven chips with hypothetical and geometry application software program and task at mind

6364 satellite connection grid is a connected alliance of satellite connection grid is a connected alliance of satellites that work and process things like communication together as a whole network

6365 paid satellite data connection grid network is a conn paid satellite data connection grid network is a connected alliance of satellites that work and process things like communication together as a whole network

6366 satellite data packet grid prefix and paid satellite satellite data packet grid prefix and paid satellite connection grid network is a connected alliance of satellites that work and process things like communication together as a whole network with the ability to send packets to and from each other

6367 paid satellite data packet grid prefix network branch paid satellite data packet grid prefix network branches and paid satellite connection grid network is a connected alliance of satellites that work and process things like communication together as a whole network with the ability to send packets to and from each other

6368 paid satellite data packet grid prefix and paid satel paid satellite data packet grid prefix and paid satellite connection grid network is a connected alliance of satellites that work and process things like communication together as a whole network with the ability to send packets to and from each other
6369 satellite to cell branches are cellular channels that satellite to cell branches are cellular channels that focus to the nearest cell reach to the nearest satellite for convenience and speed
6370 home router to cell to satellite paid satellite conne home router to cell to satellite paid satellite connection grid network is a connected alliance of satellites that work and process things like communication together as a whole network with the ability to send packets to and from each other
6371 diesel and ethel sodium nitrate fuel for diesel for t diesel and ethel sodium nitrate fuel for diesel for trucks tractor trailers and cars as well as airplanes and drones
6372 compressed alcoholasgas engine is a compromised vap compressed alcoholasgas engine is a compromised vapor ignition engine for trucks tractor trailers and cars as well as airplanes and drones
6373 in a compressed alcoholasgas engine a compromised v in a compressed alcoholasgas engine a compromised vapor ignition fuel injector is a prepared measure of vapor agitator to make a fine atomized vapor to burn and combust for trucks tractor trailers and cars as well as airplanes and drones
6374 agitated vapor fuel is the closest to flash point in agitated vapor fuel is the closest to flash point in any compound that would be important in a compressed alcoholasgas engine a compromised vapor ignition fuel injector is a prepared measure of vapor agitator to make a fine atomized vapor to burn and combust for trucks tractor trailers and cars as well as airplanes and drones
6375 compromised fuel aerosol is premeasured agitated vap compromised fuel aerosol is premeasured agitated vapor fuel and is the closest to flash point in any compound that would be important in a compressed alcoholasgas engine a compromised vapor ignition fuel injector is a prepared measure of vapor agitator to make a fine atomized vapor to burn and combust for trucks tractor trailers and cars as well as airplanes and drones
6376 compromised fuel aerosol engine will use premeasured compromised fuel aerosol engine will use premeasured agitated vapor fuel and is the closest to flash point in any compound that would be important in a compressed alcoholasgas engine a compromised vapor ignition fuel injector is a prepared measure of vapor agitator to make a fine atomized vapor to burn and combust for trucks tractor trailers and cars as well as airplanes and drones
6377 atomized and vapor hybrid engine will use premeasure atomized and vapor hybrid engine will use premeasured agitated vapor fuel and is the closest to flash point in any compound that would be important in a compressed alcoholasgas engine a compromised vapor ignition fuel injector is a prepared measure of vapor agitator to make a fine atomised vapor to burn and combust for trucks tractor trailers and cars as well as airplanes and drones
6378 atomized fuel and vapor hybrid engine will use preme atomized fuel and vapor hybrid engine will use premeasured agitated vapor fuel and is the closest to flash point in any compound that would be important in a compressed alcoholasgas engine a compromised vapor ignition fuel injector is a prepared measure of vapor agitator to make a fine atomised vapor to burn and combust for trucks tractor trailers and cars as well as airplanes and drones
6379 smart fuel is pre respirated gasoline in a volatile smart fuel is pre respirated gasoline in a

volatile vapor to burn and combust for trucks tractor trailers and cars as well as airplanes and drones

6380 pre respirated gasoline in a volatile vapor calculat pre respirated gasoline in a volatile vapor calculator that finds the fuels top flash point automatically and in a few cycles adjusts it to any gas for the engine

6381 vapor compressor is a exciter and pre respirator for vapor compressor is a exciter and pre respirator for gasoline in a volatile vapor calculator that finds the fuels top flash point automatically and in a few cycles adjusts it to any gas for the engine

6382 smart fuel system in conjunction with vapor compresso smart fuel system in conjunction with vapor compressor is an exciter and pre respirated gasoline fuel in a volitile vapor calculator that finds the mixes top flash point automatically and in a few cycles adjusts it to any gas for the proper efficiency

6383 law bureau of investigation to seek and find corrupti law bureau of investigation to seek and find corruption in government would be a branch of law directed at politics and make a political transition from the public service to the private administration of law and free us from pay offs and contract breaks

6384 virtual search of power is a learning method to compu virtual search of power is a learning method to compute the most powerful solution to run tomorrows cars and every day engines motors and energy motions of any kind while measuring the possibilities of the content to make that energy and the worth of the out come as well as the potency of that worth to the foot print and the regeneration of the properties

6385 software that looks and learns the cost of a fuel or software that looks and learns the cost of a fuel or substance and compares that to a starch and the mineral to make that energy with the combinations of other properties of value in a computational way of virtual search of power is a learning method to compute the most powerful solution to run tomorrows cars and every day engines motors and energy motions of any kind while measuring the possibilities of the content to make that energy and the worth of the out come as well as the potency of that worth to the foot print and the regeneration of the properties

6386 virtual search of power library for a data start with virtual search of power library for a data start with software that looks and learns the cost of a fuel or substance and compares that to a starch and the mineral to make that energy with the combinations of other properties of value in a computational way of virtual search of power is a learning method to compute the most powerful solution to run tomorrows cars and every day engines motors and energy motions of any kind while measuring the possibilities of the content to make that energy and the worth of the out come as well as the potency of that worth to the foot print and the regeneration of the properties

6387 bureau of lawyer investigation is a simple investigat bureau of lawyer investigation is a simple investigation to condone or condemn the laws by a specific lawyer

6388 large scale software overwrites are the overwritten o large scale software overwrites are the overwritten os and programs apps and unlocked formats of devices and the user agreement broken by opposing software and reclaiming a device based on ownership

6389 drone operating system and the library functions of t drone operating system and the library functions of that data

6390 virtual drone navigational operating system and the l virtual drone navigational operating system and the library functions of that data including geo navigation satellite location and local weather conditions as in corporate in a system of methods that conclude a operation inside a alternate virtual use _

6391 a global connected cloud resource of data and targets a global connected cloud resource of data and targets to compromise the enemy and their assets as a concluded end to a means the satellites and the data location in a sense of war over internet protocol

6392 virtual calculated energy verses for profit formula t virtual calculated energy verses for profit formula table software is a search and input library of values and methods of constants and catalysts that react with one another in a virtual unreal way of study to mathematically search and find any such data as an inquiry to a means

6393 wireless through gateway ping router is a device that wireless through gateway ping router is a device that allows computers to connect and share files thru software and a single router essentially a very small internet by wifi network hardware and software

6394 wireless computer to wireless computer wireless computer to wireless computer

6395 wireless phone to wireless phone direct wireless phone to wireless phone direct

6396 multiple external modular format is a hardware driven multiple external modular format is a hardware driven by driver format that excludes the chassis location and provides ports that transfer the data in and out in thread cables

6397 hiroshima latin invasion spawn hiroshima latin invasion spawned by leftists

6398 data center secure wireless multiple external modular data center secure wireless multiple external modular format is a hardware driven by driver format that excludes the chassis location and provides ports that transfer the data in and out wireless with a header data packet that includes a specific device for inclusion in a data center for wireless alliance computing

6399 multi signal wireless receiver is a receiver for mult multi signal wireless receiver is a receiver for multiple managed wireless signals and incorporating wireless devices

6400 processor driven wifi signal receiver for multiple ma processor driven wifi signal receiver for multiple managed wireless signals and incorporating wireless devices processors and computations as a whole in a multitude of receiving and processing of a signal

6401 recyclable air filters patent pending recyclable air filters

6402 recyclable water filters patent pending recyclable water filters

6403 recyclable oil filters patent pending recyclable oil filters

6404 mosquito control tabs for large ponds p mosquito control tabs for large ponds patent pending

6405 multiple conjoined boards by os is a group of boards multiple conjoined boards by os is a group of boards that are essentially separated working cells that are joined by operating system patent pending

6406 wireless multiple conjoined boards by os is a group o wireless multiple conjoined boards by os is a group of boards that are essentially separated working cells that are joined by operating system without wires patent pending

6407 to learn sharing software is a program or app that ac to learn sharing software is a program or app that accepts multiple users in order to learn and teach verses one mouse and one input at a time patent pending

6408 multiple users and rules software is a program or app multiple users and rules software is a program or app that accepts multiple users in order to work and perform as a team in one mission with rules of hierarchy and ranking patent pending

6409 boronmagnesiumsulfate patent pending boronmagnesiumsulfate patent pending
6410 hydrogen oxide sulfate patent pending hydrogen oxide sulfate patent pending
6411 sodium sulfur carbonate patent pending sodium sulfur carbonate patent pending
6412 sodium carbonite aluminum sodium carbonite copyr sodium carbonite aluminum sodium carbonite patent pending
6413 zirconhydroxy isolated layer is a layer of zirconium zirconhydroxy isolated layer is a layer of zirconium which is a silicon that is more insulating and less thermal conductive than diamond carbonate this is good for making three dimensional chips and operators
6414 subtractively printed zirconhydroxy or photo laser subtractively printed zirconhydroxy or photo laser cut zirconhydroxy isolated layer is a layer of zirconium which is a silicon that is more insulating and less thermal conductive than diamond carbonate this is good for making three dimensional chips and operators
6415 subtractively printed photo laser cut layer is a la subtractively printed photo laser cut layer is a layer of conductor or isolate r which is a cut or etched by a time generated photo of energy such as burning or to degrade the photo or image into something or out of something which is good for making three dimensional chips and operators
6416 lcd stencil lens for pi co and nano active subtract lcd stencil lens for pi co and nano active subtractively printed photo laser is a laser stencil photo object to print subtractively with mediums
6417 three dimensional stencil graphic laser printer is a three dimensional stencil graphic laser printer is a pico and nano active subtractively printed photo laser is a laser stencil photo object to print and subtractively with medium for example to think that a grid of pico layered and formed photo timed generated method of stencil emulsion printing converts a flux to accept the grid of the negative print also said to use small stencils to print smaller circuits
6418 gold chromatic building microprocessors is a part of gold chromatic building microprocessors is a part of the three dimensional stencil graphic laser printer and is a pico and nano active subtractively printed photo laser is a laser stencil photo object to print and subtractively with medium for example to think that a grid of pico layered and formed photo timed generated method of stencil emulsion printing converts a flux to accept the grid of the negative print also said to use small stencils to print smaller circuits
6419 silicachromaticbuildingmicroprocessors patent chr silicachromaticbuildingmicroprocessors
6420 exterior liquid cooled computing components such as m exterior liquid cooled computing components such as microprocessors used in cell towers and more memory and other actively cooled in a climate controlled efficiency for higher performance
6421 exterior <span>meaning out side in atmosphere </span> exterior <span>meaning out side in atmosphere </span>liquid cooled motherboard is an actively cooled in a climate controlled efficiency way of cooling for higher performance
6422 exterior meaning out side in atmosphere liquid cooled exterior meaning out side in atmosphere liquid cooled memory is an actively cooled in a climate controlled efficiency way of cooling for higher performance
6423 hard drive readout is a simple lcd or led read out of hard drive readout is a simple lcd or led read out of status on hard drive functionality
6424 memory led readout is a simple lcd or led read out of memory led readout is a simple lcd or led read out of status on hard drive functionality

6425 gpu readout is a simple lcd or led read out of status gpu readout is a simple lcd or led read out of status on gpu for reference functionality
6426 company compatible hardware for reference functionali company compatible hardware for reference functionality is another way of saying that the oem source may be compatible with a company when forming an alliance in partnership and software hardware compatibility meaning in another way more universal components and higher use and less unaccepted products as well as a better way of life for information technology also said as this company a is compatible with this company b
6427 page switch browser plugin is a software internet or page switch browser plugin is a software internet or mobile web interface that takes large tall pages that run on and on and divides them into smaller and easier to download workable pages by splitting them into different views of minor pages like a tree layout in a table of contents
6428 personal data storage software is a way to keep the o personal data storage software is a way to keep the original paper mail copied and safe off line or on line in a digital world while accessing the properties of print and scan a need to fax and forward to any service like united states postal service and more is the priority of the software in question and the protection is a part of the meaning of its importance the life cycle of the person and day to day is a important function of all of us
6429 system on chip product foundation is the start of a n system on chip product foundation is the start of a new cloud format far from large servers and server racks we enter the card based system of scrolling wall panels and more
6430 system on chip wall mount boards and large card input system on chip wall mount boards and large card input panels
6431 system on chip wall mount boards and large card input system on chip wall mount boards and large card input panels that move
6432 system on chip plug and play grid and processing arra system on chip plug and play grid and processing arrangement of network wall mount boards
6433 multiple oi protocol router board is an important par multiple oi protocol router board is an important part of information in and out of any given system on chip wall mounting moving input unit this is the protocol that moves the data in and out of the section per multitude of processing systems on one wall board
6434 embedded access interface in a collection of system o embedded access interface in a collection of system on chips code is a data in and out of the section per multitude of processing systems on one wall board
6435 wireless access soc is a code access by wifi or wirel wireless access soc is a code access by wifi or wirelessethernet processing
6436 soc foundation power by usb data by usb on board ram soc foundation power by usb data by usb on board ram on board processor hard drive by compact flash made to run programmable applications
6437 wifi server foundation power by usb data by usb on bo wifi server foundation power by usb data by usb on board ram on board processor hard drive by compact flash made to run programmable applications with the access of wifi integrated
6438 system on chip server foundation power by usb data by system on chip server foundation power by usb data by usb on board ram on board processor hard drive by compact flash made to run programmable applications with the access of wifi integrated

6439 wifi alternating form access of wifi integrated is a wifi alternating form access of wifi integrated is a triplet form of one send and one receive and one group of process as a whole of one in any open signals

6440 a group of any available open form of one send and on a group of any available open form of one send and one receive and one group of process as a whole of one in any open signals

6441 certified and notary of email is a service of notary certified and notary of email is a service of notary in an email record to and from clients

6442 government serial digital copy notary document number government serial digital copy notary document number registry is a general document of recording in a digital sense

6443 serial digital copy document number registry is a gen serial digital copy document number registry is a general document of recording in a digital sense

6444 medical serial digital copy document number registry medical serial digital copy document number registry is a general document of recording in a digital sense

6445 education document server serial digital copy documen education document server serial digital copy document number registry is a general document of recording in a digital sense

6446 business document registry number and document server business document registry number and document server serial digital copy document number registry is a general document of recording in a digital sense

6447 auto pc number document registry number and document auto pc number document registry number and document server serial digital copy document number registry is a general document of recording in a digital sense for the personal computer and information of scientific origin

6448 email ping record notary registry number and informat email ping record notary registry number and information of legal origin

6449 phone ping record notary registry number and informat phone ping record notary registry number and information of legal origin

6450 ocr cursive per word and the fewest changes ocr cursive per word and the fewest changes

6451 gps road lanes are the global positioning satellites gps road lanes are the global positioning satellites way of making lanes for flying and navigating instead of yellow white stripes there could be pre designated routes by height from and in what direction

6452 gps aerial drone road lanes are the global positionin gps aerial drone road lanes are the global positioning satellites way of making lanes for flying and navigating instead of yellow white stripes there could be pre designated routes by height from and in what direction

6453 gps aerial lanes for drones are the global positionin gps aerial lanes for drones are the global positioning satellites way of making lanes for flying and navigating instead of yellow white stripes there could be pre designated routes by height from and in what direction

6454 gps aerial lanes for airplanes are the global positio gps aerial lanes for airplanes are the global positioning satellites way of making lanes for flying and navigating instead of yellow white stripes there could be pre designated routes by height from and in what direction

6455 global positioning satellite grid of ownership includ global positioning satellite grid of ownership including place in physics natural and vertical horizontal and down

6456 gps fishing zone global positioning satellite grid of gps fishing zone global positioning satellite grid of ownership including place in physics natural and vertical horizontal and

down
6457 annotation physics spatial grid including place in ph annotation physics spatial grid including place in physics natural and vertical horizontal and down mapping by global positioning satellite government or private designation place in space
6458 dual annotation physics spatial grid including place dual annotation physics spatial grid including place in physics natural and vertical horizontal and down from two origins
6459 gps navigational property and the confines of that d gps navigational property and the confines of that d property
6460 adjustable format video is a hardware rendering devic adjustable format video is a hardware rendering device application that runs a basic group of files a specific way to improve the display of any movie or music and other data projects simply said you put your project in basic adjustable format and the video player renders the adjusted final part
6461 military reverse calvin cycle air purifiers copyr military reverse calvin cycle air purifiers
6462 bids and sales for legitimate futures in project perf bids and sales for legitimate futures in project performance is the sale of a large private job for any work made in a presales term
6463 cellular foundation negotiation network is a real cha cellular foundation negotiation network is a real chance of service to any known location by selling the use of a cellular network to any under written provider for negotiation and sales
6464 hybrid connected communication network is a real chan hybrid connected communication network is a real chance of service to any known location by selling the use of a cellular to satellite hybrid service network to any under written provider for negotiation and sales
6465 a reverse reflective tunnel that magnifies the light a reverse reflective tunnel that magnifies the light and graduates the source to maximize the solar energy post
6466
6467 a energy center or building with many focused solar g a energy center or building with many focused solar generators that reverse reflective tunnel that magnifies the light and graduates the source to maximize the solar energy post
6468 ai is named wrong you have to take more into consider ai is named wrong you have to take more into consideration like the answer not the truth of the question left and right is the asymmetrical processing
6469 micro alternating circuit battery is a circuit that r micro alternating circuit battery is a circuit that recycles itself with current
6470 processor micro circuit battery is a circuit cell tha processor micro circuit battery is a circuit cell that holds current
6471 acid alkaline printed chips in a diffused solution to acid alkaline printed chips in a diffused solution to compute as a battery on chip
6472 laser printed levels of circuits and multiple cured s laser printed levels of circuits and multiple cured solvents as circuits layers laser printed chips in a diffused solution to compute as a chip
6473 ultra violet laser printed levels of circuits and mul ultra violet laser printed levels of circuits and multiple uv cured solvents as circuits layers laser printed chips in a diffused solution to compute as a chip
6474 laser printed levels of circuits and multiple photo s laser printed levels of circuits and multiple photo sensitive cured solvents as circuits layers laser printed chips in a diffused

solution to compute as a chip

6475 perpendicular laser printed levels of circuits proces perpendicular laser printed levels of circuits processors and memory in multiple photo sensitive cured solvents as circuits layers laser printed chips in a diffused solution to compute as a chip

6476 a photo reactive multiple element formula of printing a photo reactive multiple element formula of printing materials for perpendicular laser printed levels of circuits processors and memory in multiple photo sensitive cured solvents as circuits layers laser printed chips in a diffused solution to compute as a chip

6477 printing materials for perpendicular laser printed le printing materials for perpendicular laser printed levels of circuits processors and memory in multiple photo sensitive cured solvents as circuits layers laser printed chips in a diffused solution to compute as a chip in a series of different elements

6478 vertical clamp socket for chip christop vertical clamp socket for chip

6479 five sided computer chip for computations copyrig five sided computer chip for computations

6480 sided computer chip for computations sided computer chip for computations

6481 sided computer chip for computations and stacking a sided computer chip for computations and stacking arrangements for chip processing

6482 pico nano voxel and elemental compounds for chip proc pico nano voxel and elemental compounds for chip processing printing

6483 conductive and positive pico nano voxel and elemental conductive and positive pico nano voxel and elemental compounds for chip processing printing in three dimensions

6484 non conductive and negative pico nano voxel and eleme non conductive and negative pico nano voxel and elemental compounds for chip processing printing in three dimensions

6485 non conductive silica solvent white space and negativ non conductive silica solvent white space and negative pico nano voxel and elemental compounds for chip processing printing in three dimensions

6486 conductive gold and mineral solvent conductors in a p conductive gold and mineral solvent conductors in a positive pico nano voxel and elemental compound form for three dimensional chip processing printing

6487 empty space for looped inside linking conductive vect empty space for looped inside linking conductive vector for making a place for conductors in pico nano voxel and elemental compounds for chip processing printing in three dimensions

6488 connection vectors and the empty space for looped ins connection vectors and the empty space for looped inside linking conductive vector for making a place for conductors in pico nano voxel and elemental compounds for chip processing printing in three dimensions

6489 software that makes connection vectors conductors in software that makes connection vectors conductors in pico nano voxel and elemental compounds for chip processing printing in three dimensions

6490 the intellectual property management office and large the intellectual property management office and large document record for keeping trade secrets and patents safe and secured by named ownership

6491 spiral compressed reflective fiber optical cable spiral compressed reflective fiber optical cable

6492 spiral compound reflective receiver decoder processor spiral compound reflective

receiver decoder processor that reads reflective signals in fiber optic signals
6493 spiral compound reflective sending out encoder proces spiral compound reflective sending out encoder processor that codes reflective signals in fiber optic signals
6494 spiral fiberoptic splicer device and the markings th spiral fiberoptic splicer device and the markings that make a reading splicer obtain the proper place in the cable to splice or loop into with precision and accuracy for less signal loss
6495 manufacturer electric motor recycle programs and ince manufacturer electric motor recycle programs and incentives for autos and parts reclamation
6496 modified hard drive control and add on secondary hard modified hard drive control and add on secondary hard drive chips for cache and indexing
6497 air plane antivirus software system for corrupted par air plane antivirus software system for corrupted parts and software integrity
6498 part due date is a manufacturers recall date for part part due date is a manufacturers recall date for part services on life threatening parts and mandatory services made due
6499 fiber optic reflective turn connection in data to let fiber optic reflective turn connection in data to let a signal repeat and split in order to go around an object of area
6500 service time out price cut is a service interruption service time out price cut is a service interruption cost cut for minute by minute operations and service as software companies verses outage and payment service
6501 vertical threads and the property of stacking layers vertical threads and the property of stacking layers of chips
6502 light turbo focused energy is a small reflected syste light turbo focused energy is a small reflected system of cycles in the case that one or only a few light emitters generate a stronger system of a source of solar energy in amplification by reflection and the profit of energy is greater than the source
6503 three dimensional tunnel light turbo focused energy i three dimensional tunnel light turbo focused energy is a small reflected system of cycles in the case that one or only a few light emitters generate a stronger system of a source of solar energy in amplification by reflection and the profit of energy is greater than the source
6504 a one way mirror or rather said as a one sided reflec a one way mirror or rather said as a one sided reflective one side transparent solar energy glass window for building a reflective solar tunnel
6505 spiral focus energy is a one way mirror or rather sai spiral focus energy is a one way mirror or rather said as a one sided reflective one side transparent solar energy glass window for building a reflective solar tunnel spirally to amplify the source
6506 square focus energy is a one way mirror or rather sai square focus energy is a one way mirror or rather said as a one sided reflective one side transparent solar energy glass window for building a reflective solar tunnel square to amplify the source
6507 cone focus energy is a one way mirror or rather said cone focus energy is a one way mirror or rather said as a one sided reflective one side transparent solar energy glass window for building a reflective solar tunnel cone to amplify the source
6508 microwave fuse that generates solar electric energy i microwave fuse that generates solar electric energy is a mini microwave signal inside a one way mirror sphere or box with receiving solar energy cells on the outside inside another mini sphere feeding another sphere with one way mirror sphere or box with receiving solar energy cells with options to continue

the cycle or to copy the out put in more on the outside inside another mini sphere feeding another sphere with one way mirror sphere or box with receiving solar energy cells on the outside inside another mini sphere feeding another sphere with one way mirror sphere or box with receiving solar energy cells on the outside inside another mini sphere feeding another sphere with one way mirror sphere or box with receiving solar energy cell son the outside inside another mini sphere feeding another sphere with one way mirror sphere or box with receiving solar energy cells or to simply end in one or two cycles

6509 immigrated income revenue service is a service devote immigrated income revenue service is a service devoted to helping immigrants over come short falls and improve the lives of immigrants and others who are incontinent of taxes as language and citizenship problems

6510 microwave ecology and the study of light particles an microwave ecology and the study of light particles and oxygen from microwave stable and unstable optical combustion

6511 microwave combustion microwave flash point in any o microwave combustion microwave flash point in any operation as an ignition for combustion is the newest resolution here for energy.

6512 microwave vacuum combustion microwave flash point vac microwave vacuum combustion microwave flash point vacuum in any operation as an ignition for combustion is the newest resolution here for energy or force of energy

6513 satellite directional range accelerations when the ar satellite directional range accelerations when the area of interest is incorporated into a conglomerate signal of area in data within a similar location where as the area of interest is in a geopacket prefix for code accelerations

6514 gps pi navigation access is fractional pi satellite d gps pi navigation access is fractional pi satellite directional range accelerations when the area of interest is incorporated into a conglomerate signal of area in data within a similar location where as the area of interest is in a geopacket prefix for navigation acceleration for motion

6515 encrypted cellular service christoph encrypted cellular service

6516 encrypted cellular application and software encrypted cellular application and software

6517 mold detecting refrigerator christop mold detecting refrigerator

6518 optical micro lens reflector accelerator for laser us optical micro lens reflector accelerator for laser use and light particle compression

6519 tapered and threaded lens reflector accelerator for l tapered and threaded lens reflector accelerator for laser use and light particle compression

6520 dual reflective tapered and threaded lens reflector a dual reflective tapered and threaded lens reflector accelerator for laser use and light particle compression

6521 tapered and threaded tube reflector accelerator for l tapered and threaded tube reflector accelerator for laser use and light particle compression

6522 dual reflective tapered and threaded tube shaped refl dual reflective tapered and threaded tube shaped reflector accelerator for laser use and light particle compression

6523 a optical jet effect of light particle acceleration i a optical jet effect of light particle acceleration in many reflective tapered and threaded tube shaped reflector accelerator for laser use and light particle compression

6524 light particle compression by reflected layers of tub light particle compression by reflected layers of tubing and objects with alternating properties

6525 usb cpu input christopher gabriel br usb cpu input

6526 many usb cpu input christopher gabri many usb cpu input
6527 many sd usb cpu input christopher ga many sd usb cpu input
6528 many sd usb cpu input board christop many sd usb cpu input board
6529 many exchangeable sd usb cpu input board many exchangeable sd usb cpu input board
6530 d triplet pi ration map is the three dimensional pos d triplet pi ration map is the three dimensional possible notation of travel in distance to be expected by any map
6531 gps d triplet pi ration is the rational notation of gps d triplet pi ration is the rational notation of small physical or normal number physics computational relation to gps
6532 local and global participation in gps d triplet pi r local and global participation in gps d triplet pi ration is the dynamics of location for any known given computeable location
6533 rewrite able solid state micro processing chips write rewrite able solid state micro processing chips writer drive for code inscribe processors
6534 rewriteable synthetic metal micro chips rewriteable synthetic metal micro chips
6535 rewriteable solid state micro processing chips copyri rewriteable solid state micro processing chips
6536 rewrite able solid state micro processing chips write rewrite able solid state micro processing chips writer language for code inscribe processors
6537 emergency sos satellite system based on cell phone sat emergency sos satellite system based on cell phone satellite connections. sos from wikipedia
6538 real time and pure light %infinite times + %infinite= real time and pure light %infinite times + %infinite=e%uxc binom lim n toward infinity(+{ } over {n})^{n} part
6539 after market gadgets need the shape you want. build yo after market gadgets need the shape you want. build your own tablet hand held chassis and server related fabric smaller un fused working parts that equal more power and higher concentration of parts dual socket tablet with fans and inches to inches
6540 real time and pure light %infinite times + %infinite= real time and pure light %infinite times + %infinite=e%uxc binom lim n toward infinity(+{ } over {n})^{n} %infinite times + %infinite%uxc binom max xe ^{sum +infinity cdot +%uxe a {e} over x sum to{{} } x^{} %epsilon } part
6541 optical fiber paths and boards that use lens motors optical fiber paths and boards that use lens motors optical motors and optic conductors in conjunction with a optical cpu making electrons differently than an ion more sort of a ee on
6542 optical fiber paths and boards that use lens motors op optical fiber paths and boards that use lens motors optical motors and optic conductors in conjunction with a optical cpu making electrons differently than an ion more sort of a ee on
6543 architecture in cubits another way to say functions in architecture in cubits another way to say functions in written language a cubits as any other known as a path or circuit in another to build a chip out of a formed path of cubits in an alphabet of cubits and then circuits in super annotation cell of conductors and processor cores as well as circuits insulators and cell walls as the language of reading functions
6544 scramble encrypted rearranged methods of encryption fo scramble encrypted rearranged methods of encryption for multiple channels of information bridge to access any such specific need or industry specific technology to share and improve that data share market of information is a mini expanded data exchange to be said again is like the information of aero industry holding a internet of its own and the specified television

network on a different and separated internet but being serviced by the same devices only in a expansive connected channel of internet access

6545 synthetic sodiummagnesium battery technology to power synthetic sodiummagnesium battery technology to power large and expansive technology specific environments

6546 help line for any given issue and abuse mental or drug help line for any given issue and abuse mental or drug crisis being there as a cost safe alternative to police this would be a pre extreme non emergency health hotline that could elevate the police as a or similar dial code for health issues

6547 invent solutions for problematic situations in the light age part full circle invent deposion soluons for problemac situaons in the light age part it's my idea that electronic is a need. it's my concept that opcal reflecons are beer than the present electro conductors today. the issue is complicated but can be proven very simply. a light is far more impressive than electronic means. it's not stupid to think that. but let us examine why that may be. light can be seen from long and far distances. the topic at hand is technology ben efits of light (lasers) and electronic means.one of my newest invenons the micro mirror can compress light into a shape and render thatlight some where else. how small you make light into what ever you like is the goal for a problem free microprocessor. you may be able to guess where i'm headed next with this thought. please read into the code names below with thought and interest towards changing and improving the future of the light age.i want to think twice about certain things that i do before i commit to something. then i have another thought that makes me want to reexamine everything and make sure the art will survive my personal tastes through the many phases i go through. one of the most important lessons i was taught was to move on and study more than one thing at a me. i simply can't stop the different things that i do from happening. in the art sense of the meaning i want to progress and connue to improve and make more and beer things on a up and posive note. why do the software engi neers make software all the me?new ideas and more and more different ways to do things are always happening. so to conclude this short introducon i would like to persuade you to understand that in fact it is this progression that will change the world and and beer things will happen for the greater good of us all.in conclusion is this the light age is possible with smoke and mir rors after all. i would like to reiterate this how do you read something that is very small? have you ever heard that old saying

6548 invent cloud in print to cloud in touch with us invent cloud in print to cloud in touch with us

6549 touch us cloud in print to cloud in touch with usinvent deposion & theology by touch the webmy lightscribe edion of altracks was geng held up and soon enough

6550 invent what and why the internet scrolls are effective what and why the internet scrolls are effecvedeposion on theology of psychology... simple tongue twister and why i internet... with out this psychological method the internet would seem senseless. this is how to make shape and form a web site to an accessible dimension. to esmate the equivalent viewers psychology.

6551 invent (a+m=e) part fractalist to generalist next»invent deposion by christopher g. brown(a+m=e) part a fractal is the opposite of a worm hole. the enre amplitude of any enty with twice the mass will make energy that posses a general whole number that is not prime. it's plain to see but what is there to see? it's the amplitude with some form of fracon of a whole

that makes the enty a whole number that never actually is ever completed and the number is merely a infinite hypoth esis reacon
6552 invent (a+m=e) part a+m=e connued/ ? .amplitude () . / doubled mass () ? . [.] es mated energy constant weightimportance? {concepon electricity
6553 invent (a+m=e) part fractalist to generalist invent deposion by christopher g. brown(a +m=e) part short explanaon to summarizeto get everything straight is to completely understand the task at hand and contemplate the enre subject. some kind of accelerated compensaon equaon is to see that the whole is taken in to consideraon. simply put the factors like gravity and wind when a scud missile is being talked about before the patriot missile is sent to say hello. when the gulf war was on tv it was obvious to me that this was the perfect me to pracce the compensaon equaon to pin point accuracy because of the steaks at risk.so to sum up the tally is to say that first to state the maer then to put the equaon and finally to show the proof is somewhat of a geometric given. the making of all things is to understand the factors that prove the hypothesis to exact dimensions while taking all of the sums to make thefinal facts. seems hard but we start with gravity and then factor in everything else. sir isaac new ton's apple is all about weight and the other things that make a bump on the head a bump on the head. what makes how much it hurts is to understand the persons (paents) pain threshold and other things that may be hard to take into consideraon?for examples of real things like gravity and collision is to take that physical data and make something that equals a bicycle and then there are things to understand after that like why i shouldn't share the road due to the importance of traffic. personal opinion but what else is there in this world your thoughts my thoughts and someone else's understanding that there actually over a long period of me is economically truth to the h/o/v/lane we have here in georgia. it's safety of numbers and just like that birds of a feather flock together and more over that if we un derstand numbers we need to see that the number is effected by other numbers./ ? .amplitude () . / doubled mass () ? . [.] es mated energy constant weightimportance? {concepon
6554 invent open idea app a different way to internet open idea app a different way to internetinvent deposion by christopher g. brownto design a ethernet cell or satellite based cell phone applicaon that connects people's phones as pages instead of pages on a server. the main purpose is to communicate and then the other things will gradually fall into place. i think it would be perfect to pracce this in the jungles or deserts. open idea app
6555 invent modialcom machine a different way to ftp invent modialcom machine a different way to ftp
6556 modialcom machinea different way to ftpinvent deposion by christopher g. brownmodialcom machine via trust awards to find an excuse to invent more would be to make sense and fun of it all. to benefit the best of humanity and gradually get to the good stuff is what i dream of. here is my idea a universal hand held device that is essenally a flash drive with screen and intuive circle keypad. here is what i am thinking about what is the difference between people like the eccentric truth seeking radical but ethical advancement of our informaon? thats what i want to know. if the government would let us ftp files back and forth that specific individuals with trust awards of the civilian private sector why would there not be a device that is so valuable to us all like an informaon gun invented? rapid modialcom geverfire rapid conversions and mulple divide mulply add and subtract sums
6557 invent strictly confidential widget invent strictly confidential widget
6558 strictly confidenala different way to seeinvent deposion by christopher g.

brownbusiness ethics and personal values actually do make up the person who works for you. and you and i may see eye to eye for once that you dont want a drug user as your wherehouse manager so what precauons would you be willing to take? personality or drug tests? to what level can you go to insure that there isnt any problems... to me it seems that the higher the magnitude of company the level of sancty is to be seen reasonable. i wish right about now i could quote a devils advo cate line

6559 invent long data why can't we all just get along? invent long data why can't we all just get along?

6560 long datawhy cant we all just get along?invent deposion by christopher g. brown crioner.com christopher g. brown long data concept i believe that a universal computer file that will put the hard efforts and intelligence of today to work tomorrow. this is not only the best way to understand its going to be the best way to do business while sll compet ing in a hard to open market. the first hand is the image type of code image map

6561 invent two open applications simultaneously transitioning invent two open applications simultaneously transitioning

6562 two open applicaons simultaneously transioning trying to work faster.invent deposion by christopher g. browna few quesons and what to expect step one a nano motorthe need for two apps to transion through one another is really something adobe systems is good at but my queson is this

6563 invent infinite motion infinite motion lord carpentersinfinite motion how to put it all together by christopher g. browna spinning top is very similar to something you'd like to have fun and stare at forever. it was brought to my aenon that there is a need for such a thing to run/turn forever. the issue is a few things also somemes called the same thing

6564 invent fnatma fnatimg invent fnatma fnatimg

6565 fnatma fnatimg chemisty topic of anotherinvent deposion by christopher g. browna few quesons and what to expect how to charge an element using the nasa nevada experimental rail way? why would you bother them and what it means to the rest of us. i think its best put as a set charge accelerator... a queson of when and not if. there is hope but somemes we need to take a guess and then the faultswill occur. valence (chemistry) from wikipedia valence

6566 invent pulse ion trigger algebraic lens motor invent pulse ion trigger algebraic lens motor

6567 pulse ion trigger algebraic lens motor to pulse nano photonic color sensortrying to work more efficiently.invent deposion by christopher g. browna few quesons and what to expect ions the free encyclopediajump to:navigaon

6568 invent invent more skepticism invent invent more skepticism

6569 what were they thinking?does everything have to have a microchip inside? things i just dont want to happen debate of the minds.invent more skepcism by christopher g. brownwhen we get to the point that everything has a microchip inside what will that mean? is tech nology going to go too far? is there going to be a need for example to put a microchip inside a cup? or rather a cup inside the chip? when things require updates as much as my car or computer i will stop being happy.so what made methink of that possibility that there is a need and a place for everything? well heres a roundabout way of it all. portable tv sets and why did i connue when i should have stopped

6570 invent codec to dextmetrics invent codec to dextmetrics

6571 two concepts to measure it all codec to dextmetrics.invent more christopher g. brown ¢ two opposing ideas that form a scienfic outcome in computer analycal methods. to have codec applicaons and human interfaces which make all things essenally equal in to opposite ways like reverse outcome process/negave cell theory please use ¢ diodemetrics algebras (to the technology makers there is a point of two or more operang systems to understand yet there is the world of sales that makes what we buy genecally similar.) ¢ inter science open app (technology called they want their biology book back) ¢ demetrisism computer theory(a system must de tect and respond? comments of codes and conferences
6572 invent appreciation and degradation values invent appreciation and degradation values
6573 appreciaon and degradaon values theorecal business analycsto speak about ones past is sad at mes. but so to me that is all opinion and at mes facts of the case at hand. what made it great is the queson. the same goes for why it went bad and when it went bad
6574 invent digit social currency invent digit social currency
6575 digit social currency what if there was a voluntary new digit social currency card that made public bank as op posed to an fdic private bank transfers with oponal tax involvement if its oponal the rest of the uninvolved would report to the irs with enhanced scripng technology such as birth place to evade terrorisc threats and illegal immigraon threats as well as tax at a more fair rate and percent upon comsumpon lower taxes on higher comsumpon and lower interest rates on lower spending. and a four digit alternate security code. added four digits to the exisng three that are now there
6576 invent topical cause invent topical cause
6577 topical cause part & to introduce the world to the largest topical cause is my first and foremost missionto quote a line from the matrix is to describe the topic. the topic is how many mes does the ef fect of the single cause and how great can you actually make one cause that has so many differ ent effect the possibilies are endless to say that in a shorter way is that
6578 invent topical cause part invent topical cause part and became the worldwide standard under the second international radio telegraphic convention which was signed on november and became effective on july . sos remained the maritime radio distress signal until when it was replaced by the global maritime distress safety system. [ ] (with this new system in place it became illegal for a ship to signal that she is in distress in morse code. citation needed]) sos is still recognized as a visual distress signal.[] from the beginning the sos distress signal has really consisted of a continuous sequence of threeditz/threedash/threeditz all run together without letter spacing. in international morse code three ditz form the letter s and three dash make the letter o so sos became an easy way to remember the order of the ditz and dash. in modern terminology sos is a morse procedural signal or pro sign and the formal way to write it is with a bar above the letters: sos in popular usage sos became associated with such phrases as save our ship save our souls and send out succor. these may be regarded as mnemonics but sos does not stand for anything and is not an abbreviation acronym or initials. in fact sos is only one of several ways that the combination could have been written vtb for example would produce exactly the same sound but sos was chosen to describe this combination. sos is the only element signal in morse code making it more easily recognizable as no other symbol uses more than elements.
6579 i wanted to be a great artist. but besides a huge identy crisis i look ahead. the purpose of a theorecal philosophy that carries on and on... what is the next thing to come to your mind. why is that inspired by another and into a different one?

6580 topical cause part & to introduce the world to the largest topical cause is my first and foremost mission
6581 invent cuna cuna invent cuna cuna
6582 cuna cuna chemisty topic of another part invent deposion by christopher g. browna few quesons and what to expect how to charge an element using the nasa nevada experimental rail way? why would you bother them and what it means to the rest of us. i think its best put as a set charge accelera tor... a queson of when and not if. there is hope but somemes we need to take a guess and then the faults will occur. valence (chemistry) from wikipedia valence
6583 invent hour house hour house algebraic photonic time measurements the chips are a lot like a house. what i do is i conceptualize something and make up a bad name and eventually it's similar to a long horn leg horn thing. the chips are like a ranch styled house that get's boring after a while. with the current push in nanophotonics the ladders and stairs are going to happen with steps and very similar things that make analogies common place to a house. that is all i can say about that
6584 invent cloud life/birth/death cloud comparison in a frenzy part invent deposion deep blue the original cloud vs. azure my cloudcloud comparison and cloud analycs to be connued...the difference of deep blue was that it wasnt considered a cloud at the me. the focus was only on the game and the server itself. this isnt the focus of what the azure is. windows will now carry on as usual... welcome to the new long data beer
6585 invent cloud comparison invent cloud comparison
6586 cloud life/birth/death in a frenzy part invent deposion by christopher g. browni have already compared technology to biology as a whole
6587 invent time continuation equation invent time continuation equation
6588 real me and pure light part +invent deposion by christopher g. brown worm hole my riddle the free encyclopediajump to: navigaon what goes around comes around? well if it's round there should be more area to view. i missed a step but basically there is another saying that goes like this karma will get you. the machine is the invenon of mechanized labor.introducing the light age ladies and gentlemen light trigger + varied colored la ser semiconductor & microchip® aka cold light micro chip digital optics by colored micro mirrors add subtract mode to divide and multiply digital platforms color mathmatics and algorithyms based on color reflections for process control [me and light measure ment + stair case mirror chips] nanophotonics the light age
6589 invent real time and pure light part infinites invent real time and pure light part infinites
6590 %infinite times + %infinite=e sim binom lim n toward infinity(+{ } over {n})^{n} %infinite times + %infinite sim binom max xe ^{sum +infinity cdot + prop {e} over x sum to{{} } x^{}%epsilon } while on the phone to a hp tech agent i menoned ever tried to print the web moment of me excluded. web to print applicaons that make sense is the mission of all of this. wiki media foundaon donaons aside lets all make things that random thoughts can eventually get together and all jump into the same pond. in other words locate and print what if you really could. cloud and print into the next few centuries? forget that im nuts and remember that me will tell us all that in the beginging the clouds moved aside and god said let there be light.sorry about the rounding of all corners. my name is christopher g. brown
6591 invent computer parts and musical chairs invent computer parts and musical chairs
6592 varios® computer parts and musical chairs code name vegasinvent deposion isnt it simple that if the world followed quintet and sixtet then that would mean that midi and the

mc is and will always be the way that math in dance is sincronized and transfixate and then beat spliced into pure mathimacal mad ness and its all equal to beats like mine. and to esmate the whole effect of that number)/ ? .amplitude () . / doubled mass () ? . [.] es mated energy constant weightimportance? {concepon lighng electricity etc.}from wikipedia / ? ?
6593 invent white noise to bass line code name atlantis invent white noise to bass line code name atlantis etc.}from wikipedia / ? ?? (somemes wrien pi) is a mathemacal constant whose value is the rao of any circle's circum ference to its diameter in euclidean space this is the same value as the rao of a circle's area to the square of its radius. it is approximately equal to . in the usual decimal notaon (see the table for its representaon in some other bases). the constant is also known as archimedes constant although this name is rather uncommon in modern western englishspeaking contexts. many formulae from mathemacs science and engineering involve ? which is one of the most importantmathemacal and physical constants. []/ ? .amplitude () . / doubled mass () ? . [.] es mated energy constant weightimportance? {concepon lighng electricity etc.}from wikipedia / ? ?
6594 tb white noise to bass line code name atlantisinvent deposion in a class of me and its all in a lile white lie. the is a mop up of a noise. the pitch decay and use of s main mix of the midi will make a bass sound that makes mad people happy. lighng electricity etc.}from wikipedia / ? ?
6595 invent ajax rss search invent ajax rss search
6596 ajax rss search seek & search code name apacheinvent deposion simply a extened plaorm of exisng searches and database files that make a thing simple even more simple. something that records me and searches for changes..
6597 invent help me walk? invent help me walk? like { (instance)+ (second instance)=code } thus the proper encrypon code is known to the recipient.
6598 help me walk?some organic/ some post organic measureinvent deposion electronic muscle pulse therapy for atrophy paents step super infomercial for medicalif i saw it on tv it has to be realdisabled tendon repair and extensions step chicken cat transferalternate cartalige transplantorganic fiber opc nerve conductors step non evasive nerologicalwhere do you have troubleand electronic pulse for prolonged wheel chair paents
6599 invent spool effect of data data translation invent spool effect of data data translation
6600 mp < spool effect of data – data translaoninvent deposion spool effect of data – data translaon one way in and two ways out is beer than only one way in and one way out. logical translaon is that a queson of danger comes into guess work. a modificaon of compression is only a peg. modified mpeg... sounds like an alice in wonderland piece. the ability to read and write and well as read writes and translates. the compression of the mp is a queson of a fact of desire... crioner.com
6601 invent plystyro < synthetic compound invent plystyro < synthetic compound as well as a long history of previous things such as revisions and other instances like undo data and authors date and other things to pass along the data that may make informaon archeolo gists study how to make more money and or why there was a loss of money. to summarize what im thinking of is to make files that have such close code and scripts as well as alternate informaon added that could be readable by things like for example internet browsers or phone apps.
6602 poly carbonate to a styro carbonate compound for use in interesng and problemac situa ons more to be found. invent deposion many carbonates into heat as catalyst

6603 invent inventing a cloud inventing inventions invent inventing a cloud inventing inventions can the computer {hardware or software} conduct two or more ions from a micro spark generator and then somehow keep those two ions making switches go off and on while not colliding and at the same me act as a nerve to control the computer as a whole to es senally make a mulion and eventually a mulplying micro spark generator the way that this diagram demonstrates in an abstract transion.
6604 ai thought invenng a cloud inventing inventionsthe real reason is to continue work on a daily basis as intendedinvent deposion amplitude infinity and other infinites all makes for an arficial intelligence with some or less than a real opinion for itself
6605 invent for the shear fun of music invent for the shear fun of music
6606 for the shear fun of musicanother reason is to connue work on a daily basis as intendedinvent deposion its a fact of life that to be propelled into a unfair and non respect form of work is not only detrimental and confusing to the arst it degrades the work and makes the arst suffer. from the beginning the underground of house and techno makes what we call self indie arsts self publishing... its companies like amazon.com that are making it happen today by extreme mea sures and interesng methods... to upgrade any kind of plaorm and obtain service counsel as well be kind to call crioner.com at the number below. also known as valency or valency number is a measure of the number of chemical bonds formed by the atoms of a given element. over the last century the concept of valence evolved into a range of ap proaches for describing the chemical bond including lewis structures ( ) valence bond theory ( ) molecular orbitals ( ) valence shell electron pair repulsion theory ( ) and all the advanced methods of quantum chemistry.
6607 invent comma separated encryption invent comma separated encryption
6608 comma separated encrypon another reason is to connue work on a daily basis as intended securelyinvent deposion strange brew is only a reason to understand that everyone is csv. styled now and excel my mi crosoft is no reason to degrade the graphical keys to encrypon... imagine.... search nanohub.org is sci ence cyberinfrastructure[ ] comprising communitycontributed resources and geared toward educaonal applicaons professional networking and interacve simulaon tools for nano technology. funded by the naonal science foundaon (nsf) it is a product of the network for computaonal nanotechnology (ncn) a muluniversity iniave of eight member instuons including purdue university the university of california at berkeley the university of illinois at urbanachampaign the molecular foundry at lawrence berkeley naonal laboratory norfolk state university northwestern university and the university of texas at el paso. ncn was estab lished to create a resource for nanoscience and nanotechnology via online services for research educaon and professional collaboraon. ncn supports research efforts in nanoelectronics nano electromechanical systems or nems nanofluidics nanomedicine/biology and nanophotonics.
6609 invent speechless while in love invent speechless while in love
6610 speechless while in loveapplicaons that text and how to make it as small as one or two opons that have a greater click appeal paraphrase quesons with proper context all while scripng invent deposion how do we go from ugly misshapen clouds to something that has more than only a tech savvy appeal? why cant we find words that mean what we say when we are in love? everybody knows what they feel when they are in love just somemes it is so much easier to give up and say allot rather than nothing or even rather than one thing that people usually say. for exam ple to use a phrase that makes grammacally correct quesons like

the way that large com panies have with telephone services like for example would you like to buy now? or connue shopping with this product that is like something you just saw but there are beer colors in this other product? how to go from mulple choices that dont make sense to a more exact link that makes intent complete? applicaons that text and how to make it as small as one or two opons that have a greater click appeal paraphrase with proper context... the light age. the man and his nucleus to quote nacho libre. it just seems funny. why does everything have to advance day after day why cant it just stay the same? may be this is just my birthday coming and my age is speaking.

6611 invent inspiration to grow your business invent inspiration to grow your business

6612 when you decide to have another baby inspiraon to grow your businesswhen lile families become big business... or rather when big business becomes a bigger family to maintain a reliable structure takes a lot of planning and its judgment that puts hard work to use when it is me or when it needs to happen... growth in business starts with a lile inspiraon.

6613 invent the basic eight invent the basic eight

6614 the basic eight| next»invent deposion successful data sharing perceptual image ocr codes and translaon scripts and security file extending import export applicaons support and help why the things made it fall from popularity may atmes be opinion or merely poecal jusce. what goes up must come down. to translate the simple things in business are always from intuion. to hire people with posive ethical spirit and atude is the most important thing to start with.

6615 invent question and concept part page of quesiton and concept part next»queson and concept part i see you asking for some kind of revoluonary help that is a mental curse. the data will not work if the data is only in the air. the data and technology i have already submied will work but

6616 invent likely hood of an emergency invent likely hood of an emergency

6617 likelyhood of an emergency simple est is a solar cellphone recharger my aeroplane crashed and lets say im stranded who would i call first?

6618 invent ssds invent ssds to be smart enough that meanness and arrogance comes into play that somehow that end result is a beer life. however audacity is not acknowledgeable so to that i bid you a due. the real queson at hand is exactly what cause makes the largest difference in the lives we have share and love with? for ex ample a mate matching website the ethics are there in good and bad. but all in all to me they are what im after. however if you consider a large corporaon that has triggers and switches at their disposal and nothing happens without someone making a cause into the reacon what im saying is i need a job and a girlfriend but never the less thats not the topic at hand.to oppose a nuclear destrucve demonstraon is to simply build a topical cause with good bet ter or great may be even perfect circumstance from a super individualist {so to speak. } for ex ample the issue is the cause and effect reacon of a purpose and what kind of circumstances are there. this is simply a philosophical insight to why things happen and who or what the effects are to and vice a versa. to imagine that im just an arst is to say to the rest of the world i make art. to the rest of history i examine the mes before me and learn and then eventually i may help shape the future. that is to be in an abstract poec sense of the arstry hood im having.to compromise and go to different tears in the formula and eventually add all the things mak ing a new effect without actually hindering or dying into a catastrophic failure is something that needless to say isnt actually something that is humanly possible. for example the shear nature of nature

is to draw to a final conclusion that all things may be some kind of effect or symbiosis but more over the exact science of science to the very last fact is there is always room for error. concluding that to be perfect like my brother says is hard to do...
6619 ssds simple est is a stacked cluster of solid states invent deposion
6620 invent niacine insulin invent niacine insulin
6621 niacine insulingraphic only invent deposion phd vi
6622 invent knowing the difference invent knowing the difference
6623 knowing the differenceinvent deposion also known as valency or valency number is a measure of the number of chemical bonds formed by the atoms of a given element. over the last century the concept of valence evolved into a range of approaches for describing the chemical bond including lewis structures ( ) valence bond theory ( ) molecular orbitals ( ) valence shell electron pair repul sion theory ( ) and all the advanced methods of quantum chemistry.
6624 invent water inherited chemistry invent water inherited chemistry
6625 improved chemical actions and more compable.
6626 h / + isotopes of oxygen + medicalchemistrysearingiso na halflife dm de (mev) dp .% is stable with neutrons . % is stable with neutrons . % is stable with neutronswater inherinted chemistry
6627 invent separate equators invent separate equators
6628 separate equators the most of us would understand that children are the best thing that can happen to us as people. may be its their naive understanding that helps us learn how to describe something. i think that the most learning i have ever done was when i make music its more experimental than some accept. the adaptive ness is the way to learn effective ion based processor may be more effective is to build two separateprocessors that would go in and out like a heart valve. meaning to create two completely separate processors that are dual quad and octet each on their own separate capacity is to learn with our capacity. (l + l=)°o(ll=)°o(=) °°(=). controlled by crioner.graphic only invent deposion
6629 invent hyperactive engine invent hyperactive engine search for other uses see infinity (disambiguaon). this arcle includes a list of references or external links but its sources remain unclear because it has insufficient inline citaons. please help to improve this arcle by introducing more precise citaons where appropriate. (june) the lemniscate ˆž in several typefaces.infinity (somemes symbolically represented by ˆž) is a concept in many fields most predominantly mathemacs and physics that refers to a quanty without bound or end. people have developed various ideas throughout history about the nature of infinity. the word comes from the lan infinitas or unboundedness. in mathemacs infinity is often treated as if it were a number (i.e. it counts or measures things: an infinite number of terms) but it is not the same sort of number as the real numbers. in number systems incorporang infinitesimals the reciprocal of an infinitesimal is an infinite number i.e. a number greater than any real number. georg cantor formalized many ideas related to infinity and infinite sets during the late th and early th centuries. he also discovered that there are different kinds of infinite sets a concept called cardinality. for example the set of integers is countably infinite while the set of real num bers is uncountably infinite
6630 cylindrical rotaons with hour glass shaped impact hyperacve engine / centrifugal force energygraphic only invent deposion
6631 invent ssd drives/ with expandable states invent ssd drives/ with expandable states

6632 istatic external ssd hard drives/ with expandable statessuper contemplaon moment heavy next do you ever wonder how long it takes to make it from atlanta georgia to san diego califor nia? the intent to arrive in a far place is the task at hand. not only to arrive in a place that is somewhere but more over a contemplaon that has a different me and interest. there are people who like abstract art and there are people who prefer realisc art. this is what im talking about

6633 invent super contemplation moment stablefuse invent super contemplation moment stablefuse theoretical separated chain reaction fuse theoretical separated chain reaction fusesuper contemplation moment stablefuse graphic only invent deposition

6634 invent comparisons and amalgamations invent comparisons and amalgamations

6635 schematics of a interwoven statistical cloud. and when variables are compared using normal clients as well as abnormal clients. the mission is to compare two or more things and see if there is any such thing as a proper way to sell and keep on selling. for example how much email does a person like and how many times can you send them a request to buy before they unsubscribe. or out and out asking the right question in the proper context using good judgment and a level heading. what makes things go jump in the night and why other things like time place person or and different things exist. the optional context meaning two or more. is the real secret to any equation.

6636 invent hour house algebraic photonic time measurements invent hour house algebraic photonic time measurements

6637 hour house algebraic photonic time measurements

6638 the chips are a lot like a house. what i do is i conceptualize something and make up a bad name and eventually it's similar to a long horn leg horn thing. the chips are like a ranch styled house that get's boring after a while. with the current push in nanophotonics the ladders and stairs are going to happen with steps and very similar things that make analogies common place to a house. that is all i can say about that

6639 invent infinite motion how to put it all together infinite moon lord carpentersinfinite moon how to put it all together by christopher g. browna spinning top is very similar to something you'd like to have fun and stare at forever. it was brought to my aenon that there is a need for such a thing to run/turn forever. the issue is a few things also somemes called the same thing

6640 invent burning trash isn't as bad as it sounds beer for it burning trash isn't as bad as it soundsby christopher g. brownconnotaons of shock come to mind when things are somemes thought of a process. what i mean is when we think of how would you do that? there are so many different variables that somemes it's like turning tar into gas or water to wine. the things that technology are capable of now are more impressive than we can even guess.the cost of burning trash is unequivalent to the benefits. i have found a way to think of things. air and light is the moo of my local fire staon. the best thing to imagine is to start with two elements that are the most simple to begin some kind of abstract formula. what the public is afraid of are the contaminates in the soluons that are presented after and during and even before the spark of air and light. so let me explain in detail.it's a lot like a nuclear bomb only in reverse. instead of destroying elements we are pung them together. but more important than a superspontaneous collision we are separang the elements for recycling and purificaon. the muffler and the past catalyc converters in a car is one example of how the process is somewhat related to one another.

6641 invent cloud computing statistical virtual memory stacking invent cloud computing statistical virtual memory stacking

6642 easy to ask but i can remember christmas shopping with my parents and some times it really wasnt a good year when this situation happened your in a store grabbing a gift just because its another gift. they say that what really makes something worth giving is the thought. complicated things come in small packages. but big things can seem so far away at any given time.

6643 in a frenzy people cannot see the frenzy some times. have you ever seen a squad of year olds play soccer? every one chases the ball. if only there was a better way to cloud compute the answers of inventions then my friends i would be useless and only if that scenario was so perfect. i think that to spawn two inventions on one deposition would be point less. to give birth to imperfection is to look away from the frenzy.

6644 platform computing that measurers instance rather than current. a dream always seems brighter when you your self imagine the possibilities. cloud stat memory stacking only works when the sorting is all copasetic. stack virtual memory and ram to match the four plus chips that are now in progress

6645 invent wireless usb technology invent wireless usb technology but more a suggeson of what we could do and how itshould be done...

6646 microsoft had the goods and i needed what they had. they listened and i plainly spoke what i wanted. when where and how is the point. microsoft is no longer accepting bids for invent projects. there isn't much to say about this this was when microsoft was accepting feed back and invent depositions by way of solicitation. i emailed them that there should be wireless and input together. and i was out right sick of the wire on my mouse.

6647 invent negative microwave technology and format invent negative microwave technology and format

6648 making cold things stay cold and the same ovens that make things work for warmth can make things stay cold for a while after that. so after all their is cold fusion. the thought is that the technology that is available to consumers that makes things warm can make things cold. just softly and moderation is what we need to study for a while... but

6649 the world needs things cold. the world needs things cold for a longer time. another way to find a need where there is no need

6650 light trigger + varied colored laser s light trigger + varied colored laser semiconductor & microchip cold light micro chip add subtract mode to divide and multiply digital platforms

6651 satellite communication amp aoip the satellite communication amp aoip the communication amp is not only for talking and voip but a entertainment and communication all over internet protocol amplifier/map.

6652 [time and light measure ment + stair c [time and light measure ment + stair case mirror chips] (optical mathematic weight and scale by calculations and common studies)

6653 the infinite motion inside the first s the infinite motion inside the first sphere is made by all the rest of the batteries recharging the original battery inside. the only thing missing (magnetic electricity generating) is the method to recharge a battery with the least amount of connections

6654 it s a lot like a nuclear bomb only in it s a lot like a nuclear bomb only in reverse. instead of destroying elements we are putting them together. but more important than a super spontaneous collision we are separating the elements for recycling and purification. the

muffler and the past cat
6655 platform computing that measures insta platform computing that measures instance rather than current cloud computing statistical virtual memory stacking easy to ask but i can remember christmas shopping with my parents and some times it really wasn't a good year when this situation happened
6656 c technology wireless usb technology w c technology wireless usb technology wireless usb technology microsoft had the goods and i needed what they had. they listened and i plainly spoke what i wanted. when where and how is the point. microsoft is no longer accepting bids for invent projects. first and foremost i take a larger picture into consideraon. what is the difference with a diplomat trying to become a missionary? what is the difference between a philosopher such as myself on a mission as opposed to a supermodel trying to hand out vitamins?secon i. teach a man to fishproverb: give a man a fish he eats for a day teach a man to fish he eats for a lifeme.•communism doesn't work and democracy does. to talk to a person in a nonmilitant/non mis sionary/nongovernmental fashion and let the defined reason of history hold presidency.•a lot of my ideas and invenons will not work because the country at hand is so broken and war struck. to me my conversaonal prose is the only intent. slavery is wrong and hatred toward oneanother is evil.•in history the best thing to do is learn from it. chile adopted the us constuon and to this day they are the most successful south american country to date. this is my idea to prove right.secon ii. filled with uncertain and discernable rights.anquilology makes the possession of man illegal the taxaon only upon representaon•it's a dream that people want a miracle device that heals and finishes off anguish. it's to my self that a theoricacal just of the basic situaon starts with the ability to start at the root of the problem and understand that with all things considered the problem is their government. imag ine how we the people became great is by fore fathers that distrusted the english.•i think that to my understanding the wars inside poverty stricken countries are facing civil unjust due to huge improbable governments. to go to a country at war is not the goal. to begin is to see a country in need but not to aack the country first in the most war torn. help the one who is near the country that is close to the war and have intuion spread.•if the plan is successful the data will become unquesonably great.•taxaon and spread of united states like society to third world countries.
6657 negative microwave technology and form negative microwave technology and format making cold things stay cold and the same ovens that make things work for warmth can make things stay cold for a while after that. so after all their is cold fusion. the thought is that the technology that is avai
6658 lcus united states of america armed fo lcus united states of america armed forces aero contract winner
6659 deposition on theology of psychology deposition on theology of psychology this is the only reason why the internet web pages actually work
6660 a fractal is the opposite of a worm h a fractal is the opposite of a worm hole. (a+m=e) part a fractal is the opposite of a worm hole. the entire amplitude of any entity with twice the mass will make energy that posses a general whole number that is not prime. it's plain to see but what is t
6661 amplitude (). / doubled mass () [.] e amplitude (). / doubled mass () [.] estimated energy constant weight (a+m=e) part thinking of different things how to invent the definition of something that doesn't exist

6662 amplitude (). / doubled mass () [.] e amplitude (). / doubled mass () [.] estimated energy constant weight

6663 open idea app to design a ethernet ce open idea app to design a ethernet cell or satellite based cell phone application open idea app a different way to internet to design a ethernet cell or satellite based cell phone application that connects people's phones as pages instead of pages on a s

6664 modial comm. a different way to ftp modial comm. a different way to ftp to design a ethernet cell or satellite based cell phone application that connects people's phones as pages instead of pages on a server. the main purpose is to communicate and then the other things will gradually fall

6665 a different way to see business ethic a different way to see business ethics and personal values actually do make up the person who works for you. and you and i may see eye to eye for once that you don't want a drug user as your warehouse manager so what precautions would you be willing to t

6666 technology of the relations between f technology of the relations between files long data why can't we all just get along g. brown long data concept i believe that a universal computer file that will put the hard efforts and intelligence of today to work tomorrow. this is not only the best

6667 the need for two apps to transition t the need for two apps to transition through one another trying to work faster. a few questions and what to expectstep one a nano motor the need for two apps to transition through one another is really something adobe systems is good at but

6668 a few questions and what to expect fn a few questions and what to expect fnatma fnatimg fnatma fnatimg chemistry topic of another invent deposition a few questions and what to expecthow to charge an element using the nasa nevada experimental rail way why would you bother them and what it

6669 a few questions and what to expect pu a few questions and what to expect pulse ion trigger algebraic lens motor to pulse nano photon color sensor pulse ion trigger algebraic lens motor to pulse nano photon color sensor trying to work more efficiently. ions

6670 what were they thinking what were the what were they thinking what were they thinking does everything have to have a microchip inside things i just don t want to happen

6671 codex to diametric two opposing ideas codex to diametric two opposing ideas that form a scientific outcome in computer analytical methods two concepts to measure it all codex to dielectrics. two opposing ideas that form a scientific outcome in computer analytical methods. to have codex appli

6672 theoretical business analytic s theor theoretical business analytic s theoretical business analytic s to speak about ones past is sad at times. but

6673 digit treasury to track taxes and ter digit treasury to track taxes and terrorist threats

6674 introduce the world to the largest to introduce the world to the largest topical cause is my first and foremost mission

6675 cuna cuna next chemistry topic of ano cuna cuna next chemistry topic of another part invent deposition by g. brown a few questions and what to expect how to charge an element using the nasa nevada experimental rail way why would you bother them and what it means to the res

6676 cloud cycle to invent concept the dif cloud cycle to invent concept the difference of deep blue was that it wasn t considered a cloud at the time. the focus was only on the game and the server itself. this isn t the focus of what the azure is. windows will now carry on as usual welcome to

6677 intent to remove cuna cuna chemistr intent to remove cuna cuna chemistry topic of another part how to charge an element using the nasa nevada experimental rail way why would you bother them and what it means to the rest of us. i think it's best put as a set charge accelerator a quest

6678 another cloud cycle to invent concept another cloud cycle to invent concept the difference of deep blue was that it wasn t considered a cloud at the time. the focus was only on the game and the server itself. this isn t the focus of what the azure is. windows will now carry on as usual we

6679 real time and pure light %infinite ti real time and pure light %infinite times + %infinite=e%uxc binom lim n toward infinity(+{} over {n})^{n} part

6680 real time and pure light %infinite ti real time and pure light %infinite times + %infinite=e%uxc binom lim n toward infinity(+{} over {n})^{n} %infinite times + %infinite %uxc binom max xe ^{sum +infinity cdot +%uxea {e} over x sum to{{} } x^{}%epsilon }part

6681 varios computer parts and musical cha varios computer parts and musical chairs code name vegas isn't it simple that if the world followed quintet and sextet then that would mean that midi and the mc is and will always be the way that math in dance is synchronized and trans fixate and then be

6682 in a class of time and it s all in a in a class of time and it s all in a little white lie. the is a mop up of a noise. white noise to bass line code name atlantis in a class of time and it's all in a little white lie. the is a mop up of a noise. the pitch decay and use of 's main mix of th

6683 rss search seek & search code name ap rss search seek & search code name apache

6684 electronic muscle pulse therapy for a electronic muscle pulse therapy for atrophy patients help me walk some organic / some post organic measure electronic muscle pulse therapy for atrophy patients step super infomercial for medical if i saw it on tv it has to be real disabled tendon repair

6685 spool effect of data data translation spool effect of data data translation spool effect of data data translation one way in and two ways out is better than only one way in and one way out. logical translation is that a question of danger comes into guess work. a modification of compression

6686 many carbonates into heat as catalyst many carbonates into heat as catalyst many complex solutions to air and water with a new multiple compound of a s tyro synthetic new starch with metal poly carbonate to a s tyro carbonate compound for use in interesting and problematic situations more

6687 amplitude measurement infinity and ot amplitude measurement infinity and other infinities all makes for an artificial intelligence with some or less than a real opinion for itself but more a suggestion of what we could do and how it should be done

6688 it s a fact of life that to be propel it s a fact of life that to be propelled into a unfair and non respect form of work is not only detrimental and confusing to the artist it degrades the work and makes the artist suffer. from the beginning the underground of house and techno makes what we

6689 comma separated encryption comma sepa comma separated encryption comma separated encryption another reason is to continue work on a daily basis as intended securely strange brew is only a reason to understand that everyone is csv. styled now and excel my microsoft is no reason to degrade the

6690 speechless while in love applications speechless while in love applications that text and how to make it as small as one or two options that have a greater click appeal paraphrase questions with proper context all while scripting speechless while in love applications that text and how to mak

6691 inspiration to grow your business whe inspiration to grow your business when you decide to have another baby inspiration when little families become big business or rather when big business becomes a bigger family

6692 successful data sharing perceptual im successful data sharing perceptual image ocr codes and translation scripts and security file extending import export applications support and help

6693 theology of basic wrongs done right q theology of basic wrongs done right question and concept part i see you asking for some kind of

6694 simple est is a solar cell phone re c simple est is a solar cell phone re charger my airplane crashed and let s say i m stranded who would i call first solar cell phone re charger color mathematics and algorithms based on color reflections for processing

6695 sub scaleable sd branches and trees c sub scaleable sd branches and trees

6696 nachmv insulin chris nachmv insulin

6697 knowing the difference painting any w knowing the difference painting any way you like and knowing the difference

6698 two separate processors that are equa two separate processors that are equal and octet each on their own capacity

6699 chemical searing internal process and chemical searing internal process and reactions inherit water activated medicine

6700 cylindrical rotations with hour glass cylindrical rotations with hour glass shaped impact

6701 static sd hard drives/ with expandabl static sd hard drives/ with expandable states

6702 stable fuse (theoretical separated ch stable fuse (theoretical separated chain reaction fuse)

6703 scholastic aptitude testing like comp scholastic aptitude testing like comparisons gone wild schematics of a interwoven statistical cloud scholastic aptitude testing like comparisons gone wild schematics of a interwoven statistical cloud. and when variables are compared using normal clients

6704 retro retro retro penicillin two peni retro retro retro penicillin two penicillin two the simple minds think alike. but we progress through abstract minds that are complex yet still simple looking back is always important. why did i leave that milk out on the kitchen counter all day its

6705 extreme complex computations multiple extreme complex computations multiplex chips with multiple stairs and intelligent accelerators extreme complex computations multiplex chips with multiple stairs and intelligent accelerators extreme complex computations new computer platforms and sets for

6706 imagine a decisive moment when all co imagine a decisive moment when all computations end and a computer crashes what if the demand put us into a suspended turbo modal and a flash point of matter inside an ion created a super accelerated moment when

matter and equation is important multiplex
6707 suspended air and seed super suspende suspended air and seed super suspended fuel flow for hyper active engine part seeds and force suspended air and seed to centrifugal force included inside a hyperactive engine to generate force and energy and make a more fuel effective means for work.
6708 too much / paid in adverts program fl too much / paid in adverts program flush market tactics too much / paid in adverts program no one said you had to listen to the whole thing. flush the market strategies and convoluted scenarios of an artist and their own thought of worth. why is it that
6709 nano tetrahedron motors/period parti nano tetrahedron motors/period particles tets of a period
6710 commons unique abnormal s commons uni commons unique abnormal s commons unique abnormal
6711 nine dash nine chris nine dash nine
6712 nano motors of s tyro carbonate nano nano motors of s tyro carbonate nano motors of s tyro carbonate and in the shape of a tetrahedron
6713 theater servers hd theater experience theater servers hd theater experience hf theater data packs.
6714 from my own experience psychotic debi from my own experience psychotic debilitation from my own experience i believe that there is brain damage during a psychotic episode that may lead to serious and more permanent debilitation. this is important due to the chemical balance and the aid of re
6715 to round the estimation of a half pix to round the estimation of a half pixel closer with a pi triplet fraction.
6716 criminally insane schizophrenia crimi criminally insane schizophrenia criminally schizophrenic what is the issue with virile contributors and identity theft to compose why this is important in a short is to say that the specific context is technology. why a person will gain access to a lo
6717 led lcd or plasma theater movie scree led lcd or plasma theater movie screen plasma movie screen
6718 a pragmatic estimation pragmatic comp a pragmatic estimation pragmatic computational cloud theory
6719 let s say that there are ways to help let s say that there are ways to help others and save lives would you trust a doctor to make a interesting finding with out any long term damage if you {me some one important we both know} the patient survives
6720 a strict and compact intersection new a strict and compact intersection news cloud percents and search ability
6721 how to a essence of a subscription th how to a essence of a subscription that includes dates events and clicks. as well as notable notes and other things that require attention.
6722 to stop within a certain rule of deno to stop within a certain rule of denominations so to speak literally
6723 the difference between a friendly cod the difference between a friendly code command and an unfriendly one is the process to limit and not with out limit. vague code complex friendly vague code anamorphic script commands the difference between a friendly code command and an unfriendly one is

6724 ethel nitrogen oxide fuel diverted na ethel nitrogen oxide fuel diverted natural gas and combined salt
6725 study of sorts to understand and reas study of sorts to understand and reason geometry and other trigonometry waves with a comparative interest into measurement of statistical process. the way a cloud can help use measurement and understand other process and actually see shapes.
6726 pop fad curves intrinsic popularity c pop fad curves intrinsic popularity curves in modern culture. a. popular fadhigh arch to middle decent and small arch with gradual fade out. b. near impossiblelong high arch b. different curvegradual fade in with a small arch and middle decent to a high
6727 data compression virtual zip record k data compression virtual zip record keeping servers services platforms and scripts into a history bin folder for later recall
6728 the reasons for poetic pretense and y the reasons for poetic pretense and you. mystery of art and us the history strange or truth fiction of a future always as a surprise
6729 portable hand held server with sequen portable hand held server with sequential process to enable distant and no service areas similar to the open idea app yet more specific in titles needs like sever weather reports and how to get medicine. the people who would use such a device are patrol
6730" seriously from [] sent tuesday, may , seriously from [] sent tuesday " am to microsoft us partner team subject retro active software resale partner id hello mpn at microsoft
6731 the ability to toggle an early invent the ability to toggle an early invent toggles and switches the ability to toggle and make paths in order to compute the existing switches that need to be used and made off and on. electricity gone computational. simple but very early need in tech space.
6732 data tree multiplying data tree assis data tree multiplying data tree assistants data trees and solid state assistants the ability to toggle and make paths in order to compute the existing switches that need to be used and made off and on. electricity gone computational. simple but very earl
6733 the sum of all abstracts the sum of a the sum of all abstracts the sum of all abstracts thinking of a boomerang effect. for example the thought of a real computation being inside a reals in set theory
6734 cram data shapes things to come and w cram data shapes things to come and why data should have a shape critical random access memory
6735 a mouse with internal memory for such a mouse with internal memory for such applications as copy and paste quickly and sufficiently to increase file transfers to computer a to computer b
6736 to seek find and replace recolonize o to seek find and replace recolonize organ specific micro cell stems to seek find replace the celluloid and kill eat or replace that cell or multitude of cells to cure cancers and other age immune deficiencies and or the many diseases that peo
6737 user defined process and additions us user defined process and additions user defined process and additions vague code complex statistical comparative triplet pixel of noise with pi. computer arithmetic cannot directly operate on real numbers
6738 mouse is live christ mouse is live
6739 simple complex abstract intent to ref simple complex abstract intent to reflect process and redirect. the essence of ion and light inside a working electronic or iontronic machine

6740 easier said than done to create an en easier said than done to create an entity that interpret appreciations of science art and humanities

6741 time to get up and move. working sake time to get up and move. working sake of data conference worldwide time to get up and move. this is a concept for the sake of all data in the entire time and code for codes sake. to incorporate a sync code to share information throughout the time we will

6742 learn it and be the machine animate t learn it and be the machine animate to print artwork there is a time and a breadth. choose your battles and win in a million odds over here is my hope and dreams for this world and the intent to conceive any gain for man. script specials and the dream to

6743 nanometric microcircuit trip devic nanometric microcircuit trip device [breaker] there is a time and a breadth. choose your battles and win in a million odds over here is my hope and dreams for this world and the intent to conceive any gain for man. nanometric microcircuit trip devi

6744 vinegar essence sulfate tablets extra vinegar essence sulfate tablets extract testing actualization

6745 acetoxybenzoic acid quartiondine ligh acetoxybenzoic acid quartiondine light exposure testing actualization's ionized and ultraviolet laser chemical enhancing medicines acetoxybenzoic acid with second half exposure to make acetoxybenzoic acid quartiondine.

6746 equilibrium inside a annotation of pl equilibrium inside a annotation of place crione

6747 wireless machine adapters and person wireless machine adapters and personal wireless comps with routers mini cloud invent more deposition is here

6748 why can t my phone connect to a sate why can t my phone connect to a satellite connect the dots why can't my phone connect to a satellite instead of cell towers why can't my personal router connect to a satellite for un interrupted or rather a ±% up time and possibly easier set ups connect

6749 this invent project is based upon ph this invent project is based upon phone communication gone satellite cell tower possibilities this invent project is based upon phone communication gone satellite. the importance is that this is to equate the chance of a alternate use for cell broadcast

6750 flip the floppy with toenail in the flip the floppy with toenail in the side jamb lets examine why a solid state data format would work.again the intent to understand that size matters the free encyclopedia

6751 using oxygen to propel things in spa using oxygen to propel things in space oxygen system propel engine for use with light weight and satellite operations. the oxygen orbit engine.

6752 recycling nuclear waste into medical recycling nuclear waste into medical radiology use in a dynamic equilibrium recycling nuclear waste into medical radiology use in a dynamic equilibrium nuclear potential energy

6753 fractal math string zoom formula for fractal math string zoom formula for bio and non chemical measurements to zoom and extract dna from stem cells as we

6754 cnc (computer navigated control) mic cnc (computer navigated control) microscope for bio and chemical measurements to zoom and extract dna from stem cells

6755 computer phone a phone call that mad computer phone a phone call that made it retro active. a large smart phone book like design. large phone book like design. conference call computer a phone call that made it retro active. mixed up smart phone more channels per callvoice screen

6756 to use fractal noise as a means to f to use fractal noise as a means to find the infinite extending paths of scripts and all while using trip circuit for control

6757 to use fractal noise as a means to f to use fractal noise as a means to find the infinite extending paths of scripts and all while using trip circuits for control. boolean updates to practical scripts and vague code complex. two planes of intersection and if or a what. createspace independe

6758" more channels per callvoice, data, more channels per callvoice " screen

6759 transistor nano direction circuit na transistor nano direction circuit nano direction and a path of a y transistor nano direction circuit

6760 point a with a synchronized clock da point a with a synchronized clock daybreak compensation measurements point a with a synchronized clock to use compensation measurements like atmosphere elements and other catalyst. measurements for point b to compare and complete the time to distant li

6761 to save all sources state of our art to save all sources state of our art arch of a window to elaborate on this with full intent to save all sources. the means of any archive is how much there is to make any save or estimation of weight weight of a back up on any scale to forward or fo

6762 state of our art open market gadgets state of our art open market gadgets to elaborate on this with full intent to progress the moment of technology and processor. imagine you being able to pick the size and computational power of your own gadget and yet at the same time you yourself coul

6763 lcus united states of america armed lcus united states of america armed forces aero contract winner state of our art aero t design stealth state of our art aero t design united states of america armed forces aero contract winner

6764 things that go with poor spelling he things that go with poor spelling health invent tab state of our art things that go with poor spelling spider pill carbon stabilize reaction

6765 ask intel about it they will say the ask intel about it they will say the exact same thing server chip stacking stacking this state of our art early invent coming to light ask intel about it they will say the exact same thingserver chip stacking. createspace independent publishing platfor

6766 oem oms original equipment manufactu oem oms original equipment manufacturer optional manufacturer system oem oms state of our art open market systems to elaborate on this with full intent to progress the moment of technology and processor. imagine you being able to pick the size and comp

6767 this is a situation state of our art this is a situation state of our art woq enterprise email records archive this is a situation of one fall scenario spam and filter checks. to assign a script to this is not adequate to make a program that exports and imports files paged by person and t

6768 astro hardware satellite server stat astro hardware satellite server state of our art astro service hardware astro hardware. imagine a disillusioned space elevator that has no clue. just a satellite that has servers aboard. imagine space travel that is so successful that over a long or sh

6769 astro hardware astro size state of o astro hardware astro size state of our art astro size hardware form astro hardware. extended satellite computations. imagine space travel that is

so successful that over a long or short time we are able to store data in space itself. createspace indepe
6770 exit format expressions efe state of exit format expressions efe state of our art exit format expressions exit format expressions the intent to share all types of data or miscellaneous file types and the intent to not share or make program compatible is an interoperability challenge and p
6771 emw state of our art eject my work i emw state of our art eject my work i have always wanted to borrow someone's pc but it's a pc how come we can't eject the os the updates and the software we own as well as our work and subsequently call hard ware hardware and eject my workcreatespace in
6772 atomized ion printing atomized ion p atomized ion printing atomized ion printing state of our art atomized ion printing with ± demagnetized trionic paper atomized ion printing with ± demagnetized trionic paper uses security stripsnew optical mediasfine art printing createspace independe
6773 state of our art it sound s like tha state of our art it sound s like that in a sentence phonology the syllables founding of latin reference
6774 super high carbon conductors super h super high carbon conductors super high carbon conductors plasma molding diamond dust state of our art run on super high carbon conductors yielding welding solder heating all things carbon pure carbon with plasma into a height of super states of meta seriously i am asking for you to sell office again. treat this comment with possibilities lately you
6775 atomized electormechanical photo pr atomized electormechanical photo printing atomized electormechanical photo printing state of our art run on atomized electormechanical photo printing as opposed to ion atomized demagnetized printing this would be a simple and more consumer affordabl
6776 soft poly silicate carbonate nuclear soft poly silicate carbonate nuclear smelting
6777 state of our art hard oxide hard pol state of our art hard oxide hard poly oxide carbonate nuclear smelting or what makes it so that the other sets
6778 mission diagnose changes at dopa min mission diagnose changes at dopa mine serotonin adrenaline and histamine receptor sites in the central nervous system by using a similar method to diabetic blood testing. mission diagnose changes at dopa mine adrenaline and histamine receptor
6779 what goes up may come down finding a what goes up may come down finding a height to measure the un measurable off the grid computations and landing points by what goes up may come down. the point that we need to measure in haste is the un measurable flash point that will keep the platform
6780 hollow arc field mathematical plane hollow arc field mathematical plane plateau exit the invisible points that may connect a plane by inverse
6781 intent to covert and see the matter intent to covert and see the matter at hand. to tablet to desktop to phone ineligible document conversion wysiwyg
6782 for safe and secure as well as quick for safe and secure as well as quick and immediate transactions a card that provides service when service is only one overdraft away. to speed up the transactions posting and pending to post as a involuntary means. createspace independent publishing plat
6783 even and odd fractional status even even and odd fractional status even and odd

fractional status the improvement of multi deck processors all natural and computational binary numbers will be multiplied and divided with roots and squares only over a short time span will this happen inside

6784 pixel language em css wc intent adi pixel language em css wc intent adi adi adi

6785 fuse nano motors ch fuse nano motors

6786 atomic weight vacuum precious metal atomic weight vacuum precious metal recycling and atom mining

6787 to process code with measurement cas to process code with measurement cascading increments a certain unit of measurement . or for processing electronic measurement using my certain unit of measurement data versus the shape of media today

6788 exit comp rules that apply with each exit comp rules that apply with each process data is the progress of format in my opinion. the greatest thing to happen to anything is to negate the format itself. why do people make things in side a box of any sort. this is maddening to myself. at this

6789 electromagnetic divalent effervescen electromagnetic divalent effervescence

6790 it s funny you should but ask i m in it s funny you should but ask i m in servers severs not software web os

6791 using multiple tests compensation an using multiple tests compensation and how to provide any consistency with statistics elaborate compensations will measure the point of our art and science. using multiple tests and using all the measures known by science to study the form of art that wil

6792 nano motors and in the way of open nano motors and in the way of open and closed. aggregate verses passive for technological or medical scenarios and other processes when size does matter.

6793 can we figure out the chemistry in a can we figure out the chemistry in a healthy human can we figure out the chemistry in a healthy human

6794 to make something work sometimes siz to make something work sometimes size does matter. what i want is a fast hard drive that happens to be external for example the mystery is how to make a unique hole and a plug to do that with without loss or deterioration in cables. crioner creates

6795 intelligence and brain growth there intelligence and brain growth there is the science we all know

6796 compact hardware service compact ser compact hardware service compact server inside a series of software mods and a different way to dedicate the data position size and capabilities for allocation compact server. compact hardware service compact server inside a series of software mods and a

6797 grade b grade all in a thing called grade b grade all in a thing called hardware service cloud. to make a note there is a difference in all technology and the service of a hardware is not a change. to specify a invent called service grading and rating. compact server. compact hardware serv

6798 falling by data verses falling by da falling by data verses falling by data verses balanced data at the same measure of a chemical balanced neutral chemistry ph the best way to make us understand the falling off stature of a certain mark such as to take two or more things and measure the

6799 things that verses in terms this ver things that verses in terms this verses that in order to make another turn as well as things that verses and do not equal any such return or sense. the thought is the matter at hand. an abstract definition (ca

6800 myriad nano sphere nano sphere myria myriad nano sphere nano sphere myriad nanosphere nanosphere of myriad in reference to tension in side a molecular consistent other wise known as a very small sphere (floating of the free encyclopedia main a

6801 assemble of pre face and su face ass assemble of pre face and su face assemble of pre face and su face universal assemblage formats companies who make things for other companies to sell with their name on top and companies to sell what someone else s already made with an alternate name on t

6802 divergent decision this is a company divergent decision this is a company specific attempt to hold notes and thoughts in the air. the example of cars as compared to specific software gives precedence to a new way for profit intent. the decision to make two or more different operating system camera aio all digital comm a cloud receiver. the intent to design a complete radio tv phone data receiver. the mundane and exciting work prior to the internet to make data from radio television and voice com

6803 processors isolated semi conductors processors isolated semi conductors and their organized processing looping processors isolated semi conductors and their organized processing may be needed to comply more than two specific parts of a computer. to make a conductor for part a and part b as

6804 script dividing script patterns and script dividing script patterns and repetitive computations multiplied by a larger script. to divide or multiply one large process into sub processes for a real time application

6805 dynamic verses static web content tr dynamic verses static web content translation by use of analytical history transition content transition content translation pack the intent to take static web content and automate the content into dynamic by use of analytic patterns of use history creat

6806 three ring binder glucose incubation three ring binder glucose incubation a computer controlled molecular telescope / nan scope that can insert and impregnate new dna will consequently rebuild the cell. a computer controlled dissection will allow probability of success for great accomplishm

6807 turning off the virus virus intentio turning off the virus virus intentions to turn and transform virus intentions to turn and transform the effort of mainline to a true police operating system. to steady the intent and take the means in order to use that code for a positive purpose. for ex

6808 another comparative analogy water wa another comparative analogy water water cyclewater data cycle fresh water storagenew data server sea waterworld wide data tidesto sync data syn toxin vs bio toxin fruit fly farming. all these things can change medicine

6809 the positive intent to administer a the positive intent to administer a native formula for globalization patients

6810 to give data sending water through o to give data sending water through or not to send water. if there were a .rar equal to a need then there would be a need called .raz. to send a .raz into a receiver would be like making a scripted transition to and from a device or line. translated into

6811 synthetic currents to anchor underwa synthetic currents to anchor underwater current makers to a high middle and low temperatures and in the consistent direction to prevent stagnant water and refresh the water in a pond or reservoir. the benefits would be less insects and healthier fish cre

6812 intelligent voip s server to point a intelligent voip s server to point a server instead of a pc to magistrate commas and processes.

6813 topical antibiotic mouthwash topical topical antibiotic mouthwash topical antibiotic mouthwash (halitosis) to cure by way of rinsing and nasal spray of antibiotic solution topical antibiotic bath soak (to cure by way of bath soaking in diluted antibiotic solution createspace independent pub

6814 total year end dividend trading join total year end dividend trading joint stock companies act from wikipedia debate the joint stock companies bill was introduced to parliament by the then vice president of the board of trade mr robert lowe in doing so he proclaimed the right of createspace

6815 tired of ftp what if i didn t have t tired of ftp what if i didn t have to do it that way. what if there were new and exciting ways to engage clients data that make and hold more data than usual. for example a cloud that is low to the ground is called fog. files on the ground would make syn

6816 tired of upgrading key socket adapte tired of upgrading key socket adapter a molding cpu socket adapter that works like clay on a car key in a cool movie. working to accept all patterns. but only all the patterns present

6817 compensation chip compensation chips compensation chip compensation chips long processors vs. short and stubby. it s a uniform shape that is divided by and then multiplied with time and hardware mass. so to speak

6818 search by image to search for a topi search by image to search for a topic with an image. to find people places and things. with input from meta tags such as technical terms when where who and why. as well as to modify the photo scan or topic by perspective date and angle using the image it

6819 personal computer server personal se personal computer server personal server computer re ignite the passion for computing put one foot forward and take two steps back try installing windows eight with a server by intel use as directed and wash twice a day intel sy createspace independen

6820 my lzw algorithm isn t free a fee fo my lzw algorithm isn t free a fee for a free platform is essentially not happening. i invented the pd f and here is my quote. either trust me or don't. the fact of the matter is that like the pokemon there was a puzzle in the equation of how to market

6821 feedback note simple feed back form feedback note simple feed back form from microsoft office that wanted more vector and less bitmap in the os the things that are happening with css are incredible

6822 do they put that stuff in the air th do they put that stuff in the air the chance of the hospital itself being sick is the real issue. like the story goes how do you heal the sick inside a sick place. well there are extremely strong antibiotics and then there are subtle every day antibioti

6823 auto matron machine of reverse publi auto matron machine of reverse publisher

6824 explain this is to accumulate the ci explain this is to accumulate the circumstances this isn't a time device a folder generator that catalogs achieved cd's and cdroms into a folder on a hard drive flash card or sd and even server related temps

6825 the issue is when will a co processo the issue is when will a co processor complimentary on and off as well as different and alternate processing to explain this is to accumulate the circumstances of on and off in a larger picture. to estimate the neurological existence of two halves of o
6826 one creative step bridge parallel mo one creative step bridge parallel modern efficiency content text context parallel (email submission) assumptions of a coprocessing pattern the issue is when will a co processor understand that to full fill one creative step. it's important to duplicat
6827 who really understands better than a who really understands better than a child trying to kick a ball into the wind it may do this it may do that but what we really need to understand is there are curve anomalies that happen more than we hope that s why it s fun yet to understand them is
6828 voluntary / involuntary core process voluntary / involuntary core process stop core back user selected modes and bios updates
6829 microwave fuse content text contextm microwave fuse content text contextmelting the parts for safety or other means. with a metal and timer similar to a wave generator inside a microwave oven. with military and aero design specifics as well as fuse and exploding instances. micro wave melt s
6830 pi difference a. to b. comments ther pi difference a. to b. comments there is a point in every computation that will like light transfer to another point and time. every thing is timed with pi you can measure the distance of any computation from point a to point b with angle circumferenc
6831 to multiply comments the chances of to multiply comments the chances of using two or more mother boards and then working together with what it may hold there is a point in every computation that will like light transfer to another point and time. every thing is timed with pi you can
6832 to multiply on local network os over to multiply on local network os over os under os scenario to multiply on local network os the chances of using two or more under operating systems and concluding it to a working hierarchy of operating system +even or +odd. createspace independent publi
6833 laser wave modulation shaping a lase laser wave modulation shaping a laser with complimentary light is anyone out there shaping a laser with complimentary light for navigation and artificial energy math components (laser theoryenergyexpansion of a sum = accelerated motion
6834 as well as triangular square and cir as well as triangular square and circular properties such as vertical horizontal and spherical combinations with two or more in one process. line of sight
6835 as well as triangular square and cir as well as triangular square and circular properties such as vertical horizontal and spherical combinations with two or more in one process. line of sight as well as to inject gas and form a modulation of image appropriate for television and viewing c
6836 infrared computer screen human inter infrared computer screen human interface manipulation for laser generated d tv comments is anyone out there shaping a laser with complimentary light for navigation and artificial energy math components (laser theory energy expansion shaping a laser wi

6837 out put computers are a method of cr out put computers are a method of creation out put computers are a method of creation that people need to make things. i have decided to claim this as a separate market of intent for improvement in usability and justification of my means. there are curre
6838 glass (or poly carbonate) insulated glass (or poly carbonate) insulated gold line wire housing. needed to stack motherboards and double or more the capacity of the vertical possibilities inside that manner. as opposed to a silicon board this would connect boards to one another. createspace
6839 the intent to reactivate a flower fo the intent to reactivate a flower for a shape for extended central processing units and the possibilities to multiply and agitate the growth of a unit into more than one units a flower verses in terms. (july
6840 crystallized mother board the intent crystallized mother board the intent to reactivate a flower for a shape for extended central processing units and the possibilities to multiply and agitate the growth of a unit into more than one units a flower verses in terms. the intent to reactivate a
6841 a simple dividing trigger for electr a simple dividing trigger for electronic and dividing transistors inside a circuit path.
6842 photon fractal math which and where photon fractal math which and where rgb
6843 a=/ bh/a=pi r ^+. is versable in ter a=/ bh/a=pi r ^+. is versable in terms
6844 {to use a non primal number is the i {to use a non primal number is the in and out of a circuit if to use a prime number the sum must have a divisible cube root.} which verses and changes in terms and may be exchangeable. factorization
6845 a=/ bh/a=pi r ^+. number in fraction a=/ bh/a=pi r ^+. number in fractional os states or to abstract with the use of number [one million seven hundred and twentyfive] {to use a non primal number is the in and out of a circuit if to use a prim
6846 immune systemic insulin. insulin med immune systemic insulin. insulin medicine to magistrate through the auto immune system immune systemic insulin. insulin medicine to magistrate through the auto immune system insulin main article insulin therapy type diabetes is typically treated with a
6847 immune systemic anti psychotics anti immune systemic anti psychotics antipsychotic medicine to magistrate through the auto immune system anti psychotic medicine to magistrate through the auto immune system physiological the causes of bipolar disorder have yet to be fully uncovered
6848 emergency sos satellite system based emergency sos satellite system based on cell phone satellite connections. sos from wikipedia
6849 plastic layered electronic micro boa plastic layered electronic micro board a process defined with nano printing circuits and layers of layers of circuitry that provides depth into height of computing capabilities or alternate poly carbonate / carbonate porous compounds createspace independ
6850 outdoor hot and cold out door auto/s outdoor hot and cold out door auto/semi conductor open processors outdoor hot and cold climates need processing
6851 outdoor hot and cold climates need p outdoor hot and cold climates need processing let s imagine that there could be a cup with a microchip inside it after all open processors and the instance of virtual to real time applicable things like traffic flow energy systems police dispatch and

6852 parallel processing and my scripts p parallel processing and my scripts parallel code reprocessing divide and multiply the cell numbers from tables and other things generated by a compromise including large verses the many

6853 serial artwork number or swan to reg serial artwork number or swan to register and official works of a group of artwork printed or raw data sets for future reference and worth including any given details of certifications.

6854 bandwagon effect from wikipedia the bandwagon effect from wikipedia the free encyclopedia jump to navigation search the bandwagon effect is a well documented form of group think in behavioral science and has many applications. the general rule is that conduct or beliefs spread among peopl

6855 this is a needed attempt at making r this is a needed attempt at making real circumstances translatable into real terms of useful objects. for example if the code says up this could mean literal or non relative terms

6856 the need to place secure socket laye the need to place secure socket layers into place with a packet flaw prerequisite. to speak plainly a packet is requested from the server. the server sends a packet first with the completed file information backwards with weight and scale then loads t cr

6857 to protect the small glitches and ma to protect the small glitches and malfunctions of any surge from sensitive and expensive trips breaks and surges of electricity to protect the most valuable devices.

6858 it s true that there is a popular ac it s true that there is a popular accent in america tv and the spread of a californian accent across the united states of america is the new pink.

6859 any such right as to investigate and any such right as to investigate and with plausible cause to search for a missing person upon any premise. with unique attributes justified by law holding contrary existing census information and legitimate rights of distrust or suspicion createspace ind

6860 many other countries use the us doll many other countries use the us dollar. to equate a hypothesis is to generate a revenue inside it s self. the dollar bill with country intent for example a widget country denominated dollar with gold / silver / property / resource note. createspace indep

6861 lottery ticket cloud subscriptions c lottery ticket cloud subscriptions

6862 to initiate an add on application di to initiate an add on application different than a program but more over a specific add on to compliment code in a sense of script and all while not having a apparent app face formula. a thing to call love and work with and seemingly be the same as child

6863 to include two computers in a sense to include two computers in a sense of permanence. complete with software and hardware options and tickets of operation as well as ip address.

6864 to deliberate the sustainability of to deliberate the sustainability of a vote census or a moderated e census

6865 to publicly render the president pet to publicly render the president petitionally un available for office

6866 i am not referring to my fans here y i am not referring to my fans here you are allowed to come back and download as much as you wish to be specific the newest type of stalker is someone you know (or do not) that watches and stalks as you do not wish. people with probable cause not in

6867 ethernet fixed raid to have an ether ethernet fixed raid to have an ethernet with multiple raid fixes per connected units. using a raid modified ethernet router.
6868 parallel code jamming and encryption parallel code jamming and encryption
6869 fractal parallel memory cpu operatio fractal parallel memory cpu operations
6870 minimum displacement data alternate minimum displacement data alternate data scripting translations with quality checks
6871 walking and write ready data copyrig walking and write ready data
6872 compact disc christ compact disc
6873 turbo stopping point and alter wait turbo stopping point and alter wait
6874 choose your format sync data base mo choose your format sync data base monetary ratings and guidance
6875 to use anti psychotics and mental a to use anti psychotics and mental a b receptors to recover
6876 offering for cpu+memory in one opera offering for cpu+memory in one operation to add secondary processing and third and fourth in the memory ram itself
6877 grounded board edge for nano poly ca grounded board edge for nano poly carbonate electric conductors
6878 a means to raid activate each level a means to raid activate each level for accuracy.
6879 second first and third level server second first and third level server board management
6880 with the mass of complicated ports t with the mass of complicated ports there should be a uniform port of snap in with pin play and align to the left scenario like a find and play plug and play device that may be useful for upcoming devices and experimental utilities yet unknown. createspac
6881 my thought to amplify the core is by my thought to amplify the core is by multiplying the board and amp mechanism operations and connections during a core connection and relay amplitude marker a starting point that has a reciprocating point to relay.
6882 my intent is to change the way peopl my intent is to change the way people put the chip in and how many times you can change the chip to satisfy the craving for more speed. with extractable chips and interchangeable cpu second processing unit chip drive readers.
6883 the right to hold the representation the right to hold the representation legally bound by any means and amendments to the constitution such as a law that shall hold the branches such as even to the intellectual property rights counsel itself liable for negligence.
6884 anti histamine use to deliver anti p anti histamine use to deliver anti psychotic medication
6885 synthetic poly metallic compound cop synthetic poly metallic compound
6886 synthetic poly protein sugar concent synthetic poly protein sugar concentrates
6887 to divide odd and even fractions int to divide odd and even fractions into an encryption translation for data and other media
6888 complication computations super comp complication computations super computer built by super computer and into the abyss that is more computations virtual mathematics including fractals
6889 raid multi sd flash card device raid raid multi sd flash card device raid multiple compact flash t card holder drive addition and subtract able device
6890 neurological coherence test and cent neurological coherence test and central nervous system cognitive balance test in form of a phosphorous ion activity test. verses in turn a

hydrogen activity test.
6891 virtual predictions of translation b virtual predictions of translation bio information to a real world application producing phosphorous based medicines
6892 ecology economic recycling processes ecology economic recycling processes
6893 sodium delineation native valances a sodium delineation native valances and their properties in the brain verses muscles and other organs.
6894 involuntary finite ion tet of an org involuntary finite ion tet of an organ and voluntary control neurology
6895 creative data engineers employment s creative data engineers employment software and certificate location a business of creative judgment and relationship attributes for data
6896 machine builders and labor machine m machine builders and labor machine makers to receive incentives benefits. in local machine and robot automology
6897 pcie e os installer and configured o pcie e os installer and configured out of the box insert and run playable secondary or primary to provide higher point contact and super fast calculations.
6898 to equate the code percentages with to equate the code percentages with the persistent substantial available data needed to complete an operation
6899 making higher connections like a cab making higher connections like a cable verses in terms to a or pin circuit
6900 making isolation as easy as drop. co making isolation as easy as drop.
6901 / fractions in dynamic digital cable / fractions in dynamic digital cable frequency modulations
6902 to add an array of more inexpensive to add an array of more inexpensive chips through a port of alternate matching sets
6903 a and over frequency of compression a and over frequency of compression to trans pond and locate proper signal dials in digital computation packets
6904 how to create a true population irre how to create a true population irregularity anomaly verses a false popular anomaly in math and science chemistry and physics as well as politics and government
6905 trigonometry personal computing calc trigonometry personal computing calculations derived from the number over
6906 to compare an initial altair to tomo to compare an initial altair to tomorrows lcus it s as though there is no difference in new super computer. the assumption that all wheel drive is like four wheel drive only all the time in a balanced formation of code.
6907 geometric scripts that fractionally geometric scripts that fractionally divide and parallel the operations at hand. to use the method and source as the same path
6908 a computational script that instead a computational script that instead of one s and zeros a frequency that pairs with other waves to make a computation together
6909 under ocean jet stream path way of n under ocean jet stream path way of nuclear reactor non exchanging temperatures
6910 to add traffic conductors to overlap to add traffic conductors to overlapping circuits
6911 to theorize the assumption that ther to theorize the assumption that there will be a pathway for data to process
6912 to place multiple traffic chips insi to place multiple traffic chips inside a core of many like stop lights

6913 alternating traffic triggers and co alternating traffic triggers and coprocessors to branch overall assets between super links

6914 periodical carbon and starch biologi periodical carbon and starch biological and synthetic deluge refining separation

6915 a path to clean and process new sign a path to clean and process new signals from the core or multitude of cores

6916 fractional diverting process and app fractional diverting process and application performance amplification and coordination

6917 logical and virtual core with a crea logical and virtual core with a creative and reprocessing core

6918 located inside the logical and creat located inside the logical and creative core processes there will be a mechanism script to run the processing

6919 time unawareness and unscheduled sle time unawareness and unscheduled sleeping resulting in acute insomnia

6920 time awareness and anticipation obse time awareness and anticipation obsessiveness resulting in acute insomnia

6921 generating natural d images with two generating natural d images with two ports at one monitor

6922 to make operating over two or more d to make operating over two or more drives to one system in any os by way of a key file

6923 dmonitor led layer nano sphere pixe dmonitor led layer nano sphere pixel layer for three dimensional projection and perspective

6924 brainstorm us gov application time s brainstorm us gov application time stamp applications and concept

6925 using lasers to generate high potent using lasers to generate high potential energy in combination with solar receiving cells.

6926 using a thin transistor based liquid using a thin transistor based liquid crystal to alternate into motherboard off and on circuits and similar exchanges like cpu and memory cells

6927 horizontal/vertical motherboard sock horizontal/vertical motherboard socket intersections

6928 over non malice encryption in commun over non malice encryption in communications

6929 using many thin transistor based liq using many thin transistor based liquid crystal to alternate into motherboard off and on circuits and similar exchanges like cpu and memory cells

6930 using many thin transistor based cir using many thin transistor based circuits to alternate into motherboard off and on circuits and similar exchanges like cpu and memory cells

6931 using many thin transistor based cir using many thin transistor based circuits to alternate into pcie plug ins to make off and on circuits and similar exchanges like cpu and memory cells

6932 using octavio rhythm sequencing in c using octavio rhythm sequencing in communications to produce multiple connections in circuits applied compression as in applied calculative computations verses the term known as digital

6933 as compared to the electricity grid as compared to the electricity grid in north america using transmission and subtransmission to generate primary cores and secondary core signals as in the high to lower steps similar in cable to make any such signals computational. applied compression a

6934 to add more chips in a formation inc to add more chips in a formation including similar to a honey comb with fractional diamond central processing chip stack and assembly

6935 to give any such meaning to approxim to give any such meaning to approximate and a sum of non exact processing to result inside a estimated code or signal of will from making a stopping point and the root of pi from fractal transformations.

6936 ethel nitrogen oxide engine and the ethel nitrogen oxide engine and the parameters of intent of power.

6937 to place multiple central processing to place multiple central processing units in a way that shapes an h i like an i beam in construction methodology

6938 modular work board group chassis and modular work board group chassis and fabric to hold and join multiple it super itx boards into a new modular chassis & add for small x forms

6939 modular work board group chassis and modular work board group chassis and fabric with software cluster to hold and join multiple it super itx boards into a new modular chassis & add for small x forms

6940 miniature parallel cluster software miniature parallel cluster software to migrate processing and clusters of many boards for applications and data base processing

6941 miniature parallel cluster board and miniature parallel cluster board and bios a board that translates the management into a suitable definition of a group working together

6942 miniature cluster chassis middle for miniature cluster chassis middle form factor a chassis built to compute many different x or mini boards verses one single board

6943 smaller than previous bios chips and smaller than previous bios chips and transforming code to a digital to triad octavia signal to compute calculations and computations in a way previously unable to do with signal processors by way of transforming the signal into a code pre amplified to c

6944 triad octavia signal to grid format triad octavia signal to grid format yx with a coherent of

6945 triad octavia signal to grid format triad octavia signal to grid format yx with a coherent of a controller that modifies the signal into computations before processing into various program signals in a tet of a period machine controlled nano sphere.

6946 interleaving circuit conductor traff interleaving circuit conductor traffic signals chip sockets alternate secondary processing units that work to control processes based on a alternate path

6947 interchangeable secondary processing interchangeable secondary processing unit sockets interleaving circuit conductor traffic signals chip sockets alternate secondary processing units that work to control processes based on a alternate path

6948 variant cloud voip relay schema voic variant cloud voip relay schema voice and other data cross internet clouds to relay data communication via the internet

6949 in relation to modular servers in pr in relation to modular servers in production today this would equate a stacking server using multiple boards and modular steps

6950 to degrade plastics and harden or so to degrade plastics and harden or solvency the plastics in advance to incineration and generate electricity as well as a sooty carbon for commercial uses and energy

6951 fee based cloud sharing and cell tra fee based cloud sharing and cell transmitting between business and business. similar to cell tower property verses server property in the clouds. provider to provider to re seller to host
6952 to modify the bios on a chip verses to modify the bios on a chip verses the board via efi and presorted bios properties
6953 after market gadgets need the shape after market gadgets need the shape you want. build your own tablet hand held chassis and server related fabric smaller un fused working parts that equal more power and higher concentration of parts dual socket tablet with or without fans and inches
6954 after market gadgets need the shape after market gadgets need the shape you want. build your own tablet hand held chassis and server related fabric smaller un fused working parts that equal more power and higher concentration of parts dual socket tablet with fans and inches to inches d
6955 a pcb board to fit other boards into a pcb board to fit other boards into the conjoining board
6956 a pcb board to fit other boards into a pcb board to fit other boards into the conjoining board completed board to self modulating cell board
6957 a pcb board to fit other boards into a pcb board to fit other boards into the conjoining board completed board to self modulating cell board along side a mirror image to use parallel processing in formation
6958 mini board to board connection landi mini board to board connection landing engine micro controller board cloud connection board to board lock landing
6959 mini data to data board lock data en mini data to data board lock data engine m. form factor board receiver connection base to board lock landing
6960 real head board lock data & fabric e real head board lock data & fabric engine micro controller board cloud connection board to board lock landing connecting and operating m. form factor board receiver connection base to board lock landing
6961 to purpose propose an update to the to purpose propose an update to the current board registration and operating system scheme that will equate into more than one board opposing the hypothesis that using more than one board will over come.
6962 pcie shape operator differential geo pcie shape operator differential geometric computational processes o equate the opposing and similarities in mathematical differential calculus and integral calculus as well as linear algebra and multi linear algebra to study problems in computational ge
6963 computational fractal encryption wit computational fractal encryption with keys and lock as well a double formulas for higher security
6964 ricochet laser foresighted led energ ricochet laser foresighted led energy
6965 weakest link lcus the weakest link i weakest link lcus the weakest link is us but we are its only asset to multiply the threads in a processing formula of over lapping adjustments
6966 channel dimension process multiplyin channel dimension process multiplying such a thing to equate a size dedication to channel actualization and capacity per element channel
6967 children specific dose measurement s children specific dose measurement solvent formula
6968 second diagnosis estimate to conclud second diagnosis estimate to conclude the status of illness

6969 cpu chip drop install pliers copyrig cpu chip drop install pliers
6970 second and third level + processing second and third level + processing unit interchanging socket to compose another central based chip socket with alternate sub levels of chip sockets. generally considered non central or additional solder and molded chips for example a replaceable second
6971 a crime including the rights to just a crime including the rights to justify the truth for the greater good of humanity
6972 a multitude of cells that reflect an a multitude of cells that reflect and generate picture with only a segment of cells actually carrying data although showing partial information in the series of cells with all considered
6973 alternating step code sequencing to alternating step code sequencing to multiply and receive the signals in alternating steps
6974 focused artificial energy energy web focused artificial energy energy web energy server focused artificial energy energy web a contained web sphere that simulates a web of energy to pilot stations for distribution from a building that is a self contained focused laser generated solar energy
6975 energy server focused artificial ene energy server focused artificial energy energy server focused artificial energy energy web a contained web sphere that simulates a web of energy to pilot stations for distribution from a building that is a self contained focused laser generated solar ene
6976 energy server focused artificial ene energy server focused artificial energy energy web a contained web sphere that simulates a web of energy to pilot stations for distribution from a building that is a self contained focused laser generated solar energy structure that is on and off with se
6977 input data software multiplying proc input data software multiplying processing out put script to make a cloud state of servers work over multiplying fabric end points and signal bandwidth
6978 honeycomb board that is a wall of ar honeycomb board that is a wall of architecture upon its self. to make a glass cased gold wire fish through the board up down and over and through printed circuit boards to endup inside a printed piping board with corrugations.
6979 stacked conjoined honeycomb board th stacked conjoined honeycomb board that is a wall of architecture upon its self. to make a glass cased gold wire fish through the board up down and over and through printed circuit boards to endup inside a printed piping board with corrugations submitted
6980 to expand raid capacity to equate in to expand raid capacity to equate into pcie thunder bolt raid
6981 to expand raid capacity to equate in to expand raid capacity to equate into mobile docking temp raid and bay station for all in one in other words a docking all in one with true form technology repeated to expand raid capacity to equate into a mobile docking temp raid and bay station for al
6982 software making it all happen to exp software making it all happen to expand raid capacity to equate into a mobile docking temp raid and bay station for all in one in other words a docking all in one with true form technology essentially a computer that docs your phone or tablet repeated an
6983 another cloud cycle to invent concep another cloud cycle to invent concept the

difference of deep blue was that it wasn't considered a cloud at the time. the focus was only on the game and the server itself. this is not the focus of what the azure is. windows will now carry on as usual w

6984 local cloud temp raid system verses local cloud temp raid system verses expanded services cloud for example a local more secure way to cloud that would incorporate your existing data and media servers as well as a new local platform that may or may not synchronize as the same based upon yo

6985 a smaller less expensive way to soli a smaller less expensive way to solid state data to add layers to a existing ddr plug in and plug in more layers with new adjustable configurations for example dd r with half height extensions that run but stand up like a pcie that has layers included t

6986 to perform a movement in a fractal a to perform a movement in a fractal animation with encryption to have a double as well as a start and finish equal to a formula of change

6987 to perform a movement in a fractal w to perform a movement in a fractal with encryption to have a double as well as a start and finish equal to a formula of change and as well as to make more than one time loop in the process

6988 to expand raid capacity to equate in to expand raid capacity to equate into mobile docking temp raid and bay station for by attachment device in other words a docking by attachment device with true form technology repeated to expand raid capacity to equate into a mobile docking temp raid an

6989 amendment deficiency petitions by po amendment deficiency petitions by popular veto

6990 to declare a substance medicinally a to declare a substance medicinally addictive and harmful to ones health by overdose as in unsubscribed methods of use.

6991 denationalize of radical liberalism denationalize of radical liberalism to declare a free argument of a amendment or change in policy too liberal for the nations good and notate it un popular.

6992 to make a political state of technol to make a political state of technology different than previous and current standing into a new and updated stature of state of the art design and vote from the intended place of interest.

6993 to build a bluray or archival disc to build a bluray or archival disc mm media inside a glass or carbonate jewel case with spectrum magnified reading points with the intent of making it secure and dust free while being redundant and replaceable with the intent not confuse it and a inch

6994 reading and writing using convex and reading and writing using convex and concave lenses to build a bluray or archival disc mm media inside a glass or carbonate jewel case with spectrum magnified reading points with the intent of making it secure and dust free while being redundant and rep

6995 a device reading and writing using c a device reading and writing using convex and concave lenses to build a bluray or archival disc mm media inside a glass or carbonate jewel case with spectrum magnified reading points with the intent of making it secure and dust free while being redundan

6996 chronological passive processing ver chronological passive processing verses an active aggressor in a non sequential format of computations will help to stabilize the order of complex arrangements

6997 a cable that connects pcie to sata v a cable that connects pcie to sata verses in terms

6998 an archival free server service that an archival free server service that records history based upon proprietary intellectual property. say for example a url that is specific that includes a .doc suffix and moderated by governmental appreciations. for a good short summary a that is accessib
6999 a governmental act that may deliver a governmental act that may deliver a electronic exemplified terms of use and search document where the new cloud of information evidence applied is searched and deemed acceptable by use of lawsuit including the file process of fees and documented servic
7000 to link hard drives and with a promp to link hard drives and with a prompt configure a large local disc population in one group of windows system discs
7001 conceptual invention s and the inten conceptual invention s and the intent to inspire the thought and not hold back an inventor who cares to drift instead of dwelling into market. to things of concept in a sense to work without patent boundaries even if the process may not or may include an
7002 to enhance by way of less is more si to enhance by way of less is more situation of compatibility and less apps over programmable problems and obstacles saying that gingerbread operating systems are the way of the past and the future of os publishing is two fold a punter and a player vers
7003 market that protects and serves for market that protects and serves for the greater good of mankind
7004 market controlled by the homeland an market controlled by the homeland and intellectual protection service as well as a library of congress effort to control the property we own and would like to buy
7005 linking ram interchange is a linking linking ram interchange is a linking secondary support ram
7006 easy invent cad submit platform a pr easy invent cad submit platform a programmable interface to sort and submit inventions per company quickly in a demand and non chronological manner.
7007 laser eye surgery by way of emory un laser eye surgery by way of emory university and the hospital at midtown and the parts in side the laser surgical technique
7008 antibiotic soap chr antibiotic soap
7009 never pi /. indefinite piinfinity p never pi /. indefinite piinfinity pi pi times one equals pi indefinite pi is never ending infinite pi
7010 a program to build a series of files a program to build a series of files in order to switch mobile phone operating systems and then to install a different operating system and reload your data
7011 acrowdprocessor that will use two or acrowdprocessor that will use two or more tapes to create a crowd of itx atx mitx tx boards working to process as one board by tape and crowd presets known also as modular tx
7012 a study of any cure by way of toxic a study of any cure by way of toxic and valance testing to include but not limited to cancer and diseases like alzheimer's and substance abuse cessation aids.
7013 mandatory cloud bandwidth controlto mandatory cloud bandwidth controlto suggest that a cloud should only hold so much practical waste to the internet entirety as a application as a whole to reduce backups and compress data backups by parts.

7014 data compression cloud formatthe mea data compression cloud formatthe means to compress scrolling data that may need to move and write and read ready as well as transport to place to place

7015 securing and encryption by way of fo securing and encryption by way of format doubling for example this format is encrypted then this format is translated into this file format to read

7016 converting multiple computer motherb converting multiple computer motherboards to unify into a working system that is not parallel (matching) or odd working (not matching) into a new cabinet data of mini desktop situation and cards that tell the central processor to do what the completed mi

7017 interoperable cpu a central process interoperable cpu a central processing unit that branches your own connections how you want to build your high performance system to allow any configuration important to you and the scale of your platform

7018 interoperable building parts and bo interoperable building parts and board design free build parts designed to connect a central processing unit that branches your own connections how you want to build your high performance system to allow any configuration important to you and the scale

7019 configure this into a system with po configure this into a system with power management configure this into a system with computational control configure this into a system with data scale management a square chance chassis that fits with your own choices and arrangement. free arrangement w

7020 a hardware system that will power th a hardware system that will power that software exactly (software that estimates the hardware system that will work with that software exactly) processing and computations inside a software vessel a vessel that estimates processing and computations as an

7021 intel edison kit for arduino single intel edison kit for arduino single components ediarduin.al.k modified to control xeon phi on off and load switch

7022 when vector computations are needed when vector computations are needed there should be a precise meaning to every curve like the way pre selected sorts are generated size how many tall and wide as well as per space intensity xyz

7023 a software program that will generat a software program that will generate code for external unsorted efi batches to route any computations needed

7024 traffic cloud and perbuilt selects traffic cloud and perbuilt selects for realtime issue management

7025 police cloud and perbuilt selects f police cloud and perbuilt selects for realtime issue management

7026 syndicated media news cloud and per syndicated media news cloud and perbuilt selects for realtime issue management

7027 air bound traffic cloud and perbuil air bound traffic cloud and perbuilt selects for realtime issue management

7028 war management satellite / ground cl war management satellite / ground cloud and perbuilt selects for realtime issue management

7029 minimum sale retail price cloud and minimum sale retail price cloud and perbuilt selects for realtime issue management

7030 digital shelf price display for real digital shelf price display for real time updates from a

msrp cloud
7031 digital shelf price display for real digital shelf price display for real time updates from a msrp cloud stored planed and adjustable by demands something that would make a sale percustomer and availability
7032 synthetic liquid plastic ester and c synthetic liquid plastic ester and carbon soot energy in a single compound to make a combustible energy (incinerator biproducts and alcohol acids)
7033 educational in class os educational educational in class os educational operating system with intent to block virus and provide a safe computation platforms for age and course specific apps educational cloud system and perbuilt selects for realtime issue management
7034 rearranged tetrahedral amorphous car rearranged tetrahedral amorphous carbon with abstract particle matching to reconstituted energy sp forms diamond (cubic) lonsdaleite (hexagonal diamond) sp forms graphite graphene fullerenes (buckminsterfullerene higher fullerenes
7035 a habit release agent to alcohol abu a habit release agent to alcohol abuse patch pill gum
7036 a habit release agent to marijuana a a habit release agent to marijuana abuse patch pill gum
7037 an elaborate paging software system an elaborate paging software system that links processors for a continuous processing group of microchips dealing or complimentary in any similarity that forms an accessible shape of a shed family software
7038 an elaborate paging hardware system an elaborate paging hardware system that links processors for a continuous processing group of microchips alignend or complimentary in any similarity that forms an accessible shape of a shed family hardware to add cores to a group of processing cores and
7039 no cloud software registration a pro no cloud software registration a program specific intent to keep the software as is and with out any foreign auto updates and stripped integration from internet interference of opportunity and eula confidence trials of intent to disturb the sleeping soft
7040 alternate size spinning magnetic ele alternate size spinning magnetic electric generator lord carpenters infinite motion how to put it all together a spinning top is very similar to something you'd like to have fun and stare at forever. it was brought to my attention that there is a need fo
7041 effervescent mouth wash for serious effervescent mouth wash for serious ailments like headaches bacteria and dizziness caused by oral sickness.
7042 a thing called turbo per element tha a thing called turbo per element that can shape a path where previously there was no way to reflect perpendicular or parallel with the help of mini and per operation by a hypos thesischip alternate computational curve based algorithms aiding by another
7043 a thing called turbo per element tha a thing called turbo per element that can shape a path where previously there was no way to reflect perpendicular or parallel with the help of mini and per operation by a stressthesischip alternate computational curve based algorithms aiding by another
7044 more desktop capacity by way of modu more desktop capacity by way of modular expansions via mini modular modes non ecc or ecc yes either or intent sell a module to me and make it bigger

7045 open thread navigational embedded so open thread navigational embedded software. a software base that controls the method of navigation of a processing thread inside a cpu
7046 curriculum software for public schoo curriculum software for public schools no cloud base or cloud base data schema download and toss media vs. intent to recycle and modify in class testing by way of simple send and receive test email like online college with intuitive public school social
7047 triplet pi translation axis for comp triplet pi translation axis for compensation equation sum and path intent.
7048 triplet pi translation axis for comp triplet pi translation axis for compensation equation sum part travel pi cubed translation axis for compensation equation sum and path intent. software hardware virtual and literal intent to create and estimate any means of anno place in time points of v
7049 triplet pi translation axis for comp triplet pi translation axis for compensation equation sum part travel pi cubed translation axis for a compensation equation sum and path intent. software hardware virtual and literal intent to create and estimate any means of anno place in time points of
7050 real web a web connection that is a real web a web connection that is a retail and local web that processes alternate connections like credit cards and other information like medical records and bank transactions. a web that makes real life from day to day a positive one with higher restri
7051 real web part encryption phone chan real web part encryption phone channel a web connection that is a retail and local web that processes alternate connections like credit cards and other information like medical records and bank transactions. a web that makes real life from day to day a
7052 data archive retail pack keeping the data archive retail pack keeping the pack a retail matter when time does matter
7053 a free or sale community secure or f a free or sale community secure or friendly web source connections community web
7054 build a toy platform you submit the build a toy platform you submit the size shape and means and function and go play
7055 build a software platform you submit build a software platform you submit the size shape and means and function and go play
7056 brain temperature and intelligence i brain temperature and intelligence is the temperature related to intelligence or is intelligence only hereditary
7057 big data creative data engineers sof big data creative data engineers software client requests terms and permissions rules and exceptions reply response using terms and conditions as well as requests and permissions to translate into real life data arrangements (banking tra
7058 big data creative data engineers com big data creative data engineers compliant hardware client requests ability software wreckless replacement exceptions speed in control using test and server strength to encrypt and control critical cohesion products and services of any kind
7059 organ cell symbiosis cloning and rep organ cell symbiosis cloning and replacement organs to grow two cells into a new organ for kidney patients caner cures and bioorganic failures or positives

7060 to avoid another war use diplomatic to avoid another war use diplomatic monetary incentives and resources or not

7061 encrypted phonenumber transmitting encrypted phonenumber transmitting and receiving key's and the new enigma generator.

7062 encrypted phonesoftware transmittin encrypted phonesoftware transmitting and receiving key's and the new enigma generator.

7063 unformulated alien text formats to c unformulated alien text formats to create a unknown and previously illegible type text to keep data secure said a unknown character symbol set that will translate into some thing as known to the other receiver

7064 build your own cloud service softwar build your own cloud service software hardware and applications global functions of cloud server storage and the medium that powers that service incorporated with small large and desktop applications with input and control to manage your own stack of ser

7065 we build your cloud service architec we build your cloud service architects engineers software hardware and applications architects engineers global functions of cloud server storage and the medium that powers that service incorporated with small large and desktop applications with input an

7066 the light age of board technology la the light age of board technology layered fiber optical computer boards heat resistant and accessible to carbon fiber

7067 to search for a topic with an image. to search for a topic with an image. to find people places and things. with input from meta tags such as technical terms when where who and why. as well as to modify the photo scan or topic by perspective date and angle using the image itself and the top

7068 personal freedom to drive makes me t personal freedom to drive makes me think that taking cars and making trains out of them is against my freedom.

7069 optical fiber paths and boards that optical fiber paths and boards that use lens motors optical motors and optic conductors in conjunction with a optical cpu making electrons differently than an ion more sort of a ee on

7070 making software a virtual hardware c making software a virtual hardware controller virtual compromises in memory cores and threads memory that holds software permanently

7071 computer aided nerve sciences to reg computer aided nerve sciences to register what nerve sends and collects what with a nano scope using computer navigated control finding nerves in an optical focused laser infrared camera and thermos scope

7072 super embedding board technology usi super embedding board technology using quartered circuits and fractal inverse technology making boards flat and embedding while conducting in one motion with out attaching

7073 information satellite that pilots li information satellite that pilots like drones and may reenter the atmosphere and disperse again into the atmosphere at our control with translation receiving and sending information that holds a scale as of a self sufficient server cloud satellite a sel

7074 war ship satellite a self supported war ship satellite a self supported nuclear powered satellite that pilots like drones and may reenter the atmosphere and disperse again into the atmosphere at our control with translation receiving and sending information that holds a scale as of a self

7075 automated robotics in space to elimi automated robotics in space to eliminate the human space factor and automate the sequences of working robotics in space such as extended stay time and removal of life support systems as well as to incorporate remote control actives and war

7076 space territory political rights the space territory political rights the agreement option to register any given orbit free realm to patrol or gather records of information and scientific findings important to human survival and communication

7077" biochemical deceasedviral library, biochemical deceasedviral library "

7078 centralized satellite control networ centralized satellite control network governmental / private nanotubes nanobud

7079 build a script portable calculator a build a script portable calculator a calculator device that instead of only numerical sums it builds a computational script to make bios and other interesting things that would other wise take a very long time

7080 energy weight focus scope to weigh t energy weight focus scope to weigh the energy in a focal point with energy density and amplitude

7081 density and amplitude energy chart s density and amplitude energy chart scale a energy chart with amplitude and density comparable to the chemical elements diagram with consideration for gas solids and chemical compounds as well as their reaction to one another.

7082 translation virtual predictive densi translation virtual predictive density matter to measure and estimate the outcome of any two forms of energy together in one equation or software platform to create new and exciting forms of medicine and energy by functioning heat chemical compound or a

7083 matter mining by way of na nowaver matter mining by way of na nowaveradio signals find the element and save that element or to create more elements

7084 life by dead virus by way of na now life by dead virus by way of na nowaveradio signals to kill a virus and make an anti virus by way of very small radio waves

7085 programmable medical surgery robotic programmable medical surgery robotics by way of na nowave energy weight focus scope medical surgery device by way of laser and energy matter compensations

7086 computer controlled negative and pos computer controlled negative and positive and neutral laser and energy matter compensations

7087 poly carbonate sandwiched stacked op poly carbonate sandwiched stacked optical circuit board on plyboard technology

7088 optical data rate photon transformer optical data rate photon transformer

7089 neutral performing laser to move and neutral performing laser to move and work with out damage and neutral force.

7090 a transverse capacitor that calculat a transverse capacitor that calculates and compresses at the same time

7091 embedded hyper threading printed cir embedded hyper threading printed circuits in a measured capacity that relates to cascading increments

7092 embedded hyper threading printed cir embedded hyper threading printed circuits in a measured solid state board

7093 linking cpu interchange is a linking linking cpu interchange is a linking secondary support cpu

7094 one chip board multiple function pla one chip board multiple function platforms in solid state matter

7095 synthetic natural conventional non a synthetic natural conventional non associated gas a substance that may be clean burning and easy to make synthetic pressured gas
7096 synthetic pressurized gas turbine to synthetic pressurized gas turbine to generate electricity
7097 poly nitrate oxide ethanol carbonate poly nitrate oxide ethanol carbonate
7098 ethanol nitrogen fuel engine copyrig ethanol nitrogen fuel engine
7099 governmental cloud separated state a governmental cloud separated state and federal cloud service encryption values from logical to high performance situations of traffic to water control to records of who what and where
7100 commercial cloud separated commerce commercial cloud separated commerce and public pay for cloud service encryption values from logical to high performance situations of taxes transfers and payments who what and where
7101 switch book operation a non account switch book operation a non account related platform system is a device sensitive memory working horse that transfers accounts
7102 plasma pressurized poly oxide metal plasma pressurized poly oxide metal using plasma pressure to mold many oxidized metals back to a combined metal making a new inexpensive metal
7103 static electric poly oxide metal usi static electric poly oxide metal using electricity to mold many oxidized metals back to a combined metal making a new metal
7104 off shore ocean current electric gen off shore ocean current electric generators as opposed to land locked wind mills
7105 off shore ocean current electric gen off shore ocean current electric generator farms as opposed to land locked wind mills this would be a dedicated area of operations
7106 magnetized ions in a transformer cap magnetized ions in a transformer capacitor in a generated sequence of order
7107 off shore ocean current centrifugal off shore ocean current centrifugal force electric generator farms as opposed to land locked wind mills this would be a dedicated area of operations
7108 anything over the internet cell towe anything over the internet cell towers resident and roaming services subscribed wireless signals and encrypted channels repeater towers that drive this internet forward faster than as expected a local and populous need
7109 anything over the internet cell towe anything over the internet cell towers resident and roaming services subscribed wireless signals and encrypted channels small aoi small local repeaters boxes that drive this internet forward faster than as expected a local and less populous needs for a u
7110 atomic blood testing using alternate atomic blood testing using alternate scales of sodium and sugar as well as nitrate chlorides
7111 automated atomic blood testing machi automated atomic blood testing machine using alternate scales of sodium and sugar as well as nitrate chlorides to an extreme scale
7112 computational predictive plasma sort computational predictive plasma sorting lapidary alchemy studies in cures for cancer and virtual new materials
7113 computational predictive ultra viole computational predictive ultra violet sorting biochemical studies in cures for cancer and virtual new materials
7114 shaping chips to reflect amplify and shaping chips to reflect amplify and duplicate processing objects inside the chip binder page

7115 state of our art is never a constant state of our art is never a constant so to make a platform as on the fly as possible would be the the greatest advancing scale ever to make an engineering system that makes your service in a virtual environment and sale rate increase with redesign propos

7116 manipulative personality disorder is manipulative personality disorder is a selfish and greedy property in low importance comparison to exceptional sanctity binder page

7117 company incentives for recycling tec company incentives for recycling technology is a monetary program based on weight and recovery from the local and federal government binder page

7118 technology leasing and propagating s technology leasing and propagating specialists is a monetary program based on profit and recovery from the manufacturers post attributes binder page

7119 future of less open software and th future of less open software and the concurrent topics that it will hold such as fee based operation times and subscription updates binder page

7120 future of protected and eula softwar future of protected and eula software and the concurrent topics that it will hold such as free operation times and nonsubscription updates

7121 school student information secure da school student information secure data protection is a method of protecting the future of learning with technology flashblue ","

7122 cloud data security software is a me cloud data security software is a method of protecting the future with technology flashblue

7123 local government security bots to pr local government security bots to protect and serve with the intent to find and seek searching local criminal data through the internet using web bots

7124 single sd chip module board that sta single sd chip module board that stacks easily into a plural sd board system and controls with striping and stacking coprocessing in a chain reactive board configuration

7125 conceptual conclusion diagrams and a conceptual conclusion diagrams and acceptable means to what translates into a function or a thing and mixes and matches with proper context a diagram legend that translates by name and intuition

7126 conceptual prose and the intent to i conceptual prose and the intent to invent a time frame of any sort always carries a way of speech and sort of accentuation if you will the time frame of any given state of art is to generally gain a conceptual prose of a given time frame

7127 chip stilts form factor to stand up chip stilts form factor to stand up chips in any vertical fashion and add a plural height to perform cooling and or data exchange

7128 interval chip stilts with data bridg interval chip stilts with data bridges to efi

7129 chip stilts with data processing cal chip stilts with data processing calculating rise and run to make inside circuits happen and connecting super fine cable gold lines

7130 exchange chip stilts with data proce exchange chip stilts with data processing calculating rise and run to make inside circuits happen and connecting super fine cable gold lines and repeating octagon chip inside chips and vector resolution chips

7131 exchange chip stilts with data proce exchange chip stilts with data processing calculating rise and run to make inside circuits happen and connecting super fine cable gold lines and repeating octagon chip inside chips and vector resolution chips and conducting boards

7132 intersecting diagonal and perpendicu intersecting diagonal and perpendicular circuit threads by vector resolution chips

7133 a hardware mass array of cloud stati a hardware mass array of cloud statistics and numerical estimations for one cloud to any other cloud

7134 open data statistics offering to pro open data statistics offering to provide a starting point to compare data and the use of its properties to compare to another or any other way of stats

7135 end coordinate known vector board ci end coordinate known vector board circuit path regiment and processing boosters an end coordinate inside the terms of use of a vector board and vector conducting boards that sends signals to the circuits that make the path of processing from chip to chip

7136 cloud data security software is a me cloud data security software is a method of protecting the future with technology by foreseeing the attention of progress and code modifications including the methods in place now and the possibilities in the future of what and will be a method to consid

7137 cloud probabilities in turn concludi cloud probabilities in turn concluding any real life example situation into a consequence cloud for example the process of lend and borrow the process of land and take off the process of any registration set into a faster method with any such correspondi

7138 public for hire on demand technology public for hire on demand technology companies a company that forms any such supply built from a design that originates with out or with corporate proprietary ship and sells that with a demand for an outcome

7139 private on demand technology compani private on demand technology companies a company that forms any such supply built from a design that originates with out or with corporate proprietary ship and sells that with a demand for an outcome

7140 nano capacity electric signals when nano capacity electric signals when the wave of electricity meanders into a tip of a needle to move the vector relationships by way of nano gigawave

7141 a half value conductor that measures a half value conductor that measures half of a wave of electricity being a nano capacity electric signals when the wave of electricity meanders into a tip of a needle to move the vector relationships by way of nano gigawave

7142 tension strength of electrical curre tension strength of electrical currents in a pico nano space for connections transistors and breakers making a bridge into the future of computing and printed circuit boards with a open closed signal holding minimal power allotted

7143 pico circuit with poly carbs cerami pico circuit with poly carbs ceramic insulation and poly oxide metal as conducting circuits with power and wear as a consideration for measuring the entire tension and properties of laser made engraving by plasma soldering yielding and melting.

7144 pico circuit pico layer chip and ci pico circuit pico layer chip and circuit building segmented layers and connecting ends from bottom to upper layer for stacking interior with poly carbs ceramic insulation and poly oxide metal as conducting circuits with power and wear as a consideration

7145 pico nano micro scale reverse scena pico nano micro scale reverse scenario of heat and size rationality when the size doesn't make sense to make it that small and making multiple on board integrated circuits and cpu per system and the process of material being of more importance such as p

7146 sata mini add on compute module size sata mini add on compute module size sata that adds to the computational ability to a system.
7147 a disposable update to isolated syst a disposable update to isolated systems and the intent to improve performance and remove virus or add alternate software with out online update
7148 compact active performance software compact active performance software a disposable update to isolated systems and the intent to improve performance or add alternate software with out online update
7149 processed optical energy and the thi processed optical energy and the things that equal a light to energy including a dynamic electrode receiving liquid crystal panel and the intent to make electricity by sharing and sending and repeating
7150 processed optical energy and the thi processed optical energy and the things that equal a light to energy including a building with transparent solar liquid crystal panels / windows on the outside and the intent to make electricity transparent solar power generating windows
7151 stand along systems hardware a compl stand along systems hardware a complimentary system in a shape portable or flash matters that make bios a symbiotic relationship in a organism and computational theme of improvement and error free computing
7152 stand along systems software a compl stand along systems software a complimentary system in a shape portable or flash matters that make bios a symbiotic relationship in a organism and computational theme of improvement and error free computing
7153 exterior bios library co existing bi exterior bios library co existing bios library adjustments submissive profile programmable adjustments in a vague code and hardware environment to aid in a stand along software and hardware solution that makes a large section of addalong configurations
7154 condensation water farms the help we condensation water farms the help we need is in cooling and heating the air itself to generate water where there may be a lack of water and more oxygen than happy a large scale condensation factory
7155 condensation water generator on a co condensation water generator on a condensation water farm the help we need is in cooling and heating the air itself to generate water where there may be a lack of water and more oxygen than happy a large scale condensation factory
7156 device transferable operating system device transferable operating system platform a platform operating system that adapts to the hardware at supply and negotiates the devices properties easily
7157 extended belling vertical sd chip st extended belling vertical sd chip stack
7158 promise software building platform c promise software building platform cloud promise cloud software building platform cloud that adds and trades certain processes for a monetary value and immediate commercial release final options
7159 open software building platform clou open software building platform cloud cloud software building platform cloud that adds and trades certain processes for a non monetary value and immediate noncommercial release final options
7160 solar energy generating stickers per solar energy generating stickers per window panel with circuits inside or linked storage
7161 triplet pi d focus ranges optical an triplet pi d focus ranges optical and virtual focus calculations and equilibrium annotations for use in cloud scenarios and mobile devices
7162 predictive computations in triplet p predictive computations in triplet pi d focus ranges

optical and virtual focus calculations and equilibrium annotations for use in any situation
7163 probability statistics in everyday p probability statistics in everyday perspective dimensions with cubed and annotative physics
7164 m. electronics form factor add on co m. electronics form factor add on computational enhancement processors
7165 m. electronics form factor add on gr m. electronics form factor add on graphics computational enhancement processors
7166 msata electronics form factor add on msata electronics form factor add on computational enhancement processors
7167 msata electronics form factor add on msata electronics form factor add on graphics enhancement processors
7168 solvent sludge and the processes tha solvent sludge and the processes that make taking trash and turning it into sludge and making electricity as well as reclaimable minerals gases and metals by way of incineration and sort magnetizing
7169 dry solvent clay and the processes t dry solvent clay and the processes that make taking trash and turning it into rock and making electricity as well as reclaimable minerals gases and metals by way of incineration and sort magnetizing
7170 inverted gas sorting and reclaiming inverted gas sorting and reclaiming recycled incineration gasses by way of catalytic converter and gas humidifier for or only with a unique dry or paste wet solvent clay and the processes that make taking trash and turning it into rock or solvent sludge
7171 carbon by metallic energy signal for carbon by metallic energy signal force is the wave of energy that attracts or repels any such one carbon away and from each other in a radio magnetic force in any size obvious or microscopic force of annotative fixation including or excluding reactive pr
7172 gasses energy signal wave gas wave e gasses energy signal wave gas wave energy signal is the measure of energy that attracts or repels any such one gas or other gasses to and from each other in a energy force in any size obvious or microscopic force of annotative fixation including or exclu
7173 carbon energy signal wave carbon wav carbon energy signal wave carbon wave energy signal is the measure of energy that attracts or repels any such one oxide or other metal to and from each other in a energy force in any size obvious or microscopic force of annotative fixation including or e
7174 starch energy signal wave starch wav starch energy signal wave starch wave energy signal is the measure of energy that attracts or repels any such one starch to and from each other in a energy force in any size obvious or microscopic force of annotative fixation including or excluding react
7175 physeometric prediction energy signa physeometric prediction energy signal wave measures in scales of negative as well as positive may be used in any predictive computational data analytic such as to say that with a known and given there could be any such physeometric prediction of applied
7176 physeometric prediction data cloud a physeometric prediction data cloud a group of servers or information structure that houses a secluded or open system of predictions for the information that bases it's self on predictive measures of experimental operations with or without committing to

7177 how to realize irrational thinking f how to realize irrational thinking for an irrational person or group of people war drug part two

7178 how to loose a war is to follow thei how to loose a war is to follow their rules and drop flowers instead of bombs. when flowers don't work drop bombs

7179 how to opt out of their convention a how to opt out of their convention and still have a smile on our faces a monetary stipulation and land ownership terms and correctives in a tentative agreement that states thing in our terms and conditions at war and any such give means to attack as well

7180 state and local satellite share time state and local satellite share times shared government satellite service

7181 private and commerce satellite renta private and commerce satellite rental times rental public satellite service

7182 poly carbonate sandwiched stacked ci poly carbonate sandwiched stacked circuit board on plyboard technology

7183 to avoid a deliberate argumentative to avoid a deliberate argumentative

7184 dynamic functions of a input output dynamic functions of a input output resolution a computative functioning virtual reality of measurement cloud or software system a virtual building cloud that simulates the construction of points and volts down to a format that is appreciative and perce

7185 a breaking in trial and error when t a breaking in trial and error when the only cost is the operator the software and hardware when the physical meets a breaking point for example to include calibration of volts amps and weight and any other important variable then the trial and error of m

7186 commons unique abnormal commons uniq commons unique abnormal commons unique abnormal a + m = e (. {} over {}) %uxe a {e} over {m} %uxe b {e%delta ^{}} over {c%delta ^{}} %uxe c{e%ux } over {c%ux }

7187 commons unique abnormal commons uniq commons unique abnormal commons unique abnormal infinity x +infinity %uxe max /<=x<= xe{x^{}} %uxe %infinite %uxd + %uxea %epsilon %sigma

7188 commons unique abnormal commons uniq commons unique abnormal commons unique abnormal <p style= marginbottom in >lllint />%uxea %uxf {b%uxe sqrt{b^{}ac} } over {a} %notequal binom{%sigma }binom{{%uxeb i%uxeb m} }{ < j < n } p (i

7189 negative light waves and their post negative light waves and their post positive method of use a contrary value in rgb light and inverted light magnifications

7190 eclipse laser light magnifications a eclipse laser light magnifications and the carbon mark that shapes the radiation into the mirror of any such ecliptic or optical use of out side shapes

7191 reversed poly operative thematic lib reversed poly operative thematic library the proposal of a case where if you know a equation and then look up a similar given number then in a hypothesis of any outcome making a working summation to the question in a linear composition

7192 science calculators with calculation science calculators with calculation insert able or embedded library's of instance of information purpose calculator holding the power to answer the questions properly the first time that may do hypophysics theory or build a script and even virtual pred

7193 a rounded number of encryption based a rounded number of encryption based on a four segment of numbers to process and extract an encryptable alphanumerical code for ssl and more advanced communications
7194 duplicate cubits zeros ones and twos duplicate cubits zeros ones and twos and threes a nonargumentative physical quantitative mechanical on off state with two layers by reading twice
7195 hardware saving process by updating hardware saving process by updating cpu systems only inside a dlq duplicate layer cubits modifier and reader plain english updating the entire cloud or system by cpu and the processing of reading what the cpu is able to comprehend in terms of simple code
7196 hardware saving process by updating hardware saving process by updating cpu systems only inside a ddlq double dimension layer cubits modifier and reader plain english updating the entire cloud or system by cpu and the processing of reading what the cpu is able to comprehend in terms of sim
7197 double cubits two sequences of zeros double cubits two sequences of zeros ones and a nonargumentative physical quantitative mechanical on off state or with two layers
7198 limonene generated silicone doping t limonene generated silicone doping to degrade plastics and harden or solvency the plastics in advance to incineration and generate electricity as well as a sooty carbon for synthetic metal semiconductors
7199 pendulum generator off and on magnet pendulum generator off and on magnetic power switches and percentages to propel and generate electricity at a minimal minus and pi ratio
7200 more cubits zeros ones and twos and more cubits zeros ones and twos and threes a nonargumentative physical quantitative mechanical on off state with two layers by reading changes at a modified on series and then a modified off series in a section with in a measurement of cubits together
7201 stacking linking cpu interchange is stacking linking cpu interchange is a linking secondary support cpu
7202 synthetic metal cell drawing and sha synthetic metal cell drawing and shaping vector cubit cell dividing and cascading increments of myriads within
7203 a semi solid state social state driv a semi solid state social state drive and chip board configuration. that conjoins vectors and makes any path a routine in quantum steps
7204 repeated chemical electrode pool cop repeated chemical electrode pool
7205 application device instructions on c application device instructions on chip
7206 cubit cell off and on group of cubit cubit cell off and on group of cubits a translation of on off and signals in a group a simple yet complex method of calculation and intersect of paths for any group of information
7207 mirror sphere box laser projection l mirror sphere box laser projection lens
7208 extractable card form factor comput extractable card form factor computing by multiplying systems on a traveling boards
7209 traveling boards base chassis is a c traveling boards base chassis is a computing accessory that houses the card computer and makes the parts that are used in everyday computing optical disc drive usb support and screen and keyboard interface a possible exchangeable thing in the composition
7210 ddr system application on chip a sli ddr system application on chip a slim operating system that is dedicated to alternate functions based upon application per device including

secondary cpu and or storage and system bios.
7211 executable back up optical disc syst executable back up optical disc system disc array doing both data and program operations
7212 executable system carry across multi executable system carry across multiple storage states to return a greater number of operations per system completion of any request at a expandable operating big server
7213 is a software executable system that is a software executable system that spans across multiple storage states to return a greater number of operations per system completion of any request and per addition of more arrays will increase the operations ability
7214 application area array migration and application area array migration and control software making an exchanging array organizing the platform of executable software and control of data source and place in the so called cloud instance
7215 exchangeable cell cell card for a lo exchangeable cell cell card for a local single and separate non synchronized cloud account cell phones that is a starting point to a private phone
7216 exchangeable executable cell cell ca exchangeable executable cell cell card for a local non synchronized cloud account cell phones that is astarting point to a private phone
7217 exchangeable cell cell card for a lo exchangeable cell cell card for a local non synchronized cloud account cell phones that is a starting point to a private phone a private and under non agreement phone privacy
7218 for hire security web bots is a serv for hire security web bots is a service that will design and search for security issues with web robot search and seek code to server and repeating actions and report back to a source
7219 government data research web bots a government data research web bots a private search and possible investigative understanding that may hold evidence of any question of activity by searching communications servers and other internet references
7220 multiple wireless multiple device ba multiple wireless multiple device back up table port
7221 wireless device compatibly bluetooth wireless device compatibly bluetooth backup clone and restore software
7222 wireless backup clone and restore so wireless backup clone and restore software encryption codes
7223 phone station bluetooth magnetic bac phone station bluetooth magnetic backuprecharge wireless charge and backup clone update and restore hardware
7224 encrypted magnetic data waves to sec encrypted magnetic data waves to secure and process computing information to and from device to device phones and computers
7225 magnetic data magnetic ion capacitor magnetic data magnetic ion capacitor in use with the data signal octavia
7226 magnetic data waves of intertwined m magnetic data waves of intertwined mini signals and partial process of half and triplet pulse
7227 magnetic data and the magnetized tra magnetic data and the magnetized transducer to code and process magnetic signs of positive and negative
7228 diverse operating board magneticion diverse operating board magneticion fiberoptic and nanoelectric signals to work the large and small things into a sound well rounded machine
7229 a working complete process working s a working complete process working software is

a platform of a data base that is built on a question of fundamentals to make a transitional and schematic plan for a business with one part system

7230 a working partial process working so a working partial process working software is a platform of a data base that is built on a question of fundamentals to make a transitional and schematic plan for a business with some of part system made to work with other parts

7231 a working parts process working soft a working parts process working software is a platform of a data base that is built on a question of fundamentals to make a transitional and schematic plan for a business with many parts system built to work together

7232 flash system on chip point and landi flash system on chip point and landing a micro server that can be included on a chip and land a website with folders and replace a server for intentions of verses in terms when a server admits to a micro card and a tray of server chips that makes a serve

7233 flash system on chip point and landi flash system on chip point and landing bed fabric chassis a micro server bed that holds parts that can be included on a chip and land a website with folders and replace a server for intentions of verses in terms when a server admits to a micro card

7234 vector cubed boards exchange chip st vector cubed boards exchange chip stilts with data processing calculating rise and run to make inside circuits happen and connecting super fine cable gold lines and repeating octagon chip inside chips and vector resolution chips and conducting boards

7235 vector cubed chips exchange chip sti vector cubed chips exchange chip stilts with data processing calculating rise and run to make inside circuits happen and connecting super fine cable gold lines and repeating octagon chip inside chips and vector resolution chips and conducting boards

7236 war web bots and the scripting abili war web bots and the scripting ability to and kill enemy computers and cell phones in a local or distant area of combat or war

7237 war web safe area and the scripting war web safe area and the scripting ability to make a safe harbor for any study of attack anti attack and a command group of war

7238 a squared area of cascading incremen a squared area of cascading increments funny but real to process code with measurement cascading increments a certain unit of measurement " . or for processing electronic measurement using my certain unit of measurement data versus the shape of

7239 d electric circuit board printer a t d electric circuit board printer a three dimensional printer that intermittently uses alternate metal printing and silicon filament

7240 nano micro and pico soldering metal nano micro and pico soldering metal printing and three dimensional printer ability to grow vertically and horizontally with a moderate soldering plasma thermal flash plasma thermal printing

7241 standard popular retro active hardwa standard popular retro active hardware is a forgotten chip socket board or state of work made popular again for the fun of its performance and suggestions k again standard popular hardware

7242 multiplied and fractional diamond di multiplied and fractional diamond divided chip to assimilate the quartered and then square a shape for different angles of processing with the thought that there is a connection between the shape and the result of connections available diamond divided ch

7243 diamond divided chip properties is a diamond divided chip properties is a multiplied

and fractional divided chip to assimilate the quartered and then the square or less
7244 secured wifi wireless accessories po secured wifi wireless accessories post is a group of accessories that accompany a powered usb pairing unit as a multi interface device making all your personal computing needs wireless and only yours secured wireless accessories post
7245 automatic xeon phi platform software automatic xeon phi platform software auto pilot phi
7246 pilot per scripted gpu and a per uni pilot per scripted gpu and a per unit plan of process this is really any driven gpu per device to any single operation meaning that there is part or parts of any separated or single graphic processing unit with a process unit plan per device scripted gpu
7247 mini complete server ip/location/chi mini complete server ip/location/chip/system in a disk optical a optically read by disk that makes any such form or function such as to mirror a completed server with ip virtual optical server disk
7248 mini complete server ip/location/chi mini complete server ip/location/chip/system in a disk solid state solid state chip with a server format of completed functions of on and off and all other things any other server would function as into a cloned disk with the entire system or majority of
7249 mini complete server ip/location/chi mini complete server ip/location/chip/system in a disk pcie load this is really a pcie location intertwined with any given pci port or express location that is a translated mini completed server. mini server per pcie
7250 mini complete server ip/location/chi mini complete server ip/location/chip/system in a virtual disk folder translating into a place inside any given medium a separate window into a looping server that is in itself a mini completed sever in a folder on a disk. complete server in a virtual fo
7251 volunteer web warriors software. to volunteer web warriors software. to aid against the enemy and to fight a cyber war volunteerism with our at home devices to counter attack the enemy foes.
7252 a large rechargeable batteryplant th a large rechargeable batteryplant that has automated chemical pool recharging and sending receiving charging and re doping electron batches and storage for electricity on any large scale in acres and years suitable for the safety and health of human life
7253 a large recycled battery pool that m a large recycled battery pool that makes other small batteries with less time and higher concentrations of elementsrechargeable battery plant that has automated chemical pool recharging and sending receiving charging and re doping electron ions and neutr
7254 powder salt reaction with out combin powder salt reaction with out combing gasoline to make a neutral burning fuel that propels on impact but not exhaust only vapor oil salt powder fuel reactions
7255 powder salt reaction engine with out powder salt reaction engine with out combing gasoline to make a neutral burning fuel that propels on impact and compression with ignition
7256 tax loan government program of lien tax loan government program of lien for a loan on income tax returns
7257 dynamic compressed virtual encryptio dynamic compressed virtual encryption to encapsulate data for a certain end point protocol while compressing compressed encrypted end point protocol

7258 wireless radio patching per device i wireless radio patching per device is to patch devices with the board of a receiving serial signal easily verses a software connection wireless radio patch device serial
7259 electric catalyze sodium nitrate car electric catalyze sodium nitrate carbonate reaction engine system and motive for an alternative power source that may be able to propel from small amounts of sulfur and a powder combustion engine with sodium nitrate and spark plug and piston action powde
7260 probability is a term for business e probability is a term for business ethics compromise and ethics rules against arbitrary lying and dishonesty of information and statistics of income and profits ethics probability
7261 cell tower lending and broad cast sh cell tower lending and broad cast shares build your own cell tower with our technology and profit with our company byo cell tower
7262 critical non attached data back up r critical non attached data back up registrations and cloud clusters is a extremely secure web of servers and data bases that conclude information that is nearly irreplaceable or important more than any other data critical non attached back up
7263 a dual copy archival backup format t a dual copy archival backup format table of compare and examine the data on a large translation scale in multiple part sequence
7264 a single copy dual file archival bac a single copy dual file archival backup format table of compare and examine the data on a large translation scale in multiple part sequence
7265 secondary chip sockets that are repl secondary chip sockets that are replaceable and upgrade able adapters to chip socket changes in size and dimension to improve the performance of a system
7266 central chip sockets that are replac central chip sockets that are replaceable and upgrade able adapters to chip socket changes in size and dimension to improve the performance of a system
7267 socket to modification socket to chi socket to modification socket to chip additions and improvements by the chip maker or chip end user by large there is some thing that needs to improve socket to socket and chip layers to make a new and improved stack of chip socket to chip to chip socket
7268 sodium magnesium carbon oxide compou sodium magnesium carbon oxide compound for powdered combustion engines and fuel made with a powered process and less liquid use and waste as a chemical propellant of combustion
7269 software software please make my sof software software please make my software software what i want is a software to make software platform private copy to cloud format of come and serve a software company that builds software for people on a property ownership basis
7270 software software please make my sof software software please make my software software design software that relates in vector and code preferences that is an easy and resell able application package maker and formatted
7271 software software please make my sof software software please make my software software information and data management creation and business software that relates in vector and code preferences that is an easy and resell able application package maker and formatted
7272 software software please make my sof software software please make my software

software banking and finance software that relates in vector and code preferences that is an easy and resell able application package maker and formatted

7273 software software please make my sof software software please make my software software science computations and equations that make the physical become a reality of study and changes of any state of art including the need for any other means software that relates in vector and code prefere

7274 software software please make my sof software software please make my software software medicine medical and health of solutions and directives of care for people and problems with health software that relates in vector and code preferences that is an easy and resell able application packa

7275 processor plug in base and periphera processor plug in base and peripheral ports that have a multipart available function to attachment and configuration adjustable port noteable programmable inside the bios and what to where situation of this and that makes working parts down to the chip

7276 perbuilt selected options for proce perbuilt selected options for processor plug in base and peripheral ports that have a multipart available function to attachment and configuration adjustable port noteable programmable inside the bios and what to where situation of this and that makes

7277 open mother boardarrangement of par open mother boardarrangement of parts connected instructions perbuilt open ended selected options for processor plug in base and peripheral ports that have a multipart available function to attachment and configuration adjustable port noteable progra

7278 consumer paid open mother boardarra consumer paid open mother boardarrangement of parts connected instructions of perbuilt open ended selected options for processor plug in base and peripheral ports that have a multipart available function to attachment and configuration adjustable port

7279 specific industrial or general consu specific industrial or general consumer recycle line arrangement

7280 recycle disassemble line arrangement recycle disassemble line arrangement speed verses reuse properties

7281 recycle disassemble line arrangement recycle disassemble line arrangement shred and sort compact and incinerate and then sort and compact and re manufactured soot and gasses separated to weight and composite

7282 landfill recycle mining and disasse landfill recycle mining and disassembly starch and carbon line arrangement is a property of known practices that still a recycle tanner into a this is all we work with working with itself and reworking all the materials as a chemical to process what we

7283 recycle and cycle gas liquid and gas recycle and cycle gas liquid and gas separated mining and disassembly to material on a settle absolute table weight process take and rest into a sedimentary weight of stagnation and aggression movement and non movement improving heating resting and cool

7284 recycle and cycle solid metal and so recycle and cycle solid metal and solid mineral mining and disassembly to material on a settle absolute table weight process take and rest into a sedimentary weight of stagnation and aggression movement and non movement improving heating resting and coo

7285 pain induction and reduction testing pain induction and reduction testing for extreme cases of pain management recovery a way to eliminate tolerances and control
7286 boiling and cooling wet materials of boiling and cooling wet materials of any sort with the intent to recycle a tannery method of cycle recycle process
7287 licensed conceptual inventor status licensed conceptual inventor status and document the status of concept s based on the deposition writer themselves
7288 legally bound arbitrary capital adju legally bound arbitrary capital adjustment is if the contract is good there should be assumption of capital payment
7289 where are they now help and history where are they now help and history of any known centique centiqueology a study of honest and real un bias history encounters factual links
7290 thin form mobile you build it chassi thin form mobile you build it chassis format of parts and interconnections by scsi scsi medium and scsi small connections that overlap and up and over connections by scaleable link interface small medium and large
7291 rivet thin form mobile you build it rivet thin form mobile you build it chassis format of parts and interconnections building things essentially by a inch and by inch and inch increments of across and over by inches for conformity
7292 parts that unite by scale and connec parts that unite by scale and connections across carry interconnection circuit processors and alternate vectors of chip exchange a chip that sends a specific vector data rate to a specified place to and then to more or to reply
7293 a specified place or vector of a cub a specified place or vector of a cubit cell data that is sent to and answered by a cubit group of cells
7294 cubit alphabet sequence signals in c cubit alphabet sequence signals in code of any such on and off group including headers and spacers for instruction language in short a second generation cubit language that itself is translated as more than code and on off but letters way morse code and
7295 cell phone voip servers a tower that cell phone voip servers a tower that changes from voice data to a second generation of cubit data tower and reflection services into an endless roam into and away from the host controller satellites
7296 cell phone technology in a merge and cell phone technology in a merge and equate into a single cubit data ratio and modular tower and reflection services different than a voice over internet a distinct data into cell phone signal
7297 secured and encrypted cell phone tec secured and encrypted cell phone technology in a merge and equate into a single cubit data ratio and modular tower and reflection services different than a voice over internet a distinct data into cell phone signal
7298 solid state compressor chip is a syn solid state compressor chip is a synthetic metal conductor that holds the data at a rate and multiplies the volume per calculation to increase the density of signals per circuit in bound and accordingly
7299 solid state multiplier chip is a syn solid state multiplier chip is a synthetic metal conductor that holds the data at a rate and amplifies the volume per calculation to increase the definitions of signal per circuit in bound and accordingly
7300 fiber optic repeating solid state sy fiber optic repeating solid state system on chip is a synthetic metal conductor processing unit that examines data and security and then repeats it to continue as the intended length of optic focus
7301 system shell a system of congruent p system shell a system of congruent processors a system of a chip inside an operable compressing and multiplier system of processing system

shell inside shell inside shell

7302 secure system shell a system of encr secure system shell a system of encrypted processors a system of a chip inside an operable compressing and multiplier system of processing system shell inside shell inside shell

7303 shell to shell connecting system of shell to shell connecting system of operating code and instructions as in reference to secured and shell chips in shell the operation of cubits and second or more generations of multiple cubit instructions per chip and vector directions

7304 quartered height profile mini pcie quartered height profile mini pcie x modified graphics card format right

7305 planned limonene plastics a solvent planned limonene plastics a solvent plastic that has a specific degrade composite known and planned to recycle with a specified make and end to the solvent and finished plastic new and dead

7306 ex tractable system on chip bed of c ex tractable system on chip bed of chips storage server brick and relay board and configuration management server system graph and error correction indication led configured and manufactured system clone with data and duplication flash disc and drives on

7307 soldered down system on chip bed of soldered down system on chip bed of chips storage server brick and relay board and configuration management server system graph and error correction indication led configured and manufactured system clone with data and duplication flash disc and drives o

7308 fountain power a fountain drink comb fountain power a fountain drink combination fuel of magnesium salt powder and a mixture of alcohol for body and movement to power a combustion engine that is engineered for a powder and mixed with liquid for a concentrated fuel at a lower cost and higher

7309 water purified engine exhaust cycled water purified engine exhaust cycled cylinders used with internal combustion engines fueled by either petrol or diesel including leanburn engines as well as kerosene heaters and stoves second stem exhaust tunnel

7310 solvent purified engine exhaust cycl solvent purified engine exhaust cycled cylinders used with internal combustion engines fueled by either petrol or diesel including leanburn engines as well as kerosene heaters and stoves second stem exhaust tunnel

7311 solution purified engine exhaust cyc solution purified engine exhaust cycled cylinder and additional multiple cycles of belly and exchange filter products like an synthetic mechanized oil that is exchangeable and recycled into other product multiple stem exhaust tunnel

7312 solution purified engine exhaust cyc solution purified engine exhaust cycled cylinder absorbing particle lubricant product multiple stem exhaust tunnel

7313 epa standard recyclable exchange por epa standard recyclable exchange ports for the exhaust purified solution exhaust cycled cylinders and product multiple stem exhaust tunnel

7314 epa standard recyclable exchange fil epa standard recyclable exchange filters for the exhaust purified solution exhaust cycled cylinders and product multiple stem exhaust tunnel

7315 fractal math string zoom formula for fractal math string zoom formula for synthetic and poly chemical measurements to zoom and extract dna from stem cells

7316 properties of stagnation improper us properties of stagnation improper use of technology in a manipulative manner to conclude monetary funds verses the intent to progress for example the coprocessor verse the use of an extended automatic co processor verses a deliberate attempt to keep the

7317 improper use of the truth as a suffi improper use of the truth as a sufficient means for rules against any such corporation or notarized agreement

7318 sold as pre manufactured system on a sold as pre manufactured system on a chip of any known software such as operating systems that are adopted to the plug and play hardware or detach and fee reattached schema

7319 summit and sellathon conference kn summit and sellathon conference known as convention for sale and for the use of property

7320 international summit and sellathon international summit and sellathon at a world interest and denomination of ownership

7321 drug abuse brain damage and the inte drug abuse brain damage and the intent to make a chemical such as to snap a person into a complete dopamine narcosis and occur inside an acute non vegetative comma altering a person from any such addiction and problem

7322 planned degrading paper for consumab planned degrading paper for consumable means and the intent to make as there is an end to the beginning of a paper that is easy to sort burn and carbonize or recycle

7323 compressed thermal turbine and incin compressed thermal turbine and incinerator with condensed exhaust purified solution tunnel and absorbing solvent is a three cycle energy study by what means is there an obvious but smaller than abnormal gain in energy by energy for example synthetic and

7324 smart shoe media comm center usb and smart shoe media comm center usb and impact data exchange to find energy use activity use and mile use in order to keep up a productive life style

7325 ex tractable intelligent card for sh ex tractable intelligent card for shoe media comm center usb and impact data exchange to find energy use activity use and mile use in order to keep up a productive life style

7326 pressure wire circuits for testing a pressure wire circuits for testing athlete performance in for shoe media comm center usb and impact data exchange to find energy use activity use and mile use in order to keep up a productive life style

7327 analyzing software to compliment the analyzing software to compliment the smart shoe and the game in tow meaning that the game experiences and the turn of events i a sequenced analyzing moment of sport gone scientific video and movement software

7328 smart baseball and analyzing softwar smart baseball and analyzing software to compliment the smart practice baseball and the game in tow meaning that the game experiences and the turn of events i a sequenced analyzing moment of sport gone scientific as well as the geometric compensations of

7329 homeland security web analyzing soft homeland security web analyzing software that collects and collates the data to hot spots and sensitive areas inside the united states and abroad that acts like a nerve of intelligence and initiates ip and web activity bots to specify the targets activit

7330 corporate security web analyzing sof corporate security web analyzing software that collects and collates the data to hot spots and sensitive areas inside the united states and abroad that acts like a nerve of intelligence and initiates ip and web activity bots to specify the targets activi

7331 citizen specific security web analyz citizen specific security web analyzing software that collects and collates the data to hot spots and sensitive areas inside the united states and abroad that acts like a nerve of intelligence and initiates ip and web activity bots to specify the targets

7332 pre world war crime trial and intent pre world war crime trial and intent to issue a declaration of isolation as well as term correction to any such life interrupting country as a whole

7333 pre world war crime disciplinary cap pre world war crime disciplinary capital payment and just dues of damage

7334 lacquer jet fine art printer is a pr lacquer jet fine art printer is a premier collectible and fine art way of printing original fine two dimensional art

7335 layered lacquer ink is a special sol layered lacquer ink is a special solvent that is made to work with lacquer fine art printers and the technology of making a yield of ink that may be layered and kept a print work special

7336 layered acrylic printing and jet spr layered acrylic printing and jet spray plasticprinting in itself is a term generalized as a two part d and d printing combined

7337 paint printing jet spray plasticprin paint printing jet spray plasticprinting in itself is a term generalized printing with paint and an opacity paint plastic solvent

7338 metal and laser printing by way of l metal and laser printing by way of layered conducting print sheets and cartridge base for circuits and synthetic metals soot carbon doping electrodes

7339 printed solid state circuits and syn printed solid state circuits and synthetic metals by way of plasma layered bonding and thermal re doping data driven circuits

7340 embedded printed solid state circuit embedded printed solid state circuits and synthetic metals by way of plasma layered bonding and thermal re doping data driven circuits

7341 raised and recircuited printed soli raised and recircuited printed solid state circuits and synthetic metals by way of plasma layered bonding and thermal re doping data driven circuits

7342 less than pin riser connections that less than pin riser connections that are a random function with applicable chip port storage identification to bridge and support a more connected board of circuits

7343 open source programmable chips and s open source programmable chips and systems that are conveniently unsecured pre mirrored

7344 open source programmable secure chip open source programmable secure chips that are conveniently encrypted for resale as mirrored

7345 open source programmable secure chip open source programmable secure chips that are conveniently encrypted for resale as mirrored and embedded with a functionality along side the less than pin riser connections that are a random function with applicable chip port storage identification to b

7346 free fall generator a generator that free fall generator a generator that works on weight and gravity mechanized a sequence of hoses filling up large tubs and dropping them a very long distance in a downward scope of gravity pull making a electric motor generate power

7347 chip bios loader and sequence and th chip bios loader and sequence and then exchange and then install per socket to hold and keep and then install out of your design

7348 circuit printer and thermal circuit circuit printer and thermal circuit board copper solder printer soft copper mess for a less expensive and more operational dynamic study of process

7349 blank chip sd and blank chip designi blank chip sd and blank chip designing acceptable circuit driven operations of a system on a chip
7350 blank chip cpu and blank chip design blank chip cpu and blank chip designing acceptable circuit driven operations of a system on a chip
7351 enscribble open chip cpu and softwa enscribble open chip cpu and software driven registration for designing acceptable circuit driven operations of a system on a chip
7352 enscribble write once open chip cpu enscribble write once open chip cpu and software driven registration for designing acceptable circuit driven operations of a system on a chip
7353 enscribble rewritable open chip cp enscribble rewritable open chip cpu and software driven registration for designing acceptable circuit driven operations of a system on a chip
7354 transformation solid state memory in transformation solid state memory into cores and threads of computational processing shapes and cram computer aided triggered layers of computational mass
7355 automatic bios correction library an automatic bios correction library and error beeping vocabulary
7356 automatic system correction maintena automatic system correction maintenance add in card with plug and play beeping error codes and other operations libraries
7357 device specific data write shape kno device specific data write shape known as a cram functioning device specified write once or multiple times in order for a finite use of solid state matter nano writes and re writes to configure a more than a cubit to a cram shape for a multitude of opera
7358 write cubit device language of shape write cubit device language of shape and form for function software to make a shape in one language and it equal to a transistor building shape in another said this way building a chip from languages of shapes to make a shape in one language equal to a t
7359 write cubit device language of shape write cubit device language of shape and form for function hardware to make a shape in one language and it equal to a transistor building shape in another said this way building a chip from languages of shapes to make a shape in one language equal to a t
7360 rewriteable cubit device language rewriteable cubit device language of shape and form for function hardware to make a shape in one language and it equal to a transistor building shape in another said this way building a chip from languages of shapes to make a shape in one language equa
7361 practice and sport smart training da practice and sport smart training data base comparison software for the smartball smart shoe and smart practice languages
7362 smart ball of impact and resistance smart ball of impact and resistance control analytical study real time information wireless transmission
7363 reverse government and capitalism on reverse government and capitalism only by representation and our nature of representative tax based economically sound capital adjustment the means for a party capital adjustment economy
7364 encrypted phone application key and encrypted phone application key and pair with to speak and decode in milliseconds as ten four
7365 privatize and modernize war on a tec privatize and modernize war on a technological software front to make any smart super tactic a flight above at all times other words to make a smart war out of dumb enemies and use any means necessary and able to create a war with

only the enemy suffered

7366 the learning tablet for children wit the learning tablet for children with program and curriculum based compact flash cards and a wireless system in a school learning technologically advanced environment

7367 technology aided learning of the uni technology aided learning of the united states should have a privatized level of integration and legal funding for all schools and states learning should be focused on traditional context and should be modernized in a equal way to unify learning as well

7368 school approved learning device is a school approved learning device is a working tablet or pc that operates when needed and is encrypted for students personal ownership works with a specific class and operates with tcompactflashor any mobile scheme including the means to submit tests an

7369 gaseous carbonized smoke with water gaseous carbonized smoke with water and electricity stabilizing the protons and electron particles for fuel and refinery in a electrical ph balance

7370 gaseous carbonized smoke with solven gaseous carbonized smoke with solvent and electricity stabilizing the protons and electron particles for fuel and refinery in a electrical ph balance

7371 gaseous carbonized smoke with solven gaseous carbonized smoke with solvent and electricity stabilizing the protons and electron particles for fuel and refinery in a electrical ph balance vapor fume tank for making compounds medicine and chemicals in a step by step process making a smoke fro

7372 single to multiple operation core fu single to multiple operation core functions in server and data center useages working as a tier based institution translations as multiple or single cell core systems on chips with connections powered by software that works as needed when the chip on a

7373 single to multiple single string cor single to multiple single string cores and data storage to power a response from any working request of information client streaming systems with the software that requests and provides expandable dimensions in demand flexibility

7374 two chip and one in out board that f two chip and one in out board that functions and works as a system on a chip with a data storage system and a controller system making a mirroring of on and off for any processing including the transfer of an operation and exchange of any single file

7375 bigger board by going smaller multip bigger board by going smaller multiple chips of storage to an embedded and exchangeable sense of connections explained as a wall of insertable systems built by rows an columns of an architecture of request and a string of systems on strings wall based o

7376 modular section server parts and pie modular section server parts and pieces with a specified error correction code per device section building a server with more parts that are replaceable verses one single modular board with upgrade able parts and version compatible parts

7377 air recovery recycle particulate sta air recovery recycle particulate stations with environmental specified control and air improvement abilities is an air recovery station that inhales polluted air and recycles that air to a percentage of clean that is acceptable to improve air quality in

7378 modular recovery stations and filter modular recovery stations and filter exhaust catalyst converters that not only control but convert bad air to good air at a conditioning level air recycling and sanitation's continued by air recovery recycle particulate stations with environmental specif
7379 geo stations of air conditions and v geo stations of air conditions and ventilator generators that catch air and control the pollutants and then exhaust with a generation of expended and recycled energy and new clean air for valley and depreciated congested stagnate environments air recycli
7380 low level back pack air cleaner and low level back pack air cleaner and ventilator generators that catch air and control the pollutants and then exhaust with a generation of expended and recycled energy and new clean air for valley and depreciated congested stagnate environments air recycl
7381 air cleaner and ventilator generator air cleaner and ventilator generators that catch air and control the pollutants and then exhaust with a generation of expended and recycled energy and new clean air for valley and depreciated congested stagnate environments air recycling and sanitation's
7382 short pay phone local cell phone tow short pay phone local cell phone towers short stations instead of blasting communications from far above why not make communication a small subscription network like the way it used to be in the pay phone days
7383 publically supported short network publically supported short network stations instead of blasting communications from far above why not make communication a small subscription network like the way it used to be in the pay phone days we could have mobile networks everywhere someone wante
7384 in a traveling pi operation the new in a traveling pi operation the new period separated computer controlled measurements of testing and software zoom mandelbrot formulas can be used to build more precise fractions of processing
7385 periods of meaning are the scales of periods of meaning are the scales of numbers followed by the numerical relations of places and points of vector annotations by giving a certain number of periods or specific symbol in a sequence to translate as an equation
7386 the easy chemistry of hydro dynamic the easy chemistry of hydro dynamic equilibrium refining and decompressed atomized oxidation with lasers and conservation techniques
7387 chemical balance relation goal is th chemical balance relation goal is the chance to achieve the proper chemicals in the brain or an organ to make it work better and function regulatory like while not poisoning the other organs in relation to the technique of ingestion or intake of the medi
7388 cell phone shut down of un friendly cell phone shut down of un friendly cell phones in war zones as well as known friendly phones allotted list
7389 electric and battery operated utensi electric and battery operated utensil exam of any battle field prior to operations and smart tracking uncontrolled devices
7390 mobile communications and hard line mobile communications and hard line encryption control for war zones and temperamental places of interest
7391 a cell phone app that tracks phrases a cell phone app that tracks phrases to anti sentimental text to linking attacks of terrorism
7392 functions of any such blockade of te functions of any such blockade of technology communications for war places and territories of conspiracy

7393 terrorist country suspension list to terrorist country suspension list to the greater good of our united states by posting actions to suspend any positive aid or commerce or like to a country with a certain negative attitude and actions against innocent people
7394 the pledge of allegiance is a nation the pledge of allegiance is a national abidance of our heritage and citizen children of public education should be noted for not having allegiance
7395 german conflicts of interest in chri german conflicts of interest in christianity and islam may incite a new world war the exemption of refugee ship should be fined and evaded by way of isolation and deportation aid to a specified area as not a national place of christianity
7396 driving tension scale of accidents a driving tension scale of accidents and incidents that conclude to an unsafe level of community relationships in driving and public behavior
7397 business alliances are a single mana business alliances are a single manager for out sourced business arrangement with multiple favorite company venture family of out sourcing scheme of business related management and the techniques of friendly business engagements with licenses abound by p
7398 chickens verses eagles the national chickens verses eagles the national challenge to build a stronger nation with chickens running the country
7399 architecture in cubits another way t architecture in cubits another way to say functions in written language a cubits as any other known as a path or circuit in another to build a chip out of a formed path of cubits in an alphabet of cubits and then circuits in super annotation cell of cond
7400 building language hardware written b building language hardware written by software as a solid state or flash based conductor processor and operator made into a cubit written composite working tool
7401 building language software written b building language software written by software hardware as a solid state or flash based conductor processor and operator made into a cubit written composite working tool
7402 poly carbonate sub species and lead poly carbonate sub species and lead interference differences in toxicity managing the traits of carbon and the differences between all other poly carbonate number makes
7403 energy studies of probable generatio energy studies of probable generation of any such source of energy verses the cost of making that energy free fall generator or incineration electricity or pendulum associated control session
7404 disposal incinerator quality control disposal incinerator quality control by modified ports of chambers and vacuum services to increase efficiency of any such known service of operation
7405 service incineration vacuum and prop service incineration vacuum and propulsion of any attached turbine while at the same moment making a chain reaction of feeding and eating
7406 simplified vacuum jet compressed inc simplified vacuum jet compressed incinerator is a service incineration vacuum and propulsion of any attached turbine while at the same moment making a chain reaction of feeding and eating from previously expended compression
7407 simplified vacuum jet compressed mot simplified vacuum jet compressed motor is a service motor vacuum and propulsion of any attached turbo turbine multiplied while at the same moment making a chain reaction of feeding and eating from previously expended

compression in a cycle
7408 phi co amplified or parallel process phi co amplified or parallel processor on flash chip with software driven function and amplitude of cooperating chips of the same process or of equal ownership of functions
7409 paid parts of parts program of indep paid parts of parts program of independent energy makers for example for this amount of money we will qualify you to make more energy to add to the existing supply for a fee of operations and connections
7410 usb alternate co processing substitu usb alternate co processing substitution and usb amp accelerator processing stand along plug and play device to improve computations
7411 usb server on chip functions and usb usb server on chip functions and usb server bed of computation devices for processing any known protocol
7412 fiber optic system connection for al fiber optic system connection for alternate co processing substitution and fiber optic system amp accelerator processing stand along plug and play device to improve computations and the transceiver relationship in that
7413 fiber optic system server on chip fu fiber optic system server on chip functions and fiber optic system server bed of computation devices for processing any known protocol and the transceiver relationship in that
7414 cell tower connected data cloud incl cell tower connected data cloud including a wireless batch of servers and data center operations
7415 wireless mini servers for a cell tow wireless mini servers for a cell tower connected data cloud including a wireless batch of servers and data center operations
7416 a service array of wireless mini ser a service array of wireless mini servers for a cell tower connected data cloud including a wireless batch of servers and data center operations
7417 co processing appliances for a wirel co processing appliances for a wireless mini servers and data center operations network
7418 co processing active software for a co processing active software for a wireless mini servers and data center operations network is a software platform that runs and completes the process of who what when and where easily by calling on a group of processes to work in unison at more than on
7419 wireless data center protocol and th wireless data center protocol and the processed cell operations inside wireless mini data servers holding a sub numerical phone number name in a send and receive order
7420 wireless data center registration gr wireless data center registration group of numbers and locations in a decimal formatted pre registered group of assigned names in any given array of a whole to respond and request information
7421 essential voip cellular combination essential voip cellular combination wireless data center and the contingency of any such known cloud operation to voice the data center in any form of cubit secondary movement
7422 laser translator for optical hard li laser translator for optical hard line is a laser inspired data field connected to a satellite or other form of transcribe optical connection
7423 laser cell translator for optical ha laser cell translator for optical hard line is a laser inspired data field connected to a tower or other form of transcribe optical connection concluding into a connected internet and data scheme privately secured or pubic nature of owner ship
7424 a focused laser receiver that holds a focused laser receiver that holds and records laser

signals as data

7425 a focused laser receiver that holds a focused laser receiver that holds and records laser signals as data in an annotation of triplet pi equilibrium is a wave of data as a signal

7426 a focused laser receiver group that a focused laser receiver group that holds and records laser signals as data in multitudes encrypted or un encrypted methods

7427 a focused laser sending group that s a focused laser sending group that sends and relays laser signals as data in multitudes encrypted or un encrypted methods

7428 range path data as wave signal in a range path data as wave signal in a focused laser sending and receiving group that sends and relays holds and records laser signals as data in multitudes encrypted or un encrypted methods in any shade of ultraviolet to white co concluding into a wireless

7429 the code and compensation required t the code and compensation required to provide a simple targeted geonautic range path data as wave signal in a focused laser sending and receiving group that sends and relays holds and records laser signals as data in multitudes encrypted or un encrypted

7430 the device transmitting code and com the device transmitting code and compensation required to provide a simple targeted geonautic range path data as wave signal in a focused laser sending and receiving group that sends and relays holds and records laser signals as data in multitudes encry

7431 array controller of process is a bra array controller of process is a brain to make all the cells of any given data center work together and perform in complete success multiple functions of operations essentially a server for other servers the instruction service server completed instructi

7432 operating system operation code kill operating system operation code kill control and array controller of process is a brain to make all the cells of any given data center work together and perform in complete success multiple functions of operations essentially a server for other servers t

7433 wifi operating system operation code wifi operating system operation code kill control and array controller of process is a brain to make all the cells of any given data center work together and perform in complete success multiple functions of operations essentially a server for other serv

7434 network ethernet operating system op network ethernet operating system operation code kill control and array controller of process is a brain to make all the cells of any given data center work together and perform in complete success multiple functions of operations essentially a server fo

7435 monarch connection operating system monarch connection operating system operation code kill control and array controller of process is a brain to make all the cells of any given data center work together and perform in complete success multiple functions of operations essentially a server

7436 lets play political jeopardy where t lets play political jeopardy where there were bank watches and monetary status alarms of insufficient and super sufficient notes that are politically motivated and controlled how to find political corruption and traces of homeland security problems of gr

7437 lets play political jeopardy and say lets play political jeopardy and say that people who run government should have a cap on income until out of office and officially audited by the

irs to have any such money g brown
7438 the light age needs to modernize gov the light age needs to modernize government and parts that require government advice and intuition may help fight crimes and wars of terror with generous offerings and divisions for improvement with the technology of our nation at risk we should help pro
7439 the live needle polygraph test to st the live needle polygraph test to study by acupuncture the truth of any such person g brown
7440 old medicine has a new study the int old medicine has a new study the integration of old ways into the new way of taking medicine antiquebiology g brown
7441 super simple small push button with super simple small push button with microphone and speaker working with voice command and no touch screen cell phone hardware to sd to no sd g brown
7442 super simple small push button micro super simple small push button microphone speaker voice command phone operating system that is network and web inclusive g brown
7443 second generation of allotted multip second generation of allotted multiple connections to any given port of operations wifi and more computational connection strings of packets and wireless information wifi two is a cubit matter that is a signal incorporated into the operation of code beyo
7444 long range laser data wave is a ligh long range laser data wave is a light wave of information that carries to point to point and holds wave signals of information similar to optical data yet without fibers g brown
7445 cellular information channel for pol cellular information channel for police that carry police data specific and confidentially secured information g brown
7446 a secured public information channel a secured public information channel for monetary transfers is a specific web application that transfers ownership and funds to other banks and balances g brown
7447 multiple channels of information bri multiple channels of information bridge to access any such specific need or industry specific technology to share and improve that data share market of information is a mini expanded data exchange to be said again is like the information of aero industry
7448 packet encryption by presiding marke packet encryption by presiding markers and suffix markers of packets for multiple channels of information bridge to access any such specific need or industry specific technology to share and improve that data share market of information is a mini expande
7449 pcie plug and play data signatures a pcie plug and play data signatures and readers for multiple channels of information bridge to access any such specific need or industry specific technology to share and improve that data share market of information is a mini expanded data exchange to be
7450 pcie plug and play data encoders and pcie plug and play data encoders and decoders and readers for multiple channels of information bridge to access any such specific need or industry specific technology g brown
7451 scramble encrypted rearranged method scramble encrypted rearranged methods of encryption for multiple channels of information bridge to access any such specific need or industry specific technology to share and improve that data share market of information is a mini expanded data exchange t

7452 electronic us treasury of banks and electronic us treasury of banks and commissions is a united states trade bank that works with commercial common banks to control federal trade and electronic fund transfers of ownership g brown
7453 optical disc cpu with functions that optical disc cpu with functions that process like cubits as circuits less expensive circuit driven optical central processing units and processing written and then used in language circuits optical cpu g brown
7454 optical disc cpu with multiple read optical disc cpu with multiple read and process lasers in rotation with the percircuit adjustment g brown
7455 optical disc cpu with multiple read optical disc cpu with multiple read and process lasers in rotation with multiple layers of architecture g brown
7456 detachable optical disc cpu with int detachable optical disc cpu with interoperable parts and changeable socket drives and bios configuration instructions to improve today's computations and sciences g brown
7457 secondary leading and transferable o secondary leading and transferable optical disc cpu with exchangeable cpu disc like a compact disc drive that holds memory and computations in and out g brown
7458 embedded solution with optical disc embedded solution with optical disc cpu holding a fixed architecture for processing computations g brown
7459 stacked solution with optical disc c stacked solution with optical disc cpu holding a fixed architecture for processing computations g brown
7460 data internet channel is a paid serv data internet channel is a paid service that originates from the phone company and media ties of per interest based data g brown
7461 public data internet channel is a pu public data internet channel is a public service for recreating the television and internet into a new all in one signal source g brown
7462 data rating internet channel is a ra data rating internet channel is a rating service that rates the restricted content of sexuality and parental guidance per internet channel g brown
7463 internet channel and the process of internet channel and the process of data per industry and good keeping of that service including ratings infrastructure and cohesiveness g brown
7464 government mimic bot is a robot sear government mimic bot is a robot search script that attaches to well known bots and reads the similar data g brown
7465 police bot is a web bot and spider s police bot is a web bot and spider searching index that finds negative platforms and collects data from their information g brown
7466 internet data over radio is a specif internet data over radio is a specified sending and receiving data connection with radio signals in cubit data information g brown
7467 encrypted internet data over radio i encrypted internet data over radio is a encrypted cubit radio signal similar to cell tower signals only wider range and broadcast g brown
7468 internet data over radio to wifi rou internet data over radio to wifi router and radio broadcast transceiver to make a wireless home network and a radio connection to the outside internet inside g brown
7469 internet data over radio to wifi rou internet data over radio to wifi router and radio broadcast transceiver to make a wireless home network and a radio connection to the outside internet inside by phone cell tower g brown
7470 supply and demand cost of inflation supply and demand cost of inflation control is a negative system of checks that control the situation of inflation and prices by market

adjustment control g brown

7471 weak influenza vaccine is a low tole weak influenza vaccine is a low tolerable flu virus antibody that works to cure by a combination of antimicrobial sodium compound and deceased virus g brown

7472 long range electric transfer is a en long range electric transfer is a energy solution that works on transportable mobile energy cells or battery arsenal by train truck or hard links g brown

7473 community future investments are fun community future investments are funds for sustainable community management and the deprecation of environmental resources and state of improvements g brown

7474 shared by payment learning by conclu shared by payment learning by conclusion work and assembly ifs are a unlimited function memory database is a software that records and keeps a library of operations for working scenarios and what to do if situations for robotic manufacturing learning g b

7475 shared by payment learning by conclu shared by payment learning by conclusion vocabulary and sound unlimited function memory database is a software that records and keeps a library of operations for working scenarios and what to do if situations for learning and voice command software g bro

7476 data connection radio signal channel data connection radio signal channel devices are a group of devices that send and receive data through channels in radio signals g brown

7477 data connection radio signal channel data connection radio signal channel services are a group of devices for services that send and receive data trough channels in radio signals g brown

7478 data connection radio signal channel data connection radio signal channel devices and integrated circuits translations with a long range radio data modulation in negative microwave nano and packet direction services dm send and digital call sign codes stored as a verbal bios compressed comm

7479 synthetic sodiummagnesium battery t synthetic sodiummagnesium battery technology to power large and expansive technology specific environments

7480 rail car battery generators that gen rail car battery generators that generate power by rolling on the track and keep it in an onboard cell for keeping and use g brown

7481 car battery generators that generate car battery generators that generate power by rolling and then keep it in an on board cell for storage and reuse g brown

7482 cycle recycle battery generators tha cycle recycle battery generators that generate power by rolling and keep it in an on board cell for keeping and use g brown

7483 wireless network of small devices th wireless network of small devices that operate together when the first available exchange of data is able to make any server operable at any given time is a wireless cloud of processing g brown

7484 wireless packet direction is a prefi wireless packet direction is a prefix of packet information that sends to a specific receiving point that may have a direct link to a subscriber g brown

7485 wireless cloud router is a regulated wireless cloud router is a regulated document that works with multiple points of receiving and operation of sending as though there could be more than one wifi router commonly known as to operate together to send massive data and internet protocol signal

7486 on off magnetic electric generator t on off magnetic electric generator that works as off and on are sequentially put in motion to generate electricity in a magnetic field off center in a path of the coil and not in a jedliks motor inside but a path of logical magnetic cycles of coil along
7487 a multiplied dimension cycle electri a multiplied dimension cycle electric generator can be used to create electricity from electricity in a cycle of recycle which is a motor moving and then after performance on the return of the motor action another set of electric commutative cycle return
7488 transient of a multiplied dimension transient of a multiplied dimension cycle electric generator can be used to create electricity from electricity in a cycle of recycle which is a motor moving and then after performance on the return of the motor action another set of electric commutative
7489 cohesive layout of a multiplied dime cohesive layout of a multiplied dimension cycle electric generator can be used to create electricity from torque in a cycle of recycle which is a motor moving and then after performance on the return of the motor action another set of electric commutativ
7490 to go backwards from computer histor to go backwards from computer history in a tech size reversed build a giant field of cohesive layout of a multiplied dimension cycle electric generator can be used to create electricity from torque in a cycle of recycle which is a motor moving and then a
7491 hardware built to compromise the ene hardware built to compromise the energy of a force and generate a recycled electricity by making a circuit working on top of a previously expended torque for example a wheel with electromagnets stimulating another wheel with electromagnets that generate
7492 to use a software to engineer a circ to use a software to engineer a circuit driven computational fractal energy and recycled electricity by commutative exciter paths simple z = z^ + c to generate electricity g brown
7493 making electricity by using a recycl making electricity by using a recycle electric motor in a combination of pi and a combined fractal percentage of operation to work with things that are in motion to re generate electricity g brown
7494 using an exciter or multiple exciter using an exciter or multiple exciters as well as making electricity by using a recycle electric motor in a combination of pi and a combined fractal percentage of operation to work with things that are in motion to re generate electricity g brown
7495 solid state cpu second cpu and third solid state cpu second cpu and third cpu and plus as to write the chip with code instead of scoring the chip as a photo g brown
7496 solid state cpu software leased or p solid state cpu software leased or paid by a fee as to pay for the concept with rights as implied intellectual property g brown
7497 solid state cpu written using cubit solid state cpu written using cubit software that writes hardware g brown
7498 solid state cpu second cpu and third solid state cpu second cpu and third cpu and plus by pcie or alternate pipe like for example a tb processor in data cubits g brown
7499 military device of statistical units military device of statistical units of motion use and location tracking g brown
7500 police device of statistical units o police device of statistical units of motion use and

location tracking of effectiveness and location statistics g brown
7501 public dentition device of statistic public dentition device of statistical units of motion use and location tracking cloud data hardware and software working together to correct and notify of the occurrences g brown
7502 satellite target tracking system wit satellite target tracking system with unique boundaries and reports g brown
7503 cellular communications target track cellular communications target tracking system with unique boundaries and reports g brown
7504 track paging system that contacts an track paging system that contacts an information base to report locations for automated data exchange and service announcements g brown
7505 information base is a data routing s information base is a data routing system used to accelerate the location of data recipients by sub packet number and prefixes by area code g brown
7506 a data exchange server is a large or a data exchange server is a large or small interface that works as a unified information through port that directs things as in a direct input form using a information base is a data routing system used to accelerate the location of data recipients by su
7507 karaoke virtual reality user extensi karaoke virtual reality user extensible software and hardware is an augmented reality focus that makes you part of your virtual reality fantasy or scheme of augmented reality g brown
7508 public slander law and outlandish st public slander law and outlandish statement is a thing that makes it a crime to state things that are not true in any such questionnaire or consent of authority g brown
7509 debate of ownership is the law that debate of ownership is the law that makes it a crime to sell something that does not belong to you or your company g brown
7510 adjusted property jump is a search o adjusted property jump is a search of audit for the illegal gain of political paid compensation and buying off of any such persons favor g brown
7511 cloud on chips is any such amplified cloud on chips is any such amplified start and finish direction of processing that holds a building echo of data such as a galaxy operation where to say in one code that the predecessor may be an expensive system that makes code and related parts of info
7512 projection video phone and the laser projection video phone and the laser stick led compact or desktop models are conference friendly g brown
7513 play along karaoke or game augmented play along karaoke or game augmented reality projection and the laser stick led compact or desktop models are entertainment friendly g brown
7514 transparent sphere television and vi transparent sphere television and video layered spectrum display is a sphere of translucent properties that can display video in a perspective g brown
7515 sphere high definition perspective r sphere high definition perspective resolution encoding for visual display and communication g brown
7516 point of view added perspective disp point of view added perspective display user to display any resolution at the users proper point of view g brown
7517 server to compact flash with the pro server to compact flash with the process of data redirection would let the data decide where to go in this there could be multiple soc on one

board g brown
7518 compact flash bed of servers on chip compact flash bed of servers on chip and including a routed path of information to exchange the rate of processing a bed of data and processing chips with an on board router appliance g brown
7519 global routing initiative is a detai global routing initiative is a detailed paid routing service data base that helps clouds route to specific areas of the world to improve connectivity g brown
7520 paid multi device operating system i paid multi device operating system is an operating system that adapts to the device used on in any way needed how many devices do you want to run this copy of this operating system plan g brown
7521 secured drive of any paid multi devi secured drive of any paid multi device operating system is an operating system that adapts to the device used on in any way needed how many devices do you want to run this copy of this operating system plan g brown
7522 compact flash os paid multi device o compact flash os paid multi device operating system is an operating system that adapts to the device used on in any way needed how many devices do you want to run this copy of this operating system plan g brown
7523 usb flash os paid multi device opera usb flash os paid multi device operating system is an operating system that adapts to the device used on in any way needed how many devices do you want to run this copy of this operating system plan g brown
7524 adaptable fiber optic short solution adaptable fiber optic short solutions adaptable short solutions in fiber optic short cables and common issues in connectivity for everyday use fiber optic short translator connections compact fiber optic solutions g brown
7525 layered depth display optic solution layered depth display optic solutions for temporal three dimensional depth perspective is to layer a perspective in color and field display with layers of led and transparent layers of display layouts in a omni layer of depth and picture g brown
7526 transparent back light opacity scale transparent back light opacity scale of the to come display optic solutions for temporal three dimensional depth perspective is to layer a perspective in color and field display with layers and transparent layers of display layouts in a omni layer of dep
7527 vertical optical display circuits to vertical optical display circuits to display a varied layer of three dimensional optic display solutions for depth perspective where the circuit is layered and in itself holds a layer of more layers with a point of view calculated g brown
7528 software that plural signal control software that plural signal control per application and multiplied signal options for a stronger signal receiving g brown
7529 display of unordinary behavior and display of unordinary behavior and public riot crime is a unexpected method of protest and public disruption g brown
7530 radical religious increments of unre radical religious increments of unrealism is the religious extreme made to be the un excepted form of ban freedom and the unfree concept of terrorism g brown
7531 telemarketer terrorism and the pill telemarketer terrorism and the pill pushers problems to fight homeland phone terrorism ftc trial of do not call list deficiency g brown
7532 user specific watching web bots that user specific watching web bots that identify and trace criminal and malicious activity by following them and then their intent to disrupt g brown

7533 group watching web bots that track a group watching web bots that track and trace a specific group of attitude and system of targets by identifying them and then following their intent g brown
7534 a regulatory system of web bot maker a regulatory system of web bot makers that make a group of police and repeat servers and stations that relate to the specific origin of a nation g brown
7535 building and reattaching method of building and reattaching method of a synthetic metal chip into a printed circuit board part that isn't soldered down and is replaceable by automatic printing control made by a shared measuring chip bridge machine that is giving to prior specified dimens
7536 universal permeasurement bonding an universal permeasurement bonding and soldering the pre measured circuit socket flashblue.gif
7537 universal bonding agent part that ac universal bonding agent part that accepts a specified dimension of micro chip for processing or storage etc also known as a socket for a socket bonded solder g brown
7538 global recycles market exchange and global recycles market exchange and welfare for the environment is a monetary substance recycle exchange for the world of today tomorrow and the future and exchange of solids starches gases and more for sale and recycling as well as patrol for safe conta
7539 assistance and acceptance of over du assistance and acceptance of over due taxes as a forgive and forget income status is a means to fight for people who work but do not make enough to pay back taxes and new taxes and a separated income bracket that provides a substitute planning verses fin
7540 magnetic key encrypted attached tech magnetic key encrypted attached technology device interface storage for data and processors
7541 enscribble stacked level micro chan enscribble stacked level micro channel architecture processors and solid state processors replaceable technology per a attached technology mega sata
7542 qfl cubit function language is a spe qfl cubit function language is a specified architecture solid state specific software written language that is transformed by a function written chip that makes the written data function after written to
7543 mqfl magnetic cubit function languag mqfl magnetic cubit function language is a specified architecture solid state specific software written language that is transformed by a function written chip that makes the written data function after written to magnetically
7544 pqfl photo cubit function language i pqfl photo cubit function language is a specified architecture solid state specific software written language that is transformed by a function written chip that makes the written data function after written to photogenically
7545 diamond emulsion printing for silico diamond emulsion printing for silicon graphic chips and transistor state data operation circuits is the laser and plasma use of a finely focused layer of solution that makes a connected circuit of printing possible with a synthesized doped carbon diamond
7546 optical data layers in transparent c optical data layers in transparent color cycles and luminescence using a color sequence to translate a higher data rate and activate phosphorescent and ultra violet materials
7547 printed circuit board printing by st printed circuit board printing by stencil layers

and photo emulsion plasma bonding over silica to make a connection on a larger scale even smaller

7548 layer of insulation to connected int layer of insulation to connected intermittent silica linking to a printed circuit board printing by stencil layers and photo emulsion plasma bonding over silica to make a connection on a larger scale even smaller

7549 embedded hyperistic chips and proce embedded hyperistic chips and processors that hold inside a layer of insulation to connected intermittent silica linking to a printed circuit board printing by stencil layers and photo emulsion plasma bonding over silica to make a connection on a larger

7550 how would anyone control artificial how would anyone control artificial intelligence so that it is not a ready made corruption of control meaning intelligence in itself is uncontrollable via the old proverb of apple of knowledge and history personal opinion of the fight of any intelligence

7551 who goes to jail or becomes fined ov who goes to jail or becomes fined over a problem with an artificially driven car and or death or accident how would anyone control artificial intelligence so that it is not a ready made corruption of control meaning intelligence in itself is uncontrollab

7552 instead of artificially stupidity in instead of artificially stupidity intelligence why don't they work on real issues like terrorism and airplane wrecks or the traffic we have to go through every day just to get to where we want don't steal my inventions and sweat my equity this is a waste

7553 shipping on a drone front needs all shipping on a drone front needs all the fixes that any other delivery path would acquire with permission a new travel rout with drone preferences

7554 safety issues and control of pathway safety issues and control of pathway control properties legal trade and international processing as shipping on a drone front needs all the fixes that any other delivery path would acquire with permission a new travel rout with drone preferences function

7555 logistical managers and shipping int logistical managers and shipping interested insurance making any drone liable shipping made right

7556 drone shipping non operating artific drone shipping non operating artificial intelligence driven system managed cloud preference and interest made good to ban the waste of non binomial if statements

7557 written cubit functions by size of t written cubit functions by size of the data on a given chip's architecture meaning that if the chip is a data driven nano meters then the cubit could be or less written by size meters and the same for a chip written in a nano meter depth of focus in opti

7558 help line for any given issue and ab help line for any given issue and abuse mental or drug crisis being there as a cost safe alternative to police this would be a pre extreme non emergency health hotline that could elevate the police as a or similar dial code for health issues

7559 marijuana cessation and the caffeine marijuana cessation and the caffeine pill using a positive for a past negative by tolerances and over balanced technique of chemistry

7560 protecting yourself from a bad fad t protecting yourself from a bad fad think realistically hold your fights and always protect your rights be happy know that help is a place and you can always get there from here know that some are good and some are not control auto content at

any costespe
7561 negative information managers as a t negative information managers as a title for the architect who writes the rules against false news and hypothetical as a software
7562 a vague statement in even number par a vague statement in even number parts
7563 gas station runoff reservoir for env gas station runoff reservoir for environment for safety water treatment and river friendly filters
7564 cell tower time share is to buy prop cell tower time share is to buy property and rights to broadcast for a fee and make money
7565 rebirth of local private companies e rebirth of local private companies energy generating infrastructure focus technology franchise based on demand rules and time shares
7566 ultra violet led wall to ultra viole ultra violet led wall to ultra violet solar green nano metric wave receiving cells to generate electricity by emitting more ultraviolet energy than consuming in a energy cycle of send and receive
7567 lens magnified and focused ultra vio lens magnified and focused ultra violet led wall to green solar crystal send and receive as a synthetic electra photosynthesis
7568 lens magnified and focused infrared lens magnified and focused infrared led wall to green solar crystal send and receive as a synthetic electra photosynthesis
7569 approved small munitions of electric approved small munitions of electric generating stores and subscribers
7570 medical suit and marijuana legal sta medical suit and marijuana legal state anti trust to un support the marijuana fed funded states why should different states support other states
7571 colored lens magnified and focused i colored lens magnified and focused infrared led wall to green solar crystal send and receive as a synthetic electra photosynthesis
7572 uv or luminescence colored lens magn uv or luminescence colored lens magnified and focused infrared led wall to green solar crystal send and receive as a synthetic electra photosynthesis
7573 multiplied uv or luminescence colore multiplied uv or luminescence colored lens magnified and focused infrared led wall to green solar crystal send and receive as a synthetic electra photosynthesis
7574 this into a light tunnel of amped re this into a light tunnel of amped reflected focused solar energy multiplied uv or luminescence colored lens magnified and focused infrared led wall to green solar crystal send and receive as a synthetic electra photosynthesis
7575 directed and fiber optic reflected f directed and fiber optic reflected focused solar energy multiplied uv or luminescence colored lens magnified and focused infrared led wall to green solar crystal send and receive as a synthetic electra photosynthesis
7576 oscillating and inverted by redirect oscillating and inverted by redirected and fiber optic reflected focused solar energy multiplied uv or luminescence colored lens magnified and focused infrared led wall to green solar crystal send and receive as a synthetic electra photosynthesis
7577 unconstitutional radical increments unconstitutional radical increments in perspective to any known issue granted by a process of multiple courts excluding the one and only court of any such state or federal system allotted to change any other court terms
7578 in case of a state of dysfunction of in case of a state of dysfunction of the former functioning laws shall be recommitted to the legislation and government shall continue as previously stated

7579 monopoly suited situation of control monopoly suited situation of control in unsafe circumstances as well as the issues of per citizen inventor verses the corporation of unincorporated inability to serve stop and dis assist as a means to help issues of infringement in any right

7580 intellectual property service is a b intellectual property service is a branch of government that takes the service of intellectual property and dues of monetary issuance as a new and joined idea branch of rights and property to help the income and advancement of proprietary capitalism of t

7581 large drone pilot operated shipping large drone pilot operated shipping crafts that are controlled at a navigation headquarters with margin able software to insure delivery

7582 drone pilot signal wave and code con drone pilot signal wave and code controlled actions of safe navigation and encrypted communication from pilot to drone

7583 approved levels of flight security f approved levels of flight security for any drone shipping piloted and non piloted software driven means

7584 software only driven drone shipping software only driven drone shipping operations and communications with auto navigation

7585 software only driven drone shipping software only driven drone shipping operations and communications with flight control parables possibilities and corrections and including improvised attended interception in probable cause

7586 flight paths of protection from dron flight paths of protection from drone traffic and flight control signal repeaters in a cellular flight pattern

7587 foreign war locally driven weapon ho foreign war locally driven weapon holding drone war landcraft and aircraft as well as watercraft for a safe death less war

7588 making the cloud today on one server making the cloud today on one server as in a cubit written at will connections in micro cloud computing making a system on chip a wireless and hard line data send and receive intent to send with wireless ac and a hard line to receive data or verses in te

7589 to change the cloud subscriptions in to change the cloud subscriptions into an derogatory of abuse of sales interest to say that cloud subscriptions are wrong and untrue in the cost of ownership

7590 free to sue the part of government t free to sue the part of government that helps people who need compensation who are unable to see the right power of law branch for improper use of intellectual property abuse and theft

7591 a formal submitter of s infringement a formal submitter of s infringement based on the intent to use with out proper or patent rights platform based on comma separated value spreadsheet

7592 a free to file online court system t a free to file online court system that works on merit and perspectives on interest

7593 forms with the probono contingency forms with the probono contingency in attendance would be to file for free but support the people who put effort by a percent of earnings

7594 focused laser to amplified reflectiv focused laser to amplified reflective tunnel solar energy and process of light by multiplying the mass and energy of any light source as a laser to magnify the out come of energy

7595 multiple focused laser to amplified multiple focused laser to amplified reflective tunnel solar energy and process of light by multiplying the mass and energy of any light source as a laser to magnify the out come of energy

7596 see saw action hydro pumping valve e see saw action hydro pumping valve electric generation and infinite unstopped water engine taking a current force and not stopping that energy but making a symbiotic source of energy

7597 see saw action synthetic gas pumping see saw action synthetic gas pumping valve electric generation and infinite force fulcrum engine taking a current force and not stopping that energy but making a symbiotic source of energy where one force over comes the other one and repeats

7598 large ocean platform of aero see saw large ocean platform of aero see saw action valve electric generation and infinite force fulcrum engine taking a current force and not stopping that energy but making a symbiotic source of energy where one force over comes the other one and repeats

7599 open chip design library can be a ri open chip design library can be a right feed on chip designs and configurations to improve the processor and the advancement of technology itself

7600 scribeable chip design library can scribeable chip design library can be a right feed on chip designs and configurations to improve the processor and the advancement of technology itself

7601 scribeable chip design can be a unl scribeable chip design can be a unlocked blank chip based on focused layers of data on chip for function ambled for on chip designs and configurations to improve the processor and the advancement of technology itself

7602 write enabled un scribe chip design write enabled un scribe chip design would be a un written chip that could be written to and can be a unlocked blank chip based on focused layers of data on chip for function ambled for on chip designs and configurations to improve the processor and the a

7603 radio data signal operations in cell radio data signal operations in cellular circumstances of wave properties and the inherited secured pci/m/flash radio tuner for data

7604 areal flash server cloud that stores areal flash server cloud that stores tickets of packets in the cell tower as compact flash micro super high compact data

7605 areal flash server cloud that stores areal flash server cloud that stores a processing and acceleration factor of signal in the cell tower as compact flash micro super high compact

7606 aerial flash server cloud that store aerial flash server cloud that stores data is encrypted as well as distributed into a faster radio directed cell tower with a communicated operating system with usage and inclusive data distribution

7607 aerial flash server cloud that store aerial flash server cloud that stores data is encrypted as well as distributed into a faster radio directed cell tower with a communicated operating system with usage and inclusive data distribution to a command center and then multiplied signals

7608 network looped all incorporated comm network looped all incorporated communication signals in a plural cubit signal scheme would be a multitude of signals inside a group of signals echoing a batch of previous signals to continue a wave of data

7609 a mechanical access signal processin a mechanical access signal processing station that answers and computes processing of communication packets and pluralizes them into a echoing batch of signals

7610 secure and amplified echoing batch r secure and amplified echoing batch receiver and encoder for incorporated communication signals in a plural cubit signal scheme
7611 chip writing drive in accordance to chip writing drive in accordance to a blank solid state synthetic metal processor with socket type preference contact points for interface
7612 blank billets for chip writing drive blank billets for chip writing drive in accordance to a blank solid state synthetic metal processor with socket type preference for soldering or fusing boards as well as incorporated or replaceable sockets
7613 a secured or profitable solution for a secured or profitable solution for chip design and acceleration as well as to load and print chip architecture in a printer software interface with a chip writing drive in accordance to a blank solid state synthetic metal processor with socket type pre
7614 open out doors chassis mod is to ena open out doors chassis mod is to enable a single cell or multi cell device operate permanently out side by routed power or solar powered operations liquid contact cooling and grounded transistors capacitors and completed shock resistant grounds
7615 open out doors chassis mod memory/gr open out doors chassis mod memory/ground is to enable a single cell or multi cell device operate permanently out side by routed power or solar powered operations liquid contact cooling and grounded transistors capacitors and completed shock resistant gro
7616 open out doors chassis mod self adju open out doors chassis mod self adjusting climate control is to enable a single cell or multi cell device operate permanently out side by routed power or solar powered operations liquid contact cooling and grounded transistors capacitors and completed sh
7617 corn gas thinner perspective and the corn gas thinner perspective and the foresight to see that the differences in ethanol and gasoline are in consistency and burn rationality in order to improve alternate fuels
7618 a plasticized combination gasoline m a plasticized combination gasoline made from sodium and petroleum
7619 a combustion engine with an alternat a combustion engine with an alternate high ethanol intake and bi burn rationality with larger viscosity engineering modified to take a higher percent of ethanol
7620 corn gas central perspective and the corn gas central perspective and the foresight to see that natural burn synthetic made corn gas can and could burn at a zero level of pollutants in according to the epa
7621 pi by rail generator using the rotat pi by rail generator using the rotation of rail wheels to generate current to store on railway car by the study of pi
7622 retrofit added rail generator using retrofit added rail generator using the rotation of rail wheels to generate current to store on railway car
7623 depot service drop for retrofit adde depot service drop for retrofit added rail generator using the rotation of rail wheels to generate current to store on railway car and would be a good alternative for automation and robotics
7624 common industrial size rechargeable common industrial size rechargeable batteries for retrofit added cycle generator using the rotation of x wheels to generate current to store on x
7625 encrypted phone service that is for encrypted phone service that is for government
7626 encrypted phone service that is for encrypted phone service that is for military

7627 encrypted phone service that is for encrypted phone service that is for public
7628 dot gov a verified news channel from dot gov a verified news channel from the us government book twit
7629 official branch of news for the gove official branch of news for the government as s patents and legalities and suits with holdings and returns
7630 narcotic information agency is the p narcotic information agency is the proposal of an entity that would watch record and track illegal narcotics in an important information tracking module of police and protection for the greater good of our country
7631 private narcotic information agency private narcotic information agency is the proposal of an entity that would watch record and track illegal narcotics in an important information tracking module of police and protection for the greater good of mankind
7632 mental illness derived from narcoti mental illness derived from narcotics including lsd is the known cause of many induced chemical imbalances to correct any such change of a long period of time would be to induce an alternative state of wellness as another chemical balance to correct the
7633 to admit that the united states nar to admit that the united states narcotic problem would be easier to overcome would be anti marijuana gatewaydrug lockdown to prepare for a conclusive issue of illegal status of drug use look into the past problems and sue the president for his veto of
7634 retro fit industrial truck transmis retro fit industrial truck transmission attached axle line rotary electrical generator for parttime hybrid trucks and long haulers with batteries or storage of current
7635 argon or hydrogen plasma chip etchi argon or hydrogen plasma chip etching by neon on rhodium bedding under and over layered chip printing all or parts
7636 under and over layered blanks for w under and over layered blanks for writing purpose and laying the path to write the functions with software innate
7637 under and over stacked layered blan under and over stacked layered blanks for writing purpose and laying the path to write the functions with software innate locking and pressing together
7638 power by alternate point of energy power by alternate point of energy torque slip by extended cam shaft would translate as a slip and grip when needed part of any motorized engine that has an alternative shaft of torque for another source of power if needed a dual performance shaft if you
7639 power by more than two points of en power by more than two points of entry to add in any such power by alternative point of energy force method
7640 battery that incorporates the use o battery that incorporates the use of an atwill performance and storage with an added electrical generator and recycle
7641 gas powered hybrid alternative poin gas powered hybrid alternative point of energy torque slip cam
7642 gas start and hybrid long run alter gas start and hybrid long run alternative highway mileage fuel economy method is when the start is the majority controlled by combustion fuel and the highway gears are controlled by electricity methods
7643 gas start and hybrid long run alter gas start and hybrid long run alternative highway mileage transmission is when the start is the majority controlled by combustion fuel and the highway gears are controlled by electricity methods

7644 gas start and hybrid long run alter gas start and hybrid long run alternative highway mileage fuel economy method is when the start is the majority controlled by combustion fuel and the highway gears are controlled by electricity methods with each gear a different volt and torque
7645 long run alternative highway mileag long run alternative highway mileage voltage economy method is when transmission gears are controlled by electricity methods with each gear a different volt and torque
7646 vertical and embedded chip stilts t vertical and embedded chip stilts to branch layered under and over stacked layered blanks to add to a multiple layered processing chip or storage
7647 nano related myriad layers of press nano related myriad layers of pressing alignment in branch layered over and under stacked layered blanks to add to the building of a layered processing chip
7648 multi layered processing chip is a multi layered processing chip is a nano related myriad layers of pressing alignment in branch layered over and under stacked layered blanks to add to the building of a layered processing chip
7649 future of less open software and th future of less open software and the concurrent topics that it will hold such as a fee based operation time and subscription updates
7650 myriad nano layer built magnified t myriad nano layer built magnified transistors bipolar transistor and grounded emitter
7651 myriad nano layer built magnified a myriad nano layer built magnified amplifier and compressor
7652 myriad nano layer built magnified r myriad nano layer built magnified resistors quantum and relative
7653 myriad nano layer built magnified c myriad nano layer built magnified capacitors and fuses in a sequence of build
7654 aftermarket hybrid fuel thinner and aftermarket hybrid fuel thinner and formulator that will take a higher level of ethanol and percentage it to your specific model of car make and run longer and more economy friendly
7655 utility permit and cell tower franc utility permit and cell tower franchise reseller authorization diy broadcasting
7656 above board solid state threading c above board solid state threading
7657 end state above board links and inp end state above board links and inputs are intermittent paths on the circuit board that provide input and through put
7658 board stacking brackets and board t board stacking brackets and board to board ports with tapes and transports using a hypotheisis board off load through put
7659 government do not share consumer in government do not share consumer information list is a list that prohibits the sale of user information and logs
7660 user browser encryption is the end user browser encryption is the end user controlled browser session as a controlled level of security of information
7661 job bot that studies trends and pro job bot that studies trends and properties in sales and up coming sale for product research
7662 job bot that makes assumptions base job bot that makes assumptions based on popularity trends and formulates new products
7663 job bot that sends email to problem job bot that sends email to problem accounts with options and help situations

7664 job bot that asks for feedback from job bot that asks for feedback from positive and negative accounts and uses that information in service
7665 directive software that is an inter directive software that is an inter operable cloud software that routes the fastest out path and in path of data in the cloud to improve performance and assets allocation
7666 virtual data center design forecast virtual data center design forecast software to build a virtual cohesive center with proper estimations
7667 educational planned curriculum fore educational planned curriculum forecast software to build a schedule and studied learning with proper estimations
7668 sheet virtual manufacturing cost an sheet virtual manufacturing cost and turn around design forecast software to build a virtual cohesive plan with proper estimations
7669 automated import business cost and automated import business cost and payments sheet expenses and asset value real time scores and the learning from predictions and history software
7670 system on chip and the divided part system on chip and the divided parts of a one system add in board are controlled by bios and eufi properties that are extensive and individually controlling in each circumstance of operation
7671 inclusive system on chip board and inclusive system on chip board and part controller could function as a bed operating controller that gives multiple instructions to each sub system on a board and help directive options for processing
7672 in a unlooped system on chip the p in a unlooped system on chip the properties of processing could be controlled by a network router or a in and out send and receive connected protocol of any kind to work separated and un connected in a secured isolation mode
7673 to ship cloud backups to the client to ship cloud backups to the client on record able media for recovery
7674 programmable chip software and the programmable chip software and the opportunity to make a chip into a performance enhancer such as a co appliance or main appliance or second appliance for processing or for storage or routing
7675 vector data path routing direction vector data path routing direction chips that tell data where and what to go or perform propagation
7676 system on chip and the divided part system on chip and the divided parts of a one system add in board are controlled by flash back dos and parameters that are extensive and individually controlling in each circumstance of operation
7677 to encode cubits in a series of par to encode cubits in a series of parameters that are extensive and individually controlling in each circumstance of operation and as well as to auto encode written software with software for example a series of events written by software that writes softw
7678 embedded software language per part embedded software language per part in a stored cubit translator which could control more bits per channel and more code per device
7679 scribble insert or image insert to scribble insert or image insert to search engine for results across the internet and likeness
7680 fossilized nuclear waste and the re fossilized nuclear waste and the renewable study of micro wave negative and positive nuclear reactive waste
7681 microwaved nuclear waste and the re microwaved nuclear waste and the renewable study of micro wave negative and positive nuclear reactive waste recycle and recharging

uranium and non depleted uranium

7682 operating system mode do not shut d operating system mode do not shut down and run specific programs

7683 visual search data shapes and curve visual search data shapes and curves symbols and references library

7684 ocr for objects drawings and images ocr for objects drawings and images including the combination of symbols and conjunctions

7685 image puzzle translation software c image puzzle translation software

7686 electric aeronautics and pilot frie electric aeronautics and pilot friendly energy efficient software

7687 electric aeronautics and the electr electric aeronautics and the electric aided recycle magnetic turbine is a spinning and rotation generate electra magnetic jet propulsion

7688 electric aeronautics and scale able electric aeronautics and scale able drone shipping enterprise as an economic solution

7689 electric aeronautics and direct cur electric aeronautics and direct current electric generating engines powered by lithium drum battery stations

7690 shaping chips to reflect amplify an shaping chips to reflect amplify and duplicate processing objects inside the chip

7691 electra magnetic compressed jet pro electra magnetic compressed jet propulsion is a software controlled on and off of electra magnetic motors that can turn propellers in a compressed modular sequence to build a jet action of energy

7692 electra magnetic compressed jet pro electra magnetic compressed jet propulsion is a software controlled on and off of electra magnetic motors that can turn propellers in a compressed modular sequence to build a jet action of energy electra magnetic compressed jet software

7693 to prove that artificial intelligen to prove that artificial intelligence is un secured and dangerous we can look at the responsibility of consequences first and foremost in pre examination routines of what if my car gets hit by a robot or what if my kid gets run over by a robot what happe

7694 to prove that the free pop art is i to prove that the free pop art is in fact a infringement

7695 to note that engineering a wireless to note that engineering a wireless network could be easy as plug and play but no company makes a plug and play school wifi network plug and play wifi network pre configured and shipped for laymen technology

7696 laymen technology smart home lights laymen technology smart home lights and sound along side pre programmed television internet and phone plugin and use configurations ready out of the box

7697 a wireless pre configured room by r a wireless pre configured room by room and service bundle software built smart all in one service for home

7698 to take dumbing it down more than a to take dumbing it down more than anything ever has a wireless pre configured solution of commercial information technology service that incorporates all the services needed to work an office of today for any company as a all in one service for work

7699 phone back up chip that stores numb phone back up chip that stores numbers and important codes

7700 computer back up chip that stores a computer back up chip that stores account

information and important authorization codes
7701 phone distress chip that can send a phone distress chip that can send an sos to a qualified number
7702 application that helps connect emer application that helps connect emergency information to help for people who don't currently have an internet connection
7703 an app that sends domestic abuse or an app that sends domestic abuse or mental health related and drug abuse issues to a counselor chat and the proper help in case of emergencies a specific need for a subtle conclusion affordable in any counsel situation related to a semi non emergency hel
7704 solid state synthetic metal soldere solid state synthetic metal soldered on motherboard ram and alternate accelerated memory by software
7705 solid state synthetic metal un sold solid state synthetic metal un soldered on mother board replaceable removable bios architectural chip
7706 sodium nickel acid design for a lar sodium nickel acid design for a larger battery size in anticipation on recycle and reuse operations included by design
7707 a secured intelligent business app a secured intelligent business app that sends important confidential information to itself and no one else by finger print proof and encrypted messaging
7708 a webbot network of data applicati a webbot network of data applications searching for the meaning of artificial intelligence con and pro
7709 the negative conclusion foresight o the negative conclusion foresight of any such research on artificial intelligence and the effects on every day life for humans and the difference between real state of the art and self driving cars etc
7710 magnetic propulsion engine an elect magnetic propulsion engine an electronically controlled on and off magnet engine generating torque and force
7711 magnetic propulsion torque an elect magnetic propulsion torque an electronically controlled on and off magnet engine generating torque and force
7712 magnetic torque transmission and ac magnetic torque transmission and accelerating interface to control the speed and rpm
7713 magnetic propulsion torque turbine magnetic propulsion torque turbine and calibration of generating electricity from a chain reaction offset
7714 humor slander judgment case of lies humor slander judgment case of lies and public media broadcasting
7715 electra magnetic torque converter a electra magnetic torque converter and acceleration board and software as a clutch operator
7716 multiple coiled electrically powere multiple coiled electrically powered magnets for the electra magnetic torque converter and acceleration board and software as a clutch operator
7717 electra magnetic cycled passing cha electra magnetic cycled passing charge of a magnet is when every turn the magnet there could be other magnets that connects a passing circuit generating a current
7718 magnetic engine and the electra coi magnetic engine and the electra coiled speed control by automatic transforming voltage regulator
7719 wind mill and the recycle electric wind mill and the recycle electric generator that provides a push to any such greater movement to be accompanied by a multiplied series of passing engines and coils

7720 combustion and the push motor to po combustion and the push motor to power a engine that in part connected to a more powerful engine
7721 developer software driven central p developer software driven central processing unit would be controlled by software verses the parameters hard wired
7722 developer software for a software d developer software for a software driven central processing unit would be controlled by software verses the parameters hard wired
7723 chip operator and compute magnetic chip operator and compute magnetic transmission for torque and propulsion of device controlling a stationary over controlled passing magnets that provide any such current
7724 mini wireless chip operatored and mini wireless chip operatored and compute magnetic transmission for torque and propulsion of device controlling a stationary over controlled passing magnets that provide any such current controlled with a wireless connection for torque magnitude intensi
7725 ecology scale landscaping will chan ecology scale landscaping will change deserts into jungles by that mountain of debree built by synthesizing a mountain and valley precipitation valve
7726 enterprise art server and the inten enterprise art server and the intent to create and master the digital frontier in a normal server used as a machine for not intended but built intentions the translated definition in a simple name thus made as a digitalartserver regiment of computers k
7727 denotation of any such specified pl denotation of any such specified platform specific as to route a version of any operating system as a true role in a non pragmatic cloud but intentionally a specified role in a company operating system for example my mother was a nurse and later in her c
7728 medical aid bar code instrument of medical aid bar code instrument of inventory and patient data input for wifi and accordance of any such links into a information ecosystem
7729 legal aid and bar code instrument o legal aid and bar code instrument of contracts and legal data input for wifi or data dump and accordance of any such links into a local or official legal information ecosystem
7730 legal aid and bar code software of legal aid and bar code software of contracts and legal data input for wifi or data dump and accordance of any such links into a local or official legal information ecosystem
7731 medical aid bar code software of in medical aid bar code software of inventory and patient data input for wifi and accordance of any such links into a information ecosystem
7732 compact battery and wifi translator compact battery and wifi translator for the smart shoe is a wifi solution that transmits data to the receiver for consideration
7733 magnetic shield barrier for the mag magnetic shield barrier for the magnetic torque engine as to accord any such other magnetic interference
7734 the updated nation of banks and lie the updated nation of banks and liens as a wealth of ownership in percent of the entire active and stable economy is a data base of ownership percents snip
7735 public verses a proprietary ownersh public verses a proprietary ownership of privileged operation is a data center that operates with little out side or un commercial activity snip
7736 a mobile war data center and the op a mobile war data center and the operations prior to any such consequences of a war zone known as a new data war with drone and air based

weapons snip
7737 the law to compete the retread situ the law to compete the retread situation of unsafe driving and open arms of retread ding semi truck tires in accordance with a safe means snip
7738 drone war remote weapons system inf drone war remote weapons system infantry low close to ground altitude and the operations prior to any such consequences of a war zone known as a new data war with drone and air based weapons
7739 short remote drone virtual reality short remote drone virtual reality warfare and an application controlled war drone based weapons
7740 vr military grade fault less warfar vr military grade fault less warfare drone controller software and hardware for a new drone war for drone based weapons
7741 self destructing military drone bas self destructing military drone based weapons
7742 drone specific artillery with a gps drone specific artillery with a gps location driven drone based weapons
7743 drone color of lights to show what drone color of lights to show what side it's on drone based weapons
7744 drone war is a bad guy gone and goo drone war is a bad guy gone and good guy life saved for a drone based weapons war the value of life is priceless technology can be created to fight war on our terms and save lives with or without a warning shot alarm or physical watching presence
7745 drone warfare can end war and make drone warfare can end war and make a safe place for freedom as we know it police driven drone will make a unmanageable place a safe place
7746 drone digital camouflage for drone drone digital camouflage for drone based weapons
7747 drone attack with non lethal chemic drone attack with non lethal chemical stunning weapons
7748 hover drone with short land air and hover drone with short land air and sea capabilities for the military war effort with weapons and target cameras
7749 playing field embedded wifi for the playing field embedded wifi for the smart shoe and training purpose as well as real play
7750 replaceable and customize able part replaceable and customize able parts for the smart shoe including chips sensors and connectors as well as and training purpose as well as real play
7751 replaceable and custom software tha replaceable and custom software that records distance force and occurrences as well as places in time as well as and training purpose as well as real play
7752 grid array tray of solid state oper grid array tray of solid state operators is a column and row defined access point of processors and chips
7753 automated robotic operated cell tow automated robotic operated cell tower elevator that accesses the components in a arranged method of distribution and installation like a robotic spider for cell communication equipment snip
7754 archive of common robotic motions a archive of common robotic motions and fixtures is a library of skills that help any or some robotic tools operate
7755 defense and war related remote any defense and war related remote any operable aircraft control system is a system that manually shifts controls and manipulates an aircraft by retro fit levers switches and indicators by a remote access system
7756 defense and war related software op defense and war related software operation is a

semi retro fix of software controlled previously known as manual operation to change the on board to remote access system of operations completely non personal aircraft to operate
7757 defense and war related remote any defense and war related remote any operable boat or submersible control system is a system that manually shifts controls and manipulates an boat or water craft by retro fit levers switches and indicators by a remote access system
7758 defense and war related software op defense and war related software operation is a semi retro fix of software controlled previously known as manual operation to change the on board to remote access system of operations completely non personal water craft to operate
7759 defense and war related remote any defense and war related remote any operable land craft control system is a system that manually shifts controls and manipulates an land craft by retro fit levers switches and indicators by a remote access system
7760 defense and war related software op defense and war related software operation is a semi retro fix of software controlled previously known as manual operation to change the on board to remote access system of operations completely non personal land craft to operate
7761 intelligent warship is a lifeless b intelligent warship is a lifeless battle ship that is an artificial war machine that wins wars defends freedom and kills bad guys
7762 drone launching warship intelligent drone launching warship intelligent warship is a lifeless battle ship that is an artificial war machine that wins wars defends freedom and kills bad guys
7763 infantry drone launching warship in infantry drone launching warship intelligent warship is a lifeless battle ship that is an artificial war machine that wins wars defends freedom and kills bad guys
7764 drone lost badge is a tracking chip drone lost badge is a tracking chip to help locate and track war data and keeps the drone from function if removed that is an artificial war machine that wins wars defends freedom and kills bad guys
7765 war data is a ultra fast format use war data is a ultra fast format used to save lives by the examples performed in the cloud to help defend freedom and dedicate sponsorship to help end war that is an artificial war machine that wins wars defends freedom and kills bad guys
7766 war drone software interface that d war drone software interface that detonates bombs shoots a gun and all works to help defend freedom and dedicate sponsorship to help end war that is an artificial war machine that wins wars defends freedom and kills bad guys
7767 the need for patented hypothetical the need for patented hypothetical theory rights is a common missed opportunity based on will and why as in a information back up right protected by schematics and red tape a duplicate protection enabled by nature
7768 ed method information is not a lega ed method information is not a legal binding attribute and should be
7769 a running circle definition of what a running circle definition of what has been said is in fact a no answer for example if someone were to propose a question to a branch of government and the return answer was a previously stated circular statement not a yes or no answer by definition the
7770 a misleading running circle definit a misleading running circle definition of what has been said is in fact a no answer for example if someone were to propose a question to a branch of government and the return answer was a previously stated circular statement not a yes or no answer by def
7771 a hypothetical definition included a hypothetical definition included as intellectual

property is the mission of a duplicate and patent case filed in both manners
7772 a chip written and in a state of re a chip written and in a state of rewritable status that can be written to and then rewritten in any sort of language for function and purpose not only standard capacity random access memory
7773 a write once chip that has a state a write once chip that has a state of permanence and will only function as a second or first capacity full function chip with architecture written by software
7774 the language of permanent or tempor the language of permanent or temporary written function cubits and the as the written code and switches as conductors that transpose into a computing functional chip
7775 the intent to create any such chip the intent to create any such chip library or write and store functional architecture for sale or for open access
7776 the intent to create any such chip the intent to create any such chip library or write and store functional architecture for sale or for open access including the scale of architecture as the written language code
7777 to understand dangerous technology to understand dangerous technology and the anti climatic autonomous era of unexpected danger the intent to improve not endanger the obvious state of a space elevator vision of autonomous intent to catapult caca and non reality of foresight
7778 to understand dangerous technology to understand dangerous technology and the anti climatic autonomous era of unexpected danger the road verses the air for travel aeroautonomous
7779 to understand dangerous technology to understand dangerous technology and the anti climatic autonomous era of unexpected danger landing pads for the autonomous air drones with automated load and unload robots
7780 to understand dangerous technology to understand dangerous technology and the anti climatic autonomous era of unexpected danger security travel and cloud based drone traffic control flight issuance
7781 to understand dangerous technology to understand dangerous technology and the anti climatic autonomous era of unexpected danger the signal control federal communication level of drone and non commercial travel patterns
7782 to understand dangerous technology to understand dangerous technology and the anti climatic autonomous era of unexpected danger the signal control federal communication level of drone and commercial travel patterns
7783 blue tooth security and the non ele blue tooth security and the non elevated signal of secure encoded blue tooth encryption
7784 aircraft take over software for mis aircraft take over software for mission critical control
7785 radio specified alpha channel is th radio specified alpha channel is the intent to focus out a specified communication with a single operative with the intent to direct with out interference of other channels during communication say for example a unit of battle or communication line is sp
7786 radio specified alpha channel softw radio specified alpha channel software is the intent to focus out a specified communication with a single operative with the intent to direct with out interference of other channels during communication say for example a unit of battle or communication l

7787 radio specified alpha channel hardw radio specified alpha channel hardware is the intent to focus out a specified communication with a single operative with the intent to direct with out interference of other channels during communication say for example a unit of battle or communication l

7788 radio specified alpha channel encry radio specified alpha channel encrypted software is the intent to focus out a specified communication with a single operative with the intent to direct with out interference of other channels during communication say for example a unit of battle or commu

7789 soft silica chip insulator film tha soft silica chip insulator film that would enable vertical chip branching and layers of no conducting parts of chips in a fashion to layer other chip parts to conduct a pseudo balanced and compressed level of conductivity

7790 vertical chip branching and layers vertical chip branching and layers of conducting parts of chips in a fashion to layer other chip parts to conduct a pseudo balanced and compressed level of conductivity

7791 vertical hyper threading chip parts vertical hyper threading chip parts to conduct a pseudo balanced and compressed level of conductivity

7792 vertical chip design software and t vertical chip design software and the congruent chips made from stacking and vertical aligned methods

7793 spindled printed vertical chip laye spindled printed vertical chip layered computer controlled and measured in nano myriads a link of layers to build with

7794 single level chip platform print an single level chip platform print and stack conductors that match a sphere and link like a socket and drive

7795 multiple level chip assembly to pri multiple level chip assembly to print and stack construction chips in a link and exchange processing manner

7796 software written multiple level chi software written multiple level chip assembly to print and stack construction chips in a link and exchange processing manner by cubit cell and cubit grid

7797 blank chips for the software writte blank chips for the software written multiple level chip assembly to print and stack construction chips in a link and exchange processing manner by cubit cell and cubit grid

7798 the software that will write the so the software that will write the software written multiple level chip assembly to print and stack construction chips in a link and exchange processing manner by cubit cell and cubit grid

7799 the hardware that helps software wr the hardware that helps software written multiple level chip assembly to print and stack construction chips in a link and exchange processing manner by cubit cell and cubit grid

7800 the connected hardware and software the connected hardware and software that software written multiple level chip assembly to print and stack construction chips in a link and exchange processing manner by cubit cell and cubit grid

7801 additional socket and secondary lev additional socket and secondary level chips of a software written multiple level chip assembly to print and stack construction chips in a link and exchange processing manner by cubit cell and cubit grid

7802 intermittent synthetic metal and os intermittent synthetic metal and oscillating cascading silica non conductive spindled printed vertical chip layered computer controlled and measured in nano myriads a link of layers to build with

7803 intermittent synthetic conductive g intermittent synthetic conductive gel and oscillating cascading silica carbon insulated spindled printed vertical chip layered computer controlled and measured in nano myriads a link of layers to build with
7804 cascading printing reproduction is cascading printing reproduction is the interprinted method of the conductive property and the insulator to generate a conductive chip
7805 after the print and the process of after the print and the process of end doping of equal molecular weight conductive and insulation printing of conductive paths and non conductive insulator in a vertical and arranged manner of myriads is essentially giving conductive working properties
7806 three dimensional printed circuit d three dimensional printed circuit design software that grows in a multiple complex of parts and structure of a place to conduct and process
7807 in chip manufacturing and printing in chip manufacturing and printing the property printing of any scale by the materials density and ionic conductive relationship is the absolute of any progress to relate
7808 gold metal conductive and silica zi gold metal conductive and silica zircon non doped circuit printing and design to assemble
7809 many layered processing cores align many layered processing cores aligned and centered vertically for conductive repetitive processing
7810 many layered and horizontally align many layered and horizontally aligned and stacked for conductive repetitive processing
7811 a liberation statement such as a do a liberation statement such as a doctrine that plainly stating the purpose and consistences of a prove means of valuable to itself in a means not a current to accurately describe why some technology may not be suitable for safe public occurrences or to p
7812 the anti liberation statement such the anti liberation statement such as any doctrine that sates why this given technology should be use
7813 synthetic metal conductive and sili synthetic metal conductive and silica zircon negatively doped circuit printing and design to assemble
7814 metal conductive ion circuits and s metal conductive ion circuits and silica zircon positively doped circuit printing and design to assemble
7815 carbon ash suet and a purified carb carbon ash suet and a purified carbon electrical doping technology is a mesh printed object of carbon and laser printed to rasterize transistors and create a circuit to process
7816 inline double triplet express hyper inline double triplet express hyper threading and the mesh vector to create a circuit to process
7817 intertwined thread to send the same intertwined thread to send the same signal to multiple places and conduct a vector resolution in sync motions
7818 intertwined hyperthread to send th intertwined hyperthread to send the same signal to multiple places and conduct a vector resolution in sync motions
7819 intertwined double triplet hyperth intertwined double triplet hyperthread to send the same signal to multiple places and conduct a vector resolution in sync motions of processing
7820 a nano printed hyperembedded direc a nano printed hyperembedded directional navigation chip that provides the path direction based on a frequency change in the signal like a flashing yellow go when clear light
7821 a nano printed hyperembedded direc a nano printed hyperembedded directional

navigation chip that provides the path direction based on a frequency change in the signal like a traffic stop light

7822 a nano printed hyperembedded direc a nano printed hyperembedded directional navigation chip that provides the path direction based on a frequency change in the signal like a way stop with traffic signs

7823 a nano printed hyperembedded direc a nano printed hyperembedded directional navigation chip that provides the path direction based on a frequency change in the signal like a way stop light intersection

7824 a nano printed hyperembedded direc a nano printed hyperembedded directional navigation end that provides the path direction based on a frequency change in the signal like a right or left lane fork in the road

7825 a hyperembedded directional vector a hyperembedded directional vector coordinate directions is to travel on any such given processor chip and micro board as well as to repeat and loop in a quantified sequence and method on any given fork traffic changes and in any such given directional

7826 a simple beat and pulse of operatin a simple beat and pulse of operating code that transforms any such sequence of in and out for a unified measurement of any such arranged pulse of computations

7827 hyper multi directional threading i hyper multi directional threading is a simple beat and pulse of operating code that transforms any such sequence of in and out for a unified measurement of any such arranged pulse of computations

7828 planned disaster is a pre planned s planned disaster is a pre planned satellite crash course of premptive action as a last resort to the beginning of the end of any satellites planned ending and to where to crash why to crash or a gliding crash

7829 satellite landing zone is a owned a satellite landing zone is a owned and operated seek and map a designated place for landing and or crashing gliding or disperse

7830 satellite expiration estimate for a satellite expiration estimate for atmosphere reentry will help people work with satellites in a new and responsible way to help the space atmosphere environment and all the other costs of satellite orbit concerns

7831 cable tap adjustment port is an inf cable tap adjustment port is an information technicians friend when confusing cables at the data center get to be too much and how hope can be gained with the signal generation and the cable tap adjustment port

7832 cable tap adjustment identification cable tap adjustment identification signal is an information technicians friend when confusing cables at the data center get to be too much and how hope can be gained with the signal generation and the cable tap adjustment port

7833 a secured password encrypted cable a secured password encrypted cable tap adjustment identification signal is an information technicians friend when confusing cables at the data center get to be too much and how hope can be gained with the signal generation and the cable tap adjustment po

7834 a cable tap adjustment reader is an a cable tap adjustment reader is an information technicians friend when confusing cables at the data center get to be too much and how hope can be gained with the signal generation and the cable tap adjustment port

7835 a signal improvement repeater is a a signal improvement repeater is a localized internet or ethernet signal packet provider focus and adjustment of coded sequences and information in a better accelerated format

7836 compressed service provider is a is compressed service provider is a isp data provider that uses a compression ratio for packet delivery
7837 encrypted compressed service provid encrypted compressed service provider is a isp data provider that uses a compression ratio for packet delivery
7838 iau is an instructional application iau is an instructional application unit that tells the ai what to do and how to do it
7839 iau is an instructional application iau is an instructional application software that tells the ai what to do and how to do it
7840 mission critical application unit m mission critical application unit mciau is an instructional application software that tells the ai what to do and how to do it with a logical back up and or raid ability to operated code and instructions by architectures
7841 instructional application machine a instructional application machine and management is an instructional application software that tells the ai what to do and how to do it with a rom and connected channel to operated code and instructions by architectures
7842 cellular control cloud is a process cellular control cloud is a processing cloud communication and accessing rights to process and direct packets to other cell towers at a higher rate of control properties for things like data and file transfers as well as send and receive
7843 software encrypted and accelerated software encrypted and accelerated cellular control cloud is a processing cloud communication and accessing rights to process and direct packets to other cell towers at a higher rate of control properties for things like data and file transfers as well a
7844 hybrid incorporated data signal to hybrid incorporated data signal to cellular expanded network is a internet origin of routing to a particular place of any such packets of information then as soon as the signal comes close enough to the target it will then convert to a wireless signal to
7845 infinite hybrid incorporated data s infinite hybrid incorporated data signal to cellular expanded network is a leaping internet origin of routing to a particular place of any such packets of information then as soon as the signal comes close enough to the target it will then convert to a w
7846 hybrid incorporated signal protocol hybrid incorporated signal protocol is a data service and expanded network access signal protocol is a internet origin of routing to a particular place of any such packets of information then as soon as the signal comes close enough to the target it will
7847 hybrid incorporated data dedicated hybrid incorporated data dedicated rental satellite service and expanded network access signal protocol is a internet origin of routing to a particular place of any such packets of information then as soon as the signal comes close enough to the target i
7848 allotted maintenance and design ope allotted maintenance and design operation is not a given known intelligence and to understand that perpetual scanning may cause over bearing and non acceptable watching is to understand that there should be a kill switch of code to mandate operation and
7849 data code kill switch agreement and data code kill switch agreement and operation adjustment cooperation is the operation agreement that there is a safety concern for data on the service cloud and this may come to a part time outage based on the security of the data

there

7850 data code kill switch of unknown ab data code kill switch of unknown ability previously known as friendly vague code and a design designation as a adjustment code

7851 a premptive agreement in a cloud d a premptive agreement in a cloud database environment that protects the entity of itself by control and data code kill switch script

7852 a data war or war data premptive a a data war or war data premptive agreement in a cloud database environment that protects the entity of itself by control and data code kill switch script cooperation and compliance of no service

7853 a zone not incorporated with data a a zone not incorporated with data and on a war or war data premptive agreement in a cloud database environment that protects the entity of itself by control and data code kill switch script cooperation and compliance of no service

7854 to use a device where the data pack to use a device where the data packets of the internet and cellular comm has stopped and a radio wave of certain freq is controlled in a zone not incorporated with data and on a war or war data premptive agreement in a cloud database environment that p

7855 to switch off a zone incorporated w to switch off a zone incorporated with data and on a war or war data premptive agreement in a cloud database environment that protects the entity of itself by control and data code kill switch script cooperation and compliance of no service

7856 answer to a questionable theory by answer to a questionable theory by a hypothetical proof may be the hope that people need to find a cure for any know disease or virus

7857 curing a virus disease by viral vac curing a virus disease by viral vaccine may be hope for another kind of artificial virus of a synthetic kind artificial anti virus

7858 a heart worm with parasitic contami a heart worm with parasitic contaminates may be the cure for other diseases with the carrying body of the intent to cure more than one infliction

7859 to point a specific targeted progra to point a specific targeted program to a chip or configuration and hardware specific software outright

7860 to ignore the first aim is to aim a to ignore the first aim is to aim at the second target first to switch off a network with a virus and then scope and probe the culprit at a second target first

7861 to find the connections that refuse to find the connections that refuse to comply with a non connective network may expose the places of occupied aggressors

7862 starch protein and sugar dna micro starch protein and sugar dna microbiologically printed antibody used to fight disease

7863 printed dna from any known starch o printed dna from any known starch or protein microbiologically printed antibody used to fight disease

7864 dna at cg nucleotide printed dna fr dna at cg nucleotide printed dna from any known starch or protein microbiologically printed antibody used to fight disease or cancer

7865 dna at cg nucleotide printed dna fr dna at cg nucleotide printed dna from any known starch or protein microbiologically printed antibody used to fight disease or cancer positively doped

7866 dna at cg nucleotide printed dna fr dna at cg nucleotide printed dna from any known starch or protein microbiologically printed antibody used to fight disease or cancer negatively doped

7867 dna at cg nucleotide printed dna fr dna at cg nucleotide printed dna from any known starch or protein microbiologically printed antibody used to fight disease or cancer positively fibrillated refibrillated infibrillated
7868 dna at cg nucleotide printed dna fr dna at cg nucleotide printed dna from any known starch or protein microbiologically printed antibody used to fight disease or cancer negatively fibrillated refibrillated infibrillated
7869 national rage helpline and the ment national rage helpline and the mental health open hot line phone number and assistance associations abstract utility
7870 nicotine narcosis is the unstable i nicotine narcosis is the unstable inherit reaction to an overdose of nicotine
7871 acute nicotine narcosis is the long acute nicotine narcosis is the long term unstable inherit reaction to a continual overdose of nicotine
7872 marijuana use and the health of any marijuana use and the health of any such stimulant turned into a constant use where the patient has an addiction base on a series of ups and downs where the drug must maintain a non equal abuse level to be considered at a normal high is also known as a e
7873 software run program applications f software run program applications for printers that uses nano / pico / triad mixed and formulated biochemical nucleotide to replicate on a recurring smaller intent to cure cancer and disease software for biochemical printers
7874 software run program applications f software run program applications for printers that uses nano/pico/triad mixed and fromulated biochemical nucleotide to replicate on a recurring smaller intent to cure cancer and disease
7875 a post lactates light solution flus a post lactates light solution flush to help cure calcium deposits to prevent cancer
7876 a presentperpost lactates light s a presentperpost lactates light salt solution check to help clean calcium deposits to prevent cancer utility
7877 a presentperpost lactates nonalk a presentperpost lactates nonalkaline solution check to help clean calcium deposits to prevent cancer
7878 a combination presentperpost lact a combination presentperpost lactates nonalkaline solution and ultrasonic abrasive shock treatment to break and to help clean calcium deposits to prevent cancer
7879 at home kit to use combination pres at home kit to use combination presentperpost lactates nonalkaline solution and ultrasonic abrasive shock treatment to break and to help clean calcium deposits to prevent cancer
7880 doors are a important secure privat doors are a important secure private office operating system that is office inside an office that works with firewalls and fences for people who operate in tiers and teams to work on productive security means that are sensitive and need doors and keys on
7881 secure private badges for using sig secure private badges for using signatures in a secure work place called doors are a important secure private office operating system that is office inside an office that works with firewalls and fences for people who operate in tiers and teams to work o
7882 an add in card memory or hardware t an add in card memory or hardware that makes a hard line like connection that holds issues and hard place port instructions and memory for a secure private badges for using signatures in a secure work place called doors are a important

secure private off
7883 an artistic judgment to copy and cu an artistic judgment to copy and cure is the obvious mission of any nucleotide printed microorganism
7884 dna and nucleotide historical libra dna and nucleotide historical library and ownership per dna finger print solution
7885 a presentperpost lactates light s a presentperpost lactates light salt solution check to help clean calcium deposits to prevent cancer
7886 software run program applications f software run program applications for printers that uses nano / pico / triad mixed and formulated biochemical nucleotide to replicate on a recurring smaller intent to cure cancer and disease formulated biochemical nucleotide dcfbc page
7887 software run program applications f software run program applications for printers that uses nano / pico / triad mixed and formulated biochemical nucleotide to replicate on a recurring smaller intent to cure cancer and disease software for biochemical printers dcfbc page
7888 to multiply the conductive threads to multiply the conductive threads in a insulated chip levels made from of with a coherence of any insulation method of stacking horizontal or vertical chip organization to build a larger chip also said as to make a non conductive layer with small outer
7889 in a insulated chip levels made fro in a insulated chip levels made from of with a coherence of any insulation method of stacking horizontal or vertical chip organization to build a larger chip also said as to make a non conductive layer with small outer inner conductive measures while ope
7890 in a insulated chip levels with a c in a insulated chip levels with a coherence of any insulation method of stacking horizontal or vertical chip organization to build a larger chip also said as to make a non conductive layer with small outer inner conductive measures while operation is pos
7891 cube processors in a insulated chip cube processors in a insulated chip levels with a coherence of any insulation method of stacking horizontal or vertical chip organization to build a larger chip also said as to make a non conductive layer with small outer inner conductive measures while
7892 stacked form of many cube processor stacked form of many cube processors in a insulated chip levels with a coherence of any insulation method of stacking horizontal or vertical chip organization to build a larger chip also said as to make a non conductive layer with small outer inner condu
7893 free orchestrated data routing is a free orchestrated data routing is a open connected network that travels data based on open frequency bandwidth abstract utility
7894 a user operated device that enters a user operated device that enters as your original line and adapts to your connection that inturns blocks all connections and or encrypts or allows connections based on a simple password protocol in another way to say is to secure a networks connection
7895 a software virus company operated d a software virus company operated device that enters as your original line and adapts to your connection that inturns blocks all connections and or encrypts or allows connections based on a simple password protocol in another way to say is to secure a n

7896 a software virus company operated d a software virus company operated device that you can insert data with a secure environment to see the data without risk abstract utility
7897 a government sponsored software vir a government sponsored software virus company operated network scanning police bot to help find and trace topic of negative nature
7898 a permit to operate and sanction an a permit to operate and sanction any such privilege of scanning police bot to help find and trace topics of negative nature and danger for man kind
7899 populated bot database the recovery populated bot database the recovery validation for sale of recovered bot data and found information as confirmed data or false data as a trade in economic value or true data
7900 the validity of a data sheet and th the validity of a data sheet and the value rating for true data and how true the data is at any capacity
7901 satellite service incorporated is a satellite service incorporated is a freelance satellite scenario that builds and sells bandwidth on demand as a service for large and small company uses with a permit to render
7902 federal satellite admin satellite s federal satellite admin satellite service incorporated is a oversee satellite scenario that manages and approves the builds and sales of bandwidth on demand as a service for large and small company uses with a permit to render
7903 a red collar crime is a high rankin a red collar crime is a high ranking official caught or suspected to be wrong in monetary just gain
7904 printed operating system is a versi printed operating system is a version of embedded code that may or may not be changed according to the write function of the system and may be printed during manufacturing
7905 war network unlinking is a unloop war network unlinking is a unlooped firewall device for security and data integrity in a war data center
7906 election network linking is a unlo election network linking is a unlooped firewall device for security and data integrity in a election data center
7907 network linking chip is a unlooped network linking chip is a unlooped firewall embedded device for security and data integrity in a data center end start point
7908 pyramid chip scheme is a scaleable pyramid chip scheme is a scaleable multi processor right of way that claims more computing ability per consumer rather than consumer per processors
7909 multiple assignment os dcfbc page c multiple assignment os dcfbc page
7910 marijuana is should not be legal du marijuana is should not be legal due to addiction issues and behavior problems
7911 wrongful legality of bitcoin due to wrongful legality of bitcoin due to security invasion and of any such coin worth or unofficially a money right as to interfere with the united states treasury
7912 options in memory and the memory at options in memory and the memory attachment of a scaled inch standard drive as a to sata connected accelerator memory drop and find add on's
7913 a chip that holds the proper bios a a chip that holds the proper bios and instruction set for the plugin itself to operate as a fail safe pre occupied set of true plug and play functions in any os and any system on chip meaning if it's not operational it does not operate
7914 to take the block ledger offline fr to take the block ledger offline from an online state of transactions would secure the worlds trade and commerce around the globe and to end crypt

o currency would help the standard trade sanctions for every one
7915 to alternate the current internet a to alternate the current internet as a second internet for commerce and create a default encrypted status as to recreate a secured internet to require a ssl or tss
7916 retro fit smart house switches and retro fit smart house switches and connectivity features for traditional homes would include things like a room to room hub and wifi central apps that negotiate lights air conditioning and blinds for privacy even the door security and room itself audio w
7917 escape the os update plugin to esc escape the os update plugin to escape operating system updates permanently or semi choice
7918 update response company is a secure update response company is a secured and devoted complaint and semi responsible negotiating proactive alliance between consumer and the operating system manufacturer
7919 block chain attacks crypt o currenc block chain attacks crypt o currency is the attack of software and hardware together to steal
7920 multi drone pilot compensation soft multi drone pilot compensation software is a air and path pi ratio that groups or navigates multiple drones
7921 multi drone pilot compensation hard multi drone pilot compensation hardware is a part that works with air and path pi ratio that groups or navigates multiple drones
7922 stealth multi drone is a radar less stealth multi drone is a radar less and radar proof satellite driven drone
7923 software operated and controlled ce software operated and controlled central processing unit as a path to an operation type or person as a personal system operated on a come and go log
7924 automatic software operated and con automatic software operated and controlled central processing unit as a negotiated per program and app as the needed comp system to the operations
7925 a negotiated batch of pre operated a negotiated batch of pre operated and defined method of hardware as well as a complimentary pre selected operating software per presentation of any combination of system and hardware built to operate in sync as the maximum performance as well as success
7926 sequential sync and a maximum perfo sequential sync and a maximum performance from hardware with the automatic preference to apply the fixes and bottleneck drops with a work ethic to improve performance and software driven hardware os for the cpu
7927 scaleable drone with features and scaleable drone with features and cell communications software for cell to cell drone flight utility captur
7928 drone cell stations protocol for sc drone cell stations protocol for scaleable drone with features and cell communications network for cell to cell drone flight and land navigation utility
7929 lost drone safe way map and navigat lost drone safe way map and navigation per satellite route and permits for lost dog drones that can find their way home utility
7930 cron job flight navigation servers cron job flight navigation servers for drone devices is a ping service that directs and corrects any such flight or road travel utility
7931 cron job flight navigation code and cron job flight navigation code and software for devices that work with ping control utility

7932 cron job flight navigation hardware cron job flight navigation hardware that incorporates the memory factor of from point a to point b in a compensation mode utility
7933 anomaly report service is a service anomaly report service is a service that helps artificial devices understand seeds of change and occurrences in the issue of a change as a compensation equation and a reference base for service like a wind pattern change to help wind mills more energy du
7934 anomaly report service is a service anomaly report service is a service hardware and translation equipment that helps artificial devices understand seeds of change and occurrences in the issue of a change as a compensation equation and a reference base for service like a wind pattern chang
7935 anomaly report service is a service anomaly report service is a service software analyzing patterns and statistics that helps artificial devices understand seeds of change and occurrences in the issue of a change as a compensation equation and a reference base for service like a wind patte
7936 dual user add on information applic dual user add on information applications that work on cache and submission processes is a working rule based program that allows more than one user at a time to use the same work place for example a spread sheet that is incorporated to other sheets and
7937 multiple user hardware that works w multiple user hardware that works with software applications that run on live cache and submission processes is a working rule based program that allows more than one user at a time to use the same work place for example a spread sheet that is incorporat
7938 watch and see user and plus applica watch and see user and plus applications that work on cache and submission processes is a working rule based program that allows more than one user at a time to use the same work place for example a air navigation tower that is interoperable with in an
7939 random seed and anomaly report clou random seed and anomaly report cloud data with dual user and plus applications that work on cache and submission processes is a working rule based program that allows more than one user at a time to use the same work place for example a spread sheet that
7940 diode printed and stacked nano metr diode printed and stacked nano metric parts utility
7941 hot chip for safety safety chip and hot chip for safety safety chip and sos communication bridge allocation software utility
7942 global for profit school learning s global for profit school learning software and tablet interface that will start with ocr textbooks and ed information sale and the room of improvisations in learning processes to help a modern school internet deploy globally and recreate learning on a ne
7943 local state wide for profit school local state wide for profit school learning software and tablet interface that will start with ocr textbooks and ed information sale and the room of improvisations in learning processes to help a modern school internet deploy state wide and recreate lear
7944 free global not for profit school l free global not for profit school learning software and tablet interface that will start with ocr textbooks and ed information sale and the room of improvisations in learning processes to help a modern school internet deploy globally and

recreate learnin
7945 ocr and translation meaning softwar ocr and translation meaning software for clear internet learning school software and beyond is a linking between shapes and meaning in a data format language language learning
7946 ocr and translation meaning softwar ocr and translation meaning software for search data and search form engine and beyond is a linking meaning between shapes and meaning in a usage data format language language learning
7947 object and meaning database ocr and object and meaning database ocr and translation meaning software for search data and search form engine and beyond is a linking meaning between shapes and meaning in a usage data format language language learning
7948 many objects and meaning database o many objects and meaning database ocr and translation meaning software for search data and search form engine and beyond is a linking meaning between shapes and meaning in a usage data format language language learning
7949 many objects and multiple meaning d many objects and multiple meaning database ocr and translation meaning software for search data and search form engine and beyond is a linking meaning between shapes and meaning in a usage data format language language learning
7950 ai laws in effect and laws to speci ai laws in effect and laws to specify the out come of ai and ai actions and ai faults and government result laws of failure compensation and punishment
7951 artificial energy is a nonspontane artificial energy is a nonspontaneous reaction to a forced digital or analog form of simulated energy in a real sense of negative or positive
7952 artificial magnetic energy is a non artificial magnetic energy is a nonspontaneous reaction to a forced magnetic form of simulated energy in a real sense of negative or positive
7953 artificial relative energy is a non artificial relative energy is a nonspontaneous reaction to a forced magnetic digital amped weight in a volatile form of simulated energy in a real sense of negative or positive
7954 negative conductive algorithms are negative conductive algorithms are the translation of current in a form that may be used to hold energy and data at the same time with a specific compression ratio per algorithm and energy source in a cold state
7955 positive with negative conductive a positive with negative conductive algorithms are the translation of current in a form that may be used to hold energy and data at the same time with a specific compression ratio per algorithm and energy source in a alternate state
7956 positive with negative conductive a positive with negative conductive algorithms cpu chips computer memory and addon processors are the translation of current in a form that may be used to hold energy and data at the same time with a specific compression ratio per algorithm and energy sou
7957 trans coding chips that make a wave trans coding chips that make a wave of energy into positive with negative conductive algorithms cpu chips computer memory and addon processors are the translation of current in a form that may be used to hold energy and data at the same time with a spec
7958 free functional addons are the add free functional addons are the additional scaleable plug and play options of any such freely to place in a location to import processing and to increase a probability of performance
7959 tiered leveled sequential multiple tiered leveled sequential multiple free functional

addons are the additional scaleable plug and play options of any such freely to place in a location to import processing and to increase a probability of performance

7960 cloud addons are the servers or vi cloud addons are the servers or virtual performance servers in data center to act as a tiered leveled sequential multiple free functional addons are the additional scaleable plug and play options of any such freely to place in a location to import proc

7961 virtual performance servers in data virtual performance servers in data center are equatable to code and scripting within folders and software allocations

7962 multiple tiered virtual performance multiple tiered virtual performance servers in data center are equatable to code and scripting within folders and software allocations in a series format

7963 virtual functional addons are the virtual functional addons are the additional scaleable plug and play software options of any such freely to place in a location to import processing and to increase a probability of performance

7964 virtual functional gpu are the addi virtual functional gpu are the additional scaleable plug and play software options of any such freely to place in a location to import processing and to increase a probability of performance

7965 gpu inside a gpu inside for virtual gpu inside a gpu inside for virtual functional gpu are the additional scaleable plug and play software options of any such freely to place in a location to import processing and to increase a probability of performance x

7966 upgrade able secondary level chips upgrade able secondary level chips that co process in an onboard secondary socket that incorporate alternate processing like the central chip but in a on board or in socket form of non graphic non central but in a second level of cache and co processing

7967 upgrade able secondary level random upgrade able secondary level random access memory that store in an onboard secondary group of sockets that incorporate alternate processing like the first level ram but in a off or on board or in socket form of non graphic non central but in a second lev

7968 retro fit smart home breaker box is retro fit smart home breaker box is a device board that is controllable by phone or computer network of links and changes for variations and add on's in power and connectivity

7969 retro fit smart home breaker os and retro fit smart home breaker os and the retro fit smart home breaker box is a device board that is controllable by phone or computer network of links and changes for variations and add on's in power and connectivity

7970 security add on with retro fit smar security add on with retro fit smart home breaker os and the retro fit smart home breaker box is a device board that is controllable by phone or computer network of links and changes for variations and add on's in power and connectivity

7971 new item embedded controller instru new item embedded controller instructions as to add operating instructions per operation and embedded vectors

7972 smart home adaptive new or retro ap smart home adaptive new or retro appliance embedded power instructions switch control for a power related control operations

7973 smart home adaptive new or retro ap smart home adaptive new or retro appliance embedded library of instructions for compound control of smart objects with embedded options and chips ram as well as ports

7974 local library object instructions i local library object instructions is the safe and unlinked local area network of a system smart home adaptive new or retro appliance embedded library of instructions for compound control of smart objects with embedded options and chips ram as well as po

7975 connected object network of instruc connected object network of instructions library object instructions is the linked local area network of a system smart home adaptive new or retro appliance embedded library of instructions for compound control of smart objects with embedded options and

7976 a deliberate method network of conn a deliberate method network of connected object network of instructions library object instructions is the paid hierarchy connection within a local area network of a system smart home adaptive new or retro appliance embedded library of instructions for c

7977 block chain audit is a method to au block chain audit is a method to audit the leaks and attacks of cyber security an a cyber currency as a whole

7978 national technology research is a t national technology research is a technology study branch of government that is similar to nasa only the change of space to technology study

7979 tax report now is the time that we tax report now is the time that we have the proper data systems to calculate all the taxes and their effectiveness it time to do a country wide tax report

7980 government data exchange is a cloud government data exchange is a cloud method of revising the current scheme of paper arranged data

7981 war data center is a principal with war data center is a principal with the intent to make a secure and break in free environment that is a near to impossible notion of a study of all things war related

7982 war data center rit is a fast green war data center rit is a fast green/red light for any such advanced motion of war in a fast real sense of approval in the war data center

7983 war data records and the short hand war data records and the short hand version per soldier in battle by bot or by live combat by a recorded notable system

7984 educational data center is a princi educational data center is a principal with the intent to make a secure and break in free environment for schools

7985 medical data center is a principal medical data center is a principal with the intent to make a secure and break in free environment that is secure to all things study related

7986 medical data center rit is a fast g medical data center rit is a fast green red light for any such advanced motion of medical cloud related issues

7987 educational data center rit is a fa educational data center rit is a fast green or red light for any such advanced motion of cloud environmental situations

7988 block chain proof of purchase is th block chain proof of purchase is the encrypted method of payment and an added method of authentication per user agent

7989 search into systems is a simple sea search into systems is a simple search engine that searches by tunnel and hidden internet protocol in the specified system with results on a different page

7990 paid search into systems is a simpl paid search into systems is a simple search engine that searches by tunnel and hidden internet protocol into the specified system with paid results on a different page

7991 paid search into systems network is paid search into systems network is a simple search engine alliance that searches by tunnel and hidden internet protocol in the specified system

with paid results on a different page
7992 roaming address is a long haul truc roaming address is a long haul truck driver or occupational address where the citizen is not contacted by postal address buy by phone and mobile email
7993 government security number remap is government security number remap is a new recorded method for securing your citizenship and voter rights as well as secondary social security number
7994 paid government security number car paid government security number card or secure id is a new recorded method for securing your citizenship and voter rights with a chip
7995 hdmi server on chip is a compliment hdmi server on chip is a complimentary part to a input bed of systems on chip by hdmi connections
7996 hdmi server input board is the hdmi hdmi server input board is the hdmi server on chip that is a part of input bed of systems on board by hdmi connections
7997 to have a fiber optic vector regist to have a fiber optic vector registered board that has a lined connective port of objects inline to work like a copper embedded circuit board
7998 system on chip optical server input system on chip optical server input board to have a fiber optic vector registered board that has a lined optical embedded circuit
7999 auto thread and processor controlle auto thread and processor controller software and scripted control chips are the automated central processor unit and the memory optimization included with all of the other parts such as gpu and or oi accelerator and even a co processor in unison as such
8000 serial recording there is a need fo serial recording there is a need for a faster paced invention deposition writing and security method with the usa to make a licensed professional is important in a serial recorded document status combined with the method of registration
8001 landfill mining and dithering mobil landfill mining and dithering mobile disassembly plant is an arranged machine that separates the material on a scale per unit of measurement first is the magnetic property of the unit second is the weight of the unit and third is the size and this metho
8002 gmvitamins are genetically modifi gmvitamins are genetically modified vitamins that encourage growth to patients with severe deficiencies in a certain vitamin or cell of the body
8003 gmantivirus are genetically modif gmantivirus are genetically modified vaccines that protect important cell growth to patients with severe deficiencies in a certain vitamin or cell of the body
8004 autonomous landfill mining and dith autonomous landfill mining and dithering mobile disassembly plant is a robotics controlled arranged machine that separates the material on a scale per unit of measurement first is the magnetic property of the unit second is the weight of the unit and th
8005 microwave reactor is a combination microwave reactor is a combination of reactions in few scenarios like for example the combination of air or water to run a turbine and create electricity or the microwaveable consideration of other reactive materials as solvents or compounds to create en
8006 fossilized and un radiated uranium fossilized and un radiated uranium through a process of microwave until negative powers are there and no heat is constant
8007 dunner and the re exam of pre exist dunner and the re exam of pre existed depleted

uranium for microwave tables and the recycled nuclear products

8008 microwave energy and the reconstitu microwave energy and the reconstituted nuclear elements for regeneration and reuse

8009 private energy farms and the mobile private energy farms and the mobile battery that can change the energy industry are easy to dream of but more difficult to consume the intent to make a plug and rechargeable system of portable electricity is in itself to create a whole industry the study

8010 vertical chip engineering software vertical chip engineering software is a software that will aid in the building of a vertical wafer of chips in a faster more compact size

8011 vertical chip engineering printers vertical chip engineering printers is a machine that will aid in the building of a vertical wafer of chips in a faster more compact size

8012 vertical chip multi compound printe vertical chip multi compound printers is a machine that will aid in the building of a vertical wafer of chips in a faster more compact size while printing in multiple stages of mediums in a series of layers

8013 chip compound direction printers is chip compound direction printers is a machine that will aid in the building of a vertical and horizontal wafer of chips in a faster more compact size while printing in multiple stages of mediums in a series of layers to print horizontal and vertical to a

8014 chip compound direction software is chip compound direction software is a machine writer that will aid in the building of a vertical and horizontal wafer of chips in a faster more compact size while printing in multiple stages of mediums in a series of layers to print horizontal and vertic

8015 compound angle chips are the chips compound angle chips are the chips that have horizontal diagonal vertical processing that will aid in the processing of a vertical and other angles including horizontal made wafer of chips in a faster more compact size while printing in multiple stages o

8016 compound chip parts are the cores compound chip parts are the cores memory and agents that have direction any compound direction of processing with building of a vertical and horizontal wafer of chips in a faster more compact size while printing in multiple stages of mediums in a series

8017 compound chip parts are the cores m compound chip parts are the cores memory and agents that have direction any compound direction of processing with building of a vertical and horizontal wafer of chips in a faster more compact size while printing in multiple stages of mediums in a series

8018 multi processing compound angel of multi processing compound angel of processing links toner compiled compound chip laser printed gold powder and cubic zircon powder printed chips

8019 laboratory do it your self rights t laboratory do it your self rights to find and cure to cancers virus and diseases is a old thing new again that the current system to practice active measures of laboratory work require unknown lengths of red tape this is an equation of experience and sch

8020 laboratory intellectual rights are laboratory intellectual rights are the rules and knowledge ownership of laboratory do it your self rights to find and cure to cancers virus and diseases is a old thing new again that the current system to practice active measures of laboratory work requi

8021 private research intellectual right private research intellectual rights lab permits are the rules and knowledge ownership of laboratory do it your self rights to find and cure to cancers virus and diseases is a old thing new again that the current system to practice active measures of lab
8022 proprietary research rights laborat proprietary research rights laboratory is a seek and find a cure for a monetary gain
8023 free rights and trade laboratory is free rights and trade laboratory is the non compete way of salable research
8024 legally bound comma separated value legally bound comma separated values and sheets for digital paper submissions are records that can be submitted by csv by any such given form for legal certified documents
8025 hope for the wire bound is a simple hope for the wire bound is a simple word for the transient of wireless driven things of the internet and the data center for a smaller more complex driven form of one os per many devices meaning one set of instructions like a web hosting instruction per
8026 part of a room is a frame of sorts part of a room is a frame of sorts for example the separation of data and the complied operation system could be an easier cloud to use meaning if the parts of any library of data has a role for the drive storage and which functions could be as simple as
8027 a travel cloud is a set of revolvin a travel cloud is a set of revolving ip addresses for data and servers
8028 a secure roaming cloud is a random a secure roaming cloud is a random set of revolving ip addresses for data and servers
8029 a secure lost cloud is a non revolv a secure lost cloud is a non revolving random resetting ip address for data and servers to help evade domain denial of service
8030 insufficient rights to claim as non insufficient rights to claim as non negligent for a purpose given is to declare a right for the damaged claim over any waiver of rights previously noted
8031 server over a system is a simple co server over a system is a simple configuration of one server per many parts and many redundant parts per many systems
8032 wrongful creation intent of ai and wrongful creation intent of ai and the false artificial intelligent proposal is simply a romantic novel
8033 to short the ai technology market i to short the ai technology market is a given rule of thumb of many
8034 alternative to ai is the instructio alternative to ai is the instructional applications ia and the provided instructions of a skynet like operation in a new meaning of the sense
8035 alternatives to artificially driven alternatives to artificially driven things are the things that are so important like the car and air planes or trains are simple pilot driven back up navigation
8036 the important things of non applied the important things of non applied artificial intelligence are to be noted meaning that there is a level to artificial intelligence that should not be applied perverted and abused
8037 positive nature is important in a r positive nature is important in a resolution for bad ai outcome and should be held responsible for its nature by the ai maker
8038 ai car insurance is the most positi ai car insurance is the most positive way for resolution

for bad ai outcome and should be held responsible for its unnatural nature
8039 ai drone insurance is the most posi ai drone insurance is the most positive way for resolution for bad ai outcome and should be held responsible for its unnatural nature
8040 artificial intelligence and learnin artificial intelligence and learning aerial and ground drone is a bot operated drone that is computed to navigate and report with a prepared version of a given set of scenarios
8041 artificial intelligence and learnin artificial intelligence and learning aerial marine and ground war drone is a bot operated drone that is computed to navigate and report with a prepared version of a given set of scenarios
8042 stealth artificial intelligence and stealth artificial intelligence and learning aerial marine and ground war drone is a bot operated drone that is computed to navigate and report with a prepared version of a given set of scenarios
8043 search and rescue ai maritime drone search and rescue ai maritime drone artificial intelligence and learning aerial marine and ground drone is a bot operated drone that is computed to navigate and report with a prepared version of a given set of scenarios
8044 optical calculation is a step in th optical calculation is a step in the optical cpu with a transposed availability to calculate a problem in a scenario of motion as opposed to a stationary circuit
8045 looping optical calculation is a st looping optical calculation is a step in the optical cpu with a transposed availability to calculate a problem in a scenario of motion as opposed to a stationary circuit
8046 multiple cycles looping optical cal multiple cycles looping optical calculation is a step in the optical cpu with a transposed availability to calculate a problem in a scenario of motion as opposed to a stationary circuit
8047 virtual transistors in optical thre virtual transistors in optical thread translated into a code specific processing object for an optical cpu
8048 optical processing language is the optical processing language is the binary equal to central processing unit code of cubits as an optical cpu
8049 magnetic optical processor is a sim magnetic optical processor is a simple name for the magnetic cubit optical media circuit written chip that is bound by optical processing language and is the binary equal to central processing unit code of cubits as an optical processor
8050 magnetic object written chip is a s magnetic object written chip is a simple name for the magnetic cubit optically written chip that is bound by a processing language and is the binary equal to central processing unit code of cubits as an circuit processor
8051 optically written magnetic object i optically written magnetic object is a simple name for the laser written optically printed chip as an circuit processor as opposed to a diffused optically printed chip (august
8052 optically written object blank is a optically written object blank is a simple name for the laser written optically printed chip blank similar to a optical media disc as an circuit processor as opposed to a diffused optically printed chip (august
8053 portable optically written object b portable optically written object blank similar to a optical media disc as an circuit processor as opposed to a diffused optically printed chip (august
8054 object writer for the portable opti object writer for the portable optically written object

blank similar to a optical media disc as an circuit processor as opposed to a diffused optically printed chip will bring circuit printing to the household markets (august

8055 paid instructions for the object wr paid instructions for the object writer for the portable optically written object blank similar to a optical media disc as an circuit processor as opposed to a diffused optically printed chip will bring circuit printing to the household diy markets (augu

8056 many optical circuit objects in ord many optical circuit objects in order on a server bed of input ports meaning a group of objects working as system on chips as portable optically written object blank similar to a optical media disc as an circuit processor as opposed to a diffused optical

8057 optical circuit focus range is the optical circuit focus range is the measurement of circuits in an optically written object blank similar to a optical media disc as an circuit processor as opposed to a diffused optically printed chip will bring circuit printing to the household diy marke

8058 in board solid state threading is t in board solid state threading is the path of computational signals traveling inside the server board for faster translation computations and processing

8059 board solid state hyperthreading i board solid state hyperthreading is the path of computational signals traveling inside the server board for faster translation computations and processing

8060 hyper threading cable is a multiple hyper threading cable is a multiple lane cable that transports signals into and from a source to another receiver

8061 hyper threading fiber optic cable i hyper threading fiber optic cable is a multiple lane cable that transports signals into and from a source to another receiver

8062 hyper threading usb cable is a mult hyper threading usb cable is a multiple lane cable that transports signals into and from a source to another receiver

8063 wireless hard drive is a two step d wireless hard drive is a two step data storage drive and wireless adapter that transports signals into and from a source to another receiver

8064 sd wireless hard drive system is a sd wireless hard drive system is a two step data storage drive and wireless adapter that transports signals into and from a source to another receiver

8065 multiplied wireless hard drive rout multiplied wireless hard drive router is a multiple signal transporter and encoder with a specified multiple places of destination

8066 multiplied wireless hd receiver is multiplied wireless hd receiver is a multiple signal wireless adapter that transports many different signals into and from a source to another router with specified multiple places in destination

8067 wireless storage network is a non p wireless storage network is a non processing cache only system of storage drives

8068 wireless computational network proc wireless computational network processing only system of processing

8069 computational network processing on computational network processing only system of scripted processing

8070 allotted memory network is a shared allotted memory network is a shared system of cache and paging system that shares a specified amount of links in memory disc space

8071 home to cell to satellite routers c home to cell to satellite routers cell branches that hold a message in the packet prefix or suffix that extends the direction of cellular channels that focus to the nearest cell reach to the nearest satellite for convenience and speed

8072 low density performance scale proce low density performance scale processing is the number in processors compared to size

8073 high density complex scale processi high density complex scale processing is the number in processors compared to size

8074 high density performance scale proc high density performance scale processing is the ratio number in processors compared to scheme of arrangements and clusters in ram and transistors a

8075 category chips are purpose driven c category chips are purpose driven chips with that program and task at mind

8076 creative category chips are purpose creative category chips are purpose driven chips with that program and task at mind

8077 calc category chips are purpose dri calc category chips are purpose driven chips with that program and task at mind

8078 category add on cards are purpose d category add on cards are purpose driven chips with that program and task at mind

8079 creative category add on cards are creative category add on cards are purpose driven chips with that program and task at mind

8080 calc category add on cards are purp calc category add on cards are purpose driven chips with that program and task at mind

8081 multiple category chips are purpose multiple category chips are purpose driven chips with that program and task at mind

8082 program categories for specified ca program categories for specified category chips are purpose driven chips with that application software program and task at mind

8083 calc program categories for specifi calc program categories for specified category chips are purpose driven chips with number and physics application software program and task at mind

8084 creative program categories for spe creative program categories for specified category chips are purpose driven chips with hypothetical and geometry application software program and task at mind

8085 satellite connection grid is a conn satellite connection grid is a connected alliance of satellites that work and process things like communication together as a whole network

8086 paid satellite data connection grid paid satellite data connection grid network is a connected alliance of satellites that work and process things like communication together as a whole network

8087 satellite data packet grid prefix a satellite data packet grid prefix and paid satellite connection grid network is a connected alliance of satellites that work and process things like communication together as a whole network with the ability to send packets to and from each other

8088 paid satellite data packet grid pre paid satellite data packet grid prefix network branches and paid satellite connection grid network is a connected alliance of satellites that work and process things like communication together as a whole network with the ability to send packets to and f

8089 paid satellite data packet grid pre paid satellite data packet grid prefix and paid satellite connection grid network is a connected alliance of satellites that work and process things like communication together as a whole network with the ability to send packets to and from each other

8090 satellite to cell branches are cell satellite to cell branches are cellular channels that focus to the nearest cell reach to the nearest satellite for convenience and speed

8091 home router to cell to satellite pa home router to cell to satellite paid satellite connection grid network is a connected alliance of satellites that work and process things like communication together as a whole network with the ability to send packets to and from each other

8092 diesel and ethel sodium nitrate fue diesel and ethel sodium nitrate fuel for diesel for trucks tractor trailers and cars as well as airplanes and drones

8093 compressed alcoholasgas engine is compressed alcoholasgas engine is a compromised vapor ignition engine for trucks tractor trailers and cars as well as airplanes and drones

8094 in a compressed alcoholasgas engi in a compressed alcoholasgas engine a compromised vapor ignition fuel injector is a prepared measure of vapor agitator to make a fine atomized vapor to burn and combust for trucks tractor trailers and cars as well as airplanes and drones

8095 agitated vapor fuel is the closest agitated vapor fuel is the closest to flash point in any compound that would be important in a compressed alcoholasgas engine a compromised vapor ignition fuel injector is a prepared measure of vapor agitator to make a fine atomized vapor to burn and c

8096 compromised fuel aerosol is premea compromised fuel aerosol is premeasured agitated vapor fuel and is the closest to flash point in any compound that would be important in a compressed alcoholasgas engine a compromised vapor ignition fuel injector is a prepared measure of vapor agitato

8097 compromised fuel aerosol engine wil compromised fuel aerosol engine will use premeasured agitated vapor fuel and is the closest to flash point in any compound that would be important in a compressed alcoholasgas engine a compromised vapor ignition fuel injector is a prepared measure of

8098 atomized and vapor hybrid engine wi atomized and vapor hybrid engine will use premeasured agitated vapor fuel and is the closest to flash point in any compound that would be important in a compressed alcoholasgas engine a compromised vapor ignition fuel injector is a prepared measure of

8099 atomized fuel and vapor hybrid engi atomized fuel and vapor hybrid engine will use premeasured agitated vapor fuel and is the closest to flash point in any compound that would be important in a compressed alcoholasgas engine a compromised vapor ignition fuel injector is a prepared measu

8100 smart fuel is pre respirated gasol smart fuel is pre respirated gasoline in a volatile vapor to burn and combust for trucks tractor trailers and cars as well as airplanes and drones

8101 pre respirated gasoline in a volat pre respirated gasoline in a volatile vapor calculator that finds the fuels top flash point automatically and in a few cycles adjusts it to any gas for the engine

8102 vapor compressor is a exciter and p vapor compressor is a exciter and pre respirator for gasoline in a volatile vapor calculator that finds the fuels top flash point automatically and in a few cycles adjusts it to any gas for the engine

8103 smart fuel system in conjunction wi smart fuel system in conjunction with vapor compressor is an exciter and pre respirated gasoline fuel in a volitile vapor calculator that finds the mixes top flash point automatically and in a few cycles adjusts it to any gas for the proper efficiency

8104 law bureau of investigation to seek law bureau of investigation to seek and find corruption in government would be a branch of law directed at politics and make a political transition from the public service to the private administration of law and free us from pay offs and contract breaks

8105 virtual search of power is a learni virtual search of power is a learning method to compute the most powerful solution to run tomorrows cars and every day engines motors and energy motions of any kind while measuring the possibilities of the content to make that energy and the worth of the

8106 software that looks and learns the software that looks and learns the cost of a fuel or substance and compares that to a starch and the mineral to make that energy with the combinations of other properties of value in a computational way of virtual search of power is a learning method to

8107 virtual search of power library for virtual search of power library for a data start with software that looks and learns the cost of a fuel or substance and compares that to a starch and the mineral to make that energy with the combinations of other properties of value in a computational w

8108 bureau of lawyer investigation is a bureau of lawyer investigation is a simple investigation to condone or condemn the laws by a specific lawyer

8109 large scale software overwrites are large scale software overwrites are the overwritten os and programs apps and unlocked formats of devices and the user agreement broken by opposing software and reclaiming a device based on ownership

8110 drone operating system and the libr drone operating system and the library functions of that data

8111 virtual drone navigational operatin virtual drone navigational operating system and the library functions of that data including geo navigation satellite location and local weather conditions as in corporate in a system of methods that conclude a operation inside a alternate virtual use (c

8112 a global connected cloud resource o a global connected cloud resource of data and targets to compromise the enemy and their assets as a concluded end to a means the satellites and the data location in a sense of war over internet protocol

8113 virtual calculated energy verses fo virtual calculated energy verses for profit formula table software is a search and input library of values and methods of constants and catalysts that react with one another in a virtual unreal way of study to mathematically search and find any such data

8114 wireless through gateway ping route wireless through gateway ping router is a device that allows computers to connect and share files thru software and a single router essentially a very small internet by wifi network hardware and software

8115 wireless computer to wireless compu wireless computer to wireless computer

8116 wireless phone to wireless phone di wireless phone to wireless phone direct

8117 multiple external modular format is multiple external modular format is a hardware driven by driver format that excludes the chassis location and provides ports that transfer the data in and out in thread cables

8118 hiroshima latin invasion spa hiroshima latin invasion spawned by leftists

8119 data center secure wireless multipl data center secure wireless multiple external modular format is a hardware driven by driver format that excludes the chassis location and provides ports that transfer the data in and out wireless with a header data packet that includes a specific device
8120 multi signal wireless receiver is a multi signal wireless receiver is a receiver for multiple managed wireless signals and incorporating wireless devices
8121 processor driven wifi signal receiv processor driven wifi signal receiver for multiple managed wireless signals and incorporating wireless devices processors and computations as a whole in a multitude of receiving and processing of a signal
8122 mosquito control tabs for large pon mosquito control tabs for large ponds
8123 multiple conjoined boards by os is multiple conjoined boards by os is a group of boards that are essentially separated working cells that are joined by operating system
8124 wireless multiple conjoined boards wireless multiple conjoined boards by os is a group of boards that are essentially separated working cells that are joined by operating system without wires
8125 to learn sharing software is a prog to learn sharing software is a program or app that accepts multiple users in order to learn and teach verses one mouse and one input at a time
8126 multiple users and rules software i multiple users and rules software is a program or app that accepts multiple users in order to work and perform as a team in one mission with rules of hierarchy and ranking
8127 boronmagnesiumsulfate boronmagnesiumsulfate
8128 sodium carbonite aluminum sodium ca sodium carbonite aluminum sodium carbonite
8129 zirconhydroxy isolated layer is a l zirconhydroxy isolated layer is a layer of zirconium which is a silicon that is more insulating and less thermal conductive than diamond carbonate this is good for making three dimensional chips and operators
8130 subtractively printed zirconhydro subtractively printed zirconhydroxy or photo laser cut zirconhydroxy isolated layer is a layer of zirconium which is a silicon that is more insulating and less thermal conductive than diamond carbonate this is good for making three dimensional chips an
8131 subtractively printed photo laser subtractively printed photo laser cut layer is a layer of conductor or isolate r which is a cut or etched by a time generated photo of energy such as burning or to degrade the photo or image into something or out of something which is good for making t
8132 lcd stencil lens for pi co and nano lcd stencil lens for pi co and nano active subtractively printed photo laser is a laser stencil photo object to print subtractively with mediums
8133 stencil graphic laser printer is a stencil graphic laser printer is a pico and nano active subtractively printed photo laser stencil photo object to print and subtractively with medium
8134 stencil graphic laser printer softw stencil graphic laser printer software is the software for the stencil graphic laser printer is a pico and nano active subtractively printed photo laser stencil grid
8135 three dimensional stencil graphic l three dimensional stencil graphic laser printer is a pico and nano active subtractively printed photo laser is a laser stencil photo object to print and subtractively with medium for example to think that a grid of pico layered and formed photo tim
8136 gold chromatic building microproces gold chromatic building microprocessors is a

part of the three dimensional stencil graphic laser printer and is a pico and nano active subtractively printed photo laser is a laser stencil photo object to print and subtractively with medium for examp

8137 silicachromaticbuildingmicropro silicachromaticbuildingmicroprocessors

8138 molecular photo printing said to us molecular photo printing said to use small stencils to print smaller circuits in an adjusted dimension with an emulsion photo fusion process

8139 printing focus stencil grid is a la printing focus stencil grid is a large grid of pixels that when compensated or reflected into a smaller size they connect and with reason to provide connections

8140 reversed printing focus stencil gri reversed printing focus stencil grid is a large grid of pixels that when compensated or reflected into a smaller size they connect and conduct as a circuit

8141 exterior liquid cooled computing co exterior liquid cooled computing components such as microprocessors used in cell towers and more memory and other actively cooled in a climate controlled efficiency for higher performance

8142 exterior <span>meaning out side in exterior <span>meaning out side in atmosphere </span>liquid cooled motherboard is an actively cooled in a climate controlled efficiency way of cooling for higher performance

8143 exterior meaning out side in atmosp exterior meaning out side in atmosphere liquid cooled memory is an actively cooled in a climate controlled efficiency way of cooling for higher performance

8144 exterior in the elements liquid coo exterior in the elements liquid cooled memory is actively cooled liquid thermal contact that aids in temperature adjustments by thermal liquid conduction

8145 hard drive readout is a simple lcd hard drive readout is a simple lcd or led read out of status on hard drive functionality

8146 memory led readout is a simple lcd memory led readout is a simple lcd or led read out of status on hard drive functionality

8147 add hardware wizard with drivers an add hardware wizard with drivers and more is a simple unique way to pre initialize the moment of pre install with how to and pre installed drivers

8148 gpu readout is a simple lcd or led gpu readout is a simple lcd or led read out of status on gpu for reference functionality

8149 company compatible hardware for ref company compatible hardware for reference functionality is another way of saying that the oem source may be compatible with a company when forming an alliance in partnership and software hardware compatibility meaning in another way more universal compon

8150 page switch browser plugin is a so page switch browser plugin is a software internet or mobile web interface that takes large tall pages that run on and on and divides them into smaller and easier to download workable pages by splitting them into different views of minor pages like a tre

8151 personal data storage software is a personal data storage software is a way to keep the original paper mail copied and safe off line or on line in a digital world while accessing the properties of print and scan a need to fax and forward to any service like united states postal service and

8152 system on chip product foundation i system on chip product foundation is the start of a new cloud format far from large servers and server racks we enter the card based system of scrolling wall panels and more
8153 system on chip wall mount boards an system on chip wall mount boards and large card input panels
8154 system on chip wall mount boards an system on chip wall mount boards and large card input panels that move
8155 system on chip plug and play grid a system on chip plug and play grid and processing arrangement of network wall mount boards
8156 multiple oi protocol router board i multiple oi protocol router board is an important part of information in and out of any given system on chip wall mounting moving input unit this is the protocol that moves the data in and out of the section per multitude of processing systems on one wal
8157 embedded access interface in a coll embedded access interface in a collection of system on chips code is a data in and out of the section per multitude of processing systems on one wall board
8158 wireless access soc is a code acces wireless access soc is a code access by wifi or wirelessethernet processing
8159 soc foundation power by usb data by soc foundation power by usb data by usb on board ram on board processor hard drive by compact flash made to run programmable applications
8160 wifi server foundation power by usb wifi server foundation power by usb data by usb on board ram on board processor hard drive by compact flash made to run programmable applications with the access of wifi integrated
8161 system on chip server foundation po system on chip server foundation power by usb data by usb on board ram on board processor hard drive by compact flash made to run programmable applications with the access of wifi integrated
8162 wifi alternating form access of wif wifi alternating form access of wifi integrated is a triplet form of one send and one receive and one group of process as a whole of one in any open signals
8163 a group of any available open form a group of any available open form of one send and one receive and one group of process as a whole of one in any open signals
8164 certified and notary of email is a certified and notary of email is a service of notary in an email record to and from clients
8165 government serial digital copy nota government serial digital copy notary document number registry is a general document of recording in a digital sense
8166 serial digital copy document number serial digital copy document number registry is a general document of recording in a digital sense
8167 medical serial digital copy documen medical serial digital copy document number registry is a general document of recording in a digital sense
8168 education document server serial di education document server serial digital copy document number registry is a general document of recording in a digital sense
8169 business document registry number a business document registry number and document server serial digital copy document number registry is a general document of recording in a digital sense
8170 auto pc number document registry nu auto pc number document registry number and

document server serial digital copy document number registry is a general document of recording in a digital sense for the personal computer and information of scientific origin
8171 email ping record notary registry n email ping record notary registry number and information of legal origin
8172 phone ping record notary registry n phone ping record notary registry number and information of legal origin
8173 ocr cursive per word and the fewest ocr cursive per word and the fewest changes
8174 gps road lanes are the global posit gps road lanes are the global positioning satellites way of making lanes for flying and navigating instead of yellow white stripes there could be pre designated routes by height from and in what direction
8175 gps aerial drone road lanes are the gps aerial drone road lanes are the global positioning satellites way of making lanes for flying and navigating instead of yellow white stripes there could be pre designated routes by height from and in what direction
8176 gps aerial lanes for drones are the gps aerial lanes for drones are the global positioning satellites way of making lanes for flying and navigating instead of yellow white stripes there could be pre designated routes by height from and in what direction
8177 gps aerial lanes for airplanes are gps aerial lanes for airplanes are the global positioning satellites way of making lanes for flying and navigating instead of yellow white stripes there could be pre designated routes by height from and in what direction
8178 global positioning satellite grid o global positioning satellite grid of ownership including place in physics natural and vertical horizontal and down
8179 gps fishing zone global positioning gps fishing zone global positioning satellite grid of ownership including place in physics natural and vertical horizontal and down
8180 annotation physics spatial grid inc annotation physics spatial grid including place in physics natural and vertical horizontal and down mapping by global positioning satellite government or private designation place in space
8181 dual annotation physics spatial gri dual annotation physics spatial grid including place in physics natural and vertical horizontal and down from two origins
8182 gps navigational property and the c gps navigational property and the confines of that d property
8183 adjustable format video is a hardwa adjustable format video is a hardware rendering device application that runs a basic group of files a specific way to improve the display of any movie or music and other data projects simply said you put your project in basic adjustable format and the vi
8184 military reverse calvin cycle air p military reverse calvin cycle air purifiers
8185 bids and sales for legitimate futur bids and sales for legitimate futures in project performance is the sale of a large private job for any work made in a presales term
8186 satellite negotiations network is a satellite negotiations network is a paid environment for services in the satellite atmosphere to make money and profit
8187 cellular foundation negotiation net cellular foundation negotiation network is a real chance of service to any known location by selling the use of a cellular network to any under written provider for negotiation and sales
8188 hybrid connected communication netw hybrid connected communication network is a real chance of service to any known location by selling the use of a cellular to satellite hybrid service network to any under written provider for negotiation and sales

8189 a reverse reflective tunnel that ma a reverse reflective tunnel that magnifies the light and graduates the source to maximize the solar energy post
8190 a energy center or building with ma a energy center or building with many focused solar generators that reverse reflective tunnel that magnifies the light and graduates the source to maximize the solar energy post
8191 ai is named wrong you have to take ai is named wrong you have to take more into consideration like the answer not the truth of the question left and right is the asymmetrical processing
8192 micro alternating circuit battery i micro alternating circuit battery is a circuit that recycles itself with current
8193 processor micro circuit battery is processor micro circuit battery is a circuit cell that holds current
8194 acid alkaline printed chips in a di acid alkaline printed chips in a diffused solution to compute as a battery on chip
8195 laser printed levels of circuits an laser printed levels of circuits and multiple cured solvents as circuits layers laser printed chips in a diffused solution to compute as a chip
8196 ultra violet laser printed levels o ultra violet laser printed levels of circuits and multiple uv cured solvents as circuits layers laser printed chips in a diffused solution to compute as a chip
8197 laser printed levels of circuits an laser printed levels of circuits and multiple photo sensitive cured solvents as circuits layers laser printed chips in a diffused solution to compute as a chip
8198 perpendicular laser printed levels perpendicular laser printed levels of circuits processors and memory in multiple photo sensitive cured solvents as circuits layers laser printed chips in a diffused solution to compute as a chip
8199 a photo reactive multiple element f a photo reactive multiple element formula of printing materials for perpendicular laser printed levels of circuits processors and memory in multiple photo sensitive cured solvents as circuits layers laser printed chips in a diffused solution to compute a
8200 printing materials for perpendicula printing materials for perpendicular laser printed levels of circuits processors and memory in multiple photo sensitive cured solvents as circuits layers laser printed chips in a diffused solution to compute as a chip in a series of different elements (c
8201 vertical clamp socket for chip copy vertical clamp socket for chip
8202 five sided computer chip for comput five sided computer chip for computations
8203 sided computer chip for computation sided computer chip for computations
8204 sided computer chip for computation sided computer chip for computations and stacking arrangements for chip processing
8205 pico nano voxel and elemental compo pico nano voxel and elemental compounds for chip processing printing
8206 conductive and positive pico nano conductive and positive pico nano voxel and elemental compounds for chip processing printingin three dimensions
8207 non conductive and negative pico na non conductive and negative pico nano voxel and elemental compounds for chip processing printingin three dimensions
8208 non conductive silica solvent whit non conductive silica solvent white space and

negative pico nano voxel and elemental compounds for chip processing printing in three dimensions
8209 conductive gold and mineral solven conductive gold and mineral solvent conductors in a positive pico nano voxel and elemental compound form for three dimensional chip processing printing
8210 empty space for looped inside linki empty space for looped inside linking conductive vector for making a place for conductors in pico nano voxel and elemental compounds for chip processing printing in three dimensions
8211 connection vectors and the empty sp connection vectors and the empty space for looped inside linking conductive vector for making a place for conductors in pico nano voxel and elemental compounds for chip processing printing in three dimensions
8212 software that makes connection vect software that makes connection vectors conductors in pico nano voxel and elemental compounds for chip processing printing in three dimensions
8213 the intellectual property manageme the intellectual property management office and large document record for keeping trade secrets and patents safe and secured by named ownership
8214 spiral compressed reflective fiber spiral compressed reflective fiber optical cable
8215 spiral compound reflective receiver spiral compound reflective receiver decoder processor that reads reflective signals in fiber optic signals
8216 spiral compound reflective sending spiral compound reflective sending out encoder processor that codes reflective signals in fiber optic signals
8217 spiral fiberoptic splicer device a spiral fiberoptic splicer device and the markings that make a reading splicer obtain the proper place in the cable to splice or loop into with precision and accuracy for less signal loss
8218 exchangeable and upgrade able camer exchangeable and upgrade able camera chassis and processor models
8219 exchangeable and upgrade able displ exchangeable and upgrade able displays and monitors for in chassis computing extensions
8220 exchangeable and upgrade able lapto exchangeable and upgrade able laptop models and ports processing addon
8221 exchangeable phone card migration s exchangeable phone card migration software and compatible memory chips
8222 report service of citizenship is a report service of citizenship is a small personalized membership to pay taxes for a limited trade for temporary immunity
8223 remote controlled automobile air co remote controlled automobile air conditioning
8224 advanced accessible wheel chair rob advanced accessible wheel chair robotics for disabled mobility and the move and position library for automation in a standard uniform parking place
8225 sewage removable ultrabiotics for sewage removable ultrabiotics for water and soil in a microbeenviroment as lead neutralizers and ph balance changers
8226 manufacturer electric motor recycle manufacturer electric motor recycle programs and incentives for autos and parts reclamation
8227 modified hard drive control and add modified hard drive control and add on secondary hard drive chips for cache and indexing

8228 air plane antivirus software system air plane antivirus software system for corrupted parts and software integrity
8229 part due date is a manufacturers re part due date is a manufacturers recall date for part services on life threatening parts and mandatory services made due
8230 fiber optic reflective turn connect fiber optic reflective turn connection in data to let a signal repeat and split in order to go around an object of area
8231 service time out price cut is a ser service time out price cut is a service interruption cost cut for minute by minute operations and service as software companies verses outage and payment service
8232 counter attack outage service are c counter attack outage service are companies as paid ddos retaliations and defense mercenaries that defend and log corporate and government interruptions and attacks like life threatening power outages in iot and flight control centers
8233 data war science is the study of wa data war science is the study of war over internet mobile and satellite
8234 data economics and the cost of info data economics and the cost of information in today's life and the sum of what it all concludes to move forward every day
8235 data tax and the data trade commiss data tax and the data trade commission and the unequal differences and adjustments in an administration of machines and cost to service
8236 security and the possible chance of security and the possible chance of corruption during a data audit is the algorithm that registers a pattern in change
8237 trends and the possible chance of p trends and the possible chance of popular opinion statistical studies in acute product research in an algorithm bot could improve more future products
8238 seek and find algorithm bot is a pr seek and find algorithm bot is a programmable model of information search and find where the first variable is combine able with more than one conjunction
8239 bureaucratic reset is the full dist bureaucratic reset is the full distress of laws of a previous state to reset the laws from another state as a legal situation similar to the gross loss in california
8240 computer system made operating code computer system made operating code in a chain of environment variables is a chain of parts that work out of symbiotic relationship like an organism
8241 a chain of parts that make the enti a chain of parts that make the entire computational platform accelerate instead of parallel they add on in chain and improve with every multiplying part
8242 computer add on theory against a pa computer add on theory against a parallel world and the core of a internet of things that don't coincide with parallel but an opposite meaning
8243 quantum raid processing is a sum of quantum raid processing is a sum of physical non theoretical group of computers that make a mission of processing
8244 quantum raid memory stack is a serv quantum raid memory stack is a service of memory or storage accessible for computing information on a group scale
8245 quantum raid service is the entire quantum raid service is the entire process of memory storage and connective processing in an entirety of a system
8246 quantum service scale is the measur quantum service scale is the measure of quantum raid service and is the entire process of memory storage and connective processing in an

entirety of a system

8247 laser cut cpu chri laser cut cpu

8248 trapezoid zirconium (cubic zircon) trapezoid zirconium (cubic zircon) laser focus angle is a use of chemically cooked carbon cut to a shape that makes a reflective magnified focus of light energy or mass

8249 spiral zirconium (cubic zircon) las spiral zirconium (cubic zircon) laser focus angle is a use of chemically cooked carbon cut to a shape that makes a reflective magnified focus of light energy or mass

8250 spectral reflective scale and the c spectral reflective scale and the contributing spiral zirconium (cubic zircon) laser focus angle is a use of chemically cooked carbon cut to a shape that makes a reflective magnified focus of light energy or mass

8251 to define the scale of reflective f to define the scale of reflective focus and light combined in an energy spent verses the energy obtained is a study of solar refraction

8252 the process of making electricity w the process of making electricity with the mention of reflective focus and light combined in an energy spent verses the energy obtained is a study of solar refraction and to incorporate the less to make more is the mission of solar energy recycle as well

8253 to magnify and amplify the process to magnify and amplify the process of making electricity with the mention of reflective focus and light combined in an energy spent verses the energy obtained is a study of solar refraction and to incorporate the less to make more is the mission of solar

8254 solar recycle center is a place tha solar recycle center is a place that magnify and amplify the process of making electricity with the mention of reflective focus and light combined in an energy spent verses the energy obtained is a study of solar refraction and to incorporate the less to

8255 to artificially cross dna and uncro to artificially cross dna and uncross dna is not a gain or operation i myself would condone utility

8256 an artistic judgment to copy and cu an artistic judgment to copy and cure is the obvious mission of any nucleotide printed microorganism utility

8257 dna and nucleotide historical libra dna and nucleotide historical library and ownership per dna finger print solution utility

8258 software run program applications f software run program applications for printers that uses nano / pico / triad mixed and formulated biochemical nucleotide to replicate on a recurring smaller intent to cure cancer and disease utility formulated biochemical nucleotide

8259 insulated chip levels made from of insulated chip levels made from of with a coherence of any insulation method of stacking horizontal or vertical chip organization to build a larger chip also said as to make a non conductive layer with small outer inner conductive measures while operatio

8260 vertical threads and the property o vertical threads and the property of stacking layers of chips utility

8261 watch smart phones with solar panel watch smart phones with solar panels utility

8262 data board is a separated connectio data board is a separated connection of data from power by changing the data ports to optical and the power ports to electrical for a faster schema utility

8263 solid data board is a separated con solid data board is a separated connection of data from power by changing the data ports to solid state and the power ports to electrical for a faster schema utility

8264 electronic power and signal with fi electronic power and signal with fiber optical data and threads as well as solid state memory as threads and data signal carriers and power conduction in a computational system board for interseeding connections and processing nodes util

8265 add in transformer for data that pr add in transformer for data that precedes the cpu if there is a optical data connection to lead to a processing opposing in signal operations utility

8266 add in exporter for data that supe add in exporter for data that supersedes the cpu if there is a optical data connection to lead to a processing opposing in signal operations utility

8267 add in transforming chip for data t add in transforming chip for data that uses two different kinds of bios and can process in two different signals like optical and electronic noise utility

8268 ability of many sets of bios and th ability of many sets of bios and their respective parts working together in a system optical magnetic data and electronic utility

8269 bios rules and operations script in bios rules and operations script in a working environment over of many other bios and their respective parts working together in a system utility

8270 water proof smart shoe is a shoe wi water proof smart shoe is a shoe with calculative software connected or embedded with data out put in a water proof situation with size of mechanics and memory instances utility

8271 wifi gaming smart shoe is a shoe wi wifi gaming smart shoe is a shoe with calculative software connected or embedded with data out put in a gaming or practice situation with size of mechanics and memory instances utility

8272 sport smart shoe is a shoe with cal sport smart shoe is a shoe with calculative software connected or embedded with data out put in a gaming or practice situation with size of mechanics and memory instances utility

8273 patent cloud and search platform f patent cloud and search platform for ecommerce utility

8274 cloud and search platform for ecom cloud and search platform for ecommerce utility

8275 government cellular service for sec government cellular service for security purposes utility

8276 government satellite combat service government satellite combat service for security purposes utility

8277 soldier watch makes the watching of soldier watch makes the watching of a soldier in combat a function of a matter of life or death the service would follow a soldier into and out of a combat zone and record all of the data of the battle in progress and keep record of the out comings as a

8278 student watch makes the watching of student watch makes the watching of a student in school a function of a matter of win or loose the service would measure a students rates and learning process and record all of the data of the experience utility

8279 clay building bricks recycled to r clay building bricks recycled to resolve ph balance in lead heavy ground as a counter product in a process of saturation utility

8280 high speed transcoding encoding st high speed transcoding encoding station is a fiber optical resolution station that transforms signals into a compressed code for travel into a

network utility
8281 high speed encryption station is a high speed encryption station is a fiber optical resolution station that transforms signals into a encryptedcode for travel into a network utility
8282 high speed compression station is a high speed compression station is a fiber optical resolution station that transforms signals into acompressed code for travel into a network utility
8283 high speed block transfer highway s high speed block transfer highway station is a fiber optical resolution station that transforms signals into a code for travel into a different network utility
8284 high speed aerospace statellite to high speed aerospace statellite to satellite to ground encrypted processed and compressed signal data station is a resolution station that transforms signals into aencrypted code for travel into a different network utility
8285 high speed sata gpu chip connection high speed sata gpu chip connections and formats utility
8286 high speed micro sd performance ch high speed micro sd performance chips are alternate and inclusive functioning chips in a ecosystem of a computer utility
8287 downloadable code for high speed m downloadable code for high speed micro sd performance chips utility
8288 a blank transistor chip that holds a blank transistor chip that holds no instructions and the user builds and makes the bios by code instructions and navigation paths utility
8289 many blank transistor chips that ho many blank transistor chips that holds no instructions and the user builds and makes the bios by code instructions and navigation paths to build a performance chip group with alternate and inclusive functioning chips in a ecosystem of a computer patent
8290 parallel many blank transistor chip parallel many blank transistor chips that holds no instructions and the user builds and makes the bios by code instructions and navigation paths to build a performance chip group with alternate and inclusive functioning chips in a ecosystem of a computer
8291 inprecievable compression is a un inprecievable compression is a un noticeable time difference loss to assist in compression and data lag of operations and conduction in code or conversion utility
8292 room focused energy is a large refl room focused energy is a large reflected system of cycles in the case that one or only a few light emitters generate a large system of a source of solar energy in amplification by reflection and the profit of energy is greater than the source patent abst
8293 formula for thought combination for formula for thought combination formula of commons unique and abnormal the theory is a function of indefinite sums and energy in the mass of that sum with the longevity of that same sum a + m = e (. {} over {}) %uxea {e} over {m} %uxe b {e%delta ^{}} ov
8294 autonomous software anti malware is autonomous software anti malware is the added safety measure of autonomous software security utility
8295 light turbo focused energy is a sma light turbo focused energy is a small reflected system of cycles in the case that one or only a few light emitters generate a stronger system of a source of solar energy in amplification by reflection and the profit of energy is greater than

the source p

8296 three dimensional tunnel light turb three dimensional tunnel light turbo focused energy is a small reflected system of cycles in the case that one or only a few light emitters generate a stronger system of a source of solar energy in amplification by reflection and the profit of energy is

8297 a one way mirror or rather said as a one way mirror or rather said as a one sided reflective one side transparent solar energy glass window for building a reflective solar tunnel utility

8298 spiral focus energy is a one way mi spiral focus energy is a one way mirror or rather said as a one sided reflective one side transparent solar energy glass window for building a reflective solar tunnel spirally to amplify the source utility

8299 square focus energy is a one way mi square focus energy is a one way mirror or rather said as a one sided reflective one side transparent solar energy glass window for building a reflective solar tunnel square to amplify the source utility

8300 cone focus energy is a one way mirr cone focus energy is a one way mirror or rather said as a one sided reflective one side transparent solar energy glass window for building a reflective solar tunnel cone to amplify the source utility

8301 microwave fuse that generates solar microwave fuse that generates solar electric energy is a mini microwave signal inside a one way mirror sphere or box with receiving solar energy cells on the outside inside another mini sphere feeding another sphere with one way mirror sphere or box with

8302 immigrated income revenue service i immigrated income revenue service is a service devoted to helping immigrants over come short falls and improve the lives of immigrants and others who are incontinent of taxes as language and citizenship problems utility

8303 microwave ecology and the study of microwave ecology and the study of light particles and oxygen from microwave stable and unstable optical combustion utility

8304 microwave combustion microwave fl microwave combustion microwave flash point in any operation as an ignition for combustion is the newest resolution here for energy. utility

8305 microwave vacuum combustion microwa microwave vacuum combustion microwave flash point vacuum in any operation as an ignition for combustion is the newest resolution here for energy or force of energy utility

8306 satellite directional range acceler satellite directional range accelerations when the area of interest is incorporated into a conglomerate signal of area in data within a similar location where as the area of interest is in a geopacket prefix for code accelerations

8307 gps pi navigation access is fractio gps pi navigation access is fractional pi satellite directional range accelerations when the area of interest is incorporated into a conglomerate signal of area in data within a similar location where as the area of interest is in a geopacket prefix for

8308 encrypted cellular service cop encrypted cellular service

8309 encrypted cellular application and encrypted cellular application and software

8310 mold detecting refrigerator copyrig mold detecting refrigerator

8311 optical micro lens reflector accele optical micro lens reflector accelerator for laser use and light particle compression

8312 tapered and threaded lens reflector tapered and threaded lens reflector accelerator for laser use and light particle compression

8313 dual reflective tapered and threade dual reflective tapered and threaded lens reflector accelerator for laser use and light particle compression
8314 tapered and threaded tube reflector tapered and threaded tube reflector accelerator for laser use and light particle compression
8315 dual reflective tapered and threade dual reflective tapered and threaded tube shaped reflector accelerator for laser use and light particle compression
8316 a optical jet effect of light parti a optical jet effect of light particle acceleration in many reflective tapered and threaded tube shaped reflector accelerator for laser use and light particle compression
8317 light particle compression by refle light particle compression by reflected layers of tubing and objects with alternating properties
8318 usb cpu input chri usb cpu input
8319 many sd usb cpu input board copyrig many sd usb cpu input board
8320 many exchangeable sd usb cpu input many exchangeable sd usb cpu input board
8321 d triplet pi ration map is the thre d triplet pi ration map is the three dimensional possible notation of travel in distance to be expected by any map
8322 gps d triplet pi ration is the rati gps d triplet pi ration is the rational notation of small physical or normal number physics computational relation to gps
8323 local and global participation in g local and global participation in gps d triplet pi ration is the dynamics of location for any known given computeable location
8324 rewriteable synthetic metal micro c rewriteable synthetic metal micro chips
8325 rewriteable solid state micro proce rewriteable solid state micro processing chips
8326 rewrite able solid state micro proc rewrite able solid state micro processing chips writer language for code inscribe processors
8327 rewrite able solid state micro proc rewrite able solid state micro processing chips writer drive for code inscribe processors
8328 gaming software for war data scienc gaming software for war data science scenarios and real world ai scripted drones
8329 data center and other data driven s data center and other data driven strategy operations for study gaming software for war data science and real world ai scripted drones
8330 ai war software from gaming softwar ai war software from gaming software for war data science strategy and ai scripted drones
8331 ai driving software derived from ga ai driving software derived from gaming software for ai scripted drones
8332 fiber optical conducting boards and fiber optical conducting boards and insert cards for processing in a optical environment of computations fiber embedded processing on gpu
8333 fiber optical conducting boards and fiber optical conducting boards and insert cards for processing in a optical environment of computations fiber embedded processing on cpu
8334 fiber embedded processing on sd int fiber embedded processing on sd interupt fiber optical conducting boards and insert cards for processing in a optical environment of computations fiber embedded processing on solid data pcie and also ssd
8335 compact optical processor signal tr compact optical processor signal translator for embedded fiber signal optical boards and analog solid data synthetic sd
8336 printed optical circuit board is an printed optical circuit board is an embedded fiber optical conducting signal board of calculation

8337 optical ram is an embedded fiber op optical ram is an embedded fiber optical conducting signal of nano batteries that display a function in a stored time for input into a board of calculation
8338 compact optical power supply is an compact optical power supply is an conducting signal of a source that changes a function in a stored time for input into a board of calculation
8339 board splice chip optical power swi board splice chip optical power switch is an alternating signal of a source that changes a function in a stored time for input into a board of calculation
8340 female directional optical transiti female directional optical transition connections are radial shaped to linear shaped optical data signal bridges
8341 male directional optical transition male directional optical transition connections are radial shaped to linear shaped optical data signal bridges with pins and replaceable optical connections
8342 boosting directional optical transi boosting directional optical transition connections are radial shaped to linear shaped optical data signal bridges with pins and replaceable optical connections with incorporating power operators
8343 optical signal break vector is a br optical signal break vector is a broken link detection location of directional optical transition connections are radial shaped to linear shaped optical data signal bridges with pins and replaceable optical connections with incorporating power operators
8344 bar coded location chips of a loop bar coded location chips of a loop series in fiber optical line to help find breaks and leaks as well as loss in splices
8345 vagrant law of profane loitering an vagrant law of profane loitering and illegal dwelling
8346 chip invitational design outsourcin chip invitational design outsourcing we print your chip for fees and rights
8347 advanced patent law is an exact and advanced patent law is an exact and more specific ownership control library of means and ownership of sciences
8348 a squared area of cascading increme a squared area of cascading increments funny but real to process code with measurement cascading increments a certain unit of measurement . or for processing electronic measurement using my certain unit of measurement data versus the shape of medi
8349 quantum frequency processing group quantum frequency processing group is a quantity calculated to process at a certain frequency when grouped
8350 embedded processor administration i embedded processor administration is an editable administrationto the processor and the instructions per core
8351 power over fiber and processors is power over fiber and processors is an acceleration method that injects processing on point of entry to point of process and back again
8352 exchangable gpu sockets on pcie boa exchangable gpu sockets on pcie boards
8353 a programmable frequency chip copyr a programmable frequency chip
8354 many signal code thread sequences c many signal code thread sequences
8355 miniture signal code thread sequenc miniture signal code thread sequences
8356 signal compression on thread theory signal compression on thread theory
8357 autophi on microsd autophi on sd co autophi on microsd autophi on sd
8358 intellegent software on device that intellegent software on device that adopts the connection and applies the executable in any form acceptable

8359 programmable intellegent software o programmable intellegent software on device that adopts the connection and writes the executable in any form acceptable
8360 computer phone accelerators are use computer phone accelerators are user identified and applied hand held computer operating system that connects on cellular networks verses in terms different than smart phone and includes navigational preprogramming and runs the use of accelerator defined
8361 adaptable software that is as large adaptable software that is as large as the device and adapts to the open ports and ability of any such connected processors and data controllers and data out ins
8362 there is a new compute of perceptua there is a new compute of perceptual computing that scales the periods to human values of time and complexity that a human will notice
8363 probable shutdown is a noted reason probable shutdown is a noted reason for legal and absent mission of right for action
8364 goal computing is the specific way goal computing is the specific way to orient methods of calling processing and machine learning
8365 magnified optical etching is a uniq magnified optical etching is a unique method of point and burn processor production of magnified focal processor
8366 optical subtractive transistor cons optical subtractive transistor construction is the process of removing parts to engineer a processing transistor
8367 atomic qubit library and annotation atomic qubit library and annotation of transistorized molecular instructions
8368 the attributes and schematic langua the attributes and schematic language of a library in any dynamic form needed to use the atomic qubit library and annotation of transistorized molecular instructions
8369 infadecimal and the rights of occu infadecimal and the rights of occurrences in the quantum physical atomic molecular library instructions for processing
8370 infamechanical is the infadecimal infamechanical is the infadecimal growth for fractions
8371 guardian drug rehab the eyeful watc guardian drug rehab the eyeful watch of a person who takes privlage and worth for a drug users well being from a set date and time to become drug free
8372 buy invent records request is the e buy invent records request is the entire record in pdf form of any document received to from the united states patent and trademark office as well as the united states of america office.
8373 do you know of patent infringement buy the right to follow suit and get a letter of permission to do so.
8374 scramble encrypted rearranged metho scramble encrypted rearranged methods of encryption for multiple channels of information bridge to access any such specific need or industry specific technology to share and improve that data share market of information is a mini expanded data exchange to
8375 electronic us treasury of banks and electronic us treasury of banks and commissions is a united states trade bank that works with commercial common banks to control federal trade and electronic fun d transfers of ownership
8376 optical disc cpu with functions tha optical disc cpu with functions that process like cubits as circuits less expensive circuit driven optical central processing un its and processing

written and then used in language circuits optical cpu
8377 optical disc cpu with multiple read optical disc cpu with multiple read and process lasers in rotation with the pre circuit adjustment
8378 optical disc cpu with multiple read optical disc cpu with multiple read and process lasers in rotation with multiple layers of architecture
8379 data tree multiplying data tree ass data tree multiplying data tree assistants data trees and solid state assistants the ability to toggle and make paths in order to compute the existing switches that need to be used and made off and on electricity gone computational simple but very early n
8380 detachable optical disc cpu with in detachable optical disc cpu with inter operable parts and changeable socket drives and bios configuration instructions to improve today's computations and sciences
8381 secondary leading and transferable secondary leading and transferable optical disc cpu with exchangeable cpu disc like a compact disc drive that holds memory and computations in and out
8382 embedded solution with optical disc embedded solution with optical disc cpu holding a fixed architecture for processing computations
8383 stacked solution with optical disc stacked solution with optical disc cpu holding a fixed architecture for processing computations
8384 data internet channel is a paid ser data internet channel is a paid service that originates from the phone company and media ties of per interest based data
8385 public data internet channel is a p public data internet channel is a public service for recreating the television radio and internet into a new all in one signal source
8386 data rating internet channel is a r data rating internet channel is a rating service that rates the restricted content of sexuality and parental guidance per internet channel
8387 internet channel and the process of internet channel and the process of data per industry and good keeping of that service including ratings infrastructure and cohesiveness
8388 government mimic bot is a robot sea government mimic bot is a robot search script that attaches to well known bots and reads the similar data
8389 police bot is a web bot and spider police bot is a web bot and spider searching index that finds negative platforms and collects data from their information
8390 the sum of all abstracts the sum of the sum of all abstracts the sum of all abstracts mathematical comp when does something come back thinking of a boomerang effect for example the thought of a real computation being inside a reals in set theory or what makes it so that the other sets of na
8391 internet data over radio is a speci internet data over radio is a specified sending and receiving data connection with radio signals in cubit data information
8392 encrypted internet data over radio encrypted internet data over radio is an encrypted cubit radio signal similar to cell tower signals only wider range and broadcast
8393 internet data over radio to wifi ro internet data over radio to wifi router and radio broadcast transceiver to make a wireless home network and a radio connection to the outside internet inside
8394 internet data over radio to wifi ro internet data over radio to wifi router and radio broadcast transceiver to make a wireless home network and a radio connection to the outside internet inside by phone cell tower

8395 supply and demand cost of inflation supply and demand cost of inflation control is a negative system of checks that control the situation of inflation and prices by market adjustment control
8396 weak influenza vaccine is a low tol weak influenza vaccine is a low tolerable flu virus antibody that works to cure by a combination of antimicrobial sodium compound and deceased virus
8397 long range electric transfer is an long range electric transfer is an energy solution that works on transportable mobile energy cells or battery arsenal by train truck or hard links
8398 community future investments are fu community future investments are fun ds for sustainable community management and the deprecation of environmental resources and state of improvements
8399 shared by payment learning by concl shared by payment learning by conclusion work and assembly ifs are a un limited function memory database is a software that records and keeps a library of operations for working scenarios and what to do if situations for robotic manufacturing learning
8400 shared by payment learning by concl shared by payment learning by conclusion vocabulary and so un d un limited function memory database is a software that records and keeps a library of operations for working scenarios and what to do if situations for learning and voice command software
8401 data connection radio signal channe data connection radio signal channel devices are a group of devices that send and receive data through channels in radio signals
8402 data connection radio signal channe data connection radio signal channel services are a group of devices for services that send and receive data trough channels in radio signals
8403 data connection radio signal channe data connection radio signal channel devices and integrated circuits translations with a long range radio data modulation in negative microwave nano and packet direction services dm send and digital call sign codes stored as verbal bios compressed commu
8404 synthetic sodium magnesium battery synthetic sodium magnesium battery technology to power large and expansive technology specific environments
8405 rail car battery generators that ge rail car battery generators that generate power by rolling on the track and keep it in an onboard cell for keeping and use
8406 car battery generators that generat car battery generators that generate power by rolling and then keep it in an on board cell for storage and reuse
8407 cycle recycle battery generators th cycle recycle battery generators that generate power by rolling and keep it in an on board cell for keeping and use
8408 wireless network of small devices t wireless network of small devices that operate together when the first available exchange of data is able to make any server operable at any given time is a wireless cloud of processing
8409 wireless packet direction is a pref wireless packet direction is a prefix of packet information that sends to a specific receiving point that may have a direct link to a subscriber
8410 wireless cloud router is a regulate wireless cloud router is a regulated document that works with multiple points of receiving and operation of sending as though there could be more than one wifi router commonly known as to operate together to send massive data and internet protocol signals
8411 on off magnetic electric generator on off magnetic electric generator that works as off

and on are sequentially put in motion to generate electricity in a magnetic field off center in a path of the coil and not in a jedliks motor inside but a path of logical magnetic cycles of coil along t

8412 a multiplied dimension cycle electr a multiplied dimension cycle electric generator can be used to create electricity from electricity in a cycle of recycle which is a motor moving and then after performance on the return of the motor action another set of electric commutative cycle returni

8413 cohesive layout of a multiplied dim cohesive layout of a multiplied dimension cycle electric generator can be used to create electricity from torque in a cycle of recycle which is a motor moving and then after performance on the return of the motor action another set of electric commutative

8414 to go backwards from computer histo to go backwards from computer history in a tech size reversed build a giant field of cohesive layout of a multiplied dimension cycle electric generator can be used to create electricity from torque in a cycle of recycle which is a motor moving and then af

8415 hardware built to compromise the en hardware built to compromise the energy of a force and generate a recycled electricity by making a circuit working on top of a previously expended torque for example a wheel with electromagnets stimulating another wheel with electromagnets that generate e

8416 to use a software to engineer a cir to use a software to engineer a circuit driven computational fractal energy and recycled electricity by commutative exciter paths simple z = z^ + c to generate electricity

8417 making electricity by using a recyc making electricity by using a recycle electric motor in a combination of pi and a combined fractal percentage of operation to work with things that are in motion to re generate electricity

8418 using an exciter or multiple excite using an exciter or multiple exciters as well as making electricity by using a recycle electric motor in a combination of pi and a combined fractal percentage of operation to work with things that are in motion to re generate electricity

8419 solid state cpu second cpu and thir solid state cpu second cpu and third cpu and plus as to write the chip with code instead of scoring the chip as photo

8420 to seek find and replace recolonize to seek find and replace recolonize organ specific micro cell stems to seek find replace the celluloid and kill eat or replace that cell or multitude of cells to cure cancers and other age syndromes immune deficiencies and or the many diseases that people

8421 solid state cpu software leased or solid state cpu software leased or paid by a fee as to pay for the concept with rights as implied intellectual property

8422 solid state cpu written using cubit solid state cpu written using cubit software that writes hardware

8423 solid state cpu second cpu and thir solid state cpu second cpu and third cpu and plus by pcie or alternate pipe like for example a tb processor in data cubits

8424 military device of statistical un i military device of statistical un its of motion use and location tracking

8425 police device of statistical un its police device of statistical un its of motion use and location tracking of effectiveness and location statistics

8426 public dentition device of statisti public dentition device of statistical un its of motion

use and location tracking cloud data hardware and software working together to correct and notify of the occurrences
8427 satellite target tracking system wi satellite target tracking system with unique boundaries and reports
8428 cellular communications target trac cellular communications target tracking system with unique boundaries and reports
8429 track paging system that contacts a track paging system that contacts an information base to report locations for automated data exchange and service
8430 information base is a data routing information base is a data routing system used to accelerate the location of data recipients by sub packet number and prefixes by area code
8431 user defined process and additions user defined process and additions user defined process and additions vague code complex statistical comparative triplet pixel of noise with pi computer arithmetic cannot directly operate on real numbers the process here of the three or more statistics wi
8432 a data exchange server is a large o a data exchange server is a large or small interface that works as unified information through port that directs things as in a direct input form using a information base is a data routing system used to accelerate the location of data recipients by sub
8433 karaoke virtual reality user extens karaoke virtual reality user extensible software and hardware is an augmented reality focus that makes you part of your virtual reality fantasy or scheme of augmented reality
8434 public slander law and outlandish s public slander law and outlandish statement is a thing that makes it a crime to state things that are not true in any such questionnaire or consent of authority
8435 debate of ownership is the law that debate of ownership is the law that makes it a crime to sell something that does not belong to you or your company
8436 adjusted property jump is a search adjusted property jump is a search of audit for the illegal gain of political paid compensation and buying off of any such persons favor
8437 cloud on chips is any such amplifie cloud on chips is any such amplified start and finish direction of processing that holds a building echo of data such as galaxy operation where to say in one code that the predecessor may be an expensive system that makes code and related parts of infor
8438 projection video phone and the lase projection video phone and the laser stick led compact or desktop models are conference friendly
8439 play along karaoke or game augmente play along karaoke or game augmented reality projection and the laser stick led compact or desktop models are entertainment friendly
8440 transparent sphere television and v transparent sphere television and video layered spectrum display is a sphere of translucent properties that can display video in a perspective
8441 sphere high definition perspective sphere high definition perspective resolution encoding for visual display and communication
8442 lcus united states of america armed lcus united states of america armed forces ro contract winner
8443 point of view added perspective dis point of view added perspective display user to display any resolution at the users proper point of view
8444 server to compact flash with the pr server to compact flash with the process of data

redirection would let the data decide where to go in this there could be multiple soc on one board
8445 compact flash bed of servers on chi compact flash bed of servers on chip and including a routed path of information to exchange the rate of processing a bed of data and processing chips with an on board router appliance
8446 global routing initiative is a deta global routing initiative is a detailed paid routing service data base that helps clouds route to specific are as of the world to improve connectivity
8447 paid multi device operating system paid multi device operating system is an operating system that adapts to the device used on in any way needed how many devices do you want to run this copy of this operating system plan
8448 secured drive of any paid multi dev secured drive of any paid multi device operating system is an operating system that adapts to the device used on in any way needed how many devices do you want to run this copy of this operating system plan
8449 compact flash os paid multi device compact flash os paid multi device operating system is an operating system that adapts to the device used on in any way needed how many devices do you want to run this copy of this operating system plan
8450 usb flash os paid multi device oper usb flash os paid multi device operating system is an operating system that adapts to the device used on in any way needed how many devices do you want to run this copy of this operating system plan
8451 adaptable fiber optic short solutio adaptable fiber optic short solutions adaptable short solutions in fiber optic short cables and common issues in connectivity for everyday use fiber optic short translator connections compact fiber optic solutions
8452 layered depth display optic solutio layered depth display optic solutions for temporal three dimensional depth perspective is to layer a perspective in color and field display with layers of led and transparent layers of display layouts in a omni layer of depth and picture
8453 simple complex abstract intent to r simple complex abstract intent to reflect process and redirect the essence of ion and light inside a working electronic or iontronic machine
8454 transparent back light opacity scal transparent back light opacity scale of the to come display optic solutions for temporal three dimensional depth perspective is to layer a perspective in color and field display with layers and transparent layers of display layouts in a omni layer of dept
8455 vertical optical display circuits t vertical optical display circuits to display a varied layer of three dimensional optic display solutions for depth perspective where the circuit is layered and in itself holds a layer of more layers with a point of view calculated
8456 software that plural signal control software that plural signal control per application and multiplied signal options for a stronger signal receiving
8457 display of un ordinary behavior and display of un ordinary behavior and public riot crime is a un expected method of protest and public disruption
8458 radical religious increments of un radical religious increments of un real ism is the religious extreme made to be the un excepted form of ban freedom and the un free concept of terrorism
8459 telemarketer terrorism and the pill telemarketer terrorism and the pill pushers problems to fight homeland phone terrorism ftc trial of do not call list deficiency
8460 user specific watching web bots tha user specific watching web bots that identify and

trace criminal and malicious activity by following them and then their intent to disrupt

8461 group watching web bots that track group watching web bots that track and trace a specific group of attitude and system of targets by identifying them and then following their intent

8462 a regulatory system of web bot make a regulatory system of web bot makers that make a group of police and repeat servers and stations that relate to the specific origin of a nation

8463 building and re attaching method of building and re attaching method of a synthetic metal chip into a printed circuit board part that isn't soldered down and is replaceable by automatic printing control made by a shared measuring chip bridge machine that is giving to prior specified dimensi

8464 universal pre measurement bonding a universal pre measurement bonding and soldering the pre measured circuit socket

8465 universal bonding agent part that a universal bonding agent part that accepts a specified dimension of micro chip for processing or storage etc also known as socket for a socket bonded solder

8466 global recycles market exchange and global recycles market exchange and welfare for the environment is a monetary substance recycle exchange for the world of today tomorrow and the future and exchange of solids starches gases and more for sale and recycling as well as patrol for safe contam

8467 assistance and acceptance of over d assistance and acceptance of over due taxes as forgive and forget income status is a means to fight for people who work but do not make enough to pay back taxes and new taxes and a separated income bracket that provides a substitute planning verses fine

8468 en scribble stacked level micro cha en scribble stacked level micro channel architecture processors and solid state processors replaceable technology per a attached technology mega sata

8469 embedded hyperistic chips and proce embedded hyperistic chips and processors that hold inside a layer of insulation to connected intermittent silica linking to a printed circuit board printing by stencil layers and photo emulsion plasma bonding over silica to make a connection on a larger s

8470 how would anyone control artificial how would anyone control artificial intelligence so that it is not a ready made corruption of control meaning intelligence in itself is un controllable via the old proverb of apple of knowledge and history personal opinion of the fight of any intelligence

8471 who goes to jail or becomes fined o who goes to jail or becomes fined over a problem with an artificially driven car and or death or accident how would anyone control artificial intelligence so that it is not a ready made corruption of control meaning intelligence in itself is un controllab

8472 instead of artificially stupidity i instead of artificially stupidity intelligence why don't they work on real issues like terrorism and airplane wrecks or the traffic we have to go through every day just to get to where we want don't steal my inventions and sweat my equity this is a wasted

8473 safety issues and control of pathwa safety issues and control of pathway control properties legal trade and international processing as shipping on a drone front needs all the fixes that any other delivery path would acquire with permission a new travel rout with drone preferences functions

8474 time to get up and move working sak time to get up and move working sake of data conference worldwide time to get up and move this is a concept for the sake of all data in the entire time and code for codes sake to incorporate a sync code to share information throughout the time we will hav

8475 written cubit functions by size of written cubit functions by size of the data on a given chip's architecture meaning that if the chip is a data driven nano meters then the cubit could be or less written by size meters and the same for a chip written in a nano meter depth of focus in optic

8476 help line for any given issue and a help line for any given issue and abuse mental or drug crisis being there as cost safe alternative to police this would be a pre extreme non emergency health hot line that could elevate the police as or similar dial code for health issues

8477 protecting yourself from a bad fad protecting yourself from a bad fad think realistically hold your fights and always protect your rights be happy know that help is a place and you can always get there from here know that some are good and some are not control auto content at any cost espe

8478 negative information managers as ti negative information managers as title for the architect who writes the rules against false news and hypothetical as software

8479 gas station run off reservoir for e gas station run off reservoir for environment for safety water treatment and river friendly filters

8480 learn it and be the machine animate learn it and be the machine animate to print artwork there is a time and a breadth choose your battles and win in a million odds over here is my hope and dreams for this world and the intent to conceive any gain for man script specials and the dream to an

8481 lens magnified and focused ultra vi lens magnified and focused ultra violet led wall to green solar crystal send and receive as synthetic electro photosynthesis

8482 lens magnified and focused infrared lens magnified and focused infrared led wall to green solar crystal send and receive as synthetic electro photosynthesis

8483 medical suit and marijuana legal st medical suit and marijuana legal state anti trust to un support the marijuana fed fun ded states why should different states support other states

8484 colored lens magnified and focused colored lens magnified and focused infrared led wall to green solar crystal send and receive as synthetic electro photosynthesis

8485 uv or luminescence colored lens mag uv or luminescence colored lens magnified and focused infrared led wall to green solar crystal send and receive as synthetic electro photosynthesis

8486 multiplied uv or luminescence color multiplied uv or luminescence colored lens magnified and focused infrared led wall to green solar crystal send and receive as synthetic electro photosynthesis

8487 this into a light tunnel of amped r this into a light tunnel of amped reflected focused solar energy multiplied uv or luminescence colored lens magnified and focused infrared led wall to green solar crystal send and receive as synthetic electro photosynthesis

8488 directed and fiber optic reflected directed and fiber optic reflected focused solar energy multiplied uv or luminescence colored lens magnified and focused infrared led wall to green solar crystal send and receive as synthetic electro photosynthesis

8489 na no metric micro circuit trip dev na no metric micro circuit trip device [breaker] there is a time and a breadth choose your battles and win in a million odds over here is my hope and dreams for this world and the intent to conceive any gain for man na no metric micro circuit trip device

8490 oscillating and inverted by redirec oscillating and inverted by redirected and fiber optic reflected focused solar energy multiplied uv or luminescence colored lens magnified and focused infrared led wall to green solar crystal send and receive as synthetic electro photosynthesis

8491 un constitutional radical increment un constitutional radical increments in perspective to any known issue granted by a process of multiple courts excluding the one and only court of any such state or federal system allotted to change any other court terms

8492 monopoly suited situation of contro monopoly suited situation of control in un safe circumstances as well as the issues of per citizen inventor verses the corporation of un incorporated inability to serve stop and dis assist as means to help issues of infringement in any right

8493 intellectual property service is a intellectual property service is a branch of government that takes the service of intellectual property and dues of monetary issuance as new and joined idea branch of rights and property to help the income and advancement of proprietary capitalism of th

8494 foreign war locally driven weapon h foreign war locally driven weapon holding drone war land craft and aircraft as well as watercraft for a safe death less war

8495 making the cloud today on one serve making the cloud today on one server as in a cubit written at will connections in micro cloud computing making a system on chip a wireless and hard line data send and receive intent to send with wireless ac and a hard line to receive data or verses in ter

8496 to change the cloud subscriptions i to change the cloud subscriptions into an derogatory of abuse of sales interest to say that cloud subscriptions are wrong and un true in the cost of ownership

8497 free to sue the part of government free to sue the part of government that helps people who need compensation who are un able to see the right power of law branch for improper use of intellectual property abuse and theft

8498 a formal submitter ofs infringement a formal submitter ofs infringement based on the intent to use with out properor rights platform based on comma separated value spreadsheet

8499 a formal submitter ofs infringement a formal submitter ofs infringement based on the intent to use with out proper or rights platform based on comma separated value spreadsheet

8500 forms with the pro bono contingency forms with the pro bono contingency in attendance would be to file for free but support the people who put effort by a percent of earnings

8501 focused laser to amplified reflecti focused laser to amplified reflective tunnel solar energy and process of light by multiplying the mass and energy of any light source as laser to magnify the out come of energy

8502 acetoxybenzoic acid quartiondine li acetoxybenzoic acid quartiondine light exposure testing actualization's ionized and ultraviolet laser chemical enhancing medicines acetoxybenzoic acid with second exposure to make acetoxybenzoic acid quartiondine

8503 multiple focused laser to amplified multiple focused laser to amplified reflective tunnel solar energy and process of light by multiplying the mass and energy of any light source as laser to magnify the out come of energy

8504 see saw action hydro pumping valve see saw action hydro pumping valve electric generation and infinite un stopped water engine taking a current force and not stopping that energy but making a symbiotic source of energy

8505 large ocean platform of ro see saw large ocean platform of ro see saw action valve electric generation and infinite force fulcrum engine taking a current force and not stopping that energy but making a symbiotic source of energy where one force over comes the other one and repeats

8506 scribe able chip design library can scribe able chip design library can be a right feed on chip designs and configurations to improve the processor and the advancement of technology itself

8507 scribe able chip design can be a un scribe able chip design can be a unlocked blank chip based on focused layers of data on chip for functional for on chip designs and configurations to improve the processor and the advancement of technology itself

8508 write en abled un scribed chip desi write en abled un scribed chip design would be a un written chip that could be written to and can be a unlocked blank chip based on focused layers of data on chip for functional for on chip designs and configurations to improve the processor and the a

8509 write enabled un scribe chip design write enabled un scribe chip design would be a un written chip that could be written to and can be a unlocked blank chip based on focused layers of data on chip for function ambled for on chip designs and configurations to improve the processor and the ad

8510 radio data signal operations in cel radio data signal operations in cellular circumstances of wave properties and the inherited secured pci m flash radio tuner for data

8511 aerial flash server cloud that stor aerial flash server cloud that stores tickets of packets in the cell tower as compact flash micro super high compact data

8512 equilibrium inside a annotation of equilibrium inside a annotation of place

8513 aerial flash server cloud that stor aerial flash server cloud that stores a processing and acceleration factor of signal in the cell tower as compact flash micro super high compact

8514 network looped all incorporated com network looped all incorporated communication signals in a plural cubit signal scheme would be a multitude of signals inside a group of signals echoing a batch of previous signals to continue a wave of data a mechanical access signal processing station th

8515 a secured or profitable solution fo a secured or profitable solution for chip design and acceleration as well as to load and print chip architecture in a printer software interface with a chip writing drive in accordance to a blank solid state synthetic metal processor with socket type pref

8516 a series of events vector graphics a series of events vector graphics the first time i learned how to boot up a computer w as in elementary school and to my dis may it w as a very un exciting moment but luckily we actually had computers in school and it w as in the early eighties! so that

8517 chris any words of advice why the c chris any words of advice why the company ford motors is doing so well this is a long time coming in the year un known and kept secretive the point is to never take what you can't pay back as you and i both know the government of any country will be as ma

8518 chris i need a platform so i answer chris i need a platform so i answer the phone in twice in a row two different people call and say if you know what i mean so out of the three i have successfully used two of them myself but i have yet to use and complete blue nile as sale but i'm good j

8519 do you ever try to get out of payin do you ever try to get out of paying a bill no you wouldn't do that would you well i did i had a call and then i returned that call and then i paid my bill but before i paid the bill i said to capital one that there should be a alternate way of paying so

8520 fog begins to roll in as inventor t fog begins to roll in as inventor the biggest part of conceptualizing any thing is how to show the people what hewlett packard did w as set aside some engineers and scientists aside to resolve the details brilliant and the greatest thing any people have

8521 i am not really old but i am how ev i am not really old but i am how ever older than the company google as for the $ billion dollars suggested buying price for google incorporated recently that brings joy to my ears when i w as doing my early artwork the phone w as constantly ringing and on

8522 i designed the adobe logo by entry i designed the adobe logo by entry to an in design competition and won rights as superlative analyst there w as a time during my recovery that i w as un ruled and divided so much that i called and wrote adobe systems quite a few times and ended up helping

8523 i don't remember the details and i i don't remember the details and i probably shouldn't tell any one those matters but the fact of the matter is that the retro car has reached heights of un imaginable proportions fact one day i w as minding my own business and i received the call from a g

8524 the reason for this short opinionat the reason for this short opinionated essay is this looking back w as it a good idea and w as the result a positive one the divided monopoly is what it w as still only now in two different legalities they make more money this year than they did last year

8525 there is one thing that this entire there is one thing that this entire world needs to understand and it's all translated with in a few commands google listens! point encase i along with so many others have written and requested favorite things with favorite companies google music google

8526 power by alternate point of energy power by alternate point of energy torque slip by extended cam shaft would translate as slip and grip when needed part of any motorized engine that has an alternative shaft of torque for another source of power if needed a dual performance shaft if you

8527 future of less open software and th future of less open software and the concurrent topics that it will hold such as fee based operation time and subscription updates

8528 to take dumbing it down more than a to take dumbing it down more than anything ever has a wireless pre configured solution of commercial information technology service that incorporates all the services needed to work an office of today for any company as all in one service for work

8529 mini wireless chip operated and mini wireless chip operated and compute magnetic transmission for torque and propulsion of device controlling a stationary over controlled passing magnets that provide any such current controlled with a wireless connection for

torque magnitude intensi
8530 drone launching warship intelli drone launching warship intelligent warship is a lifeless battle ship that is an artificial war machine that wins wars defends freedom and kills bad guys </iframe>
8531 a running circle definition of what a running circle definition of what has been said is in fact a no answer for example if someone were to propose a question to a branch of government and the return answer w as a previously stated circular statement not a yes or no answer by definition the
8532 a misleading running circle definit a misleading running circle definition of what has been said is in fact a no answer for example if someone were to propose a question to a branch of government and the return answer w as a previously stated circular statement not a yes or no answer by def
8533 a write once chip that has a state a write once chip that has a state of permanence and will only function as second or first capacity full function chip with architecture written by software
8534 astro hardware satellite server sta astro hardware satellite server state of our art astro service hardware astro hardware imagine a disillusioned space elevator that has no clue just a satellite that has servers aboard imagine space travel that is so successful that over a long or short ti
8535 to use a device where the data pack to use a device where the data packets of the internet and cellular comm has stopped and a radio wave of certain freq is controlled in a zone not incorporated with data and on a war or war data premptive agreement in a cloud data base environment that pr
8536 marijuana use and the health of any marijuana use and the health of any such stimulant turned into a constant use where the patient has an addiction base on a series of ups and downs where the drug must maintain a non equal abuse level to be considered at a normal high is also known as em
8537 system on chip optical server input system on chip optical server input board to have a fiber optic vector registered board that has a lined connective port of objects inline to work like a copper embedded circuit board
8538 microwave reactor is a combination microwave reactor is a combination of reactions in few scenarios like for example the combination of air or water to run a turbine and create electricity or the microwaveable consideration of other reactive materials as solvents or compounds to create ene
8539 compound angle chips are the chips compound angle chips are the chips that have horizontal diagonal vertical processing that will aid in the processing of a vertical and other angles including horizontal made wafer of chips in a faster more compact size while printing in multiple stages of
8540 compound chip parts are the cores m compound chip parts are the cores memory and agents that have direction any compound direction of processing with building of a vertical and horizontal wafer of chips in a faster more compact size while printing in multiple stages of mediums in a series o
8541 its fun ny you should but ask i m i its fun ny you should but ask i m in servers severs not software web os
8542 compressed alcohol as gas engine is compressed alcohol as gas engine is a compromised

vapor ignition engine for trucks tractor trailers and cars as well as airplanes and drones

8543 in a compressed alcohol as gas engi in a compressed alcohol as gas engine a compromised vapor ignition fuel injector is a prepared measure of vapor agitator to make a fine atomized vapor to burn and combust for trucks tractor trailers and cars as well as airplanes and drones

8544 in a compressed alcohol as gas engi in a compressed alcohol as gas engine a compromised vapor ignition fuel injector is a prepared measure of vapor agitator to make a fine mistified vapor to burn and combust for trucks tractor trailers and cars as well as airplanes and drones

8545 agitated vapor fuel is the closest agitated vapor fuel is the closest to flash point in any compound that would be important in a compressed alcohol as gas engine a compromised vapor ignition fuel injector is a prepared measure of vapor aggitator to make a fine mistified vapor to burn and

8546 agitated vapor fuel is the closest agitated vapor fuel is the closest to flash point in any compound that would be important in a compressed alcohol as gas engine a compromised vapor ignition fuel injector is a prepared measure of vapor agitator to make a fine atomized vapor to burn and co

8547 compromised fuel aerosol is pre mea compromised fuel aerosol is pre measured agitated vapor fuel and is the closest to flash point in any compound that would be important in a compressed alcohol as gas engine a compromised vapor ignition fuel injector is a prepared measure of vapor agitator

8548 compromised fuel aerosol engine wil compromised fuel aerosol engine will use pre measured agitated vapor fuel and is the closest to flash point in any compound that would be important in a compressed alcohol as gas engine a compromised vapor ignition fuel injector is a prepared measure of v

8549 atomized and vapor hybrid engine wi atomized and vapor hybrid engine will use pre measured agitated vapor fuel and is the closest to flash point in any compound that would be important in a compressed alcohol as gas engine a compromised vapor ignition fuel injector is a prepared measure of

8550 pre respirated gasoline in a volati pre respirated gasoline in a volatile vapor calculator that finds the fuels top flash point automatically and in a few cycles adjusts it to any gas for the engine

8551 vapor compressor is an exciter and vapor compressor is an exciter and pre respirator for gasoline in a volatile vapor calculator that finds the fuels top flash point automatically and in a few cycles adjusts it to any gas for the engine

8552 smart fuel system in conjunction wi smart fuel system in conjunction with vapor compressor is an exciter and pre respirated gasoline fuel in a volatile vapor calculator that finds the mixes top flash point automatically and in a few cycles adjusts it to any gas for the proper efficiency

8553 grade all in a thing called hardwar grade all in a thing called hardware service cloud to make a note there is a difference in all technology and the service of a hardware is not a change to specify a invent called service grading and rating compact server compact hardware service c

8554 subtractively printed zirconhyd subtractively printed zirconhydroxy or photo laser cut zirconhydroxy isolated layer is a layer of zirconium which is a silicon that is more insulating and less thermal conductive than diamond carbonate this is good for making three dimensional chips a

8555 exterior gas meaning out side in at exterior gas meaning out side in atmosphere gas liquid cooled motherboard is an actively cooled in a climate controlled efficiency way of cooling for higher performance

8556 a reverse reflective tunnel that ma a reverse reflective tunnel that magnifies the light and graduates the source to maximize the solar energy

8557 a energy center or building with ma a energy center or building with many focused solar generators that reverse reflective tunnel that magnifies the light and graduates the source to maximize the solar energy

8558 mo dial comm a different way to ftp mo dial comm a different way to ftp to design a ethernet cell or satellite based cell phone application that connects people's phones as pages instead of pages on a server the main purpose is to communicate and then the other things will gradually fall in

8559 printing materials for perpendicula printing materials for perpendicular laser printed levels of circuits processors and memory in multiple photo sensitive cured solvents as circuits layers laser printed chips in a diffused solution to compute as chip in a series of different elements

8560 four sided computer chip for comput four sided computer chip for computations

8561 eight sided computer chip for compu eight sided computer chip for computations and stacking arrangements for chip processing

8562 conductive and positive pico nano v conductive and positive pico nano voxel and elemental compounds for chip processing printing in three dimensions

8563 non conductive and negative pico na non conductive and negative pico nano voxel and elemental compounds for chip processing printing in three dimensions

8564 non conductive silica solvent white non conductive silica solvent white space and negative pico nano voxel and elemental compounds for chip processing printing in three dimensions

8565 synthetic currents to anchor underw synthetic currents to anchor underwater current makers to a high middle and low temperatures and in the consistent direction to prevent stagnant water and refresh the water in a pond or reservoir the benefits would be less insects and healthier fish

8566 clay building bricks recycled to re clay building bricks recycled to resolve ph balance in lead heavy ground as counter product in a process of saturation

8567 high speed aerospace satellite to s high speed aerospace satellite to satellite to ground encrypted processed and compressed signal data station is a resolution station that transforms signals into a encrypted code for travel into a different network

8568 microwave ecology and the study of microwave ecology and the study of light particles and oxygen from microwave stable and unstable optical combustion

8569 explain this is to accumulate the c explain this is to accumulate the circumstances this isn't a time device it's only a cd publishing system in reverse a folder generator that catalogs achieved cd's and cd rom into a folder on a hard drive flash card or sd and even server related temps so

8570 who really understands better than who really understands better than a child trying to kick a ball into the wind it may do this it may do that but what we really need to understand is there are curve anomalies that happen more than we hope thats why its fun yet to understand them is

8571 to multiply on local network os ove to multiply on local network os over os under os scenario to multiply on local network os the chances of using two or more under operating systems and concluding it to a working hierarchy of operating system +even or +odd

8572 as well as triangular square and ci as well as triangular square and circular properties such as vertical horizontal and spherical combinations with two or more in one process line of sight as well as to inject gas and form a modulation of image appropriate for television and viewing commen

8573 immune systemic insulin insulin med immune systemic insulin insulin medicine to magistrate through the auto immune system immune systemic insulin insulin medicine to magistrate through the auto immune system insulin main article insulin therapy type diabetes is typically treated with a com

8574 immune systemic anti psychotics ant immune systemic anti psychotics anti psychotic medicine to magistrate through the auto immune system anti psychotic medicine to magistrate through the auto immune system physiological the causes of bipolar disorder have yet to be fully un covered but ther

8575 emergency sos satellite system base emergency sos satellite system based on cell phone satellite connections sos from wikipedia the free encyclopedia sos is the commonly used description for the international morse code distress signal (æ'†¿½¿½¿½¿½ ¿½¿½¿½¿½ ¿½¿½¿½¿½¿½¿½¿½¿½ ¿½¿½¿½¿½ ¿½¿½¿½¿½ åj, ¿½¿½¿½¿½ æ'†' ¿½¿½¿½¿½ ¿½¿½¿½¿½¿½¿½¿½¿½ ¿½¿½¿½¿½ ¿½¿½¿½¿½ åj, ¿½¿½¿½¿½ æ'†' ¿½¿½¿½¿½ ¿½¿½¿½¿½¿½¿½¿½¿½ ¿½¿½¿½¿½ ¿½¿½¿½¿½ ¿½¿½¿½¿½

8576 emergency sos satellite system base emergency sos satellite system based on cell phone satellite connections sos from wikipedia the free encyclopedia sos is the commonly used description for the international morse code distress signal (, , , ,) this distress signal w as first adop

8577 plastic layered electronic micro bo plastic layered electronic micro board a process defined with nano printing circuits and layers of layers of circuitry that provides depth into height of computing capabilities or alternate poly carbonate carbonate porous compounds

8578 outdoor hot and cold climates need outdoor hot and cold climates need processing lets imagine that there could be a cup with a microchip inside it after all open processors and the instance of virtual to real time applicable things like traffic flow energy systems police dispatch and

8579 serial artwork number or swan to re serial artwork number or swan to register andofficial works of a group of artwork printed or raw data sets for future reference and worth including any given details of certifications

8580 serial artwork number or swan to re serial artwork number or swan to register and official works of a group of artwork printed or raw data sets for future reference and worth including any given details of certifications

8581 bandwagon effect from wikipedia the bandwagon effect from wikipedia the free encyclopedia jump to navigation search the bandwagon effect is a well documented form of group think in behavioral science and has many applications the general rule is that conduct or beliefs spread among people

8582 a few questions and what to expect a few questions and what to expect pulse ion trigger algebraic lens motor to pulse nano photon color sensor pulse ion trigger algebraic lens motor to pulse nano photon color sensor trying to work more efficiently ions nano photon and other things like the

8583 pulse na no photonic sensor copyrig pulse na no photonic sensor

8584 this is a needed attempt at making this is a needed attempt at making real circumstances translatable into real terms of useful objects for example if the code says up this could mean literal or non relative terms

8585 the need to place secure socket lay the need to place secure socket layers into place with a packet flaw prerequisite to speak plainly a packet is requested from the server the server sends a packet first with the completed file information backwards with weight and scale then loads t

8586 to protect the small glitches and m to protect the small glitches and malfunctions of any surge from sensitive and expensive trips breaks and surges of electricity to protect the most valuable devices

8587 its true that there is a popular ac its true that there is a popular accent in america tv and the spread of a californian accent across the united states of america is the new pink

8588 any such right as to investigate an any such right as to investigate and with plausible cause to search for a missing person upon any premise with unique attributes justified by law holding contrary existing census information and legitimate rights of distrust or suspicion

8589 many other co un tries use the us d many other co un tries use the us dollar to equate a hypothesis is to generate a revenue inside its self the dollar bill with country intent for example a widget country denominated dollar with gold silver property resource note

8590 to initiate an add on application d to initiate an add on application different than a program but more over a specific add on to compliment code in a sense of script and all while not having a apparent app face formula a thing to call love and work with and seemingly be the same as child

8591 to include two computers in a sense to include two computers in a sense of permanence complete with software and hardware options and tickets of operation as well as ip address

8592 my thought to amplify the core is b my thought to amplify the core is by multiplying the board and amp mechanism operations and connections during a core connection and relay amplitude marker a starting point that has a reciprocating point to relay

8593 d monitor led layer nano sphere pix d monitor led layer nano sphere pixel layer for three dimensional projection and perspective

8594 using lasers to generate high poten using lasers to generate high potential energy in combination with solar receiving cells

8595 horizontal vertical motherboard soc horizontal vertical motherboard socket intersections

8596 intent to remove cuna cuna chemis intent to remove cuna cuna chemistry topic of another part how to charge an element using the nasa nevada experimental rail way why would you bother them and what it means to the rest of us i think it's best put as set charge accelerator a question of

8597 as compared to the electricity grid as compared to the electricity grid in north america using transmission and sub transmission to generate primary cores and secondary core signals as in the high to lower steps similar in cable to make any such signals computational applied compression as

8598 to give any such meaning to approxi to give any such meaning to approximate and a sum of non exact processing to result inside a estimated code or signal of will from making a stopping point and the root of pi from fractal transformations
8599 ethel nitrogen oxide engine and the ethel nitrogen oxide engine and the parameters of intent of power
8600 to place multiple central processin to place multiple central processing un its in a way that shapes an h i like an i beam in construction methodology
8601 another cloud cycle to invent conce another cloud cycle to invent concept the difference of deep blue w as that it wasn't considered a cloud at the time the focus w as only on the game and the server itself this isn t the focus of what the azure is windows will now carry on as usual wel
8602 smaller than previous bios chips an smaller than previous bios chips and transforming code to a digital to triad octavia signal to compute calculations and computations in a way previously un able to do with signal processors by way of transforming the signal into a code pre amplified to c
8603 triad octavia signal to grid format triad octavia signal to grid format y x with a coherent of a controller that modifies the signal into computations before processing into various program signals in a tet of a period machine controlled nano sphere
8604 interleaving circuit conductor traf interleaving circuit conductor traffic signals chip sockets alternate secondary processing un its that work to control processes based on a alternate path
8605 interchangeable secondary processin interchangeable secondary processing unit sockets interleaving circuit conductor traffic signals chip sockets alternate secondary processing un its that work to control processes based on a alternate path
8606 a smaller less expensive way to sol a smaller less expensive way to solid state data to add layers to a existing ddr plug in and plug in more layers with new adjustable configurations for example dd r with half height extensions that run but stand up like a pcie that has layers included to
8607 to build a blu ray or archival disc to build a blu ray or archival disc mm media inside a glass or carbonate jewel case with spectrum magnified reading points with the intent of making it secure and dust free while being redundant and replaceable with the intent not confuse it and a inch ha
8608 reading and writing using convex an reading and writing using convex and concave lenses to build a blu ray or archival disc mm media inside a glass or carbonate jewel case with spectrum magnified reading points with the intent of making it secure and dust free while being redundant and repl
8609 electronic muscle pulse therapy for electronic muscle pulse therapy for atrophy patients help me walk some organic some post organic measure electronic muscle pulse therapy for atrophy patients step super infomercial for medical if i saw it on tv it has to be real disabled tendon repair and
8610 converting multiple computer mother converting multiple computer motherboards to unify into a working system that is not parallel (matching) or odd working (not matching) into a new cabinet data of mini desktop situation and cards that tell the central processor to do what the completed mis
8611 dominate media a path to communicat dominate media a path to communicate with

other devices using the identity of which one is passive and which one is the dominate one why you could borrow a phone or buy a new one at a moments notice and hold the things like number and email address as wel
8612 dominate server cloud a path to com dominate server cloud a path to communicate with other devices using the identity of which one is passive and which one is the dominate one why you could borrow a phone or buy a new one at a moments notice and hold the things like number and email address
8613 an elaborate paging hardware system an elaborate paging hardware system that links processors for a continuous processing group of microchips aligned or complimentary in any similarity that forms an accessible shape of a shed family hardware to add cores to a group of processing cores and
8614 alternate size spinning magnetic el alternate size spinning magnetic electric generator lord carpenters infinite motion how to put it all together a spinning top is very similar to something you'd like to have fun and stare at forever it w as brought to my attention that there is a need for
8615 centralized satellite control netwo centralized satellite control network governmental private
8616 density and amplitude energy chart density and amplitude energy chart scale a energy chart with amplitude and density comparable to the chemical elements diagram with consideration for gas solids and chemical compounds as well as their reaction to one another
8617 translation virtual predictive dens translation virtual predictive density matter to measure and estimate the outcome of any two forms of energy together in one equation or software platform to create new and exciting forms of medicine and energy by functioning heat chemical compound or a c
8618 matter mining by way of na no wave matter mining by way of na no wave radio signals find the element and save that element or to create more elements
8619 life by dead virus by way of na no life by dead virus by way of na no wave radio signals to kill a virus and make an anti virus by way of very small radio waves
8620 programmable medical surgery roboti programmable medical surgery robotics by way of na no wave energy weight focus scope medical surgery device by way of laser and energy matter compensations
8621 simple est is a solar cell phone re simple est is a solar cell phone re charger my airplane crashed and lets say i m stranded who would i call first solar cell phone re charger
8622 poly carbonate sandwiched stacked o poly carbonate sandwiched stacked optical circuit board on ply board technology
8623 neutral performing laser to move an neutral performing laser to move and work with out damage and neutral force
8624 synthetic pressurized gas turbine t synthetic pressurized gas turbine to generate electricity
8625 sub scalable sd branches and trees sub scalable sd branches and trees
8626 governmental cloud separated state governmental cloud separated state and federal cloud service encryption values from logical to high performance situations of traffic to water control to records of who what and where
8627 plasma pressurized poly oxide metal plasma pressurized poly oxide metal using plasma pressure to mold many oxidized metals back to a combined metal making a new inexpensive

metal
8628 static electric poly oxide metal us static electric poly oxide metal using electricity to mold many oxidized metals back to a combined metal making a new metal
8629 anything over the internet cell tow anything over the internet cell towers resident and roaming services subscribed wireless signals and encrypted channels small aoi small local repeaters boxes that drive this internet forward faster than as expected a local and less populous needs for a ut
8630 state of our art is never a constan state of our art is never a constant so to make a platform as on the fly as possible would be the the greatest advancing scale ever to make an engineering system that makes your service in a virtual environment and sale rate increase with redesign proposi
8631 manipulative personality disorder i manipulative personality disorder is a selfish and greedy property in low importance comparison to exceptional sanctity
8632 company incentives for recycling te company incentives for recycling technology is a monetary program based on weight and recovery from the local and federal government
8633 technology leasing and propagating technology leasing and propagating specialists is a monetary program based on profit and recovery from the manufacturers post attributes
8634 future of less open software and th future of less open software and the concurrent topics that it will hold such as fee based operation times and subscription updates
8635 future of protected and eula softwa future of protected and eula software and the concurrent topics that it will hold such as free operation times and non subscription updates
8636 school student information secure d school student information secure data protection is a method of protecting the future of learning with technology
8637 cloud data security software is a m cloud data security software is a method of protecting the future with technology
8638 a rounded number of encryption a rounded number of encryption based on a four segment of numbers to process and extract an encrypt able alpha numerical code for ssl and more advanced communications </iframe>
8639 a squared area of cascading inc a squared area of cascading increments funny but real to process code with measurement cascading increments a certain unit of measurement or for processing electronic measurement using my certain unit of measurement data versus the shape of media t </
8640 a large rechargeable battery plant a large rechargeable battery plant that has automated chemical pool recharging and sending receiving charging and re doping electron batches and storage for electricity on any large scale in acres and years suitable for the safety and health of human life
8641 a large recycled battery pool that a large recycled battery pool that makes other small batteries with less time and higher concentrations of elements rechargeable battery plant that has automated chemical pool recharging and sending receiving charging and re doping electron ions and neutr
8642 parts that unite by scale and c parts that unite by scale and connections across carry inter connection circuit processors and alternate vectors of chip exchange a chip that sends a specific vector data rate to a specified place to and then to more or to reply </iframe>
8643 old medicine has a new study the in old medicine has a new study the integration of old ways into the new way of taking medicine antique biology

8644 sodium delineation native valances sodium delineation native valances and their properties in the brain verses muscles and other organs
8645 laymen technology smart home lights laymen technology smart home lights and so un d along side pre programmed television internet and phone plug in and use configurations ready out of the box
8646 machine builders and labor machine machine builders and labor machine makers to receive incentives benefits in local machine and robot automology
8647 pcie e os installer and configured pcie e os installer and configured out of the box insert and run playable secondary or primary to provide higher point contact and super fast calculations
8648 making isolation as easy as drop co making isolation as easy as drop
8649 fractions in dynamic digital cable fractions in dynamic digital cable frequency modulations
8650 a wireless pre configured room by r a wireless pre configured room by room and service b un dle software built smart all in one service for home
8651 to compare an initial altair to tom to compare an initial altair to tomorrows lcus its as though there is no difference in new super computer the assumption that all wheel drive is like four wheel drive only all the time in a balanced formation of code
8652 geometric scripts that fractionally geometric scripts that fractionally divide and parallel the operations at hand to use the method and source as the same path
8653 a computational script that instead a computational script that instead of ones and zeros a frequency that pairs with other waves to make a computation together
8654 un der ocean jet stream path way of un der ocean jet stream path way of nuclear reactor non exchanging temperatures
8655 c un a c un a next chemistry topic c un a c un a next chemistry topic of another part invent deposition a few questions and what to expect how to charge an element using the nasa nevada experimental rail way why would you bother them and what it means to the res
8656 to take dumbing it down more than a to take dumbing it down more than anything ever h as a wireless pre configured solution of commercial information technology service that incorporates all the services needed to work an office of today for any company as all in one service for work
8657 alternating traffic triggers and co alternating traffic triggers and co processors to branch overall assets between super links
8658 time un awareness and un scheduled time un awareness and un scheduled sleeping resulting in acute insomnia
8659 cloud cycle to invent concept the d cloud cycle to invent concept the difference of deep blue w as that it wasn t considered a cloud at the time the focus w as only on the game and the server itself this isn t the focus of what the azure is windows will now carry on as usual welcome to
8660 cloud cycle to invent concept the d cloud cycle to invent concept the difference of deep blue w as that it wasn't considered a cloud at the time the focus w as only on the game and the server itself this isn t the focus of what the azure is windows will now carry on as usual welcome to
8661 real time and pure light %infinite real time and pure light %infinite times + %infinite=e %uxc binom lim n toward infinity(+{} over {n})^{n} %infinite times + %infinite%uxc binom

max xe ^{sum + infinity cdot +%uxea {e} over x sum to{{} } x^{}%epsilon } part
8662 mini data to data board lock data e mini data to data board lock data engine m form factor board receiver connection base to board lock landing
8663 real head board lock data & fabric real head board lock data & fabric engine micro controller board cloud connection board to board lock landing connecting and operating m form factor board receiver connection base to board lock landing
8664 to purpose propose an update to the to purpose propose an update to the current board registration and operating system scheme that will equate into more than one board opposing the hypothesis that using more than one board will over come
8665 varios computer parts and musical c varios computer parts and musical chairs code name veg as isn't it simple that if the world followed quintet and sextet then that would mean that midi and the mc is and will always be the way that math in dance is synchronized and trans fixate and then b
8666 second and third level + processing second and third level + processing unit interchanging socket to compose another central based chip socket with alternate sub levels of chip sockets generally considered non central or additional solder and molded chips for example a replaceable second a
8667 focused artificial energy energy we focused artificial energy energy web energy server focused artificial energy energy web a contained web sphere that simulates a web of energy to pilot stations for distribution from a building that is a self contained focused laser generated solar energy
8668 energy server focused artificial en energy server focused artificial energy energy server focused artificial energy energy web a contained web sphere that simulates a web of energy to pilot stations for distribution from a building that is a self contained focused laser generated solar ene
8669 honeycomb board that is a wall of a honeycomb board that is a wall of architecture upon its self to make a glass cased gold wire fish through the board up down and over and through printed circuit boards to end up inside a printed piping board with corrugations
8670 in a class of time and its all in a in a class of time and its all in a little white lie the is a mop up of a noise white noise to bass line code name atlantis in a class of time and it's all in a little white lie the is a mop up of a noise the pitch decay and use of 's main mix of the mid
8671 stacked conjoined honeycomb board t stacked conjoined honeycomb board that is a wall of architecture upon its self to make a glass cased gold wire fish through the board up down and over and through printed circuit boards to end up inside a printed piping board with corrugations
8672 to expand raid capacity to equate i to expand raid capacity to equate into pcie th under bolt raid
8673 to expand raid capacity to equate i to expand raid capacity to equate into mobile docking temp raid and bay station for all in one in other words a docking all in one with true form technology repeated to expand raid capacity to equate into a mobile docking temp raid and bay station for al
8674 another cloud cycle to invent conce another cloud cycle to invent concept the difference of deep blue w as that it wasn't considered a cloud at the time the focus w as only on the game and the server itself this is not the focus of what the azure is windows will now carry on as usual wel

8675 local cloud temp raid system verses local cloud temp raid system verses expanded services cloud for example a local more secure way to cloud that would incorporate your existing data and media servers as well as new local platform that may or may not synchronize as the same based upon you
8676 real time and pure light %infinite real time and pure light %infinite times + %infinite=e %uxc binom lim n toward infinity(+{} over {n})^{n} part
8677 to degrade plastics and harden or s to degrade plastics and harden or solvency the plastics in advance to incineration and generate electricity as well as sooty carbon for commercial uses and energy
8678 fee based cloud sharing and cell tr fee based cloud sharing and cell transmitting between business and business similar to cell tower property verses server property in the clouds provider to provider to re seller to host
8679 after market gadgets need the shape after market gadgets need the shape you want build your own tablet hand held chassis and server related fabric smaller un fused working parts that equal more power and higher concentration of parts dual socket tablet with or without fans and inches
8680 after market gadgets need the shape after market gadgets need the shape you want build your own tablet hand held chassis and server related fabric smaller un fused working parts that equal more power and higher concentration of parts dual socket tablet with fans and inches to inches days p
8681 an app that sends domestic abuse or an app that sends domestic abuse or mental health related and drug abuse issues to a co un selor chat and the proper help in case of emergencies a specific need for a subtle conclusion affordable in any co un sel situation related to a semi non emergency
8682 after market gadgets need the shape after market gadgets need the shape you want build your own tablet hand held chassis and server related fabric smaller un fused working parts that equal more power and higher concentration of parts dual socket tablet with fans and inches to inches
8683 computer phone a phone call that ma computer phone a phone call that made it retro active a large smart phone book like design large phone book like design conference call computer a phone call that made it retro active mixed up smart phone more channels per call voice data screen camera a
8684 honeycomb board that is a wall of a honeycomb board that is a wall of architecture upon its self to make a glass cased gold wire fish through the board up down and over and through printed circuit boards to endup inside a printed piping board with corrugations
8685 stacked conjoined honeycomb board t stacked conjoined honeycomb board that is a wall of architecture upon its self to make a glass cased gold wire fish through the board up down and over and through printed circuit boards to endup inside a printed piping board with corrugations
8686 to expand raid capacity to equate i to expand raid capacity to equate into pcie th un der bolt raid
8687 a smaller less expensive way to sol a smaller less expensive way to solid state data to add layers to a existing ddr plug in and plug in more layers with new adjustable configurations for example dd r with half height extensions that run but stand up like a pcie that h as layers included t

8688 a smaller less expensive way to sol a smaller less expensive way to solid state data to add layers to a existing ddr plug in and plug in more layers with new adjustable configurations for example ddr with height extensions that run but stand up like a pcie that h as layers included to expa

8689 to perform a movement in a fractal to perform a movement in a fractal animation with encryption to have a double as well as start and finish equal to a formula of change

8690 to perform a movement in a fractal to perform a movement in a fractal with encryption to have a double as well as start and finish equal to a formula of change and as well as to make more than one time loop in the process

8691 to expand raid capacity to equate i to expand raid capacity to equate into mobile docking temp raid and bay station for by attachment device in other words a docking by attachment device with true form technology repeated to expand raid capacity to equate into a mobile docking temp raid an

8692 amendment deficiency petitions by p amendment deficiency petitions by popular veto to change a recently voted amendment into a declared state of ruin by petition

8693 to declare a substance medicinally to declare a substance medicinally addictive and harmful to ones health by overdose as in un subscribed methods of use

8694 denationalize of radical liberalism denationalize of radical liberalism to declare a free argument of a amendment or change in policy too liberal for the nations good and notate it un popular

8695 to make a political state of techno to make a political state of technology different than previous and current standing into a new and updated stature of state of the art design and vote from the intended place of interest

8696 to build a blu ray or archival disc to build a blu ray or archival disc mm media inside a glass or carbonate jewel case with spectrum magnified reading points with the intent of making it secure and dust free while being red un dant and replaceable with the intent not confuse it and a inch

8697 reading and writing using convex an reading and writing using convex and concave lenses to build a blu ray or archival disc mm media inside a glass or carbonate jewel case with spectrum magnified reading points with the intent of making it secure and dust free while being red un dant and r

8698 a device reading and writing using a device reading and writing using convex and concave lenses to build a blu ray or archival disc mm media inside a glass or carbonate jewel case with spectrum magnified reading points with the intent of making it secure and dust free while being red un d

8699 an archival free server service tha an archival free server service that records history based upon proprietary intellectual property say for example a url that is specific that includes a doc suffix and moderated by governmental appreciations for a good short summary a that is accessible

8700 electronic muscle pulse therapy for electronic muscle pulse therapy for atrophy patients help me walk some organic some post organic measure electronic muscle pulse therapy for atrophy patients step super infomercial for medical if i saw it on tv it h as to be real disabled tendon repair a

8701 conceptual inventions and the inten conceptual inventions and the intent to inspire the thought and not hold back an inventor who cares to drift instead of dwelling into market tothings of concept in a sense to work without boundaries even if the process may not or may include an

8702 conceptual inventions and the inten conceptual inventions and the intent to inspire the thought and not hold back an inventor who cares to drift instead of dwelling into market to things of concept in a sense to work without boundaries even if the process may not or may include an image am

8703 to enhance by way of less is more s to enhance by way of less is more situation of compatibility and less apps over programmable problems and obstacles saying that gingerbread operating systems are the way of the past and the future of os publishing is two fold a p un ter and a player vers

8704 a web bot network of data applicati a web bot network of data applications searching for the meaning of artificial intelligence con and pro

8705 market controlled by the homeland a market controlled by the homeland and intellectual protection service as well as library of congress effort to control the property we own and would like to buy

8706 easy invent cad submit platform a p easy invent cad submit platform a programmable interface to sort and submit inventions per company quickly in a demand and non chronological manner

8707 laser eye surgery by way of emory u laser eye surgery by way of emory un iversity and the hospital at midtown and the parts in side the laser surgical technique

8708 spool effect of data data translati spool effect of data data translation spool effect of data data translation one way in and two ways out is better than only one way in and one way out logical translation is that a question of danger comes into guess work a modification of compression is

8709 never pi indefinite pi infinity pi never pi indefinite pi infinity pi pi times one equals pi never pi is pi times zero to equal zero indefinite pi is never ending infinite pi

8710 a crowd processor that will use two a crowd processor that will use two or more tapes to create a crowd of itx atx mitx tx boards working to process as one board by tape and crowd presets known also as modular tx

8711 tx plural crowd ch tx plural crowd

8712 a study of any cure by way of toxic a study of any cure by way of toxic and valance testing to include but not limited to cancer and diseases like alzheimer's and substance abuse cessation aids

8713 mandatory cloud bandwidth control t mandatory cloud bandwidth control to suggest that a cloud should only hold so much practical waste to the internet entirety as application as whole to reduce backups and compress data backups by parts

8714 data compression cloud format the m data compression cloud format the means to compress scrolling data that may need to move and write and read ready as well as transport to place to place

8715 converting multiple computer mother converting multiple computer motherboards to un ify into a working system that is not parallel (matching) or odd working (not matching) into a new cabinet data of mini desktop situation and cards that tell the central processor to do what the completed m

8716 inter operable cpu a central proces inter operable cpu a central processing unit that branches your own connections how you want to build your high performance system to

allow any configuration important to you and the scale of your platform
8717 inter operable building parts and b inter operable building parts and board design free build parts designed to connect a central processing unit that branches your own connections how you want to build your high performance system to allow any configuration important to you and the scale
8718 many carbonates into heat as cataly many carbonates into heat as catalyst many complex solutions to air and water with a new multiple compound of as tyro synthetic new starch with metal poly carbonate to as tyro carbonate compound for use in interesting and problematic situations more to
8719 many carbonates into heat as cataly many carbonates into heat as catalyst many complex solutions to air and water with a new multiple compound of a styro synthetic new starch with metal poly carbonate to a styro carbonate compound for use in interesting and problematic situations more to b
8720 configure this into a system with p configure this into a system with power management configure this into a system with computational control configure this into a system with data scale management a square chance chassis that fits with your own choices and arrangement free arrangement wi
8721 magnetic propulsion engine electron magnetic propulsion engine electronically controlled on and off magnet engine generating torque and force
8722 intel edison kit for arduino single intel edison kit for arduino single components ediarduinalk modified to control xeon phi on off and load switch
8723 a software program that will genera a software program that will generate code for external un sorted efi batches to route any computations needed
8724 traffic cloud and pre built selects traffic cloud and pre built selects for real time issue management using technology and real life scenarios to aid in the life of every day a synchronicity b path of popular traffic c safety management
8725 police cloud and pre built selects police cloud and pre built selects for real time issue management using technology and real life scenarios to aid in the life of every day a most wanted b history crimes c issues present past
8726 syndicated media news cloud and pre syndicated media news cloud and pre built selects for real time issue management using technology and real life scenarios to aid in the life of every day a selling and registration b station receptions c blocking and censors
8727 air bound traffic cloud and pre bui air bound traffic cloud and pre built selects for real time issue management using technology and real life scenarios to aid in the life of every day a to place b from place
8728 war management satellite ground clo war management satellite ground cloud and pre built selects for real time issue management using technology and real life scenarios to aid in the life of every day a target compensation b friendly non targets c aggressive mission d defensive mission
8729 magnetic propulsion engine by an el magnetic propulsion engine by an electronically controlled on and off magnet engine generating torque and force
8730 minimum sale retail price cloud and minimum sale retail price cloud and pre built selects for real time issue management using technology and real life scenarios to aid in the life of every day
8731 digital shelf price display for rea digital shelf price display for real time updates from a

msrp cloud stored planed and adjustable by demands something that would make a sale pre customer and availability

8732 synthetic liquid plastic ester and synthetic liquid plastic ester and carbon soot energy in a single compound to make a combustible energy (incinerator bi products and alcohol acids)

8733 educational in class os educational educational in class os educational operating system with intent to block virus and provide a safe computation platforms for age and course specific apps educational cloud system and pre built selects for real time issue management using technology and r

8734 rearranged tetrahedral amorphous ca rearranged tetrahedral amorphous carbon with abstract particle matching to reconstituted energy sp forms diamond (cubic) lonsdaleite (hexagonal diamond) sp forms graphite graphene fullerenes (buckminsterfullerene c higher fullerenes nanotubes nanobu

8735 dominate media a path to comm un ic dominate media a path to comm un icate with other devices using the identity of which one is passive and which one is the dominate one why you could borrow a phone or buy a new one at a moments notice and hold the things like number and email address as

8736 magnetic propulsion torque electron magnetic propulsion torque electronically controlled on and off magnet engine generating torque and force

8737 the infinite motion inside the firs the infinite motion inside the first sphere is made by all the rest of the batteries recharging the original battery inside the only thing missing (magnetic electricity generating) is the method to recharge a battery with the least amount of connections

8738 its a fact of life that to be prope its a fact of life that to be propelled into a un fair and non respect form of work is not only detrimental and confusing to the artist it degrades the work and makes the artist suffer from the beginning the un derground of house and techno makes what we

8739 dominate server cloud a path to com dominate server cloud a path to comm un icate with other devices using the identity of which one is passive and which one is the dominate one why you could borrow a phone or buy a new one at a moments notice and hold the things like number and email addr

8740 an elaborate paging software system an elaborate paging software system that links processors for a continuous processing group of microchips aligned or complimentary in any similarity that forms an accessible shape of a shed family software

8741 pragmatic data clarification who wh pragmatic data clarification who what where when importance and bi as to easily negotiate the promise of any data platform in this term of versable means the pragmatic translates as universal or non motivational on an agenda basis of improvement to any m

8742 no cloud software registration a pr no cloud software registration a program specific intent to keep the software as is and with out any foreign auto updates and stripped integration from internet interference of opportunity and uela confidence trials of intent to disturb the sleeping soft

8743 alternate size spinning magnetic el alternate size spinning magnetic electric generator lord carpenters infinite motion how to put it all together a spinning top is very similar to something you'd like to have f un and stare at forever it w as brought to my attention that there is a need f

8744 effervescent mouth wash for serious effervescent mouth wash for serious ailments like headaches bacteria and dizziness caused by oral sickness

8745 a thing called turbo per element th a thing called turbo per element that can shape a path where previously there w as no way to reflect perpendicular or parallel with the help of mini and per operation by a hypos thesis chip alternate computational curve based algorithms aiding by another

8746 comma separated encryption comma se comma separated encryption comma separated encryption another reason is to continue work on a daily basis as intended securely strange brew is only a reason to understand that everyone is csv styled now and excel my microsoft is no reason to degrade the

8747 a thing called turbo per element th a thing called turbo per element that can shape a path where previously there w as no way to reflect perpendicular or parallel with the help of mini and per operation by a stress thesis chip alternate computational curve based algorithms aiding by anothe

8748 more desktop capacity by way of mod more desktop capacity by way of modular expansions via mini modular modes non ecc or ecc yes either or intent sell a module to me and make it bigger make a module chassis and make it better and smaller hot swap able compute modules trans posable tx and s

8749 more desktop capacity by way of mod more desktop capacity by way of modular expansions via mini modular modes non ecc or ecc yes either or intent sell a module to me and make it bigger make a module chassis and make it better and smaller hot swap able compute modules transpose tx and slim

8750 open thread navigational embedded s open thread navigational embedded software a software base that controls the method of navigation of a processing thread inside a cpu

8751 curriculum software for public scho curriculum software for public schools no cloud base or cloud base data schema download and toss media vs intent to recycle and modify in class testing by way of simple send and receive test email like online college with intuitive public school social c

8752 triplet pi translation axis for com triplet pi translation axis for compensation equation sum and path intent

8753 triplet pi translation axis for com triplet pi translation axis for compensation equation sum part travel pi cubed translation axis for compensation equation sum and path intent software hardware virtual and literal intent to create and estimate any means of anno place in time points of ve

8754 three dimensional vector resolution three dimensional vector resolution fractional format

8755 triplet pi translation axis for com triplet pi translation axis for compensation equation sum part travel pi cubed translation axis for a compensation equation sum and path intent software hardware virtual and literal intent to create and estimate any means of anno place in time points of

8756 real web a web connection that is a real web a web connection that is a retail and local web that processes alternate connections like credit cards and other information like medical records and bank transactions a web that makes real life from day to day a positive one with higher restric

8757 real web part encryption phone chan real web part encryption phone channel a web connection that is a retail and local web that processes alternate connections like credit cards and other information like medical records and bank transactions a web that makes real life from day to day a po

8758 data archive retail pack keeping th data archive retail pack keeping the pack a retail matter when time does matter

8759 deposition on theology of psycholog deposition on theology of psychology this is the only reason why the internet web pages actually work gestalt psychology

8760 big data creative data engineers so big data creative data engineers software client requests terms and permissions rules and exceptions reply response using terms and conditions as well as requests and permissions to translate into real life data arrangements (banking flight control traff

8761 big data creative data engineers co big data creative data engineers compliant hardware client requests ability software wreck less replacement exceptions speed in control using test and server strength to encrypt and control critical cohesion products and services of any kind

8762 organ cell symbiosis cloning and re organ cell symbiosis cloning and replacement organs to grow two cells into a new organ for kidney patients caner cures and bio organic failures or positives

8763 to avoid another war use diplomatic to avoid another war use diplomatic monetary incentives and resources or not always state your political agenda

8764 inspiration to grow your business w inspiration to grow your business when you decide to have another baby inspiration when little families become big business or rather when big business becomes a bigger family a simple question to ponder over and when two things are made so special it ma

8765 encrypted phone number transmitting encrypted phone number transmitting and receiving key's and the new enigma generator

8766 encrypted phone software transmitti encrypted phone software transmitting and receiving key's and the new enigma generator

8767 un formulated alien text formats to un formulated alien text formats to create a un known and previously illegible type text to keep data secure said a un known character symbol set that will translate into some thing as known to the other receiver

8768 to use fractal noise as means to fi to use fractal noise as means to find the infinite extending paths of scripts and all while using trip circuit for control

8769 to search for a topic with an image to search for a topic with an image to find people places and things with input from meta tags such as technical terms when where who and why as well as to modify the photo scan or topic by perspective date and angle using the image itself and the topic

8770 personal freedom to drive makes me personal freedom to drive makes me think that taking cars and making trains out of them is against my freedom

8771 super embedding board technology us super embedding board technology using quartered circuits and fractal inverse technology making boards flat and embedding while conducting in one motion with out attaching

8772 information satellite that pilots l information satellite that pilots like drones and may re enter the atmosphere and disperse again into the atmosphere at our control with translation receiving and sending information that holds a scale as of a self sufficient server cloud satellite a sel

8773 war ship satellite a self supported war ship satellite a self supported nuclear powered satellite that pilots like drones and may re enter the atmosphere and disperse again into the atmosphere at our control with translation receiving and sending information that holds a scale as of a self

8774 automated robotics in space to elim automated robotics in space to eliminate the human space factor and automate the sequences of working robotics in space such as extended stay time and removal of life support systems as well as to incorporate remote control actives and war information an

8775 theology of basic wrongs done right theology of basic wrongs done right question and concept part grand challenges explorations application theology of basic wrongs done right when i go to the bm gates foundation website i see africans i see you asking for some k

8776 biochemical deceased viral library biochemical deceased viral library a study of living from the reversed immunization of virus properties and the work of today tomorrow and the future making medicine a thing on the shelf

8777 single sd chip module board that st single sd chip module board that stacks easily into a plural sd board system and controls with striping and stacking co processing in a chain reactive board configuration

8778 single ssd chip module board that s single ssd chip module board that stacks easily into a plural ssd board system and controls with striping and stacking co processing in a chain reactive board configuration

8779 electro magnetic torque converter a electro magnetic torque converter and acceleration board and software as clutch operator

8780 its a lot like a nuclear bomb only its a lot like a nuclear bomb only in reverse instead of destroying elements we are putting them together but more important than a super spontaneous collision we are separating the elements for recycling and purification the muffler and the past cata bu

8781 multiple coiled electrically powere multiple coiled electrically powered magnets for the electro magnetic torque converter and acceleration board and software as clutch operator

8782 na no capacity electric signals whe na no capacity electric signals when the wave of electricity meanders into a tip of a needle to move the vector relationships by way of nano gigawave

8783 electro magnetic cycled passing cha electro magnetic cycled passing charge of a magnet is when every turn the magnet there could be other magnets that connects a passing circuit generating a current

8784 a value conductor that measures of a value conductor that measures of a wave of electricity being a nano capacity electric signals when the wave of electricity meanders into a tip of a needle to move the vector relationships by way of nano gigawave

8785 pi co circuit with poly carb cerami pi co circuit with poly carb ceramic insulation and poly oxide metal as conducting circuits with power and wear as consideration for measuring the entire tension and properties of laser made engraving by plasma soldering yielding and melting

8786 pi co circuit pico layer chip and c pi co circuit pico layer chip and circuit building segmented layers and connecting ends from bottom to upper layer for stacking interior with poly carb ceramic insulation and poly oxide metal as conducting circuits with power and wear as consideration f

8787 pi co nano micro scale reverse scen pi co nano micro scale reverse scenario of heat and size rationality when the size doesn't make sense to make it that small and making multiple on board integrated circuits and cpu per system and the process of material being of more importance such as p
8788 sata mini add on compute module siz sata mini add on compute module size sata that adds to the computational ability to a system
8789 sata mini add on compute module a m sata mini add on compute module a module in size sata that adds to the computational ability to a system
8790 sata mini add on compute module by sata mini add on compute module by size sata that adds to the computational ability to a system
8791 magnetic engine and the electro coi magnetic engine and the electro coiled speed control by automatic transforming voltage regulator
8792 processed optical energy and the th processed optical energy and the things that equal a light to energy including a building with transparent solar liquid crystal panels windows on the outside and the intent to make electricity transparent solar power generating windows
8793 exterior bios library co existing b exterior bios library co existing bios library adjustments submissive profile programmable adjustments in a vague code and hardware environment to aid in a stand along software and hardware solution that makes a large section of add along configurations
8794 static sd hard drives with expandab static sd hard drives with expandable states
8795 static ssd hard drives with expanda static ssd hard drives with expandable states
8796 condensation water generator on a c condensation water generator on a condensation water farm the help we need is in cooling and heating the air itself to generate water where there may be a lack of water and more oxygen than happy a large scale condensation factory
8797 promise software building platform promise software building platform cloud promise cloud software building platform cloud that adds and trades certain processes for a monetary value and immediate commercial release final options
8798 promise software building platform promise software building platform cloud by promise cloud software building platform cloud that adds and trades certain processes for a monetary value and immediate commercial release final options
8799 promise software building platform promise software building platform cloud promise cloud software building platform cloud that adds and trades certain processes for a monetary value and commercial release final options
8800 open software building platform clo open software building platform cloud cloud software building platform cloud that adds and trades certain processes for a non monetary value and immediate non commercial release final options
8801 open software building platform clo open software building platform cloud by cloud software building platform cloud that adds and trades certain processes for a non monetary value and immediate non commercial release final options
8802 open software building platform clo open software building platform cloud cloud software building platform cloud that adds and trades certain processes for a non monetary value and immanent non commercial release final options
8803 m electronics form factor add on co m electronics form factor add on computational enhancement processors
8804 m electronics form factor add on gr m electronics form factor add on graphics

computational enhancement processors
8805 msata electronics form factor add o msata electronics form factor add on graphics enhancement processors
8806 inverted gas sorting and reclaiming inverted gas sorting and reclaiming recycled incineration gasses by way of catalytic converter and gas humidifier for or only with a unique dry or paste wet solvent clay and the processes that make taking trash and turning it into rock or solvent sludge
8807 carbon by metallic energy signal fo carbon by metallic energy signal force is the wave of energy that attracts or repels any such one carbon away and from each other in a radio magnetic force in any size obvious or microscopic force of annotative fixation including or excluding reactive pr
8808 gasses energy signal wave gas wave gasses energy signal wave gas wave energy signal is the measure of energy that attracts or repels any such one gas or other gasses to and from each other in a energy force in any size obvious or microscopic force of annotative fixation including or exclu
8809 gasses energy signal wave by gas wa gasses energy signal wave by gas wave energy signal is the measure of energy that attracts or repels any such one gas or other gasses to and from each other in a energy force in any size obvious or microscopic force of annotative fixation including or ex
8810 carbon energy signal wave carbon wa carbon energy signal wave carbon wave energy signal is the measure of energy that attracts or repels any such one oxide or other metal to and from each other in a energy force in any size obvious or microscopic force of annotative fixation including or e
8811 carbon energy signal wave by carbon carbon energy signal wave by carbon wave energy signal is the measure of energy that attracts or repels any such one oxide or other metal to and from each other in a energy force in any size obvious or microscopic force of annotative fixation including o
8812 starch energy signal wave starch wa starch energy signal wave starch wave energy signal is the measure of energy that attracts or repels any such one starch to and from each other in a energy force in any size obvious or microscopic force of annotative fixation including or excluding react
8813 starch energy signal wave by starch starch energy signal wave by starch wave energy signal is the measure of energy that attracts or repels any such one starch to and from each other in a energy force in any size obvious or microscopic force of annotative fixation including or excluding re
8814 scholastic aptitude testing like co scholastic aptitude testing like comparisons gone wild schematics of a interwoven statistical cloud scholastic aptitude testing like comparisons gone wild schematics of a interwoven statistical cloud and when variables are compared using normal clients a
8815 physeometric prediction by energy s physeometric prediction by energy signal wave measures in scales of negative as well as positive may be used in any predictive computational data analytic such as to say that with a known and given there could be any such physeometric prediction of appli
8816 physeometric prediction data cloud physeometric prediction data cloud a group of servers or information structure that houses a secluded or open system of predictions for the

information that bases it's self on predictive measures of experimental operations with or with out committing to

8817 physeometric prediction data cloud physeometric prediction data cloud by a group of servers or information structure that houses a secluded or open system of predictions for the information that bases it's self on predictive measures of experimental operations with or with out committing

8818 how to loose a war is to follow the how to loose a war is to follow their rules and drop flowers instead of bombs when flowers don't work drop bombs

8819 poly carbonate sandwiched stacked c poly carbonate sandwiched stacked circuit board on ply board technology

8820 dynamic functions of a input output dynamic functions of a input output resolution a com putative functioning virtual reality of measurement cloud or software system a virtual building cloud that simulates the construction of points and volts down to a format that is appreciative and perce

8821 retro retro retro penicillin two pe retro retro retro penicillin two penicillin two the simple minds think alike but we progress through abstract minds that are complex yet still simple looking back is always important why did i leave that milk out on the kitchen counter all day its an un

8822 commons unique abnormal commons uni commons unique abnormal commons unique abnormal a + m = e ({} over {}) %uxe a {e} over {m} %uxe b {e%delta ^{}} over {c%delta ^{}} %uxe c{e%ux } over {c%ux }

8823 commons unique abnormal commons uni commons unique abnormal commons unique abnormal infinity x +infinity %uxe max <=x<= xe{ x^{}} %uxe %infinite %uxd + %uxea %epsilon %sigma

8824 commons unique abnormal commons uni commons unique abnormal commons unique abnormal <p style=margin bottom in >lllint >%uxea %uxf { b%uxe sqrt{b^{} ac} } over {a} %notequal binom{%sigma }binom{{%uxeb i%uxeb m} }{ < j < n } p (i j) <p style=margin bottom in >

8825 science calculators with calculatio science calculators with calculation insert able or embedded library's of instance of information purpose calculator holding the power to answer the questions properly the first time that may do hypo physics theory or build a script and even virtual pred

8826 a rounded number of encryption base a rounded number of encryption based on a four segment of numbers to process and extract an encrypt able alpha numerical code for ssl and more advanced communications

8827 to use fractal noise as means to fi to use fractal noise as means to find the infinite extending paths of scripts and all while using trip circuits for control boolean updates to practical scripts and vague code complex two planes of intersection and if or a what

8828 duplicate cubits zeros ones and two duplicate cubits zeros ones and twos and threes a non argumentative physical quantitative mechanical on off state with two layers by reading twice

8829 double cubits two sequences of zero double cubits two sequences of zeros ones and a non argumentative physical quantitative mechanical on off state or with two layers

8830 limonene generated silicone doping limonene generated silicone doping to degrade plastics and harden or solvency the plastics in advance to incineration and generate electricity as well as sooty carbon for synthetic metal semiconductors

8831 more cubits zeros ones and twos and more cubits zeros ones and twos and threes a non argumentative physical quantitative mechanical on off state with two layers by reading changes at a modified on series and then a modified off series in a section with in a measurement of cubits together

8832 mini wireless chip operator ed and mini wireless chip operator ed and compute magnetic transmission for torque and propulsion of device controlling a stationary over controlled passing magnets that provide any such current controlled with a wireless connection for torque magnitude intensi

8833 synthetic metal cell drawing and sh synthetic metal cell drawing and shaping vector cubit cell dividing and cascading increments of myriads with in

8834 a semi solid state social state dri a semi solid state social state drive and chip board configuration that conjoins vectors and makes any path a routine in quantum steps

8835 ex tractable card form factor compu ex tractable card form factor computing by multiplying systems on a traveling boards

8836 ecology scale landscaping will chan ecology scale landscaping will change deserts into jungles by that mountain of debre built by synthesizing a mountain and valley precipitation valve

8837 ddr system application on chip a sl ddr system application on chip a slim operating system that is dedicated to alternate functions based upon application per device including secondary cpu and or storage and system bios

8838 suspended air and seed super suspen suspended air and seed super suspended fuel flow for hyper active engine part seeds and force suspended air and seed to centrifugal force included inside a hyperactive engine to generate force and energy and make a more fuel effective means for work

8839 exchangeable executable cell cell c exchangeable executable cell cell card for a local non synchronized cloud account cell phones that is a starting point to a private phone

8840 enterprise art server and the inten enterprise art server and the intent to create and master the digital frontier in a normal server used as machine for not intended but built intentions the translated definition in a simple name thus made as digital art server regiment of computers kn

8841 multiple wireless multiple device b multiple wireless multiple device back up table port

8842 platform computing that measures in platform computing that measures instance rather than current cloud computing statistical virtual memory stacking easy to ask but i can remember christm as shopping with my parents and some times it really wasn't a good year when this situation happened

8843 too much paid in adverts program fl too much paid in adverts program flush market tactics too much paid in adverts program no one said you had to listen to the whole thing flush the market strategies and convoluted scenarios of an artist and their own thought of worth why is it that people

8844 phone station bluetooth magnetic ba phone station bluetooth magnetic backup recharge wireless charge and backup clone update and restore hardware

8845 denotation of any such specified pl denotation of any such specified platform specific as to route a version of any operating system as true role in a non pragmatic cloud but intentionally a specified role in a company operating system for example my mother w as a nurse and later in her ca

8846 diverse operating board magnetic io diverse operating board magnetic ion fiber optic and nano electric signals to work the large and small things into a so un d well rounded machine

8847 a working parts process working sof a working parts process working software is a platform of a data base that is built on a question of fundamentals to make a transitional and schematic plan for a business with many parts system built to work together

8848 na no tetrahedron motors period par na no tetrahedron motors period particles tets of a period

8849 a squared area of cascading increme a squared area of cascading increments fun ny but real to process code with measurement cascading increments a certain unit of measurement

8850 a squared area of cascading increme a squared area of cascading increments funny but real to process code with measurement cascading increments a certain unit of measurement or for processing electronic measurement using my certain unit of measurement data versus the shape of media t

8851 na no micro and pico soldering meta na no micro and pico soldering metal printing and three dimensional printer ability to grow vertically and horizontally with a moderate soldering plasma thermal flash plasma thermal printing

8852 commons unique abnormals commons un commons unique abnormals commons unique abnormal

8853 to assimilate the quartered and the to assimilate the quartered and then square a shape for different angles of processing with the thought that there is a connection between the shape and the result of connections available triangle divided chip properties

8854 secured wifi wireless accessories p secured wifi wireless accessories post is a group of accessories that accompany a powered usb pairing unit as multi interface device making all your personal computing needs wireless and only yours secured wireless accessories post

8855 mini complete server ip location ch mini complete server ip location chip system in a disk optical a optically read by disk that makes any such form or function such as to mirror a completed server with ip virtual optical server disk

8856 mini complete server ip location ch mini complete server ip location chip system in a disk solid state solid state chip with a server format of completed functions of on and off and all other things any other server would function as into a cloned disk with the entire system or majority of

8857 mini complete server ip location ch mini complete server ip location chip system in a disk pcie load this is really a pcie location intertwined with any given pci port or express location that is a translated mini completed server mini server per pcie

8858 mini complete server ip location ch mini complete server ip location chip system in a virtual disk folder translating into a place inside any given medium a separate window into a looping server that is in itself a mini completed sever in a folder on a disk complete server in a virtual fol

8859 volunteer web warriors software to volunteer web warriors software to aid against the enemy and to fight a cyber war vol un teerism with our at home devices to counter attack the enemy foes

8860 a large rechargeable battery plant a large rechargeable battery plant that h as automated chemical pool recharging and sending receiving charging and re doping electron batches and storage for electricity on any large scale in acres and years suitable for the safety and health of human li

8861 why can t my phone connect to a sat why can t my phone connect to a satellite connect the dots why can't my phone connect to a satellite instead of cell towers why can't my personal router connect to a satellite for un interrupted or rather a % up time and possibly easier set ups connect t

8862 a large recycled battery pool that a large recycled battery pool that makes other small batteries with less time and higher concentrations of elements rechargeable battery plant that h as automated chemical pool recharging and sending receiving charging and re doping electron ions and neu

8863 dynamic compressed virtual encrypti dynamic compressed virtual encryption to encapsulate data for a certain end point protocol while compressing compressed encrypted end point protocol

8864 dynamic compressed virtual encrypti dynamic compressed virtual encryption to encapsulate data for a certain end point protocol while compressing compressed encrypted end point protocol by

8865 wireless radio patching per device wireless radio patching per device is to patch devices with the board of a receiving serial signal easily verses a software connection wireless radio patch device serial

8866 wireless radio patching per device wireless radio patching per device is to patch devices with the board of a receiving serial signal easily verses a software connection wireless radio patch device serial by

8867 electric catalyze sodium nitrate ca electric catalyze sodium nitrate carbonate reaction engine system and motive for an alternative power source that may be able to propel from small amo un ts of sulfur and a powder combustion engine with sodium nitrate and spark plug and piston action pow

8868 probability is a term for business probability is a term for business ethics compromise and ethics rules against arbitrary lying and dishonesty of information and statistics of income and profits ethics probability by

8869 cell tower lending and broad cast s cell tower lending and broad cast shares build your own cell tower with our technology and profit with our company byo cell tower by

8870 na no motors ofs tyro carbonate nan na no motors ofs tyro carbonate nano motors ofs tyro carbonate and in the shape of a tetrahedron

8871 na no motors of styro carbonate nan na no motors of styro carbonate nano motors of styro carbonate and in the shape of a tetrahedron

8872 critical non attached data back up critical non attached data back up registrations and cloud clusters is an extremely secure web of servers and data bases that conclude information that is nearly irreplaceable or important more than any other data critical non attached back up

8873 sodium magnesium carbon oxide compo sodium magnesium carbon oxide compound for powdered combustion engines and fuel made with a powered process and less liquid use and waste as chemical propellant of combustion

8874 software software please make my so software software please make my software software design software that relates in vector and code preferences that is an easy and re sell able application package maker and formatted

8875 software software please make my so software software please make my software software information and data management creation and business software that relates in vector and code preferences that is an easy and re sell able application package maker and formatted

8876 theater servers hd theater experien theater servers hd theater experience hf theater theater data server data packs

8877 software software please make my so software software please make my software software banking and finance software that relates in vector and code preferences that is an easy and re sell able application package maker and formatted

8878 software software please make my so software software please make my software software medicine medical and health of solutions and directives of care for people and problems with health software that relates in vector and code preferences that is an easy and re sell able application packa

8879 processor plug in base and peripher processor plug in base and peripheral ports that have a multi part available function to attachment and configuration adjustable port note able programmable inside the bios and what to where situation of this and that makes working parts down to the chip

8880 pre built selected options for proc pre built selected options for processor plug in base and peripheral ports that have a multi part available function to attachment and configuration adjustable port note able programmable inside the bios and what to where situation of this and that makes

8881 open mother board arrangement of pa open mother board arrangement of parts connected instructions pre built open ended selected options for processor plug in base and peripheral ports that have a multi part available function to attachment and configuration adjustable port note able progra

8882 consumer paid open mother board arr consumer paid open mother board arrangement of parts connected instructions of pre built open ended selected options for processor plug in base and peripheral ports that have a multi part available function to attachment and configuration adjustable port

8883 from my own experience psychotic de from my own experience psychotic debilitation from my own experience i believe that there is brain damage during a psychotic episode that may lead to serious and more permanent debilitation this is important due to the chemical balance and the aid of rec

8884 landfill recycle mining and dis ass landfill recycle mining and dis assembly starch and carbon line arrangement is a property of known practices that still a recycle tanner into a this is all we work with working with itself and reworking all the materials as chemical to process what we p

8885 recycle and cycle gas liquid and ga recycle and cycle gas liquid and gas separated mining and dis assembly to material on a settle absolute table weight process take and rest into a sedimentary weight of stagnation and aggression movement and non movement improving heating resting and cool

8886 recycle and cycle solid metal and s recycle and cycle solid metal and solid mineral mining and dis assembly to material on a settle absolute table weight process take and rest into a sedimentary weight of stagnation and aggression movement and non movement improving heating resting and coo

8887 more channels per call voice data s more channels per call voice data screen camera aio all digital comm a cloud receiver the intent to design a complete radio tv phone data receiver the m un dane and exciting work prior to the internet to make data from radio television and voice comm un
8888 licensed conceptual inventor status licensed conceptual inventor status and document the status of concepts based on the deposition writer themselves
8889 where are they now help and history where are they now help and history of any known centique centique ology a study of honest and real unbias history encounters factual links
8890 thin form mobile you build it chass thin form mobile you build it chassis format of parts and interconnections by scsi scsi medium and scsi small connections that overlap and up and over connections by scalable link interface small medium and large
8891 to round the estimation of a half p to round the estimation of a half pixel closer with a pi triplet fraction
8892 to round the estimation of a pixel to round the estimation of a pixel closer with a pi triplet fraction
8893 parts that unite by scale and conne parts that unite by scale and connections across carry inter connection circuit processors and alternate vectors of chip exchange a chip that sends a specific vector data rate to a specified place to and then to more or to reply
8894 the updated nation of banks and lie the updated nation of banks and liens as wealth of ownership in percent of the entire active and stable economy is a data base of ownership percents snip
8895 solid state multiplier chip is a sy solid state multiplier chip is a synthetic metal conductor that holds the data at a rate and amplifies the volume per calculation to increase the definitions of signal per circuit in bound and accordingly
8896 system shell a system of congruent system shell a system of congruent processors a system of a chip inside an operable compressing and multiplier system of processing system shell inside shell inside shell
8897 criminally insane schizophrenia cri criminally insane schizophrenia criminally schizophrenic what is the issue with virile contributors and identity theft to compose why this is important in a short is to say that the specific context is technology why a person will gain access to a log in
8898 the updated nation of banks and lie the updated nation of banks and liens as wealth of ownership in percent of the entire active and stable economy is a data base of ownership percents
8899 secure system shell a system of enc secure system shell a system of encrypted processors a system of a chip inside an operable compressing and multiplier system of processing system shell inside shell inside shell
8900 planned limonene plastics a solvent planned limonene plastics a solvent plastic that h as a specific degrade composite known and planned to recycle with a specified make and end to the solvent and finished plastic new and dead
8901 soldered down system on chip bed of soldered down system on chip bed of chips storage server brick and relay board and configuration management server system graph and error correction indication led configured and manufactured system clone with data and duplication flash disc and drives o
8902 fo un tain power a fo un tain drink fo un tain power a fo un tain drink combination

fuel of magnesium salt powder and a mixture of alcohol for body and movement to power a combustion engine that is engineered for a powder and mixed with liquid for a concentrated fuel at a lower cost and hi

8903 water purified engine exhaust cycle water purified engine exhaust cycled cylinders used with internal combustion engines fueled by either petrol or diesel including lean burn engines as well as kerosene heaters and stoves second stem exhaust tunnel

8904 solvent purified engine exhaust cyc solvent purified engine exhaust cycled cylinders used with internal combustion engines fueled by either petrol or diesel including lean burn engines as well as kerosene heaters and stoves second stem exhaust tunnel

8905 fractal math string zoom formula fo fractal math string zoom formula for synthetic and poly chemical measurements to zoom and extract dna from stem cells as well as dna strings to zoom and measure solid state data or solid state memory cells uses ! to zoom and extract dna from stem cells a

8906 properties of stagnation improper u properties of stagnation improper use of technology in a manipulative manner to conclude monetary fun ds verses the intent to progress for example the co processor verse the use of an extended automatic co processor verses a deliberate attempt to keep th

8907 improper use of the truth as suffic improper use of the truth as sufficient means for rules against any such corporation or notarized agreement

8908 summit and sell a thon conference k summit and sell a thon conference known as convention for sale and for the use of property

8909 international summit and sell a tho international summit and sell a thon at a world interest and denomination of ownership

8910 public verses a proprietary ownersh public verses a proprietary ownership of privileged operation is a data center that operates with little out side or un commercial activity

8911 c technology wireless usb technolog c technology wireless usb technology wireless usb technology microsoft had the goods and i needed what they had they listened and i plainly spoke what i wanted when where and how is the point microsoft is no longer accepting bids for invent projects ther

8912 a mobile war data center and the op a mobile war data center and the operations prior to any such consequences of a war zone known as new data war with drone and air based weapons snip

8913 homeland security web analyzing sof homeland security web analyzing software that collects and collates the data to hot spots and sensitive are as inside the united states and abroad that acts like a nerve of intelligence and initiates ip and web activity bots to specify the targets activi

8914 corporate security web analyzing so corporate security web analyzing software that collects and collates the data to hot spots and sensitive are as inside the united states and abroad that acts like a nerve of intelligence and initiates ip and web activity bots to specify the targets activ

8915 citizen specific security web analy citizen specific security web analyzing software that collects and collates the data to hot spots and sensitive are as inside the united states and abroad that acts like a nerve of intelligence and initiates ip and web activity bots to specify the target

8916 lets say that there are ways to hel lets say that there are ways to help others and save lives would you trust a doctor to make a interesting finding with out any long term damage if you {me some one important we both know} the patient survives

8917 pre world war crime trial and inten pre world war crime trial and intent to issue a declaration of isolation as well as term correction to any such life interrupting country as whole

8918 layered acrylic printing and jet sp layered acrylic printing and jet spray plastic printing in itself is a term generalized as two part d and d printing combined

8919 paint printing jet spray plastic pr paint printing jet spray plastic printing in itself is a term generalized printing with paint and an opacity paint plastic solvent

8920 a mobile war data center and the op a mobile war data center and the operations prior to any such consequences of a war zone known as new data war with drone and air based weapons

8921 raised and re circuited printed sol raised and re circuited printed solid state circuits and synthetic metals by way of plasma layered bonding and thermal re doping data driven circuits

8922 open source programmable chips and open source programmable chips and systems that are conveniently un secured pre mirrored

8923 the law to compete the retread situ the law to compete the retread situation of un safe driving and open arms of retread ding semi truck tires in accordance with a safe means snip

8924 en scribble open chip cpu and softw en scribble open chip cpu and software driven registration for designing acceptable circuit driven operations of a system on a chip

8925 how to a essence of a subscription how to a essence of a subscription that includes dates events and clicks as well as notable notes and other things that require attention

8926 en scribble write once open chip cp en scribble write once open chip cpu and software driven registration for designing acceptable circuit driven operations of a system on a chip

8927 en scribble re writable open chip c en scribble re writable open chip cpu and software driven registration for designing acceptable circuit driven operations of a system on a chip

8928 the law to compete the retread situ the law to compete the retread situation of un safe driving and open arms of retread ding semi truck tires in accordance with a safe means

8929 automatic system correction mainten automatic system correction maintenance add in card with plug and play beeping error codes and other operations libraries

8930 device specific data write shape kn device specific data write shape known as cram functioning device specified write once or multiple times in order for a finite use of solid state matter nano writes and re writes to configure a more than a cubit to a cram shape for a multitude of operat

8931 re write able cubit device language re write able cubit device language of shape and form for function hardware to make a shape in one language and it equal to a transistor building shape in another said this way building a chip from languages of shapes to make a shape in one language equa

8932 to stop within a certain rule of de to stop within a certain rule of denominations literally

8933 practice and sport smart training d practice and sport smart training data base comparison software for the smart ball smart shoe and smart practice languages

8934 drone war remote weapons system inf drone war remote weapons system infantry low close to ground altitude and the operations prior to any such consequences of a war zone known as new data war with drone and air based weapons

8935 school approved learning device is school approved learning device is a working tablet or pc that operates when needed and is encrypted for students personal ownership works with a specific class and operates with t compact flash or any mobile scheme including the means to submit tests an

8936 the difference between a friendly c the difference between a friendly code command and an un friendly one is the process to limit and not with out limit vague code complex friendly vague code anamorphic script commands the difference between a friendly code command and an un friendly one i

8937 single to multiple operation core f single to multiple operation core functions in server and data center use ages working as tier based institution translations as multiple or single cell core systems on chips with connections powered by software that works as needed when the chip on a s

8938 two chip and one in out board that two chip and one in out board that functions and works as system on a chip with a data storage system and a controller system making a mirroring of on and off for any processing including the transfer of an operation and exchange of any single file

8939 bigger board by going smaller multi bigger board by going smaller multiple chips of storage to an embedded and exchangeable sense of connections explained as wall of insert able systems built by rows an columns of an architecture of request and a string of systems on strings wall based op

8940 satellite by cell cell by satellite satellite by cell cell by satellite and secure satellite connected short remote drone virtual reality warfare drone based weapons

8941 public ally supported short network public ally supported short network stations instead of blasting communications from far above why not make communication a small subscription network like the way it used to be in the pay phone days we could have mobile networks everywhere someone wante

8942 study of sorts to understand and re study of sorts to understand and reason geometry and other trigonometry waves with a comparative interest into measurement of statistical process the way a cloud can help use measurement and understand other process and actually see shapes

8943 electric and battery operated utens electric and battery operated utensil exam of any battle field prior to operations and smart tracking un controlled devices

8944 driving tension scale of accidents driving tension scale of accidents and incidents that conclude to an un safe level of community relationships in driving and public behavior

8945 pop fad curves intrinsic popularity pop fad curves intrinsic popularity curves in modern culture a popular fad high arch to middle decent and small arch with gradual fade out b near impossible long high arch b different curve gradual fade in with a small arch and middle decent to a high ar

8946 architecture in cubits another way architecture in cubits another way to say functions in written language a cubits as any other known as path or circuit in another to build a chip out of a formed path of cubits in an alphabet of cubits and then circuits in super annotation cell of condu

8947 building language hardware written building language hardware written by software as solid state or flash based conductor processor and operator made into a cubit written composite working tool

8948 building language software written building language software written by software hardware as solid state or flash based conductor processor and operator made into a cubit written composite working tool

8949 fiber optic system connection for a fiber optic system connection for alternate co processing substitution and fiber optic system amp accelerator processing stand along plug and play device to improve computations and the transceiver relationship in that

8950 negative microwave technology and f negative microwave technology and format making cold things stay cold and the same ovens that make things work for warmth can make things stay cold for a while after that so after all their is cold fusion the thought is that the technology that is availa

8951 the reasons for poetic pretense and the reasons for poetic pretense and you mystery of art and us the history strange or truth fiction of a future always as surprise

8952 transistor nano direction circuit n transistor nano direction circuit na no direction and a path of a y transistor nano direction circuit a direction that may be pointed by a fractalized section of code in order to direct a correct pathway to make a working model redirected nano pathway ci

8953 co processing active software for a co processing active software for a wireless mini servers and data center operations network is a software platform that runs and completes the process of who what when and where easily by calling on a group of processes to work in un ison at more than o

8954 a focused laser receiver that holds a focused laser receiver that holds and records laser signals as data in an annotation of triplet pi equilibrium is a wave of data as signal

8955 portable hand held server with sequ portable hand held server with sequential process to enable distant and no service are as similar to the open idea app yet more specific in titles needs like sever weather reports and how to get medicine the people who would use such a device are patrol

8956 the code and compensation required the code and compensation required to provide a simple targeted geo nautic range path data as wave signal in a focused laser sending and receiving group that sends and relays holds and records laser signals as data in multitudes encrypted or un encrypted

8957 the device transmitting code and co the device transmitting code and compensation required to provide a simple targeted geo nautic range path data as wave signal in a focused laser sending and receiving group that sends and relays holds and records laser signals as data in multitudes encry

8958 seriously from [] sent tuesday may seriously from [] sent tuesday may am to microsoft us partner team subject retro active software resale partner id hello mpn at microsoft seriously i am asking for you to sell office again treat this comment with possibilities lately you are getti

8959 lets play political jeopardy and sa lets play political jeopardy and say that people who run government should have a cap on income un til out of office and officially audited by the irs to have any such money

8960 to withhold governmental breaks cop to withhold governmental breaks

8961 the live needle polygraph test to s the live needle polygraph test to study by acup un cture the truth of any such person

8962 old medicine h as a new study the i old medicine h as a new study the integration of old ways into the new way of taking medicine antique biology

8963 super simple small push button with super simple small push button with microphone

and speaker working with voice command and no touch screen cell phone hardware to sd to no sd
8964 super simple small push button micr super simple small push button microphone speaker voice command phone operating system that is network and web inclusive
8965 long range laser data wave is a lig long range laser data wave is a light wave of information that carries to point to point and holds wave signals of information similar to optical data yet with out fibers
8966 drone warfare can end war and make drone warfare can end war and make a safe place for freedom as we know it police driven drone will make a un manageable place a safe place
8967 cellular information channel for po cellular information channel for police that carry police data specific and confidentially secured information
8968 the ability to toggle an early inve the ability to toggle an early invent toggles and switches the ability to toggle and make paths in order to compute the existing switches that need to be used and made off and on electricity gone computational simple but very early need in tech space
8969 a secured public information channe a secured public information channel for monetary transfers is a specific web application that transfers ownership and fun ds to other banks and balances
8970 multiple channels of information br multiple channels of information bridge to access any such specific need or industry specific technology to share and improve that data share market of information is a mini expanded data exchange to be said again is like the information of ro industry
8971 pcie plug and play data encoders an pcie plug and play data encoders and decoders and readers for multiple channels of information bridge to access any such specific need or industry specific technology
8972 pcie plug and play data encoders an pcie plug and play data encoders and decoders and readers for multiple channels of information bridge to access any such specific need or industry specific technology to share and improve that data share market of information is a mini expanded data exch
8973 point a with a synchronized clock d point a with a synchronized clock daybreak compensation measurements point a with a synchronized clock to use compensation measurements like atmosphere elements and other catalyst measurements for point b to compare and complete the time to distant light
8974 automated robotic operated cell tow automated robotic operated cell tower elevator that accesses the components in a arranged method of distribution and installation like a robotic spider for cell communication equipment
8975 encrypted phone service that is for encrypted phone service that is for business
8976 drone la un ching warship intellige drone la un ching warship intelligent warship is a lifeless battle ship that is an artificial war machine that wins wars defends freedom and kills bad guys
8977 i don't remember the details and i i don't remember the details and i probably shouldn't tell any one those matters but the fact of the matter is that the retro car h as reached heights of un imaginable proportions fact one day i w as minding my own business and i received the call from a
8978 to save all sources state of our ar to save all sources state of our art arch of a window

to elaborate on this with full intent to save all sources the means of any archive is how much there is to make any save or estimation of weight weight of a back up on any scale to forward or foretell

8979 g as station run off reservoir for g as station run off reservoir for environment for safety water treatment and river friendly filters

8980 medical suit and marijuana legal st medical suit and marijuana legal state anti trust to un support the marijuana fed f un ded states why should different states support other states

8981 infantry drone la un ching warship infantry drone la un ching warship intelligent warship is a lifeless battle ship that is an artificial war machine that wins wars defends freedom and kills bad guys

8982 war drone software interface that d war drone software interface that detonates bombs shoots a g un and all works to help defend freedom and dedicate sponsorship to help end war that is an artificial war machine that wins wars defends freedom and kills bad guys

8983 the need for ed hypothetical theory the need for ed hypothetical theory rights is a common missed opportunity based on will and why as in a information back up right protected by schematics and red tape a duplicate protection enabled by nature

8984 a running circle definition of what a running circle definition of what h as been said is in fact a no answer for example if someone were to propose a question to a branch of government and the return answer w as a previously stated circular statement not a yes or no answer by definition t

8985 a misleading running circle definit a misleading running circle definition of what h as been said is in fact a no answer for example if someone were to propose a question to a branch of government and the return answer w as a previously stated circular statement not a yes or no answer by d

8986 a hypothetical definition included a hypothetical definition included as intellectual property is the mission of a duplicate and case filed in both manners

8987 state of our art open market gadget state of our art open market gadgets to elaborate on this with full intent to progress the moment of technology and processor imagine you being able to pick the size and computational power of your own gadget and yet at the same time you yourself could c

8988 a chip written and in a state of re a chip written and in a state of re writable status that can be written to and then rewritten in any sort of language for function and purpose not only standard capacity random access memory

8989 a write once chip that h as a state a write once chip that h as a state of permanence and will only function as second or first capacity full function chip with architecture written by software

8990 to understand dangerous technology to understand dangerous technology and the anti climatic autonomous era of un expected danger the intent to improve not endanger the obvious state of a space elevator vision of autonomous intent to catapult caca and non reality of foresight

8991 touch the web print the web my ligh touch the web print the web my light scribe edition of altracks w as getting held up and soon enough while on the phone to a hp tech agent i mentioned ever tried to print the web moment of time excluded web to print applications that make sense is the mi

8992 to understand dangerous technology to understand dangerous technology and the anti climatic autonomous era of un expected danger the road verses the air for travel ro autonomous

8993 to understand dangerous technology to understand dangerous technology and the anti climatic autonomous era of un expected danger landing pads for the autonomous air drones with automated load and un load robots

8994 to understand dangerous technology to understand dangerous technology and the anti climatic autonomous era of un expected danger security travel and cloud based drone traffic control flight issuance

8995 to understand dangerous technology to understand dangerous technology and the anti climatic autonomous era of un expected danger the signal control federal communication level of drone and non commercial travel patterns

8996 lcus united states of america armed lcus united states of america armed forces ro contract winner state of our art ro t design stealth state of our art ro t design united states of america armed forces ro contract winner

8997 to understand dangerous technology to understand dangerous technology and the anti climatic autonomous era of un expected danger the signal control federal communication level of drone and commercial travel patterns

8998 radio specified alpha channel encry radio specified alpha channel encrypted software is the intent to focus out a specified communication with a single operative with the intent to direct with out interference of other channels during communication say for example a unit of battle or comm

8999 things that go with poor spelling h things that go with poor spelling health invent tab state of our art things that go with poor spelling spider pill elemental subtraction method carbon stabilize reaction syn toxin vs bio toxin fruit fly farming all these things can change medicine by the

9000 ask intel about it they will say th ask intel about it they will say the exact same thing server chip stacking stacking this state of our art early invent coming to light ask intel about it they will say the exact same thing server chip stacking

9001 intermittent synthetic conductive g intermittent synthetic conductive gel and oscillating cascading poly carbon insulated spindled printed vertical chip layered computer controlled and measured in nano myriads a link of layers to build with

9002 cascading printing reproduction is cascading printing reproduction is the inter printed method of the conductive property and the insulator to generate a conductive chip

9003 a fractal is the opposite of a worm a fractal is the opposite of a worm hole (a+m=e) part a fractal is the opposite of a worm hole the entire amplitude of any entity with twice the mass will make energy that posses a general whole number that is not prime it's plain to see but what is ther

9004 oem oms original equipment manufact oem oms original equipment manufacturer optional manufacturer system oem oms state of our art open market systems to elaborate on this with full intent to progress the moment of technology and processor imagine you being able to pick the size and computa

9005 a liberation statement such as doct a liberation statement such as doctrine that plainly stating the purpose and consistences of a prove means of valuable to itself in a means not a current to accurately describe why some technology may not be suitable for safe public occurrences or to pr

9006 intertwined hyper thread to send th intertwined hyper thread to send the same signal to multiple places and conduct a vector resolution in sync motions
9007 intertwined double triplet hyper th intertwined double triplet hyper thread to send the same signal to multiple places and conduct a vector resolution in sync motions of processing
9008 a nano printed hyper embedded direc a nano printed hyper embedded directional navigation chip that provides the path direction based on a frequency change in the signal like a flashing yellow go when clear light
9009 this is a situation state of our ar this is a situation state of our art woq enterprise email records archive this is a situation of one fall scenario spam and filter checks to assign a script to this is not adequate to make a program that exports and imports files paged by person and tabb
9010 a nano printed hyper embedded direc a nano printed hyper embedded directional navigation chip that provides the path direction based on a frequency change in the signal like a traffic stop light
9011 a nano printed hyper embedded direc a nano printed hyper embedded directional navigation chip that provides the path direction based on a frequency change in the signal like a way stop with traffic signs
9012 a nano printed hyper embedded direc a nano printed hyper embedded directional navigation chip that provides the path direction based on a frequency change in the signal like a way stop light intersection
9013 a nano printed hyper embedded direc a nano printed hyper embedded directional navigation end that provides the path direction based on a frequency change in the signal like a right or left lane fork in the road
9014 a hyper embedded directional vector a hyper embedded directional vector coordinate directions is to travel on any such given processor chip and micro board as well as to repeat and loop in a quantified sequence and method on any given fork traffic changes and in any such given directional
9015 planned disaster is a pre planned s planned disaster is a pre planned satellite crash course of premptive action as last resort to the beginning of the end of any satellites planned ending and to where to crash why to crash or a gliding crash
9016 preplanned disaster is a pre planne preplanned disaster is a pre planned satellite crash course of premptive action as last resort to the beginning of the end of any satellites planned ending and to where to crash why to crash or a gliding crash
9017 this invent project is based upon p this invent project is based upon phone communication gone satellite cell tower possibilities this invent project is based upon phone communication gone satellite the importance is that this is to equate the chance of a alternate use for cell broadcast s
9018 satellite expiration estimate for a satellite expiration estimate for atmosphere re entry will help people work with satellites in a new and responsible way to help the space atmosphere environment and all the other costs of satellite orbit concerns
9019 astro hardware satellite server sta astro hardware satellite server state of our art astro service hardware astro hardware imagine a disillusioned space elevator that h as no clue just a satellite that h as servers aboard imagine space travel that is so successful that over a long or short
9020 astro hardware astro size state of astro hardware astro size state of our art astro size

hardware form astro hardware extended satellite computations imagine space travel that is so successful that over a long or short time we are able to store data in space itself

9021 argon or hydrogen plasma chip etchi argon or hydrogen plasma chip etching by neon on rhodium bedding un der and over layered chip printing all or parts

9022 exit format expressions efe state o exit format expressions efe state of our art exit format expressions exit format expressions the intent to share all types of data or miscellaneous file types and the intent to not share or make program compatible is an interoperability challenge and pro

9023 data code kill switch of un known a data code kill switch of un known ability previously known as friendly vague code and a design designation as adjustment code

9024 a premptive agreement in a cloud da a premptive agreement in a cloud data base environment that protects the entity of itself by control and data code kill switch script

9025 a data war or war data premptive ag a data war or war data premptive agreement in a cloud data base environment that protects the entity of itself by control and data code kill switch script cooperation and compliance of no service

9026 a zone not incorporated with data a a zone not incorporated with data and on a war or war data premptive agreement in a cloud data base environment that protects the entity of itself by control and data code kill switch script cooperation and compliance of no service

9027 to use a device where the data pack to use a device where the data packets of the internet and cellular comm h as stopped and a radio wave of certain freq is controlled in a zone not incorporated with data and on a war or war data premptive agreement in a cloud data base environment that p

9028 to switch off a zone incorporated w to switch off a zone incorporated with data and on a war or war data premptive agreement in a cloud data base environment that protects the entity of itself by control and data code kill switch script cooperation and compliance of no service

9029 un der and over layered blanks for un der and over layered blanks for writing purpose and laying the path to write the functions with software innate

9030 emw state of our art eject my work emw state of our art eject my work i have always wanted to borrow someone's pc but it's a pc how come we can't eject the os the updates and the software we own as well as our work and subsequently call hard ware hardware and eject my work

9031 starch protein and sugar dna micro starch protein and sugar dna micro biologically printed antibody used to fight disease

9032 printed dna from any known starch o printed dna from any known starch or protein micro biologically printed antibody used to fight disease

9033 dna at cg nucleotide printed dna fr dna at cg nucleotide printed dna from any known starch or protein micro biologically printed antibody used to fight disease or cancer

9034 un der and over layered blanks by f un der and over layered blanks by for writing purpose and laying the path to write the functions with software innate

9035 dna at cg nucleotide printed dna fr dna at cg nucleotide printed dna from any known starch or protein micro biologically printed antibody used to fight disease or cancer positively doped

9036 dna at cg nucleotide printed dna fr dna at cg nucleotide printed dna from any known starch or protein micro biologically printed antibody used to fight disease or cancer negatively doped

9037 dna at cg nucleotide printed dna fr dna at cg nucleotide printed dna from any known starch or protein micro biologically printed antibody used to fight disease or cancer positively fibrillated re fibrillated in fibrillated

9038 dna at cg nucleotide printed dna fr dna at cg nucleotide printed dna from any known starch or protein micro biologically printed antibody used to fight disease or cancer negatively fibrillated re fibrillated in fibrillated

9039 national rage helpline and the ment national rage helpline and the mental health open hot line phone number and assistance associations

9040 nucleotide miscalculated effects ar nucleotide miscalculated effects are the slowly growing organisms that are synthetically printed or fibula ted with a drone dna this should be avoided to erode the heredity of any such illness

9041 atomized ion printing atomized ion atomized ion printing atomized ion printing state of our art atomized ion printing with demagnetized tr ionic paper atomized ion printing with demagnetized tr ionic paper uses security strips new optical medi as fine art printing

9042 nicotine narcosis is the un stable nicotine narcosis is the un stable inherit reaction to an overdose of nicotine

9043 acute nicotine narcosis is the long acute nicotine narcosis is the long term un stable inherit reaction to a continual overdose of nicotine

9044 marijuana use and the health of any marijuana use and the health of any such stimulant turned into a constant use where the patient h as an addiction base on a series of ups and downs where the drug must maintain a non equal abuse level to be considered at a normal high is also known as em

9045 un der and over stacked layered bla un der and over stacked layered blanks for writing purpose and laying the path to write the functions with software innate locking and pressing together

9046 to sponsor the abuse of any dna at to sponsor the abuse of any dna at cg nucleotide printed dna from any known starch or protein micro biologically printed antibody used to make people is a bad thing

9047 software run program applications f software run program applications for printers that uses nano pico triad mixed and formulated biochemical nucleotide to replicate on a recurring smaller intent to cure cancer and disease software for biochemical printers

9048 software run program applications f software run program applications for printers that uses nano pico triad mixed and formulated biochemical nucleotide to replicate on a recurring smaller intent to cure cancer and disease biochemical nucleotide printers

9049 software run program applications f software run program applications for printers that uses nano pico triad mixed and formulated biochemical nucleotide to replicate on a recurring smaller intent to cure cancer and disease

9050 a post lactus light solution flush a post lactus light solution flush to help cure calcium deposits to prevent cancer

9051 a present pre post lactates light s a present pre post lactates light salt solution check to help clean calcium deposits to prevent cancer

9052 insulated chip levels made from of insulated chip levels made from of with a coherence of any insulation method of stacking horizontal or vertical chip organization to build a larger chip also said as to make a no conductive layer with small outer inner conductive measures while operation

9053 insulated chip levels made from of insulated chip levels made from of with a coherence of any insulation method of stacking horizontal or vertical chip organization to build a larger chip also said as to make a non conductive layer with small outer and inner conductive measures while oper

9054 a present pre post lactates non alk a present pre post lactates non alkaline solution check to help clean calcium deposits to prevent cancer

9055 un der and over stacked layered bla un der and over stacked layered blanks by for writing purpose and laying the path to write the functions with software innate locking and pressing together

9056 a combination present pre post lact a combination present pre post lactates non alkaline solution and ultrasonic abrasive shock treatment to break and to help clean calcium deposits to prevent cancer

9057 to multiply the conductive threads to multiply the conductive threads in a insulated chip levels made from of with a coherence of any insulation method of stacking horizontal or vertical chip organization to build a larger chip

9058 at home kit to use combination pres at home kit to use combination present pre post lactates non alkaline solution and ultrasonic abrasive shock treatment to break and to help clean calcium deposits to prevent cancer

9059 veritcal threads multi threaded cop veritcal threads multi threaded

9060 state of our art it so un ds like t state of our art it so un ds like that in a sentence phonology the syllables fo un ding of latin reference

9061 an artistic judgment to copy and cu an artistic judgment to copy and cure is the obvious mission of any nucleotide printed micro organism

9062 power by alternate point of energy power by alternate point of energy torque slip by extended cam shaft would translate as slip and grip when needed part of any motorized engine that h as an alternative shaft of torque for another source of power if needed a dual performance shaft if you

9063 a present pre post lactus light sal a present pre post lactus light salt solution check to help clean calcium deposits to prevent cancer

9064 software run program applications f software run program applications for printers that uses nano pico triad mixed and formulated biochemical nucleotide to replicate on a recurring smaller intent to cure cancer and disease formulated biochemical nucleotide

9065 super high carbon conductors super super high carbon conductors super high carbon conductors plasma molding diamond dust state of our art run on super high carbon conductors yielding welding solder heating all things carbon pure carbon with plasma into a height of super states of metal or

9066 stacked form of many processors in stacked form of many processors in a insulated chip levels with a coherence of any insulation method of stacking horizontal or vertical chip organization to build a larger chip also said as to make a non conductive layer with small outer inner conductive

9067 free orchestrated data routing is a free orchestrated data routing is a open connected network that travels data based on open frequency bandwidth

9068 many stacked cube processors stacke many stacked cube processors stacked form of many cube processors in a insulated chip levels with a coherence of any insulation method of stacking horizontal or vertical chip organization to build a larger chip also said as to make a non conductive layer

9069 a user operated device that enters a user operated device that enters as your original line and adapts to your connection that in turns blocks all connections and or encrypts or allows connections based on a simple password protocol in another way to say is to secure a networks connection

9070 a software virus company operated d a software virus company operated device that enters as your original line and adapts to your connection that in turns blocks all connections and or encrypts or allows connections based on a simple password protocol in another way to say is to secure a n

9071 a software virus company operated d a software virus company operated device that you can insert data with a secure environment to see the data without risk

9072 atomized elector mechanical photo p atomized elector mechanical photo printing atomized elector mechanical photo printing state of our art run on atomized elector mechanical photo printing as opposed to ion atomized demagnetized printing this would be a simple and more consumer affordable

9073 atomized electro mechanical photo p atomized electro mechanical photo printing atomized electro mechanical photo printing state of our art run on atomized electro mechanical photo printing as opposed to ion atomized demagnetized printing this would be a simple and more consumer affordable

9074 populated bot database the recovery populated bot database the recovery validation for sale of recovered bot data and fo un d information as confirmed data or false data as trade in economic value or true data

9075 battery that incorporates the use o battery that incorporates the use of an at will performance and storage with an added electrical generator and recycler

9076 satellite service incorporated is a satellite service incorporated is a freelance satellite scenario that builds and sells bandwidth on demand as service for large and small company uses with a permit to render

9077 federal satellite admin satellite s federal satellite admin satellite service incorporated is a oversee satellite scenario that manages and approves the builds and sales of bandwidth on demand as service for large and small company uses with a permit to render

9078 war network un linking is a un loop war network un linking is a un looped firewall device for security and data integrity in a war data center

9079 election network linking is a un lo election network linking is a un looped firewall device for security and data integrity in a election data center

9080 network linking chip is a un looped network linking chip is a un looped firewall embedded device for security and data integrity in a data center end start point

9081 amplitude () doubled mass () [] est amplitude () doubled mass () [] estimated energy constant weight (a+m=e) part thinking of different things how to invent the definition of something that doesn't exist

9082 amplitude () doubled mass () [] est amplitude () doubled mass () [] estimated energy constant weight (a+m=e) part thinking of different things how to invent the definition of something that doesn't exist time and motion in tandem with out physical being and some of everything at the same t

9083 g as powered hybrid alternative poi g as powered hybrid alternative point of energy

torque slip cam
9084 pyramid chip scheme is a scale able pyramid chip scheme is a scale able multi processor right of way that claims more computing ability per consumer rather than consumer per processors
9085 smart software is a software that c smart software is a software that can use more of any part attached to the system per computation node as cloud operated single system module with one purpose to increase productivity
9086 wrongful legality of bitcoin due to wrongful legality of bitcoin due to security invasion and of any such coin worth or un officially a money right as to interfere with the united states treasury
9087 options in memory and the memory at options in memory and the memory attachment of a scaled inch standard drive as to sata connected accelerator memory drop and find add on's
9088 a chip that holds the proper bios a a chip that holds the proper bios and instruction set for the plugin itself to operate as fail safe pre occupied set of true plug and play functions in any os and any system on chip meaning if it's not operational it does not operate
9089 to take the block ledger offline fr to take the block ledger offline from an online state of transactions would secure the worlds trade and commerce aro un d the globe and to end crypt o currency would help the standard trade sanctions for every one
9090 to take the block ledger offline fr to take the block ledger offline from an online state of transactions would secure the worlds trade and commerce aro un d the globe and to end crypto currency would help the standard trade sanctions for every one
9091 to alternate the current internet a to alternate the current internet as second internet for commerce and create a default encrypted status as to recreate a secured internet to require a ssl or tss
9092 g as start and hybrid long run alte g as start and hybrid long run alternative highway mileage fuel economy method is when the start is the majority controlled by combustion fuel and the highway gears are controlled by electricity methods
9093 soft poly silicate carbonate nuclea soft poly silicate carbonate nuclear smelting and energy rod recycle fission soft poly silicate carbonate hard poly oxide carbonate in reference to smelting of metal nuclear smelting regeneration o (the decomposition of limestone in the middle zones of t
9094 data loss and the kill update blank data loss and the kill update blanket this is evident of any such blanket consumer rights to agree or not agree with property of any such malicious terms from a known consumer issuance discrepancy
9095 escape the os update plug in to esc escape the os update plug in to escape operating system updates permanently or semi choice
9096 block chain attacks crypto currency block chain attacks crypto currency is the attack of software and hardware together to steal
9097 multi drone pilot system is a many multi drone pilot system is a many to one scenario to drone navigation
9098 g as start and hybrid long run alte g as start and hybrid long run alternative highway mileage transmission is when the start is the majority controlled by combustion fuel and the highway gears are controlled by electricity methods
9099 software operated and controlled ce software operated and controlled central processing unit as path to an operation type or person as personal system operated on a come

and go log
9100 state of our art hard oxide hard po state of our art hard oxide hard poly oxide carbonate nuclear smelting and energy rod recycle fission soft poly silicate carbonate hard poly oxide carbonate in reference to smelting of metal nuclear smelting regeneration o (the decomposition of limestone
9101 automatic software operated and con automatic software operated and controlled central processing unit as negotiated per program and app as the needed comp system to the operations
9102 a negotiated batch of pre operated a negotiated batch of pre operated and defined method of hardware as well as complimentary pre selected operating software per presentation of any combination of system and hardware built to operate in sync as the maximum performance as well as success
9103 scale able drone with features and scale able drone with features and cell communications software for cell to cell drone flight
9104 scale able drone with features and scale able drone with features and cell communications software for cell to cell drone flight captur
9105 drone cell stations protocol for sc drone cell stations protocol for scale able drone with features and cell communications network for cell to cell drone flight and land navigation
9106 flip the floppy with toenail in the flip the floppy with toenail in the side jamb lets examine why a solid state data format would work again the intent to understand that size matters and when study of density of a disc form is the goal why not!
9107 lost drone safe way map and navigat lost drone safe way map and navigation per satellite route and permits for lost dog drones that can find their way home
9108 cron job flight navigation servers cron job flight navigation servers for drone devices is a ping service that directs and corrects any such flight or road travel
9109 cron job flight navigation code and cron job flight navigation code and software for devices that work with ping control
9110 cron job flight navigation hardware cron job flight navigation hardware that incorporates the memory factor of from point a to point b in a compensation mode
9111 anomaly report service is a service anomaly report service is a service that helps artificial devices understand seeds of change and occurrences in the issue of a change as compensation equation and a reference base for service like a wind pattern change to help wind mills more energy dur
9112 mission diagnose changes at dopa mi mission diagnose changes at dopa mine serotonin adrenaline and histamine receptor sites in the central nervous system by using a similar method to diabetic blood testing mission diagnose changes at dopa mine
9113 anomaly report service is a service anomaly report service is a service hardware and translation equipment that helps artificial devices understand seeds of change and occurrences in the issue of a change as compensation equation and a reference base for service like a wind pattern change
9114 anomaly report service is a service anomaly report service is a service software analyzing patterns and statistics that helps artificial devices understand seeds of change and occurrences in the issue of a change as compensation equation and a reference base for service like a wind patter
9115 open out doors chassis mod memory g open out doors chassis mod memory ground

is to enable a single cell or multi cell device operate permanently out side by routed power or solar powered operations liquid contact cooling and grounded transistors capacitors and completed shock resistant gro

9116 flip the floppy with toenail in the flip the floppy with toenail in the side jamb lets examine why a solid state data format would work again the intent to understand that size matters and when study of density of a disc form is the goal why not! from wikipedia the free encyclopedia (redir

9117 watch and see user and plus applica watch and see user and plus applications that work on cache and submission processes is a working rule based program that allows more than one user at a time to use the same work place for example a air navigation tower that is inter operable with in an

9118 diode printed and stacked nano metr diode printed and stacked nano metric parts

9119 hot chip for safety safety chip and hot chip for safety safety chip and sos communication bridge allocation software

9120 global for profit school learning s global for profit school learning software and tablet interface that will start with ocr textbooks anded information sale and the room of improvisations in learning processes to help a modern school internet deploy globally and recreate learning

9121 local state wide for profit school local state wide for profit school learning software and tablet interface that will start with ocr textbooks anded information sale and the room of improvisations in learning processes to help a modern school internet deploy state wide and recre

9122 what goes up may come down finding what goes up may come down finding a height to measure the un measurable off the grid computations and landing points by what goes up may come down the point that we need to measure in haste is the un measurable flash point that will keep the platform fr

9123 free global not for profit school l free global not for profit school learning software and tablet interface that will start with ocr textbooks anded information sale and the room of improvisations in learning processes to help a modern school internet deploy globally and recreate

9124 g as start and hybrid long run alte g as start and hybrid long run alternative highway mileage fuel economy method is when the start is the majority controlled by combustion fuel and the highway gears are controlled by electricity methods with each gear a different volt and torque

9125 artificial energy is a non spontane artificial energy is a non spontaneous reaction to a forced digital or analog form of simulated energy in a real sense of negative or positive

9126 artificial magnetic energy is a non artificial magnetic energy is a non spontaneous reaction to a forced magnetic form of simulated energy in a real sense of negative or positive

9127 artificial relative energy is a non artificial relative energy is a non spontaneous reaction to a forced magnetic digital amped weight in a volatile form of simulated energy in a real sense of negative or positive

9128 positive with negative conductive a positive with negative conductive algorithms cpu chips computer memory and add on processors are the translation of current in a form that may be used to hold energy and data at the same time with a specific compression ratio per algorithm and energy sou

9129 trans coding chips that make a wave trans coding chips that make a wave of energy into positive with negative conductive algorithms cpu chips computer memory and add on processors are the translation of current in a form that may be used to hold energy and data at the same time with a spec

9130 hyper multi lane transcoding chips hyper multi lane transcoding chips that make a wave of energy into postive with negative conductive algorithms cpu chips computer memory and add on processors are the translation of current in a form that may be used to hold energy and data at the same t

9131 free functional addons are the addi free functional addons are the additional scalable plug and play options of any such freely to place in a location to import processing and to increase a probability of performance

9132 tiered leveled sequential multiple tiered leveled sequential multiple free functional addons are the additional scalable plug and play options of any such freely to place in a location to import processing and to increase a probability of performance

9133 cloud addons are the servers or vir cloud addons are the servers or virtual performance servers in data center to act as tiered leveled sequential multiple free functional addons are the additional scalable plug and play options of any such freely to place in a location to import proce

9134 cloud addons are the servers or vir cloud addons are the servers or virtual performance servers in data center to act as tiered leveled sequential multiple free functional addons are the additional scalable plug and play options of any such freely to place in a location to import processi

9135 intent to covert and see the matter intent to covert and see the matter at hand to tablet to desktop to phone ineligible document conversion wysiwyg

9136 virtual functional addons are the a virtual functional addons are the additional scalable plug and play software options of any such freely to place in a location to import processing and to increase a probability of performance

9137 virtual functional gpu are the addi virtual functional gpu are the additional scalable plug and play software options of any such freely to place in a location to import processing and to increase a probability of performance

9138 gpu inside a gpu inside for virtual gpu inside a gpu inside for virtual functional gpu are the additional scalable plug and play software options of any such freely to place in a location to import processing and to increase a probability of performance

9139 gpu inside a gpu inside for virtual gpu inside a gpu inside for virtual functional gpu are the additional scalable plug and play software options of any such freely to place in a location to import processing and to increase a probability of performance x

9140 for safe and secure as well as quic for safe and secure as well as quick and immediate transactions a card that provides service when service is only one overdraft away to speed up the transactions posting and to post as involuntary means

9141 local library object instructions i local library object instructions is the safe and un linked local area network of a system smart home adaptive new or retro appliance embedded library of instructions for compound control of smart objects with embedded options and chips ram as well as po

9142 multi layered processing chip is a multi layered processing chip is a nano related myriad layers of pressing alignment in branch layered over and un der stacked layered blanks to add

to the building of a layered processing chip
9143 block chain audit is a method to au block chain audit is a method to audit the leaks and attacks of cyber security an a cyber currency as whole
9144 block chain audit is a method to au block chain audit is a method to audit the leaks and attacks of cyber security and cyber currency as whole by governmental or private issuance
9145 national technology research is a t national technology research is a technology study branch of government that is similar to nasa only the change of focus from space to general technology study
9146 tax report now is the time that we tax report now is the time that we have the proper data systems to calculate all the taxes and their effectiveness its time to do a country wide tax report census
9147 government data exchange is a cloud government data exchange is a cloud method of revising the current scheme of paper arranged data folders into a data driven dynamically accessible and protected base of terms agreements and licenses by paid per use
9148 war data center right is a fast gre war data center right is a fast green red light for any such advanced motion of war in a fast real sense of approval in the war data center is principal with the intent to make a secure and break in free environment that is a near to impossible notion of
9149 war data center rit is a fast green war data center rit is a fast green red light for any such advanced motion of war in a fast real sense of approval in the war data center
9150 educational data center is a princi educational data center is a principal with the intent to make a secure and break in free environment that is a near to impossible notion of a study of all things related
9151 medical data center is a principal medical data center is a principal with the intent to make a secure and break in free environment that is a near to impossible notion of a study of all things related
9152 medical data center right is a fast medical data center right is a fast green red light for any such advanced motion in a fast real sense of approval in the data center is principal with the intent to make a secure and break in free environment that is a near to impossible notion of a stud
9153 educational data center right is a educational data center right is a fast green red light for any such advanced motion in a fast real sense of approval in the data center is principal with the intent to make a secure and break in free environment that is a near to impossible notion of a
9154 search into systems is a simple sea search into systems is a simple search engine that searches by tunnel and hidden internet protocol into the specified system with results on a different page
9155 paid search into systems network is paid search into systems network is a simple search engine alliance that searches by tunnel and hidden internet protocol into the specified system with paid results on a different page
9156 roaming address is a long haul truc roaming address is a long haul truck driver or occupational address where the citizen is not contacted by postal address but by phone and mobile email
9157 government security number remap ca government security number remap card is a new recorded method for securing your citizenship and voter rights as well as secondary

social security number
9158 to have a fiber optic vector regist to have a fiber optic vector registered board that h as a lined connective port of objects inline to work like a copper embedded circuit board
9159 system on chip optical server input system on chip optical server input board to have a fiber optic vector registered board that h as a lined connective port of objects inline to work like a copper embedded circuit board
9160 system on chip optical server input system on chip optical server input board to have a fiber optic vector registered board that h as a lined optical embedded circuit
9161 auto thread and processor controlle auto thread and processor controller software and scripted control chips are the automated central processor unit and the memory optimization included with all of the other parts such as gpu and or io accelerator and even a co processor in un ison as suc
9162 landfill mining and dithering mobil landfill mining and dithering mobile dis assembly plant is an arranged machine that separates the material on a scale per unit of measurement first is the magnetic property of the unit second is the weight of the unit and third is the size and this metho
9163 myriad nano layer built magnified a myriad nano layer built magnified amplifier compressor
9164 g m vitamins are genetically modifi g m vitamins are genetically modified vitamins that encourage growth to patients with severe deficiencies in a certain vitamin or cell of the body
9165 amplitude () doubled mass () [] est amplitude () doubled mass () [] estimated energy constant weight
9166 g m antivirus are genetically modif g m antivirus are genetically modified vaccines that protect important cell growth to patients with severe deficiencies in a certain vitamin or cell of the body
9167 autonomous landfill mining and dith autonomous landfill mining and dithering mobile dis assembly plant is a robotics controlled arranged machine that separates the material on a scale per unit of measurement first is the magnetic property of the unit second is the weight of the unit and th
9168 microwave reactor is a combination microwave reactor is a combination of reactions in few scenarios like for example the combination of air or water to run a turbine and create electricity or the microwaveable consideration of other reactive materials as solvents or compo un ds to create
9169 fossilized and un radiated uranium fossilized and un radiated uranium through a process of microwave un til negative powers are there and no heat is constant
9170 d un ner and the re exam of pre exi d un ner and the re exam of pre existed depleted uranium for microwave tables and the recycled nuclear products
9171 compo un d angle chips are the chip compo un d angle chips are the chips that have horizontal diagonal vertical processing that will aid in the processing of a vertical and other angles including horizontal made wafer of chips in a faster more compact size while printing in multiple stages
9172 compo un d chip parts are the cores compo un d chip parts are the cores memory and agents that have direction any compound direction of processing with building of a vertical and horizontal wafer of chips in a faster more compact size while printing in multiple stages of mediums in a serie

9173 laboratory do it your self rights t laboratory do it your self rights to find and cure to cancers virus and diseases is a old thing new again that the current system to practice active measures of laboratory work require un known lengths of red tape this is an equation of experience and sc
9174 to process code with measurement ca to process code with measurement cascading increments a certain unit of measurement or for processing electronic measurement using my certain unit of measurement data versus the shape of media today {}
9175 part of a room is a frame of sorts part of a room is a frame of sorts for example the separation of data and the complied operation system could be an easier cloud to use meaning if the parts of any library of data h as a role for the drive storage and which functions could be as simple a
9176 using oxygen to propel things in sp using oxygen to propel things in space oxygen system propel engine for use with light weight and satellite operations the oxygen orbit engine
9177 server over a system is a simple co server over a system is a simple configuration of one server per many parts and many red un dant parts per many systems
9178 exit comp rules that apply with eac exit comp rules that apply with each process data is the progress of format in my opinion the greatest thing to happen to anything is to negate the format itself why do people make things in side a box of any sort this is maddening to myself at this poin
9179 alternative to ai is the instructio alternative to ai is the instructional applications ia and the provided instructions of a sky net like operation in a new meaning of the sense
9180 ai car insurance is the most positi ai car insurance is the most positive way for resolution for bad ai outcome and should be held responsible for its un natural nature
9181 ai drone insurance is the most posi ai drone insurance is the most positive way for resolution for bad ai outcome and should be held responsible for its un natural nature
9182 utility permit and cell tower franc utility permit and cell tower franchise re seller authorization diy broadcasting
9183 optically written magnetic object i optically written magnetic object is a simple name for the laser written optically printed chip as an circuit processor as opposed to a diffused optically printed chip
9184 optically written object blank is a optically written object blank is a simple name for the laser written optically printed chip blank similar to a optical media disc as an circuit processor as opposed to a diffused optically printed chip
9185 its f un ny you should but ask i m its f un ny you should but ask i m in servers severs not software web os
9186 portable optically written object b portable optically written object blank similar to a optical media disc as an circuit processor as opposed to a diffused optically printed chip
9187 object writer for the portable opti object writer for the portable optically written object blank similar to a optical media disc as an circuit processor as opposed to a diffused optically printed chip will bring circuit printing to the household markets
9188 paid instructions for the object wr paid instructions for the object writer for the portable optically written object blank similar to a optical media disc as an circuit processor as opposed to a diffused optically printed chip will bring circuit printing to the household diy markets

9189 board solid state hyper threading i board solid state hyper threading is the path of computational signals traveling inside the server board for faster translation computations and processing
9190 using multiple tests compensation a using multiple tests compensation and how to provide any consistency with statistics elaborate compensations will measure the point of our art and science using multiple tests and using all the measures known by science to study the form of art that will
9191 cached satellite camera is a shared cached satellite camera is a shared system of cache and paging system that shares a specified amount of links in memory disc space
9192 arson cached satellite camera is a arson cached satellite camera is a shared system of cache and paging system that shares a specified amount of links in memory disc space
9193 na no motors and in the way of open na no motors and in the way of open and closed aggregate verses passive for technological or medical scenarios and other processes when size does matter
9194 war cached satellite camera is a sh war cached satellite camera is a shared system of cache and paging system that shares a specified amount of links in memory disc space
9195 high density performance scale proc high density performance scale processing is the ratio number in processors compared to scheme of arrangements and clusters in ram and transistors
9196 vertical hyperthreading chip is a s vertical hyperthreading chip is a simple direction to the thread in change and direction as well as elevation and density within the chip or memory
9197 vertical stepping hyperthreading ch vertical stepping hyperthreading chip is a simple direction to the thread in change and direction as well as elevation and density within the chip or memory
9198 can we figure out the chemistry in can we figure out the chemistry in a healthy human can we figure out the chemistry in a healthy human
9199 can we figure out the chemistry in can we figure out the chemistry in a healthy human can we figure out the chemistry in a healthy human then make a ph balance inside each organ including the brain and thus making chemistry balance to help the new and exciting way of working with illness
9200 satellite connection grid is a conn satellite connection grid is a connected alliance of satellites that work and process things like communication together as whole network
9201 paid satellite data connection grid paid satellite data connection grid network is a connected alliance of satellites that work and process things like communication together as whole network
9202 user browser encryption is the end user browser encryption is the end user controlled browser session as controlled level of security of information
9203 satellite data packet grid prefix a satellite data packet grid prefix and paid satellite connection grid network is a connected alliance of satellites that work and process things like communication together as whole network with the ability to send packets to and from each other
9204 satellite data packet grid prefix a satellite data packet grid prefix and paid satellite connection grid network is a connected alliance of satellites that work and process things like communication together as whole network with the ablilty to send packets to and from each other

9205 paid satellite data packet grid pre paid satellite data packet grid prefix and paid satellite connection grid network is a connected alliance of satellites that work and process things like communication together as whole network with the ablilty to send packets to and from each other
9206 paid satellite data packet grid pre paid satellite data packet grid prefix network branches and paid satellite connection grid network is a connected alliance of satellites that work and process things like communication together as whole network with the ability to send packets to and fr
9207 home router to cell to satellite pa home router to cell to satellite paid satellite connection grid network is a connected alliance of satellites that work and process things like communication together as whole network with the ablilty to send packets to and from each other
9208 paid satellite data packet grid pre paid satellite data packet grid prefix and paid satellite connection grid network is a connected alliance of satellites that work and process things like communication together as whole network with the ability to send packets to and from each other
9209 satellite to cell branches satellit satellite to cell branches satellite paid satellite connection grid network is a connected alliance of satellites that work and process things like communication together as whole network with the ablilty to send packets to and from each other
9210 diesel and electric motor engines f diesel and electric motor engines for trucks tractor trailers and cars as well as airplanes and drones
9211 home router to cell to satellite pa home router to cell to satellite paid satellite connection grid network is a connected alliance of satellites that work and process things like communication together as whole network with the ability to send packets to and from each other
9212 corn g as thinner perspective and t corn g as thinner perspective and the foresight to see that the differences in ethanol and gasoline are in consistency and burn rationality in order to improve alternate fuels
9213 to make something work sometimes si to make something work sometimes size does matter what i want is a fast hard drive that happens to be external for example the mystery is how to make a unique hole and a plug to do that with without loss or deterioration in cablescrioner
9214 to make something work sometimes si to make something work sometimes size does matter what i want is a fast hard drive that happens to be external for example the mystery is how to make a unique hole and a plug to do that with without loss or deterioration in cables crioner
9215 compressed alcohol as g as engine i compressed alcohol as g as engine is a compromised vapor ignition engine for trucks tractor trailers and cars as well as airplanes and drones
9216 in a compressed alcohol as g as eng in a compressed alcohol as g as engine a compromised vapor ignition fuel injector is a prepared measure of vapor agitator to make a fine atomized vapor to burn and combust for trucks tractor trailers and cars as well as airplanes and drones
9217 in a compressed alcohol as g as eng in a compressed alcohol as g as engine a compromised vapor ignition fuel injector is a prepared measure of vapor agitator to make

a fine mistified vapor to burn and combust for trucks tractor trailers and cars as well as airplanes and drones

9218 agitated vapor fuel is the closest agitated vapor fuel is the closest to flash point in any compound that would be important in a compressed alcohol as g as engine a compromised vapor ignition fuel injector is a prepared measure of vapor aggitator to make a fine mistified vapor to burn an

9219 agitated vapor fuel is the closest agitated vapor fuel is the closest to flash point in any compound that would be important in a compressed alcohol as g as engine a compromised vapor ignition fuel injector is a prepared measure of vapor agitator to make a fine atomized vapor to burn and

9220 compromised fuel aerosol is pre mea compromised fuel aerosol is pre measured agitated vapor fuel and is the closest to flash point in any compound that would be important in a compressed alcohol as g as engine a compromised vapor ignition fuel injector is a prepared measure of vapor agitat

9221 compromised fuel aerosol engine wil compromised fuel aerosol engine will use pre measured agitated vapor fuel and is the closest to flash point in any compound that would be important in a compressed alcohol as g as engine a compromised vapor ignition fuel injector is a prepared measure of

9222 atomized and vapor hybrid engine wi atomized and vapor hybrid engine will use pre measured agitated vapor fuel and is the closest to flash point in any compound that would be important in a compressed alcohol as g as engine a compromised vapor ignition fuel injector is a prepared measure o

9223 smart fuel is pre respirated gasoli smart fuel is pre respirated gasoline in a volatile vapor to burn and combust for trucks tractor trailers and cars as well as airplanes and drones

9224 pre respirated gasoline in a volati pre respirated gasoline in a volatile vapor calculator that finds the fuels top flash point automatically and in a few cycles adjusts it to any g as for the engine

9225 vapor compressor is an exciter and vapor compressor is an exciter and pre respirator for gasoline in a volatile vapor calculator that finds the fuels top flash point automatically and in a few cycles adjusts it to any g as for the engine

9226 open idea app to design a ethernet open idea app to design a ethernet cell or satellite based cell phone application open idea app a different way to internet to design a ethernet cell or satellite based cell phone application that connects people's phones as pages instead of pages on a s

9227 intelligence and brain growth there intelligence and brain growth there is the science we all know then there is a mystery in the science we think we know intelligence and brain growth a thought of selfishness is not always as shallow as we may think sometimes it's not emotions and why the

9228 smart fuel system in conjunction wi smart fuel system in conjunction with vapor compressor is an exciter and pre respirated gasoline fuel in a volatile vapor calculator that finds the mixes top flash point automatically and in a few cycles adjusts it to any g as for the proper efficiency

9229 law bureau of investigation to seek law bureau of investigation to seek and find corruption in government would be a branch of law directed at politics and make a political transition from the public service to the private administration of law and free us from pay offs and contract break

9230 virtual search of power is a learni virtual search of power is a learning method to compute the most powerful solution to run tomorrows cars and every day engines motors and energy motions of any kind while measuring the possiblities of the content to make that energy and the worth of the

9231 virtual drone navigational operatin virtual drone navigational operating system and the library functions of that data including geo navigation satellite location and local weather conditions as incorporated in a system of methods that conclude a operation inside a alternate virtual use

9232 a global connected cloud resource o a global connected cloud resource of data and targets to compromise the enemy and their assets as concluded end to a means the satellites and the data location in a sense of war over internet protocol

9233 compact hardware service compact se compact hardware service compact server inside a series of software mods and a different way to dedicate the data position size and capabilities for allocation compact server compact hardware service compact server inside a series of software mods and a

9234 recycling nuclear waste into medica recycling nuclear waste into medical radiology use in a dynamic equilibrium recycling nuclear waste into medical radiology use in a dynamic equilibrium nuclear potential energy the potential energy of the particles inside an atomic nucleus nuclear power

9235 virtual calculated energy verses fo virtual calculated energy verses for profit formula table software is a search and input library of values and methods of constants and catalysts that react with one another in a virtual un real way of study to mathematically search and find any such dat

9236 virtual calculated reactive formula virtual calculated reactive formula table is a search and input library of values and methods of constants and catalysts that react with one another in a virtual un real way of study to mathematically search and find any such data as an enquiry to a mean

9237 virtual calculated reactive formula virtual calculated reactive formula table software is a search and input library of values and methods of constants and catalysts that react with one another in a virtual un real way of study to mathematically search and find any such data as an enquiry

9238 hiroshima latin invasion spawned by hiroshima latin invasion spawned by leftists

9239 grade b grade all in a thing called grade b grade all in a thing called hardware service cloud to make a note there is a difference in all technology and the service of a hardware is not a change to specify a invent called service grading and rating compact server compact hardware service

9240 processor driven wifi signal receiv processor driven wifi signal receiver for multiple managed wireless signals and incorporating wireless devices processors and computations as whole in a multitude of receiving and processing of a signal

9241 multiple users and rules software i multiple users and rules software is a program or app that accepts multiple users in order to work and perform as team in one mission with rules of hierarchy and ranking

9242 falling by data verses falling by d falling by data verses falling by data verses balanced data at the same measure of a chemical balanced neutral chemistry ph the best way to make us understand the falling off stature of a certain mark such as to take two or more things and measure the im

9243 sub tr actively printed zirconhydro sub tr actively printed zirconhydroxy or photo laser cut zirconhydroxy isolated layer is a layer of zirconium which is a silicon that is more insulating and less thermal conductive than diamond carbonate this is good for making three dimensional chips an

9244 sub tr actively printed photo laser sub tr actively printed photo laser cut layer is a layer of conductor or isolate r which is a cut or etched by a time generated photo of energy such as burning or to degrade the photo or image into something or out of something which is good for making t

9245 lcd stencil lens for pi co and nano lcd stencil lens for pi co and nano active sub tr actively printed photo laser is a laser stencil photo object to print sub tr actively with mediums

9246 stencil graphic laser printer is a stencil graphic laser printer is a pi co and nano active sub tr actively printed photo laser stencil photo object to print and sub tr actively with medium

9247 stencil graphic laser printer softw stencil graphic laser printer software is the software for the stencil graphic laser printer is a pi co and nano active sub tr actively printed photo laser stencil grid

9248 three dimensional stencil graphic l three dimensional stencil graphic laser printer is a pi co and nano active sub tr actively printed photo laser is a laser stencil photo object to print and sub tr actively with medium for example to think that a grid of pi co layered and formed photo tim

9249 things that verses in terms this ve things that verses in terms this verses that in order to make another turn as well as things that verses and do not equal any such return or sense the thought is the matter at hand an abstract definition

9250 gold chromatic building microproces gold chromatic building microprocessors is a part of the three dimensional stencil graphic laser printer and is a pi co and nano active sub tr actively printed photo laser is a laser stencil photo object to print and sub tr actively with medium for examp

9251 silica chromatic building microproc silica chromatic building microprocessors

9252 reversed printing focus stencil gri reversed printing focus stencil grid is a large grid of pixels that when compensated or reflected into a smaller size they connect and conduct as circuit

9253 exterior <span>meaning out side in exterior <span>meaning out side in atmosphere < span>liquid cooled motherboard is an actively cooled in a climate controlled efficiency way of cooling for higher performance

9254 exterior meaning out side in atmosp exterior meaning out side in atmosphere liquid cooled motherboard is an actively cooled in a climate controlled efficiency way of cooling for higher performance

9255 myriad nano sphere nano sphere myri myriad nano sphere nano sphere myriad nano sphere nano sphere of myriad in reference to tension in side a molecular consistent other wise known as very small sphere (floating of)abstract definition myriad from wikipedia the free encyclopedia main artic

9256 page switch browser plug in is a so page switch browser plug in is a software internet or mobile web interface that takes large tall pages that run on and on and divides them

into smaller and easier to download workable pages by splitting them into different views of minor pages like a tre
9257 sheet virtual manufacturing cost an sheet virtual manufacturing cost and turn aro un d design forecast software to build a virtual cohesive plan with proper estimations
9258 assemble of pre face and su face as assemble of pre face and su face assemble of pre face and su face universal assemblage formats companies who make things for other companies to sell with their name on top and companies to sell what someone elses already made with an alternate name on t
9259 multiple oi protocol router board i multiple oi protocol router board is an important part of information in and out of any given system on chip wall mo un ting moving input unit this is the protocol that moves the data in and out of the section per multitude of processing systems on one w
9260 wireless access soc is a code acces wireless access soc is a code access by wifi or wireless ethernet processing
9261 wifi alternating form access of wif wifi alternating form access of wifi integrated is a triplet form of one send and one receive and one group of process as whole of one in any open signals
9262 a group of any available open form a group of any available open form of one send and one receive and one group of process as whole of one in any open signals
9263 divergent decision this is a compan divergent decision this is a company specific attempt to hold notes and thoughts in the air the example of cars as compared to specific software gives precedence to a new way for profit intent the decision to make two or more different operating systems
9264 system on chip and the divided part system on chip and the divided parts of a one system add in board are controlled by bios and uefi properties that are extensive and individually controlling in each circumstance of operation
9265 processors isolated semi conductors processors isolated semi conductors and their organized processing looping processors isolated semi conductors and their organized processing may be needed to comply more than two specific parts of a computer to make a conductor for part a and part b as
9266 inclusive system on chip board and inclusive system on chip board and part controller could function as bed operating controller that gives multiple instructions to each sub system on a board and help directive options for processing
9267 bids and sales for legitimate futur bids and sales for legitimate futures in project performance is the sale of a large private job for any work made in a pre sales term
9268 script dividing script patterns and script dividing script patterns and repetitive computations multiplied by a larger script to divide or multiply one large process into sub processes for a real time application
9269 in a un looped system on chip the p in a un looped system on chip the properties of processing could be controlled by a network router or a in and out send and receive connected protocol of any kind to work separated and un connected in a secured isolation mode
9270 cellular foundation negotiation net cellular foundation negotiation network is a real chance of service to any known location by selling the use of a cellular network to any un der written provider for negotiation and sales
9271 hybrid connected communication netw hybrid connected communication network is a

real chance of service to any known location by selling the use of a cellular to satellite hybrid service network to any un der written provider for negotiation and sales
9272 a reverse reflective tunnel that ma a reverse reflective tunnel that magnifies the light and graduates the source to maximize the solar energypost
9273 a reverse reflective tunnel that ma a reverse reflective tunnel that magnifies the light and graduates the source to maximize the solar energy by post
9274 a energy center or building with ma a energy center or building with many focused solar generators that reverse reflective tunnel that magnifies the light and graduates the source to maximize the solar energy by post
9275 acid alkaline printed chips in a di acid alkaline printed chips in a diffused solution to compute as battery on chip
9276 laser printed levels of circuits an laser printed levels of circuits and multiple cured solvents as circuits layers laser printed chips in a diffused solution to compute as chip
9277 mo dial comm a different way to ftp mo dial comm a different way to ftp to design a ethernet cell or satellite based cell phone application that connects people's phones as pages instead of pages on a server the main purpose is to comm un icate and then the other things will gradually fall
9278 dynamic verses static web content t dynamic verses static web content translation by use of analytical history transition content transition content translation pack the intent to take static web content and automate the content into dynamic by use of analytic patterns of use history
9279 ultra violet laser printed levels o ultra violet laser printed levels of circuits and multiple uv cured solvents as circuits layers laser printed chips in a diffused solution to compute as chip
9280 laser printed levels of circuits an laser printed levels of circuits and multiple photo sensitive cured solvents as circuits layers laser printed chips in a diffused solution to compute as chip
9281 perpendicular laser printed levels perpendicular laser printed levels of circuits processors and memory in multiple photo sensitive cured solvents as circuits layers laser printed chips in a diffused solution to compute as chip
9282 printing materials for perpendicula printing materials for perpendicular laser printed levels of circuits processors and memory in multiple photo sensitive cured solvents as circuits layers laser printed chips in a diffused solution to compute as chip in a series of different elementsdays
9283 printing materials for perpendicula printing materials for perpendicular laser printed levels of circuits processors and memory in multiple photo sensitive cured solvents as circuits layers laser printed chips in a diffused solution to compute as chip in a series of different elements day
9284 fractal math string zoom formula fo fractal math string zoom formula for bio and non chemical measurements to zoom and extract dna from stem cells as well as dna strings to zoom and measure solid state data or solid state memory cells uses ! to zoom and extract dna from stem cells as well
9285 pico nano voxel and elemental compo pico nano voxel and elemental compo un ds for chip processing printing
9286 three ring binder glucose incubatio three ring binder glucose incubation a computer

controlled molecular telescope nan scope that can insert and impregnate new dna will consequently rebuild the cell a computer controlled dissection will allow probability of success for great accomplishment

9287 conductive and positive pico nano v conductive and positive pico nano voxel and elemental compo un ds for chip processing printing in three dimensions

9288 non conductive and negative pico na non conductive and negative pico nano voxel and elemental compo un ds for chip processing printing in three dimensions

9289 non conductive silica solvent white non conductive silica solvent white space and negative pico nano voxel and elemental compo un ds for chip processing printing in three dimensions

9290 empty space for looped inside linki empty space for looped inside linking conductive vector for making a place for conductors in pico nano voxel and elemental compo un ds for chip processing printing in three dimensions

9291 programmable chip software and the programmable chip software and the opportunity to make a chip into a performance enhancer such as co appliance or main appliance or second appliance for processing or for storage or routing

9292 connection vectors and the empty sp connection vectors and the empty space for looped inside linking conductive vector for making a place for conductors in pico nano voxel and elemental compo un ds for chip processing printing in three dimensions

9293 software that makes connection vect software that makes connection vectors conductors in pico nano voxel and elemental compo un ds for chip processing printing in three dimensions

9294 the intellectual property managemen the intellectual property management office and large document record for keeping trade secrets ands safe and secured by named ownership

9295 turning off the virus virus intenti turning off the virus virus intentions to turn and transform virus intentions to turn and transform the effort of mainline to a true police operating system to steady the intent and take the means in order to use that code for a positive purpose for exam

9296 spiral fiber optic splicer device a spiral fiber optic splicer device and the markings that make a reading splicer obtain the proper place in the cable to splice or loop into with precision and accuracy for less signal loss

9297 exchangeable and upgrade able lapto exchangeable and upgrade able laptop models and ports processing add on

9298 bios rules and operations script in bios rules and operations script in a working environment over of many other bios and their respective parts working together in a system

9299 intelligent voips server to point a intelligent voips server to point a server instead of a pc to magistrate comm as and processes

9300 add in transformer for data that pr add in transformer for data that precedes the cpu if there is a optical data connection to lead to a processing opposing in signal operations

9301 data tax and the data trade commiss data tax and the data trade commission and the un equal differences and adjustments in an administration of machines and cost to service

9302 vertical threads and the property o vertical threads and the property of stacking layers of chips

9303 add in transforming chip for data t add in transforming chip for data that uses two different kinds of bios and can process in two different signals like optical and electronic noise

9304 sewage removable ultra bio tics for sewage removable ultra bio tics for water and soil in a microbe enviroment as lead neutralizers and ph balance changers
9305 watch smart phones with solar panel watch smart phones with solar panels
9306 add in exporter for data that super add in exporter for data that supersedes the cpu if there is a optical data connection to lead to a processing opposing in signal operations
9307 co un ter attack outage service are co un ter attack outage service are companies as paid ddos retaliations and defense mercenaries that defend and log corporate and government interruptions and attacks like life threatening power outages in iot and flight control centers
9308 sport smart shoe is a shoe with cal sport smart shoe is a shoe with calculatives
9309 electronic power nd signal with fib electronic power nd signal with fiber optical data and threads as well as solid state memory as threads and data signal carriers and power conduction in a computational system board for inter seeding connections and processing nodes
9310 to give data sending water through to give data sending water through or not to send water if there were a rar equal to a need then there would be a need called raz to send a raz into a receiver would be like making a scripted transition to and from a device or line translated into a
9311 synthetic currents to anchor un der synthetic currents to anchor un derwater current makers to a high middle and low temperatures and in the consistent direction to prevent stagnant water and refresh the water in a pond or reservoir the benefits would be less insects and healthier fish
9312 to artificially cross dna and un cr to artificially cross dna and un cross dna is not a gain or operation i myself would condone
9313 bureaucratic reset is the full dist bureaucratic reset is the full distress of laws of a previous state to reset the laws from another state as legal situation similar to the gross loss in california
9314 cloud and search platform for ecomm cloud and search platform for ecommerce
9315 ability of many sets of bios and th ability of many sets of bios and their respective parts working together in a system optical magnetic data and electronic
9316 watch phones with solar panels copy watch phones with solar panels
9317 add in transfromer for data that pr add in transfromer for data that precedes the cpu if there is a optical data connection to lead a processing opposing in signal operations
9318 data board is a separated connectio data board is a separated connection of data from power by changing the data ports to optical and the power ports to electrical for a faster schema
9319 report service of citizenship is a report service of citizenship is a small personalized membership to pay taxes for a limited trade for temporary imm un ity
9320 another comparative analogy water w another comparative analogy water water cycle water data cycle fresh water storage new data server sea water world wide data tides to sync data
9321 fiber optic reflective turn connect fiber optic reflective turn connection in data to let a signal repeat and split in order to go aro un d an object of area
9322 solid data board is a separated con solid data board is a separated connection of data from power by changing the data ports to solid state and the power ports to electrical for a faster schema

9323 water proof smart shoe is a shoe wi water proof smart shoe is a shoe with calculative software connected or embedded with data out put in a water proof situation with size of mechanics and memory instances
9324 electronic power and signal with fi electronic power and signal with fiber optical data and threads as well as solid state memory as threads and data signal carriers and power conduction in a computational system board for inter seeding connections and processing nodes
9325 wifi gaming smart shoe is a shoe wi wifi gaming smart shoe is a shoe with calculative software connected or embedded with data out put in a gaming or practice situation with size of mechanics and memory instances
9326 sport smart shoe is a shoe with cal sport smart shoe is a shoe with calculative software connected or embedded with data out put in a gaming or practice situation with size of mechanics and memory instances
9327 microwaved nuclear waste and the re microwaved nuclear waste and the renewable study of micro wave negative and positive nuclear reactive waste recycle and re charging uranium and non depleted uranium
9328 government cellular service for sec government cellular service for security purposes
9329 topical antibiotic mouthwash topica topical antibiotic mouthwash topical antibiotic mouthwash (halitosis) to cure by way of rinsing and nasal spray of antibiotic solution topical antibiotic bath soak (to cure by way of bath soaking in diluted antibiotic solution
9330 government satellite combat service government satellite combat service for security purposes
9331 soldier watch makes the watching of soldier watch makes the watching of a soldier in combat a function of a matter of life or death the service would follow a soldier into and out of a combat zone and record all of the data of the battle in progress and keep record of the out comings as s
9332 student watch makes the watching of student watch makes the watching of a student in school a function of a matter of win or loose the service would measure a students rates and learning process and record all of the data of the experience
9333 clay building bricks recycled to re clay building bricks recycled to resolve ph balance in lead heavy ground as co un ter product in a process of saturation
9334 high speed trans coding encoding st high speed trans coding encoding station is a fiber optical resolution station that transforms signals into a compressed code for travel into a network
9335 high speed encryption station is a high speed encryption station is a fiber optical resolution station that transforms signals into a encrypted code for travel into a network
9336 high speed compression station is a high speed compression station is a fiber optical resolution station that transforms signals into a compressed code for travel into a network
9337 high speed block transfer highway s high speed block transfer highway station is a fiber optical resolution station that transforms signals into a code for travel into a different network
9338 high speed rospace statellite to sa high speed rospace statellite to satellite to ground encrypted processed and compressed signal data station is a resolution station that transforms signals into a encrypted code for travel into a different network
9339 high speed sata gpu chip connection high speed sata gpu chip connections and formats

9340 total year end dividend trading joi total year end dividend trading joint stock companies act from wikipedia debate the joint stock companies bill w as introduced to parliament by the then vice president of the board of trade mr robert lowe in doing so he proclaimed the right of
9341 high speed micro sd performance chi high speed micro sd performance chips are alternate and inclusive functioning chips in a ecosystem of a computer
9342 downloadable code for high speed mi downloadable code for high speed micro sd performance chips
9343 a blank transistor chip that holds a blank transistor chip that holds no instructions and the user builds and makes the bios by code instructions and navigation paths
9344 many blank transistor chips that ho many blank transistor chips that holds no instructions and the user builds and makes the bios by code instructions and navigation paths to build a performance chip group with alternate and inclusive functioning chips in a ecosystem of a computer abstract
9345 in precievable compression is a un in precievable compression is a un noticeable time difference loss to assist in compression and data lag of operations and conduction in code or conversion
9346 room focused energy is a large refl room focused energy is a large reflected system of cycles in the case that one or only a few light emitters generate a large system of a source of solar energy in amplification by reflection and the profit of energy is greater than the source abstract ut
9347 formula for thought combination for formula for thought combination formula of commons unique and abnormal the theory is a function of indefinite sums and energy in the mass of that sum with the longevity of that same sum a + m = e ({} over {}) %uxe a {e} over {m} %uxe b {e%delta ^{}} ov
9348 autonomous software anti malware is autonomous software anti malware is the added safety measure of autonomous software security
9349 light turbo focused energy is a sma light turbo focused energy is a small reflected system of cycles in the case that one or only a few light emitters generate a stronger system of a source of solar energy in amplification by reflection and the profit of energy is greater than the source a
9350 a different way to see business eth a different way to see business ethics and personal values actually do make up the person who works for you and you and i may see eye to eye for once that you don't want a drug user as your warehouse manager so what precautions would you be willing to ta
9351 tired of ftp what if i didn t have tired of ftp what if i didn t have to do it that way what if there were new and exciting ways to engage clients data that make and hold more data than usual for example a cloud that is low to the ground is called fog files on the ground would make sync
9352 tired of ftp what if i didn't have tired of ftp what if i didn't have to do it that way what if there were new and exciting ways to engage clients data that make and hold more data than usual for example a cloud that is low to the ground is called fog files on the ground would make sync
9353 a one way mirror or rather said as a one way mirror or rather said as one sided reflective one side transparent solar energy glass window for building a reflective solar tunnel
9354 spiral focus energy is a one way mi spiral focus energy is a one way mirror or rather said

as one sided reflective one side transparent solar energy glass window for building a reflective solar tunnel spirally to amplify the source
9355 cnc (computer navigated control) mi cnc (computer navigated control) microscope for bio and chemical measurements to zoom and extract dna from stem cells as well as dna strings to zoom and measure solid state data or solid state memory cells
9356 square focus energy is a one way mi square focus energy is a one way mirror or rather said as one sided reflective one side transparent solar energy glass window for building a reflective solar tunnel square to amplify the source
9357 cone focus energy is a one way mirr cone focus energy is a one way mirror or rather said as one sided reflective one side transparent solar energy glass window for building a reflective solar tunnel cone to amplify the source
9358 immigrated income revenue service i immigrated income revenue service is a service devoted to helping immigrants over come short falls and improve the lives of immigrants and others who are incontinent of taxes as language and citizenship problems
9359 microwave ecology and the study of microwave ecology and the study of light particles and oxygen from microwave stable and un stable optical combustion
9360 microwave combustion microwave flas microwave combustion microwave flash point in any operation as an ignition for combustion is the newest resolution here for energy
9361 microwave vacuum combustion microwa microwave vacuum combustion microwave flash point vacuum in any operation as an ignition for combustion is the newest resolution here for energy or force of energy
9362 tired of upgrading key socket adapt tired of upgrading key socket adapter a molding cpu socket adapter that works like clay on a car key in a cool movie working to accept all patterns but only all the patterns present
9363 satellite directional range acceler satellite directional range accelerations when the area of interest is incorporated into a conglomerate signal of area in data within a similar location where as the area of interest is in a geo packet prefix for code accelerations
9364 satellite directional range acceler satellite directional range accelerations when the area of interest is incorporated into a conglomerate signal of area in data within a similar location where as the area of interest is in a geo packet prefix for code accelerations by
9365 gps pi navigation access is fractio gps pi navigation access is fractional pi satellite directional range accelerations when the area of interest is incorporated into a conglomerate signal of area in data within a similar location where as the area of interest is in a geo packet prefix for
9366 encrypted cellular service copyrigh encrypted cellular service
9367 encrypted cellular service by copyr encrypted cellular service by
9368 encrypted cellular application and encrypted cellular application and software by
9369 compensation chip compensation chip compensation chip compensation chips long processors vs short and stubby its a uniform shape that is divided by and then multiplied with time and hardware mass
9370 search by image to search for a top search by image to search for a topic with an image to find people places and things with input from meta tags such as technical terms when where who and why as well as to modify the photo scan or topic by perspective date and angle using the image its
9371 gaming software for war data scienc gaming software for war data science scenarios

and real world ai scripted drones
9372 ai war software from gaming softwar ai war software from gaming software for war data science strategy and ai scripted drones
9373 electric aeronautics and the electr electric aeronautics and the electric aided recycle magnetic turbine is a spinning and rotation generate electro magnetic jet propulsion
9374 ai driving software derived from ga ai driving software derived from gaming software for ai scripted drones
9375 personal computer server personal s personal computer server personal server computer re ignite the passion for computing put one foot forward and take two steps back try installing windows eight with a server by intel use as directed and wash twice a day intel sy
9376 fiber embedded processing on sd int fiber embedded processing on sd interupt fiber optical conducting boards and insert cards for processing in a optical environment of computations fiber embedded processing on solid data pcie and also ssd
9377 compact optical power supply is an compact optical power supply is an conducting signal of a source that changes a function in a stored time for input into a board of calculation
9378 corn g as central perspective and t corn g as central perspective and the foresight to see that natural burn synthetic made corn g as can and could burn at a zero level of pollutants in according to the epa
9379 compact optical power supply is an compact optical power supply is an conducting signal of a source that changes a function in a stored time for input into a board of calculation sub
9380 board splice chip optical power swi board splice chip optical power switch is an alternating signal of a source that changes a function in a stored time for input into a board of calculation
9381 male directional optical transition male directional optical transition connections are radial shaped to linear shaped optical data signal bridges with pins and replaceable optical connections g
9382 boosting directional optical transi boosting directional optical transition connections are radial shaped to linear shaped optical data signal bridges with pins and replaceable optical connections with incorporating power operators chri
9383 my lzw algorithm isn t free a fee f my lzw algorithm isn t free a fee for a free platform is essentially not happening i invented the pd f and here is my quote either trust me or don't the fact of the matter is that like the pokemon there w as a puzzle in the equation of how to market the
9384 optical signal break vector is a br optical signal break vector is a broken link detection location of directional optical transition connections are radial shaped to linear shaped optical data signal bridges with pins and replaceable optical connections with incorporating power operat
9385 advanced law is an exact and more s advanced law is an exact and more specific ownership control library of means and ownership of sciences
9386 do they put that stuff in the air t do they put that stuff in the air the chance of the hospital itself being sick is the real issue like the story goes how do you heal the sick inside a sick place well there are extremely strong antibiotics and then there are subtle every day antibiotics

9387 explain this is to accumulate the c explain this is to accumulate the circumstances this isn't a time device it's only a cd publishing system in reverse a folder generator that catalogs achieved cd's and cd rom into a folder on a hard drive flash card or ssd and even server related temps s

9388 explain this is to accumulate the c explain this is to accumulate the circumstances this isn't a time device it's only a cd publishing system in reverse a folder generator that catalogs achieved cd's and cd roms into a folder on a hard drive flash card or sd and even server related temps s

9389 technology of the relations between technology of the relations between files long data why can't we all just get along long data concept i believe that a universal computer file that will put the hard efforts and intelligence of today to work tomorrow this is not only t

9390 the issue is when will a co process the issue is when will a co processor complimentary on and off as well as different and alternate processing to explain this is to accumulate the circumstances of on and off in a larger picture to estimate the neurological existence of two halves of our

9391 one creative step bridge parallel m one creative step bridge parallel modern efficiency content text context parallel (email submission) assumptions of a co processing pattern the issue is when will a co processor understand that to full fill one creative step it's important to duplicate t

9392 who really un derstands better than who really un derstands better than a child trying to kick a ball into the wind it may do this it may do that but what we really need to understand is there are curve anomalies that happen more than we hope thats why its f un yet to understand them is

9393 voluntary involuntary core process voluntary involuntary core process stop core back user selected modes and bios updates

9394 microwave fuse content text context microwave fuse content text context melting the parts for safety or other means with a metal and timer similar to a wave generator inside a microwave oven with military and ro design specifics as well as fuse and exploding instances micro wave melt swit

9395 pi difference a to b comments there pi difference a to b comments there is a point in every computation that will like light transfer to another point and time every thing is timed with pi you can measure the distance of any computation from point a to point b with angle circumference

9396 to multiply comments the chances of to multiply comments the chances of using two or more mother boards and then working together with what it may hold there is a point in every computation that will like light transfer to another point and time every thing is timed with pi you can measure

9397 electro magnetic compressed jet pro electro magnetic compressed jet propulsion is a software controlled on and off of electro magnetic motors that can turn propellers in a compressed modular sequence to build a jet action of energy

9398 to multiply on local network os ove to multiply on local network os over os un der os scenario to multiply on local network os the chances of using two or more un der operating systems and concluding it to a working hierarchy of operating system +even or +odd

9399 laser wave modulation shaping a las laser wave modulation shaping a laser with complimentary light is anyone out there shaping a laser with complimentary light for

navigation and artificial energy math components (laser theory energy expansion of a sum = accelerated motion amplified by mas
9400 as well as triangular square and ci as well as triangular square and circular properties such as vertical horizontal and spherical combinations with two or more in one process line of sight
9401 the need for two apps to transition the need for two apps to transition through one another trying to work faster a few questions and what to expect step one a nano motor the need for two apps to transition through one another is really something adobe systems is good at but to transform t
9402 as well as triangular square and ci as well as triangular square and circular properties such as vertical horizontal and spherical combinations with two or more in one process line of sight as well as to inject g as and form a modulation of image appropriate for television and viewing comm
9403 infrared computer screen human inte infrared computer screen human interface manipulation for laser generated d tv comments is anyone out there shaping a laser with complimentary light for navigation and artificial energy math components (laser theory energy expansion shaping a laser with
9404 out put computers are a method of c out put computers are a method of creation out put computers are a method of creation that people need to make things i have decided to claim this as separate market of intent for improvement in usability and justification of my means there are currentl
9405 glass (or poly carbonate) insulated glass (or poly carbonate) insulated gold line wire housing needed to stack motherboards and double or more the capacity of the vertical possibilities inside that manner as opposed to a silicon board this would connect boards to one another
9406 the intent to reactivate a flower f the intent to reactivate a flower for a shape for extended central processing un its and the possibilities to multiply and agitate the growth of a unit into more than one un its a flower verses in terms
9407 crystallized mother board the inten crystallized mother board the intent to reactivate a flower for a shape for extended central processing un its and the possibilities to multiply and agitate the growth of a unit into more than one un its a flower verses in terms the intent to reactivate
9408 electro magnetic compressed jet pro electro magnetic compressed jet propulsion is a software controlled on and off of electro magnetic motors that can turn propellers in a compressed modular sequence to build a jet action of energy electro magnetic compressed jet software
9409 a simple dividing trigger for elect a simple dividing trigger for electronic and dividing transistors inside a circuit path
9410 photonic fractal math which and whe photonic fractal math which and where rgb
9411 a= bh a=pi r ^+ is versable in term a= bh a=pi r ^+ is versable in terms
9412 {to use a non primal number is the {to use a non primal number is the in and out of a circuit if to use a prime number the sum must have a divisible cube root} which verses and changes in terms and may be exchangeable factorization divisors co un t of divisors sum of divisors prime nu
9413 satellite communication amp aoip satellite communication amp aoip the

communication amp is not only for talking and voip but a entertainment and communication all over internet protocol amplifier map

9414 a few questions and what to expect a few questions and what to expect fnatma fnatimg fnatma fnatimg chemistry topic of another invent deposition a few questions and what to expect how to charge an element using the nasa nevada experimental rail way why would you bother them and what it

9415 a= bh a=pi r ^+ number in fractiona a= bh a=pi r ^+ number in fractional os states or to abstract with the use of number [one million one h un dred and seventy seven thousand seven h un dred and twenty five] {to use a non primal number is the in and out of a circuit if to use a prime num

9416 imm un e systemic insulin insulin m imm un e systemic insulin insulin medicine to magistrate through the auto imm un e system imm un e systemic insulin insulin medicine to magistrate through the auto imm un e system insulin main article insulin therapy type diabetes is typically treated w

9417 electro magnetic compressed jet pro electro magnetic compressed jet propulsion is a software controlled on and off of electro magnetic motors that can turn propellers in a compressed modular sequence to build a jet action of energy by electro magnetic compressed jet software

9418 emergency sos satellite system base emergency sos satellite system based on cell phone satellite connections sos from wikipedia the free encyclopedia sos is the commonly used description for the international morse code distress signal (, , ,) this distress signal w as first a

9419 plastic layered electronic micro bo plastic layered electronic micro board a process defined with nano printing circuits and layers of layers of circuitry that provides depth into height of computing capabilities or alternate poly carbonate carbonate porous compo un ds

9420 outdoor hot and cold out door auto outdoor hot and cold out door auto semi conductor open processors outdoor hot and cold climates need processing let's imagine that there could be a cup with a microchip inside it after all open processors more out door auto semi conductor open processors

9421 with the mass of complicated ports with the mass of complicated ports there should be a uniform port of snap in with pin play and align to the left scenario like a find and play plug and play device that may be useful for upcoming devices and experimental utilities yet un known

9422 my thought to amplify the core is b my thought to amplify the core is by multiplying the board and amp mechanism operations and connections during a core connection and relay amplitude marker a starting point that h as a reciprocating point to relay

9423 my intent is to change the way peop my intent is to change the way people put the chip in and how many times you can change the chip to satisfy the craving for more speed with ex tractable chips and interchangeable cpu second processing unit chip drive readers

9424 the right to hold the representatio the right to hold the representation legally bound by any means and amendments to the constitution such as law that shall hold the branches such as even to the intellectual property rights co un sel itself liable for negligence

9425 theoretical business analytics theo theoretical business analytics theoretical business analytics to speak about ones past is sad at times but in the professional sense to reminisce is important the variables must contain a few transitional attempts of experimentation and study the most w

9426 complication computations super com complication computations super computer built by super computer and into the abyss that is more computations virtual mathematics including fractals

9427 raid multi sd flash card device rai raid multi sd flash card device raid multiple compact flash t card holder drive addition and subtract able device

9428 neurological coherence test and cen neurological coherence test and central nervous system cognitive balance test in form of a phosphorous ion activity test verses in turn a hydrogen activity test

9429 to publicly render the president pe to publicly render the president petition ally un available for office

9430 i am not referring to my fans here i am not referring to my fans here you are allowed to come back and download as much as you wish to be specific the newest type of stalker is someone you know (or do not) that watches and stalks as you do not wish people with probable cause not inc

9431 ethernet fixed raid to have an ethe ethernet fixed raid to have an ethernet with multiple raid fixes per connected un its using a raid modified ethernet router

9432 codex to diametric two opposing ide codex to diametric two opposing ide as that form a scientific outcome in computer analytical methods two concepts to measure it all codex to dielectrics two opposing ide as that form a scientific outcome in computer analytical methods to have codex appli

9433 a means to raid activate each board a means to raid activate each board level for accuracy

9434 a means to raid activate each level a means to raid activate each level for accuracy

9435 to prove that the free pop art is i to prove that the free pop art is in fact a infringement issue that needs to be contained coz it does that is why

9436 synthetic poly metallic compo un d synthetic poly metallic compo un d

9437 transistorized chip with empty inst transistorized chip with empty instruction sets that you could progrma and control for yourself and your business for rights and privilages

9438 exchangable gpu sockets on mother b exchangable gpu sockets on mother boards

9439 popup autophi computational targets popup autophi computational targets autophi on sd

9440 processor on a programmable sd or p processor on a programmable sd or phy over sd

9441 there is a new compute of machine c there is a new compute of machine computing that scales the periods to machine values of time and complexity that a machine will notice

9442 friendly attach process software is friendly attach process software is an easier way to attach processing leverage to any goal

9443 a supercosmic optical processor wi a supercosmic optical processor with atomic annotations would be a written amendment in a instruction set of processing for all computations in a atom sized library of annotations in a on off position

9444 infarelational is the language of infarelational is the language of mechanics and decimals of processing in a related form from the instructions and library of atomic molecular compute

9445 forced substance abuse incarceratio forced substance abuse incarceration how are we supposed to deal with drug addictions nationwide there are a few options but none are going to be happy since people manipulate others on drugs. are we supposed to make drug rehab

centers forced incarcerat
9446 light trigger + varied colored lase light trigger + varied colored laser semiconductor & microchip cold light micro chip digital optics by colored micro mirrors add subtract mode to divide and multiply digital platforms color mathematics and algorithms based on color reflections for proces
9447 brainstorm usgov applicationtime st brainstorm usgov applicationtime stamp applications and concept
9448 intent to remove c un a c un a ch intent to remove c un a c un a chemistry topic of another part how to charge an element using the nasa nevada experimental rail way why would you bother them and what it means to the rest of us i think it's best put as set charge accelerator a question
9449 [time and light measure ment + stai [time and light measure ment + stair case mirror chips] (optical ma thematic weight and scale by calculations and common studies)
9450 another cloud cycle to invent conce another cloud cycle to invent concept the difference of deep blue w as that it wasn t considered a cloud at the time the focus w as only on the game and the server itself this isn t the focus of what the azure is windows will now carry on as usual wel
9451 triad octavia signal to grid format triad octavia signal to grid format y x with a coherent of
9452 to use fractal noise as a means to to use fractal noise as a means to find the infinite extending paths of scripts and all while using trip circuits for control. boolean updates to practical scripts and vague code complex. two planes of intersection and if or a what.
9453 ask intel about it they will say th ask intel about it they will say the exact same thing server chip stacking stacking this state of our art early invent coming to light ask intel about it they will say the exact same thingserver chip stacking.
9454 astro hardware astro size state of astro hardware astro size state of our art astro size hardware form astro hardware. extended satellite computations. imagine space travel that is so successful that over a long or short time we are able to store data in space itself.
9455 density and amplitude energy chart density and amplitude energy chart scale a energy chart with amplitude and density comparable to the chemical elements diagram with consideration for g as solids and chemical compo un ds as well as their reaction to one another
9456 to switch off a zone incorporated w to switch off a zone incorporated with data and on a war or war data premptive agreement in a cloud database environment that protects the entity of itself by control and data code kill switch script cooperation and compliance of no service patent pend
9457 synthetic natural conventional non synthetic natural conventional non associated g as a substance that may be clean burning and easy to make synthetic pressured gas
9458 synthetic pressurized g as turbine synthetic pressurized g as turbine to generate electricity
9459 sub scalable ssd branches and trees sub scalable ssd branches and trees
9460 atomized ion printing atomized ion atomized ion printing atomized ion printing state of our art atomized ion printing with ± demagnetized trionic paper atomized ion printing with ± demagnetized trionic paper uses security stripsnew optical mediasfine art printing
9461 its a lot like a nuclear bomb only its a lot like a nuclear bomb only in reverse instead of destroying elements we are putting them together but more important than a super

spontaneous collision we are separating the elements for recycling and purification the muffler and the past catalyt

9462 mini wireless chip operated and com mini wireless chip operated and compute magnetic transmission for torque and propulsion of device controlling a stationary over controlled passing magnets that provide any such current controlled with a wireless connection for torque magnitude intensit

9463 pi co circuit with poly carbs ceram pi co circuit with poly carbs ceramic insulation and poly oxide metal as conducting circuits with power and wear as consideration for measuring the entire tension and properties of laser made engraving by plasma soldering yielding and melting

9464 pi co circuit pico layer chip and c pi co circuit pico layer chip and circuit building segmented layers and connecting ends from bottom to upper layer for stacking interior with poly carbs ceramic insulation and poly oxide metal as conducting circuits with power and wear as consideration

9465 arounded number of encryption based arounded number of encryption based on a four segment of numbers to process and extract an encrypt able alpha numerical code for ssl and more advanced communications

9466 extended belling vertical ssd chip extended belling vertical ssd chip stack

9467 artificial energy is a nonspontane artificial energy is a nonspontaneous reaction to a forced digital or analog form of simulated energy in a real sense of negative or positive ae

9468 artificial magnetic energy is a non artificial magnetic energy is a nonspontaneous reaction to a forced magnetic form of simulated energy in a real sense of negative or positive ae

9469 artificial relative energy is a non artificial relative energy is a nonspontaneous reaction to a forced magnetic digital amped weight in a volatile form of simulated energy in a real sense of negative or positive ae

9470 inverted g as sorting and reclaimin inverted g as sorting and reclaiming recycled incineration gasses by way of catalytic converter and g as humidifier for or only with a unique dry or paste wet solvent clay and the processes that make taking trash and turning it into rock or solvent sludg

9471 gasses energy signal wave g as wave gasses energy signal wave g as wave energy signal is the measure of energy that attracts or repels any such one g as or other gasses to and from each other in a energy force in any size obvious or microscopic force of annotative fixation including or exc

9472 gasses energy signal wave by g as w gasses energy signal wave by g as wave energy signal is the measure of energy that attracts or repels any such one g as or other gasses to and from each other in a energy force in any size obvious or microscopic force of annotative fixation including or

9473 for safe and secure as well as quic for safe and secure as well as quick and immediate transactions a card that provides service when service is only one overdraft away. to speed up the transactions posting and pending to post as a involuntary means.

9474 retro retro retro penicillin two pe retro retro retro penicillin two penicillin two the simple minds think alike but we progress through abstract minds that are complex yet still simple looking back is always important why did i leave that milk out on the kitchen co un ter all day its an u

9475 a squared area of cascading increme a squared area of cascading increments fun ny but real to process code with measurement cascading increments a certain unit of measurement or for processing electronic measurement using my certain unit of measurement data versus the shape of media t
9476 a ro un ded number of encryption ba a ro un ded number of encryption based on a four segment of numbers to process and extract an encrypt able alpha numerical code for ssl and more advanced communications
9477 cubit cell off and on group of cubi cubit cell off and on group of cubits by a translation of on off and signals in a group a simple yet complex method of calculation and intersect of paths for any group of information
9478 exchangeable cell cell card for a l exchangeable cell cell card for a local non synchronized cloud account cell phones that is a starting point to a private phone a private and un der non agreement phone privacy
9479 to process code with measurement ca to process code with measurement cascading increments a certain unit of measurement . or for processing electronic measurement using my certain unit of measurement data versus the shape of media today
9480 phone station bluetooth magnetic ba phone station bluetooth magnetic backup recharge by wireless charge and backup clone update and restore hardware
9481 magnetic data waves of intertwined magnetic data waves of intertwined mini signals and partial process of and triplet pulse
9482 diverse operating board magnetic io diverse operating board magnetic ion fiber optic and nano electric signals to work the large and small things into a so un d well ro un ded machine
9483 a working partial process working s a working partial process working software is a platform of a data base that is built on a question of fundamentals to make a transitional and schematic plan for a business with some of part system made to work with other parts
9484 a squared area of cascading increme a squared area of cascading increments f un ny but real to process code with measurement cascading increments a certain unit of measurement
9485 a squared area of cascading increme a squared area of cascading increments f un ny but real to process code with measurement cascading increments a certain unit of measurement or for processing electronic measurement using my certain unit of measurement data versus the shape of media t
9486 standard popular retro active hardw standard popular retro active hardware is a forgotten chip socket board or state of work made popular again for the f un of its performance and suggestions k again standard popular hardware
9487 parts that un ite by scale and conn parts that un ite by scale and connections across carry inter connection circuit processors and alternate vectors of chip exchange a chip that sends a specific vector data rate to a specified place to and then to more or to reply
9488 paid instructions for the object wr paid instructions for the object writer for the portable optically written object blank similar to a optical media disc as an circuit processor as opposed to a diffused optically printed chip will bring circuit printing to the household diy markets (aug
9489 volunteer web warriors software to volunteer web warriors software to aid against the enemy and to fight a cyber war vol un teerism with our at home devices to co un ter attack the enemy foes

9490 critical non attached data back up critical non attached data back up registrations and cloud clusters is an extremely secure web of servers and data bases that conclude information that is nearly irreplaceable or important more than any other data critical non attached back up by

9491 to make something work sometimes si to make something work sometimes size does matter. what i want is a fast hard drive that happens to be external for example the mystery is how to make a unique hole and a plug to do that with without loss or deterioration in cables. crioner

9492 recycle and cycle g as liquid and g recycle and cycle g as liquid and g as separated mining and dis assembly to material on a settle absolute table weight process take and rest into a sedimentary weight of stagnation and aggression movement and non movement improving heating resting and co

9493 virtual drone navigational operatin virtual drone navigational operating system and the library functions of that data including geo navigation satellite location and local weather conditions as in corporate in a system of methods that conclude a operation inside a alternate virtual use

9494 to ro un d the estimation of a half to ro un d the estimation of a half pixel closer with a pi triplet fraction

9495 to ro un d the estimation of a pixe to ro un d the estimation of a pixel closer with a pi triplet fraction

9496 properties of stagnation improper u properties of stagnation improper use of technology in a manipulative manner to conclude monetary f un ds verses the intent to progress for example the co processor verse the use of an extended automatic co processor verses a deliberate attempt to keep t

9497 things that verses in terms this ve things that verses in terms this verses that in order to make another turn as well as things that verses and do not equal any such return or sense. the thought is the matter at hand. an abstract definition

9498 silicachromaticbuildingmicroproc silicachromaticbuildingmicroprocessors

9499 layered acrylic printing and jet sp layered acrylic printing and jet spray plasticprinting in itself is a term generalized as two part d and d printing combined

9500 blank chip ssd and blank chip desig blank chip ssd and blank chip designing acceptable circuit driven operations of a system on a chip

9501 technology aided learning of the un technology aided learning of the united states should have a privatized level of integration and legal funding for all schools and states learning should be focused on traditional context and should be modernized in a equal way to un ify learning as well

9502 gaseous carbonized smoke with solve gaseous carbonized smoke with solvent and electricity stabilizing the protons and electron particles for fuel and refinery in a electrical ph balance vapor fume tank for making compo un ds medicine and chemicals in a step by step process making a smoke f

9503 printing materials for perpendicula printing materials for perpendicular laser printed levels of circuits processors and memory in multiple photo sensitive cured solvents as circuits layers laser printed chips in a diffused solution to compute as a chip in a series of different elements da

9504 ethel nitrogen oxide fuel diverted ethel nitrogen oxide fuel diverted natural g as and combined salt

9505 building language software written building language software written by software hardware by as solid state or flash based conductor processor and operator made into a cubit written composite working tool

9506 synthetic currents to anchor underw synthetic currents to anchor underwater current makers to a high middle and low temperatures and in the consistent direction to prevent stagnant water and refresh the water in a pond or reservoir. the benefits would be less insects and healthier fish

9507 a secured public information channe a secured public information channel for monetary transfers is a specific web application that transfers ownership and f un ds to other banks and balances

9508 total year end dividend trading joi total year end dividend trading joint stock companies act from wikipedia debate the joint stock companies bill was introduced to parliament by the then vice president of the board of trade mr robert lowe in doing so he proclaimed the right of

9509 electronic us treasury of banks and electronic us treasury of banks and commissions is a united states trade bank that works with commercial common banks to control federal trade and electronic f un d transfers of ownership

9510 microwave combustion microwave flas microwave combustion microwave flash point in any operation as an ignition for combustion is the newest resolution here for energy. utility

9511 community future investments are f community future investments are f un ds for sustainable community management and the deprecation of environmental resources and state of improvements

9512 gps d triplet pi ration is the rati gps d triplet pi ration is the rational notation of small physical or normal number physics computational relation to gps december

9513 local and global participation in g local and global participation in gps d triplet pi ration is the dynamics of location for any known given computeable location decem

9514 fiber embedded processing on sd int fiber embedded processing on sd interupt fiber optical conducting boards and insert cards for processing in a optical environment of computations fiber embedded processing on solid data pcie and also ssd pat

9515 to seek find and replace recolonize to seek find and replace recolonize organ specific micro cell stems to seek find replace the celluloid and kill eat or replace that cell or multitude of cells to cure cancers and other age syndromes imm un e deficiencies and or the many diseases that peo

9516 compact optical power supply is an compact optical power supply is an conducting signal of a source that changes a function in a stored time for input into a board of calculation sub

9517 boosting directional optical transi boosting directional optical transition connections are radial shaped to linear shaped optical data signal bridges with pins and replaceable optical connections with incorporating power operators patent chri

9518 universal pre measurement bonding a universal pre measurement bonding and soldering by the pre measured circuit socket

9519 universal pre measurement bonding a universal pre measurement bonding and solderingthe pre measured circuit socket

9520 embedded hyper istic chips and proc embedded hyper istic chips and processors that hold inside a layer of insulation to connected intermittent silica linking to a printed circuit board printing by stencil layers and photo emulsion plasma bonding over silica to make a connection on a larger

9521 approved small m un itions of elect approved small m un itions of electric generating stores and subscribers

9522 see saw action synthetic g as pumpi see saw action synthetic g as pumping valve electric generation and infinite force fulcrum engine taking a current force and not stopping that energy but making a symbiotic source of energy where one force over comes the other one and repeats

9523 to multiply on local network os ove to multiply on local network os over os under os scenario to multiply on local network os the chances of using two or more under operating systems and concluding it to a working hierarchy of operating system +even or +odd.

9524 encrypted phone service that is for encrypted phone service that is for government to public or government to military or public to government

9525 glass (or poly carbonate) insulated glass (or poly carbonate) insulated gold line wire housing. needed to stack motherboards and double or more the capacity of the vertical possibilities inside that manner. as opposed to a silicon board this would connect boards to one another.

9526 the intent to reactivate a flower f the intent to reactivate a flower for a shape for extended central processing units and the possibilities to multiply and agitate the growth of a unit into more than one units a flower verses in terms.

9527 {to use a non primal number is the {to use a non primal number is the in and out of a circuit if to use a prime number the sum must have a divisible cube root.} which verses and changes in terms and may be exchangeable. factorization ** ** ** ** divisors

9528 plastic layered electronic micro bo plastic layered electronic micro board a process defined with nano printing circuits and layers of layers of circuitry that provides depth into height of computing capabilities or alternate poly carbonate / carbonate porous compounds

9529 official branch of news for the gov official branch of news for the government and legalities and suits with holdings and returns

9530 the need to place secure socket lay the need to place secure socket layers into place with a packet flaw prerequisite. to speak plainly a packet is requested from the server. the server sends a packet first with the completed file information backwards with weight and scale then loads t

9531 any such right as to investigate an any such right as to investigate and with plausible cause to search for a missing person upon any premise. with unique attributes justified by law holding contrary existing census information and legitimate rights of distrust or suspicion

9532 many other countries use the us dol many other countries use the us dollar. to equate a hypothesis is to generate a revenue inside it s self. the dollar bill with country intent for example a widget country denominated dollar with gold / silver / property / resource note.

9533 with the mass of complicated ports with the mass of complicated ports there should be a uniform port of snap in with pin play and align to the left scenario like a find and play plug and play device that may be useful for upcoming devices and experimental utilities yet unknown.

9534 to admit that the united states nar to admit that the united states narcotic problem would be easier to overcome would be anti marijuana gateway drug lock down to prepare for a conclusive issue of illegal status of drug use look into the past problems and sue the president

for his veto of
9535 retro fit industrial truck transmis retro fit industrial truck transmission attached axle line rotary electrical generator for part time hybrid trucks and long haulers with batteries or storage of current
9536 wireless machine adapters and perso wireless machine adapters and personal wireless comps with routers mini cloud invent more deposition is here think of a dream and add sugar a technology gadget that removes wires and picks up a signal of your own link something that we could benefit and
9537 after market gadgets need the shape after market gadgets need the shape you want. build your own tablet hand held chassis and server related fabric smaller un fused working parts that equal more power and higher concentration of parts dual socket tablet with fans and inches to inches days
9538 stacked conjoined honeycomb board t stacked conjoined honeycomb board that is a wall of architecture upon its self. to make a glass cased gold wire fish through the board up down and over and through printed circuit boards to endup inside a printed piping board with corrugations
9539 syndicated media news cloud and per syndicated media news cloud and perbuilt selects for realtime issue management
9540 big data creative data engineers co big data creative data engineers compliant hardware client requests ability software wreckless replacement exceptions speed in control using test and server strength to encrypt and control critical cohesion products and services of any kind
9541 vertical and embedded chip stilts t vertical and embedded chip stilts to branch layered un der and over stacked layered blanks to add to a multiple layered processing chip or storage
9542 nano related myriad layers of press nano related myriad layers of pressing alignment in branch layered over and un der stacked layered blanks to add to the building of a layered processing chip
9543 subtractively printed zirconhydroxy subtractively printed zirconhydroxy or photo laser cut zirconhydroxy isolated layer is a layer of zirconium which is a silicon that is more insulating and less thermal conductive than diamond carbonate this is good for making three dimensional chips and
9544 emergency sos satellite system base emergency sos satellite system based on cell phone satellite connections sos from wikipedia the free encyclopedia sos is the commonly used description for the international morse code distress signal ( ) this distress signal w as first adop
9545 emergency sos satellite system based on cell emergency sos satellite system based on cell phone satellite connections sos from wikipedia the free encyclopedia sos is the commonly used description for the international morse code distress signal (, , ,) this distress signal w as first adop
9546 bandwagon effect bandwagon effect from wikipedia the free encyclopedia jump to navigation search the bandwagon effect is a well documented form of group think in behavioral science and h as many applications the general rule is that conduct or beliefs spread among peopl
9547 imm un e systemic anti psychotics imm un e systemic anti psychotics anti psychotic medicine to magistrate through the auto imm un e system anti psychotic medicine to magistrate through the auto imm un e system physiological the causes of bipolar disorder

have yet to be fully un covered b

9548 emergency sos satellite system emergency sos satellite system based on cell phone satellite connections sos from wikipedia the free encyclopedia sos is the commonly used description for the international morse code distress signal ( ) this distress signal w as first adopted by the ger

9549 varios computer parts and musical chairs code n varios computer parts and musical chairs code name vegas isn't it simple that if the world followed quintet and sextet then that would mean that midi and the mc is and will always be the way that math in dance is synchronized and trans fixate and then beat spliced into pure mathematical mad ness and it's all equal to beats like mine. < i beg to differ the year was > roland tb : defined the acid sound of house music. note that tb is not the origin of this type product. for example of precedence from others the free encyclopedia jump to: navigation

9550 in a class of time and it s all in a little whi in a class of time and it s all in a little white lie. the is a mop up of a noise. white noise to bass line code name atlantis in a class of time and it's all in a little white lie. the is a mop up of a noise. the pitch decay and use of 's main mix of the midi will make a bass sound that makes mad people happy. < i beg to differ the year was > roland tb : defined the acid sound of house music. note that tb is not the origin of this type product. for example of precedence from others resulting in only

9551 transistor nano direction circuit nano direct transistor nano direction circuit nano direction and a path of a y transistor nano direction circuit a direction that may be pointed by a fractalized section of code. in order to direct a re correcting pathway to make a working model

9552 point a with a synchronized clock daybreak co point a with a synchronized clock daybreak compensation measurements point a with a synchronized clock to use compensation measurements like atmosphere elements and other catalyst. measurements for point b to compare and complete the time to distant light which may be only different by the smallest or nearest neighbor of a atomic weight calculation to play interesting studies with. important things such as sea level

9553 to save all sources state of our art arch of to save all sources state of our art arch of a window to elaborate on this with full intent to save all sources. the means of any archive is how much there is to make any save or estimation of weight... weight of a back up on any scale to forward or foretell the means of any given size of data on it's way to improve the function of a crash or safety mode back up. to estimate the archive size.

9554 state of our art open market gadgets to elab state of our art open market gadgets to elaborate on this with full intent to progress the moment of technology and processor. imagine you being able to pick the size and computational power of your own gadget and yet at the same time you yourself could choose oem options of os reach/mobility the size of the gadget and what you need it to do. large or small. pocket this and think that things aren't exactly the way that they should be... let's change every thing!

9555 lcus united states of america armed forces aer lcus united states of america armed forces aero contract winner state of our art aero t design stealth state of our art aero t design united states of america armed forces aero contract winner

9556 things that go with poor spelling health inven things that go with poor spelling health invent tab state of our art things that go with poor spelling spider pill carbon stabilize reaction

9557 ask intel about it they will say the exact sam ask intel about it they will say the exact same thing server chip stacking stacking this state of our art early invent coming to light ask intel about it they will say the exact same thing server chip stacking.
9558 oem oms original equipment manufacturer option oem oms original equipment manufacturer optional manufacturer system oem oms state of our art open market systems to elaborate on this with full intent to progress the moment of technology and processor. imagine you being able to pick the size and computational power of your own gadget and yet at the same time you yourself could choose oem options of os reach/mobility the size of the gadget and what you need it to do. large or small. pocket this and think that things aren't exactly the way that they should be... let's change every thing! oem oms original equipment manufacturer optional manufacturer system
9559 this is a situation state of our art woq ent this is a situation state of our art woq enterprise email records archive this is a situation of one fall scenario spam and filter checks. to assign a script to this is not adequate to make a program that exports and imports files paged by person and tabbed by content of importance is the issue... this is beyond web mail.
9560 astro hardware satellite server state of our a astro hardware satellite server state of our art astro service hardware astro hardware. imagine a disillusioned space elevator that has no clue. just a satellite that has servers aboard. imagine space travel that is so successful that over a long or short time we are able to store data in space itself.
9561 astro hardware astro size state of our art astro hardware astro size state of our art astro size hardware form astro hardware. extended satellite computations. imagine space travel that is so successful that over a long or short time we are able to store data in space itself.
9562 exit format expressions efe state of our art exit format expressions efe state of our art exit format expressions exit format expressions the intent to share all types of data or miscellaneous file types and the intent to not share or make program compatible is an interoperability challenge and program miss interpretation of sorts. my idea is a strict intersection of two formats to not share files or to share files with an easy add in plainly stating that the files must or must not be shared. either for security or profit mobility.
9563 emw state of our art eject my work i have al emw state of our art eject my work i have always wanted to borrow someone's pc but it's a pc how come we can't eject the os the updates and the software we own as well as our work and subsequently call hard ware hardware and eject my work
9564 atomized ion printing atomized ion printing st atomized ion printing atomized ion printing state of our art atomized ion printing with ± demagnetized trionic paper atomized ion printing with ± demagnetized trionic paper uses security strips new optical medias fine art printing
9565 super high carbon conductors super high carbon super high carbon conductors super high carbon conductors plasma molding diamond dust state of our art run on super high carbon conductors yielding welding solder heating all things carbon pure carbon with plasma into a height of super states of metal or ceramic carbon. wire circuits nano breaks all things lode plasma molding diamond dust
9566 atomized electormechanical photo printing ato atomized electormechanical photo printing atomized electormechanical photo printing state of our art run on atomized electormechanical photo printing as opposed to ion atomized demagnetized printing this would be a simple and more consumer affordable way to print in minute detail and still hold

the highest quality printing method to come. something that could eventually print metallic s and or super carbon signature marking inks. for safety security

9567" soft poly silicate carbonate nuclear smelting, soft poly silicate carbonate nuclear smelting " to form a fayalitic slag which is essentially calcium silicate

9568 state of our art hard oxide hard poly oxide ca state of our art hard oxide hard poly oxide carbonate nuclear smelting to form a fayalitic slag which is essentially calcium silicate

9569 what goes up may come down finding a height to what goes up may come down finding a height to measure the un measurable off the grid computations and landing points by what goes up may come down. the point that we need to measure in haste is the un measurable flash point that will keep the platform from crashing when landing. hollow arc field mathematical plane plateau exit the invisible points that may connect a plane by inverse

9570 to process code with measurement . cascading to process code with measurement . cascading increments . a certain unit of measurement . or . for processing electronic measurement using my certain unit of measurement data versus the shape of media today

9571 exit comp rules that apply with each process d exit comp rules that apply with each process data is the progress of format in my opinion. the greatest thing to happen to anything is to negate the format itself. why do people make things in side a box of any sort. this is maddening to myself. at this point in history the dvd is still popular only because the use of that decoder and the dvd player itself is the only reason. we have essentially been forced into it. take it or leave it type of modsi pita . the way to promote everything is to make it plain and simple. the publishing schema as we know it for example doesn't need a box. when you put it in only one format it is essentially only one format so without being rhetorical hey

9572 myriad nano sphere nano sphere myriad nanosph myriad nano sphere nano sphere myriad nanosphere nanosphere of myriad in reference to tension in side a molecular consistent other wise known as a very small sphere (floating of the free encyclopedia main article: (number) a myriad is primarily a singular cardinal number just as the thousand in four thousand is singular (one does not write four thousands people) the word myriad is used in the same way: there are four myriad people outside . when used as a noun

9573 my lzw algorithm isn t free a fee for a free my lzw algorithm isn t free a fee for a free platform is essentially not happening. i invented the pd f and here is my quote. either trust me or don't. the fact of the matter is that like the pokemon there was a puzzle in the equation of how to market the product and make people interested in their service. for the pokemon there was a unique game that was interesting to children

9574 do they put that stuff in the air the chance do they put that stuff in the air the chance of the hospital itself being sick is the real issue. like the story goes how do you heal the sick inside a sick place. well there are extremely strong antibiotics and then there are subtle every day antibiotics. my guess is that there could be a scenario that provides a perfect healing environment and therefore is related to unlimited healing possibilities... to make a solution that purifies the air and substitutes a antibiotic supplement in the hospitals and other sick situations.

9575 the issue is when will a co processor complim the issue is when will a co processor complimentary on and off as well as different and alternate processing to explain this is to accumulate the circumstances of on and off in a larger picture. to estimate the neurological existence of two halves of our human brain is the essence of why and when this is important... not only to have the power in two halves but to use those two halves to alternate and

differentiate the reason to compute... as a logical and scientific method for processing. for example a left and right coprocessors transparent multiple duplicate pattern processing
9576 one creative step bridge parallel modern e one creative step bridge parallel modern efficiency content text context parallel (email submission) assumptions of a coprocessing pattern the issue is when will a co processor understand that to full fill one creative step. it's important to duplicate that first step. in this attempt to be creative there are more patterns than the first second and so on. to insure a pattern of non creative circumstance like a pattern and a distinction of a mathematical number such as pi
9577 to multiply on local network os over os under to multiply on local network os over os under os scenario to multiply on local network os the chances of using two or more under operating systems and concluding it to a working hierarchy of operating system +even or +odd.
9578 laser wave modulation shaping a laser with com laser wave modulation shaping a laser with complimentary light is anyone out there? shaping a laser with complimentary light for navigation and artificial energy... math components (laser theory energy expansion of a sum = accelerated motion horizontal
9579 as well as triangular square and circular prop as well as triangular square and circular properties such as vertical horizontal and spherical combinations... with two or more in one process. line of sight as well as to inject gas and form a modulation of image appropriate for television and viewing comments is anyone out there? shaping a laser with complimentary light for navigation and artificial energy... math components (laser theory energy expansion of a sum = accelerated motion horizontal
9580 infrared computer screen human interface manip infrared computer screen human interface manipulation for laser generated d tv comments is anyone out there shaping a laser with complimentary light for navigation and artificial energy... math components (laser theory energy expansion shaping a laser with complimentary light for navigation and artificial energy... math components (laser theory energy expansion of a sum = accelerated motion horizontal
9581 out put computers are a method of creation out out put computers are a method of creation out put computers are a method of creation that people need to make things. i have decided to claim this as a separate market of intent for improvement in usability and justification of my means. there are currently confusing situations in reading or writing platforms. i think that the server of today is the workstation that people dream of making and creating content... although a blog may be ingenious looping music videos and so on. yet the people who divide their time such as myself to create content get stuck with apps that are rubbish. if only it were as simple as pointing a finger and saying don't make it harder to use while making it easier to read... i want my pc to make my dreams come true again and out put this painting of life together with . ghz yes and a teraflop of coprocessing! like number said i need more input!!!
9582 immune systemic anti psychotics antipsychotic immune systemic anti psychotics antipsychotic medicine to magistrate through the auto immune system anti psychotic medicine to magistrate through the auto immune system physiological the causes of bipolar disorder have yet to be fully uncovered globus pallidus and increase in the rates of deep white matter hyper intensities.[][][ ] functional mri findings suggest that abnormal modulation between ventral prefrontal and limbic regions

9583 emergency sos satellite system based on cell p emergency sos satellite system based on cell phone satellite connections. sos from wikipedia
9584 outdoor hot and cold out door auto/semi conduc outdoor hot and cold out door auto/semi conductor open processors outdoor hot and cold climates need processing let's imagine that there could be a cup with a microchip inside it after all... open processors and the instance of virtual to real time applicable things like traffic flow
9585 to enhance by way of less is more situation of to enhance by way of less is more situation of compatibility and less apps over programmable problems and obstacles saying that gingerbread operating systems are the way of the past and the future of os publishing is two fold a punter and a player verses in terms as a recorder and a viewer to create a two fold operating scheme minimal and coherently elaborate in one os with two different settings
9586 no cloud software registration a program s no cloud software registration a program specific intent to keep the software as is and with out any foreign auto updates and stripped integration from internet interference of opportunity and eula confidence trials of intent to disturb the sleeping software wintel <a href= http://crione.com/index.php?route=product/product&product_id=&search=&category_id= ></a>
9587 triplet pi translation axis for compensation e triplet pi translation axis for compensation equation sum part travel pi cubed translation axis for compensation equation sum and path intent. software hardware virtual and literal intent to create and estimate any means of anno place in time points of vector registration per annotation software hardware virtual and literal intent to create and estimate any means of anno place in time points of vector registration per annotation to start with the equation of two that is cubed and then translation inside travel. to multiply and intensify _/+/? cloud compute (server or software) the matters into a higher computational sum of what when where how and why
9588 commons unique abnormal commons unique abnorma commons unique abnormal commons unique abnormal <p style= marginbottom: in >lllint />%uxe a %ux f {b%uxe sqrt{b^{}ac} } over {a} %notequal binom{%sigma }binom{{ %uxe b i%uxe b m} }{ < j < n } p (i
9589 encrypted phone service that is for business... encrypted phone service that is for business
9590 insulated chip levels to make a non conductive layer insulated chip levels made from of with a coherence of any insulation method of stacking horizontal or vertical chip organization to build a larger chip also said as to make a non conductive layer with small outer and inner conductive measures while operation is possible
9591 exterior spanmeaning out side in atmosphere exterior meaning out side in atmosphere liquid cooled motherboard is an actively cooled in a climate controlled efficiency way of cooling for higher performance
9592 a reverse reflective tunnel that magnifies th a reverse reflective tunnel that magnifies the light and graduates the source to maximize the solar energy post
9593 a energy center or building with many focused a energy center or building with many focused solar generators that reverse reflective tunnel that magnifies the light and graduates the source to maximize the solar energy post search varios manufactured by roland dates present technical specifications polyphony voices timbrality part oscillator {{{oscillator}}} synthesis type openended system module after touch yes velocity sensitive yes input/output keyboard {{{keyboard}}} external control midi/ usb [edit] overview the roland varios is a rackmounted openended variable system module released by roland in . it is essentially a

production environment with audio editing and sample playback based on the technology from the oftoverlooked vp variphrase processor. it is possible to independently manipulate the pitch time and formant of a sample add effects and even build complete audiobased arrangements,¬all in a realtime environment and without cpu drain. in addition it will emulate analogue synthesizers such as the roland jupiter . while the varios can operate as a standalone tool it also works alongside digital audio sequencers using midi clock and mtc sync. vproducer arrangements can also be saved as a standard midi file and processed audio files can be exported in .wav or aiff format for use in other editors and software. [edit] expansion cards two expansion cards were released for the varios the vc which emulates a roland d and the vc which allowed vocal processing with an external microphone with effects such as a vocoder and choir. much to the disappointment of varios owners who spent considerable amounts of money (albeit on a powerful unit) it appears roland have no plans to release any future expansion cards. furthermore it appears the vc is now out of production with various sources claiming that roland made a set number of cards in an estimation of demand.

9594 ai is named wrong you have to take more into ai is named wrong you have to take more into consideration like the answer not the truth of the question left and right is the asymmetrical processing units. it was not until the mid to late s that dj and electronic musicians in chicago found a use for the machine in the context of the newly developing house music genre. in the early 's as new acid styles emerged the tb was often overdrive producing a harsher sound. examples of this technique include hard floor's ep acperience and interlect 's ep volcano. the wellknown acid sound is typically produced by playing a repeating note pattern on the tb while altering the filter's cutoff frequency resonance and envelope modulation. the tb 's accent control modifies a note's volume filter resonance and envelope modulation allowing further variations in timbre. a distortion effect either by using a guitar effects pedal or over driving the input of an audio mixer is commonly used to give the tb a denser noisier timbre,¬as the resulting sound is much richer in harmonics. the head designer of the tb tadao kikumoto was also responsible for leading design of the tr drum machine.

9595 formula for thought combination formula of co formula for thought combination formula of commons unique and abnormal the theory is a function of indefinite sums and energy in the mass of that sum with the longevity of that same sum a + m = e (. {} over {}) %uxe a {e} over {m} %uxe b {e%delta ^{}} over {c%delta ^{}} %uxe c{e %ux } over {c %ux }lllint /> %uxe a %uxe d {b%uxe sqrt{b^{}ac} } over {a} %notequal binom{%sigma } binom{{ %uxe b i%uxe b m} }{ < j < n } p (i

9596 d triplet pi ration map d triplet pi ration map is the three dimensional possible notation of travel in distance to be expected by any map

9597 gps d triplet pi ration gps d triplet pi ration is the rational notation of small physical or normal number physics computational relation to gps

9598 gps d triplet pi ration_ local and global participation in gps d triplet pi ration is the dynamics of location for any known given computeable location submitted on decem

9599 ai war software in data data center and other data driven strategy operations for study gaming software for war data science and real world ai scripted drones submitted o

9600 compact optical processor translator compact optical processor signal translator for embedded fiber signal optical boards and analog solid data synthetic sd syn toxin vs bio toxin fruit fly farming. all these things can change medicine by themselves of to make things

interesting
9601 pocb printed optical circuit board is an embedded fiber optical conducting signal board of calculation
9602 optical ram optical ram is an embedded fiber optical conducting signal of nano batteries that display a function in a stored time for input into a board of calculation christopher
9603 board splice chip board splice chip optical power switch is an alternating signal of a source that changes a function in a stored time for input into a board of calculation christopher
9604 chip rights and fees chip invitational design outsourcing we print your chip for fees and rights
9605 satellite communication amp aoip the communication amp is not only for talking and voip but a entertainment and communication all over internet protocol amplifier/map.
9606 light trigger + varied colored laser semiconductor & microchip cold light micro chip add subtract mode to divide and multiply digital platforms
9607 [time and light measure ment + stair case mirror chips] (optical mathematic weight and scale by calculations and common studies)
9608 the infinite motion inside the first sphere is made by all the rest of the batteries recharging the original battery inside. the only thing missing (magnetic electricity generating) is the method to recharge a battery with the least amount of connections for less resistance for more force magnetic motion generator
9609 it s a lot like a nuclear bomb only in reverse. instead of destroying elements we are putting them together. but more important than a super spontaneous collision we are separating the elements for recycling and purification. the muffler and the past catalytic transformer burning trash isn't as bad as it sounds connotations of shock come to mind when things are sometimes thought of a process. what i mean is when we think of how would you do that? there are so many different variables that sometimes it's like turning tar into gas or water to wine. the things that technology are capable of now are more impressive than we can even guess. the cost of burning trash is unequivalent to the benefits. i have found a way to think of things. air and light is the motto of my local fire station. the best thing to imagine is to start with two elements that are the most simple to begin some kind of abstract formula. what the public is afraid of are the contaminates in the solutions that are presented after and during and even before the spark of air and light. so let me explain in detail. it's a lot like a nuclear bomb only in reverse. instead of destroying elements we are putting them together. but more important than a superspontaneous collision we are separating the elements for recycling and purification. the muffler and the past catalytic converters in a car is one example of how the process is somewhat related to one another. the carburetor was invented by karl benz in pressure
9610 platform computing that measures instance rather than current cloud computing statistical virtual memory stacking easy to ask but i can remember christmas shopping with my parents and some times it really wasn't a good year when this situation happened? your in a store grabbing a gift just because it's another gift. they say that what really makes something worth giving is the thought. complicated things come in small packages. but big things can seem so far away at any given time. in a frenzy people cannot see the frenzy some times. have you ever seen a squad of year old play soccer? every one chases the ball. if only there was a better way to cloud compute the answers of inventions? then my friends i would be

useless and only if that scenario was so perfect. i think that to spawn two inventions on one deposition would be point less. to give birth to imperfection is to look away from the frenzy. platform computing that measures instance rather than current. a dream always seems brighter when you your self imagine the possibilities. cloud stat memory stacking only works when the sorting is all copacetic stack virtual memory and ram to match the four plus chips that are now in progress cloud computation with real analogies to relate each and every real could form with a computational analogy. alto high cirrus lock of hair cumulus heap nimbus precipitationbearing (latin for rain cloud) stratus layer (latin for spread out) or high quality printing. metallic ink copy intent carbon signature marking inks copy intent

9611 c technology wireless usb technology wireless usb technology microsoft had the goods and i needed what they had. they listened and i plainly spoke what i wanted. when where and how is the point. microsoft is no longer accepting bids for invent projects. there isn't much to say about this this was when microsoft was accepting feed back and invent depositions by way of solicitation. i emailed them that there should be wireless and input together. and i was out right sick of the wire on my mouse. casio :[ ] sio + cao ? casio[])from wikipedia http://en.wikipedia.org/wiki/blast_furnace#chemistry in reference to damages during refining how to recreate ozone (reduction to ozonides reduction of ozone gives the ozonide anion o . derivatives of this anion are explosive and must be stored at cryogenic temperatures. ozonides for all the alkali metals are known. ko rbo and cso can be prepared from their respective super oxides: ko + o ? ko + o although ko can be formed as above it can also be formed from potassium hydroxide and ozone:[ ] koh + o ? ko + o + ho)from wikipedia http://en.wikipedia.org/wiki/ozone#with_metals ","

9612 negative microwave technology and format making cold things stay cold and the same ovens that make things work for warmth can make things stay cold for a while after that. so after all their is cold fusion. the thought is that the technology that is available to consumers that makes things warm can make things cold. just softly and moderation is what we need to study for a while... but yet. so stay tuned and keep your eyes peeled for an after market method that not only bartenders can use. to ramble on about the needs and uses would be pointless at this time. to really see a carefully practice is one of estimation. some times people really like things cold. casio :[ ] sio + cao ? casio[])from wikipedia http://en.wikipedia.org/wiki/blast_furnace#chemistry in reference to damages during refining how to recreate ozone (reduction to ozonides reduction of ozone gives the ozonide anion o . derivatives of this anion are explosive and must be stored at cryogenic temperatures. ozonides for all the alkali metals are known. ko rbo and cso can be prepared from their respective super oxides: ko + o ? ko + o although ko can be formed as above it can also be formed from potassium hydroxide and ozone:[ ] koh + o ? ko + o + ho)from wikipedia http://en.wikipedia.org/wiki/ozone#with_metals

9613 lcus united states of america armed forces aero contract winner

9614 touch the web my light scribe edition of altracks was getting held up and soon enough

9615 deposition on theology of psychology this is the only reason why the internet web pages actually work can you download that movie with paper through the air? not at this moment but for example what about a universal and translatable script that will encode and decode music books movies gps info and for the matter itself data! it's my idea to promote data not necessarily the format to put the data inside with a noteable unit of measurement that is described only as .. to process code with measurement with a use of sd and scripting into a form of data.

9616 a fractal is the opposite of a worm hole. (a+m=e) part a fractal is the opposite of a worm hole. the entire amplitude of any entity with twice the mass will make energy that posses a general whole number that is not prime. it's plain to see but what is there to see? it's the amplitude with some form of fraction of a whole that makes the entity a whole number that never actually is ever completed and the number is merely a infinite hypothesis reaction meaning a large number it follows the same rules as that phrase. however that is not the case originally in greek where there is plural.

9617 amplitude () . / doubled mass () . [.] estimated energy constant weight (a+m=e) part thinking of different things how to invent the definition of something that doesn't exist war games the movie and why tic tack toe is an improbable but necessary medium to quote

9618 amplitude () . / doubled mass () . [.] estimated energy constant weight

9619 open idea app to design a ethernet cell or satellite based cell phone application open idea app a different way to internet to design a ethernet cell or satellite based cell phone application that connects people's phones as pages instead of pages on a server. the main purpose is to communicate and then the other things will gradually fall into place. i think it would be perfect to practice this in the jungles or deserts.

9620 modial comm. a different way to ftp to design a ethernet cell or satellite based cell phone application that connects people's phones as pages instead of pages on a server. the main purpose is to communicate and then the other things will gradually fall into place. i think it would be perfect to practice this in the jungles or deserts.

9621 a different way to see business ethics and personal values actually do make up the person who works for you. and you and i may see eye to eye for once that you don't want a drug user as your warehouse manager so what precautions would you be willing to take? personality or drug tests? to what level can you go to insure that there isn't any problems... to me it seems that the higher the magnitude of company the level of sanctity is to be seen reasonable. i wish right about now i could quote a devils advocate line

9622 technology of the relations between files long data why can't we all just get along? christopher g. brown long data concept i believe that a universal computer file that will put the hard efforts and intelligence of today to work tomorrow. this is not only the best way to understand it's going to be the best way to do business while still competing in a hard to open market. the first hand is the image type of code image map and spherical combinations... with two or more in one process. line of sight

9623 the need for two apps to transition through one another trying to work faster. a few questions and what to expect step one a nano motor the need for two apps to transition through one another is really something adobe systems is good at but my question is this and spherical combinations... with two or more in one process. line of sight as well as to inject gas and form a modulation of image appropriate for television and viewing as such... infrared computer screen human interface manipulation for laser generated d tv

9624 a few questions and what to expect fnatma fnatimg fnatma fnatimg chemistry topic of another invent deposition a few questions and what to expect how to charge an element using the nasa nevada experimental rail way? why would you bother them and what it means to the rest of us. i think it's best put as a set charge accelerator... a question of when and not if. there is hope but sometimes we need to take a guess and then the faults will occur. valence (chemistry) from wikipedia valence and spherical combinations... with two or more in one process. line of sight as well as to inject gas and form a modulation of image appropriate for television and viewing as such... as well as to combine and properties the human interface with controlled manipulation of direction and spheres as opposed to windows with the infrared detection.

9625 a few questions and what to expect pulse ion trigger algebraic lens motor to pulse nano photon color sensor pulse ion trigger algebraic lens motor to pulse nano photon color sensor trying to work more efficiently. ions the free encyclopedia jump to:navigation

9626 what were they thinking what were they thinking does everything have to have a microchip inside things i just don t want to happen especially the amygdala likely contribute to poor emotional regulation and mood symptoms.[ ] according to the kindling hypothesis when people who are genetically predisposed toward bipolar disorder experience stressful events the stress threshold at which mood changes occur becomes progressively lower until the episodes eventually start (and recur) spontaneously. there is evidence of hypothalamipituitaryadrenal axis (hpa axis) abnormalities in bipolar disorder due to stress.[] [][][] http://en.wikipedia.org/wiki/bipolar_disorder

9627 codex to diametric two opposing ideas that form a scientific outcome in computer analytical methods two concepts to measure it all codex to dielectrics. two opposing ideas that form a scientific outcome in computer analytical methods. to have codex applications and human interfaces which make all things essentially equal in to opposite ways like reverse outcome process/negative cell theory please use diode metrics algebras (to the technology makers there is a point of two or more operating systems to understand yet there is the world of sales that makes what we buy genetically similar.) inter science open app (technology called they want their biology book back) dielectrics computer theory(a system must detect and respond? comments of codes and conferences and became the worldwide standard under the second international radio telegraphic convention which was signed on november and became effective on july . sos remained the maritime radio distress signal until when it was replaced by the global maritime distress safety system. [ ] (with this new system in place it became illegal for a ship to signal that she is in distress in morse code. citation needed]) sos is still recognized as a visual distress signal.[] from the beginning the sos distress signal has really consisted of a continuous sequence of threeditz/threedash/threeditz all run together without letter spacing. in international morse code three ditz form the letter s and three dash make the letter o so sos became an easy way to remember the order of the ditz and dash. in modern terminology sos is a morse procedural signal or pro sign and the formal way to write it is with a bar above the letters: sos in popular usage sos became associated with such phrases as save our ship save our souls and send out succor . these may be regarded as mnemonics but sos does not stand for anything and is not an abbreviation acronym or initials. in fact sos is only one of several ways that the combination could have been written vtb for example would produce exactly the same sound but sos was chosen to describe this combination. sos is the only element signal in morse code making it more easily recognizable as no other symbol uses more than elements.

9628 theoretical business analytic s theoretical business analytic s to speak about ones past is sad at times. but so to me that is all opinion and at times facts of the case at hand. what made it great is the question. the same goes for why it went bad and when it went bad energy systems police dispatch and flight control situations modified with integers and boolean if's.

9629 digit treasury to track taxes and terrorist threats

9630 introduce the world to the largest topical cause is my first and foremost mission
9631 cuna cuna next chemistry topic of another part invent deposition a few questions and what to expect how to charge an element using the nasa nevada experimental rail way why would you bother them and what it means to the res
9632 cloud cycle to invent concept the difference of deep blue was that it wasn t considered a cloud at the time. the focus was only on the game and the server itself. this isn t the focus of what the azure is. windows will now carry on as usual... welcome to
9633 intent to remove cuna cuna chemistry topic of another part how to charge an element using the nasa nevada experimental rail way? why would you bother them and what it means to the rest of us. i think it's best put as a set charge accelerator... a question of when and not if. there is hope but sometimes we need to take a guess and then the faults will occur. valence (chemistry) from wikipedia valence
9634 another cloud cycle to invent concept the difference of deep blue was that it wasn t considered a cloud at the time. the focus was only on the game and the server itself. this isn t the focus of what the azure is. windows will now carry on as usual... wel
9635 real time and pure light %infinite times + %infinite=e%uxc binom lim n toward infinity(+{ } over {n})^{n} part
9636 real time and pure light %infinite times + %infinite=e%uxc binom lim n toward infinity(+{ } over {n})^{n} %infinite times + %infinite%uxc binom max xe ^{sum +infinity cdot +%uxe a {e} over x sum to{{} } x^{}%epsilon } part
9637 varios computer parts and musical chairs code name vegas isn't it simple that if the world followed quintet and sextet then that would mean that midi and the mc is and will always be the way that math in dance is synchronized and trans fixate and then beat spliced into pure mathematical mad ness and it's all equal to beats like mine. < i beg to differ the year was > roland tb : defined the acid sound of house music. note that tb is not the origin of this type product. for example of precedence from others the free encyclopedia jump to: navigation
9638 in a class of time and it s all in a little white lie. the is a mop up of a noise. white noise to bass line code name atlantis in a class of time and it's all in a little white lie. the is a mop up of a noise. the pitch decay and use of 's main mix of the midi will make a bass sound that makes mad people happy. < i beg to differ the year was > roland tb : defined the acid sound of house music. note that tb is not the origin of this type product. for example of precedence from others resulting in only
9639 rss search seek & search code name apache
9640 electronic muscle pulse therapy for atrophy patients help me walk? some organic / some post organic measure electronic muscle pulse therapy for atrophy patients step super infomercial for medical if i saw it on tv it has to be real disabled tendon repair and extensions step chicken cat transfer alternate cartilage transplant organic fiber optic nerve conductors step non evasive neurological where do you have trouble and electronic pulse for prolonged wheel chair patients
9641 spool effect of data data translation spool effect of data data translation one way in and two ways out is better than only one way in and one way out. logical translation is that a question of danger comes into guess work. a modification of compression is only a peg. modified m peg? sounds like an alice in wonderland piece. the ability to read and write and well as read writes and translates. the compression of the mp is a question of a fact of desire?

9642 many carbonates into heat as catalyst many complex solutions to air and water with a new multiple compound of a s tyro synthetic new starch with metal poly carbonate to a s tyro carbonate compound? for use in interesting and problematic situations? more to be found. many carbonates into heat as catalyst
9643 amplitude measurement infinity and other infinities all makes for an artificial intelligence with some or less than a real opinion for itself but more a suggestion of what we could do and how it should be done...
9644 it s a fact of life that to be propelled into a unfair and non respect form of work is not only detrimental and confusing to the artist it degrades the work and makes the artist suffer. from the beginning the underground of house and techno makes what we
9645 comma separated encryption comma separated encryption another reason is to continue work on a daily basis as intended securely strange brew is only a reason to understand that everyone is csv. styled now and excel my microsoft is no reason to degrade the graphical keys to encryption... imagine
9646 speechless while in love applications that text and how to make it as small as one or two options that have a greater click appeal paraphrase questions with proper context all while scripting speechless while in love applications that text and how to make it as small as one or two options that have a greater click appeal paraphrase questions with proper context all while scripting how do we go from ugly misshapen clouds to something that has more than only a tech savvy appeal? why can't we find words that mean what we say when we are in love? everybody knows what they feel when they are in love just sometimes it is so much easier to give up and say allot rather than nothing or even rather than one thing that people usually say. for example to use a phrase that makes grammatically correct questions like the way that large companies have with telephone services like for example would you like to buy now? or continue shopping with this product that is like something you just saw but there are better colors in this other product? how to go from multiple choices that don't make sense to a more exact link that makes intent complete? applications that text and how to make it as small as one or two options that have a greater click appeal paraphrase with proper context...
9647 inspiration to grow your business when you decide to have another baby inspiration when little families become big business... or rather when big business becomes a bigger family to maintain a reliable structure takes a lot of planning and it's judgment that puts hard work to use when it is time or when it needs to happen... growth in business starts with a little inspiration.
9648 successful data sharing perceptual image ocr codes and translation scripts and security file extending import export applications support and help
9649 theology of basic wrongs done right question and concept part i see you asking for some kind of revolutionary help that is a mental curse. the data will not work if the data is only in the air. the data and technology i have already submitted will work but
9650 simple est is a solar cell phone re charger my airplane crashed and let s say i m stranded who would i call first solar cell phone re charger color mathematics and algorithms based on color reflections for process control [time and light measure ment + stair case mirror chips] nanophotonics the light age
9651 sub scaleable sd branches and trees
9652 nachmv insulin
9653 knowing the difference painting any way you like and knowing the difference and

different composites that make up all of the properties of fire when the trash is burned to reclaim the mediums.
9654 two separate processors that are equal and octet each on their own capacity
9655 chemical searing internal process and reactions inherit water activated medicine
9656 cylindrical rotations with hour glass shaped impact
9657 static sd hard drives/ with expandable states
9658 stable fuse (theoretical separated chain reaction fuse) while on the phone to a hp tech agent i mentioned ever tried to print the web? moment of time excluded. web to print applications that make sense is the mission of all of this. wiki media foundation donations aside lets all make things that random thoughts can eventually get together and all jump into the same pond. in other words locate and print? what if you really could. cloud and print into the next few centuries? sorry about the rounding of all corners.
9659 scholastic aptitude testing like comparisons gone wild schematics of a interwoven statistical cloud scholastic aptitude testing like comparisons gone wild schematics of a interwoven statistical cloud. and when variables are compared using normal clients as well as abnormal clients. the mission is to compare two or more things and see if there is any such thing as a proper way to sell and keep on selling. for example how much email does a person like and how many times can you send them a request to buy before they unsubscribe. or out and out asking the right question in the proper context using good judgment and a level heading. what makes things go jump in the night and why other things like time place person or and different things exist. the optional context meaning two or more is the real secret to any equation.
9660 retro retro retro penicillin two penicillin two the simple minds think alike. but we progress through abstract minds that are complex yet still simple... looking back is always important. why did i leave that milk out on the kitchen counter all day? its an unintentional thing that led from not seeing that jug of milk there. sometimes if people cannot see what is there more than likely it will hide in plain sight. here is why the reason for all the things that occur in any invention is only retroactive and progression through looking back. the contemplation experiments are drawing to and end in my own self but and to estimate the whole effect of that number)
9661 extreme complex computations multiplex chips with multiple stairs and intelligent accelerators extreme complex computations multiplex chips with multiple stairs and intelligent accelerators extreme complex computations new computer platforms and sets for extreme complex computations pulse ion electron generators and how to make it a complex extreme state nano photon and process control to nan mo motors that switch off and on as well as redirect nan mo motors are generated and transformed by a solid state of matter multiplex chips with multiple stairs and intelligent accelerators with end outcome flash point of matter extreme complex computations part imagine a decisive moment when all computations end and a computer crashes what if the demand put us into a suspended turbo modal and a flash point of matter inside an ion created a super accelerated moment when matter and equation is important would you like to play a game? sometimes the complete understanding is giving a understanding that there is such a thing as blind faith. complete trust only because someone tells you the history and the mysterious ways that there is faith and a cause for a better way of existence. to coexist and understand that beyond some compensation of arithmetic that there is in fact a calculation that is endless. to say something

that is of an eternal entity is like someone who knows that pi is the estimation compensation standard of the start of amplitude. the amplitude equation is something that makes all standards of measurement work against pi. / . amplitude () . / doubled mass () . [.] estimated energy constant weight importance? {conception lighting electricity etc.}

9662 imagine a decisive moment when all computations end and a computer crashes what if the demand put us into a suspended turbo modal and a flash point of matter inside an ion created a super accelerated moment when matter and equation is important multiplex chips with multiple stairs and intelligent accelerators extreme complex computations new computer platforms and sets for extreme complex computations pulse ion electron generators and how to make it a complex extreme state nano photon and process control to nan mo motors that switch off and on as well as redirect nan mo motors are generated and transformed by a solid state of matter multiplex chips with multiple stairs and intelligent accelerators with end outcome flash point of matter extreme complex computations part imagine a decisive moment when all computations end and a computer crashes what if the demand put us into a suspended turbo modal and a flash point of matter inside an ion created a super accelerated moment when matter and equation is important

9663 suspended air and seed super suspended fuel flow for hyper active engine part seeds and force suspended air and seed to centrifugal force included inside a hyperactive engine to generate force and energy and make a more fuel effective means for work.

9664 too much / paid in adverts program flush market tactics too much / paid in adverts program no one said you had to listen to the whole thing. flush the market strategies and convoluted scenarios of an artist and their own thought of worth. why is it that people dream large and yet still nothing happens... my ploy and your place or rather my place and your intent are the things that make me want to do this. why is it that people conjure a data disc as a rudimentary leap and jump into hyper space of nowhere. this is about the place i'm in and why i'm here doing what i think is right. i've been branded and so have you.

9665 nano tetrahedron motors/period particles tets of a period

9666 commons unique abnormal s commons unique abnormal as well as a long history of previous things such as revisions and other instances like undo data and authors date and other things to pass along the data that may make information archaeologists study how to make more money and or why there was a loss of money. to summarize what i'm thinking of is to make files that have such close code and scripts as well as alternate information added that could be readable by things like for example internet browsers or phone apps.

9667 nine dash nine can the computer {hardware or software} conduct two or more ions from a micro spark generator and then somehow keep those two ions making switches go off and on while not colliding and at the same time act as a nerve to control the computer as a whole to essentially make a multiion and eventually a multiplying micro spark generator the way that this diagram demonstrates in an abstract transition.

9668 nano motors of s tyro carbonate nano motors of s tyro carbonate and in the shape of a tetrahedron also known as valency or valency number is a measure of the number of chemical bonds formed by the atoms of a given element. over the last century the concept of valence evolved into a range of approaches for describing the chemical bond including lewis structures ( ) valence bond theory ( ) molecular orbitals ( ) valence shell electron pair repulsion theory ( ) and all the advanced methods of quantum chemistry.

9669 theater servers hd theater experience hf theater data packs. search nanohub.org is science cyberinfrastructure[ ] comprising communitycontributed resources and geared toward educational applications professional networking and interactive simulation tools for nanotechnology. funded by the national science foundation (nsf) it is a product of the network for computational nanotechnology (ncn) a multiuniversity initiative of eight member institutions including purdue university the university of california at berkeley the university of illinois at urbana campaign the molecular foundry at lawrence berkeley national laboratory norfolk state university northwestern university and the university of texas at el paso. ncn was established to create a resource for nanoscience and nanotechnology via online services for research education and professional collaboration. ncn supports research efforts in nanoelectronics nano electormechanical systems or nems nanofluidics nanomedicine/ biology and nanophotonics.

9670 from my own experience psychotic debilitation from my own experience i believe that there is brain damage during a psychotic episode that may lead to serious and more permanent debilitation. this is important due to the chemical balance and the aid of recovery to locate the impartial negative neurological synapses and prevent future reoccurrences also to prevent this episode change in patients more likely to develop later in life.

9671 to round the estimation of a half pixel closer with a pi triplet fraction.

9672 criminally insane schizophrenia criminally schizophrenic what is the issue with virile contributors and identity theft... to compose why this is important in a short is to say that the specific context is technology. why a person will gain access to a log in and cause either unsafe terms or to steal a sum of information. my guess is that people have leaped into a mental illness and somehow conceited to the possible chance that what they are doing is going to result in gain. for example some person steals money through a password or online portal why the things made it fall from popularity may at times be opinion or merely poetical justice. what goes up must come down. to translate the simple things in business are always from intuition. to hire people with positive ethical spirit and attitude is the most important thing to start with.

9673 led lcd or plasma theater movie screen plasma movie screen

9674 a pragmatic estimation pragmatic computational cloud theory

9675 let s say that there are ways to help others and save lives would you trust a doctor to make a interesting finding with out any long term damage if you {me some one important we both know} the patient survives

9676 a strict and compact intersection news cloud percents and search ability

9677 how to a essence of a subscription that includes dates events and clicks. as well as notable notes and other things that require attention. also known as valency or valency number is a measure of the number of chemical bonds formed by the atoms of a given element. over the last century the concept of valence evolved into a range of approaches for describing the chemical bond including lewis structures ( ) valence bond theory ( ) molecular orbitals ( ) valence shell electron pair repulsion theory ( ) and all the advanced methods of quantum chemistry. from wikipedia the free encyclopedia is the natural number following and preceding . since = + + = it is the smallest cube that's also the sum of three cubes (plato was among the first to notice this and mentioned it in book viii of republic). it is also the sum of a twin prime (+). but since there is no way to express it as the sum of the proper divisors of any other integer it is an untouchable number. this multiplicative magic square has magic constant . in base it is a harshad number. there are fixed hexominoes the polynomials made

from squares. is a friedman number
9678 to stop within a certain rule of denominations... so to speak literally
9679 the difference between a friendly code command and an unfriendly one is the process to limit and not with out limit. vague code complex friendly vague code anamorphic script commands the difference between a friendly code command and an unfriendly one is the process to limit and not with out limit.
9680 ethel nitrogen oxide fuel diverted natural gas and combined salt
9681 study of sorts to understand and reason geometry and other trigonometry waves with a comparative interest into measurement of statistical process. the way a cloud can help use measurement and understand other process and actually see shapes. search varios manufactured by roland dates present technical specifications polyphony voices timbrality part oscillator {{{oscillator}}} synthesis type openended system module after touch yes velocity sensitive yes input/output keyboard {{{keyboard}}} external control midi/ usb [edit] overview the roland varios is a rackmounted openended variable system module released by roland in . it is essentially a production environment with audio editing and sample playback based on the technology from the oftoverlooked vp variphrase processor. it is possible to independently manipulate the pitch time and formant of a sample add effects and even build complete audiobased arrangements—all in a realtime environment and without cpu drain. in addition it will emulate analogue synthesizers such as the roland jupiter . while the varios can operate as a standalone tool it also works alongside digital audio sequencers using midi clock and mtc sync. vproducer arrangements can also be saved as a standard midi file and processed audio files can be exported in .wav or aiff format for use in other editors and software. [edit] expansion cards two expansion cards were released for the varios the vc which emulates a roland d and the vc which allowed vocal processing with an external microphone with effects such as a vocoder and choir. much to the disappointment of varios owners who spent considerable amounts of money (albeit on a powerful unit) it appears roland have no plans to release any future expansion cards. furthermore it appears the vc is now out of production with various sources claiming that roland made a set number of cards in an estimation of demand.
9682 pop fad curves intrinsic popularity curves in modern culture. a. popular fad high arch to middle decent and small arch with gradual fade out. b. near impossible long high arch b. different curve gradual fade in with a small arch and middle decent to a high arch. units. it was not until the mid to late s that dj and electronic musicians in chicago found a use for the machine in the context of the newly developing house music genre. in the early 's as new acid styles emerged the tb was often overdrive producing a harsher sound. examples of this technique include hard floor's ep acperience and interlect 's ep volcano. the wellknown acid sound is typically produced by playing a repeating note pattern on the tb while altering the filter's cutoff frequency resonance and envelope modulation. the tb 's accent control modifies a note's volume filter resonance and envelope modulation allowing further variations in timbre. a distortion effect either by using a guitar effects pedal or over driving the input of an audio mixer is commonly used to give the tb a denser noisier timbre—as the resulting sound is much richer in harmonics. the head designer of the tb tadao kikumoto was also responsible for leading design of the tr drum machine.
9683 data compression virtual zip record keeping servers services platforms and scripts into a history bin folder for later recall

9684 the reasons for poetic pretense and you. mystery of art and us the history strange or truth fiction of a future always as a surprise

9685 portable hand held server with sequential process to enable distant and no service areas similar to the open idea app yet more specific in titles needs like sever weather reports and how to get medicine. the people who would use such a device are patrol

9686 seriously from: [] sent: tuesday : am to: microsoft us partner team subject: retro active software resale? partner id: hello mpn at microsoft

9687 the ability to toggle an early invent toggles and switches the ability to toggle and make paths in order to compute the existing switches that need to be used and made off and on. electricity gone computational. simple but very early need in tech space.

9688 data tree multiplying data tree assistants data trees and solid state assistants the ability to toggle and make paths in order to compute the existing switches that need to be used and made off and on. electricity gone computational. simple but very early need in tech space. now even more important with dynamic solid state trees.

9689 the sum of all abstracts the sum of all abstracts thinking of a boomerang effect. for example the thought of a real computation being inside a reals in set theory

9690 cram data shapes things to come and why data should have a shape critical random access memory

9691 a mouse with internal memory for such applications as copy and paste quickly and sufficiently to increase file transfers to computer a to computer b

9692 to seek find and replace recolonize organ specific micro cell stems to seek find replace the celluloid and kill eat or replace that cell or multitude of cells to cure cancers and other age immune deficiencies and or the many diseases that people wish to cure.

9693 user defined process and additions user defined process and additions . vague code complex . statistical comparative . triplet pixel of noise with pi. computer arithmetic cannot directly operate on real numbers with similar scales only with other mathematically known values. the results will make a stick shift for example into a automatic transmission for all. this may explain problems in computational flash points {or crashes} that need to be overcome. similar to a run all script command made possible by using percents of operation. first and foremost i take a larger picture into consideration. what is the difference with a diplomat trying to become a missionary? what is the difference between a philosopher such as myself on a mission as opposed to a supermodel trying to hand out vitamins? section i. teach a man to fish proverb: give a man a fish he eats for a day teach a man to fish he eats for a lifetime. communism doesn't work and democracy does. to talk to a person in a nonmilitant/ non missionary/ nongovernmental fashion and let the defined reason of history hold presidency. a lot of my ideas and inventions will not work because the country at hand is so broken and war struck. to me my conversational prose is the only intent. slavery is wrong and hatred toward one another is evil. in history the best thing to do is learn from it. chile adopted the us constitution and to this day they are the most successful south american country to date. this is my idea to prove right. section ii. filled with uncertain and discernible rights. antiquilology makes the possession of man illegal the taxation only upon representation it's a dream that people want a miracle device that heals and finishes off anguish. it's to myself that a theoretical just of the basic situation starts with the ability to start at the root of the problem and understand that with all things considered the problem is their government. imagine how we the people became great is by fore fathers that distrusted the english i think that to my understanding the wars inside poverty stricken countries are facing civil unjust due to huge improbable governments. to go to a country at war is not the goal. to begin is to see a country in need but not to attack the country first in the most war torn. help the one who is near the country that is close to the war and have intuition spread. if the plan is successful the data will become unquestionably great. taxation and spread of united states like society to third world countries.

9694 mouse is live

9695 simple complex abstract intent to reflect process and redirect. the essence of ion and light inside a working electronic or iontronic machine

9696 data and the diamond

9697 easier said than done to create an entity that interpret appreciations of science art and humanities

9698 time to get up and move. working sake of data conference worldwide time to get up and move. this is a concept for the sake of all data in the entire time and code for codes sake. to incorporate a sync code to share information throughout the time we will have. the data we have now and forever. some universal parts of script that will make sense today and tomorrow. a thing called intelligent data sharing and encryption. one for all and all for one.

9699 learn it and be the machine animate to print artwork there is a time and a breadth. choose your battles and win in a million odds over here is my hope and dreams for this world and the intent to conceive any gain for man. script specials and the dream to animate

9700 nanometric microcircuit trip device [breaker] there is a time and a breadth. choose your battles and win in a million odds over here is my hope and dreams for this world and the intent to conceive any gain for man. nanometric microcircuit trip device

9701 vinegar essence sulfate tablets extract testing actualization

9702 acetoxybenzoic acid quartiondine light exposure testing actualization's ionized and ultraviolet laser chemical enhancing medicines acetoxybenzoic acid with second half exposure to make acetoxybenzoic acid quartiondine.

9703 equilibrium inside a annotation of place crione

9704 wireless machine adapters and personal wireless comps with routers mini cloud invent more deposition is here

9705 why can t my phone connect to a satellite connect the dots why can't my phone connect to a satellite instead of cell towers why can't my personal router connect to a satellite for un interrupted or rather a ±% up time and possibly easier set ups connect to a satellite... so here i am. satellite providerphone service freesatellite tv service

9706 this invent project is based upon phone communication gone satellite cell tower possibilities this invent project is based upon phone communication gone satellite. the importance is that this is to equate the chance of a alternate use for cell broadcast stations in an attempt to save the resources we have and will maintain. cell tv public media access servers

9707 flip the floppy with toenail in the side jamb lets examine why a . solid state data format would work. again the intent to understand that size matters the free encyclopedia (redirected from floppy disc) jump to: navigation

9708 using oxygen to propel things in space oxygen system propel engine for use with light weight and satellite operations. the oxygen orbit engine.

9709 recycling nuclear waste into medical radiology use in a dynamic equilibrium recycling nuclear waste into medical radiology use in a dynamic equilibrium nuclear potential energy the use of sustained nuclear fission to generate heat and do useful work. depleted uranium main article: depleted uranium uranium enrichment produces many tons of depleted uranium (du) which consists of u with most of the easily fissile u isotope removed. u is a tough metal with several commercial uses for example

9710 fractal math string zoom formula for bio and non chemical measurements to zoom and extract dna from stem cells as well as dna strings. to zoom and measure solid state data or solid state memory cells. a. fractal

9711 cnc (computer navigated control) microscope for bio and chemical measurements · to zoom and extract dna from stem cells

9712 conference call computer

9713 computer phone a phone call that made it retro active. a large smart phone book like design. large phone book like design. conference call computer a phone call that made it retro active. mixed up smart phone more channels per call voice screen

9714 to use fractal noise as a means to find the infinite extending paths of scripts and all while using trip circuit for control

9715 to use fractal noise as a means to find the infinite extending paths of scripts and all while using trip circuits for control. boolean updates to practical scripts and vague code complex. two planes of intersection and if or a what.

9716 more channels per call voice screen

9717 transistor nano direction circuit nano direction and a path of a y transistor nano direction circuit a direction that may be pointed by a fractalized section of code. in order to direct a re correcting pathway to make a working model

9718 point a with a synchronized clock daybreak compensation measurements point a with a synchronized clock to use compensation measurements like atmosphere elements and other catalyst. measurements for point b to compare and complete the time to distant light which may be only different by the smallest or nearest neighbor of a atomic weight calculation to play interesting studies with. important things such as sea level

9719 to save all sources state of our art arch of a window to elaborate on this with full intent to save all sources. the means of any archive is how much there is to make any save or estimation of weight... weight of a back up on any scale to forward or foretell the means of any given size of data on it's way to improve the function of a crash or safety mode back up. to estimate the archive size.

9720 state of our art open market gadgets to elaborate on this with full intent to progress the moment of technology and processor. imagine you being able to pick the size and computational power of your own gadget and yet at the same time you yourself could choose oem options of os reach/mobility the size of the gadget and what you need it to do. large or small. pocket this and think that things aren't exactly the way that they should be... let's change every thing!

9721 lcus united states of america armed forces aero contract winner state of our art aero t design stealth state of our art aero t design united states of america armed forces aero contract winner

9722 things that go with poor spelling health invent tab state of our art things that go with poor spelling spider pill carbon stabilize reaction

9723 ask intel about it they will say the exact same thing server chip stacking stacking this state of our art early invent coming to light ask intel about it they will say the exact same

thing server chip stacking.
9724 oem oms original equipment manufacturer optional manufacturer system oem oms state of our art open market systems to elaborate on this with full intent to progress the moment of technology and processor. imagine you being able to pick the size and computational power of your own gadget and yet at the same time you yourself could choose oem options of os reach/mobility the size of the gadget and what you need it to do. large or small. pocket this and think that things aren't exactly the way that they should be... let's change every thing! oem oms original equipment manufacturer optional manufacturer system
9725 this is a situation state of our art woq enterprise email records archive this is a situation of one fall scenario spam and filter checks. to assign a script to this is not adequate to make a program that exports and imports files paged by person and tabbed by content of importance is the issue... this is beyond web mail.
9726 astro hardware satellite server state of our art astro service hardware astro hardware. imagine a disillusioned space elevator that has no clue. just a satellite that has servers aboard. imagine space travel that is so successful that over a long or short time we are able to store data in space itself.
9727 astro hardware astro size state of our art astro size hardware form astro hardware. extended satellite computations. imagine space travel that is so successful that over a long or short time we are able to store data in space itself.
9728 exit format expressions efe state of our art exit format expressions exit format expressions the intent to share all types of data or miscellaneous file types and the intent to not share or make program compatible is an interoperability challenge and program miss interpretation of sorts. my idea is a strict intersection of two formats to not share files or to share files with an easy add in plainly stating that the files must or must not be shared. either for security or profit mobility.
9729 emw state of our art eject my work i have always wanted to borrow someone's pc but it's a pc how come we can't eject the os the updates and the software we own as well as our work and subsequently call hard ware hardware and eject my work
9730 atomized ion printing atomized ion printing state of our art atomized ion printing with ± demagnetized trionic paper atomized ion printing with ± demagnetized trionic paper uses security strips new optical medias fine art printing seriously i am asking for you to sell office again. treat this comment with possibilities... lately you are getting too complicated and some people are moving into an open office... now is the time that take a risk on something that was so awesome. i just installed and like it better than . sorry but as for me ease is an em or rather an accessibility issue... chris
9731 state of our art it sound s like that in a sentence phonology the syllables founding of latin reference
9732 super high carbon conductors super high carbon conductors plasma molding diamond dust state of our art run on super high carbon conductors yielding welding solder heating all things carbon pure carbon with plasma into a height of super states of metal or ceramic carbon. wire circuits nano breaks all things lode plasma molding diamond dust
9733 atomized electormechanical photo printing atomized electormechanical photo printing state of our art run on atomized electormechanical photo printing as opposed to ion atomized demagnetized printing this would be a simple and more consumer affordable way to print

in minute detail and still hold the highest quality printing method to come. something that could eventually print metallic s and or super carbon signature marking inks. for safety security or what makes it so that the other sets of natural numbers integers rational numbers real numbers complex numbers can work in a cloud and configure estimates and alt sums. to use colors and reference points shapes and names for places.

9734 recycled nuclear waste

9735 soft poly silicate carbonate nuclear smelting to form a fayalitic slag which is essentially calcium silicate

9736 state of our art hard oxide hard poly oxide carbonate nuclear smelting to form a fayalitic slag which is essentially calcium silicate

9737 mission diagnose changes at dopa mine serotonin adrenaline and histamine receptor sites in the central nervous system by using a similar method to diabetic blood testing. mission diagnose changes at dopa mine adrenaline and histamine receptor sites in the central nervous system by using a similar method to diabetic blood testing. in reference to signal receptors and d d and d in use of an atypical anti psychotic

9738 what goes up may come down finding a height to measure the un measurable off the grid computations and landing points by what goes up may come down. the point that we need to measure in haste is the un measurable flash point that will keep the platform from crashing when landing. hollow arc field mathematical plane plateau exit the invisible points that may connect a plane by inverse

9739 hollow arc field mathematical plane plateau exit the invisible points that may connect a plane by inverse

9740 intent to covert and see the matter at hand. to tablet to desktop to phone ineligible document conversion wysiwyg

9741 for safe and secure as well as quick and immediate transactions a card that provides service when service is only one overdraft away. to speed up the transactions posting and pending to post as a involuntary means.

9742 even and odd fractional status even and odd fractional status the improvement of multi deck processors all natural and computational binary numbers will be multiplied and divided with roots and squares only over a short time span will this happen inside a brick mold if you will of an environment that knows which way to go. using common math geometry calculus thrums'

9743 pixel language em css wc intent adi adi adi

9744 fuse nano motors

9745 atomic weight vacuum precious metal recycling and atom mining

9746 to process code with measurement . cascading increments . a certain unit of measurement . or . for processing electronic measurement using my certain unit of measurement data versus the shape of media today

9747 exit comp rules that apply with each process data is the progress of format in my opinion. the greatest thing to happen to anything is to negate the format itself. why do people make things in side a box of any sort. this is maddening to myself. at this point in history the dvd is still popular only because the use of that decoder and the dvd player itself is the only reason. we have essentially been forced into it. take it or leave it type of modsi pita . the way to promote everything is to make it plain and simple. the publishing schema as we know it for example doesn't need a box. when you put it in only one format it is essentially only one

format so without being rhetorical hey
9748 electromagnetic divalent effervescence
9749 it s funny you should but ask i m in servers severs not software web os
9750 using multiple tests compensation and how to provide any consistency with statistics elaborate compensations will measure the point of our art and science. using multiple tests and using all the measures known by science to study the form of art that will lead to a perfect arch or a perfect line. which both are very far away in terms. governmental servers for data reach and military security intelligence communication servers. why can't my phone connect to a satellite instead of cell towers why can't my personal router connect to a satellite for un interrupted or rather a ±% up time and possibly easier set ups connect to a satellite... so here i am. satellite providerphone service satellite mynetwork service freesatellite tv service
9751 nano motors and in the way of open and closed. aggregate verses passive for technological or medical scenarios and other processes when size does matter. search floppy redirects here. for other uses see floppy (disambiguation). inch inch and inch floppy disks inch inch (full height) and inch drives a floppy disk is a disk storage medium composed of a disk of thin and flexible magnetic storage medium sealed in a rectangular plastic carrier lined with fabric that removes dust particles. they are read and written by a floppy disk drive (fdd). invented by ibm floppy disks in .inch (mm) .inch (mm) and inch (mm) forms were a ubiquitous form of data storage and exchange from the mid s to the s.[ ] while floppy disk drives still have some limited uses especially with legacy industrial computer equipment they have been superseded by data storage methods with much greater capacity such as usb flash drives portable external hard disk drives optical discs memory cards and computer networks.
9752 can we figure out the chemistry in a healthy human can we figure out the chemistry in a healthy human
9753 to make something work sometimes size does matter. what i want is a fast hard drive that happens to be external... for example... the mystery is how to make a unique hole and a plug to do that with without loss or deterioration in cables. crioner aircraft production radiation shielding and armor as it has a higher density than lead. depleted uranium is also controversially used in munitions
9754 intelligence and brain growth there is the science we all know the brain receptors need to work and they want to work. nightmares and why they are good set choice mandelbrot z = z^ + c b. fractal set choice mandelbrot z = z^ + c a. mandelbrot x y . magnification b. mandelbrot x. y . magnification a. julia x y post x . y . b. julia x . y . magnification . post x y .
9755 compact hardware service compact server inside a series of software mods and a different way to dedicate the data position size and capabilities for allocation compact server. compact hardware service compact server inside a series of software mods and a different way to dedicate the data position size and capabilities for allocation. a grade b grade all in a thing called hardware service cloud make a note there is a difference in all technology and the service of a hardware is not a change. to specify a invent called service grading and rating.
9756 grade b grade all in a thing called hardware service cloud. to make a note there is a difference in all technology and the service of a hardware is not a change. to specify a invent called service grading and rating. compact server. compact hardware service compact server inside a series of software mods and a different way to dedicate the data position size and capabilities for allocation. a grade b grade all in a thing called hardware service cloud make a note there is a difference in all technology and the service of a hardware is not a change. to

specify a invent called service grading and rating.

9757 falling by data verses falling by data verses balanced data at the same measure of a chemical balanced neutral chemistry ph the best way to make us understand the falling off stature of a certain mark... such as to take two or more things and measure the importance or the proposition at hand. the abstract way to say this would be this way... which data to disregard which to archive and which to make a note of at a later time. or the most wisest decision would be to catalog the entire mass and then recall all data by user/product such as interference. camera aio business os and situation communication computations cordial os or situation for unsecured communications comps

9758 things that verses in terms this verses that in order to make another turn as well as things that verses and do not equal any such return or sense. the thought is the matter at hand. an abstract definition...

9759 myriad nano sphere nano sphere myriad nanosphere nanosphere of myriad in reference to tension in side a molecular consistent other wise known as a very small sphere (floating of the free encyclopedia main article: (number) a myriad is primarily a singular cardinal number just as the thousand in four thousand is singular (one does not write four thousands people) the word myriad is used in the same way: there are four myriad people outside . when used as a noun

9760 assemble of pre face and su face assemble of pre face and su face universal assemblage formats companies who make things for other companies to sell with their name on top and companies to sell what someone else s already made with an alternate name on t camera aio all digital comm a cloud receiver. the intent to design a complete radio tv phone data receiver. the mundane and exciting work prior to the internet to make data from radio television and voice communications into ones and zeros. first for function then for data quality improvement. imagine if you will a device that would receive what ever you like as long as its okay with you. transforming all things into a receiving end user experience of sorts.

9761 divergent decision this is a company specific attempt to hold notes and thoughts in the air. the example of cars as compared to specific software gives precedence to a new way for profit intent. the decision to make two or more different operating systems and agendas are non exceptionally unanimous. to speak more clearly the decision to make a two motif platform is contagious. yet at the same time undone as to a codex to dielectrics after all. strict intent to remain computational verses intent to perceive to set an example would be to make a personality test of the intent holding from the crowd of corresponding architects. to take the analytic personalities and make a platform while a intuitive and non working informational pragmatic platform of their different colleagues asses alternate differences. so to plainly speak the differences in side windows xp ie verses windows *new

9762 processors isolated semi conductors and their organized processing looping processors isolated semi conductors and their organized processing may be needed to comply more than two specific parts of a computer. to make a conductor for part a and part b as well as c and d.

9763 script dividing script patterns and repetitive computations multiplied by a larger script. to divide or multiply one large process into sub processes for a real time application

9764 dynamic verses static web content translation by use of analytical history transition content transition content translation pack the intent to take static web content and automate the content into dynamic by use of analytic patterns of use history

9765 three ring binder glucose incubation a computer controlled molecular telescope / nan scope that can insert and impregnate new dna will consequently rebuild the cell. a computer controlled dissection will allow probability of success for great accomplishment

9766 turning off the virus virus intentions to turn and transform virus intentions to turn and transform the effort of mainline to a true police operating system. to steady the intent and take the means in order to use that code for a positive purpose. for example to hack a hack is to make a bucket full of drinking water instead of used oil. this is accordance with the vague code complex and the intent to run a attack in to a greeting like a knock at the door from an old friend. turning off the virus syn toxin vs bio toxin fruit fly farming. all these things can change medicine by themselves of to make things interesting

9767 another comparative analogy water . water cycle water data cycle . fresh water storage new data server . sea water world wide data . tides to sync data

9768 the positive intent to administer a native formula for globalization patients

9769 to give data sending water through or not to send water. if there were a .rar equal to a need then there would be a need called .raz. to send a .raz into a receiver would be like making a scripted transition to and from a device or line. translated into a

9770 synthetic currents to anchor underwater current makers to a high middle and low temperatures and in the consistent direction to prevent stagnant water and refresh the water in a pond or reservoir. the benefits would be less insects and healthier fish

9771 intelligent voip s server to point a server instead of a pc to magistrate commas and processes.

9772 topical antibiotic mouthwash topical antibiotic mouthwash (halitosis) to cure by way of rinsing and nasal spray of antibiotic solution topical antibiotic bath soak (to cure by way of bath soaking in diluted antibiotic solution

9773 total year end dividend trading joint stock companies act from wikipedia debate the joint stock companies bill was introduced to parliament by the then vice president of the board of trade mr robert lowe in doing so he proclaimed the right of

9774 tired of ftp what if i didn t have to do it that way. what if there were new and exciting ways to engage clients data that make and hold more data than usual. for example a cloud that is low to the ground is called fog. files on the ground would make sync

9775 tired of upgrading key socket adapter a molding cpu socket adapter that works like clay on a car key in a cool movie. working to accept all patterns. but only all the patterns present

9776 compensation chip compensation chips long processors vs. short and stubby. it s a uniform shape that is divided by and then multiplied with time and hardware mass. so to speak...

9777 search by image to search for a topic with an image. to find people places and things. with input from meta tags such as technical terms when where who and why. as well as to modify the photo scan or topic by perspective date and angle using the image its or high quality printing. metallic ink copy intent carbon signature marking inks copy intent

9778 personal computer server personal server computer re ignite the passion for computing put one foot forward and take two steps back try installing windows eight with a server by intel use as directed and wash twice a day... intel sy

9779 my lzw algorithm isn t free a fee for a free platform is essentially not happening. i invented the pd f and here is my quote. either trust me or don't. the fact of the matter is that like the pokemon there was a puzzle in the equation of how to market the product and make people interested in their service. for the pokemon there was a unique game that was interesting to children casio :[ ] sio + cao ? casio[])from wikipedia http://en.wikipedia.org/wiki/blast_furnace#chemistry in reference to damages during refining how to recreate ozone (reduction to ozonides reduction of ozone gives the ozonide anion o . derivatives of this anion are explosive and must be stored at cryogenic temperatures. ozonides for all the alkali metals are known. ko rbo and cso can be prepared from their respective super oxides: ko + o ? ko + o although ko can be formed as above it can also be formed from potassium hydroxide and ozone:[ ] koh + o ? ko + o + ho)from wikipedia http://en.wikipedia.org/wiki/ozone#with_metals

9780 feedback note simple feed back form from microsoft office that wanted more vector and less bitmap in the os the things that are happening with css are incredible casio :[ ] sio + cao ? casio[])from wikipedia http://en.wikipedia.org/wiki/blast_furnace#chemistry in reference to damages during refining how to recreate ozone (reduction to ozonides reduction of ozone gives the ozonide anion o . derivatives of this anion are explosive and must be stored at cryogenic temperatures. ozonides for all the alkali metals are known. ko rbo and cso can be prepared from their respective super oxides: ko + o ? ko + o although ko can be formed as above it can also be formed from potassium hydroxide and ozone:[ ] koh + o ? ko + o + ho)from wikipedia http://en.wikipedia.org/wiki/ozone#with_metals

9781 do they put that stuff in the air the chance of the hospital itself being sick is the real issue. like the story goes how do you heal the sick inside a sick place. well there are extremely strong antibiotics and then there are subtle every day antibiotics. my guess is that there could be a scenario that provides a perfect healing environment and therefore is related to unlimited healing possibilities... to make a solution that purifies the air and substitutes a antibiotic supplement in the hospitals and other sick situations.

9782 auto matron machine of reverse publisher

9783 explain this is to accumulate the circumstances this isn't a time device a folder generator that catalogs achieved cd's and cdroms into a folder on a hard drive flash card or sd and even server related temps. so let's recap an automaton that loads prepares and saves the files music pictures and data to another method of folders and date marks the items. scientific complimentary processing

9784 the issue is when will a co processor complimentary on and off as well as different and alternate processing to explain this is to accumulate the circumstances of on and off in a larger picture. to estimate the neurological existence of two halves of our human brain is the essence of why and when this is important... not only to have the power in two halves but to use those two halves to alternate and differentiate the reason to compute... as a logical and scientific method for processing. for example a left and right coprocessors transparent multiple duplicate pattern processing

9785 one creative step bridge parallel modern efficiency content text context parallel (email submission) assumptions of a coprocessing pattern the issue is when will a co processor understand that to full fill one creative step. it's important to duplicate that first step. in this attempt to be creative there are more patterns than the first second and so on. to insure a pattern of non creative circumstance like a pattern and a distinction of a mathematical number such as pi

9786 who really understands better than a child trying to kick a ball into the wind it may do this it may do that but what we really need to understand is there are curve anomalies that happen more than we hope that s why it s fun... yet to understand them is

9787 voluntary / involuntary core process stop core back user selected modes and bios updates
9788 microwave fuse content text context melting the parts for safety or other means. with a metal and timer similar to a wave generator inside a microwave oven. with military and aero design specifics as well as fuse and exploding instances. micro wave melt switch
9789 pi difference a. to b. comments there is a point in every computation that will like light transfer to another point and time. every thing is timed... with pi you can measure the distance of any computation from point a to point b with angle circumference
9790 to multiply comments the chances of using two or more mother boards and then working together with what it may hold... there is a point in every computation that will like light transfer to another point and time. every thing is timed... with pi you can measure the distance of any computation from point a to point b with angle circumference and distance. along side this is many different ways to also say
9791 to multiply on local network os over os under os scenario to multiply on local network os the chances of using two or more under operating systems and concluding it to a working hierarchy of operating system +even or +odd. can you download that movie with paper through the air? not at this moment but for example what about a universal and translatable script that will encode and decode music books movies gps info and for the matter itself data! it's my idea to promote data not necessarily the format to put the data inside with a noteable unit of measurement that is described only as .. to process code with measurement with a use of sd and scripting into a form of data.
9792 laser wave modulation shaping a laser with complimentary light is anyone out there? shaping a laser with complimentary light for navigation and artificial energy... math components (laser theory energy expansion of a sum = accelerated motion horizontal
9793 as well as triangular square and circular properties such as vertical horizontal and spherical combinations... with two or more in one process. line of sight
9794 as well as triangular square and circular properties such as vertical horizontal and spherical combinations... with two or more in one process. line of sight as well as to inject gas and form a modulation of image appropriate for television and viewing comments is anyone out there? shaping a laser with complimentary light for navigation and artificial energy... math components (laser theory energy expansion of a sum = accelerated motion horizontal
9795 infrared computer screen human interface manipulation for laser generated d tv comments is anyone out there shaping a laser with complimentary light for navigation and artificial energy... math components (laser theory energy expansion shaping a laser with complimentary light for navigation and artificial energy... math components (laser theory energy expansion of a sum = accelerated motion horizontal
9796 out put computers are a method of creation out put computers are a method of creation that people need to make things. i have decided to claim this as a separate market of intent for improvement in usability and justification of my means. there are currently confusing situations in reading or writing platforms. i think that the server of today is the workstation that people dream of making and creating content... although a blog may be ingenious looping music videos and so on. yet the people who divide their time such as myself to create content get stuck with apps that are rubbish. if only it were as simple as pointing a finger and saying don't make it harder to use while making it easier to read... i want my pc to make my dreams come true again and out put this painting of life together with . ghz yes and a teraflop

of coprocessing! like number said i need more input!!!
9797 glass (or poly carbonate) insulated gold line wire housing. needed to stack motherboards and double or more the capacity of the vertical possibilities inside that manner. as opposed to a silicon board this would connect boards to one another.
9798 the intent to reactivate a flower for a shape for extended central processing units and the possibilities to multiply and agitate the growth of a unit into more than one units a flower verses in terms. the brain receptors need to work and they want to work.
9799 crystallized mother board the intent to reactivate a flower for a shape for extended central processing units and the possibilities to multiply and agitate the growth of a unit into more than one units a flower verses in terms. the intent to reactivate a root system for a shape specifically extending the circuits and the possibilities to multiply and agitate the growth of a unit into more than one units. (a plant root verses in terms) in unison to fractal function organize a mother board to the interest for d printing and layer sorting a glass insulated board that would form a recyclable product worth going and building .... building a small flower
9800 a simple dividing trigger for electronic and dividing transistors inside a circuit path.
9801 photon fractal math which and where rgb
9802 a= / bh/a=pi r ^+. . is versable in terms
9803 {to use a non primal number is the in and out of a circuit... if to use a prime number the sum must have a divisible cube root.} which verses and changes in terms and may be exchangeable. factorization: * * * * divisors: meaning a large number it follows the same rules as that phrase. however that is not the case originally in greek where there is plural.
9804 a= / bh/a=pi r ^+. number . in fractional os states or to abstract with the use of number [one million seven hundred and twentyfive] {to use a non primal number is the in and out of a circuit... if to use a prime number the sum must have a divisible cuberoot. } which verses and changes in terms and may be exchangeable. (one million
9805 immune systemic insulin. insulin medicine to magistrate through the auto immune system immune systemic insulin. insulin medicine to magistrate through the auto immune system insulin main article: insulin therapy type diabetes is typically treated with a combinations of regular and nph insulin a longacting formulation is usually added initially
9806 immune systemic anti psychotics antipsychotic medicine to magistrate through the auto immune system anti psychotic medicine to magistrate through the auto immune system physiological the causes of bipolar disorder have yet to be fully uncovered globus pallidus and increase in the rates of deep white matter hyper intensities.[][][ ] functional mri findings suggest that abnormal modulation between ventral prefrontal and limbic regions
9807 emergency sos satellite system based on cell phone satellite connections. sos from wikipedia
9808 plastic layered electronic micro board a process defined with nano printing circuits and layers of layers of circuitry that provides depth into height of computing capabilities or alternate poly carbonate / carbonate porous compounds
9809 outdoor hot and cold out door auto/semi conductor open processors outdoor hot and cold climates need processing let's imagine that there could be a cup with a microchip inside it after all... open processors and the instance of virtual to real time applicable things like traffic flow
9810 outdoor hot and cold climates need processing let s imagine that there could be a cup with a microchip inside it after all... open processors and the instance of virtual to real time

applicable things like traffic flow energy systems police dispatch and
9811 parallel processing and my scripts parallel code reprocessing divide and multiply the cell numbers from tables and other things generated by a compromise including large verses the many
9812 serial artwork number or swan to register and official works of a group of artwork printed or raw data sets for future reference and worth including any given details of certifications.
9813 bandwagon effect from wikipedia the free encyclopedia jump to: navigation search the bandwagon effect is a well documented form of group think in behavioral science and has many applications. the general rule is that conduct or beliefs spread among people
9814 this is a needed attempt at making real circumstances translatable into real terms of useful objects. for example if the code says up this could mean literal or non relative terms
9815 the need to place secure socket layers into place with a packet flaw prerequisite. to speak plainly a packet is requested from the server. the server sends a packet first with the completed file information backwards with weight and scale then loads t
9816 to protect the small glitches and malfunctions of any surge from sensitive and expensive trips breaks and surges of electricity to protect the most valuable devices.
9817 it s true that there is a popular accent in america tv and the spread of a californian accent across the united states of america is the new pink.
9818 any such right as to investigate and with plausible cause to search for a missing person upon any premise. with unique attributes justified by law holding contrary existing census information and legitimate rights of distrust or suspicion
9819 many other countries use the us dollar. to equate a hypothesis is to generate a revenue inside it s self. the dollar bill with country intent for example a widget country denominated dollar with gold / silver / property / resource note.
9820 lottery ticket cloud subscriptions
9821 to initiate an add on application different than a program but more over a specific add on to compliment code in a sense of script and all while not having a apparent app face formula. a thing to call love and work with and seemingly be the same as child
9822 to include two computers in a sense of permanence. complete with software and hardware options and tickets of operation as well as ip address.
9823 to deliberate the sustainability of a vote census or a moderated e census
9824 to publicly render the president petitionally un available for office
9825 i am not referring to my fans... here you are allowed to come back and download as much as you wish... to be specific the newest type of stalker is someone you know (or do not) that watches and stalks as you do not wish. people with probable cause not inc
9826 ethernet fixed raid to have an ethernet with multiple raid fixes per connected units. using a raid modified ethernet router.
9827 parallel code jamming and encryption
9828 fractal parallel memory cpu operations
9829 segmented lean processing
9830 minimum displacement data alternate data scripting translations with quality checks
9831 walking and write ready data
9832 compact disc
9833 turbo stopping point and alter wait

9834 choose your format sync data base monetary ratings and guidance
9835 to use anti psychotics and mental a b receptors to recover
9836 offering for cpu+memory in one operation to add secondary processing and third and fourth in the memory ram itself and spherical combinations... with two or more in one process. line of sight
9837 grounded board edge for nano poly carbonate electric conductors
9838 a means to raid activate each level for accuracy. and spherical combinations... with two or more in one process. line of sight as well as to inject gas and form a modulation of image appropriate for television and viewing as such... infrared computer screen human interface manipulation for laser generated d tv
9839 second first and third level server board management and spherical combinations... with two or more in one process. line of sight as well as to inject gas and form a modulation of image appropriate for television and viewing as such... as well as to combine and properties the human interface with controlled manipulation of direction and spheres as opposed to windows with the infrared detection.
9840 with the mass of complicated ports there should be a uniform port of snap in with pin play and align to the left scenario like a find and play plug and play device that may be useful for upcoming devices and experimental utilities yet unknown.
9841 my thought to amplify the core is by multiplying the board and amp mechanism operations and connections during a core connection and relay amplitude marker a starting point that has a reciprocating point to relay.
9842 my intent is to change the way people put the chip in and how many times you can change the chip to satisfy the craving for more speed. with extractable chips and interchangeable cpu second processing unit chip drive readers.
9843 the right to hold the representation legally bound by any means and amendments to the constitution such as a law that shall hold the branches such as even to the intellectual property rights counsel itself liable for negligence.
9844 anti histamine use to deliver anti psychotic medication
9845 ethel nitrogen oxide fuel
9846 synthetic poly metallic compound
9847 synthetic poly protein sugar concentrates count of divisors: sum of divisors: prime number? no fibonacci number? no base (binary): base (ternary): base (quaternary): base (quint): base (octal): base (hexadecimal): fd base : ut sin( ). cos( ) . tan( ) . sqrt( ) . http://numberworld.info/ . is " versable in terms"
9848 to divide odd and even fractions into an encryption translation for data and other media one hundred and seventyseven thousand seven hundred and twentyfive) is a very special number. the cross sum of is . if you factorize the number you will get these result * * * * . has divisors ( ) which a sum of . is not a prime number. is not a fibonacci number. the conversion of to base (binary) is . the conversion of to base (ternary) is . the conversion of to base (quaternary) is . the conversion of to base (quint) is . the conversion of to base (octal) is . the conversion of to base (hexadecimal) is fd. the conversion of to base is ut. the sine of is.. the cosine of is . . the tangent of is . . the root of is . . i hope that you now know that is an amazing number! properties of number
9849 complication computations super computer built by super computer and into the abyss that is more computations virtual mathematics including fractals while continuing oral

medications.[] doses of insulin are then increased to effect.[] http://en.wikipedia.org/wiki/diabetic

9850 raid multi sd flash card device raid multiple compact flash t card holder drive addition and subtract able device especially the amygdala likely contribute to poor emotional regulation and mood symptoms.[ ] according to the kindling hypothesis when people who are genetically predisposed toward bipolar disorder experience stressful events the stress threshold at which mood changes occur becomes progressively lower until the episodes eventually start (and recur) spontaneously. there is evidence of hypothalamipituitaryadrenal axis (hpa axis) abnormalities in bipolar disorder due to stress.[][][][] http://en.wikipedia.org/wiki/bipolar_disorder

9851 fractal digital encryption and became the worldwide standard under the second international radio telegraphic convention which was signed on november and became effective on july . sos remained the maritime radio distress signal until when it was replaced by the global maritime distress safety system. [ ] (with this new system in place it became illegal for a ship to signal that she is in distress in morse code. citation needed]) sos is still recognized as a visual distress signal.[] from the beginning the sos distress signal has really consisted of a continuous sequence of threeditz/threedash/threeditz all run together without letter spacing. in international morse code three ditz form the letter s and three dash make the letter o so sos became an easy way to remember the order of the ditz and dash. in modern terminology sos is a morse procedural signal or pro sign and the formal way to write it is with a bar above the letters: sos in popular usage sos became associated with such phrases as save our ship save our souls and send out succor . these may be regarded as mnemonics but sos does not stand for anything and is not an abbreviation acronym or initials. in fact sos is only one of several ways that the combination could have been written vtb for example would produce exactly the same sound but sos was chosen to describe this combination. sos is the only element signal in morse code making it more easily recognizable as no other symbol uses more than elements.

9852 neurological coherence test and central nervous system cognitive balance test in form of a phosphorous ion activity test. verses in turn a hydrogen activity test.

9853 virtual predictions of translation bio information to a real world application producing phosphorous based medicines energy systems police dispatch and flight control situations modified with integers and boolean if's.

9854 ecology economic recycling processes

9855 sodium delineation native valances and their properties in the brain verses muscles and other organs.

9856 involuntary finite ion tet of an organ and voluntary control neurology

9857 creative data engineers employment software and certificate location a business of creative judgment and relationship attributes for data

9858 machine builders and labor machine makers to receive incentives benefits. in local machine and robot automology

9859 pcie e os installer and configured out of the box insert and run playable secondary or primary to provide higher point contact and super fast calculations.

9860 to equate the code percentages with the persistent substantial available data needed to complete an operation

9861 making higher connections like a cable verses in terms to a or pin circuit

9862 making isolation as easy as drop.
9863 / fractions in dynamic digital cable frequency modulations
9864 to add an array of more inexpensive chips through a port of alternate matching sets
9865 a and over frequency of compression to trans pond and locate proper signal dials in digital computation packets
9866 how to create a true population irregularity anomaly verses a false popular anomaly in math and science chemistry and physics as well as politics and government
9867 trigonometry personal computing calculations derived from the number over
9868 to compare an initial altair to tomorrows lcus it s as though there is no difference in new super computer. the assumption that all wheel drive is like four wheel drive only all the time in a balanced formation of code.
9869 geometric scripts that fractionally divide and parallel the operations at hand. to use the method and source as the same path
9870 a computational script that instead of one s and zeros a frequency that pairs with other waves to make a computation together
9871 under ocean jet stream path way of nuclear reactor non exchanging temperatures
9872 to add traffic conductors to overlapping circuits
9873 to theorize the assumption that there will be a pathway for data to process
9874 to place multiple traffic chips inside a core of many like stop lights
9875 alternating traffic triggers and coprocessors to branch overall assets between super links
9876 periodical carbon and starch biological and synthetic deluge refining separation
9877 a path to clean and process new signals from the core or multitude of cores
9878 fractional diverting process and application performance amplification and coordination
9879 logical and virtual core with a creative and reprocessing core
9880 located inside the logical and creative core processes there will be a mechanism script to run the processing
9881 time unawareness and unscheduled sleeping resulting in acute insomnia
9882 time awareness and anticipation obsessiveness resulting in acute insomnia
9883 generating natural d images with two ports at one monitor
9884 to make operating over two or more drives to one system in any os by way of a key file
9885 dmonitor led layer nano sphere pixel layer for three dimensional projection and perspective
9886 brainstorm us gov application time stamp applications and concept
9887 using lasers to generate high potential energy in combination with solar receiving cells.
9888 using a thin transistor based liquid crystal to alternate into motherboard off and on circuits and similar exchanges like cpu and memory cells
9889 horizontal/vertical motherboard socket intersections
9890 over non malice encryption in communications
9891 using many thin transistor based liquid crystal to alternate into motherboard off and on circuits and similar exchanges like cpu and memory cells
9892 using many thin transistor based circuits to alternate into motherboard off and on circuits and similar exchanges like cpu and memory cells
9893 using many thin transistor based circuits to alternate into pcie plug ins to make off and on circuits and similar exchanges like cpu and memory cells

9894 using octavio rhythm sequencing in communications to produce multiple connections in circuits applied compression as in applied calculative computations verses the term known as digital
9895 as compared to the electricity grid in north america using transmission and subtransmission to generate primary cores and secondary core signals as in the high to lower steps similar in cable to make any such signals computational. applied compression as
9896 to add more chips in a formation including similar to a honey comb with fractional diamond central processing chip stack and assembly
9897 to give any such meaning to approximate and a sum of non exact processing to result inside a estimated code or signal of will from making a stopping point and the root of pi from fractal transformations.
9898 ethel nitrogen oxide engine and the parameters of intent of power.
9899 to place multiple central processing units in a way that shapes an h i like an i beam in construction methodology
9900 modular work board group chassis and fabric to hold and join multiple it super itx boards into a new modular chassis & add for small . x . forms
9901 modular work board group chassis and fabric with software cluster to hold and join multiple it super itx boards into a new modular chassis & add for small . x . forms
9902 miniature parallel cluster software to migrate processing and clusters of many boards for applications and data base processing
9903 miniature parallel cluster board and bios a board that translates the management into a suitable definition of a group working together
9904 miniature cluster chassis middle form factor a chassis built to compute many different x or mini boards verses one single board
9905 smaller than previous bios chips and transforming code to a digital to triad octavia signal to compute calculations and computations in a way previously unable to do with signal processors by way of transforming the signal into a code pre amplified to c
9906 triad octavia signal to grid format yx with a coherent of .
9907 triad octavia signal to grid format yx with a coherent of . a controller that modifies the signal into computations before processing into various program signals in a tet of a period machine controlled nano sphere.
9908 interleaving circuit conductor traffic signals chip sockets alternate secondary processing units that work to control processes based on a alternate path
9909 interchangeable secondary processing unit sockets interleaving circuit conductor traffic signals chip sockets alternate secondary processing units that work to control processes based on a alternate path
9910 variant cloud voip relay schema voice and other data cross internet clouds to relay data communication via the internet
9911 in relation to modular servers in production today this would equate a stacking server using multiple boards and modular steps
9912 to degrade plastics and harden or solvency the plastics in advance to incineration and generate electricity as well as a sooty carbon for commercial uses and energy
9913 fee based cloud sharing and cell transmitting between business and business. similar to cell tower property verses server property in the clouds. provider to provider to re seller to host

9914 to modify the bios on a chip verses the board via efi and presorted bios properties
9915 after market gadgets need the shape you want. build your own tablet hand held chassis and server related fabric smaller un fused working parts that equal more power and higher concentration of parts dual socket tablet with or without fans and inches
9916 after market gadgets need the shape you want. build your own tablet hand held chassis and server related fabric smaller un fused working parts that equal more power and higher concentration of parts dual socket tablet with fans and inches to inches
9917 a pcb board to fit other boards into the conjoining board
9918 a pcb board to fit other boards into the conjoining board completed board to self modulating cell board
9919 a pcb board to fit other boards into the conjoining board completed board to self modulating cell board along side a mirror image to use parallel processing in formation
9920 mini board to board connection landing engine micro controller board cloud connection board to board lock landing
9921 mini data to data board lock data engine m. form factor board receiver connection base to board lock landing
9922 real head board lock data & fabric engine micro controller board cloud connection board to board lock landing connecting and operating m. form factor board receiver connection base to board lock landing
9923 to purpose propose an update to the current board registration and operating system scheme that will equate into more than one board opposing the hypothesis that using more than one board will over come.
9924 pcie shape operator differential geometric computational processes o equate the opposing and similarities in mathematical differential calculus and integral calculus as well as linear algebra and multi linear algebra to study problems in computational geo
9925 computational fractal encryption with keys and lock as well a double formulas for higher security
9926 ricochet laser foresighted led energy
9927 weakest link lcus the weakest link is us but we are its only asset to multiply the threads in a processing formula of over lapping adjustments
9928 channel dimension process multiplying such a thing to equate a size dedication to channel actualization and capacity per element channel
9929 children specific dose measurement solvent formula
9930 second diagnosis estimate to conclude the status of illness
9931 cpu chip drop install pliers
9932 second and third level + processing unit interchanging socket to compose another central based chip socket with alternate sub levels of chip sockets. generally considered non central or additional solder and molded chips for example a replaceable second a
9933 a crime including the rights to justify the truth for the greater good of humanity
9934 a multitude of cells that reflect and generate picture with only a segment of cells actually carrying data although showing partial information in the series of cells with all considered
9935 alternating step code sequencing to multiply and receive the signals in alternating steps
9936 focused artificial energy energy web energy server focused artificial energy energy web a contained web sphere that simulates a web of energy to pilot stations for distribution from

a building that is a self contained focused laser generated solar energy structure that is on and off with servers as to aid in private energy sources adding to the already existing power supply
9937 energy server focused artificial energy energy server focused artificial energy energy web a contained web sphere that simulates a web of energy to pilot stations for distribution from a building that is a self contained focused laser generated solar energy structure that is on and off with servers as to aid in private energy sources adding to the already existing power supply
9938 energy server focused artificial energy energy web a contained web sphere that simulates a web of energy to pilot stations for distribution from a building that is a self contained focused laser generated solar energy structure that is on and off with servers as to aid in private energy sources adding to the already existing power supply
9939 input data software multiplying processing out put script to make a cloud state of servers work over multiplying fabric end points and signal bandwidth
9940 honeycomb board that is a wall of architecture upon its self. to make a glass cased gold wire fish through the board up down and over and through printed circuit boards to end?up inside a printed piping board with corrugations.
9941 stacked conjoined honeycomb board that is a wall of architecture upon its self. to make a glass cased gold wire fish through the board up down and over and through printed circuit boards to end?up inside a printed piping board with corrugations
9942 to expand raid capacity to equate into pcie thunder bolt raid
9943 to expand raid capacity to equate into mobile docking temp raid and bay station for all in one in other words a docking all in one with true form technology repeated to expand raid capacity to equate into a mobile docking temp raid and bay station for all in one in other words a docking all in one with true form technology essentially a computer that docs your phone or tablet
9944 software making it all happen to expand raid capacity to equate into a mobile docking temp raid and bay station for all in one in other words a docking all in one with true form technology essentially a computer that docs your phone or tablet repeated an operator to expand raid capacity to equate into a mobile docking temp raid and bay station for all in one in other words a docking all in one with true form technology essentially a computer that docs your phone or tablet by software.
9945 another cloud cycle to invent concept the difference of deep blue was that it wasn't considered a cloud at the time. the focus was only on the game and the server itself. this is not the focus of what the azure is. windows will now carry on as usual... wel
9946 local cloud temp raid system verses expanded services cloud for example a local more secure way to cloud that would incorporate your existing data and media servers as well as a new local platform that may or may not synchronize as the same based upon your choice.
9947 a smaller less expensive way to solid state data to add layers to a existing ddr plug in and plug in more layers with new adjustable configurations for example dd r with half height extensions that run but stand up like a pcie that has layers included to expand up and over for microprocessor sd and co processor integration's
9948 to perform a movement in a fractal animation with encryption to have a double as well as a start and finish equal to a formula of change
9949 to perform a movement in a fractal with encryption to have a double as well as a start and finish equal to a formula of change and as well as to make more than one time loop in the

process
9950 to expand raid capacity to equate into mobile docking temp raid and bay station for by attachment device in other words a docking by attachment device with true form technology repeated to expand raid capacity to equate into a mobile docking temp raid and bay station for by attachment device in other words a docking by attachment device with true form technology essentially a computer that docs your phone or tablet by attachment device
9951 amendment deficiency petitions by popular veto
9952 to declare a substance medicinally addictive and harmful to ones health by overdose as in unsubscribed methods of use.
9953 denationalize of radical liberalism to declare a free argument of a amendment or change in policy too liberal for the nations good and notate it un popular.
9954 to make a political state of technology different than previous and current standing into a new and updated stature of state of the art design and vote from the intended place of interest.
9955 to build a bluray or archival disc mm media inside a glass or carbonate jewel case with spectrum magnified reading points with the intent of making it secure and dust free while being redundant and replaceable with the intent not confuse it and a . inch hard drive with a similar yet less expensive case for data writes and rewrites such as to compare it with more expensive solid state drive for data storage.
9956 reading and writing using convex and concave lenses to build a bluray or archival disc mm media inside a glass or carbonate jewel case with spectrum magnified reading points with the intent of making it secure and dust free while being redundant and replaceable with the intent not confuse it and a . inch hard drive with a similar yet less expensive case for data writes and rewrites such as to compare it with more expensive solid state drive for data storage.
9957 a device reading and writing using convex and concave lenses to build a bluray or archival disc mm media inside a glass or carbonate jewel case with spectrum magnified reading points with the intent of making it secure and dust free while being redundant and replaceable with the intent not confuse it and a . inch hard drive with a similar yet less expensive case for data writes and rewrites such as to compare it with more expensive solid state drive for data storage.
9958 chronological passive processing verses an active aggressor in a non sequential format of computations will help to stabilize the order of complex arrangements
9959 a cable that connects pcie to sata verses in terms
9960 an archival free server service that records history based upon proprietary intellectual property. say for example a url that is specific that includes a .doc suffix and moderated by governmental appreciations. for a good short summary a that is accessible by internet and or free status of service
9961 a governmental act that may deliver a electronic exemplified terms of use and search document where the new cloud of information evidence applied is searched and deemed acceptable by use of lawsuit including the file process of fees and documented services to simplify the included purposed of hidden individuals whom seem to elude the you have been served an affidavit short e affidavit
9962 to link hard drives and with a prompt configure a large local disc population in one group of windows system discs

9963 conceptual invention s and the intent to inspire the thought and not hold back an inventor who cares to drift instead of dwelling into market. to things of concept in a sense to work without patent boundaries even if the process may not or may include an image amendment to intellectual property and rules of international sanctions of property worth value
9964 to enhance by way of less is more situation of compatibility and less apps over programmable problems and obstacles saying that gingerbread operating systems are the way of the past and the future of os publishing is two fold a punter and a player verses in terms as a recorder and a viewer to create a two fold operating scheme minimal and coherently elaborate in one os with two different settings
9965 market that protects and serves for the greater good of mankind
9966 market controlled by the homeland and intellectual protection service as well as a library of congress effort to control the property we own and would like to buy
9967 linking ram interchange is a linking secondary support ram
9968 easy invent cad submit platform a programmable interface to sort and submit inventions per company quickly in a demand and non chronological manner.
9969 laser eye surgery by way of emory university and the hospital at midtown and the parts in side the laser surgical technique
9970 antibiotic soap
9971 never pi /. indefinite pi infinity pi pi times one equals pi indefinite pi is never ending infinite pi
9972 a program to build a series of files in order to switch mobile phone operating systems and then to install a different operating system and reload your data
9973 a crowd processor that will use two or more tapes to create a crowd of itx atx mitx tx boards working to process as one board by tape and crowd presets known also as modular tx
9974 a study of any cure by way of toxic and valance testing to include but not limited to cancer and diseases like alzheimer's and substance abuse cessation aids.
9975 mandatory cloud bandwidth control to suggest that a cloud should only hold so much practical waste to the internet entirety as a application as a whole to reduce backups and compress data backups by parts.
9976 data compression cloud format the means to compress scrolling data that may need to move and write and read ready as well as transport to place to place
9977 securing and encryption by way of format doubling for example this format is encrypted then this format is translated into this file format to read
9978 converting multiple computer motherboards to unify into a working system that is not parallel (matching) or odd working (not matching) into a new cabinet data of mini desktop situation and cards that tell the central processor to do what the completed mission of computing would be in short by software.
9979 interoperable cpu a central processing unit that branches your own connections how you want to build your high performance system to allow any configuration important to you and the scale of your platform
9980 interoperable building parts and board design free build parts designed to connect a central processing unit that branches your own connections how you want to build your high performance system to allow any configuration important to you and the scale of your platform with extended and non duplicate or duplicate ports that make sense to everyone

similar to concurrent motherboards that are free standing and removable such as replaceable transistors capacitors and third and secondary chips as to replace a single motherboard with multiple boards with a top level processing chip

9981 configure this into a system with power management configure this into a system with computational control configure this into a system with data scale management a square chance chassis that fits with your own choices and arrangement. free arrangement with thermal vents and common connections ports that are unobtrusive beyond the rack. continued a space for this cpu with ports

9982 a hardware system that will power that software exactly (software that estimates the hardware system that will work with that software exactly) processing and computations inside a software vessel a vessel that estimates processing and computations as an artist and inventor it comes to my attention that there are some programs that don't require endless size and resource values

9983 intel edison kit for arduino single components edi arduin.al.k modified to control xeon phi on off and load switch

9984 when vector computations are needed there should be a precise meaning to every curve like the way pre selected sorts are generated size how many tall and wide as well as per space intensity xyz

9985 a software program that will generate code for external unsorted efi batches to route any computations needed

9986 traffic cloud and perbuilt selects for realtime issue management

9987 police cloud and perbuilt selects for realtime issue management

9988 syndicated media news cloud and perbuilt selects for realtime issue management

9989 air bound traffic cloud and perbuilt selects for realtime issue management

9990 war management satellite / ground cloud and perbuilt selects for realtime issue management

9991 minimum sale retail price cloud and perbuilt selects for realtime issue management

9992 digital shelf price display for real time updates from a msrp cloud

9993 digital shelf price display for real time updates from a msrp cloud stored planed and adjustable by demands something that would make a sale percustomer and availability

9994 synthetic liquid plastic ester and carbon soot energy in a single compound to make a combustible energy (incinerator biproducts and alcohol acids)

9995 educational in class os educational operating system with intent to block virus and provide a safe computation platforms for age and course specific apps educational cloud system and perbuilt selects for realtime issue management

9996 rearranged tetrahedral amorphous carbon with abstract particle matching to reconstituted energy sp forms diamond (cubic) · lonsdaleite (hexagonal diamond) sp forms graphite · graphene · fullerenes (buckminsterfullerene higher fullerenes

9997 a habit release agent to alcohol abuse patch pill gum

9998 a habit release agent to marijuana abuse patch pill gum

9999 dominate media

10000 dominate server cloud

10001 an elaborate paging software system that links processors for a continuous processing group of microchips dealing or complimentary in any similarity that forms an accessible shape of a shed family software

10002 an elaborate paging hardware system that links processors for a continuous processing group of microchips alignend or complimentary in any similarity that forms an accessible shape of a shed family hardware to add cores to a group of processing cores and multiplying threads in a desired format chipcloud co chips
10003 an elaborate paging hardware system that links processors for a continuous processing group of microchips alignend or complimentary in any similarity that forms an accessible shape of a shed family hardware to add cores to a group of processing cores and multiplying threads in a desired format chipcloud co chips board and socket exchange
10004 pragmatic data clarification importance and bias to easily negotiate the promise of any data platform
10005 no cloud software registration a program specific intent to keep the software as is and with out any foreign auto updates and stripped integration from internet interference of opportunity and eula confidence trials of intent to disturb the sleeping software wintel <a href= http://crione.com/index.php?route=product/product&product_id=&search=&category_id= ></a>
10006 alternate size spinning magnetic electric generator lord carpenters infinite motion how to put it all together a spinning top is very similar to something you'd like to have fun and stare at forever. it was brought to my attention that there is a need for such a thing to run/turn forever. the issue is a few things also sometimes called the same thing the sidereal day is shorter than the solar day. at time
10007 effervescent mouth wash for serious ailments like headaches bacteria and dizziness caused by oral sickness.
10008 a thing called turbo per element that can shape a path where previously there was no way to reflect perpendicular or parallel with the help of mini and per operation by a hypos thesischip alternate computational curve based algorithms aiding by another chip
10009 a thing called turbo per element that can shape a path where previously there was no way to reflect perpendicular or parallel with the help of mini and per operation by a stressthesischip alternate computational curve based algorithms aiding by another chip in a chain reaction processing
10010 more desktop capacity by way of modular expansions via mini modular modes non ecc or ecc yes either or intent sell a module to me and make it bigger
10011 open thread navigational embedded software. a software base that controls the method of navigation of a processing thread inside a cpu
10012 curriculum software for public schools no cloud base or cloud base data schema download and toss media vs. intent to recycle and modify in class testing by way of simple send and receive test email like online college with intuitive public school social connections
10013 triplet pi translation axis for compensation equation sum and path intent.
10014 triplet pi translation axis for compensation equation sum part travel pi cubed translation axis for compensation equation sum and path intent. software hardware virtual and literal intent to create and estimate any means of anno place in time points of vector registration per annotation
10015 triplet pi translation axis for compensation equation sum part travel pi cubed translation axis for a compensation equation sum and path intent. software hardware virtual and literal intent to create and estimate any means of anno place in time points of vector registration per annotation software hardware virtual and literal intent to create and

estimate any means of anno place in time points of vector registration per annotation to start with the equation of two that is cubed and then translation inside travel

10016 triplet pi translation axis for compensation equation sum part travel pi cubed translation axis for compensation equation sum and path intent. software hardware virtual and literal intent to create and estimate any means of anno place in time points of vector registration per annotation software hardware virtual and literal intent to create and estimate any means of anno place in time points of vector registration per annotation to start with the equation of two that is cubed and then translation inside travel. to multiply and intensify _/+/? cloud compute (server or software) the matters into a higher computational sum of what when where how and why

10017 real web a web connection that is a retail and local web that processes alternate connections like credit cards and other information like medical records and bank transactions. a web that makes real life from day to day a positive one with higher restricted content and in contrast to the global internet application itself this is a connection with either a satellite or direct phone number that is not connected globally or may eventually be titled the real web. /c ri on e .com

10018 real web part encryption phone channel a web connection that is a retail and local web that processes alternate connections like credit cards and other information like medical records and bank transactions. a web that makes real life from day to day a positive one with higher restricted content and in contrast to the global internet application itself this is a connection with either a satellite or direct phone number that is not connected globally or may eventually be titled the real web. /c ri on e .com

10019 data archive retail pack keeping the pack a retail matter when time does matter

10020 a free or sale community secure or friendly web source connections community web

10021 build a toy platform you submit the size shape and means and function and go play

10022 build a software platform you submit the size shape and means and function and go play

10023 brain temperature and intelligence is the temperature related to intelligence? or is intelligence only hereditary?

10024 big data creative data engineers software client requests terms and permissions rules and exceptions reply response using terms and conditions as well as requests and permissions to translate into real life data arrangements (banking traffic control

10025 big data creative data engineers compliant hardware client requests ability software wreckless replacement exceptions speed in control using test and server strength to encrypt and control critical cohesion products and services of any kind

10026 organ cell symbiosis cloning and replacement organs to grow two cells into a new organ for kidney patients caner cures and bioorganic failures or positives

10027 to avoid another war use diplomatic monetary incentives and resources or not

10028 encrypted phonenumber transmitting and receiving key's and the new enigma generator.

10029 encrypted phonesoftware transmitting and receiving key's and the new enigma generator.

10030 unformulated alien text formats to create a unknown and previously illegible type text to keep data secure said a unknown character symbol set that will translate into some thing as known to the other receiver

10031 build your own cloud service software hardware and applications global functions of cloud server storage and the medium that powers that service incorporated with small large and desktop applications with input and control to manage your own stack of servers that have a mission to provide a decisive constitution on off and critical cohesion.
10032 we build your cloud service architects engineers software hardware and applications architects engineers global functions of cloud server storage and the medium that powers that service incorporated with small large and desktop applications with input and control to manage your own stack of servers that have a mission to provide a decisive constitution on off and critical cohesion.
10033 the light age of board technology layered fiber optical computer boards heat resistant and accessible to carbon fiber
10034 to search for a topic with an image. to find people places and things. with input from meta tags such as technical terms when where who and why. as well as to modify the photo scan or topic by perspective date and angle using the image itself and the topic to search with. the intent is to exactly find the right thing at the right time while using visual content and with proper context.
10035 personal freedom to drive makes me think that taking cars and making trains out of them is against my freedom.
10036 optical fiber paths and boards that use lens motors optical motors and optic conductors in conjunction with a optical cpu making electrons differently than an ion more sort of a ee on
10037 a mental shortage of sugar
10038 making software a virtual hardware controller virtual compromises in memory cores and threads memory that holds software permanently
10039 computer aided nerve sciences to register what nerve sends and collects what with a nano scope using computer navigated control finding nerves in an optical focused laser infrared camera and thermos scope
10040 super embedding board technology using quartered circuits and fractal inverse technology making boards flat and embedding while conducting in one motion with out attaching nanotubes nanobuds) · glassy carbon sp forms linear acetylenic carbon
10041 information satellite that pilots like drones and may reenter the atmosphere and disperse again into the atmosphere at our control with translation receiving and sending information that holds a scale as of a self sufficient server cloud satellite a self supported nuclear powered satellite
10042 war ship satellite a self supported nuclear powered satellite that pilots like drones and may reenter the atmosphere and disperse again into the atmosphere at our control with translation receiving and sending information that holds a scale as of a self sufficient server war satellite
10043 automated robotics in space to eliminate the human space factor and automate the sequences of working robotics in space such as extended stay time and removal of life support systems as well as to incorporate remote control actives and war and important scientific discoveries.
10044 space territory political rights the agreement option to register any given orbit free realm to patrol or gather records of information and scientific findings important to human survival and communication

10045 biochemical deceasedviral library

10046 centralized satellite control network governmental / private

10047 build a script portable calculator a calculator device that instead of only numerical sums it builds a computational script to make bios and other interesting things that would other wise take a very long time

10048 energy weight focus scope to weigh the energy in a focal point with energy density and amplitude

10049 density and amplitude energy chart scale a energy chart with amplitude and density comparable to the chemical elements diagram with consideration for gas solids and chemical compounds as well as their reaction to one another.

10050 translation virtual predictive density matter to measure and estimate the outcome of any two forms of energy together in one equation or software platform to create new and exciting forms of medicine and energy by functioning heat chemical compound or a catalyst of desire including the laser and sodium and sugar in this term of versable means the pragmatic translates as universal or non motivational on an agenda basis of improvement to any means or a goal of motivation. for example i submitted a to a company and they told me to submit it to the forums when i said i wanted to keep the s specifically. in this attempt i am assuming that they wanted to release me of my . wintel <a href= http://crione.com/index.php?route=product/product&product_id= &search= target= _blank ></a>.

10051 matter mining by way of na nowaveradio signals find the element and save that element or to create more elements

10052 life by dead virus by way of na nowaveradio signals to kill a virus and make an anti virus by way of very small radio waves the sun and a certain distant star are both overhead. at time the planet has rotated ° and the distant star is overhead again but the sun is not (? = one sidereal day). it is not until a little later at time that the sun is overhead again (? = one solar day).earth's rotation period relative to the sun (its mean solar day) is seconds of mean solar time. each of these seconds is slightly longer than an si second because earth's solar day is now slightly longer than it was during the th century due to tidal acceleration. the mean solar second between and was chosen in by simon new comb as the independent unit of time in his tables of the sun. these tables were used to calculate the world's ephemerides between and so this second became known as the ephemeris second. the si second was made equal to the ephemeris second in .[ ] earth's rotation period relative to the fixed stars called its stellar day by the international earth rotation and reference systems service (iers) is . seconds of mean solar time (ut) (h m . s).[][n] earth's rotation period relative to the precessing or moving mean vernal equinox misnamed its sidereal day[n] is . seconds of mean solar time (ut) (h m . s).[] thus the sidereal day is shorter than the stellar day by about . ms.[] the length of the mean solar day in si seconds is available from the iers for the periods [] and .[] from wikipedia

10053 programmable medical surgery robotics by way of na nowave energy weight focus scope medical surgery device by way of laser and energy matter compensations

10054 computer controlled negative and positive and neutral laser and energy matter compensations

10055 poly carbonate sandwiched stacked optical circuit board on plyboard technology

10056 optical data rate photon transformer

10057 neutral performing laser to move and work with out damage and neutral force.

10058 a transverse capacitor that calculates and compresses at the same time

10059 embedded hyper threading printed circuits in a measured capacity that relates to cascading increments
10060 embedded hyper threading printed circuits in a measured solid state board
10061 linking cpu interchange is a linking secondary support cpu
10062 one chip board multiple function platforms in solid state matter
10063 synthetic natural conventional non associated gas a substance that may be clean burning and easy to make synthetic pressured gas
10064 synthetic pressurized gas turbine to generate electricity
10065 poly nitrate oxide ethanol carbonate
10066 ethanol nitrogen fuel
10067 ethanol nitrogen fuel engine
10068 governmental cloud separated state and federal cloud service encryption values from logical to high performance situations of traffic to water control to records of who what and where
10069 commercial cloud separated commerce and public pay for cloud service encryption values from logical to high performance situations of taxes transfers and payments who what and where
10070 switch book operation a non account related platform system is a device sensitive memory working horse that transfers accounts
10071 plasma pressurized poly oxide metal using plasma pressure to mold many oxidized metals back to a combined metal making a new inexpensive metal warfare any other means incorporating system interrupts
10072 static electric poly oxide metal using electricity to mold many oxidized metals back to a combined metal making a new metal
10073 off shore ocean current electric generators as opposed to land locked wind mills
10074 off shore ocean current electric generator farms as opposed to land locked wind mills this would be a dedicated area of operations
10075 magnetized ions in a transformer capacitor in a generated sequence of order
10076 off shore ocean current centrifugal force electric generator farms as opposed to land locked wind mills this would be a dedicated area of operations
10077 anything over the internet cell towers resident and roaming services subscribed wireless signals and encrypted channels repeater towers that drive this internet forward faster than as expected a local and populous need
10078 anything over the internet cell towers resident and roaming services subscribed wireless signals and encrypted channels small aoi small local repeaters boxes that drive this internet forward faster than as expected a local and less populous needs for a utility post that links other posts wireless continuously linking
10079 atomic blood testing using alternate scales of sodium and sugar as well as nitrate chlorides
10080 automated atomic blood testing machine using alternate scales of sodium and sugar as well as nitrate chlorides to an extreme scale
10081 computational predictive plasma sorting lapidary alchemy studies in cures for cancer and virtual new materials
10082 computational predictive ultra violet sorting biochemical studies in cures for cancer and virtual new materials

10083 shaping chips to reflect amplify and duplicate processing objects inside the chip binder _page_

10084 state of our art is never a constant so to make a platform as on the fly as possible would be the the greatest advancing scale ever to make an engineering system that makes your service in a virtual environment and sale rate increase with redesign propositions binder _page_

10085 manipulative personality disorder is a selfish and greedy property in low importance comparison to exceptional sanctity binder _page_

10086 company incentives for recycling technology is a monetary program based on weight and recovery from the local and federal government binder _page_

10087 technology leasing and propagating specialists is a monetary program based on profit and recovery from the manufacturers post attributes binder _page_

10088 future of less open software and the concurrent topics that it will hold such as fee based operation times and subscription updates binder _page_

10089 future of protected and eula software and the concurrent topics that it will hold such as free operation times and nonsubscription updates

10090 school student information secure data protection is a method of protecting the future of learning with technology flashblue

10091 cloud data security software is a method of protecting the future with technology flashblue

10092 local government security bots to protect and serve with the intent to find and seek searching local criminal data through the internet using web bots

10093 single sd chip module board that stacks easily into a plural sd board system and controls with striping and stacking coprocessing in a chain reactive board configuration

10094 conceptual conclusion diagrams and acceptable means to what translates into a function or a thing and mixes and matches with proper context a diagram legend that translates by name and intuition

10095 conceptual prose and the intent to invent a time frame of any sort always carries a way of speech and sort of accentuation if you will the time frame of any given state of art is to generally gain a conceptual prose of a given time frame

10096 chip stilts form factor to stand up chips in any vertical fashion and add a plural height to perform cooling and or data exchange

10097 interval chip stilts with data bridges to efi

10098 chip stilts with data processing calculating rise and run to make inside circuits happen and connecting super fine cable gold lines

10099 exchange chip stilts with data processing calculating rise and run to make inside circuits happen and connecting super fine cable gold lines and repeating octagon chip inside chips and vector resolution chips

10100 exchange chip stilts with data processing calculating rise and run to make inside circuits happen and connecting super fine cable gold lines and repeating octagon chip inside chips and vector resolution chips and conducting boards

10101 intersecting diagonal and perpendicular circuit threads by vector resolution chips

10102 a hardware mass array of cloud statistics and numerical estimations for one cloud to any other cloud

10103 open data statistics offering to provide a starting point to compare data and the use of

its properties to compare to another or any other way of stats
10104 end coordinate known vector board circuit path regiment and processing boosters an end coordinate inside the terms of use of a vector board and vector conducting boards that sends signals to the circuits that make the path of processing from chip to chip a greater complex computation simulating an extension cord.
10105 cloud data security software is a method of protecting the future with technology by foreseeing the attention of progress and code modifications including the methods in place now and the possibilities in the future of what and will be a method to consider cloud processing software that sees and fixes security problems
10106 cloud probabilities in turn concluding any real life example situation into a consequence cloud for example the process of lend and borrow the process of land and take off the process of any registration set into a faster method with any such corresponding input information at the start of the situation
10107 public for hire on demand technology companies a company that forms any such supply built from a design that originates with out or with corporate proprietary ship and sells that with a demand for an outcome
10108 private on demand technology companies a company that forms any such supply built from a design that originates with out or with corporate proprietary ship and sells that with a demand for an outcome
10109 nano capacity electric signals when the wave of electricity meanders into a tip of a needle to move the vector relationships by way of nano gigawave
10110 a half value conductor that measures half of a wave of electricity being a nano capacity electric signals when the wave of electricity meanders into a tip of a needle to move the vector relationships by way of nano gigawave
10111 tension strength of electrical currents in a pico nano space for connections transistors and breakers making a bridge into the future of computing and printed circuit boards with a open closed signal holding minimal power allotted
10112 pico circuit with poly carbs ceramic insulation and poly oxide metal as conducting circuits with power and wear as a consideration for measuring the entire tension and properties of laser made engraving by plasma soldering yielding and melting.
10113 pico circuit pico layer chip and circuit building segmented layers and connecting ends from bottom to upper layer for stacking interior with poly carbs ceramic insulation and poly oxide metal as conducting circuits with power and wear as a consideration for measuring the entire tension and properties of laser made engraving by plasma soldering yielding and melting.
10114 pico nano micro scale reverse scenario of heat and size rationality when the size doesn't make sense to make it that small and making multiple on board integrated circuits and cpu per system and the process of material being of more importance such as poly carbonate and poly mineral
10115 pico nano micro scale reverse scenario of heat and size rationality when the size doesn't make sense to make it that small and making multiple on board integrated circuits and cpu per system and the process of material being of more importance such as poly carbonate and poly mineral and using a graphite molding compound to bind multiple minerals into a conductive metal.
10116 . sata mini add on compute module size sata that adds to the computational ability to

a system.

10117 a disposable update to isolated systems and the intent to improve performance and remove virus or add alternate software with out online update

10118 compact active performance software a disposable update to isolated systems and the intent to improve performance or add alternate software with out online update

10119 processed optical energy and the things that equal a light to energy including a dynamic electrode receiving liquid crystal panel and the intent to make electricity by sharing and sending and repeating

10120 processed optical energy and the things that equal a light to energy including a building with transparent solar liquid crystal panels / windows on the outside and the intent to make electricity transparent solar power generating windows

10121 stand along systems hardware a complimentary system in a shape portable or flash . matters that make bios a symbiotic relationship in a organism and computational theme of improvement and error free computing

10122 stand along systems software a complimentary system in a shape portable or flash . matters that make bios a symbiotic relationship in a organism and computational theme of improvement and error free computing

10123 exterior bios library co existing bios library adjustments submissive profile programmable adjustments in a vague code and hardware environment to aid in a stand along software and hardware solution that makes a large section of addalong configurations possible a given set of bios that run to and from and along while communicating the goal overall

10124 condensation water farms the help we need is in cooling and heating the air itself to generate water where there may be a lack of water and more oxygen than happy a large scale condensation factory

10125 condensation water generator on a condensation water farm the help we need is in cooling and heating the air itself to generate water where there may be a lack of water and more oxygen than happy a large scale condensation factory

10126 device transferable operating system platform a platform operating system that adapts to the hardware at supply and negotiates the devices properties easily

10127 extended belling vertical sd chip stack

10128 promise software building platform cloud promise cloud software building platform cloud that adds and trades certain processes for a monetary value and immediate commercial release final options

10129 open software building platform cloud cloud software building platform cloud that adds and trades certain processes for a non monetary value and immediate noncommercial release final options

10130 solar energy generating stickers per window panel with circuits inside or linked storage

10131 triplet pi d focus ranges optical and virtual focus calculations and equilibrium annotations for use in cloud scenarios and mobile devices

10132 predictive computations in triplet pi d focus ranges optical and virtual focus calculations and equilibrium annotations for use in any situation

10133 probability statistics in everyday perspective dimensions with cubed and annotative physics

10134 m. electronics form factor add on computational enhancement processors
10135 m. electronics form factor add on graphics computational enhancement processors
10136 msata electronics form factor add on computational enhancement processors
10137 msata electronics form factor add on graphics enhancement processors
10138 solvent sludge and the processes that make taking trash and turning it into sludge and making electricity as well as reclaimable minerals gases and metals by way of incineration and sort magnetizing
10139 dry solvent clay and the processes that make taking trash and turning it into rock and making electricity as well as reclaimable minerals gases and metals by way of incineration and sort magnetizing
10140 inverted gas sorting and reclaiming recycled incineration gasses by way of catalytic converter and gas humidifier for or only with a unique dry or paste wet solvent clay and the processes that make taking trash and turning it into rock or solvent sludge and making electricity as well as reclaimable minerals gases and metals by way of incineration and sort magnetizing
10141 carbon by metallic energy signal force is the wave of energy that attracts or repels any such one carbon away and from each other in a radio magnetic force in any size obvious or microscopic force of annotative fixation including or excluding reactive properties
10142 gasses energy signal wave gas wave energy signal is the measure of energy that attracts or repels any such one gas or other gasses to and from each other in a energy force in any size obvious or microscopic force of annotative fixation including or excluding reactive properties
10143 carbon energy signal wave carbon wave energy signal is the measure of energy that attracts or repels any such one oxide or other metal to and from each other in a energy force in any size obvious or microscopic force of annotative fixation including or excluding reactive properties
10144 starch energy signal wave starch wave energy signal is the measure of energy that attracts or repels any such one starch to and from each other in a energy force in any size obvious or microscopic force of annotative fixation including or excluding reactive properties
10145 physeometric prediction energy signal wave measures in scales of negative as well as positive may be used in any predictive computational data analytic such as to say that with a known and given there could be any such physeometric prediction of applied science with the gradual chemical building squares of medicine and any other essential things in any quantity or sum
10146 physeometric prediction data cloud a group of servers or information structure that houses a secluded or open system of predictions for the information that bases it's self on predictive measures of experimental operations with or without committing to the real and holding virtual attempts in their system for a record of things and terms for future and immediate use with the energy signal wave calculative measurements
10147 how to realize irrational thinking for an irrational person or group of people war drug part two
10148 how to loose a war is to follow their rules and drop flowers instead of bombs. when flowers don't work drop bombs
10149 how to opt out of their convention and still have a smile on our faces a monetary stipulation and land ownership terms and correctives in a tentative agreement that states thing in our terms and conditions at war and any such give means to attack as well as take

over. the take over bid by paper to justify a means to an end to adjust an option to not opt in and a monetary consumption fee to over take an enemy on rules of any engagement opposite of a peace treaty and course of war and exceptions non included inside any preamble needs of a destructive course of action
10150 state and local satellite share times shared government satellite service
10151 private and commerce satellite rental times rental public satellite service
10152 poly carbonate sandwiched stacked circuit board on plyboard technology
10153 to avoid a deliberate argumentative
10154 dynamic functions of a input output resolution a computative functioning virtual reality of measurement cloud or software system a virtual building cloud that simulates the construction of points and volts down to a format that is appreciative and perceptual plain english
10155 a breaking in trial and error when the only cost is the operator the software and hardware when the physical meets a breaking point for example to include calibration of volts amps and weight and any other important variable then the trial and error of manufacturing and so called cost of waste and cost of profit is calculated and configured with the dynamic functions of a input output resolution a computative functioning virtual reality of measurement cloud or software system
10156 commons unique abnormal commons unique abnormal a + m = e (. {} over {}) %uxe a {e} over {m} %uxe b {e%delta ^{}} over {c%delta ^{}} %uxe c{e%ux } over {c%ux }
10157 commons unique abnormal commons unique abnormal infinity x +infinity %ux e max / <=x<= xe{x^{}} %uxe %infinite %ux d + %uxe a %epsilon %sigma
10158 commons unique abnormal commons unique abnormal <p style= marginbottom: in >lllint />%uxe a %ux f {b%uxe sqrt{b^{}ac} } over {a} %notequal binom{%sigma } binom{{ %uxe b i%uxe b m} }{ < j < n } p (i
10159 negative light waves and their post positive method of use a contrary value in rgb light and inverted light magnifications
10160 eclipse laser light magnifications and the carbon mark that shapes the radiation into the mirror of any such ecliptic or optical use of out side shapes
10161 reversed poly operative thematic library the proposal of a case where if you know a equation and then look up a similar given number then in a hypothesis of any outcome making a working summation to the question in a linear composition
10162 science calculators with calculation insert able or embedded library's of instance of information purpose calculator holding the power to answer the questions properly the first time that may do hypophysics theory or build a script and even virtual predictions of translation bio information
10163 a rounded number of encryption based on a four segment of numbers to process and extract an encryptable alphanumerical code for ssl and more advanced communications
10164 duplicate cubits zeros ones and twos and threes a nonargumentative physical quantitative mechanical on off state with two layers by reading twice
10165 hardware saving process by updating cpu systems only inside a dlq duplicate layer cubits modifier and reader plain english updating the entire cloud or system by cpu and the processing of reading what the cpu is able to comprehend in terms of simple code conduct of a chip
10166 double layer cubit cpu

10167 hardware saving process by updating cpu systems only inside a ddlq double dimension layer cubits modifier and reader plain english updating the entire cloud or system by cpu and the processing of reading what the cpu is able to comprehend in terms of simple code conduct of a chip
10168 double cubits two sequences of zeros ones and a nonargumentative physical quantitative mechanical on off state or with two layers
10169 limonene generated silicone doping to degrade plastics and harden or solvency the plastics in advance to incineration and generate electricity as well as a sooty carbon for synthetic metal semiconductors
10170 pendulum generator off and on magnetic power switches and percentages to propel and generate electricity at a minimal minus and pi ratio
10171 more cubits zeros ones and twos and threes a nonargumentative physical quantitative mechanical on off state with two layers by reading changes at a modified on series and then a modified off series in a section with in a measurement of cubits together
10172 stacking linking cpu interchange is a linking secondary support cpu
10173 synthetic metal cell drawing and shaping vector cubit cell dividing and cascading increments of myriads within
10174 a semi solid state social state drive and chip board configuration. that conjoins vectors and makes any path a routine in quantum steps
10175 repeated chemical electrode pool
10176 application device instructions on chip
10177 cubit cell off and on group of cubits a translation of on off and signals in a group a simple yet complex method of calculation and intersect of paths for any group of information
10178 mirror sphere box laser projection lens
10179 smart card system array
10180 vaccine bath and mouthwash
10181 extractable card form factor computing by multiplying systems on a traveling boards
10182 traveling boards base chassis is a computing accessory that houses the card computer and makes the parts that are used in everyday computing optical disc drive usb support and screen and keyboard interface a possible exchangeable thing in the composition of computing shape executable excludeable verses the board and chip system itself.
10183 ddr... system application on chip a slim operating system that is dedicated to alternate functions based upon application per device including secondary cpu and or storage and system bios.
10184 executable back up optical disc system disc array doing both data and program operations
10185 executable system carry across multiple storage states to return a greater number of operations per system completion of any request at a expandable operating big server
10186 is a software executable system that spans across multiple storage states to return a greater number of operations per system completion of any request and per addition of more arrays will increase the operations ability
10187 application area array migration and control software making an exchanging array organizing the platform of executable software and control of data source and place in the so called cloud instance
10188 exchangeable cell cell card for a local single and separate non synchronized cloud

account cell phones that is a starting point to a private phone
10189 exchangeable executable cell cell card for a local non synchronized cloud account cell phones that is a starting point to a private phone
10190 exchangeable cell cell card for a local non synchronized cloud account cell phones that is a starting point to a private phone a private and under non agreement phone privacy
10191 for hire security web bots is a service that will design and search for security issues with web robot search and seek code to server and repeating actions and report back to a source
10192 government data research web bots a private search and possible investigative understanding that may hold evidence of any question of activity by searching communications servers and other internet references
10193 multiple wireless multiple device back up table port
10194 wireless device compatibly bluetooth backup clone and restore software
10195 wireless backup clone and restore software encryption codes
10196 phone station bluetooth magnetic backuprecharge wireless charge and backup clone update and restore hardware
10197 encrypted magnetic data waves to secure and process computing information to and from device to device phones and computers
10198 magnetic data magnetic ion capacitor in use with the data signal octavia
10199 magnetic data waves of intertwined mini signals and partial process of half and triplet pulse
10200 magnetic data and the magnetized transducer to code and process magnetic signs of positive and negative
10201 diverse operating board magneticion fiberoptic and nanoelectric signals to work the large and small things into a sound well rounded machine
10202 a working complete process working software is a platform of a data base that is built on a question of fundamentals to make a transitional and schematic plan for a business with one part system
10203 a working partial process working software is a platform of a data base that is built on a question of fundamentals to make a transitional and schematic plan for a business with some of part system made to work with other parts
10204 a working parts process working software is a platform of a data base that is built on a question of fundamentals to make a transitional and schematic plan for a business with many parts system built to work together
10205 flash system on chip point and landing a micro server that can be included on a chip and land a website with folders and replace a server for intentions of verses in terms when a server admits to a micro card and a tray of server chips that makes a server only a system on a chip instead of a rack mountable
10206 flash system on chip point and landing bed fabric chassis a micro server bed that holds parts that can be included on a chip and land a website with folders and replace a server for intentions of verses in terms when a server admits to a micro card
10207 vector cubed boards exchange chip stilts with data processing calculating rise and run to make inside circuits happen and connecting super fine cable gold lines and repeating octagon chip inside chips and vector resolution chips and conducting boards
10208 vector cubed chips exchange chip stilts with data processing calculating rise and run to

make inside circuits happen and connecting super fine cable gold lines and repeating octagon chip inside chips and vector resolution chips and conducting boards

10209 war web bots and the scripting ability to and kill enemy computers and cell phones in a local or distant area of combat or war

10210 war web safe area and the scripting ability to make a safe harbor for any study of attack anti attack and a command group of war

10211 a squared area of cascading increments funny but real to process code with measurement . cascading increments . a certain unit of measurement " . or . for processing electronic measurement using my certain unit of measurement data versus the shape of media today

10212 d electric circuit board printer a three dimensional printer that intermittently uses alternate metal printing and silicon filament

10213 nano micro and pico soldering metal printing and three dimensional printer ability to grow vertically and horizontally with a moderate soldering plasma thermal flash plasma thermal printing

10214 standard popular retro active hardware is a forgotten chip socket board or state of work made popular again for the fun of its performance and suggestions k again standard popular hardware

10215 multiplied and fractional diamond divided chip to assimilate the quartered and then square a shape for different angles of processing with the thought that there is a connection between the shape and the result of connections available diamond divided chip properties

10216 diamond divided chip properties is a multiplied and fractional divided chip to assimilate the quartered and then the square or less

10217 secured wifi wireless accessories post is a group of accessories that accompany a powered usb pairing unit as a multi interface device making all your personal computing needs wireless and only yours secured wireless accessories post

10218 automatic xeon phi platform software auto pilot phi

10219 pilot per scripted gpu and a per unit plan of process this is really any driven gpu per device to any single operation meaning that there is part or parts of any separated or single graphic processing unit with a process unit plan per device scripted gpu

10220 mini complete server ip/location/chip/system in a disk optical a optically read by disk that makes any such form or function such as to mirror a completed server with ip virtual optical server disk

10221 mini complete server ip/location/chip/system in a disk solid state solid state chip with a server format of completed functions of on and off and all other things any other server would function as into a cloned disk with the entire system or majority of a system. mini server per solid state

10222 mini complete server ip/location/chip/system in a disk pcie load this is really a pcie location intertwined with any given pci port or express location that is a translated mini completed server. mini server per pcie

10223 mini complete server ip/location/chip/system in a virtual disk folder translating into a place inside any given medium a separate window into a looping server that is in itself a mini completed sever in a folder on a disk. complete server in a virtual folder captuer

10224 volunteer web warriors software. to aid against the enemy and to fight a cyber war volunteerism with our at home devices to counter attack the enemy foes.

10225 a large rechargeable battery plant that has automated chemical pool recharging and sending receiving charging and re doping electron batches and storage for electricity on any large scale in acres and years suitable for the safety and health of human life

10226 a large recycled battery pool that makes other small batteries with less time and higher concentrations of elements rechargeable battery plant that has automated chemical pool recharging and sending receiving charging and re doping electron ions and neutron batches for refining and element source reclaiming and storage for electricity on any large or small scale in acres or inches and years or instance of positive or negative charge to make it a recycle instead of a single cycle.

10227 powder salt reaction with out combing gasoline to make a neutral burning fuel that propels on impact but not exhaust only vapor oil salt powder fuel reactions

10228 powder salt reaction engine with out combing gasoline to make a neutral burning fuel that propels on impact and compression with ignition

10229 tax loan government program of lien for a loan on income tax returns

10230 dynamic compressed virtual encryption to encapsulate data for a certain end point protocol while compressing compressed encrypted end point protocol

10231 wireless radio patching per device is to patch devices with the board of a receiving serial signal easily verses a software connection wireless radio patch device serial

10232 electric catalyze sodium nitrate carbonate reaction engine system and motive for an alternative power source that may be able to propel from small amounts of sulfur and a powder combustion engine with sodium nitrate and spark plug and piston action powder combustion engine with sodium nitrate

10233 probability is a term for business ethics compromise and ethics rules against arbitrary lying and dishonesty of information and statistics of income and profits ethics probability

10234 cell tower lending and broad cast shares build your own cell tower with our technology and profit with our company byo cell tower

10235 critical non attached data back up registrations and cloud clusters is a extremely secure web of servers and data bases that conclude information that is nearly irreplaceable or important more than any other data critical non attached back up

10236 a dual copy archival backup format table of compare and examine the data on a large translation scale in multiple part sequence

10237 a single copy dual file archival backup format table of compare and examine the data on a large translation scale in multiple part sequence

10238 secondary chip sockets that are replaceable and upgrade able adapters to chip socket changes in size and dimension to improve the performance of a system

10239 central chip sockets that are replaceable and upgrade able adapters to chip socket changes in size and dimension to improve the performance of a system

10240 socket to modification socket to chip additions and improvements by the chip maker or chip end user by large there is some thing that needs to improve socket to socket and chip layers to make a new and improved stack of chip socket to chip to chip socket adapter to chip layered adapter and stacked chip

10241 sodium magnesium carbon oxide compound for powdered combustion engines and fuel made with a powered process and less liquid use and waste as a chemical propellant of combustion

10242 software software please make my software software what i want is a software to make

software platform private copy to cloud format of come and serve a software company that builds software for people on a property ownership basis
10243 software software please make my software software design software that relates in vector and code preferences that is an easy and resell able application package maker and formatted
10244 software software please make my software software information and data management creation and business software that relates in vector and code preferences that is an easy and resell able application package maker and formatted
10245 software software please make my software software banking and finance software that relates in vector and code preferences that is an easy and resell able application package maker and formatted
10246 software software please make my software software science computations and equations that make the physical become a reality of study and changes of any state of art including the need for any other means software that relates in vector and code preferences that is an easy and resell able application package maker and formatted
10247 software software please make my software software medicine medical and health of solutions and directives of care for people and problems with health software that relates in vector and code preferences that is an easy and resell able application package maker and formatted
10248 processor plug in base and peripheral ports that have a multipart available function to attachment and configuration adjustable port noteable programmable inside the bios and what to where situation of this and that makes working parts down to the chip direction user modified instructions per part and piece inside the arrangement of parts connected
10249 perbuilt selected options for processor plug in base and peripheral ports that have a multipart available function to attachment and configuration adjustable port noteable programmable inside the bios and what to where situation of this and that makes working parts down to the chip direction user modified instructions per part and piece inside the arrangement of parts connected
10250 open mother boardarrangement of parts connected instructions perbuilt open ended selected options for processor plug in base and peripheral ports that have a multipart available function to attachment and configuration adjustable port noteable programmable inside the bios and what to where situation of this and that makes working parts down to the chip direction user modified instructions per part and piece inside the arrangement of parts connected
10251 consumer paid open mother boardarrangement of parts connected instructions of perbuilt open ended selected options for processor plug in base and peripheral ports that have a multipart available function to attachment and configuration adjustable port noteable programmable inside the bios and what to where situation of this and that makes working parts down to the chip direction user modified instructions per part and piece inside the arrangement of parts connected
10252 specific industrial or general consumer recycle line arrangement
10253 recycle disassemble line arrangement speed verses reuse properties
10254 recycle disassemble line arrangement shred and sort compact and incinerate and then sort and compact and re manufactured soot and gasses separated to weight and composite
10255 landfill recycle mining and disassembly starch and carbon line arrangement is a

property of known practices that still a recycle tanner into a this is all we work with working with itself and reworking all the materials as a chemical to process what we process process funny but in a tanning sense of natural curing chemicals of positive breakdown ability to adjust and re consume the previous shred and sort to magnetite and incinerate and then re compact and re manufacture materials and minerals and gas reclaiming and separating into everything we started with

10256 recycle and cycle gas liquid and gas separated mining and disassembly to material on a settle absolute table weight process take and rest into a sedimentary weight of stagnation and aggression movement and non movement improving heating resting and cooling

10257 recycle and cycle solid metal and solid mineral mining and disassembly to material on a settle absolute table weight process take and rest into a sedimentary weight of stagnation and aggression movement and non movement improving heating resting and cooling

10258 pain induction and reduction testing for extreme cases of pain management recovery a way to eliminate tolerances and control

10259 boiling and cooling wet materials of any sort with the intent to recycle a tannery method of cycle recycle process

10260 licensed conceptual inventor status and document the status of concept s based on the deposition writer themselves

10261 legally bound arbitrary capital adjustment is if the contract is good there should be assumption of capital payment

10262 where are they now help and history of any known centique centiqueology a study of honest and real un bias history encounters factual links

10263 thin form mobile you build it chassis format of parts and interconnections by scsi scsi medium and scsi small connections that overlap and up and over connections by scaleable link interface small medium and large

10264 rivet thin form mobile you build it chassis format of parts and interconnections building things essentially by a inch and by inch and inch increments of across and over by inches for conformity

10265 parts that unite by scale and connections across carry interconnection circuit processors and alternate vectors of chip exchange a chip that sends a specific vector data rate to a specified place to and then to more or to reply

10266 a specified place or vector of a cubit cell data that is sent to and answered by a cubit group of cells

10267 cubit alphabet sequence signals in code of any such on and off group including headers and spacers for instruction language in short a second generation cubit language that itself is translated as more than code and on off but letters way morse code and triad octavio signals that work to make a more eloquent and higher capacity dimension

10268 cell phone voip servers a tower that changes from voice data to a second generation of cubit data tower and reflection services into an endless roam into and away from the host controller satellites

10269 cell phone technology in a merge and equate into a single cubit data ratio and modular tower and reflection services different than a voice over internet a distinct data into cell phone signal

10270 secured and encrypted cell phone technology in a merge and equate into a single cubit data ratio and modular tower and reflection services different than a voice over internet a

distinct data into cell phone signal
10271 solid state compressor chip is a synthetic metal conductor that holds the data at a rate and multiplies the volume per calculation to increase the density of signals per circuit in bound and accordingly
10272 solid state multiplier chip is a synthetic metal conductor that holds the data at a rate and amplifies the volume per calculation to increase the definitions of signal per circuit in bound and accordingly
10273 fiber optic repeating solid state system on chip is a synthetic metal conductor processing unit that examines data and security and then repeats it to continue as the intended length of optic focus
10274 system shell a system of congruent processors a system of a chip inside an operable compressing and multiplier system of processing system shell inside shell inside shell
10275 secure system shell a system of encrypted processors a system of a chip inside an operable compressing and multiplier system of processing system shell inside shell inside shell
10276 shell to shell connecting system of operating code and instructions as in reference to secured and shell chips in shell the operation of cubits and second or more generations of multiple cubit instructions per chip and vector directions
10277 quartered height profile mini pcie x modified graphics card format right
10278 planned limonene plastics a solvent plastic that has a specific degrade composite known and planned to recycle with a specified make and end to the solvent and finished plastic new and dead
10279 ex tractable system on chip bed of chips storage server brick and relay board and configuration management server system graph and error correction indication led configured and manufactured system clone with data and duplication flash disc and drives on chips and sas
10280 soldered down system on chip bed of chips storage server brick and relay board and configuration management server system graph and error correction indication led configured and manufactured system clone with data and duplication flash disc and drives on chips and sass
10281 fountain power a fountain drink combination fuel of magnesium salt powder and a mixture of alcohol for body and movement to power a combustion engine that is engineered for a powder and mixed with liquid for a concentrated fuel at a lower cost and higher availability and lower emissions and preexisting carbon foot prints in ecology energy such as coal mining
10282 water purified engine exhaust cycled cylinders used with internal combustion engines fueled by either petrol or diesel including leanburn engines as well as kerosene heaters and stoves second stem exhaust tunnel
10283 solvent purified engine exhaust cycled cylinders used with internal combustion engines fueled by either petrol or diesel including leanburn engines as well as kerosene heaters and stoves second stem exhaust tunnel
10284 solution purified engine exhaust cycled cylinder and additional multiple cycles of belly and exchange filter products like an synthetic mechanized oil that is exchangeable and recycled into other product multiple stem exhaust tunnel
10285 solution purified engine exhaust cycled cylinder absorbing particle lubricant product

multiple stem exhaust tunnel
10286 epa standard recyclable exchange ports for the exhaust purified solution exhaust cycled cylinders and product multiple stem exhaust tunnel
10287 epa standard recyclable exchange filters for the exhaust purified solution exhaust cycled cylinders and product multiple stem exhaust tunnel
10288 fractal math string zoom formula for synthetic and poly chemical measurements to zoom and extract dna from stem cells as well as dna strings. to zoom and measure solid state data or solid state memory cells. a. fractal
10289 properties of stagnation improper use of technology in a manipulative manner to conclude monetary funds verses the intent to progress for example the coprocessor verse the use of an extended automatic co processor verses a deliberate attempt to keep the i in the sky the profit cow
10290 improper use of the truth as a sufficient means for rules against any such corporation or notarized agreement
10291 sold as pre manufactured system on a chip of any known software such as operating systems that are adopted to the plug and play hardware or detach and fee reattached schema
10292 summit and sellathon conference known as convention for sale and for the use of property
10293 international summit and sellathon at a world interest and denomination of ownership
10294 drug abuse brain damage and the intent to make a chemical such as to snap a person into a complete dopamine narcosis and occur inside an acute non vegetative comma altering a person from any such addiction and problem
10295 planned degrading paper for consumable means and the intent to make as there is an end to the beginning of a paper that is easy to sort burn and carbonize or recycle
10296 compressed thermal turbine and incinerator with condensed exhaust purified solution tunnel and absorbing solvent is a three cycle energy study by what means is there an obvious but smaller than abnormal gain in energy by energy for example synthetic and incineration and recycled gas the first stage is burning waste product and then turning a turbine and sending the remaining thermal energy of hot air and exhaust through a pipe and into a tunnel of absorbing solvents and refining the pollutants to a extremely fine degree of reusable means
10297 smart shoe media comm center usb and impact data exchange to find energy use activity use and mile use in order to keep up a productive life style
10298 ex tractable intelligent card for shoe media comm center usb and impact data exchange to find energy use activity use and mile use in order to keep up a productive life style
10299 pressure wire circuits for testing athlete performance in for shoe media comm center usb and impact data exchange to find energy use activity use and mile use in order to keep up a productive life style
10300 analyzing software to compliment the smart shoe and the game in tow meaning that the game experiences and the turn of events i a sequenced analyzing moment of sport gone scientific video and movement software
10301 smart baseball and analyzing software to compliment the smart practice baseball and the game in tow meaning that the game experiences and the turn of events i a sequenced analyzing moment of sport gone scientific as well as the geometric compensations of the

place in the playing field turns and location in the game or moment of routine

10302 homeland security web analyzing software that collects and collates the data to hot spots and sensitive areas inside the united states and abroad that acts like a nerve of intelligence and initiates ip and web activity bots to specify the targets activities and movements

10303 corporate security web analyzing software that collects and collates the data to hot spots and sensitive areas inside the united states and abroad that acts like a nerve of intelligence and initiates ip and web activity bots to specify the targets activities and movements

10304 citizen specific security web analyzing software that collects and collates the data to hot spots and sensitive areas inside the united states and abroad that acts like a nerve of intelligence and initiates ip and web activity bots to specify the targets activities and movements

10305 pre world war crime trial and intent to issue a declaration of isolation as well as term correction to any such life interrupting country as a whole

10306 pre world war crime disciplinary capital payment and just dues of damage

10307 lacquer jet fine art printer is a premier collectible and fine art way of printing original fine two dimensional art

10308 layered lacquer ink is a special solvent that is made to work with lacquer fine art printers and the technology of making a yield of ink that may be layered and kept a print work special

10309 layered acrylic printing and jet spray plastic?printing in itself is a term generalized as a two part d and d printing combined

10310 paint printing jet spray plastic?printing in itself is a term generalized printing with paint and an opacity paint plastic solvent

10311 metal and laser printing by way of layered conducting print sheets and cartridge base for circuits and synthetic metals soot carbon doping electrodes

10312 printed solid state circuits and synthetic metals by way of plasma layered bonding and thermal re doping data driven circuits

10313 embedded printed solid state circuits and synthetic metals by way of plasma layered bonding and thermal re doping data driven circuits

10314 raised and recircuited printed solid state circuits and synthetic metals by way of plasma layered bonding and thermal re doping data driven circuits

10315 less than pin riser connections that are a random function with applicable chip port storage identification to bridge and support a more connected board of circuits

10316 open source programmable chips and systems that are conveniently unsecured pre mirrored

10317 open source programmable secure chips that are conveniently encrypted for resale as mirrored

10318 open source programmable secure chips that are conveniently encrypted for resale as mirrored and embedded with a functionality along side the less than pin riser connections that are a random function with applicable chip port storage identification to bridge and support a more connected board of circuits

10319 free fall generator a generator that works on weight and gravity mechanized a sequence of hoses filling up large tubs and dropping them a very long distance in a downward scope of gravity pull making a electric motor generate power

10320 chip bios loader and sequence and then exchange and then install per socket to hold and keep and then install out of your design

10321 circuit printer and thermal circuit board copper solder printer soft copper mess for a less expensive and more operational dynamic study of process

10322 blank chip sd and blank chip designing acceptable circuit driven operations of a system on a chip

10323 blank chip cpu and blank chip designing acceptable circuit driven operations of a system on a chip

10324 enscribble open chip cpu and software driven registration for designing acceptable circuit driven operations of a system on a chip

10325 enscribble write once open chip cpu and software driven registration for designing acceptable circuit driven operations of a system on a chip

10326 enscribble rewritable open chip cpu and software driven registration for designing acceptable circuit driven operations of a system on a chip

10327 transformation solid state memory into cores and threads of computational processing shapes and cram computer aided triggered layers of computational mass

10328 automatic bios correction library and error beeping vocabulary

10329 automatic system correction maintenance add in card with plug and play beeping error codes and other operations libraries

10330 device specific data write shape known as a cram functioning device specified write once or multiple times in order for a finite use of solid state matter nano writes and re writes to configure a more than a cubit to a cram shape for a multitude of operators and function devices in a language of write and function said in lameman terms a shape of x in one language will equal an off in a reading function of a device where the outre or intro is the devices method of use

10331 device specific data write shape known as a cram functioning device specified write once or multiple times in order for a finite use of solid state matter nano writes and re writes to configure a more than a cubit to a cram shape for a multitude of operators and function devices in a language of write and function said in lameman terms a shape of x in one language will equal an off in a reading function of a device where the outre or intro is the devices method of use or as also to make a shape in one language and it equal to a transistor building shape in another said this way building a chip from languages of shapes to make a shape in one language equal to a transistor in another nano peta language of in and out

10332 write cubit device language of shape and form for function software to make a shape in one language and it equal to a transistor building shape in another said this way building a chip from languages of shapes to make a shape in one language equal to a transistor in another nano peta language of in and out

10333 write cubit device language of shape and form for function hardware to make a shape in one language and it equal to a transistor building shape in another said this way building a chip from languages of shapes to make a shape in one language equal to a transistor in another nano peta language of in and out

10334 rewriteable cubit device language of shape and form for function hardware to make a shape in one language and it equal to a transistor building shape in another said this way building a chip from languages of shapes to make a shape in one language equal to a transistor in another nano peta language of in and out

10335 practice and sport smart training data base comparison software for the smartball smart shoe and smart practice languages set choice mandelbrot z = z^ + c b. fractal set choice mandelbrot z = z^ + c a. mandelbrot x y . magnification b. mandelbrot x. y . magnification a. julia x y post x . y . b. julia x . y . magnification . post x y .

10336 smart ball of impact and resistance control analytical study real time information wireless transmission

10337 reverse government and capitalism only by representation and our nature of representative tax based economically sound capital adjustment the means for a party capital adjustment economy

10338 encrypted phone application key and pair with to speak and decode in milliseconds as ten four

10339 privatize and modernize war on a technological software front to make any smart super tactic a flight above at all times other words to make a smart war out of dumb enemies and use any means necessary and able to create a war with only the enemy suffered dead and smart tactics of warn and bomb

10340 the learning tablet for children with program and curriculum based compact flash cards and a wireless system in a school learning technologically advanced environment

10341 technology aided learning of the united states should have a privatized level of integration and legal funding for all schools and states learning should be focused on traditional context and should be modernized in a equal way to unify learning as well as share knowledge and information and human rights of people

10342 school approved learning device is a working tablet or pc that operates when needed and is encrypted for students personal ownership works with a specific class and operates with tcompactflashor any mobile scheme including the means to submit tests and homework from home the road abroad or inside class tests could be modified or encryption signatures in the submission could be succinct with the owner of a finger print

10343 gaseous carbonized smoke with water and electricity stabilizing the protons and electron particles for fuel and refinery in a electrical ph balance

10344 gaseous carbonized smoke with solvent and electricity stabilizing the protons and electron particles for fuel and refinery in a electrical ph balance

10345 gaseous carbonized smoke with solvent and electricity stabilizing the protons and electron particles for fuel and refinery in a electrical ph balance vapor fume tank for making compounds medicine and chemicals in a step by step process making a smoke from sulfur and iron carbon oxide and then tainting the smoke with solvent or water and then electrically charging the compounds as they are atomized in the air to perform an electrical doping in the solvent as it is in the air as an equilibrium in balanced form

10346 single to multiple operation core functions in server and data center useages working as a tier based institution translations as multiple or single cell core systems on chips with connections powered by software that works as needed when the chip on a single in and out string

10347 single to multiple single string cores and data storage to power a response from any working request of information client streaming systems with the software that requests and provides expandable dimensions in demand flexibility

10348 two chip and one in out board that functions and works as a system on a chip with

a data storage system and a controller system making a mirroring of on and off for any processing including the transfer of an operation and exchange of any single file
10349 bigger board by going smaller multiple chips of storage to an embedded and exchangeable sense of connections explained as a wall of insertable systems built by rows an columns of an architecture of request and a string of systems on strings wall based operations literally
10350 modular section server parts and pieces with a specified error correction code per device section building a server with more parts that are replaceable verses one single modular board with upgrade able parts and version compatible parts
10351 air recovery recycle particulate stations with environmental specified control and air improvement abilities is an air recovery station that inhales polluted air and recycles that air to a percentage of clean that is acceptable to improve air quality in any place by using a strained air and low temperature catalyst converters recycling and oxidizing any specified carbon to a new sanitation level by lowtemperature carbon ion oxidation catalyst
10352 modular recovery stations and filter exhaust catalyst converters that not only control but convert bad air to good air at a conditioning level air recycling and sanitation's continued by air recovery recycle particulate stations with environmental specified control and air improvement abilities is an air recovery station that inhales polluted air and recycles that air to a percentage of clean that is acceptable to improve air quality in any place by using a strained air and low temperature catalyst converters recycling and oxidizing any specified carbon sodium to a new sanitation level
10353 geo stations of air conditions and ventilator generators that catch air and control the pollutants and then exhaust with a generation of expended and recycled energy and new clean air for valley and depreciated congested stagnate environments air recycling and sanitation's for a government and private industrial level of effort to sanitize the environment by lowtemperature carbon oxidation catalyst
10354 low level back pack air cleaner and ventilator generators that catch air and control the pollutants and then exhaust with a generation of expended and recycled energy and new clean air for valley and depreciated congested stagnate environments air recycling and sanitation's for a personalized level of effort to sanitize the environment by lowtemperature sodium oxidation catalyst
10355 air cleaner and ventilator generators that catch air and control the pollutants and then exhaust with a generation of expended and recycled energy and new clean air for valley and depreciated congested stagnate environments air recycling and sanitation's for a personalized level of effort to sanitize the environment by lowtemperature sugar oxidation catalyst called a reversed calvin cycle powered by way of microwave fuse with water and sugar
10356 short pay phone local cell phone towers short stations instead of blasting communications from far above why not make communication a small subscription network like the way it used to be in the pay phone days
10357 publically supported short network stations instead of blasting communications from far above why not make communication a small subscription network like the way it used to be in the pay phone days we could have mobile networks everywhere someone wanted a connection
10358 in a traveling pi operation the new period separated computer controlled measurements of testing and software zoom mandelbrot formulas can be used to build more

precise fractions of processing

10359 periods of meaning are the scales of numbers followed by the numerical relations of places and points of vector annotations by giving a certain number of periods or specific symbol in a sequence to translate as an equation

10360 the easy chemistry of hydro dynamic equilibrium refining and decompressed atomized oxidation with lasers and conservation techniques

10361 chemical balance relation goal is the chance to achieve the proper chemicals in the brain or an organ to make it work better and function regulatory like while not poisoning the other organs in relation to the technique of ingestion or intake of the medicine by finding all the complex differences in any reaction to the medicine and make a indirect correction of the known changes

10362 cell phone shut down of un friendly cell phones in war zones as well as known friendly phones allotted list

10363 electric and battery operated utensil exam of any battle field prior to operations and smart tracking uncontrolled devices

10364 mobile communications and hard line encryption control for war zones and temperamental places of interest

10365 a cell phone app that tracks phrases to anti sentimental text to linking attacks of terrorism

10366 functions of any such blockade of technology communications for war places and territories of conspiracy

10367 terrorist country suspension list to the greater good of our united states by posting actions to suspend any positive aid or commerce or like to a country with a certain negative attitude and actions against innocent people

10368 the pledge of allegiance is a national abidance of our heritage and citizen children of public education should be noted for not having allegiance

10369 german conflicts of interest in christianity and islam may incite a new world war the exemption of refugee ship should be fined and evaded by way of isolation and deportation aid to a specified area as not a national place of christianity

10370 driving tension scale of accidents and incidents that conclude to an unsafe level of community relationships in driving and public behavior

10371 business alliances are a single manager for out sourced business arrangement with multiple favorite company venture family of out sourcing scheme of business related management and the techniques of friendly business engagements with licenses abound by privileges

10372 chickens verses eagles the national challenge to build a stronger nation with chickens running the country

10373 architecture in cubits another way to say functions in written language a cubits as any other known as a path or circuit in another to build a chip out of a formed path of cubits in an alphabet of cubits and then circuits in super annotation cell of conductors and processor cores

10374 architecture in cubits another way to say functions in written language a cubits as any other known as a path or circuit in another to build a chip out of a formed path of cubits in an alphabet of cubits and then circuits in super annotation cell of conductors and processor cores as well as circuits insulators and cell walls

10375 architecture in cubits another way to say functions in written language a cubits as any other known as a path or circuit in another to build a chip out of a formed path of cubits in an alphabet of cubits and then circuits in super annotation cell of conductors and processor cores as well as circuits insulators and cell walls as the language of reading functions
10376 building language hardware written by software as a solid state or flash based conductor processor and operator made into a cubit written composite working tool
10377 building language software written by software hardware as a solid state or flash based conductor processor and operator made into a cubit written composite working tool
10378 poly carbonate sub species and lead interference differences in toxicity managing the traits of carbon and the differences between all other poly carbonate number makes
10379 energy studies of probable generation of any such source of energy verses the cost of making that energy free fall generator or incineration electricity or pendulum associated control session
10380 disposal incinerator quality control by modified ports of chambers and vacuum services to increase efficiency of any such known service of operation
10381 service incineration vacuum and propulsion of any attached turbine while at the same moment making a chain reaction of feeding and eating
10382 simplified vacuum jet compressed incinerator is a service incineration vacuum and propulsion of any attached turbine while at the same moment making a chain reaction of feeding and eating from previously expended compression
10383 simplified vacuum jet compressed motor is a service motor vacuum and propulsion of any attached turbo turbine multiplied while at the same moment making a chain reaction of feeding and eating from previously expended compression in a cycle
10384 phi co amplified or parallel processor on flash chip with software driven function and amplitude of cooperating chips of the same process or of equal ownership of functions
10385 paid parts of parts program of independent energy makers for example for this amount of money we will qualify you to make more energy to add to the existing supply for a fee of operations and connections
10386 usb alternate co processing substitution and usb amp accelerator processing stand along plug and play device to improve computations
10387 usb server on chip functions and usb server bed of computation devices for processing any known protocol
10388 fiber optic system connection for alternate co processing substitution and fiber optic system amp accelerator processing stand along plug and play device to improve computations and the transceiver relationship in that
10389 fiber optic system server on chip functions and fiber optic system server bed of computation devices for processing any known protocol and the transceiver relationship in that
10390 cell tower connected data cloud including a wireless batch of servers and data center operations
10391 wireless mini servers for a cell tower connected data cloud including a wireless batch of servers and data center operations
10392 a service array of wireless mini servers for a cell tower connected data cloud including a wireless batch of servers and data center operations
10393 co processing appliances for a wireless mini servers and data center operations

network
10394 co processing active software for a wireless mini servers and data center operations network is a software platform that runs and completes the process of who what when and where easily by calling on a group of processes to work in unison at more than one task
10395 wireless data center protocol and the processed cell operations inside wireless mini data servers holding a sub numerical phone number name in a send and receive order
10396 wireless data center registration group of numbers and locations in a decimal formatted pre registered group of assigned names in any given array of a whole to respond and request information
10397 essential voip cellular combination wireless data center and the contingency of any such known cloud operation to voice the data center in any form of cubit secondary movement
10398 laser translator for optical hard line is a laser inspired data field connected to a satellite or other form of transcribe optical connection
10399 laser cell translator for optical hard line is a laser inspired data field connected to a tower or other form of transcribe optical connection concluding into a connected internet and data scheme privately secured or pubic nature of owner ship
10400 a focused laser receiver that holds and records laser signals as data
10401 a focused laser receiver that holds and records laser signals as data in an annotation of triplet pi equilibrium is a wave of data as a signal
10402 a focused laser receiver group that holds and records laser signals as data in multitudes encrypted or un encrypted methods
10403 a focused laser sending group that sends and relays laser signals as data in multitudes encrypted or un encrypted methods
10404 range path data as wave signal in a focused laser sending and receiving group that sends and relays holds and records laser signals as data in multitudes encrypted or un encrypted methods in any shade of ultraviolet to white co concluding into a wireless optical data connection
10405 the code and compensation required to provide a simple targeted geonautic range path data as wave signal in a focused laser sending and receiving group that sends and relays holds and records laser signals as data in multitudes encrypted or un encrypted methods in any shade of ultraviolet to white co concluding into a wireless optical data connection christopher g brown
10406 the device transmitting code and compensation required to provide a simple targeted geonautic range path data as wave signal in a focused laser sending and receiving group that sends and relays holds and records laser signals as data in multitudes encrypted or un encrypted methods in any shade of ultraviolet to white co concluding into a wireless optical data connection christopher g brown
10407 array controller of process is a brain to make all the cells of any given data center work together and perform in complete success multiple functions of operations essentially a server for other servers the instruction service server completed instruction can result in a duplicate system of more servers over servers for elaborated control indefinitely stated christopher g brown
10408 operating system operation code kill control and array controller of process is a brain to make all the cells of any given data center work together and perform in complete success

multiple functions of operations essentially a server for other servers the instruction service server completed instruction can result in a duplicate system of more servers over servers for elaborated control indefinitely stated christopher g brown

10409 wifi operating system operation code kill control and array controller of process is a brain to make all the cells of any given data center work together and perform in complete success multiple functions of operations essentially a server for other servers the instruction service server completed instruction can result in a duplicate system of more servers over servers for elaborated control indefinitely stated christopher g brown

10410 network ethernet operating system operation code kill control and array controller of process is a brain to make all the cells of any given data center work together and perform in complete success multiple functions of operations essentially a server for other servers the instruction service server completed instruction can result in a duplicate system of more servers over servers for elaborated control indefinitely stated christopher g brown

10411 monarch connection operating system operation code kill control and array controller of process is a brain to make all the cells of any given data center work together and perform in complete success multiple functions of operations essentially a server for other servers the instruction service server completed instruction can result in a duplicate system of more servers over servers for elaborated control indefinitely stated christopher g brown

10412 lets play political jeopardy where there were bank watches and monetary status alarms of insufficient and super sufficient notes that are politically motivated and controlled how to find political corruption and traces of homeland security problems of great stature the government watches bank accounts of low income status citizens why not the opposite christopher g brown

10413 lets play political jeopardy and say that people who run government should have a cap on income until out of office and officially audited by the irs to have any such money christopher g brown

10414 the light age needs to modernize government and parts that require government advice and intuition may help fight crimes and wars of terror with generous offerings and divisions for improvement with the technology of our nation at risk we should help protect people who protect us christopher g brown

10415 the live needle polygraph test to study by acupuncture the truth of any such person christopher g brown

10416 old medicine has a new study the integration of old ways into the new way of taking medicine antiquebiology christopher g brown

10417 super simple small push button with microphone and speaker working with voice command and no touch screen cell phone hardware to sd to no sd christopher g brown

10418 super simple small push button microphone speaker voice command phone operating system that is network and web inclusive christopher g brown

10419 second generation of allotted multiple connections to any given port of operations wifi and more computational connection strings of packets and wireless information wifi two is a cubit matter that is a signal incorporated into the operation of code beyond the os holding a cubit cell instruction in a wireless connection christopher g brown

10420 long range laser data wave is a light wave of information that carries to point to point and holds wave signals of information similar to optical data yet without fibers christopher g brown

10421 cellular information channel for police that carry police data specific and confidentially secured information christopher g brown

10422 a secured public information channel for monetary transfers is a specific web application that transfers ownership and funds to other banks and balances christopher g brown

10423 multiple channels of information bridge to access any such specific need or industry specific technology to share and improve that data share market of information is a mini expanded data exchange to be said again is like the information of aero industry holding a internet of its own and the specified television network on a different and separated internet but being serviced by the same devices only in a expansive connected channel of internet access christopher g brown

10424 packet encryption by presiding markers and suffix markers of packets for multiple channels of information bridge to access any such specific need or industry specific technology to share and improve that data share market of information is a mini expanded data exchange to be said again is like the information of aero industry holding a internet of its own and the specified television network on a different and separated internet but being serviced by the same devices only in a expansive connected channel of internet access christopher g brown

10425 pcie plug and play data signatures and readers for multiple channels of information bridge to access any such specific need or industry specific technology to share and improve that data share market of information is a mini expanded data exchange to be said again is like the information of aero industry holding a internet of its own and the specified television network on a different and separated internet but being serviced by the same devices only in a expansive connected channel of internet access christopher g brown

10426 pcie plug and play data encoders and decoders and readers for multiple channels of information bridge to access any such specific need or industry specific technology christopher g brown

10427 scramble encrypted rearranged methods of encryption for multiple channels of information bridge to access any such specific need or industry specific technology to share and improve that data share market of information is a mini expanded data exchange to be said again is like the information of aero industry holding a internet of its own and the specified television network on a different and separated internet but being serviced by the same devices only in a expansive connected channel of internet access

10428 electronic us treasury of banks and commissions is a united states trade bank that works with commercial common banks to control federal trade and electronic fund transfers of ownership christopher g brown

10429 optical disc cpu with functions that process like cubits as circuits less expensive circuit driven optical central processing units and processing written and then used in language circuits optical cpu christopher g brown

10430 optical disc cpu with multiple read and process lasers in rotation with the percircuit adjustment christopher g brown

10431 optical disc cpu with multiple read and process lasers in rotation with multiple layers of architecture christopher g brown

10432 detachable optical disc cpu with interoperable parts and changeable socket drives and bios configuration instructions to improve today's computations and sciences christopher g brown

10433 secondary leading and transferable optical disc cpu with exchangeable cpu disc like a compact disc drive that holds memory and computations in and out christopher g brown

10434 embedded solution with optical disc cpu holding a fixed architecture for processing computations christopher g brown

10435 stacked solution with optical disc cpu holding a fixed architecture for processing computations christopher g brown

10436 data internet channel is a paid service that originates from the phone company and media ties of per interest based data christopher g brown

10437 public data internet channel is a public service for recreating the television and internet into a new all in one signal source christopher g brown

10438 data rating internet channel is a rating service that rates the restricted content of sexuality and parental guidance per internet channel christopher g brown

10439 internet channel and the process of data per industry and good keeping of that service including ratings infrastructure and cohesiveness christopher g brown

10440 government mimic bot is a robot search script that attaches to well known bots and reads the similar data christopher g brown

10441 police bot is a web bot and spider searching index that finds negative platforms and collects data from their information christopher g brown

10442 internet data over radio is a specified sending and receiving data connection with radio signals in cubit data information christopher g brown

10443 encrypted internet data over radio is a encrypted cubit radio signal similar to cell tower signals only wider range and broadcast christopher g brown

10444 internet data over radio to wifi router and radio broadcast transceiver to make a wireless home network and a radio connection to the outside internet inside christopher g brown

10445 internet data over radio to wifi router and radio broadcast transceiver to make a wireless home network and a radio connection to the outside internet inside by phone cell tower christopher g brown

10446 supply and demand cost of inflation control is a negative system of checks that control the situation of inflation and prices by market adjustment control christopher g brown

10447 weak influenza vaccine is a low tolerable flu virus antibody that works to cure by a combination of antimicrobial sodium compound and deceased virus christopher g brown

10448 long range electric transfer is a energy solution that works on transportable mobile energy cells or battery arsenal by train truck or hard links christopher g brown

10449 community future investments are funds for sustainable community management and the deprecation of environmental resources and state of improvements christopher g brown

10450 shared by payment learning by conclusion work and assembly ifs are a unlimited function memory database is a software that records and keeps a library of operations for working scenarios and what to do if situations for robotic manufacturing learning christopher g brown

10451 shared by payment learning by conclusion vocabulary and sound unlimited function memory database is a software that records and keeps a library of operations for working scenarios and what to do if situations for learning and voice command software christopher g brown

10452 data connection radio signal channel devices are a group of devices that send and receive data through channels in radio signals christopher g brown

10453 data connection radio signal channel services are a group of devices for services that send and receive data trough channels in radio signals christopher g brown

10454 data connection radio signal channel devices and integrated circuits translations with a long range radio data modulation in negative microwave nano and packet direction services dm send and digital call sign codes stored as a verbal bios compressed communication operation system christopher g brown

10455 synthetic sodiummagnesium battery technology to power large and expansive technology specific environments

10456 rail car battery generators that generate power by rolling on the track and keep it in an onboard cell for keeping and use christopher g brown

10457 car battery generators that generate power by rolling and then keep it in an on board cell for storage and reuse christopher g brown

10458 cycle recycle battery generators that generate power by rolling and keep it in an on board cell for keeping and use christopher g brown

10459 wireless network of small devices that operate together when the first available exchange of data is able to make any server operable at any given time is a wireless cloud of processing christopher g brown

10460 wireless packet direction is a prefix of packet information that sends to a specific receiving point that may have a direct link to a subscriber christopher g brown

10461 wireless cloud router is a regulated document that works with multiple points of receiving and operation of sending as though there could be more than one wifi router commonly known as to operate together to send massive data and internet protocol signals abroad christopher g brown

10462 on off magnetic electric generator that works as off and on are sequentially put in motion to generate electricity in a magnetic field off center in a path of the coil and not in a jedliks motor inside but a path of logical magnetic cycles of coil along the path of cycle christopher g brown revised cycle electric motor

10463 a multiplied dimension cycle electric generator can be used to create electricity from electricity in a cycle of recycle which is a motor moving and then after performance on the return of the motor action another set of electric commutative cycle returning electricity to be revised christopher g brown

10464 transient of a multiplied dimension cycle electric generator can be used to create electricity from electricity in a cycle of recycle which is a motor moving and then after performance on the return of the motor action another set of electric commutative cycle returning electricity to be revised christopher g brown

10465 cohesive layout of a multiplied dimension cycle electric generator can be used to create electricity from torque in a cycle of recycle which is a motor moving and then after performance on the return of the motor action another set of electric commutative cycle returning electricity like a pre exciter to exciter to exciter operation christopher g brown

10466 to go backwards from computer history in a tech size reversed build a giant field of cohesive layout of a multiplied dimension cycle electric generator can be used to create electricity from torque in a cycle of recycle which is a motor moving and then after

performance on the return of the motor action another set of electric commutative cycle returning electricity like a pre exciter to exciter to exciter operation christopher g brown
10467 hardware built to compromise the energy of a force and generate a recycled electricity by making a circuit working on top of a previously expended torque for example a wheel with electromagnets stimulating another wheel with electromagnets that generate electricity to use christopher g brown
10468 to use a software to engineer a circuit driven computational fractal energy and recycled electricity by commutative exciter paths simple z = z^ + c to generate electricity christopher g brown
10469 making electricity by using a recycle electric motor in a combination of pi and a combined fractal percentage of operation to work with things that are in motion to re generate electricity christopher g brown
10470 using an exciter or multiple exciters as well as making electricity by using a recycle electric motor in a combination of pi and a combined fractal percentage of operation to work with things that are in motion to re generate electricity christopher g brown
10471 solid state cpu second cpu and third cpu and plus as to write the chip with code instead of scoring the chip as a photo christopher g brown
10472 solid state cpu software leased or paid by a fee as to pay for the concept with rights as implied intellectual property christopher g brown
10473 solid state cpu written using cubit software that writes hardware christopher g brown
10474 solid state cpu second cpu and third cpu and plus by pcie or alternate pipe like for example a tb processor in data cubits christopher g brown
10475 military device of statistical units of motion use and location tracking christopher g brown
10476 police device of statistical units of motion use and location tracking of effectiveness and location statistics christopher g brown
10477 public dentition device of statistical units of motion use and location tracking cloud data hardware and software working together to correct and notify of the occurrences christopher g brown
10478 satellite target tracking system with unique boundaries and reports christopher g brown
10479 cellular communications target tracking system with unique boundaries and reports christopher g brown
10480 track paging system that contacts an information base to report locations for automated data exchange and service announcements christopher g brown
10481 information base is a data routing system used to accelerate the location of data recipients by sub packet number and prefixes by area code christopher g brown
10482 a data exchange server is a large or small interface that works as a unified information through port that directs things as in a direct input form using a information base is a data routing system used to accelerate the location of data recipients by sub packet number and prefixes by area code this is the utensil that makes the pipe work to control the flow from place to place christopher g brown
10483 karaoke virtual reality user extensible software and hardware is an augmented reality focus that makes you part of your virtual reality fantasy or scheme of augmented reality christopher g brown

10484 public slander law and outlandish statement is a thing that makes it a crime to state things that are not true in any such questionnaire or consent of authority christopher g brown
10485 debate of ownership is the law that makes it a crime to sell something that does not belong to you or your company christopher g brown
10486 adjusted property jump is a search of audit for the illegal gain of political paid compensation and buying off of any such persons favor christopher g brown
10487 cloud on chips is any such amplified start and finish direction of processing that holds a building echo of data such as a galaxy operation where to say in one code that the predecessor may be an expensive system that makes code and related parts of information that goes down river for other processing christopher g brown
10488 projection video phone and the laser stick led compact or desktop models are conference friendly christopher g brown
10489 play along karaoke or game augmented reality projection and the laser stick led compact or desktop models are entertainment friendly christopher g brown
10490 transparent sphere television and video layered spectrum display is a sphere of translucent properties that can display video in a perspective christopher g brown
10491 sphere high definition perspective resolution encoding for visual display and communication christopher g brown
10492 point of view added perspective display user to display any resolution at the users proper point of view christopher g brown
10493 server to compact flash with the process of data redirection would let the data decide where to go in this there could be multiple soc on one board christopher g brown
10494 compact flash bed of servers on chip and including a routed path of information to exchange the rate of processing a bed of data and processing chips with an on board router appliance christopher g brown
10495 global routing initiative is a detailed paid routing service data base that helps clouds route to specific areas of the world to improve connectivity christopher g brown
10496 paid multi device operating system is an operating system that adapts to the device used on in any way needed how many devices do you want to run this copy of this operating system plan christopher g brown
10497 secured drive of any paid multi device operating system is an operating system that adapts to the device used on in any way needed how many devices do you want to run this copy of this operating system plan christopher g brown
10498 compact flash os paid multi device operating system is an operating system that adapts to the device used on in any way needed how many devices do you want to run this copy of this operating system plan christopher g brown
10499 usb flash os paid multi device operating system is an operating system that adapts to the device used on in any way needed how many devices do you want to run this copy of this operating system plan christopher g brown
10500 adaptable fiber optic short solutions adaptable short solutions in fiber optic short cables and common issues in connectivity for everyday use fiber optic short translator connections compact fiber optic solutions christopher g brown
10501 layered depth display optic solutions for temporal three dimensional depth perspective is to layer a perspective in color and field display with layers of led and transparent

layers of display layouts in a omni layer of depth and picture christopher g brown

10502 transparent back light opacity scale of the to come display optic solutions for temporal three dimensional depth perspective is to layer a perspective in color and field display with layers and transparent layers of display layouts in a omni layer of depth and picture christopher g brown

10503 vertical optical display circuits to display a varied layer of three dimensional optic display solutions for depth perspective where the circuit is layered and in itself holds a layer of more layers with a point of view calculated christopher g brown

10504 software that plural signal control per application and multiplied signal options for a stronger signal receiving christopher g brown

10505 display of unordinary behavior and public riot crime is a unexpected method of protest and public disruption christopher g brown

10506 radical religious increments of unrealism is the religious extreme made to be the un excepted form of ban freedom and the unfree concept of terrorism christopher g brown

10507 telemarketer terrorism and the pill pushers problems to fight homeland phone terrorism ftc trial of do not call list deficiency christopher g brown

10508 user specific watching web bots that identify and trace criminal and malicious activity by following them and then their intent to disrupt christopher g brown

10509 group watching web bots that track and trace a specific group of attitude and system of targets by identifying them and then following their intent christopher g brown

10510 a regulatory system of web bot makers that make a group of police and repeat servers and stations that relate to the specific origin of a nation christopher g brown

10511 building and reattaching method of a synthetic metal chip into a printed circuit board part that isn't soldered down and is replaceable by automatic printing control made by a shared measuring chip bridge machine that is giving to prior specified dimensions of metrics and universally accepted christopher g brown

10512 universal permeasurement bonding and soldering the pre measured circuit socket flashblue.gif

10513 universal bonding agent part that accepts a specified dimension of micro chip for processing or storage etc also known as a socket for a socket bonded solder christopher g brown

10514 global recycles market exchange and welfare for the environment is a monetary substance recycle exchange for the world of today tomorrow and the future and exchange of solids starches gases and more for sale and recycling as well as patrol for safe contaminates and bio hazards as a legal from of trade christopher g brown

10515 assistance and acceptance of over due taxes as a forgive and forget income status is a means to fight for people who work but do not make enough to pay back taxes and new taxes and a separated income bracket that provides a substitute planning verses fines or criminal punishment a credential workmanship

10516 magnetic key encrypted attached technology device interface storage for data and processors

10517 enscribble stacked level micro channel architecture processors and solid state processors replaceable technology per a attached technology mega sata

10518 qfl cubit function language is a specified architecture solid state specific software written language that is transformed by a function written chip that makes the written data function after written to

10519 mqfl magnetic cubit function language is a specified architecture solid state specific software written language that is transformed by a function written chip that makes the written data function after written to magnetically

10520 pqfl photo cubit function language is a specified architecture solid state specific software written language that is transformed by a function written chip that makes the written data function after written to photogenically

10521 diamond emulsion printing for silicon graphic chips and transistor state data operation circuits is the laser and plasma use of a finely focused layer of solution that makes a connected circuit of printing possible with a synthesized doped carbon diamond solution ink

10522 optical data layers in transparent color cycles and luminescence using a color sequence to translate a higher data rate and activate phosphorescent and ultra violet materials

10523 printed circuit board printing by stencil layers and photo emulsion plasma bonding over silica to make a connection on a larger scale even smaller

10524 layer of insulation to connected intermittent silica linking to a printed circuit board printing by stencil layers and photo emulsion plasma bonding over silica to make a connection on a larger scale even smaller

10525 embedded hyperistic chips and processors that hold inside a layer of insulation to connected intermittent silica linking to a printed circuit board printing by stencil layers and photo emulsion plasma bonding over silica to make a connection on a larger scale even smaller

10526 how would anyone control artificial intelligence so that it is not a ready made corruption of control meaning intelligence in itself is uncontrollable via the old proverb of apple of knowledge and history personal opinion of the fight of any intelligence that is supersynthetic and binomial incorrect in assessment of morality and negative reality ai should be a banned practice and modified into a

10527 who goes to jail or becomes fined over a problem with an artificially driven car and or death or accident how would anyone control artificial intelligence so that it is not a ready made corruption of control meaning intelligence in itself is uncontrollable via the old proverb of apple of knowledge and history personal opinion of the fight of any intelligence that is supersynthetic and binomial incorrect in assessment of morality and negative reality ai should be a banned practice and modified into a supersituational programmable software

10528 instead of artificially stupidity intelligence why don't they work on real issues like terrorism and airplane wrecks or the traffic we have to go through every day just to get to where we want don't steal my inventions and sweat my equity this is a wasted time and wrongfully spent money companies that fund the ai should be pointed out for unintelligent intelligence

10529 shipping on a drone front needs all the fixes that any other delivery path would acquire with permission a new travel rout with drone preferences

10530 safety issues and control of pathway control properties legal trade and international processing as shipping on a drone front needs all the fixes that any other delivery path would acquire with permission a new travel rout with drone preferences functions of an everyday operating shipping company with information technicians and software writers an all other needs

10531 logistical managers and shipping interested insurance making any drone liable shipping made right

10532 drone shipping non operating artificial intelligence driven system managed cloud preference and interest made good to ban the waste of non binomial if statements

10533 written cubit functions by size of the data on a given chip's architecture meaning that if the chip is a data driven nano meters then the cubit could be or less written by size meters and the same for a chip written in a nano meter depth of focus in optical measurements of cubits

10534 help line for any given issue and abuse mental or drug crisis being there as a cost safe alternative to police this would be a pre extreme non emergency health hotline that could elevate the police as a or similar dial code for health issues

10535 marijuana cessation and the caffeine pill using a positive for a past negative by tolerances and over balanced technique of chemistry

10536 protecting yourself from a bad fad think realistically hold your fights and always protect your rights be happy know that help is a place and you can always get there from here know that some are good and some are not control auto content at any cost especially if it may loose value on your brand name managers templates for rules against false news and hypothetical

10537 negative information managers as a title for the architect who writes the rules against false news and hypothetical as a software

10538 a vague statement in even number parts

10539 gas station runoff reservoir for environment for safety water treatment and river friendly filters

10540 cell tower time share is to buy property and rights to broadcast for a fee and make money

10541 rebirth of local private companies energy generating infrastructure focus technology franchise based on demand rules and time shares

10542 ultra violet led wall to ultra violet solar green nano metric wave receiving cells to generate electricity by emitting more ultraviolet energy than consuming in a energy cycle of send and receive

10543 lens magnified and focused ultra violet led wall to green solar crystal send and receive as a synthetic electra photosynthesis

10544 lens magnified and focused infrared led wall to green solar crystal send and receive as a synthetic electra photosynthesis

10545 approved small munitions of electric generating stores and subscribers

10546 medical suit and marijuana legal state anti trust to un support the marijuana fed funded states why should different states support other states

10547 colored lens magnified and focused infrared led wall to green solar crystal send and receive as a synthetic electra photosynthesis

10548 uv or luminescence colored lens magnified and focused infrared led wall to green solar crystal send and receive as a synthetic electra photosynthesis

10549 multiplied uv or luminescence colored lens magnified and focused infrared led wall to green solar crystal send and receive as a synthetic electra photosynthesis

10550 this into a light tunnel of amped reflected focused solar energy multiplied uv or luminescence colored lens magnified and focused infrared led wall to green solar crystal send and receive as a synthetic electra photosynthesis

10551 directed and fiber optic reflected focused solar energy multiplied uv or luminescence colored lens magnified and focused infrared led wall to green solar crystal send and receive as a synthetic electra photosynthesis

10552 oscillating and inverted by redirected and fiber optic reflected focused solar energy multiplied uv or luminescence colored lens magnified and focused infrared led wall to green solar crystal send and receive as a synthetic electra photosynthesis

10553 unconstitutional radical increments in perspective to any known issue granted by a process of multiple courts excluding the one and only court of any such state or federal system allotted to change any other court terms

10554 in case of a state of dysfunction of the former functioning laws shall be recommitted to the legislation and government shall continue as previously stated

10555 monopoly suited situation of control in unsafe circumstances as well as the issues of per citizen inventor verses the corporation of unincorporated inability to serve stop and dis assist as a means to help issues of infringement in any right

10556 intellectual property service is a branch of government that takes the service of intellectual property and dues of monetary issuance as a new and joined idea branch of rights and property to help the income and advancement of proprietary capitalism of the united states of america to assist inventors where the and patent offices differentiate

10557 large drone pilot operated shipping crafts that are controlled at a navigation headquarters with margin able software to insure delivery

10558 drone pilot signal wave and code controlled actions of safe navigation and encrypted communication from pilot to drone

10559 approved levels of flight security for any drone shipping piloted and non piloted software driven means

10560 software only driven drone shipping operations and communications with auto navigation

10561 software only driven drone shipping operations and communications with flight control parables possibilities and corrections and including improvised attended interception in probable cause

10562 flight paths of protection from drone traffic and flight control signal repeaters in a cellular flight pattern

10563 foreign war locally driven weapon holding drone war landcraft and aircraft as well as watercraft for a safe death less war

10564 making the cloud today on one server as in a cubit written at will connections in micro cloud computing making a system on chip a wireless and hard line data send and receive intent to send with wireless ac and a hard line to receive data or verses in terms at change in software as though there is a grid flash memory system chassis with the intent to be an entire cloud in a microscopic form only in systems

10565 making the cloud today on one server as in a cubit written at will connections in micro cloud computing making a system on chip a wireless and hard line data send and receive intent to send with wireless ac and a hard line to receive data or verses in terms at change in software as though there is a grid flash memory system chassis with the intent to be an entire cloud in a microscopic form only in systems miniature inclusive cloud architecture software

10566 to change the cloud subscriptions into an derogatory of abuse of sales interest to say that cloud subscriptions are wrong and untrue in the cost of ownership

10567 free to sue the part of government that helps people who need compensation who are unable to see the right power of law branch for improper use of intellectual property abuse and theft
10568 a formal submitter of s infringement based on the intent to use with out proper or patent rights platform based on comma separated value spreadsheet
10569 a free to file online court system that works on merit and perspectives on interest
10570 forms with the probono contingency in attendance would be to file for free but support the people who put effort by a percent of earnings
10571 focused laser to amplified reflective tunnel solar energy and process of light by multiplying the mass and energy of any light source as a laser to magnify the out come of energy
10572 multiple focused laser to amplified reflective tunnel solar energy and process of light by multiplying the mass and energy of any light source as a laser to magnify the out come of energy
10573 see saw action hydro pumping valve electric generation and infinite unstopped water engine taking a current force and not stopping that energy but making a symbiotic source of energy
10574 see saw action synthetic gas pumping valve electric generation and infinite force fulcrum engine taking a current force and not stopping that energy but making a symbiotic source of energy where one force over comes the other one and repeats
10575 large ocean platform of aero see saw action valve electric generation and infinite force fulcrum engine taking a current force and not stopping that energy but making a symbiotic source of energy where one force over comes the other one and repeats
10576 open chip design library can be a right feed on chip designs and configurations to improve the processor and the advancement of technology itself
10577 scribeable chip design library can be a right feed on chip designs and configurations to improve the processor and the advancement of technology itself
10578 scribeable chip design can be a unlocked blank chip based on focused layers of data on chip for function ambled for on chip designs and configurations to improve the processor and the advancement of technology itself
10579 write enabled un scribe chip design would be a un written chip that could be written to and can be a unlocked blank chip based on focused layers of data on chip for function ambled for on chip designs and configurations to improve the processor and the advancement of technology itself
10580 radio data signal operations in cellular circumstances of wave properties and the inherited secured pci/m/flash radio tuner for data
10581 areal flash server cloud that stores tickets of packets in the cell tower as compact flash micro super high compact data
10582 areal flash server cloud that stores a processing and acceleration factor of signal in the cell tower as compact flash micro super high compact
10583 aerial flash server cloud that stores data is encrypted as well as distributed into a faster radio directed cell tower with a communicated operating system with usage and inclusive data distribution
10584 aerial flash server cloud that stores data is encrypted as well as distributed into a faster radio directed cell tower with a communicated operating system with usage and inclusive

data distribution to a command center and then multiplied signals
10585 network looped all incorporated communication signals in a plural cubit signal scheme would be a multitude of signals inside a group of signals echoing a batch of previous signals to continue a wave of data
10586 a mechanical access signal processing station that answers and computes processing of communication packets and pluralizes them into a echoing batch of signals
10587 secure and amplified echoing batch receiver and encoder for incorporated communication signals in a plural cubit signal scheme
10588 chip writing drive in accordance to a blank solid state synthetic metal processor with socket type preference contact points for interface
10589 blank billets for chip writing drive in accordance to a blank solid state synthetic metal processor with socket type preference for soldering or fusing boards as well as incorporated or replaceable sockets
10590 a secured or profitable solution for chip design and acceleration as well as to load and print chip architecture in a printer software interface with a chip writing drive in accordance to a blank solid state synthetic metal processor with socket type preference
10591 open out doors chassis mod is to enable a single cell or multi cell device operate permanently out side by routed power or solar powered operations liquid contact cooling and grounded transistors capacitors and completed shock resistant grounds
10592 open out doors chassis mod memory/ground is to enable a single cell or multi cell device operate permanently out side by routed power or solar powered operations liquid contact cooling and grounded transistors capacitors and completed shock resistant grounds
10593 open out doors chassis mod self adjusting climate control is to enable a single cell or multi cell device operate permanently out side by routed power or solar powered operations liquid contact cooling and grounded transistors capacitors and completed shock resistant grounds
10594 corn gas thinner perspective and the foresight to see that the differences in ethanol and gasoline are in consistency and burn rationality in order to improve alternate fuels
10595 a plasticized combination gasoline made from sodium and petroleum
10596 a combustion engine with an alternate high ethanol intake and bi burn rationality with larger viscosity engineering modified to take a higher percent of ethanol
10597 corn gas central perspective and the foresight to see that natural burn synthetic made corn gas can and could burn at a zero level of pollutants in according to the epa
10598 pi by rail generator using the rotation of rail wheels to generate current to store on railway car by the study of pi
10599 retrofit added rail generator using the rotation of rail wheels to generate current to store on railway car
10600 depot service drop for retrofit added rail generator using the rotation of rail wheels to generate current to store on railway car and would be a good alternative for automation and robotics
10601 common industrial size rechargeable batteries for retrofit added cycle generator using the rotation of x wheels to generate current to store on x
10602 encrypted phone service that is for government
10603 encrypted phone service that is for military
10604 encrypted phone service that is for public

10605 dot gov a verified news channel from the us government book twit
10606 official branch of news for the government as s patents and legalities and suits with holdings and returns
10607 narcotic information agency is the proposal of an entity that would watch record and track illegal narcotics in an important information tracking module of police and protection for the greater good of our country
10608 private narcotic information agency is the proposal of an entity that would watch record and track illegal narcotics in an important information tracking module of police and protection for the greater good of mankind
10609 mental illness derived from narcotics including lsd is the known cause of many induced chemical imbalances to correct any such change of a long period of time would be to induce an alternative state of wellness as another chemical balance to correct the first balance over time this is concluded with out of balance and in balance times of medication and wellness a study of my own kind
10610 to admit that the united states narcotic problem would be easier to overcome would be anti marijuana gatewaydrug lockdown to prepare for a conclusive issue of illegal status of drug use look into the past problems and sue the president for his veto of the issue on any occurrence
10611 retro fit industrial truck transmission attached axle line rotary electrical generator for parttime hybrid trucks and long haulers with batteries or storage of current
10612 argon or hydrogen plasma chip etching by neon on rhodium bedding under and over layered chip printing all or parts
10613 under and over layered blanks for writing purpose and laying the path to write the functions with software innate
10614 under and over stacked layered blanks for writing purpose and laying the path to write the functions with software innate locking and pressing together
10615 power by alternate point of energy torque slip by extended cam shaft would translate as a slip and grip when needed part of any motorized engine that has an alternative shaft of torque for another source of power if needed a dual performance shaft if you will
10616 power by more than two points of entry to add in any such power by alternative point of energy force method
10617 battery that incorporates the use of an atwill performance and storage with an added electrical generator and recycle
10618 gas powered hybrid alternative point of energy torque slip cam
10619 gas start and hybrid long run alternative highway mileage fuel economy method is when the start is the majority controlled by combustion fuel and the highway gears are controlled by electricity methods
10620 gas start and hybrid long run alternative highway mileage transmission is when the start is the majority controlled by combustion fuel and the highway gears are controlled by electricity methods
10621 gas start and hybrid long run alternative highway mileage fuel economy method is when the start is the majority controlled by combustion fuel and the highway gears are controlled by electricity methods with each gear a different volt and torque
10622 long run alternative highway mileage voltage economy method is when transmission gears are controlled by electricity methods with each gear a different volt and torque

10623 vertical and embedded chip stilts to branch layered under and over stacked layered blanks to add to a multiple layered processing chip or storage
10624 nano related myriad layers of pressing alignment in branch layered over and under stacked layered blanks to add to the building of a layered processing chip
10625 multi layered processing chip is a nano related myriad layers of pressing alignment in branch layered over and under stacked layered blanks to add to the building of a layered processing chip
10626 future of less open software and the concurrent topics that it will hold such as a fee based operation time and subscription updates
10627 myriad nano layer built magnified transistors bipolar transistor and grounded emitter
10628 myriad nano layer built magnified amplifier and compressor
10629 myriad nano layer built magnified resistors quantum and relative
10630 myriad nano layer built magnified capacitors and fuses in a sequence of build
10631 aftermarket hybrid fuel thinner and formulator that will take a higher level of ethanol and percentage it to your specific model of car make and run longer and more economy friendly
10632 utility permit and cell tower franchise reseller authorization diy broadcasting
10633 above board solid state threading
10634 end state above board links and inputs are intermittent paths on the circuit board that provide input and through put
10635 board stacking brackets and board to board ports with tapes and transports using a hypotheisis board off load through put
10636 government do not share consumer information list is a list that prohibits the sale of user information and logs
10637 user browser encryption is the end user controlled browser session as a controlled level of security of information
10638 job bot that studies trends and properties in sales and up coming sale for product research
10639 job bot that makes assumptions based on popularity trends and formulates new products
10640 job bot that sends email to problem accounts with options and help situations
10641 job bot that asks for feedback from positive and negative accounts and uses that information in service
10642 directive software that is an inter operable cloud software that routes the fastest out path and in path of data in the cloud to improve performance and assets allocation
10643 virtual data center design forecast software to build a virtual cohesive center with proper estimations
10644 educational planned curriculum forecast software to build a schedule and studied learning with proper estimations
10645 sheet virtual manufacturing cost and turn around design forecast software to build a virtual cohesive plan with proper estimations
10646 automated import business cost and payments sheet expenses and asset value real time scores and the learning from predictions and history software
10647 system on chip and the divided parts of a one system add in board are controlled by bios and eufi properties that are extensive and individually controlling in each circumstance

of operation
10648 inclusive system on chip board and part controller could function as a bed operating controller that gives multiple instructions to each sub system on a board and help directive options for processing
10649 in a unlooped system on chip the properties of processing could be controlled by a network router or a in and out send and receive connected protocol of any kind to work separated and un connected in a secured isolation mode
10650 to ship cloud backups to the client on record able media for recovery
10651 programmable chip software and the opportunity to make a chip into a performance enhancer such as a co appliance or main appliance or second appliance for processing or for storage or routing
10652 vector data path routing direction chips that tell data where and what to go or perform propagation
10653 system on chip and the divided parts of a one system add in board are controlled by flash back dos and parameters that are extensive and individually controlling in each circumstance of operation
10654 to encode cubits in a series of parameters that are extensive and individually controlling in each circumstance of operation and as well as to auto encode written software with software for example a series of events written by software that writes software
10655 embedded software language per part in a stored cubit translator which could control more bits per channel and more code per device
10656 scribble insert or image insert to search engine for results across the internet and likeness
10657 fossilized nuclear waste and the renewable study of micro wave negative and positive nuclear reactive waste
10658 microwaved nuclear waste and the renewable study of micro wave negative and positive nuclear reactive waste recycle and recharging uranium and non depleted uranium
10659 operating system mode do not shut down and run specific programs
10660 visual search data shapes and curves symbols and references library
10661 ocr for objects drawings and images including the combination of symbols and conjunctions
10662 image puzzle translation software
10663 electric aeronautics and pilot friendly energy efficient software
10664 electric aeronautics and the electric aided recycle magnetic turbine is a spinning and rotation generate electra magnetic jet propulsion
10665 electric aeronautics and scale able drone shipping enterprise as an economic solution
10666 electric aeronautics and direct current electric generating engines powered by lithium drum battery stations
10667 shaping chips to reflect amplify and duplicate processing objects inside the chip
10668 electra magnetic compressed jet propulsion is a software controlled on and off of electra magnetic motors that can turn propellers in a compressed modular sequence to build a jet action of energy
10669 electra magnetic compressed jet propulsion is a software controlled on and off of electra magnetic motors that can turn propellers in a compressed modular sequence to build a jet action of energy electra magnetic compressed jet software

10670 to prove that artificial intelligence is un secured and dangerous we can look at the responsibility of consequences first and foremost in pre examination routines of what if my car gets hit by a robot or what if my kid gets run over by a robot what happens to the operator and owner of either or in any circumstance and to know that there are and will be rules and law suits
10671 to prove that the free pop art is in fact a infringement
10672 to note that engineering a wireless network could be easy as plug and play but no company makes a plug and play school wifi network plug and play wifi network pre configured and shipped for laymen technology
10673 laymen technology smart home lights and sound along side pre programmed television internet and phone plugin and use configurations ready out of the box
10674 a wireless pre configured room by room and service bundle software built smart all in one service for home
10675 to take dumbing it down more than anything ever has a wireless pre configured solution of commercial information technology service that incorporates all the services needed to work an office of today for any company as a all in one service for work
10676 phone back up chip that stores numbers and important codes
10677 computer back up chip that stores account information and important authorization codes
10678 phone distress chip that can send an sos to a qualified number
10679 application that helps connect emergency information to help for people who don't currently have an internet connection
10680 an app that sends domestic abuse or mental health related and drug abuse issues to a counselor chat and the proper help in case of emergencies a specific need for a subtle conclusion affordable in any counsel situation related to a semi non emergency helpline
10681 solid state synthetic metal soldered on motherboard ram and alternate accelerated memory by software
10682 solid state synthetic metal un soldered on mother board replaceable removable bios architectural chip
10683 sodium nickel acid design for a larger battery size in anticipation on recycle and reuse operations included by design
10684 a secured intelligent business app that sends important confidential information to itself and no one else by finger print proof and encrypted messaging
10685 a webbot network of data applications searching for the meaning of artificial intelligence con and pro
10686 the negative conclusion foresight of any such research on artificial intelligence and the effects on every day life for humans and the difference between real state of the art and self driving cars etc
10687 magnetic propulsion engine an electronically controlled on and off magnet engine generating torque and force
10688 magnetic propulsion torque an electronically controlled on and off magnet engine generating torque and force
10689 magnetic torque transmission and accelerating interface to control the speed and rpm
10690 magnetic propulsion torque turbine and calibration of generating electricity from a chain reaction offset

10691 humor slander judgment case of lies and public media broadcasting
10692 electra magnetic torque converter and acceleration board and software as a clutch operator
10693 multiple coiled electrically powered magnets for the electra magnetic torque converter and acceleration board and software as a clutch operator
10694 electra magnetic cycled passing charge of a magnet is when every turn the magnet there could be other magnets that connects a passing circuit generating a current
10695 magnetic engine and the electra coiled speed control by automatic transforming voltage regulator
10696 wind mill and the recycle electric generator that provides a push to any such greater movement to be accompanied by a multiplied series of passing engines and coils
10697 combustion and the push motor to power a engine that in part connected to a more powerful engine
10698 developer software driven central processing unit would be controlled by software verses the parameters hard wired
10699 developer software for a software driven central processing unit would be controlled by software verses the parameters hard wired
10700 chip operator and compute magnetic transmission for torque and propulsion of device controlling a stationary over controlled passing magnets that provide any such current
10701 mini wireless chip operatored and compute magnetic transmission for torque and propulsion of device controlling a stationary over controlled passing magnets that provide any such current controlled with a wireless connection for torque magnitude intensity
10702 ecology scale landscaping will change deserts into jungles by that mountain of debree built by synthesizing a mountain and valley precipitation valve
10703 enterprise art server and the intent to create and master the digital frontier in a normal server used as a machine for not intended but built intentions the translated definition in a simple name thus made as a digitalartserver regiment of computers known as servers
10704 denotation of any such specified platform specific as to route a version of any operating system as a true role in a non pragmatic cloud but intentionally a specified role in a company operating system for example my mother was a nurse and later in her career they tried to make her into an information technical nurse but what they should have done was hired a tune of information engineers to better transition the paper trail nursing into the big data volume of data that could be received as a smart app on any such phone or bar code incorporated nursing instrument of data
10705 medical aid bar code instrument of inventory and patient data input for wifi and accordance of any such links into a information ecosystem
10706 legal aid and bar code instrument of contracts and legal data input for wifi or data dump and accordance of any such links into a local or official legal information ecosystem
10707 legal aid and bar code software of contracts and legal data input for wifi or data dump and accordance of any such links into a local or official legal information ecosystem
10708 medical aid bar code software of inventory and patient data input for wifi and accordance of any such links into a information ecosystem
10709 compact battery and wifi translator for the smart shoe is a wifi solution that transmits data to the receiver for consideration
10710 magnetic shield barrier for the magnetic torque engine as to accord any such other

magnetic interference
10711 the updated nation of banks and liens as a wealth of ownership in percent of the entire active and stable economy is a data base of ownership percents snip
10712 public verses a proprietary ownership of privileged operation is a data center that operates with little out side or un commercial activity snip
10713 a mobile war data center and the operations prior to any such consequences of a war zone known as a new data war with drone and air based weapons snip_
10714 the law to compete the retread situation of unsafe driving and open arms of retread ding semi truck tires in accordance with a safe means snip
10715 drone war remote weapons system infantry low close to ground altitude and the operations prior to any such consequences of a war zone known as a new data war with drone and air based weapons
10716 short remote drone virtual reality warfare and an application controlled war drone based weapons
10717 satellite by cell
10718 vr military grade fault less warfare drone controller software and hardware for a new drone war for drone based weapons
10719 self destructing military drone based weapons
10720 drone specific artillery with a gps location driven drone based weapons
10721 drone color of lights to show what side it's on drone based weapons
10722 drone war is a bad guy gone and good guy life saved for a drone based weapons war the value of life is priceless technology can be created to fight war on our terms and save lives with or without a warning shot alarm or physical watching presence
10723 drone warfare can end war and make a safe place for freedom as we know it police driven drone will make a unmanageable place a safe place
10724 drone digital camouflage for drone based weapons
10725 drone attack with non lethal chemical stunning weapons
10726 hover drone with short land air and sea capabilities for the military war effort with weapons and target cameras
10727 playing field embedded wifi for the smart shoe and training purpose as well as real play
10728 replaceable and customize able parts for the smart shoe including chips sensors and connectors as well as and training purpose as well as real play
10729 replaceable and custom software that records distance force and occurrences as well as places in time as well as and training purpose as well as real play
10730 grid array tray of solid state operators is a column and row defined access point of processors and chips
10731 automated robotic operated cell tower elevator that accesses the components in a arranged method of distribution and installation like a robotic spider for cell communication equipment snip_
10732 archive of common robotic motions and fixtures is a library of skills that help any or some robotic tools operate
10733 defense and war related remote any operable aircraft control system is a system that manually shifts controls and manipulates an aircraft by retro fit levers switches and indicators by a remote access system
10734 defense and war related software operation is a semi retro fix of software controlled

previously known as manual operation to change the on board to remote access system of operations completely non personal aircraft to operate

10735 defense and war related remote any operable boat or submersible control system is a system that manually shifts controls and manipulates an boat or water craft by retro fit levers switches and indicators by a remote access system

10736 defense and war related software operation is a semi retro fix of software controlled previously known as manual operation to change the on board to remote access system of operations completely non personal water craft to operate

10737 defense and war related remote any operable land craft control system is a system that manually shifts controls and manipulates an land craft by retro fit levers switches and indicators by a remote access system

10738 defense and war related software operation is a semi retro fix of software controlled previously known as manual operation to change the on board to remote access system of operations completely non personal land craft to operate

10739 intelligent warship is a lifeless battle ship that is an artificial war machine that wins wars defends freedom and kills bad guys

10740 drone launching warship intelligent warship is a lifeless battle ship that is an artificial war machine that wins wars defends freedom and kills bad guys

10741 infantry drone launching warship intelligent warship is a lifeless battle ship that is an artificial war machine that wins wars defends freedom and kills bad guys

10742 drone lost badge is a tracking chip to help locate and track war data and keeps the drone from function if removed that is an artificial war machine that wins wars defends freedom and kills bad guys

10743 war data is a ultra fast format used to save lives by the examples performed in the cloud to help defend freedom and dedicate sponsorship to help end war that is an artificial war machine that wins wars defends freedom and kills bad guys

10744 war drone software interface that detonates bombs shoots a gun and all works to help defend freedom and dedicate sponsorship to help end war that is an artificial war machine that wins wars defends freedom and kills bad guys

10745 the need for patented hypothetical theory rights is a common missed opportunity based on will and why as in a information back up right protected by schematics and red tape a duplicate protection enabled by nature

10746 ed method information is not a legal binding attribute and should be

10747 a running circle definition of what has been said is in fact a no answer for example if someone were to propose a question to a branch of government and the return answer was a previously stated circular statement not a yes or no answer by definition the answer is no

10748 a misleading running circle definition of what has been said is in fact a no answer for example if someone were to propose a question to a branch of government and the return answer was a previously stated circular statement not a yes or no answer by definition the answer is yes

10749 a hypothetical definition included as intellectual property is the mission of a duplicate and patent case filed in both manners

10750 a chip written and in a state of rewritable status that can be written to and then rewritten in any sort of language for function and purpose not only standard capacity random access memory

10751 a write once chip that has a state of permanence and will only function as a second or first capacity full function chip with architecture written by software
10752 the language of permanent or temporary written function cubits and the as the written code and switches as conductors that transpose into a computing functional chip
10753 the intent to create any such chip library or write and store functional architecture for sale or for open access
10754 the intent to create any such chip library or write and store functional architecture for sale or for open access including the scale of architecture as the written language code
10755 to understand dangerous technology and the anti climatic autonomous era of unexpected danger the intent to improve not endanger the obvious state of a space elevator vision of autonomous intent to catapult caca and non reality of foresight
10756 to understand dangerous technology and the anti climatic autonomous era of unexpected danger the road verses the air for travel aeroautonomous
10757 to understand dangerous technology and the anti climatic autonomous era of unexpected danger landing pads for the autonomous air drones with automated load and unload robots
10758 to understand dangerous technology and the anti climatic autonomous era of unexpected danger security travel and cloud based drone traffic control flight issuance
10759 to understand dangerous technology and the anti climatic autonomous era of unexpected danger the signal control federal communication level of drone and non commercial travel patterns
10760 to understand dangerous technology and the anti climatic autonomous era of unexpected danger the signal control federal communication level of drone and commercial travel patterns
10761 blue tooth security and the non elevated signal of secure encoded blue tooth encryption
10762 aircraft take over software for mission critical control
10763 radio specified alpha channel is the intent to focus out a specified communication with a single operative with the intent to direct with out interference of other channels during communication say for example a unit of battle or communication line is specified by one channel and every one on that same channel can hear each other at the same time verses hearing each other at separate times
10764 radio specified alpha channel software is the intent to focus out a specified communication with a single operative with the intent to direct with out interference of other channels during communication say for example a unit of battle or communication line is specified by one channel and every one on that same channel can hear each other at the same time verses hearing each other at separate times
10765 radio specified alpha channel hardware is the intent to focus out a specified communication with a single operative with the intent to direct with out interference of other channels during communication say for example a unit of battle or communication line is specified by one channel and every one on that same channel can hear each other at the same time verses hearing each other at separate times
10766 radio specified alpha channel encrypted software is the intent to focus out a specified communication with a single operative with the intent to direct with out interference of other channels during communication say for example a unit of battle or communication line

is specified by one channel and every one on that same channel can hear each other at the same time verses hearing each other at separate times

10767 soft silica chip insulator film that would enable vertical chip branching and layers of no conducting parts of chips in a fashion to layer other chip parts to conduct a pseudo balanced and compressed level of conductivity

10768 vertical chip branching and layers of conducting parts of chips in a fashion to layer other chip parts to conduct a pseudo balanced and compressed level of conductivity

10769 vertical hyper threading chip parts to conduct a pseudo balanced and compressed level of conductivity

10770 vertical chip design software and the congruent chips made from stacking and vertical aligned methods

10771 spindled printed vertical chip layered computer controlled and measured in nano myriads a link of layers to build with

10772 single level chip platform print and stack conductors that match a sphere and link like a socket and drive

10773 multiple level chip assembly to print and stack construction chips in a link and exchange processing manner

10774 software written multiple level chip assembly to print and stack construction chips in a link and exchange processing manner by cubit cell and cubit grid

10775 blank chips for the software written multiple level chip assembly to print and stack construction chips in a link and exchange processing manner by cubit cell and cubit grid

10776 the software that will write the software written multiple level chip assembly to print and stack construction chips in a link and exchange processing manner by cubit cell and cubit grid

10777 the hardware that helps software written multiple level chip assembly to print and stack construction chips in a link and exchange processing manner by cubit cell and cubit grid

10778 the connected hardware and software that software written multiple level chip assembly to print and stack construction chips in a link and exchange processing manner by cubit cell and cubit grid

10779 additional socket and secondary level chips of a software written multiple level chip assembly to print and stack construction chips in a link and exchange processing manner by cubit cell and cubit grid

10780 intermittent synthetic metal and oscillating cascading silica non conductive spindled printed vertical chip layered computer controlled and measured in nano myriads a link of layers to build with

10781 intermittent synthetic conductive gel and oscillating cascading silica carbon insulated spindled printed vertical chip layered computer controlled and measured in nano myriads a link of layers to build with

10782 cascading printing reproduction is the interprinted method of the conductive property and the insulator to generate a conductive chip

10783 after the print and the process of end doping of equal molecular weight conductive and insulation printing of conductive paths and non conductive insulator in a vertical and arranged manner of myriads is essentially giving conductive working properties

10784 three dimensional printed circuit design software that grows in a multiple complex of parts and structure of a place to conduct and process

10785 in chip manufacturing and printing the property printing of any scale by the materials density and ionic conductive relationship is the absolute of any progress to relate
10786 gold metal conductive and silica zircon non doped circuit printing and design to assemble
10787 many layered processing cores aligned and centered vertically for conductive repetitive processing
10788 many layered and horizontally aligned and stacked for conductive repetitive processing
10789 a liberation statement such as a doctrine that plainly stating the purpose and consistences of a prove means of valuable to itself in a means not a current to accurately describe why some technology may not be suitable for safe public occurrences or to prove why this technology should be used
10790 the anti liberation statement such as any doctrine that sates why this given technology should be use
10791 synthetic metal conductive and silica zircon negatively doped circuit printing and design to assemble
10792 metal conductive ion circuits and silica zircon positively doped circuit printing and design to assemble
10793 carbon ash suet and a purified carbon electrical doping technology is a mesh printed object of carbon and laser printed to rasterize transistors and create a circuit to process
10794 inline double triplet express hyper threading and the mesh vector to create a circuit to process
10795 intertwined thread to send the same signal to multiple places and conduct a vector resolution in sync motions
10796 intertwined hyperthread to send the same signal to multiple places and conduct a vector resolution in sync motions
10797 intertwined double triplet hyperthread to send the same signal to multiple places and conduct a vector resolution in sync motions of processing
10798 a nano printed hyperembedded directional navigation chip that provides the path direction based on a frequency change in the signal like a flashing yellow go when clear light
10799 a nano printed hyperembedded directional navigation chip that provides the path direction based on a frequency change in the signal like a traffic stop light
10800 a nano printed hyperembedded directional navigation chip that provides the path direction based on a frequency change in the signal like a way stop with traffic signs
10801 a nano printed hyperembedded directional navigation chip that provides the path direction based on a frequency change in the signal like a way stop light intersection
10802 a nano printed hyperembedded directional navigation end that provides the path direction based on a frequency change in the signal like a right or left lane fork in the road
10803 a hyperembedded directional vector coordinate directions is to travel on any such given processor chip and micro board as well as to repeat and loop in a quantified sequence and method on any given fork traffic changes and in any such given directional return vector frequency of travel
10804 a simple beat and pulse of operating code that transforms any such sequence of in and out for a unified measurement of any such arranged pulse of computations
10805 hyper multi directional threading is a simple beat and pulse of operating code that

transforms any such sequence of in and out for a unified measurement of any such arranged pulse of computations

10806 planned disaster is a pre planned satellite crash course of premptive action as a last resort to the beginning of the end of any satellites planned ending and to where to crash why to crash or a gliding crash

10807 satellite landing zone is a owned and operated seek and map a designated place for landing and or crashing gliding or disperse

10808 satellite expiration estimate for atmosphere reentry will help people work with satellites in a new and responsible way to help the space atmosphere environment and all the other costs of satellite orbit concerns

10809 cable tap adjustment port is an information technicians friend when confusing cables at the data center get to be too much and how hope can be gained with the signal generation and the cable tap adjustment port

10810 cable tap adjustment identification signal is an information technicians friend when confusing cables at the data center get to be too much and how hope can be gained with the signal generation and the cable tap adjustment port

10811 a secured password encrypted cable tap adjustment identification signal is an information technicians friend when confusing cables at the data center get to be too much and how hope can be gained with the signal generation and the cable tap adjustment port

10812 a cable tap adjustment reader is an information technicians friend when confusing cables at the data center get to be too much and how hope can be gained with the signal generation and the cable tap adjustment port

10813 a signal improvement repeater is a localized internet or ethernet signal packet provider focus and adjustment of coded sequences and information in a better accelerated format

10814 compressed service provider is a isp data provider that uses a compression ratio for packet delivery

10815 encrypted compressed service provider is a isp data provider that uses a compression ratio for packet delivery

10816 iau is an instructional application unit that tells the ai what to do and how to do it

10817 iau is an instructional application software that tells the ai what to do and how to do it

10818 mission critical application unit mciau is an instructional application software that tells the ai what to do and how to do it with a logical back up and or raid ability to operated code and instructions by architectures

10819 instructional application machine and management is an instructional application software that tells the ai what to do and how to do it with a rom and connected channel to operated code and instructions by architectures

10820 cellular control cloud is a processing cloud communication and accessing rights to process and direct packets to other cell towers at a higher rate of control properties for things like data and file transfers as well as send and receive

10821 software encrypted and accelerated cellular control cloud is a processing cloud communication and accessing rights to process and direct packets to other cell towers at a higher rate of control properties for things like data and file transfers as well as send and receive

10822 hybrid incorporated data signal to cellular expanded network is a internet origin of routing to a particular place of any such packets of information then as soon as the signal comes close enough to the target it will then convert to a wireless signal to broadcast to the receiver

10823 infinite hybrid incorporated data signal to cellular expanded network is a leaping internet origin of routing to a particular place of any such packets of information then as soon as the signal comes close enough to the target it will then convert to a wireless signal to broadcast to the receiver

10824 hybrid incorporated signal protocol is a data service and expanded network access signal protocol is a internet origin of routing to a particular place of any such packets of information then as soon as the signal comes close enough to the target it will then convert to a wireless signal to broadcast to the receiver and back again through a combination routing utility

10825 hybrid incorporated data dedicated rental satellite service and expanded network access signal protocol is a internet origin of routing to a particular place of any such packets of information then as soon as the signal comes close enough to the target it will then convert to a wireless signal to broadcast to the receiver and back again through a combination routing utility

10826 allotted maintenance and design operation is not a given known intelligence and to understand that perpetual scanning may cause over bearing and non acceptable watching is to understand that there should be a kill switch of code to mandate operation and non operation inside any such known data control

10827 data code kill switch agreement and operation adjustment cooperation is the operation agreement that there is a safety concern for data on the service cloud and this may come to a part time outage based on the security of the data there

10828 data code kill switch of unknown ability previously known as friendly vague code and a design designation as a adjustment code

10829 a premptive agreement in a cloud database environment that protects the entity of itself by control and data code kill switch script

10830 a data war or war data premptive agreement in a cloud database environment that protects the entity of itself by control and data code kill switch script cooperation and compliance of no service

10831 a zone not incorporated with data and on a war or war data premptive agreement in a cloud database environment that protects the entity of itself by control and data code kill switch script cooperation and compliance of no service

10832 to use a device where the data packets of the internet and cellular comm has stopped and a radio wave of certain freq is controlled in a zone not incorporated with data and on a war or war data premptive agreement in a cloud database environment that protects the entity of itself by control and data code kill switch script cooperation and compliance of no service

10833 to switch off a zone incorporated with data and on a war or war data premptive agreement in a cloud database environment that protects the entity of itself by control and data code kill switch script cooperation and compliance of no service

10834 answer to a questionable theory by a hypothetical proof may be the hope that people need to find a cure for any know disease or virus

10835 curing a virus disease by viral vaccine may be hope for another kind of artificial virus of a synthetic kind artificial anti virus

10836 a heart worm with parasitic contaminates may be the cure for other diseases with the carrying body of the intent to cure more than one infliction
10837 to point a specific targeted program to a chip or configuration and hardware specific software outright
10838 to ignore the first aim is to aim at the second target first to switch off a network with a virus and then scope and probe the culprit at a second target first
10839 to find the connections that refuse to comply with a non connective network may expose the places of occupied aggressors
10840 starch protein and sugar dna microbiologically printed antibody used to fight disease
10841 printed dna from any known starch or protein microbiologically printed antibody used to fight disease
10842 dna at cg nucleotide printed dna from any known starch or protein microbiologically printed antibody used to fight disease or cancer
10843 dna at cg nucleotide printed dna from any known starch or protein microbiologically printed antibody used to fight disease or cancer positively doped
10844 dna at cg nucleotide printed dna from any known starch or protein microbiologically printed antibody used to fight disease or cancer negatively doped
10845 dna at cg nucleotide printed dna from any known starch or protein microbiologically printed antibody used to fight disease or cancer positively fibrillated refibrillated infibrillated
10846 dna at cg nucleotide printed dna from any known starch or protein microbiologically printed antibody used to fight disease or cancer negatively fibrillated refibrillated infibrillated
10847 national rage helpline and the mental health open hot line phone number and assistance associations patent pending abstract utility _
10848 nicotine narcosis is the unstable inherit reaction to an overdose of nicotine
10849 acute nicotine narcosis is the long term unstable inherit reaction to a continual overdose of nicotine
10850 marijuana use and the health of any such stimulant turned into a constant use where the patient has an addiction base on a series of ups and downs where the drug must maintain a non equal abuse level to be considered at a normal high is also known as a emotional maletrauma
10851 software run program applications for printers that uses nano / pico / triad mixed and formulated biochemical nucleotide to replicate on a recurring smaller intent to cure cancer and disease software for biochemical printers _
10852 software run program applications for printers that uses nano/pico/triad mixed and fromulated biochemical nucleotide to replicate on a recurring smaller intent to cure cancer and disease
10853 a post lactates light solution flush to help cure calcium deposits to prevent cancer
10854 a presentperpost lactates light salt solution check to help clean calcium deposits to prevent cancer
10855 a presentperpost lactates nonalkaline solution check to help clean calcium deposits to prevent cancer
10856 a combination presentperpost lactates nonalkaline solution and ultrasonic abrasive shock treatment to break and to help clean calcium deposits to prevent cancer
10857 at home kit to use combination presentperpost lactates nonalkaline solution and ultrasonic abrasive shock treatment to break and to help clean calcium deposits to prevent

cancer
10858 doors are a important secure private office operating system that is office inside an office that works with firewalls and fences for people who operate in tiers and teams to work on productive security means that are sensitive and need doors and keys on a professional logged and improved structure for government military private offices and a means to identify issues that people create
10859 secure private badges for using signatures in a secure work place called doors are a important secure private office operating system that is office inside an office that works with firewalls and fences for people who operate in tiers and teams to work on productive security means that are sensitive and need doors and keys on a professional logged and improved structure for government military private offices and a means to identify issues that people create
10860 an add in card memory or hardware that makes a hard line like connection that holds issues and hard place port instructions and memory for a secure private badges for using signatures in a secure work place called doors are a important secure private office operating system that is office inside an office that works with firewalls and fences for people who operate in tiers and teams to work on productive security means that are sensitive and need doors and keys on a professional logged and improved structure for government military private offices and a means to identify issues that people create
10861 an artistic judgment to copy and cure is the obvious mission of any nucleotide printed microorganism
10862 dna and nucleotide historical library and ownership per dna finger print solution _
10863 a presentperpost lactates light salt solution check to help clean calcium deposits to prevent cancer _
10864 software run program applications for printers that uses nano / pico / triad mixed and formulated biochemical nucleotide to replicate on a recurring smaller intent to cure cancer and disease formulated biochemical nucleotide dcfbc _page_
10865 software run program applications for printers that uses nano / pico / triad mixed and formulated biochemical nucleotide to replicate on a recurring smaller intent to cure cancer and disease software for biochemical printers dcfbc _page_
10866 marijuana use and the health of any such stimulant turned into a constant use where the patient has an addiction base on a series of ups and downs where the drug must maintain a non equal abuse level to be considered at a normal high is also known as a emotional maletrauma _
10867 to multiply the conductive threads in a insulated chip levels made from of with a coherence of any insulation method of stacking horizontal or vertical chip organization to build a larger chip also said as to make a non conductive layer with small outer inner conductive measures while operation is possible with vertical threads _
10868 in a insulated chip levels made from of with a coherence of any insulation method of stacking horizontal or vertical chip organization to build a larger chip also said as to make a non conductive layer with small outer inner conductive measures while operation is possible with vertical threads _
10869 in a insulated chip levels with a coherence of any insulation method of stacking horizontal or vertical chip organization to build a larger chip also said as to make a non conductive layer with small outer inner conductive measures while operation is possible with

vertical threads and vertical processing and cube processors

10870 cube processors in a insulated chip levels with a coherence of any insulation method of stacking horizontal or vertical chip organization to build a larger chip also said as to make a non conductive layer with small outer inner conductive measures while operation is possible with vertical threads and vertical processing and cube processors

10871 stacked form of many cube processors in a insulated chip levels with a coherence of any insulation method of stacking horizontal or vertical chip organization to build a larger chip also said as to make a non conductive layer with small outer inner conductive measures while operation is possible with vertical threads and vertical processing and cube processors

10872 free orchestrated data routing is a open connected network that travels data based on open frequency bandwidth patent pending abstract utility

10873 a user operated device that enters as your original line and adapts to your connection that inturns blocks all connections and or encrypts or allows connections based on a simple password protocol in another way to say is to secure a networks connection based on a encryption box and also known as a hard line encrypted router firewall box patent pending abstract utility

10874 a software virus company operated device that enters as your original line and adapts to your connection that inturns blocks all connections and or encrypts or allows connections based on a simple password protocol in another way to say is to secure a networks connection based on a encryption box and also known as a hard line encrypted router firewall box patent pending abstract utility _

10875 a software virus company operated device that you can insert data with a secure environment to see the data without risk patent pending abstract utility

10876 a government sponsored software virus company operated network scanning police bot to help find and trace topic of negative nature

10877 a permit to operate and sanction any such privilege of scanning police bot to help find and trace topics of negative nature and danger for man kind

10878 populated bot database the recovery validation for sale of recovered bot data and found information as confirmed data or false data as a trade in economic value or true data

10879 the validity of a data sheet and the value rating for true data and how true the data is at any capacity

10880 satellite service incorporated is a freelance satellite scenario that builds and sells bandwidth on demand as a service for large and small company uses with a permit to render

10881 federal satellite admin satellite service incorporated is a oversee satellite scenario that manages and approves the builds and sales of bandwidth on demand as a service for large and small company uses with a permit to render

10882 a red collar crime is a high ranking official caught or suspected to be wrong in monetary just gain

10883 printed operating system is a version of embedded code that may or may not be changed according to the write function of the system and may be printed during manufacturing

10884 war network unlinking is a unlooped firewall device for security and data integrity in a war data center

10885 election network linking is a unlooped firewall device for security and data integrity in a election data center

10886 network linking chip is a unlooped firewall embedded device for security and data integrity in a data center end start point
10887 pyramid chip scheme is a scaleable multi processor right of way that claims more computing ability per consumer rather than consumer per processors
10888 multiple assignment os
10889 multiple assignment os dcfbc _page_
10890 marijuana is should not be legal due to addiction issues and behavior problems _
10891 wrongful legality of bitcoin due to security invasion and . of any such coin worth or unofficially a money right as to interfere with the united states treasury
10892 options in memory and the memory attachment of a scaled . inch standard drive as a to sata connected accelerator memory drop and find add on's
10893 a chip that holds the proper bios and instruction set for the plugin itself to operate as a fail safe pre occupied set of true plug and play functions in any os and any system on chip meaning if it's not operational it does not operate
10894 to take the block ledger offline from an online state of transactions would secure the worlds trade and commerce around the globe and to end crypt o currency would help the standard trade sanctions for every one
10895 to alternate the current internet as a second internet for commerce and create a default encrypted status as to recreate a secured internet to require a ssl or tss
10896 retro fit smart house switches and connectivity features for traditional homes would include things like a room to room hub and wifi central apps that negotiate lights air conditioning and blinds for privacy even the door security and room itself audio with a one time base to circuit transforming upgradeable port
10897 escape the os update plugin to escape operating system updates permanently or semi choice
10898 data loss and the kill update blanket this is evident of any such blanket consumer rights to agree or not agree with property of any such malicious terms from a known consumer issuance discrepancy
10899 update response company is a secured and devoted complaint and semi responsible negotiating proactive alliance between consumer and the operating system manufacturer
10900 block chain attacks crypt o currency is the attack of software and hardware together to steal
10901 multi drone pilot compensation software is a air and path pi ratio that groups or navigates multiple drones
10902 multi drone pilot compensation hardware is a part that works with air and path pi ratio that groups or navigates multiple drones
10903 stealth multi drone is a radar less and radar proof satellite driven drone
10904 international ip market
10905 software operated and controlled central processing unit as a path to an operation type or person as a personal system operated on a come and go log
10906 automatic software operated and controlled central processing unit as a negotiated per program and app as the needed comp system to the operations
10907 a negotiated batch of pre operated and defined method of hardware as well as a complimentary pre selected operating software per presentation of any combination of system and hardware built to operate in sync as the maximum performance as well as success

adjustments for your data direction
10908 sequential sync and a maximum performance from hardware with the automatic preference to apply the fixes and bottleneck drops with a work ethic to improve performance and software driven hardware os for the cpu
10909 scaleable drone with features and cell communications software for cell to cell drone flight captur
10910 drone cell stations protocol for scaleable drone with features and cell communications network for cell to cell drone flight and land navigation
10911 lost drone safe way map and navigation per satellite route and permits for lost dog drones that can find their way home
10912 cron job flight navigation servers for drone devices is a ping service that directs and corrects any such flight or road travel
10913 cron job flight navigation code and software for devices that work with ping control
10914 cron job flight navigation hardware that incorporates the memory factor of from point a to point b in a compensation mode
10915 anomaly report service is a service that helps artificial devices understand seeds of change and occurrences in the issue of a change as a compensation equation and a reference base for service like a wind pattern change to help wind mills more energy during the windiest part of the day from what direction
10916 anomaly report service is a service hardware and translation equipment that helps artificial devices understand seeds of change and occurrences in the issue of a change as a compensation equation and a reference base for service like a wind pattern change to help wind mills more energy during the windiest part of the day from what direction
10917 anomaly report service is a service software analyzing patterns and statistics that helps artificial devices understand seeds of change and occurrences in the issue of a change as a compensation equation and a reference base for service like a wind pattern change to help wind mills more energy during the windiest part of the day from what direction
10918 dual user add on information applications that work on cache and submission processes is a working rule based program that allows more than one user at a time to use the same work place for example a spread sheet that is incorporated to other sheets and linked by a pseudo data connection and plural mouse movements
10919 multiple user hardware that works with software applications that run on live cache and submission processes is a working rule based program that allows more than one user at a time to use the same work place for example a spread sheet that is incorporated to other sheets and linked by a pseudo data connection and plural mouse movements
10920 watch and see user and plus applications that work on cache and submission processes is a working rule based program that allows more than one user at a time to use the same work place for example a air navigation tower that is interoperable with in an area of operation seeing working and using plural mouse movements commands and operations in formulas
10921 random seed and anomaly report cloud data with dual user and plus applications that work on cache and submission processes is a working rule based program that allows more than one user at a time to use the same work place for example a spread sheet that is incorporated to other sheets and linked by a pseudo data connection and plural mouse movements
10922 diode printed and stacked nano metric parts

10923 hot chip for safety safety chip and sos communication bridge allocation software
10924 global for profit school learning software and tablet interface that will start with ocr textbooks and ed information sale and the room of improvisations in learning processes to help a modern school internet deploy globally and recreate learning on a new level as well as trouble shooting and learning curves in students and problems in software company from ed text to learning and certificate graduates of learning scales
10925 local state wide for profit school learning software and tablet interface that will start with ocr textbooks and ed information sale and the room of improvisations in learning processes to help a modern school internet deploy state wide and recreate learning on a new level as well as trouble shooting and learning curves in students and problems in software company from ed text to learning and certificate graduates of learning scales
10926 free global not for profit school learning software and tablet interface that will start with ocr textbooks and ed information sale and the room of improvisations in learning processes to help a modern school internet deploy globally and recreate learning on a new level as well as trouble shooting and learning curves in students and problems in software company from ed text to learning and certificate graduates of learning scales
10927 ocr and translation meaning software for clear internet learning school software and beyond is a linking between shapes and meaning in a data format language language learning
10928 ocr and translation meaning software for search data and search form engine and beyond is a linking meaning between shapes and meaning in a usage data format language language learning
10929 object and meaning database ocr and translation meaning software for search data and search form engine and beyond is a linking meaning between shapes and meaning in a usage data format language language learning
10930 many objects and meaning database ocr and translation meaning software for search data and search form engine and beyond is a linking meaning between shapes and meaning in a usage data format language language learning
10931 many objects and multiple meaning database ocr and translation meaning software for search data and search form engine and beyond is a linking meaning between shapes and meaning in a usage data format language language learning
10932 ai laws in effect and laws to specify the out come of ai and ai actions and ai faults and government result laws of failure compensation and punishment
10933 artificial energy is a nonspontaneous reaction to a forced digital or analog form of simulated energy in a real sense of negative or positive ae
10934 artificial magnetic energy is a nonspontaneous reaction to a forced magnetic form of simulated energy in a real sense of negative or positive ae
10935 artificial relative energy is a nonspontaneous reaction to a forced magnetic digital amped weight in a volatile form of simulated energy in a real sense of negative or positive ae
10936 negative conductive algorithms are the translation of current in a form that may be used to hold energy and data at the same time with a specific compression ratio per algorithm and energy source in a cold state
10937 positive with negative conductive algorithms are the translation of current in a form that may be used to hold energy and data at the same time with a specific compression ratio per algorithm and energy source in a alternate state
10938 positive with negative conductive algorithms cpu chips computer memory and addon

processors are the translation of current in a form that may be used to hold energy and data at the same time with a specific compression ratio per algorithm and energy source in a alternate state

10939 trans coding chips that make a wave of energy into positive with negative conductive algorithms cpu chips computer memory and addon processors are the translation of current in a form that may be used to hold energy and data at the same time with a specific compression ratio per algorithm and energy source in a alternate state

10940 free functional addons are the additional scaleable plug and play options of any such freely to place in a location to import processing and to increase a probability of performance

10941 tiered leveled sequential multiple free functional addons are the additional scaleable plug and play options of any such freely to place in a location to import processing and to increase a probability of performance

10942 cloud addons are the servers or virtual performance servers in data center to act as a tiered leveled sequential multiple free functional addons are the additional scaleable plug and play options of any such freely to place in a location to import processing and to increase a probability of performance

10943 virtual performance servers in data center are equatable to code and scripting within folders and software allocations

10944 multiple tiered virtual performance servers in data center are equatable to code and scripting within folders and software allocations in a series format

10945 virtual functional addons are the additional scaleable plug and play software options of any such freely to place in a location to import processing and to increase a probability of performance

10946 virtual functional gpu are the additional scaleable plug and play software options of any such freely to place in a location to import processing and to increase a probability of performance

10947 gpu inside a gpu inside for virtual functional gpu are the additional scaleable plug and play software options of any such freely to place in a location to import processing and to increase a probability of performance x

10948 upgrade able secondary level chips that co process in an onboard secondary socket that incorporate alternate processing like the central chip but in a on board or in socket form of non graphic non central but in a second level of cache and co processing formation of working computational additions far from a memory take away but a embedded solution market

10949 upgrade able secondary level random access memory that store in an onboard secondary group of sockets that incorporate alternate processing like the first level ram but in a off or on board or in socket form of non graphic non central but in a second level of cache formation of working computational additions like a memory take away but a embedded solution market

10950 retro fit smart home breaker box is a device board that is controllable by phone or computer network of links and changes for variations and add on's in power and connectivity

10951 retro fit smart home breaker os and the retro fit smart home breaker box is a device board that is controllable by phone or computer network of links and changes for variations and add on's in power and connectivity

10952 security add on with retro fit smart home breaker os and the retro fit smart home breaker box is a device board that is controllable by phone or computer network of links and

changes for variations and add on's in power and connectivity
10953 new item embedded controller instructions as to add operating instructions per operation and embedded vectors
10954 smart home adaptive new or retro appliance embedded power instructions switch control for a power related control operations
10955 smart home adaptive new or retro appliance embedded library of instructions for compound control of smart objects with embedded options and chips ram as well as ports
10956 local library object instructions is the safe and unlinked local area network of a system smart home adaptive new or retro appliance embedded library of instructions for compound control of smart objects with embedded options and chips ram as well as ports
10957 connected object network of instructions library object instructions is the linked local area network of a system smart home adaptive new or retro appliance embedded library of instructions for compound control of smart objects with embedded options and chips ram as well as ports
10958 a deliberate method network of connected object network of instructions library object instructions is the paid hierarchy connection within a local area network of a system smart home adaptive new or retro appliance embedded library of instructions for compound control of smart objects with embedded options and chips ram as well as ports
10959 block chain audit is a method to audit the leaks and attacks of cyber security an a cyber currency as a whole
10960 national technology research is a technology study branch of government that is similar to nasa only the change of space to technology study
10961 tax report now is the time that we have the proper data systems to calculate all the taxes and their effectiveness it time to do a country wide tax report
10962 government data exchange is a cloud method of revising the current scheme of paper arranged data
10963 war data center is a principal with the intent to make a secure and break in free environment that is a near to impossible notion of a study of all things war related
10964 war data center rit is a fast green/red light for any such advanced motion of war in a fast real sense of approval in the war data center
10965 war data records and the short hand version per soldier in battle by bot or by live combat by a recorded notable system
10966 educational data center is a principal with the intent to make a secure and break in free environment for schools
10967 medical data center is a principal with the intent to make a secure and break in free environment that is secure to all things study related
10968 medical data center rit is a fast green red light for any such advanced motion of medical cloud related issues
10969 educational data center rit is a fast green or red light for any such advanced motion of cloud environmental situations
10970 block chain proof of purchase is the encrypted method of payment and an added method of authentication per user agent
10971 search into systems is a simple search engine that searches by tunnel and hidden internet protocol in the specified system with results on a different page
10972 paid search into systems is a simple search engine that searches by tunnel and hidden

internet protocol into the specified system with paid results on a different page
10973 paid search into systems network is a simple search engine alliance that searches by tunnel and hidden internet protocol in the specified system with paid results on a different page
10974 roaming address is a long haul truck driver or occupational address where the citizen is not contacted by postal address buy by phone and mobile email
10975 government security number remap is a new recorded method for securing your citizenship and voter rights as well as secondary social security number
10976 paid government security number card or secure id is a new recorded method for securing your citizenship and voter rights with a chip
10977 hdmi server on chip is a complimentary part to a input bed of systems on chip by hdmi connections
10978 hdmi server input board is the hdmi server on chip that is a part of input bed of systems on board by hdmi connections
10979 to have a fiber optic vector registered board that has a lined connective port of objects inline to work like a copper embedded circuit board
10980 system on chip optical server input board to have a fiber optic vector registered board that has a lined optical embedded circuit
10981 auto thread and processor controller software and scripted control chips are the automated central processor unit and the memory optimization included with all of the other parts such as gpu and or oi accelerator and even a co processor in unison as such as to work uniformly as fast as possible
10982 serial recording there is a need for a faster paced invention deposition writing and security method with the usa to make a licensed professional is important in a serial recorded document status combined with the method of registration
10983 landfill mining and dithering mobile disassembly plant is an arranged machine that separates the material on a scale per unit of measurement first is the magnetic property of the unit second is the weight of the unit and third is the size and this method is repeated over and over again to a sufficient level of recycled property
10984 gmvitamins are genetically modified vitamins that encourage growth to patients with severe deficiencies in a certain vitamin or cell of the body
10985 gmantivirus are genetically modified vaccines that protect important cell growth to patients with severe deficiencies in a certain vitamin or cell of the body
10986 autonomous landfill mining and dithering mobile disassembly plant is a robotics controlled arranged machine that separates the material on a scale per unit of measurement first is the magnetic property of the unit second is the weight of the unit and third is the size and this method is repeated over and over again to a sufficient level of recycled property
10987 microwave reactor is a combination of reactions in few scenarios like for example the combination of air or water to run a turbine and create electricity or the microwaveable consideration of other reactive materials as solvents or compounds to create energy as the catalyst as the microwave the converter or electric generation and then the recycle of the reaction
10988 fossilized and un radiated uranium through a process of microwave until negative powers are there and no heat is constant
10989 dunner and the re exam of pre existed depleted uranium for microwave tables and the

recycled nuclear products
10990 microwave energy and the reconstituted nuclear elements for regeneration and reuse
10991 private energy farms and the mobile battery that can change the energy industry are easy to dream of but more difficult to consume the intent to make a plug and rechargeable system of portable electricity is in itself to create a whole industry the study of and arrangement of a recycle system with acceptable awareness for the environment can be achieved as easy as the difference in a propane tank and the electrical battery exchange
10992 vertical chip engineering software is a software that will aid in the building of a vertical wafer of chips in a faster more compact size
10993 vertical chip engineering printers is a machine that will aid in the building of a vertical wafer of chips in a faster more compact size
10994 vertical chip multi compound printers is a machine that will aid in the building of a vertical wafer of chips in a faster more compact size while printing in multiple stages of mediums in a series of layers
10995 chip compound direction printers is a machine that will aid in the building of a vertical and horizontal wafer of chips in a faster more compact size while printing in multiple stages of mediums in a series of layers to print horizontal and vertical to arrange in a more efficient manner
10996 chip compound direction software is a machine writer that will aid in the building of a vertical and horizontal wafer of chips in a faster more compact size while printing in multiple stages of mediums in a series of layers to print horizontal and vertical to arrange in a more efficient manner
10997 compound angle chips are the chips that have horizontal diagonal vertical processing that will aid in the processing of a vertical and other angles including horizontal made wafer of chips in a faster more compact size while printing in multiple stages of mediums in a series of layers to print horizontal and vertical to arrange in a more efficient manner
10998 compound chip parts are the cores memory and agents that have direction any compound direction of processing with building of a vertical and horizontal wafer of chips in a faster more compact size while printing in multiple stages of mediums in a series of layers to print horizontal and vertical to arrange in a more efficient manner
10999 multi processing compound angel of processing links toner compiled compound chip laser printed gold powder and cubic zircon powder printed chips
11000 laboratory do it your self rights to find and cure to cancers virus and diseases is a old thing new again that the current system to practice active measures of laboratory work require unknown lengths of red tape this is an equation of experience and scholarship to include the diy and proprietary rights for work and operation of private labs
11001 laboratory intellectual rights are the rules and knowledge ownership of laboratory do it your self rights to find and cure to cancers virus and diseases is a old thing new again that the current system to practice active measures of laboratory work require unknown lengths of red tape this is an equation of experience and scholarship to include the diy and proprietary rights for work and operation of private labs
11002 private research intellectual rights lab permits are the rules and knowledge ownership of laboratory do it your self rights to find and cure to cancers virus and diseases is a old thing new again that the current system to practice active measures of laboratory work require unknown lengths of red tape this is an equation of experience and scholarship to include the

diy and proprietary rights for work and operation of private labs
11003 proprietary research rights laboratory is a seek and find a cure for a monetary gain
11004 free rights and trade laboratory is the non compete way of salable research
11005 legally bound comma separated values and sheets for digital paper submissions are records that can be submitted by csv by any such given form for legal certified documents
11006 hope for the wire bound is a simple word for the transient of wireless driven things of the internet and the data center for a smaller more complex driven form of one os per many devices meaning one set of instructions like a web hosting instruction per many devices
11007 part of a room is a frame of sorts for example the separation of data and the complied operation system could be an easier cloud to use meaning if the parts of any library of data has a role for the drive storage and which functions could be as simple as a read and play part of access which could be a stored part of a program for saving resources and processing some where else
11008 a travel cloud is a set of revolving ip addresses for data and servers
11009 a secure roaming cloud is a random set of revolving ip addresses for data and servers
11010 a secure lost cloud is a non revolving random resetting ip address for data and servers to help evade domain denial of service
11011 insufficient rights to claim as non negligent for a purpose given is to declare a right for the damaged claim over any waiver of rights previously noted
11012 server over a system is a simple configuration of one server per many parts and many redundant parts per many systems
11013 wrongful creation intent of ai and the false artificial intelligent proposal is simply a romantic novel
11014 to short the ai technology market is a given rule of thumb of many
11015 alternative to ai is the instructional applications ia and the provided instructions of a skynet like operation in a new meaning of the sense
11016 alternatives to artificially driven things are the things that are so important like the car and air planes or trains are simple pilot driven back up navigation
11017 the important things of non applied artificial intelligence are to be noted meaning that there is a level to artificial intelligence that should not be applied perverted and abused
11018 positive nature is important in a resolution for bad ai outcome and should be held responsible for its nature by the ai maker
11019 ai car insurance is the most positive way for resolution for bad ai outcome and should be held responsible for its unnatural nature
11020 ai drone insurance is the most positive way for resolution for bad ai outcome and should be held responsible for its unnatural nature
11021 artificial intelligence and learning aerial and ground drone is a bot operated drone that is computed to navigate and report with a prepared version of a given set of scenarios
11022 artificial intelligence and learning aerial marine and ground war drone is a bot operated drone that is computed to navigate and report with a prepared version of a given set of scenarios
11023 stealth artificial intelligence and learning aerial marine and ground war drone is a bot operated drone that is computed to navigate and report with a prepared version of a given set of scenarios
11024 search and rescue ai maritime drone artificial intelligence and learning aerial marine

and ground drone is a bot operated drone that is computed to navigate and report with a prepared version of a given set of scenarios
11025 optical calculation is a step in the optical cpu with a transposed availability to calculate a problem in a scenario of motion as opposed to a stationary circuit
11026 looping optical calculation is a step in the optical cpu with a transposed availability to calculate a problem in a scenario of motion as opposed to a stationary circuit
11027 multiple cycles looping optical calculation is a step in the optical cpu with a transposed availability to calculate a problem in a scenario of motion as opposed to a stationary circuit
11028 virtual transistors in optical thread translated into a code specific processing object for an optical cpu
11029 optical processing language is the binary equal to central processing unit code of cubits as an optical cpu
11030 magnetic optical processor is a simple name for the magnetic cubit optical media circuit written chip that is bound by optical processing language and is the binary equal to central processing unit code of cubits as an optical processor
11031 magnetic object written chip is a simple name for the magnetic cubit optically written chip that is bound by a processing language and is the binary equal to central processing unit code of cubits as an circuit processor
11032 optically written magnetic object is a simple name for the laser written optically printed chip as an circuit processor as opposed to a diffused optically printed chip
11033 optically written object blank is a simple name for the laser written optically printed chip blank similar to a optical media disc as an circuit processor as opposed to a diffused optically printed chip
11034 portable optically written object blank similar to a optical media disc as an circuit processor as opposed to a diffused optically printed chip
11035 object writer for the portable optically written object blank similar to a optical media disc as an circuit processor as opposed to a diffused optically printed chip will bring circuit printing to the household markets
11036 paid instructions for the object writer for the portable optically written object blank similar to a optical media disc as an circuit processor as opposed to a diffused optically printed chip will bring circuit printing to the household diy markets
11037 many optical circuit objects in order on a server bed of input ports meaning a group of objects working as system on chips as portable optically written object blank similar to a optical media disc as an circuit processor as opposed to a diffused optically printed chip will bring circuit printing to the household diy markets
11038 optical circuit focus range is the measurement of circuits in an optically written object blank similar to a optical media disc as an circuit processor as opposed to a diffused optically printed chip will bring circuit printing to the household diy markets
11039 in board solid state threading is the path of computational signals traveling inside the server board for faster translation computations and processing
11040 board solid state hyperthreading is the path of computational signals traveling inside the server board for faster translation computations and processing
11041 hyper threading cable is a multiple lane cable that transports signals into and from a source to another receiver
11042 hyper threading fiber optic cable is a multiple lane cable that transports signals into

and from a source to another receiver
11043 hyper threading usb cable is a multiple lane cable that transports signals into and from a source to another receiver
11044 wireless hard drive is a two step data storage drive and wireless adapter that transports signals into and from a source to another receiver
11045 sd wireless hard drive system is a two step data storage drive and wireless adapter that transports signals into and from a source to another receiver
11046 multiplied wireless hard drive router is a multiple signal transporter and encoder with a specified multiple places of destination
11047 multiplied wireless hd receiver is a multiple signal wireless adapter that transports many different signals into and from a source to another router with specified multiple places in destination
11048 wireless storage network is a non processing cache only system of storage drives
11049 wireless computational network processing only system of processing
11050 computational network processing only system of scripted processing
11051 allotted memory network is a shared system of cache and paging system that shares a specified amount of links in memory disc space
11052 home to cell to satellite routers cell branches that hold a message in the packet prefix or suffix that extends the direction of cellular channels that focus to the nearest cell reach to the nearest satellite for convenience and speed
11053 low density performance scale processing is the number in processors compared to size
11054 high density complex scale processing is the number in processors compared to size
11055 high density performance scale processing is the ratio number in processors compared to scheme of arrangements and clusters in ram and transistors a
11056 category chips are purpose driven chips with that program and task at mind
11057 creative category chips are purpose driven chips with that program and task at mind
11058 calc category chips are purpose driven chips with that program and task at mind
11059 category add on cards are purpose driven chips with that program and task at mind
11060 creative category add on cards are purpose driven chips with that program and task at mind
11061 calc category add on cards are purpose driven chips with that program and task at mind
11062 multiple category chips are purpose driven chips with that program and task at mind
11063 program categories for specified category chips are purpose driven chips with that application software program and task at mind
11064 calc program categories for specified category chips are purpose driven chips with number and physics application software program and task at mind
11065 creative program categories for specified category chips are purpose driven chips with hypothetical and geometry application software program and task at mind
11066 satellite connection grid is a connected alliance of satellites that work and process things like communication together as a whole network
11067 paid satellite data connection grid network is a connected alliance of satellites that work and process things like communication together as a whole network
11068 satellite data packet grid prefix and paid satellite connection grid network is a

connected alliance of satellites that work and process things like communication together as a whole network with the ability to send packets to and from each other

11069 paid satellite data packet grid prefix network branches and paid satellite connection grid network is a connected alliance of satellites that work and process things like communication together as a whole network with the ability to send packets to and from each other

11070 paid satellite data packet grid prefix and paid satellite connection grid network is a connected alliance of satellites that work and process things like communication together as a whole network with the ability to send packets to and from each other

11071 satellite to cell branches are cellular channels that focus to the nearest cell reach to the nearest satellite for convenience and speed

11072 home router to cell to satellite paid satellite connection grid network is a connected alliance of satellites that work and process things like communication together as a whole network with the ability to send packets to and from each other

11073 diesel and ethel sodium nitrate fuel for diesel for trucks tractor trailers and cars as well as airplanes and drones

11074 compressed alcoholasgas engine is a compromised vapor ignition engine for trucks tractor trailers and cars as well as airplanes and drones

11075 in a compressed alcoholasgas engine a compromised vapor ignition fuel injector is a prepared measure of vapor agitator to make a fine atomized vapor to burn and combust for trucks tractor trailers and cars as well as airplanes and drones

11076 agitated vapor fuel is the closest to flash point in any compound that would be important in a compressed alcoholasgas engine a compromised vapor ignition fuel injector is a prepared measure of vapor agitator to make a fine atomized vapor to burn and combust for trucks tractor trailers and cars as well as airplanes and drones

11077 compromised fuel aerosol is premeasured agitated vapor fuel and is the closest to flash point in any compound that would be important in a compressed alcoholasgas engine a compromised vapor ignition fuel injector is a prepared measure of vapor agitator to make a fine atomized vapor to burn and combust for trucks tractor trailers and cars as well as airplanes and drones

11078 compromised fuel aerosol engine will use premeasured agitated vapor fuel and is the closest to flash point in any compound that would be important in a compressed alcoholasgas engine a compromised vapor ignition fuel injector is a prepared measure of vapor agitator to make a fine atomized vapor to burn and combust for trucks tractor trailers and cars as well as airplanes and drones

11079 atomized and vapor hybrid engine will use premeasured agitated vapor fuel and is the closest to flash point in any compound that would be important in a compressed alcoholasgas engine a compromised vapor ignition fuel injector is a prepared measure of vapor agitator to make a fine atomised vapor to burn and combust for trucks tractor trailers and cars as well as airplanes and drones

11080 atomized fuel and vapor hybrid engine will use premeasured agitated vapor fuel and is the closest to flash point in any compound that would be important in a compressed alcoholasgas engine a compromised vapor ignition fuel injector is a prepared measure of vapor agitator to make a fine atomised vapor to burn and combust for trucks tractor trailers and cars as well as airplanes and drones

11081 smart fuel is pre respirated gasoline in a volatile vapor to burn and combust for trucks tractor trailers and cars as well as airplanes and drones

11082 pre respirated gasoline in a volatile vapor calculator that finds the fuels top flash point automatically and in a few cycles adjusts it to any gas for the engine

11083 vapor compressor is a exciter and pre respirator for gasoline in a volatile vapor calculator that finds the fuels top flash point automatically and in a few cycles adjusts it to any gas for the engine

11084 smart fuel system in conjunction with vapor compressor is an exciter and pre respirated gasoline fuel in a volitile vapor calculator that finds the mixes top flash point automatically and in a few cycles adjusts it to any gas for the proper efficiency

11085 law bureau of investigation to seek and find corruption in government would be a branch of law directed at politics and make a political transition from the public service to the private administration of law and free us from pay offs and contract breaks

11086 virtual search of power is a learning method to compute the most powerful solution to run tomorrows cars and every day engines motors and energy motions of any kind while measuring the possibilities of the content to make that energy and the worth of the out come as well as the potency of that worth to the foot print and the regeneration of the properties

11087 software that looks and learns the cost of a fuel or substance and compares that to a starch and the mineral to make that energy with the combinations of other properties of value in a computational way of virtual search of power is a learning method to compute the most powerful solution to run tomorrows cars and every day engines motors and energy motions of any kind while measuring the possibilities of the content to make that energy and the worth of the out come as well as the potency of that worth to the foot print and the regeneration of the properties

11088 virtual search of power library for a data start with software that looks and learns the cost of a fuel or substance and compares that to a starch and the mineral to make that energy with the combinations of other properties of value in a computational way of virtual search of power is a learning method to compute the most powerful solution to run tomorrows cars and every day engines motors and energy motions of any kind while measuring the possibilities of the content to make that energy and the worth of the out come as well as the potency of that worth to the foot print and the regeneration of the properties

11089 bureau of lawyer investigation is a simple investigation to condone or condemn the laws by a specific lawyer

11090 large scale software overwrites are the overwritten os and programs apps and unlocked formats of devices and the user agreement broken by opposing software and reclaiming a device based on ownership

11091 drone operating system and the library functions of that data

11092 virtual drone navigational operating system and the library functions of that data including geo navigation satellite location and local weather conditions as in corporate in a system of methods that conclude a operation inside a alternate virtual use _

11093 a global connected cloud resource of data and targets to compromise the enemy and their assets as a concluded end to a means the satellites and the data location in a sense of war over internet protocol

11094 virtual calculated energy verses for profit formula table software is a search and input library of values and methods of constants and catalysts that react with one another in a virtual unreal way of study to mathematically search and find any such data as an inquiry to a means

11095 wireless through gateway ping router is a device that allows computers to connect and share files thru software and a single router essentially a very small internet by wifi network hardware and software

11096 wireless computer to wireless computer

11097 wireless phone to wireless phone direct

11098 multiple external modular format is a hardware driven by driver format that excludes the chassis location and provides ports that transfer the data in and out in thread cables

11099 hiroshima latin invasion spawned by leftists

11100 data center secure wireless multiple external modular format is a hardware driven by driver format that excludes the chassis location and provides ports that transfer the data in and out wireless with a header data packet that includes a specific device for inclusion in a data center for wireless alliance computing

11101 multi signal wireless receiver is a receiver for multiple managed wireless signals and incorporating wireless devices

11102 processor driven wifi signal receiver for multiple managed wireless signals and incorporating wireless devices processors and computations as a whole in a multitude of receiving and processing of a signal

11103 recyclable air filters

11104 recyclable water filters

11105 recyclable oil filters

11106 mosquito control tabs for large ponds patent pending

11107 multiple conjoined boards by os is a group of boards that are essentially separated working cells that are joined by operating system patent pending

11108 wireless multiple conjoined boards by os is a group of boards that are essentially separated working cells that are joined by operating system without wires patent pending

11109 to learn sharing software is a program or app that accepts multiple users in order to learn and teach verses one mouse and one input at a time patent pending

11110 multiple users and rules software is a program or app that accepts multiple users in order to work and perform as a team in one mission with rules of hierarchy and ranking patent pending

11111 boronmagnesiumsulfate patent pending

11112 hydrogen oxide sulfate patent pending

11113 sodium sulfur carbonate patent pending

11114 sodium carbonite aluminum sodium carbonite patent pending

11115 zirconhydroxy isolated layer is a layer of zirconium which is a silicon that is more insulating and less thermal conductive than diamond carbonate this is good for making three dimensional chips and operators

11116 subtractively printed zirconhydroxy or photo laser cut zirconhydroxy isolated layer is a layer of zirconium which is a silicon that is more insulating and less thermal conductive than diamond carbonate this is good for making three dimensional chips and operators

11117 subtractively printed photo laser cut layer is a layer of conductor or isolate r which is a cut or etched by a time generated photo of energy such as burning or to degrade the photo or image into something or out of something which is good for making three dimensional chips

and operators
11118 lcd stencil lens for pi co and nano active subtractively printed photo laser is a laser stencil photo object to print subtractively with mediums
11119 stencil graphic laser printer is a pico and nano active subtractively printed photo laser stencil photo object to print and subtractively with medium
11120 stencil graphic laser printer software is the software for the stencil graphic laser printer is a pico and nano active subtractively printed photo laser stencil grid
11121 three dimensional stencil graphic laser printer is a pico and nano active subtractively printed photo laser is a laser stencil photo object to print and subtractively with medium for example to think that a grid of pico layered and formed photo timed generated method of stencil emulsion printing converts a flux to accept the grid of the negative print also said to use small stencils to print smaller circuits
11122 gold chromatic building microprocessors is a part of the three dimensional stencil graphic laser printer and is a pico and nano active subtractively printed photo laser is a laser stencil photo object to print and subtractively with medium for example to think that a grid of pico layered and formed photo timed generated method of stencil emulsion printing converts a flux to accept the grid of the negative print also said to use small stencils to print smaller circuits
11123 silicachromaticbuildingmicroprocessors
11124 molecular photo printing said to use small stencils to print smaller circuits in an adjusted dimension with an emulsion photo fusion process
11125 printing focus stencil grid is a large grid of pixels that when compensated or reflected into a smaller size they connect and with reason to provide connections
11126 reversed printing focus stencil grid is a large grid of pixels that when compensated or reflected into a smaller size they connect and conduct as a circuit
11127 exterior liquid cooled computing components such as microprocessors used in cell towers and more memory and other actively cooled in a climate controlled efficiency for higher performance
11128 exterior <span>meaning out side in atmosphere </span>liquid cooled motherboard is an actively cooled in a climate controlled efficiency way of cooling for higher performance
11129 exterior meaning out side in atmosphere liquid cooled memory is an actively cooled in a climate controlled efficiency way of cooling for higher performance
11130 exterior in the elements liquid cooled memory is actively cooled liquid thermal contact that aids in temperature adjustments by thermal liquid conduction
11131 hard drive readout is a simple lcd or led read out of status on hard drive functionality
11132 memory led readout is a simple lcd or led read out of status on hard drive functionality
11133 add hardware wizard with drivers and more is a simple unique way to pre initialize the moment of pre install with how to and pre installed drivers
11134 gpu readout is a simple lcd or led read out of status on gpu for reference functionality
11135 company compatible hardware for reference functionality is another way of saying that the oem source may be compatible with a company when forming an alliance in partnership and software hardware compatibility meaning in another way more universal components and higher use and less unaccepted products as well as a better way of life for information technology also said as this company a is compatible with this company b
11136 page switch browser plugin is a software internet or mobile web interface that takes

large tall pages that run on and on and divides them into smaller and easier to download workable pages by splitting them into different views of minor pages like a tree layout in a table of contents

11137 personal data storage software is a way to keep the original paper mail copied and safe off line or on line in a digital world while accessing the properties of print and scan a need to fax and forward to any service like united states postal service and more is the priority of the software in question and the protection is a part of the meaning of its importance the life cycle of the person and day to day is a important function of all of us

11138 system on chip product foundation is the start of a new cloud format far from large servers and server racks we enter the card based system of scrolling wall panels and more

11139 system on chip wall mount boards and large card input panels

11140 system on chip wall mount boards and large card input panels that move

11141 system on chip plug and play grid and processing arrangement of network wall mount boards

11142 multiple oi protocol router board is an important part of information in and out of any given system on chip wall mounting moving input unit this is the protocol that moves the data in and out of the section per multitude of processing systems on one wall board

11143 embedded access interface in a collection of system on chips code is a data in and out of the section per multitude of processing systems on one wall board

11144 wireless access soc is a code access by wifi or wirelessethernet processing

11145 soc foundation power by usb data by usb on board ram on board processor hard drive by compact flash made to run programmable applications

11146 wifi server foundation power by usb data by usb on board ram on board processor hard drive by compact flash made to run programmable applications with the access of wifi integrated

11147 system on chip server foundation power by usb data by usb on board ram on board processor hard drive by compact flash made to run programmable applications with the access of wifi integrated

11148 wifi alternating form access of wifi integrated is a triplet form of one send and one receive and one group of process as a whole of one in any open signals

11149 a group of any available open form of one send and one receive and one group of process as a whole of one in any open signals

11150 certified and notary of email is a service of notary in an email record to and from clients

11151 government serial digital copy notary document number registry is a general document of recording in a digital sense

11152 serial digital copy document number registry is a general document of recording in a digital sense

11153 medical serial digital copy document number registry is a general document of recording in a digital sense

11154 education document server serial digital copy document number registry is a general document of recording in a digital sense

11155 business document registry number and document server serial digital copy document number registry is a general document of recording in a digital sense

11156 auto pc number document registry number and document server serial digital copy

document number registry is a general document of recording in a digital sense for the personal computer and information of scientific origin
11157 email ping record notary registry number and information of legal origin
11158 phone ping record notary registry number and information of legal origin
11159 ocr cursive per word and the fewest changes
11160 gps road lanes are the global positioning satellites way of making lanes for flying and navigating instead of yellow white stripes there could be pre designated routes by height from and in what direction
11161 gps aerial drone road lanes are the global positioning satellites way of making lanes for flying and navigating instead of yellow white stripes there could be pre designated routes by height from and in what direction
11162 gps aerial lanes for drones are the global positioning satellites way of making lanes for flying and navigating instead of yellow white stripes there could be pre designated routes by height from and in what direction
11163 gps aerial lanes for airplanes are the global positioning satellites way of making lanes for flying and navigating instead of yellow white stripes there could be pre designated routes by height from and in what direction
11164 global positioning satellite grid of ownership including place in physics natural and vertical horizontal and down
11165 gps fishing zone global positioning satellite grid of ownership including place in physics natural and vertical horizontal and down
11166 annotation physics spatial grid including place in physics natural and vertical horizontal and down mapping by global positioning satellite government or private designation place in space
11167 dual annotation physics spatial grid including place in physics natural and vertical horizontal and down from two origins
11168 gps navigational property and the confines of that d property
11169 adjustable format video is a hardware rendering device application that runs a basic group of files a specific way to improve the display of any movie or music and other data projects simply said you put your project in basic adjustable format and the video player renders the adjusted final part
11170 military reverse calvin cycle air purifiers
11171 bids and sales for legitimate futures in project performance is the sale of a large private job for any work made in a presales term
11172 satellite negotiations network is a paid environment for services in the satellite atmosphere to make money and profit
11173 cellular foundation negotiation network is a real chance of service to any known location by selling the use of a cellular network to any under written provider for negotiation and sales
11174 hybrid connected communication network is a real chance of service to any known location by selling the use of a cellular to satellite hybrid service network to any under written provider for negotiation and sales
11175 a reverse reflective tunnel that magnifies the light and graduates the source to maximize the solar energy post
11176 a energy center or building with many focused solar generators that reverse reflective

tunnel that magnifies the light and graduates the source to maximize the solar energy post
11177 ai is named wrong you have to take more into consideration like the answer not the truth of the question left and right is the asymmetrical processing
11178 micro alternating circuit battery is a circuit that recycles itself with current
11179 processor micro circuit battery is a circuit cell that holds current
11180 acid alkaline printed chips in a diffused solution to compute as a battery on chip
11181 laser printed levels of circuits and multiple cured solvents as circuits layers laser printed chips in a diffused solution to compute as a chip
11182 ultra violet laser printed levels of circuits and multiple uv cured solvents as circuits layers laser printed chips in a diffused solution to compute as a chip
11183 laser printed levels of circuits and multiple photo sensitive cured solvents as circuits layers laser printed chips in a diffused solution to compute as a chip
11184 perpendicular laser printed levels of circuits processors and memory in multiple photo sensitive cured solvents as circuits layers laser printed chips in a diffused solution to compute as a chip
11185 a photo reactive multiple element formula of printing materials for perpendicular laser printed levels of circuits processors and memory in multiple photo sensitive cured solvents as circuits layers laser printed chips in a diffused solution to compute as a chip
11186 printing materials for perpendicular laser printed levels of circuits processors and memory in multiple photo sensitive cured solvents as circuits layers laser printed chips in a diffused solution to compute as a chip in a series of different elements
11187 vertical clamp socket for chip
11188 five sided computer chip for computations
11189 sided computer chip for computations
11190 sided computer chip for computations and stacking arrangements for chip processing
11191 pico nano voxel and elemental compounds for chip processing printing
11192 conductive and positive pico nano voxel and elemental compounds for chip processing printing in three dimensions
11193 non conductive and negative pico nano voxel and elemental compounds for chip processing printing in three dimensions
11194 non conductive silica solvent white space and negative pico nano voxel and elemental compounds for chip processing printing in three dimensions
11195 conductive gold and mineral solvent conductors in a positive pico nano voxel and elemental compound form for three dimensional chip processing printing
11196 empty space for looped inside linking conductive vector for making a place for conductors in pico nano voxel and elemental compounds for chip processing printing in three dimensions
11197 connection vectors and the empty space for looped inside linking conductive vector for making a place for conductors in pico nano voxel and elemental compounds for chip processing printing in three dimensions
11198 software that makes connection vectors conductors in pico nano voxel and elemental compounds for chip processing printing in three dimensions
11199 the intellectual property management office and large document record for keeping trade secrets and patents safe and secured by named ownership
11200 spiral compressed reflective fiber optical cable

11201 spiral compound reflective receiver decoder processor that reads reflective signals in fiber optic signals
11202 spiral compound reflective sending out encoder processor that codes reflective signals in fiber optic signals
11203 spiral fiberoptic splicer device and the markings that make a reading splicer obtain the proper place in the cable to splice or loop into with precision and accuracy for less signal loss
11204 exchangeable and upgrade able camera chassis and processor models
11205 exchangeable and upgrade able displays and monitors for in chassis computing extensions
11206 exchangeable and upgrade able laptop models and ports processing addon
11207 exchangeable phone card migration software and compatible memory chips
11208 report service of citizenship is a small personalized membership to pay taxes for a limited trade for temporary immunity
11209 remote controlled automobile air conditioning
11210 advanced accessible wheel chair robotics for disabled mobility and the move and position library for automation in a standard uniform parking place
11211 sewage removable ultrabiotics for water and soil in a microbeenviroment as lead neutralizers and ph balance changers
11212 manufacturer electric motor recycle programs and incentives for autos and parts reclamation
11213 modified hard drive control and add on secondary hard drive chips for cache and indexing
11214 air plane antivirus software system for corrupted parts and software integrity
11215 part due date is a manufacturers recall date for part services on life threatening parts and mandatory services made due
11216 fiber optic reflective turn connection in data to let a signal repeat and split in order to go around an object of area
11217 service time out price cut is a service interruption cost cut for minute by minute operations and service as software companies verses outage and payment service
11218 counter attack outage service are companies as paid ddos retaliations and defense mercenaries that defend and log corporate and government interruptions and attacks like life threatening power outages in iot and flight control centers
11219 data war science is the study of war over internet mobile and satellite
11220 data economics and the cost of information in today's life and the sum of what it all concludes to move forward every day
11221 data tax and the data trade commission and the unequal differences and adjustments in an administration of machines and cost to service
11222 security and the possible chance of corruption during a data audit is the algorithm that registers a pattern in change
11223 trends and the possible chance of popular opinion statistical studies in acute product research in an algorithm bot could improve more future products
11224 seek and find algorithm bot is a programmable model of information search and find where the first variable is combine able with more than one conjunction
11225 bureaucratic reset is the full distress of laws of a previous state to reset the laws from another state as a legal situation similar to the gross loss in california

11226 computer system made operating code in a chain of environment variables is a chain of parts that work out of symbiotic relationship like an organism
11227 a chain of parts that make the entire computational platform accelerate instead of parallel they add on in chain and improve with every multiplying part
11228 computer add on theory against a parallel world and the core of a internet of things that don't coincide with parallel but an opposite meaning
11229 quantum raid processing is a sum of physical non theoretical group of computers that make a mission of processing
11230 quantum raid memory stack is a service of memory or storage accessible for computing information on a group scale
11231 quantum raid service is the entire process of memory storage and connective processing in an entirety of a system
11232 quantum service scale is the measure of quantum raid service and is the entire process of memory storage and connective processing in an entirety of a system
11233 laser cut cpu
11234 trapezoid zirconium (cubic zircon) laser focus angle is a use of chemically cooked carbon cut to a shape that makes a reflective magnified focus of light energy or mass
11235 spiral zirconium (cubic zircon) laser focus angle is a use of chemically cooked carbon cut to a shape that makes a reflective magnified focus of light energy or mass
11236 spectral reflective scale and the contributing spiral zirconium (cubic zircon) laser focus angle is a use of chemically cooked carbon cut to a shape that makes a reflective magnified focus of light energy or mass
11237 to define the scale of reflective focus and light combined in an energy spent verses the energy obtained is a study of solar refraction
11238 the process of making electricity with the mention of reflective focus and light combined in an energy spent verses the energy obtained is a study of solar refraction and to incorporate the less to make more is the mission of solar energy recycle as well as artificial solar led recycle
11239 to magnify and amplify the process of making electricity with the mention of reflective focus and light combined in an energy spent verses the energy obtained is a study of solar refraction and to incorporate the less to make more is the mission of solar energy recycle as well as artificial solar led recycle amplified
11240 solar recycle center is a place that magnify and amplify the process of making electricity with the mention of reflective focus and light combined in an energy spent verses the energy obtained is a study of solar refraction and to incorporate the less to make more is the mission of solar energy recycle as well as artificial solar led recycle amplified
11241 to artificially cross dna and uncross dna is not a gain or operation i myself would condone
11242 dna and nucleotide historical library and ownership per dna finger print solution
11243 software run program applications for printers that uses nano / pico / triad mixed and formulated biochemical nucleotide to replicate on a recurring smaller intent to cure cancer and disease formulated biochemical nucleotide
11244 insulated chip levels made from of with a coherence of any insulation method of stacking horizontal or vertical chip organization to build a larger chip also said as to make a non conductive layer with small outer inner conductive measures while operation is possible

11245 vertical threads and the property of stacking layers of chips
11246 watch smart phones with solar panels
11247 data board is a separated connection of data from power by changing the data ports to optical and the power ports to electrical for a faster schema
11248 solid data board is a separated connection of data from power by changing the data ports to solid state and the power ports to electrical for a faster schema
11249 electronic power and signal with fiber optical data and threads as well as solid state memory as threads and data signal carriers and power conduction in a computational system board for interseeding connections and processing nodes
11250 add in transformer for data that precedes the cpu if there is a optical data connection to lead to a processing opposing in signal operations
11251 add in exporter for data that supersedes the cpu if there is a optical data connection to lead to a processing opposing in signal operations
11252 add in transforming chip for data that uses two different kinds of bios and can process in two different signals like optical and electronic noise
11253 ability of many sets of bios and their respective parts working together in a system optical magnetic data and electronic
11254 bios rules and operations script in a working environment over of many other bios and their respective parts working together in a system
11255 water proof smart shoe is a shoe with calculative software connected or embedded with data out put in a water proof situation with size of mechanics and memory instances
11256 wifi gaming smart shoe is a shoe with calculative software connected or embedded with data out put in a gaming or practice situation with size of mechanics and memory instances
11257 sport smart shoe is a shoe with calculative software connected or embedded with data out put in a gaming or practice situation with size of mechanics and memory instances
11258 patent cloud and search platform for ecommerce
11259 cloud and search platform for ecommerce
11260 government cellular service for security purposes
11261 government satellite combat service for security purposes
11262 soldier watch makes the watching of a soldier in combat a function of a matter of life or death the service would follow a soldier into and out of a combat zone and record all of the data of the battle in progress and keep record of the out comings as a satellite and soldier the obvious security links are unquestionable in importance and the data would be encrypted
11263 student watch makes the watching of a student in school a function of a matter of win or loose the service would measure a students rates and learning process and record all of the data of the experience
11264 clay building bricks recycled to resolve ph balance in lead heavy ground as a counter product in a process of saturation
11265 high speed transcoding encoding station is a fiber optical resolution station that transforms signals into a compressed code for travel into a network
11266 high speed encryption station is a fiber optical resolution station that transforms signals into a encrypted code for travel into a network
11267 high speed compression station is a fiber optical resolution station that transforms signals into a compressed code for travel into a network

11268 high speed block transfer highway station is a fiber optical resolution station that transforms signals into a code for travel into a different network

11269 high speed aerospace satellite to satellite to ground encrypted processed and compressed signal data station is a resolution station that transforms signals into a encrypted code for travel into a different network

11270 high speed sata gpu chip connections and formats

11271 high speed micro sd performance chips are alternate and inclusive functioning chips in a ecosystem of a computer

11272 downloadable code for high speed micro sd performance chips

11273 a blank transistor chip that holds no instructions and the user builds and makes the bios by code instructions and navigation paths

11274 many blank transistor chips that holds no instructions and the user builds and makes the bios by code instructions and navigation paths to build a performance chip group with alternate and inclusive functioning chips in a ecosystem of a computer

11275 parallel many blank transistor chips that holds no instructions and the user builds and makes the bios by code instructions and navigation paths to build a performance chip group with alternate and inclusive functioning chips in a ecosystem of a computer

11276 inprecievable compression is a un noticeable time difference loss to assist in compression and data lag of operations and conduction in code or conversion

11277 room focused energy is a large reflected system of cycles in the case that one or only a few light emitters generate a large system of a source of solar energy in amplification by reflection and the profit of energy is greater than the source

11278 formula for thought combination formula of commons unique and abnormal the theory is a function of indefinite sums and energy in the mass of that sum with the longevity of that same sum a + m = e (. {} over {}) %uxe a {e} over {m} %uxe b {e%delta ^{}} over {c %delta ^{}} %uxe c{e %ux } over {c%ux }lllint /> %uxe a %uxe d {b%uxe sqrt{b^{}ac} } over {a} %notequal binom{%sigma }binom{{ %uxe b i%uxe b m} }{ < j < n } p (i

11279 autonomous software anti malware is the added safety measure of autonomous software security

11280 light turbo focused energy is a small reflected system of cycles in the case that one or only a few light emitters generate a stronger system of a source of solar energy in amplification by reflection and the profit of energy is greater than the source

11281 three dimensional tunnel light turbo focused energy is a small reflected system of cycles in the case that one or a few light emitters generate a stronger system of a source of solar energy in amplification by reflection and the profit of energy is greater than the source

11282 a one way mirror or rather said as a one sided reflective one side transparent solar energy glass window for building a reflective solar tunnel

11283 spiral focus energy is a one way mirror or rather said as a one sided reflective one side transparent solar energy glass window for building a reflective solar tunnel spirally to amplify the source

11284 square focus energy is a one way mirror or rather said as a one sided reflective one side transparent solar energy glass window for building a reflective solar tunnel square to amplify the source

11285 cone focus energy is a one way mirror or rather said as a one sided reflective one side transparent solar energy glass window for building a reflective solar tunnel cone to amplify

the source
11286 microwave fuse that generates solar electric energy is a mini microwave signal inside a one way mirror sphere or box with receiving solar energy cells on the outside inside another mini sphere feeding another sphere with one way mirror sphere or box with receiving solar energy cells with options to continue the cycle or to copy the out put in more on the outside inside another mini sphere feeding another sphere with one way mirror sphere or box with receiving solar energy cells on the outside inside another mini sphere feeding another sphere with one way mirror sphere or box with receiving solar energy cells on the outside inside another mini sphere feeding another sphere with one way mirror sphere or box with receiving solar energy cell son the outside inside another mini sphere feeding another sphere with one way mirror sphere or box with receiving solar energy cells or to simply end in one or two cycles
11287 immigrated income revenue service is a service devoted to helping immigrants over come short falls and improve the lives of immigrants and others who are incontinent of taxes as language and citizenship problems
11288 microwave ecology and the study of light particles and oxygen from microwave stable and unstable optical combustion
11289 microwave combustion microwave flash point in any operation as an ignition for combustion is the newest resolution here for energy.
11290 microwave vacuum combustion microwave flash point vacuum in any operation as an ignition for combustion is the newest resolution here for energy or force of energy
11291 satellite directional range accelerations when the area of interest is incorporated into a conglomerate signal of area in data within a similar location where as the area of interest is in a geopacket prefix for code accelerations
11292 gps pi navigation access is fractional pi satellite directional range accelerations when the area of interest is incorporated into a conglomerate signal of area in data within a similar location where as the area of interest is in a geopacket prefix for navigation acceleration for motion
11293 encrypted cellular service
11294 encrypted cellular applicaton and software
11295 mold detecting refrigerator
11296 invent retro retro retro retro retro penicillin two next protected by crioner.com and lcusthe simple minds think alike. but we progress through abstract minds that are complex yet sll simple... looking back is always important. why did i leave that milk out on the kitchen counter all day? it's an unintenonal thing that led from not seeing that jug of milk there. somemes if people cannot see what is there more than likely it will hide in plain sight. here is why the reason for all the things that occur in any invenon is only retroacve and progression through looking back. the contemplaon experiments are drawing to and end in my own self but
11297 invent extreme complex computations new computer plaorms and sets for extreme complex computaons pulse ion electron generators and how to make it a complex extreme state nano photonics and process control to nanmo motors that switch off and on as well as redirect nanmo motors are generated and transformed by a solid state of maer mulplex chips with mulple stairs and intelligent accelerators with end outcome.
11298 invent extreme complex computations part invent extreme complex computations

part imagine a decisive moment when all computaons end and a computer crashes... what if the demand put us into a suspended turbo modal and a flashpoint of maer inside an ion created a super accelerated moment when maer and equaon is important. crioner.com
11299 invent super suspened fuel super suspended fuel flow for hyper acve engine part next protected by crioner.com and lcusseedsandforcesuspended air and seed to centrifical force included inside a hyperacve engine to generate force and engery and make a more fuel effecve means for work.
11300 invent tet of period invent tet of period s: a riddle of sorts my algebra teacher used to say that the only actual true definion of a work is when you move something... so if you were to change around words like see and look it would be like work and job... what is a job and what is work? if you were to change a name for example period for smaller parcales as a metaphorical me algebraic formal as words and work the word works is a strange way. the object is to make a motor that holds four sides to {point
11301 invent commons uniques abnormal (a + m = e (. {} over {}) approx a {e} over {m} approx b {e %delta ^{}} over {c %delta ^{}} approx c{e uparrow } over {c uparrow })commons (infinity x +infinity sim max / < =x< = xe{x^{}} + %infinite times + %uxe a %epsilon %sigma)uniques(lllint / > %uxe a div % {b+ sqrt{b^{}ac} } over {a} %notequal binom{%sigma }binom{{ < = i < = m} }{ < j < n } p (i
11302 invent nano motors of styro carbonate nano motors of styro carbonate and in the shape of a tetrahedron next>>
11303 invent satellite communication amp aoip invent satellite communication amp aoip
11304 the communication amp is not only for talking and voip but a entertainment and communication all over internet protocol amplifier/map. the reason for topical seclusion is the need for a surprise in the market. places like canada mexico and alaska will be able to do things more affordably. that is all i can say about that
11305 invent question and concept the cold war is won invent question and concept the cold war is won
11306 im writing this opinion editorial because i feel that i have a small but very dangerous experience with russians. at least online dating and the women of the russian federation. first of all im attracted to russians because out of the cold war my hate was not hate it was an attraction because i knew that there had to be some kind of light at the end of the tunnel some how and some way. the fact of the matter is that there is plenty to be happy about.
11307 the russian federation is a very beautiful and magnificent place. they even from time to time visit my web site. and you dont have to log in to visit my web site. this is an open place that tries to ride all of the arguments no matter what who and when you come with that being said this is a very simple place. for a long time even i was enabling a translator to expand my visiting patrons to their own language. so i am hiding nothing only a few confidential things that are just that.
11308 to make a long story short im writing this to warn the men who are like me. lonely hopeful and among other things and i intend this as a compliment do not want to lower their standards and want a beautiful and brilliant russian woman as their companion. i think that the russians are a great and very cultured people. its just that a few of them are scamming men like me into giving them money. i have sent nothing and i will not send anything but
11309 this essay is one of humor but its true. ask any one if they are into russian women and they would totally ignore the question. i just wish that there were more men who are willing

to say that russians are beautiful and so are we. it goes along the lines of im boss your boss we are both boss.

11310 invent hd theater triple invent hd theater triple

11311 invent psychoc debilitation invent psychoc debilitation from my own experience i believe that there is brain damage during a psychoc episode that may lead to serious and more permanent debilitaon. this is important due to the chemical bal ance and the aid of recovery to locate the imparal negave neurological synapses and prevent future reoccurrences. also to prevent this episode change in paents more likely to develop later in life

11312 invent triplet pixel invent triplet pixel

11313 invent criminally schizophrenic criminally schizophrenic next protected by crioner.com and lcuswhat is the issue with viri contributors and identy theft... to compose why this is important in a short is to say that the specific context is technology. why a person will gain access to a log in and cause either unsafe terms or to steal a sum of informaon. my guess is that people have leaped into a mental illness and somehow conceited to the possible chance that what they are doing is going to result in gain. for example – some person steals money through a password or online portal

11314 invent plasma movie screen plasma movie screen next protected by crioner.com and lcusrollable and mathemac capable within the theather triplet g and funcons. a canvas like mate rial that is flexible and aslo transparent to illuminate with pixel per demension resoluon using plasma crystals or other material controlled by crioner.com

Buy Invent

EPILOGUE

%infinite times 1 + %infinite=E sim binom lim n toward infinity(1+{1} over {n})^{n} %infinite times 1 + %infinite sim binom max xe ^{sum +-infinity cdot 1+1 prop {E} over x sum to{{} } - x^{2}%EPSILON }

AFTERWORD

thank you

ACKNOWLEDGEMENT

63/552,008

ABOUT THE AUTHOR

Christopher G Brown

The music I make is electronic. And the Technology music I make is as varied as my interests are. I like to create many things like house, breaks, Techno, and trance. The list goes on but it's best put this way, "I make Techno." the kind of art I create is also just as varied. With a computer I find it very easy to make different things all the time and what I enjoy is to be humorous. Clip art in a way is descriptive for the moment that you may be experiencing. In other words I use humor and a touch of clip art to bring my concept to you. There are many moments when humor and personal things should be kept to a minimum but the best thing is to think of a need.

When we provide a service it's out of perception that our conclusion is made from. So, to bring my judgment and contemplation on the subject matter is the approach of our services. We have made many confidential things and we are glad to keep every thing that way. The promise of our business terms are our guiding light. "We haven't let down any one yet." this is our goal. The and old inventions I have created are special and dear. They are brilliant and resounding, as well as revolutionary and to put it in itself inventive. The best thing I do is think of first hand experience and my own knowledge and find the problem and then utilize a creative sense to discover a solution. And I could even make a solution that has no problem but, as the Romans we could conquer and multiply or we could conserve our issues. Either way the world understands long after and only long after.

The problem is that with even the best music, art, services, and inventions the LCUS Crioner Co is still a one person company. The reason is to stay responsible and reliable with reputation at stake I try to keep things all together in my own little way. I out source all of the important things and that leaves room for my head to roam and drift into happiness. Whether that is creating inventions or making enough art to fill up a Blu-ray, my mission is to make things that will provide for every one. The worst thing I think that could happen is to be lost in myself and never to fully recover. But as the time tells us all it's always a good time to move on into something better.

PRAISE FOR AUTHOR

"A LUCKY BREAK" Artist HAS FIRST EXHIBITION AT ST. EDWARD'S
Atlanta Journal and Constitution News Article Date: SATURDAY, SEPT. 16 1995

By Celia Sibley
"Lawrenceville resident Chris Brown, 20, was a senior not long ago at Central Gwinnett High School. Now he is a full-time painter getting ready for his first exhibition. Brown's works will be on display from Sunday through Nov. 18 at the art gallery of St. Edward's Episcopal Church in Lawrenceville, one of the few galleries offered by a church in metro Atlanta.
Brown and the artist who oversees the gallery, Mikki Dillon, an active member of the Georgia Pastel Society, plan to hang between 15 to 20 of his works today so that they will be ready to greet church goers Sunday morning. Each of the paintings in the Brown exhibition is an abstract in his favorite medium — spray paint.

The young artist is mostly self-taught, having quit his studies at the Atlanta College of Art to devote himself to painting full time in his studio at his parents' home. In addition to painting, he has written a book, "I Love You," which relates his theories of how art and life exist.

He is getting a break that many people in the art community would "turn handsprings" to get, Dillion said. "For the past several years St. Edward's Gallery has been a showcase for well-known and not-yet-well-known Gwinnett artists," she said. "Some of them are members of the congregation but that is never a requirement." The Gwinnett Visual Artists Association once used the room for meetings and as exhibit space."

mostly self-taught
although my favorite teacher was a woman named Susan Harlan

- TAKEN FROM THE ATLANTA JOURNAL AND CONSTITUTION.

Made in the USA
Columbia, SC
09 May 2024

c7c362c1-0f0a-4911-b9b3-c15f6c204e0aR03